THE
ADVISORY FUNCTION
OF THE
INTERNATIONAL COURT
IN THE LEAGUE AND U.N. ERAS

MICHLA POMERANCE

THE JOHNS HOPKINS UNIVERSITY PRESS

BALTIMORE AND LONDON

The Johns Hopkins University Press, Baltimore, Maryland 21218
The Johns Hopkins University Press Ltd., London

Library of Congress Catalog Card Number 72-4024
ISBN 0-8018-1291-7
Manufactured in the United States of America

Library of Congress Cataloging in Publication Data

Pomerance, Michla.
    The advisory function of the International Court in the League and UN eras.

    Includes bibliographical references.
    1. Hague.   International Court of Justice.
I. Title.
JX1971.6.P64   341.5'5   72-4024
ISBN 0-8018-1291-7

TO MY PARENTS

CONTENTS

THE ADVISORY
FUNCTION OF THE
INTERNATIONAL COURT

FOREWORD

Those who believe that the rule of law should prevail in the world community have been disappointed and troubled by the very modest role that the International Court of Justice has been allowed to play in international affairs. The Court is one of the principal organs of the United Nations. Its Statute assigns to it two functions: adjudicating disputes between states and rendering advisory opinions on legal questions submitted to it by certain international organizations. In this respect, it is very similar to its predecessor, the Permanent Court of International Justice. Yet, compared with the latter, the International Court has not increased the volume of its activity or its influence in the affairs of states or international organizations. In fact, the last ten years have witnessed a further diminution in the activity of the Court. As these lines are being written, only one contentious case appears on its calendar. Of the fourteen advisory opinions rendered by it, only two have been requested and given in the last ten years.

What have been the causes of the evident reluctance of states, and of international organizations composed of states, to use the Court? The answer must be sought in the policies of the various governments and in their estimates of the relation of the functions of the Court to their interests. The Court's functions, despite the often-heard facile dichotomy between "law" and "politics," have political implications. Its decisions and opinions cannot but affect the political relations between states. The more important a "legal" issue is to a state, the greater that issue's political significance is likely to be. For this reason, as many observers have noted, the disputes submitted to the Court for adjudication have for the most part been of little moment from the standpoint of international politics. States are reluctant to risk having their vital interests affected by judicial proceedings in which their bargaining power cannot be brought to bear on the outcome and which afford little room for accommodation and compromise.

Of somewhat greater political consequence have been certain questions submitted to the Court for advisory opinions. Potentially the most important advisory opinion has been that rendered in 1962 in the *Expenses* case. Yet, despite its formal acceptance by the General Assembly, the actual significance of the case fell far short of expectations as a result of the failure of the General Assembly to compel two powerful members to pay their share of the expenses of the United Nations peace-keeping operations in the Middle East and in the Congo. The last advisory opinion—that given in June 1971 at the request of the Security Council on the legal consequences for states of the continued presence of South Africa in Namibia (South West Africa)—is so recent that it would be premature to assess its political significance.

In order to appraise the true significance of the advisory function of the Court in the contemporary world political process and to understand the reasons for the infrequency of resort to this function, it is necessary to inquire into the antecedents and consequences of each decision of an international organ to request or not to request an advisory opinion. This is the task that Dr. Pomerance performs superbly well in this volume. Her analysis throws much needed light on the attitudes of states as members of international organizations toward the international judicial process, their motivations in deciding to resort or not to resort to the advisory function, and the role played by advisory opinions in their subsequent actions. She discloses considerable differences in the significance of the advisory function between the League of Nations era and that of the United Nations. Her admirably thorough, skillful, and lucid analysis of the advisory function as actually performed by the International Court of Justice, as well as by its predecessor, is an outstanding contribution to the study of the role of law and judicial process in the world community.

OLIVER J. LISSITZYN

ACKNOWLEDGMENTS

Various scholars were kind enough to read and comment upon this study and I wish to record my profound gratitude to each of them. They are Leland M. Goodrich, Oliver J. Lissitzyn, Louis Henkin, Jacob W. Landynski, Shabtai Rosenne, Julius Stone, the late Francis Deák, and the late Wolfgang Friedmann. Their comments saved me from many an error of omission and commission, and, in general, enhanced this study greatly. I am obliged to single out Professor Oliver J. Lissitzyn, not only for his unstinting help and encouragement over the years, but also for his kind consent to contribute a foreword to this volume.

I am deeply grateful to Columbia University, the Social Science Faculty of The Hebrew University of Jerusalem, and the Nechama Robinson Fund of the Hebrew University for generous financial assistance which enabled me to undertake the necessary research. Professor Saul Friedlander and Dr. Elisheva Yaron were most instrumental in arranging for special grants toward the completion of this work and I thank them warmly.

In the course of my research, I had occasion to make extensive use of the facilities of the International Law Library at Columbia University, and I wish to record my appreciation to librarians Mr. Tom Popovich, Mr. Lee, and Mrs. Maria Sanchez, for their cheerful and gracious help.

In the preparation of this manuscript, I was extremely fortunate to have benefited from the services of an unusually alert and expert typist, Mrs. Maryann Barrett. To her and to Mrs. Frummie Geldzahler Cohen and Mrs. Rozzy Pomerantz—both mainstays during some of the most trying periods in the preparation of this volume—go my sincerest thanks.

Mr. Kenneth Arnold and Miss Penny James of The Johns Hopkins University Press were more than considerate and helpful in bringing this book to production, and I warmly thank each of them.

Finally, my deepest debt of gratitude is undoubtedly due to my husband, Shlomo, but for whom this volume would never have seen the light of print.

The usual disclaimer, though by now perhaps trite, is still necessary. Despite the many helpful comments made on this study by others, I alone am responsible for the views expressed herein.

The Hebrew University of Jerusalem   MICHLA POMERANCE

LIST OF
ABBREVIATIONS

a.i.	agenda item
AJIL	*American Journal of International Law*
BYIL	*British Year Book of International Law*
Documents on Adoption of PCIJ Statute	*Documents concerning the Action Taken by the Council of the League of Nations under Article 14 of the Covenant and the Adoption by the Assembly of the Statute of the Permanent Court*, LN Doc. V.Legal.1920, vol. 3
ECOSOCOR	Economic and Social Council, *Official Records*
FAO	Food and Agricultural Organization
GA	General Assembly
GAOR	General Assembly, *Official Records*
GAOR (VIII), 5th Ctte., 425th Mtg.	General Assembly, *Official Records*, 8th Session, 5th Committee, 425th Meeting
Goodrich and Hambro, *Charter*	Leland M. Goodrich and Edvard Hambro, *Charter of the United Nations: Commentary and Documents*, 2nd rev. ed. (Boston: World Peace Foundation, 1949)
Hudson, *Permanent Court*	Manley O. Hudson, *The Permanent Court of International Justice, 1920–1942* (New York: Macmillan, 1943)
IAEA	International Atomic Energy Agency
IBRD	International Bank for Reconstruction and Development
ICAO	International Civil Aviation Organization
ICJ	International Court of Justice
ICJ Pleadings	International Court of Justice: *Pleadings, Oral Arguments, and Documents*
ICJ Reports	International Court of Justice: *Reports of Judgments, Advisory Opinions, and Orders*

ICLQ	*International and Comparative Law Quarterly*
IDA	International Development Association
IFC	International Finance Corporation
ILC	International Law Commission
ILO	International Labor Organization
IMCO	Intergovernmental Maritime Consultative Organization
IMF	International Monetary Fund
IO	*International Organization*
ITU	International Telecommunication Union
Lauterpacht, *International Court*	Sir Hersch Lauterpacht, *The Development of International Law by the International Court* (London: Stevens, 1958)
Lissitzyn, *International Court*	Oliver J. Lissitzyn, *The International Court of Justice: Its Role in the Maintenance of International Peace and Security* (New York: Carnegie Endowment for International Peace, 1951)
LN	League of Nations
LNOJ	League of Nations, *Official Journal*
LNTS	League of Nations, *Treaty Series*
Miller, *Covenant*	David Hunter Miller, *The Drafting of the Covenant*, 2 vols. (New York: Putnam, 1928)
Minutes of the 1926 Conf. of Signatories	*Minutes of the Conference of States Signatories of the Protocol of Signature of the Permanent Court of International Justice, 1–23 September 1926*, LN Doc. V.Legal.1926.V.26
Minutes of the 1929 Conf. of Signatories	*Minutes of the Conference regarding the Revision of the Statute of the Permanent Court of International Justice and the Accession of the United States of America to the Protocol of Signature of that Statute, 4–12 September 1929*, LN Doc. C.514.M.173.1929.V
Minutes of the 1929 Ctte. of Jurists	Committee of Jurists on the Statute of the Permanent Court of International Justice, *Minutes of the Session Held at Geneva, 11–19 March 1929*, LN Doc. C.166.M.66.1929.V
OR	Official Records
Pcdgs., 1920 Adv. Ctte. of Jurists	Advisory Committee of Jurists, *Procés-Verbaux of the Proceedings of the Committee*, LN Doc. V.Legal.1920, vol. 2
PCIJ	Permanent Court of International Justice
PCIJ, Ser. A	Permanent Court of International Justice, *Publications*, Series A: *Judgments and Orders*, Nos. 1–24 (1922–30)
_____, Ser. B	_____, Series B: *Advisory Opinions*, Nos. 1–18 (1922–30)

_____, Ser. A/B	_____, Series A/B: *Judgments, Orders, and Advisory Opinions*, Nos. 40–80 (1931–40)
_____, Ser. C	_____, Series C: *Acts and Documents relating to Judgments and Advisory Opinions*, Nos. 1–19 (1922–30); Nos. 52–87 (1931–39)
_____, Ser. D	_____, Series D: *Acts and Documents concerning the Organization of the Court*, Nos. 1–6 (1922–40)
_____, Ser. E	_____, Series E: *Annual Reports*, Nos. 1–15 (1925–39)
PMC	Permanent Mandates Commission
RC	Académie de Droit International, *Recueil des Cours*
Rosenne, *Law and Practice*	Shabtai Rosenne, *The Law and Practice of the International Court*, 2 vols. (Leiden: Sijthoff, 1965)
SC	Security Council
SCOR	Security Council, *Official Records*
SC Repertoire	*Repertoire of the Practice of the Security Council, 1946–1951* (1954); Supp. No. 1, 1952–1955 (1958); Supp. No. 2, 1956–1958 (1959); Supp. No. 3, 1959–1963 (1965); Supp. No. 4, 1964–1965 (1968); Supp. No. 5, 1966–1968 (1971)
TCOR	Trusteeship Council, *Official Records*
UNCIO Documents	*Documents of the United Nations Conference on International Organization, San Francisco, 1945*, 16 vols. (New York and London: United Nations Information Organizations, 1945–46)
UNESCO	United Nations Educational, Scientific, and Cultural Organization
UN Repertory	*Repertory of Practice of United Nations Organs*, 6 vols. (1955); Supp. No. 1, 2 vols. (1958); Supp. No. 2, 3 vols. (1963); Supp. No. 3, 2 vols. (1971)
UPU	Universal Postal Union
Verzijl, *World Court*	J. H. W. Verzijl, *The Jurisprudence of the World Court: A Case by Case Commentary*, 2 vols. (Leiden: Sijthoff, 1965)
WHO	World Health Organization
WMO	World Meteorological Organization

INTRODUCTION

As part of the elaborate peace-keeping scheme designed at Versailles in 1919, provision was made for the establishment of a Permanent Court of International Justice (PCIJ), whose primary task would be to settle "legal" disputes brought before it directly by states. Side by side with its contentious jurisdiction, the Court was to have the secondary function of rendering advisory opinions upon the request of the Council or Assembly of the League of Nations.

In practice, the advisory jurisdiction proved to be of far greater utility than originally anticipated. The advisory avenue to the Court frequently served as an alternative to the contentious, and a measure of interchangeability developed between the two jurisdictions. Moreover, in its advisory capacity, the Court elucidated problems facing not only the League Council (the League Assembly never exercised its right to request advisory opinions) but also other international bodies, especially the International Labor Organization (ILO).

When, in 1945, a new structure for world order was erected on the rubble of the old, a new Court, the International Court of Justice (ICJ) was established as well. The new Court would have an organic relationship to the general world organization which its predecessor never formally possessed. In most other respects, however, it was to be the same Court, functioning with an almost identical Statute. The two types of jurisdiction—the contentious and the advisory—were maintained in their former outlines. But, in the light of the League experience with the advisory jurisdiction, the decision was taken to extend direct access to that jurisdiction to a wider circle of organs and agencies.

If the decision by the draftsmen at San Francisco to retain, and even broaden, the advisory function of the Court was premised on the expectation that the League experience with advisory opinions would be duplicated and expanded, this expectation has been largely disappointed. For the advisory jurisdiction has been employed far differently and far less extensively in the UN period than in the League period. Indeed, in the period between 1962 and 1970, it was not employed at all.

The present study seeks to explore and analyze the elements of similarity and difference in the use of the advisory function in the two periods. In contrast to most other studies of the advisory jurisdiction, which have focused on that jurisdiction from the perspective of the Court, the primary vantage point of the present study is that of the organization. The advisory function is herein viewed as an instrument available to the political organs for the purpose of solving problems that come before them for settlement. Whether the instrument will be used at all and how it will be used are chiefly matters for decision by the political organs.

Once the advisory function is viewed in this manner, the contextual elements surrounding each advisory opinion assume vital importance. Both the pre-request and post-opinion phases are central in this regard: the former, for the light it sheds on the considerations that prompted the request and on the hopes pinned upon recourse to the Court; the latter, for an appreciation of the reception and practical effects of the Court's pronouncement.

Nor is it enough to focus solely upon the decisions to grant a role to the Court in its advisory capacity. It is equally important to examine the instances in which the Court was deliberately *denied* a role—the *missed* opportunities for recourse to the Court, the "stillborn," rather than the actual, requests. An examination of this kind serves to highlight the self-imposed restrictions placed by the relevant organs on their employment of the advisory jurisdiction and, in so doing, helps to explain the failure to use the Court's advisory function more extensively.

Since the study's perspective is "organizational," the substance of individual advisory opinions is not discussed except as required for an elucidation of the organization's attitudes and actions.[1] Nevertheless, it was deemed necessary to deal, in an over-all way, with the Court's own view of its advisory function. The manner in which the Court has regarded and exercised its advisory jurisdiction creates expectations for the future, and thus has significant implications for organs contemplating requests for advisory opinions.

As the decade of the 1970s was ushered in, a sense of crisis regarding the future of the Court was evident both within the UN[2] and among professional

[1] Comprehensive bibliographies on the cases are to be found in the yearbooks of the two Courts, in the bibliographies of the ICJ (issued as separate fascicles since 1965), and in J. Douma, *Bibliography on the International Court, including the Permanent Court, 1918-1964* (Leiden: Sijthoff, 1966).

[2] On the initiative of the United States and eleven other states, debate was begun during the twenty-fifth Assembly session on the item "Review of the Role of the

groups dedicated to the enshrinement of the rule of law in world affairs.[3] (By that time the "out of business" sign on the Court's advisory "door" had been tacked onto the contentious "door" as well.)[4] True, the Security Council's request of July 1970 for an advisory opinion on the question of Namibia (South West Africa) had temporarily redeemed the Court from the state of "august indolence"[5] to which it had involuntarily been confined; but this fact did little to mitigate the prevailing sense of crisis. In one respect, the very disenchantment with the present role of the Court produced some encouraging developments. Studies to determine "ways and means" to improve the situation were initiated; and, as one distinguished former judge has noted, this development was certainly preferable to the "indifference and neglect" from which the Court suffered during the preceding decade.[6] At least the Court's ills were no longer to be dismissed as incurable, and an active search for remedies was launched. Clearly, however, the prospective cures will have to be sought in awareness of the causes of the past malaise. It is hoped that the present study may make a modest contribution to such awareness in relation to the Court's advisory function. Perhaps the experience of the past—in both the League and UN eras—can help to throw light on the factors responsible for the atrophy of the Court's advisory role and the conditions necessary for a revival—more important, for a constructive revival—of that role.

International Court of Justice" (UN Doc. A/8042 and Add. 1 and 2). See the subsequent General Assembly discussions in the 25th Sess. (on a.i. 96) and in the 26th Sess. (on a.i. 90); see esp. the debates in the 6th Ctte., Mtgs. 1210-18, 29 October-5 November 1970, and Mtgs. 1224-30, 12-18 November 1970. See also GA Resolutions 2723 (XXV), 15 December 1970, and 2818, 15 December 1971, as well as the report of the Secretary-General on the role of the Court, UN Doc. A/8382 and Add. 1-4.

It should be noted that, for its part, the Court, in 1967, set out to revise its rules of procedure—a task it completed in May 1972.

[3] The American Society of International Law, e.g., established a panel on "The Future of the International Court of Justice."

[4] From the time that the judgment in the *Barcelona Traction* case (Second Phase) was delivered on 5 February 1970 until the Indian application against Pakistan was filed in Court on 30 August 1971, the Court had no contentious cases on its docket.

[5] The term is borrowed from Inis L. Claude, Jr., "States and the World Court: The Politics of Neglect," *Virginia Journal of International Law*, 11 (1971): 344.

[6] Philip C. Jessup, "The International Court of Justice Revisited," *ibid.*, p. 309.

I
PROVISIONS GOVERNING THE COURT'S ADVISORY JURISDICTION

The advisory jurisdiction of the Permanent Court of International Justice was a controversial innovation in international practice introduced by Article 14 of the Covenant of the League of Nations. Further elaboration of that jurisdiction was provided by the original Rules of Court, the successive revisions of the Rules, and the amended Statute of the Court.

Creation of the new Court, the International Court of Justice, was attended by few changes in the pre-established pattern of advisory jurisdiction. To the extent that modifications were made, these were in the direction of broadening the availability of the Court's advisory function.

For an appreciation of the legal framework within which the advisory function of each Court operated, as well as the conceptions surrounding the Court's advisory jurisdiction at each stage, it is necessary to examine the history of the governing provisions in the League and UN periods, respectively.[1]

THE LEAGUE PERIOD: THE PCIJ

Article 14 of the Covenant

As finally drafted, the third sentence of Article 14 of the League Covenant provided: "The Court may also give an advisory opinion upon any dispute or question referred to it by the Council or by the Assembly." The genesis of this provision offers some indication of the intentions of its framers.

---

[1] For further discussion of the manner in which the Court interpreted and applied some of the relevant provisions, see Chapter V.

The numeration of the ICJ Rules employed in this study follows that of the 1946 Rules. Revised Rules of Court were adopted in May 1972 and entered into force in September 1972. In regard to advisory jurisdiction, it may be noted, no significant changes of substance were effected by the revision.

Four early drafts of the Covenant would have permitted reference to the Court of questions submitted by one or more organs of the League. In chronological order, these drafts were: the draft of the French Ministerial Commission of 8 June 1918;[2] the draft of Colonel House of 16 July 1918;[3] the British draft convention of 20 January 1919;[4] and the Italian draft of 3 February 1919.[5] None of the four drafts, however, employed the term "advisory opinion." In fact, as will be seen presently, that term was not introduced until the very end of the drafting process. It was the British draft which foreshadowed most closely the final provision adopted, particularly by its emphasis on the *advisory* nature of the proposed reference. The Italian scheme clearly envisaged reference by the Council as an alternative method of invoking the Court's *compulsory* jurisdiction, while the drafts of the French Ministerial Commission and of Colonel House gave no indication whatever as to the binding force of the contemplated judicial pronouncement. The French and House drafts were equally vague as to the types of questions to be referred. In the British and Italian schemes, the questions were clearly related to disputes brought before the League for pacific settlement. Under the British plan, the dispute as a whole or "any particular question involved in the dispute" might be referred. The Italian draft provided for submission of a dispute brought before the Council by application of one of the parties and deemed by the Council as more suitable for judicial than political determination.

[2]The relevant provision read: "The International Tribunal shall pronounce on all questions submitted to it, either by the International Body or by a State having any dispute with another." Miller, *Covenant*, 2: 239.

[3]"The Delegates may at their discretion submit to the Court such other questions as may seem to them advisable." *Ibid.*, p. 8.

[4]"Where the Conference or the Council finds that *the dispute* can with advantage be submitted to a court of international law, *or that any particular question involved in the dispute* can with advantage be referred to a court of international law, it may submit the dispute or the particular question accordingly, and may formulate the questions for decision, and may give such directions as to procedure as it may think desirable. *In such case, the decision of the Court shall have no force or effect unless it is confirmed by the Report of the Conference or Council.*" *Ibid.*, p. 111; italics added.

[5]Article 14 of this draft scheme read: "If the dispute has been submitted to the Council by one only of the parties, and the other has either not approached it on the matter or considers that the dispute should be decided by a legal judgment, the Council shall examine the nature of the question, and if, in its opinion, either by reason of its intrinsic character or of the existence of previous agreements which there is no reason to set aside, the matter is one which should properly be solved according to the principles of international law rather than on grounds of equity or political expediency, it shall refer the question to the Court of International Justice." Article 22 provided that "the Court of International Justice shall hear: (a) All cases submitted to it by formal compromise between the parties to the dispute. (b) Cases referred to it by the Council and brought forward by one of the parties only, as laid down in Article 14; in such cases compromise shall not be necessary." *Ibid.*, pp. 250, 252.

Although the seeds of the Court's advisory function were already planted in these early drafts—and especially in the British draft—the idea very nearly fell by the wayside. It did not appear in any of the early working drafts of the League Commission. Only on 18 March 1919 did the idea re-emerge in the form of a Wilson-Cecil proposal to add to the text then under consideration[6] the words "and also any issue referred to it by the Executive Council or Body of Delegates."[7] It was this provision which, after a series of drafting changes, formed the basis of the Court's advisory jurisdiction.

The new proposal, unlike the earlier British one, did not specify that the Court's pronouncement would differ, in any way, from an actual judgment. This omission led Miller to object:

> This goes the whole length of permitting the Executive Council or the Body of Delegates to compel arbitration. . . . [C]ompulsory arbitration [would] depend solely upon the vote of the Executive Council, a vote from which the parties to the dispute would be presumably excluded.[8]

[6]"The Executive Council shall formulate plans for the establishment of a Permanent Court of International Justice and this Court shall, when established, be competent to hear and determine any matter which the parties recognize as suitable for submission to it for arbitration under the foregoing Article." *Ibid.*, p. 311.

[7]*Ibid.*, p. 585.

[8]*Ibid.*, 1: 290. A rather interesting suggestion intended precisely to establish the sort of compulsory arbitration Miller objected to and to make the Permanent Court the final arbiter of the League Covenant was raised by M. Larnaude, the French delegate, at the League Commission's meeting of 24 March 1919. The Court's jurisdiction would have extended to: "(a) any matter which is submitted to it by the Body of Delegates or the Executive Council, (b) any matter arising out of the interpretation of the Covenant establishing the League, (c) any dispute which, with the consent of the Court and the Executive Council, any of the parties may wish to have submitted to it." *Ibid.*, 2: 353. (This proposal followed closely the recommendation of an unofficial Inter-Allied League of Nations Conference held in London 11–13 March 1919. See Hudson, *Permanent Court*, p. 99, n. 26; and Clasina A. Kluyver, *Documents on the League of Nations* [Leiden: Sijthoff, 1920], p. 309.)

The only part of Larnaude's suggestion to be favored by the Commission was the first paragraph; this, along with the earlier Wilson-Cecil proposal, which it closely resembled, was sent to the drafting committee. Paragraph (b), which would have explicitly conferred Covenant-interpretation powers on the Court, was not adopted. The analogy of the United States Supreme Court, invoked by M. Larnaude, was considered misplaced. The opinion of Mr. Orlando, supported by Lord Cecil, was that "this definition of functions would be dangerous," and that questions of interpretation might best be left to the Covenant-applying organs. Paragraph (c) was adopted in an emasculated form, so as to require the explicit consent of both parties. Miller, *Covenant*, 2: 348–49. (The foregoing account of the fate of Larnaude's suggestion corresponds with that recorded in the English minutes, to whose accuracy Miller attests. The French minutes record that the amendment was withdrawn entirely. *Ibid.*, p. 516, and 1: 329–30.)

Rejection of paragraph (b) has considerable historical significance. In the League period, it left open the question whether the Court was, indeed, competent to interpret the Covenant. The issue was discussed in connection with several "stillborn" requests. (See the discussion of the Corfu aftermath, the Lithuanian-Polish dispute, and the nature

To meet this objection, the Hurst-Miller draft of 31 March 1919 revised the earlier provision to read: "and also to *advise upon* any legal questions referred to it by the Council or by the Body of Delegates."[9]

A later British proposal of 1 April 1919 reformulated the clause as follows: "and also to advise upon any dispute or question referred to it by the Council or by the Body of Delegates."[10] The specification "any dispute or question," which was later incorporated in Article 14, would seem to hark back to the earlier British draft convention, which differentiated between "the dispute" and "any particular question involved in the dispute." The substitution of "any dispute or question" for "any legal questions" is considered by Miller to have improved the text, by avoiding a construction that would have made the Court "the legal adviser of the Council and of the Assembly, a duty which its function of rendering advisory opinions does not involve."[11]

From the drafting committee came the final text, wherein the term "advisory opinion" was introduced and the power to give advisory opinions was stated in a separate sentence.[12] The significance of these changes was, according to Miller, twofold: the term "advisory opinion" underscored the *judicial* nature of the proposed function; at the same time, incorporation of advisory jurisdiction in a separate sentence indicated that that jurisdiction was to be distinct from the Court's *primary* jurisdiction (thus, presumably, allaying fears that compulsory adjudication was being introduced by circuitous means).[13]

The conclusions which may be drawn from this history of the framing of Article 14 of the Covenant are as follows.

The advisory jurisdiction was intended to be a secondary function of the Court, distinguishable in two principal ways from its primary function of

---

of the vote required for requests in Chapter IV. Specific allusions to the fate of Larnaude's amendment were made by the French representative in the Lithuanian-Polish issue [LNOJ, 1923, p. 586].) While the PCIJ was never asked to interpret the Covenant in the abstract, it had occasion, several times, to interpret Covenant provisions in the course of determining concrete issues (e.g., in the *Eastern Carelia* and *Mosul* cases).

The controversy aroused by rejection of the Larnaude suggestion foreshadowed the much more heated debate in the early UN period which resulted, in part, from rejection of a similar proposal to give the ICJ jurisdiction to interpret the UN Charter. A number of UN requests called for interpretation of Charter provisions in the abstract. See Chapters III and V.

[9] Miller, *Covenant*, 2: 662. Although the term "advisory opinion" still was not used, Miller's memorandum on this revision explains: "This article has been rewritten in order to exclude any idea of compulsory arbitration and at the same time permit the Court . . . to give advisory opinions." *Ibid.*, 1: 393.

[10] *Ibid.*, 2: 670.

[11] *Ibid.*, 1: 391–92.

[12] *Ibid.*, 2: 676.

[13] *Ibid.*, 1: 406. See also the British delegation's comment on the final draft. *Ibid.*, p. 416.

deciding disputes brought directly by states: first, the initiative of activating the Court's advisory jurisdiction was to appertain exclusively to the two political organs of the League;[14] second, the Court's advisory opinions were to be precisely that—advisory and nonbinding pronouncements. The purpose of the advisory jurisdiction was to aid the League in the peaceful settlement of disputes.[15] As for the distinction between "disputes" and "questions"—a matter which assumed significance later on—it appears not to have been discussed at all. However, the evidence in the preparatory work points to the conclusion that the distinction was in the nature of a "whole-part" distinction—namely, the dispute as a whole, as against a particular question related to the dispute.[16]

To what extent was the analogy of advisory opinions in national courts uppermost in the minds of the draftsmen of the Covenant? This is a difficult question to answer. Hudson concludes that "in view of the history of Article 14 . . . it cannot be said that the provision . . . was due to the experience of national courts,"[17] but that "this experience may have been in the minds of the draftsmen."[18] It is generally acknowledged that, during the League period, the advisory function, *as it developed in practice*, contrasted markedly with the advisory function of most national courts.[19] However, some of the contrasts had already been adumbrated at the drafting stage. Thus, "national" opinions are usually sought by the executive or legislative branch with reference to *proposed* administrative or legislative measures and in the absence of specific facts or actual litigants.[20] But, *at the very outset*, the purpose of the Permanent Court's advisory function was to aid the League in the settlement of disputes that had already arisen. Hence, the involvement of specific sets of facts and of actual parties—not merely vague opposing in-

---

[14] Both organs were probably equal in this respect. See Hudson, *Permanent Court*, p. 488. For the view that certain categories of requests might be made only by the Assembly, see the dissenting opinion of Judge Anzilotti in the case of *Danzig and the ILO*, PCIJ, Ser. B, No. 18, p. 20; and the remarks of M. Osusky (Czechoslovakia), Minutes of the 1926 Conf. of Signatories, p. 27.

[15] See, especially, the explanatory note of the British delegation in Miller, *Covenant*, 1: 416.

[16] Subsequently, there was a tendency to construe the term "question" to mean a question *unrelated* to any existing dispute. See, in particular, the discussion of the drafting of the original PCIJ Statute and of the 1936 Rules of Court below.

[17] *Permanent Court*, p. 485. See also *ibid.*, pp. 107–8, where Hudson cites as evidence the very belated introduction of the term "advisory opinion" in the drafting process and the absence of any extended consideration of the term.

[18] *Ibid.*, p. 485.

[19] On this point, see Leland M. Goodrich, "The Nature of the Advisory Opinions of the Permanent Court of International Justice," *AJIL*, 32 (1938): 738–58.

[20] On the advisory function of national courts, see Felix Frankfurter, "Advisory Opinions," *Encyclopedia of the Social Sciences*, 1: 475–78; Goodrich, *op. cit.*, pp. 754–58; Manley O. Hudson, "Advisory Opinions of National and International Courts," *Harvard Law Review*, 37 (1924): 970–1001.

terests—was to be expected. And a Court seeking to give a firmly grounded opinion might, understandably, desire to hear the arguments of the real "parties" in the case; it might wish to go beyond a lawyer-client relationship between itself and the requesting organ and to adjudicate the real interests in conflict. Seen in this light, the subsequent progressive assimilation of advisory to contentious procedure appears as a natural, though, admittedly, not inevitable, evolution from the germinal ideas already contained in Article 14. It was for later draftsmen to bring the germinal ideas to full fruition, however.

The Original PCIJ Statute

Curiously enough, the original Statute contained no express provisions concerning advisory jurisdiction.[21] In the attempt to put flesh on the skeleton provision in Article 14 of the Covenant, profound hesitations and uncertainties regarding the advisory jurisdiction, particularly its effect on the Court's primary—contentious—jurisdiction and on the Court's judicial character, were laid bare. These uncertainties were reflected in the draft article on advisory opinions submitted by the 1920 Advisory Committee of Jurists and in the decision of the first Assembly of the League of Nations to delete that article altogether.

The text of the proposed article was as follows:

> The Court shall give an advisory opinion upon any question or dispute of an international nature referred to it by the Council or Assembly.
> When the Court shall give an opinion on a question of an international nature which does not refer to any dispute that may have arisen, it shall appoint a special Commission of from three to five members.
> When it shall give an opinion upon a question which forms the subject of an existing dispute, it shall do so under the same conditions as if the case had been actually submitted to it for decision.[22]

Thus, the method proffered by the Committee of Jurists for reconciling the advisory function with the Court's judicial nature contemplated the establishment of two distinct advisory procedures, depending upon whether the question posed "forms the subject of an existing dispute" or "does not refer to any dispute that may have arisen."[23] Only in the first case was the Court qua

---

[21] This omission was not made good until 1936, when the amended statute came into force. On the legal basis of the Court's advisory jurisdiction prior to 1936, see n. 36 below.

[22] Pcdgs., 1920 Adv. Ctte. of Jurists, p. 732.

[23] The two categories would appear to be based on the "dispute-question" differentiation of Article 14 of the Covenant. But, while in Article 14 the distinction was in the nature of a "whole-part" distinction (see above), the scheme of the draft article was somewhat ambiguous. The "dispute" category was indeed interpreted to mean the dispute *in its entirety*, in the form in which it was brought before the Council. (The

Court to be implicated; in the second case, the Court would, in effect, constitute itself into a committee of jurists. Only in the first case, too, was advisory procedure to be assimilated to contentious procedure, but in such case the assimilation was to be complete.[24] Further, in the first case, the resultant opinion, while technically only advisory, would have for the Court a precedential value equal to that of a judgment and for the parties "the moral force attaching to all its [the Court's] decisions."[25] In the second case, however, the opinion would in no way bind the Court for the future,[26] and its non-binding nature for the requesting organ and for states would be obvious. In brief, in accordance with the scheme envisaged in the draft article, the Court

---

Council, it was explained, might decide "to re-establish the true character of the case and send it to the Court." [Report of the Advisory Committee of Jurists, *ibid.*, p. 731.]) However, the "question" in the second category was not a question related to only part of the dispute (the obvious counterpart of the first category) but was rather "a question . . . which *does not refer* to any dispute." Thus, the differentiation in the draft scheme was neither clearly a "whole-part" nor a "dispute–non-dispute" one; it was rather an amalgamation (or, perhaps, confusion) of both. In addition, the assumption was made at the time that, while a dispute would be "concrete," a question would be "abstract" and "general." But a question might easily *refer* to a dispute, while constituting merely *one aspect* of the dispute brought before the Council or the Assembly. Such a question might be quite "concrete" (though, perhaps, more "abstract" and generalized than the entire dispute). In fact, most questions submitted to arbitration or judicial settlement may be viewed as aspects of larger disputes. There would seem to be little logic in adopting a procedure on such questions different from that adopted in relation to larger disputes. The distinction between a question relating to an existing dispute and one not so relating (the criterion employed in the 1927 revision of Article 71 of the Rules of Court) is, perhaps, more justified (though even this distinction is fraught with theoretical and practical difficulties). That this was *not* the distinction contemplated by the Advisory Committee of Jurists is borne out by the records of the drafting of the Statute and attested to by the Registrar of the Court in his report of June 1933 reviewing the history of the various provisions of the Rules. The Registrar concluded that, "when the Advisory Committee of Jurists suggested . . . that advisory opinions on existing disputes should be considered as forming a special category, it used the expression 'existing dispute' in a much narrower sense than that which the expression has acquired since its insertion in Article 71, in 1927: in reality, the Committee had only in mind disputes which, though they had in fact been submitted to the Council, 'ought to have' been settled by judicial procedure. Accordingly, the Committee did not contemplate advisory opinions on isolated aspects of disputes pending before the Council." PCIJ, Ser. D, No. 2 (3rd Add.), p. 838.

[24] The appointment of judges *ad hoc* was definitely envisaged. Pcdgs., 1920 Adv. Ctte. of Jurists, p. 731.

[25] *Ibid.* Cf. remarks of M. de Lapradelle, *ibid.*, p. 225, who concluded that Article 14 allowed "the possibility of suing a State before the Court, whether it were willing or not," for, despite the theoretical differences between an advisory opinion and a judgment, "in practice both would have the same force." But see the objections of M. Ricci-Busatti, *ibid.*, p. 226, and later Italian amendments to the draft scheme based on these objections. Documents on Adoption of PCIJ Statute, pp. 29–30.

[26] Technically, the Court is not bound even by its judgments, there being no rule of stare decisis. Nevertheless, a court is normally reluctant to overrule outright its own previous pronouncements.

would have possessed three kinds of jurisdiction: contentious, quasi-contentious advisory, and truly advisory.

The motivation behind this proposal is illuminated by the following excerpts from the Report of the Advisory Committee of Jurists:

> If an advisory opinion is to be given which does not refer to any actually existing dispute, as the question may subsequently be brought before the Court in its judicial capacity . . . the Court must be so constituted that the opinion given in the abstract . . . does not restrict the freedom of its decision, should the question come before it later . . . as a concrete case and not merely in the abstract. . . .
>
> It may, however, happen that the dispute referred to the Court . . . is of the nature of an actual case, since it concerns a dispute which actually exists. This dispute has not been submitted by the parties to arbitration . . . but, nevertheless, it is of such a nature that the best method of solving it is, undoubtedly, by an international judicial procedure. It may even happen that the case in question is of a legal nature and should therefore be submitted to arbitration but that the parties mutually agree to transfer it from the judicial procedure which ought normally to be applied to it, to a procedure of conciliation which, in addition to its greater adaptability, offers to the parties the advantage of requiring a unanimous decision in the Council or a decision by the majority in the Assembly . . . instead of a decision by the majority in the Court. . . . To avoid the possibility of the latter, the parties may be tempted to alter the real character of their dispute, by mutual agreement. Under such circumstances the Council should be able to re-establish the true character of the case and send it to the Court. Of course the Court can only take judicial cognisance of a case brought by the contesting parties, and not by the Council or Assembly; but if the parties have decided to bring it before the Council or Assembly, they must not be surprised if the Council or Assembly refer the case to the Court.[27] The advisory opinion given by the Court, under such circumstances, would not have the force of a sentence binding upon the two parties. But the Court's decision would nevertheless have the moral force attaching to all its decisions; and if the Council or Assembly adopt it, it would have the same wholesome effect on public opinion. Whenever therefore, an existing dispute is in question, the Court must take its decision in the same manner as if an action had actually been brought before it.[28]

---

[27]The foregoing reasoning would seem to be based on the rather simplistic notion that disputes come already tagged "political" or "legal," and, if the Council or Assembly recognizes the "mislabeling" involved, it should be able to "re-establish the true character of the case and send it to the Court," the obvious addressee on the "label." For a discussion of political and legal questions, see pp. 296–303 below.

Another questionable assumption made here is that requests for advisory opinions would not require the consent of the parties. In fact, the question of the vote required for requests remained controversial throughout the League period. See pp. 213–21.

[28]Pcdgs., 1920 Adv. Ctte. of Jurists, p. 731.

There does not appear to have been much discussion in the Advisory Committee of the dual procedure or the bases for differentiating the two categories of requests.[29] When the draft article came before the subcommittee of the Assembly's Third Committee for closer scrutiny, however, doubts were expressed regarding the validity and practicability of the proposed scheme.[30] Some objected to the too full assimilation to judgments of one category of opinions; contrariwise, others opposed the apparently non-judicial character of the other category of opinions. All deemed the criteria for differentiating the two categories as "lacking in clearness and likely to give rise to practical difficulties."[31] An Italian amendment[32] to delete the third paragraph of the draft article[33] and to modify the second paragraph so as to leave the establishment of special committees for advisory cases to the discretion of the Court was adopted by the subcommittee in principle, but the final text of a substitute article was left to the Drafting Committee.[34] For its part, the Drafting Committee unanimously recommended suppression of the entire article, and this recommendation was unanimously approved by the subcommittee.[35] The latter, in its report to the parent (Third) committee, based its recommendation on the view that all opinions should be given by the same quorum of judges, that the draft scheme's proposed distinction was vague and impracticable, and that the draft had "entered into details which concerned rather the rules of procedure of the Court."[36] There was no

[29] The absence of thorough discussion of the article led M. Ricci-Busatti to abstain in the vote.

[30] Documents on Adoption of PCIJ Statute, p. 146.

[31] *Ibid.*, p. 211.

[32] *Ibid.*, pp. 40–41.

[33] The Italian objection to this paragraph was based mainly on the apparent attribution of an obligatory character to some of the Court's opinions. *Ibid.*, pp. 29–30. It is interesting to contrast the Italian attitude with the Italian draft covenant submitted at Paris (see above), in which submission of disputes by the Council was to be an alternative method of invoking the Court's compulsory jurisdiction.

[34] Documents on Adoption of PCIJ Statute, p. 146.

[35] *Ibid.*, p. 156. Proposals by Argentina to empower states to request advisory opinions (*ibid.*, p. 68) and by the International Labor Office to authorize ILO organs (*ibid.*, p. 79) were rejected by the subcommittee on the grounds that "such provisions would involve a considerable extension of the duties of the members of the Court and might lead to consequences difficult to calculate in advance." *Ibid.*, p. 211. An additional objection to the Argentine proposal was that it might result in the introduction of compulsory jurisdiction by unilateral application. *Ibid.*, p. 156.

[36] *Ibid.*, p. 211. At the time, the view was also expressed that mention of the advisory jurisdiction in the Statute was unnecessary, since, in accordance with Article 14 of the Covenant, "the Court could not refuse to give advisory opinions." *Ibid.*, p. 156. This assumes that even in the absence of an express Statute provision, the Court had both the power and the obligation to render advisory opinions. Neither point, however, is obvious. As noted by Hudson (*Permanent Court*, p. 483), Article 14 of the Covenant was not directly binding on the Court. Unlike the UN Charter and the ICJ Statute, which form one instrument, the League Covenant and the PCIJ Statute were separate instru-

further discussion of the recommendation for deletion either in the Third Committee or in Plenary.

The foregoing history of the deletion of the draft article led Hudson to conclude that "the draftsmen of the original Statute failed to appreciate the importance of the Court's advisory jurisdiction."[37] On the other hand, Judge Huber, himself a participant in the drafting of the original Statute, later attributed the deletion to lack of experience with advisory jurisdiction and the desire "not to hamper the future business of the Court by provisions the full scope of which it was impossible to foresee."[38] The two explanations are not, in fact, mutually exclusive. As noted above, the motivation behind the deletion was a rather complex one. Above all, it would appear, the uncertainty regarding the place of advisory opinions within the over-all framework of the Court's jurisdiction prompted the Statute's draftsmen to "pass the buck" to the Court, and compelled the latter to grapple with all the unresolved questions when the time came to draft the Rules of Court.

The 1922 Rules of Court

Many of the earlier uncertainties and reservations concerning the advisory function were mirrored in the Court itself during the framing of the 1922 Rules of Court. In the end, however, four articles (71-74) on advisory procedure were adopted, which had the effect of affirming the judicial character of the advisory function and of paving the way for the later, fuller assimilation of advisory to contentious procedure.

The gravest misgivings regarding the advisory function were voiced by Judge Moore.[39] The rendering of nonbinding advice, he argued, was incom-

---

ments, each with its separate set of adherents. The Court derived its powers from the Statute and not from the Covenant, except to the extent that any Covenant provision was expressly incorporated in the Statute. What, then, was the basis of the Court's advisory jurisdiction prior to 1936? According to most commentators, incorporation of Article 14 of the Covenant in the Statute by reference—whether by virtue of Article 1, Article 36(1), or the title of the Statute—provided that basis. Hudson, *Permanent Court*, pp. 406, 483-84; and Alexander P. Fachiri, *The Permanent Court of International Justice*, 2nd ed. (London: Oxford University Press, 1932), p. 78. See also the views of Judges Loder and Negulesco, PCIJ, Ser. D, No. 2, p. 502; *ibid.* (3rd Add.), pp. 679, 784. The Court, when framing its Rules in 1922, looked to Article 14 of the Covenant as the governing text and apparently entertained no doubts regarding its power to render advisory opinions. Judge Moore, however, questioned the *obligation* of the Court to render opinions, basing his view, *inter alia*, on the absence of any express Statute provision and the permissive language of Article 14 of the Covenant.

[37] *Permanent Court*, p. 212.

[38] Minutes of the 1929 Ctte. of Jurists, p. 68.

[39] PCIJ, Ser. D, No. 2, pp. 383-98, 509-13. Earlier, in the 1920 Advisory Committee of Jurists, Elihu Root had expressed opposition to the rendering of advisory opinions with reference to existing disputes. Pcdgs., 1920 Adv. Ctte. of Jurists, p. 584. The attitudes of both Moore and Root can be traced, in part, to a traditionally suspicious American attitude toward advisory opinions dating back to the United States

patible with the judicial character of *any* court and, in the case of the PCIJ, would tend to frustrate the realization of its primary function of adjudicating disputes and developing international law. While the Court undoubtedly had the *power* to render advisory opinions, there could be no question of any *obligation* to do so, particulary in view of the absence of any provision on advisory jurisdiction in the Statute and the "permissive" nature of Article 14 of the Covenant.[40] In order to discourage requests, Moore proposed omitting any reference to advisory opinions in the Rules and leaving the Court to deal with individual applications for opinions on the merits.

The Court did not accept Moore's suggestions. Neither, however, did it accept proposals which would have had the effect of sharply distinguishing the Court's advisory jurisdiction from its ordinary judicial functions. Thus, the possibility of secret requests and secret opinions was ruled out,[41] as was the possibility of opinions given by less than a full quorum of judges.[42] In accordance with the provisions actually adopted, opinions were to be given after deliberation by the full Court (Article 71); notice of the request was to be given to members of the Court, members of the League, states mentioned in the annex to the Covenant, and any international organization likely to be able to furnish information on the question (Article 73); and advisory opinions were to be published in a special collection (Article 74).

Supreme Court's refusal in 1793 to answer questions submitted by President Washington on the ground that giving the desired opinions would not be a proper exercise of the "judicial power." Frankfurter, *op. cit.*, pp. 475–78. (Several states of the Union do, however, allow advisory opinions.) Both Moore and Root subsequently modified their positions on the PCIJ's advisory function.

[40] In this respect, Judge Moore relied primarily on the English text of Article 14 ("*may* also give"), since the French text ("*Elle donnera aussi*") allows a contrary interpretation. Cf. PCIJ, Ser. D, No. 2 (3rd Add.), p. 788, however, for the conclusion that the permissive language employed in the English text related only to the power of the Council or Assembly to *request* advisory opinions and did not affect the Court's obligation to *render* such opinions.

The Court did not accept a suggestion that it specifically reserve to itself in the Rules the discretionary right not to render an opinion requested. Such a discretion was, however, considered to be implied in Article 74 as originally framed ("Any advisory opinion which *may* be given by the Court . . . shall be printed and published . . .). PCIJ, Ser. D, No. 2, p. 161. When, in 1931, Article 65 of the Rules was amended to include reference to publication of advisory opinions, separate mention in Article 74 was no longer necessary and was, therefore, deleted. This deletion automatically eliminated any allusion—even by implication—in the Rules to the Court's right not to render an opinion asked of it.

[41] See, e.g., the draft provision in *ibid.*, p. 414. Judge Anzilotti argued for allowing secret advice in the interests of world peace, but the views of Judges Moore and Finlay that secret advice would be incompatible with the Statute and would constitute a "death-blow to the Court as a judicial body" prevailed. *Ibid.*, p. 160.

[42] The Court's decision on this point was unanimous. *Ibid.*, p. 98. Some drafts had contemplated a dual procedure similar to that outlined in the 1920 draft scheme. *Ibid.*, pp. 280, 358.

The measure of assimilation to contentious procedure thus provided fell short of that envisaged for "disputes" in the draft scheme of the 1920 Advisory Committee of Jurists and that later adopted by the Court for all advisory opinions. But the steps taken were crucial in determining the character of advisory jurisdiction in the future. The "judicial" nature of the advisory function was established, and the measure of assimilation which *was* provided clearly applied to *all* advisory opinions. In no case was consultation of the Court to be equivalent to consultation of a committee of jurists. Moreover, the rules adopted were flexible enough to permit closer assimilation, should the Court find, on the basis of experience, that this was necessary or desirable.

The 1926 Revision of the Rules

By 1926, the Court had already established a well-defined advisory practice, in accordance with which many provisions of the Statute and Rules relating to contentious cases were applied by analogy to advisory cases.[43] In the 1926 revision of its Rules, the Court merely codified some of that advisory practice.

Thus, notice of the request was now to be given to the additional category of "any States entitled to appear before the Court";[44] and, besides the general notice, "a special and direct communication" was to be sent to any state "admitted to appear before the Court," or to any international organization considered "as likely to be able to furnish information on the question," as notification that the Court would be prepared to receive written statements and to hear oral statements relating to the question.[45] A State which failed to receive such a communication might "express a desire to submit a written statement, or to be heard," and the Court would decide.[46] States and organ-

[43] The important pronouncement of the Court in 1923 in the *Eastern Carelia* case (a landmark case in many respects) is notable also for the degree of assimilation to contentious proceedings which it implied. This case is discussed in more detail in subsequent chapters.

[44] From the very beginning, notice was sent to such interested states as Germany and Hungary, though they were neither members of the League nor states mentioned in the Annex to the Covenant. The Court did not view the enumeration in the original Article 73 as exhaustive. See the Registrar's answer to Poland's objection regarding the notice sent to Germany in the *German Settlers in Poland* case. PCIJ, Ser. E, No. 1, p. 263.

[45] The 1922 Rules made no mention of written and oral proceedings in advisory cases, though this was probably implied in the provision for notice in Article 73. Such proceedings were instituted by the Court from the very outset.

The practice of giving special notice to interested states was also developed early. In the *Mosul* case, the Court also applied by analogy the principle embodied in Article 63 of the Statute. In addition to the general notice, members of the League were informed that, in view of the possible bearing of the questions on the interpretation of the Covenant, the Court would be prepared to receive favorably any member's application to be allowed to furnish information. *Ibid.*, Ser. B, No. 12, pp. 7-8.

[46] This provision is analogous to Article 63 of the Statute.

izations which had presented statements were to be admitted to comment on the statements of other states or organizations, and, to this end, the Registrar was to communicate those statements to them.[47]

In adopting the limited revision of its Rules, the Court rejected, on the one hand, suggestions that it reverse its course of assimilation and establish a clearer distinction between the advisory and contentious functions,[48] and, on the other hand, the suggestion that it crystallize its previous practice more fully by enumerating the articles of the Statute and Rules which were applicable by analogy to advisory procedure.[49] The Court also stopped short of

---

In the *Acquisition of Polish Nationality* case, the Court rejected Rumania's *specific* invocation of Articles 62 and 63 of the Statute and the corresponding articles of the Rules relating to the right of intervention in contentious proceedings. While apparently considering that there was no analogous *right* to intervention in advisory cases, the Court *was* prepared, as a matter of its *discretion*, to hear the Rumanian representative under Article 73 of the Rules. *Ibid.*, Ser. E, No. 1, p. 252; see also Judge Moore's explanation of Rumania's action, *ibid.*, Ser. D, No. 2 (Add.), p. 295.

[47] This, too, followed established Court practice. Exceptionally, in the *Tunis-Morocco* case, the two governments concerned exchanged memoranda directly between themselves.

The above modifications—all introduced in Article 73—were the most significant. Article 71, as revised, required that the opinion mention the number of judges constituting the majority. The new Article 74 applied Article 58 of the Statute by analogy, substituting notice to the League's Secretary-General and to the representatives of states and organizations immediately concerned for notice to agents of the parties in contentious cases.

[48] This course was most forcefully urged by Judge Altamira. In a 1923 proposal, he argued the need for re-establishing the distinctive nature of the advisory function and reverting to the purposes which, in his view, that function was originally intended to serve—namely, to allow private consultations between the League organs and the Court. To this end, it was necessary to eliminate public hearings, the communication of documents to interested states (save in exceptional cases), and the public announcement of the opinion (unless the requesting organ so desired). *Ibid.*, pp. 293-94. See also Altamira's objections to the 1926 Rules, *ibid.*, pp. 286-88; and cf. his objections to the 1936 Rules, *ibid.* (3rd Add.), p. 925. Although the 1923 proposal was withdrawn (*ibid.* [Add.], p. 184) and was never officially discussed, the Court implicitly repudiated Altamira's view of the advisory function. Apparently, the Court shared the views of Judge Moore, who credited the Court's advisory practice with having inspired confidence in the Court and having enhanced its prestige (as evidenced by the abundance of the Court's advisory business). *Ibid.*, pp. 294-96. See also the statement of Judge Anzilotti to the effect that the nature of the advisory function, and, in particular, whether or not the function was to be exercised in secret, were no longer open questions. *Ibid.*, pp. 288-89.

A proposal which would have reversed some of the Court's advisory practice (while leaving the 1922 Rules intact) was made by Judge Yovanovitch, who recommended dispensing with oral proceedings in advisory cases. The reasoning behind this proposal, however, was different from Altamira's. *Ibid.*, pp. 290-91. Yovanovitch's suggestion was later abandoned. *Ibid.*, pp. 198-99.

[49] The suggestion was put forward by the Court's Registrar. *Ibid.*, p. 315. The aim of the proposal was to codify the Court's practice and thereby offer some guidance to interested parties. *Ibid.*, p. 226. Although the Court recognized that the enumeration did, in fact, represent a codification of past practice and that, moreover, the specified provisions would probably continue to be applied in the future, it was considered prefer-

extending its practice of assimilation to the inclusion of judges *ad hoc* in advisory cases which related to actual disputes.[50] In general, in 1926 the Court manifested satisfaction with the way it had handled its advisory function in the past and the desire to maintain a measure of freedom and flexibility in the future.

The 1927 Addition to the Rules

Although the proposal to admit judges *ad hoc* in certain advisory cases was defeated in 1926 by a substantial majority,[51] the Court reversed itself one year later by an even greater majority[52] and added the following paragraph to Article 71 of the Rules:

> On a question relating to an existing dispute between two or more States or Members of the League of Nations, Article 31 of the Statute shall apply. In case of doubt, the Court shall decide.

The Court's change of heart was probably attributable mainly to the problem presented in the *Danube Commission* case in 1927. Although the ques-

---

able to maintain for the Court the discretion it had hitherto enjoyed. It was also feared that any enumeration might give the impression that the articles excluded would be inapplicable. *Ibid.*, pp. 226–27.

[50] A proposal by President Huber would have permitted national judges in cases where the advisory opinion concerned proceedings "pending before the Council . . . or before some arbitration or conciliation tribunal, and in which States or Members of the League of Nations appear as Parties." *Ibid.*, pp. 253–54. Thus, while the proposal was similar to that put forward by the 1920 Advisory Committee of Jurists, the criterion employed in the Huber proposal was clearer. In defense of the proposal, special emphasis was placed on the compulsory character which Article 5 of the Geneva Protocol would have attributed to some of the Court's opinions. In opposition, doubts were expressed with regard to both the desirability and constitutionality of the proposed revision. Thus, e.g., some judges maintained that the proposal involved a constitutional rather than a procedural question and was, therefore, outside the Court's competence. *Ibid.*, pp. 184–94 *passim*. As noted by the Registrar (*ibid.*, pp. 188–89), in deleting the draft article on advisory opinions in 1920, the First Assembly had made the opposite assumption: that the issue of the Court's composition for advisory cases was a matter of detail to be governed by the Court's Rules.

The Huber proposal was rejected. So too was a substitute proposal to apply Article 24 (regarding the withdrawal of judges) in certain cases. *Ibid.*, pp. 193–94; see also LN, Records of the 5th Ass., Plenary, 1924, pp. 486, 488.

Another proposal rejected in 1926 would have eliminated dissenting opinions in advisory cases. Proponents and opponents of this recommendation were, it appears, equally concerned with safeguarding the authority of the Court's opinions; they merely disagreed about the effect of dissenting opinions on that authority. PCIJ, Ser. D, No. 2 (Add.), pp. 195–98. Nevertheless, had the proposal been accepted, it would undoubtedly have tended to sharpen the distinction between judgments and advisory opinions.

[51] The vote was 7 to 3, with Judges Huber, Moore, and Anzilotti alone voting in favor. *Ibid.*, p. 193.

[52] A proposal to this effect was introduced by Judge Anzilotti and was adopted overwhelmingly (with only Judges Altamira and Bustamante voting against) following a

tion of admitting judges *ad hoc* in advisory cases relating to existing disputes had arisen in several previous instances,[53] the *Danube Commission* case raised the question of equality of the parties in an acute form.[54] In that case, the problem was resolved without the necessity of taking a decision on the question of principle involved,[55] but it was felt that in the future "the solution of a matter of such farreaching importance should not . . . be left to chance."[56]

By accepting this proposal, the Court introduced a measure of assimilation to contentious procedure for advisory cases relating to existing disputes as complete as that envisaged for such cases in the 1920 draft scheme.[57] It manifested a willingness to treat the states concerned as true parties and not merely as *informateurs*. The justification for such assimilation is forcefully expressed in the following extract from the report of the specially appointed committee of the Court:

> Such prestige as the Court to-day enjoys as a judicial tribunal is largely due to the amount of its advisory business and the judicial way in which it has dealt with such business. In reality, where there are in fact contending parties, the difference between contentious cases and advisory cases is only nominal. The main difference is the way in which the case comes before the Court, and even this difference may virtually disappear. . . . So the view that advisory opinions are not binding is more theoretical than real.[58]

The Amended PCIJ Statute

The amended Statute of the Court, which came into force on 1 February 1936, contained four articles on advisory opinions (65–68), thus filling the gap left in the original Statute in 1920. In the main, the new articles, drafted by the 1929 Committee of Jurists[59] and slightly modified by the 1929 Conference of Signatories,[60] simply reproduced provisions contained in Articles

---

report on the question by a judicial committee of three (Judges Loder, Moore, and Anzilotti). *Ibid.*, Ser. E, No. 4, pp. 72–78.

[53] See *ibid.*, No. 3, pp. 223–24.

[54] Each of the three states opposing Rumania in the dispute had judges of its nationality on the bench; Rumania had none.

[55] Deputy Judge Negulesco, a Rumanian national, was summoned to sit in place of an absent regular judge. PCIJ, Ser. E, No. 4, p. 77.

[56] *Ibid.*

[57] However, as noted above, the criterion employed in 1927 was less ambiguous.

[58] *Ibid.*, p. 76.

[59] The Committee was appointed by Council resolutions of 13 and 14 December 1928 to study the question of revision of the PCIJ Statute. By a resolution of 9 March 1929, the Committee was also requested to consider the question of American accession to the Protocol of Signature.

[60] The wording of Article 68 was modified, and references to international organizations (in Articles 66 and 67) which had been deleted by the Committee of Jurists in the process of transference from Rules to Statute, were reincorporated by the Conference.

72–74 of the 1926 Rules. Article 68 alone was totally new. In its final form, it read:

> In the exercise of its advisory functions, the Court shall further be guided by the provisions of the Statute which apply in contentious cases to the extent to which it recognises them to be applicable.

Even this new article merely served to establish a firm legal basis for the Court's past practice of assimilating advisory to contentious procedure.

Undoubtedly, the principal motivation behind the proposed changes was the desire to facilitate United States accession to the Protocol of Signature. Transference from Rules to Statute would lend the relevant provisions "a permanent character," thereby allaying the fears expressed in the first part of the Senate's fifth reservation; while Article 68, by implicitly incorporating the *Eastern Carelia* principle into the Statute,[61] would go far toward quieting the fears expressed in the second part of the same reservation.[62]

---

[61] See the Registrar's report in *ibid.*, Ser. D, No. 2 (3rd Add.), p. 837. See also *ibid.*, pp. 374, 880; and the remarks of M. Fromageot at the 1929 Conference of Signatories (endorsed by the Conference), Minutes of the 1929 Conf. of Signatories, pp. 48, 79. Cf. the explanation given to the United States Senate on 1 January 1932. U.S., 72nd Cong., 1st Sess., Sen. Report No. 758, p. 9.

[62] The first part of the fifth reservation stipulated that "the Court shall not render any advisory opinion except publicly after due notice to all States adhering to the Court and to all interested States and after public hearing or opportunity for hearing given to any State concerned." U.S., 69th Cong., 1st Sess., Sen. Doc. No. 45, p. 2. No difficulty was experienced by the 1926 Conference of Signatories in accepting this part of the reservation, since all the enumerated points were held to be covered by the established practice of the Court and the 1926 Rules. Minutes of the 1926 Conf. of Signatories, pp. 19, 77.

It was the second part of the same reservation which presented the 1926 Conference (as well as the 1929 Committee of Jurists and Conference of Signatories) with the most difficulty. Its terms were as follows: "nor shall it, without the consent of the United States, entertain any request for an advisory opinion touching any dispute or question in which the United States has or claims an interest." Even here, the most important category of requests alluded to (those involving *disputes* in which the United States actually *had* an interest) was thought by the 1926 Conference to present no difficulty. The Conference contented itself with referring to the *Eastern Carelia* precedent. Minutes of the 1926 Conf. of Signatories, p. 79. However, the other three categories (requests relating to disputes in which the United States merely *claims* an interest and questions in which the United States either has or claims an interest) provided the main snag, since the controversial question of the vote required for requests was implicated. This major impediment to American accession was left to be dealt with in a special Protocol of Accession.

The new articles proposed for inclusion in the Statute in 1929 were designed to meet American objections that even the Rules of Court and the *Eastern Carelia* precedent (both of which, taken together, were thought by the 1926 Conference to dispose of most of the fifth reservation satisfactorily) were "subject to change at any time." U.S. Government to the Secretary-General of the League of Nations, 19 February 1929, Minutes of the 1929 Ctte. of Jurists, Annex 2, p. 97.

But other considerations also contributed to the decision to consecrate the Court's practice by incorporating it into the Statute. The situation confronting the 1929 draftsmen was radically different from that faced by their 1920 counterparts. By 1929, the fears and doubts regarding the advisory function which had been prevalent in 1920 had given way to a well-established advisory practice which had met with widespread acceptance and favor. There was, therefore, no longer any real opposition to codification of that advisory practice.[63] Nor was the Court's discretion, even now, to be as limited as that envisaged in the rejected 1920 draft article. Rigid classification of requests into two categories (a cause for some hesitation in 1920) was avoided. Under the new Article 68, which was admittedly intended to allow for almost complete assimilation to contentious procedure in advisory cases relating to "disputes,"[64] application by analogy was, nevertheless, left to the discretion of the Court.[65] Rather than establish any dual procedure, the provisions, as framed, allowed for a multiplicity of procedures, depending on the Court's assessment of how much assimilation was necessary or desirable in a particular case. Also unlike the 1920 scheme, no opinions were to be totally excluded from the sphere of application of judicial procedure. A minimum measure of assimilation to contentious procedure was maintained for *all* advisory opinions.

The 1936 Rules of Court

On 11 March 1936, the Court proceeded to adopt a new set of Rules, principally in order to bring the Rules into line with the revised Statute, which had entered into force on 1 February 1936.[66] With regard to advisory

For further discussion of the *Eastern Carelia* precedent, see Chapter V. On the question of the vote required for League requests, see Chapter IV, pp. 213–21.

[63] See remarks of Judge Huber, Minutes of 1929 Ctte. of Jurists, p. 68.

[64] See Report of the 1929 Ctte. of Jurists, *ibid.*, p. 125; and cf. the remarks of M. Fromageot, Minutes of the 1929 Conf. of Signatories, pp. 48, 79. See also the subsequent citation of these passages by members of the Court, PCIJ, Ser. D, No. 2 (3rd Add.), pp. 410, 680, 787.

[65] The extent of the discretion implied in Article 68 has been variously interpreted, since the article contains language which is both imperative ("shall be guided") and discretionary ("to the extent to which it recognises them to be applicable"). In the *Peace Treaties* case, the ICJ (whose Statute contains an almost identical Article 68) emphasized the discretionary aspect of the provision. ICJ Reports, 1950, p. 72. Judges Winiarski and Zoričić, on the other hand, interpreted this discretion in a more limited sense. *Ibid.*, pp. 91, 100. Cf. the *Namibia* case, in which the issue of the "residual discretion" permitted by Article 68 assumed some importance. See the discussion on p. 281, n. 14, below.

[66] Preparatory work for the revision was begun as early as May 1931, in anticipation of entry into force of the amended Statute. Four commissions were set up to study various aspects of the Rules and practice of the Court. The Fourth Commission was charged with studying advisory jurisdiction. Tentative drafts, still based on the original

jurisdiction, it was decided to delete those articles of the previous Rules now incorporated in the Statute,[67] and to add a new article (82) which would correspond to the one new provision on advisory opinions in the Statute, Article 68.[68]

The text of Article 82 was as follows:

> In proceedings in regard to advisory opinions, the Court shall, in addition to the provisions of Chapter IV of the Statute of the Court, apply the provisions of the articles hereinafter set out. It shall also be guided by the provisions of the present Rules which apply in contentious cases to the extent to which it recognizes them to be applicable, according as the advisory opinion for which the Court is asked relates, in the terms of Article 14 of the Covenant of the League of Nations, to a "dispute" or to a "question."

By its explicit reference to the "dispute-question" distinction, Article 82 would appear, at first glance, to be more limitative of the Court's discretion than Article 68 of the Statute, in which the distinction is merely implied. It would also seem to go further toward establishing a dual procedure. This conclusion, however, is not borne out by the history of the provision or by a closer examination of its terms.

At various times during the Court's debates on incorporating in the Rules a provision analogous to Article 68 of the Statute, suggestions were put forward which would, indeed, have established two distinct procedures in advisory cases: one for "disputes" and one for "questions."[69] A more or less

---

Statute, were adopted at first reading in 1935. The final revision, based on the amended Statute, was adopted at second reading in March 1936. See PCIJ, Ser. D, No. 2 (3rd Add.), p. 5.

[67] *Ibid.*, p. 693.

[68] Inclusion of such an article in the Rules was considered necessary in order to sanction application by analogy of provisions of the *Rules* relating to contentious procedure; Article 68 of the Statute merely referred to the relevant provisions of the *Statute*. For a rather extensive discussion of the necessity, function, and wording of Article 82, see *ibid.*, pp. 679-93, 694-98, as well as pp. 371-77, 408-15, 799-800, 834, 854.

[69] This was the thrust of the Fourth Commission's recommendations. Its draft Article 73 *bis* (the counterpart of Article 68 of the revised Statute) included an additional paragraph enumerating those rules applicable to *all* opinions and those reserved for opinions relating to a dispute. Similarly, its proposed Article 73 *ter* would have specified in some detail those elements of contentious procedure to be applied only in "dispute" advisory opinions. *Ibid.*, pp. 782-802 *passim*. Both the additional paragraph of Article 73 *bis* and all of Article 73 *ter* were suppressed by the Coordination Commission. *Ibid.*, pp. 880-81. But when the draft rules governing advisory procedure came before the Court for a first reading, in 1935, a rather extensive discussion of the question of dual procedure ensued. *Ibid.*, pp. 371-77, 408-15. The possibility of instituting a more simplified and expeditious procedure for opinions on a "question" was supported by Judges Negulesco, Guerrero, and Schücking (who desired to elaborate in the Rules two distinct procedures) and by Judge Rostworowski (who wished, rather, to confine the

summary procedure was envisaged for "questions," which would allow much less application by analogy of provisions governing contentious jurisdiction. But the Court, not wishing to go this far, explicitly disapproved the idea of any such rigid dichotomy.[70] Nevertheless, to avoid giving the false impression that full assimilation to contentious proceedings would be the order of the day in *all* advisory cases, some indication that requests in noncontentious cases would be accorded different treatment was considered desirable. This was the origin of the final proviso in Article 82.[71] It represented a compromise between those who favored a more explicit differentiation of the two procedures and those who desired to leave the Court's discretion unencumbered by any necessity of taking the "dispute-question" distinction into account.[72]

In the last analysis, the terms of the article left the Court as unfettered as did Article 68 of the Statute.[73] Any restrictive effect which might be implied from the final proviso was more than offset by the fact that the phrase "shall be guided by" (taken from Article 68 of the Statute) was retained,[74] and by the acknowledged vagueness of the "dispute-question" distinction.[75]

---

provisions of the Rules to "dispute" cases, leaving procedure on "questions" unregulated). During the second reading of the Rules in 1936, Judge Negulesco proposed a new Article 83 *bis*, which, with a view to hastening procedure on a "question," would have allowed oral hearings only in exceptional cases. *Ibid.*, p. 700.

It should be noted, however, that none of these proposals would have placed opinions on "questions" outside the ambit of judicial procedure altogether. In this respect, they differed considerably from the 1920 draft article on advisory opinions.

[70] In 1935, the Court voted 7 to 3 against prescribing two distinct procedures for advisory opinions. *Ibid.*, p. 414. Judge Negulesco did not press his proposed Article 83 *bis* to a vote. *Ibid.*, pp. 700–701.

[71] See the explanation of Judge van Eysinga, who first introduced a proviso of this nature at the first reading of the Rules. *Ibid.*, p. 411.

[72] Judge Anzilotti was the most vociferous spokesman for the latter view. *Ibid.*, pp. 371–77, 408–15, 678–79.

[73] Indeed, the draftsmen of Article 82 considered that they were merely making explicit the distinction already implicit in Article 68. See, e.g., *ibid.*, pp. 410, 680, 787.

In the *Namibia* case it was generally assumed by judges of both the majority and the minority that Article 82 of the ICJ Rules was more restrictive in its terms than was Article 68 of the ICJ Statute. (One of the main issues in contention with respect to South Africa's application for a judge *ad hoc* was whether Article 68 allowed the Court *residual* discretion in the event that Articles 82 and 83 of the Rules were inapplicable. See p. 281, n. 14, below.) However, the wording of Article 82 of the ICJ Rules ("for this purpose it shall above all consider whether the request . . . relates to a legal question actually pending between two or more States") may be more limitative than the formula employed in Article 82 of the PCIJ Rules.

[74] It had been argued that the term "shall be guided by" was inappropriate in the Rules. Rather, the Court, following the *guidance* of Article 68 of the Statute, should "apply" the relevant provisions. PCIJ, Ser. D., No. 2 (3rd Add.), pp. 685–93, 694–98.

[75] The unsatisfactory nature of the distinction was repeatedly emphasized by Judge Anzilotti and acknowledged by several other members of the Court. *Ibid.*, pp. 375, 408–15, and 678–86 *passim*.

Other decisions taken at the same time underscored more strongly the desire to retain for the Court the discretion it had previously enjoyed in advisory matters.[76] In particular, the Court again rejected any suggestion that it enumerate, for the more complete guidance of governments, the relevant articles of the Statute and Rules applicable by analogy to advisory proceedings.[77]

In sum, the 1936 revision of the Rules followed the lines of earlier revisions in consecrating the Court's previous advisory practice while maintaining considerable latitude for the Court with regard to particular cases.

THE U.N. PERIOD: THE ICJ

Provisions in the UN Charter and ICJ Statute

Unlike the draftsmen of Article 14 of the League Covenant, the framers of Article 96 of the UN Charter were not faced with a vacuum. They built largely on the basis of League experience with the advisory function. As noted above, the early anxieties and reservations which had surrounded the advisory jurisdiction at its inception had, in the course of the years, given way to a rather general satisfaction, and this satisfaction derived, to no mean extent, from the manner in which the PCIJ had disposed of its advisory duties. When it came to framing the new Charter provisions, concern centered mainly on enhancing the usefulness of the advisory jurisdiction in a direction already indicated by League experience,—namely, by considerably extending the circle of organs and agencies empowered to request opinions of the Court. This was the origin of the major innovation in Article 96, paragraph 2. The first paragraph of the article continues, in modified form, the provisions of

---

It would appear that the criterion employed in Article 82 was intended to be the same as that employed in relation to the appointment of judges *ad hoc*—namely, the relationship of the question to an existing dispute. See, especially, the remarks of Judge van Eysinga on this point, *ibid.*, pp. 737–38. Even this test, of course, leaves much to the appreciation of the Court. Judge Negulesco's attempt to get the Court to define the term "existing dispute" more precisely was rebuffed by the President on the grounds that the Court had already adopted an interpretation in 1927 and did not need to revert to the question. *Ibid.*, pp. 693–94.

For the conclusion that Article 82 did not seriously restrict the Court, see Hudson, *Permanent Court*, p. 299; and Goodrich, *op. cit.*, p. 743. But cf. n. 73 above with respect to Article 82 of the ICJ Statute.

[76] See, e.g., the unanimous rejection of an article designed to provide more detailed rules with regard to written proceedings in advisory cases. PCIJ, Ser. D, No. 2 (3rd Add.), pp. 373–77.

[77] Such suggestions were made by the Registrar (*ibid.*, pp. 834–37) and by the Fourth Commission (*ibid.*, pp. 799–802). The danger that enumeration might lead to an argument, *a contrario*, with respect to excluded provisions (a consideration which carried some weight in 1926) was held no longer serious, in view of the very general terms used in Article 68 of the Statute.

Article 14 of the Covenant.[78] Another change introduced in the Charter—one which did not relate specifically to the advisory function but which was to influence significantly the Court's view of that function[79]—was the new status accorded the Court in Articles 7 and 92 of the Charter. The Court was established as one of "the principal organs of the United Nations" and, more specifically, as "the principal judicial organ of the United Nations."[80] As for the relevant provisions in the Statute and Rules of Court, these followed, with very few, and mainly technical, changes, those of the PCIJ in 1936. (The most notable modifications were the addition of a new paragraph in Article 65 of the Statute and a revised version of Article 82 of the Rules.)[81]

Many of the above changes were foreshadowed in proposals put forward prior to, and in anticipation of, the San Francisco Conference. Particularly significant, in this regard, were the recommendations of the Informal Inter-Allied Committee on the Future of the Permanent Court of International Justice,[82] the Dumbarton Oaks Proposals, and recommendations of the Washington Committee of Jurists.[83]

The Informal Inter-Allied Committee, despite initial hesitations voiced by some of its members regarding continuance of the advisory jurisdiction,[84]

[78] The text of Article 96 reads as follows:

1. The General Assembly or the Security Council may request the International Court of Justice to give an advisory opinion on any legal question.

2. Other organs of the United Nations and specialized agencies, which may at any time be so authorized by the General Assembly, may also request advisory opinions of the Court on legal questions arising within the scope of their activities.

[79] See Chapter V.

[80] Article 92 provides also that the Statute "forms an integral part of the present Charter." The entire provision was taken from Chapter VII of the Dumbarton Oaks Proposals.

[81] The latter included a paragraph allowing the Court to accelerate its procedure, if necessary. Other changes in the wording of Articles 82 and 83 of the Rules, which did not appear significant at the time, assumed some importance in the *Namibia* case. See nn. 73 and 119 of this chapter.

[82] The Committee began its deliberations in 1943 and issued its recommendations in February 1944. Its report (hereinafter cited as Report of the Inter-Allied Committee) was issued as British Parliamentary Paper, Cmd. 6531, Misc. No. 2 (1944), and was reproduced in *AJIL*, 39, Supp. (1945): 1–42. See also Manley O. Hudson, "The Twenty-third Year of the Permanent Court of International Justice and Its Future," *AJIL*, 39 (1945): 1–12.

[83] The Committee was convened about two weeks before the opening of the San Francisco Conference and was charged with preparing, for the consideration of the Conference, a draft of the Court's Statute. Summary records of the Committee's deliberations are contained in *UNCIO Documents*, vol. 14.

[84] These hesitations were based on grounds similar to those expressed at the inception of the Permanent Court—e.g., the advisory jurisdiction was incompatible with the true function of a court of law; its existence might diminish the Court's contentious business; and it might lead to general pronouncements insufficiently related to a particular set of facts. Additionally, and presumably based principally on dissatisfaction with the request in the *Customs Union* case (see below), the objection was raised that "the existence of

concluded that that jurisdiction should be not only retained but even enlarged, by granting the right to request opinions to "all international associa-
tions of an inter-State or inter-governmental character possessing the necessary
status" and to "any two or more States acting in concert."[85] Certain safeguards to prevent misuse of the advisory jurisdiction also were recommended.[86] These suggestions, with the notable exception of the proposal to
empower two or more states acting in concert to request opinions, were very
similar to those ultimately adopted at San Francisco.[87]

In contrast to the Informal Inter-Allied Committee's recommendations,
the Dumbarton Oaks Proposals would have restricted the right of requesting
advisory opinions to the Council alone. The provision on advisory opinions—
though the term "advisory opinion" was not employed[88]—was inserted in

---

this jurisdiction tended to encourage the use of the Court as an instrument for settling
issues which were essentially of a political rather than of a legal character." Report of
Inter-Allied Committee, par. 65.

[85]*Ibid.*, pars. 142–43. For retention of the advisory jurisdiction, it was argued that
such jurisdiction was "of undoubted utility" in many municipal systems, and that the
new general international organization would undoubtedly require authoritative legal
advice relating to the interpretation of its constitution.

The advantage of empowering states to request opinions was said to lie in the opportunity which the advisory function would afford for clarifying states' legal rights *before*
the maturation of an issue into a definite dispute; for aiding states to reach a firm basis
for negotiations; and for achieving all this without incurring the hostility often imputed
to litigant states in contentious proceedings. *Ibid.*, pars. 67–68.

[86]The questions referred were not to be "of a merely general or abstract character,"
but were to "relate to some definite issue and circumstance," lest the Court be used "for
making pronouncements on political issues, or in a semi-legislative capacity." Ex parte
applications were to be excluded in order both to avoid a species of indirect compulsory
jurisdiction and to ensure that the Court proceeded on "an agreed basis of fact." (Cf. the
PCIJ's pronouncement on this last point in the *Eastern Carelia* case, PCIJ, Ser. B, No. 5,
p. 28.) Above all, the Court itself was to be granted the requisite discretion to safeguard
the advisory jurisdiction from abuse, by rejecting, or requiring reformulation of, questions considered inappropriate. Report of Inter-Allied Committee, pars. 69–75, 144–45.

[87]Conversely, on the question of the general relationship between the Court and the
new world organization, the ideas of the Inter-Allied Committee ran directly opposite to
the scheme eventually incorporated in the Charter. The Committee, considering that
"the Court has to some extent suffered in the past from its organic connexion with the
League, which, whether logically or not, resulted in its prestige being dependent to some
extent upon the varying fortunes of the League," recommended discontinuance of that
"organic connexion." Instead, the Court was to be regarded "as part of the machinery at
the disposal of the Organisation." For criticism of the Committee's explanation of the
decline of the Court's prestige, see Hudson, "The Twenty-third Year of the Permanent
Court of International Justice," p. 3; Rosenne, *Law and Practice*, 1: 62–63. Cf. Ruth B.
Russell, assisted by Jeannette E. Muther, *A History of the United Nations Charter*
(Washington, D.C.: The Brookings Institution, 1958), p. 383, for the view that the
Committee's suggestion was probably prompted by a desire to meet earlier American
objections to the close Court-League ties.

[88]The term was similarly avoided in earlier American drafts, reflecting, presumably,
the longstanding fears of the Senate with regard to the PCIJ's advisory function. Russell
and Muther, *op. cit.*, p. 290.

Chapter VIII, Section A, which dealt with the maintenance of international peace and security. Paragraph 6 of that section read as follows:

> Justiciable disputes should normally be referred to the international court of justice. The Security Council should be empowered to refer to the court, for advice, legal questions connected with other disputes.[89]

This apparently severe contraction of the advisory function is more readily understood when it is recalled that the League Assembly never employed its right to request an opinion of the Court; that the majority of League Council requests related to disputes brought before it or other international agencies for peaceful settlement; and that, in line with the much sharper division of functions between Council and Assembly envisaged by the Dumbarton Oaks scheme, the Security Council was to be the organ primarily (if not exclusively) responsible for the maintenance of international peace and security.[90] Nevertheless, even viewed in the light of League Council experience, the Dumbarton Oaks provision would have represented a contraction of the advisory function. For while, indeed, the *dominant* purpose for which requests were made was the peaceful settlement of disputes, a considerable number of requests were unrelated to that purpose. Most prominent in the latter category were the requests merely transmitted by the League Council on behalf of the ILO. In this respect, the provisions ultimately adopted at San Francisco were based more squarely on the *entire* League experience. Nonetheless, the idea behind the Dumbarton Oaks provision was followed, at least to this extent: the *principal* purpose which the advisory jurisdiction was to serve was still thought to be to assist the political organs of the United Nations, particularly the Security Council, in the pacific settlement of disputes.[91]

When the Washington Committee of Jurists came to consider the Dumbarton Oaks Proposals, it experienced no difficulty in recommending that authorization to request advisory opinions be extended to the General Assembly as well. Many states had proposed amendments to the Dumbarton Oaks Proposals suggesting this course,[92] and a Chinese proposal to thus empower the General Assembly was carried in the Committee without objection.[93] As explained at the time, the General Assembly might usefully employ judicial advice in connection with its functions of coordinating the policies of the

---

[89] *UNCIO Documents*, 3: 14.

[90] See the statement by Hackworth, *ibid.*, 14: 179; and Russell and Muther, *op. cit.*, pp. 385, 873.

[91] On the other hand, in the matter of the relationship between the Court and the new world organization, the Dumbarton Oaks Proposals were followed in their entirety.

[92] See, e.g., the official comments of Mexico, *UNCIO Documents*, 14: 446; Norway, *ibid.*, pp. 446–47; and Venezuela, *ibid.*, pp. 431–32.

[93] *Ibid.*, p. 179.

specialized agencies and supervising the economic and social activities of the organization.[94] A further proposal was put forward by Venezuela and the United Kingdom to empower specialized agencies and states, but was not approved.[95] Objections were raised by various representatives on the grounds that the proposed authorization might overload the Court with individual applications, thus detracting from the Court's more important duties; that it would jeopardize the work of the Security Council and General Assembly in their handling of disputes; that the function of the Court was not to play the role of general adviser;[96] and that the result might be confusion and chaos.[97] The Committee decided to leave decision on the points raised by the United Kingdom-Venezuelan proposal to the San Francisco Conference, to be dealt with in the context of the general structure of the United Nations.[98]

At San Francisco, Committee IV/1[99] readily approved the recommendation of the Committee of Jurists to extend the right to request advisory opinions to the General Assembly, but rejected proposals to extend that right to states and international organizations as well.[100] The Committee also decided to insert in the chapter dealing with the Court a general provision specifying the organs empowered to request advisory opinions,[101] and to add

[94] Views of the Chinese representative, *ibid.*, p. 177.

[95] *Ibid.*, pp. 181-83. See also written proposals, *ibid.*, pp. 319, 373-74, 431-32. According to the British proposal, only states acting in agreement—not individual states—were to be authorized. No such restriction is stipulated in the Venezuelan proposal. But cf. the later Venezuelan proposal in Committee IV/1 at San Francisco, *ibid.*, 13: 496.

[96] Arguments presented by the Soviet representative, *ibid.*, 14: 181.

[97] Statement by Mr. Hackworth, *ibid.*, p. 183.

[98] *Ibid.* See the statement of the United Kingdom representative, *ibid.*, p. 182.

[99] Committee IV/1 dealt with the International Court of Justice.

[100] *Ibid.*, 13: 234.

[101] *Ibid.*, p. 241. That provision (with one minor change) became Article 96(1) of the Charter.
   The new formula—"any legal question"—was here introduced, but apparently there was no discussion of the term or of the significance of its replacing the phrase "any dispute or question" employed in Article 14 of the Covenant.
   Committee III/2, to which the original Dumbarton Oaks provision had been sent, concurred in Committee IV/1's decision to include a more general provision in the chapter on the Court and deemed any further mention in the chapter dealing with the pacific settlement of disputes unwarranted. Rosenne (*Law and Practice*, 2: 657, n. 1) points out that shifting the position of the provision had the effect of leaving undetermined the question of the applicability of Article 27(3) (regarding compulsory abstention) to Security Council requests. (In this connection, it is interesting to note that, in challenging the formal validity of the requesting resolution in the *Namibia* case, South Africa did not raise the issue of mandatory abstention [although it did do so with respect to other Council resolutions on Namibia, and the Court erroneously assumed

to Article 65 of the Court's Statute a new paragraph granting the Court the right to give opinions to duly authorized bodies.[102]

The United Kingdom later reopened in Committee II/2[103] the question of authorizing specialized agencies to request advisory opinions. This question was now to be dealt with in the context of the powers of the Assembly. The new proposal would have enabled "such international agencies as the General Assembly may authorize for that purpose, to request advisory opinions on questions of a constitutional or judicial character arising within the scope of their activities."[104] Thus, unlike earlier proposals, the new proposal worked two limitations on the projected right of specialized agencies to request

---

that it had done so with respect to the requesting resolution as well]. See Chapter V.) Apart from the mandatory abstention issue, further questions relating to the vote required for requests were left unresolved by the Charter. (E.g., is the vote to be deemed procedural or substantive in the Security Council? Must an Assembly request be approved by a two-thirds majority or does an ordinary majority suffice? The first question arose in the *Namibia* case [see p. 285, n. 23, below]; the second, in connection with the treatment of Indians in South Africa [see p. 239, n. 332, below].)

[102] *UNCIO Documents*, 13: 242. In reply to the objection that such a provision in the Statute was unnecessary, since the Statute was an integral part of the Charter, it was observed that, "while the Statute was a part of the Charter, the Charter was not a part of the Statute." It was therefore necessary to separately grant the Court power to *render* opinions. Cf. Hans Kelsen, *The Law of the United Nations* (London: Stevens, 1950), p. 547, for the view that Article 65(1) of the Statute "is, indeed, superfluous."

The final text of Article 65(1) was as follows: "The Court may give an advisory opinion on any legal question at the request of whatever body may be authorized by or in accordance with the Charter of the United Nations to make such a request." This paragraph has frequently been invoked by the Court and by individual judges as evidence that the Court may refuse to comply with a request for an opinion, Article 65 being "permissive." And, unlike the French version of Article 14 of the Covenant ("*Elle donnera aussi*"), which did not correspond with the discretionary language of the English, the French version of Article 65(1) is equally permissive. This new clarification in the French text is noted in some individual opinions. See, e.g., ICJ Reports, 1948, pp. 94–95; and 1956, p. 112.

[103] Committee II/2 dealt with the General Assembly's political and security functions.

[104] Memorandum of the United Kingdom Delegation, *UNCIO Documents*, 9: 357–59. The suggestion was undoubtedly fashioned with the ILO experience in mind. Five PCIJ opinions had involved interpretation of the ILO Constitution, and one required interpretation of a convention concluded under ILO auspices. Since the League's earliest days, the ILO had waged a campaign to be empowered to request opinions directly from the Court without the necessity of Council intermediacy. See, e.g., the proposal of the International Labor Office at the time of the drafting of the original PCIJ Statute, Documents on Adoption of PCIJ Statute, p. 68; the Office's memorandum to the 1929 Committee of Jurists, Minutes of the 1929 Ctte. of Jurists, pp. 102–4; and the communication of the Acting Director-General to the Secretary-General of the League on 2 June 1944, LN Doc. C.20.M.20.1944.V.

In its memorandum, the United Kingdom explained that application through the UN's political organs would not be a practical alternative in the future, because the matters in question would probably be outside the scope of the Security Council's competence, and application through the General Assembly would involve considerable delay.

opinions—the first, by more narrowly defining the category of questions upon which they could request opinions;[105] the second, by making the right dependent on prior authorization by the Assembly, which, in turn, was to consider the case of each specialized agency on its merits. Committee II/2 adopted this proposal and decided to further extend the right to request advisory opinions to "other organs of the United Nations."[106]

After being notified of this decision, Committee IV/1 added a provision in conformity with Committee II/2's recommendations. This provision, with slight modifications, became paragraph 2 of Article 96 of the Charter.[107]

Before leaving this discussion of the San Francisco Conference, brief note should be made of several proposals which failed to be adopted at San Francisco, for their very rejection subsequently gave rise to debates—before the Court and other UN organs—regarding the proper limits of the advisory function. More specifically, these proposals would have established the Court in the following roles: Official Interpreter of the Charter; Interpreter of the Domestic Jurisdiction clause of the Charter, in particular; Administrative Court of Appeal; and Arbiter of Jurisdictional Conflicts among International Organizations.

The Charter, unlike the constitutions of many specialized agencies, contains no compromissory clause. Nor was such a clause included in the Dumbarton Oaks Proposals.[108] In Committee IV/2 at San Francisco, the question "How and by what organ or organs of the organization should the Charter be interpreted?" was discussed extensively.[109] In the end, the Committee endorsed the following conclusions submitted to it by a special subcommittee appointed to study the question.

[105] The limiting words "within the scope of their activities" were probably intended to prevent the specialized agencies from bringing general "political" issues before the Court by means of their newly acquired right. Russell and Muther, *op. cit.*, p. 891.

[106] *UNCIO Documents*, 9: 161. The Committee also concurred in Committee IV/1's decision to empower the General Assembly to make requests.

[107] *Ibid.*, 13: 297–99. The original British draft had referred to "questions of a constitutional or judicial character." This was changed in Committee IV/1, first to "questions of a juridical character," and later to "legal questions."

[108] The United States Staff Charter, drafted during the summer of 1943, would, indeed, have made the Court the official agency of Charter interpretation. Russell and Muther record that the idea was subsequently abandoned by higher officials in the State Department. *Op. cit.*, p. 290.

[109] Some favored granting the right of authoritative interpretation to the General Assembly, on the grounds, *inter alia*, that, since the power to interpret was equivalent to the power to legislate, it should be exercised by the most democratic body of the organization. Others favored recourse to either the Court's compulsory or advisory jurisdiction. Still others recommended constituting joint conferences between organs, or referring questions to a committee of experts. Some favored insertion of a Charter provision; others, citing the League precedent, thought that interpretation should be governed by practice. *UNCIO Documents*, 13: 633–34.

In the course of the operations from day to day of the various organs of the Organization, it is inevitable that each organ will interpret such parts of the Charter as are applicable to its particular functions. This process is inherent in the functioning of any body which operates under an instrument defining its functions and powers. It will be manifested in the functioning of such a body as the General Assembly, the Security Council, or the International Court of Justice. Accordingly, it is not necessary to include in the Charter a provision either authorizing or approving the normal operation of this principle.

Difficulties may conceivably arise in the event that there should be a difference of opinion among the organs of the Organization concerning the correct interpretation of a provision of the Charter. Thus, two organs may conceivably hold and may express or even act upon different views. Under unitary forms of national government the final determination of such a question may be vested in the highest court or in some other national authority. However, the nature of the Organization and of its operation would not seem to be such as to invite the inclusion in the Charter of any provision of this nature. If two member states are at variance concerning the correct interpretation of the Charter, they are of course free to submit the dispute to the International Court of Justice as in the case of any other treaty. Similarly, it would always be open to the General Assembly or to the Security Council, in appropriate circumstances, to ask the International Court of Justice for an advisory opinion concerning the meaning of a provision of the Charter. Should the General Assembly or the Security Council prefer another course, an *ad hoc* committee of jurists might be set up to examine the question and report its views, or recourse might be had to a joint conference. In brief, the members or the organs of the Organization might have recourse to various expedients in order to obtain an appropriate interpretation. It would appear neither necessary nor desirable to list or to describe in the Charter the various possible expedients.

It is to be understood, of course, that if an interpretation made by any organ of the Organization or by a committee of jurists is not generally acceptable it will be without binding force. In such circumstances, or in cases where it is desired to establish an authoritative interpretation as a precedent for the future, it may be necessary to embody the interpretation in an amendment to the Charter. This may always be accomplished by recourse to the procedure provided for amendment.[110]

But before the Committee's final vote, a Belgian suggestion to make referral of disagreements between organs on Charter interpretation to the Court "an established procedure" was rejected.[111]

---

[110]*Ibid.*, pp. 709–10.

[111]*Ibid.*, p. 645. Subsequent arguments which sought to base the Court's incompetence to interpret the Charter on rejection of this Belgian proposal overlooked the qualifying words in the text. To reject recourse to the Court "as an established procedure" is far different from rejecting it in any circumstances. Moreover, the report of

Apart from the general question of Charter interpretation, there was considerable sentiment at San Francisco for granting the Court a determinative role in the interpretation of the domestic jurisdiction clause.[112] This was in line with the generally strong support in favor of compulsory jurisdiction. Despite rejection of compulsory jurisdiction as a general principle in Committee IV/1, a proposal which would have allowed disputes concerning the application of Article 2(7) to be determined by the Court was introduced in Committee I/1. This proposal was not adopted, having failed to receive the requisite two-thirds majority.[113] Presumably, then, the general considerations with respect to Charter interpretation, put forward in the report of Committee IV/2, are equally applicable to Article 2(7)—i.e., each organ may interpret the provision for itself, but recourse to the Court is not precluded.[114]

The roles of Administrative Court of Appeal and Arbiter of Jurisdictional Conflicts among International Organizations were envisaged for the Court in a Venezuelan amendment to Article 34 of the Court's Statute.[115] Both parts of the Venezuelan amendment were rejected by Committee IV/1.[116]

In their final form, the provisions governing the advisory function in the Charter and the new Statute differed in a number of ways from those in the

---

Committee IV/2 clearly lists recourse to the Court—both in its contentious and advisory capacities—as one means of resolving disputes over Charter interpretation.

For an earlier recommendation to refer questions of Charter interpretation to the Court, see the official comments of Norway, *ibid.*, 3: 356 and 14: 446–47. Cf. Larnaude's proposal, submitted at Paris in 1919, to grant Covenant-interpretation powers to the PCIJ.

[112] See, e.g., the comments of Mexico (*UNCIO Documents*, 3: 186); Czechoslovakia (*ibid.*, p. 468); and Peru (*ibid.*, 14: 428). These, it should be noted, contemplated binding judgments, not advisory opinions.

[113] *Ibid.*, 6: 509. Simultaneously, an amendment to reinsert the standard of international law in Article 2(7) was also rejected. Mr. Dulles, the United States delegate, argued forcefully against both proposals. To make the Court the determining organ with respect to Article 2(7) would, he maintained, be to give the Court a general authority to interpret the Charter. *Ibid.*, pp. 507–9.

Cf. Article 5 of the abortive Geneva Protocol, in accordance with which the League Council was to submit the question of domestic jurisdiction to the Court for a binding opinion, in the event that one of the parties claimed the dispute to be domestic. LN, Records of the 5th Ass., Plenary, 1924, pp. 488, 499.

[114] See Goodrich and Hambro, *Charter*, p. 114. On numerous occasions, in connection with disputes before the General Assembly and the Security Council, proposals were put forward to refer questions relating to the interpretation of Article 2(7) to the Court for an advisory opinion. None of these was ever accepted. See Chapter IV.

[115] *UNCIO Documents*, 13: 480. International organizations were to be permitted to appear as parties to a dispute, apart from any right they might possess to request advisory opinions. *Ibid.*, 14: 139.

[116] *Ibid.*, pp. 270–71, 282. Rejection of the Venezuelan proposal to make the Court an administrative court of appeal was cited by two judges in the *UNESCO* case as

League Covenant and the Statute of the Permanent Court: the term "any legal question" in Article 96(1) replaced the former "any dispute or question"; paragraph 2 of Article 96 was an innovation, having no counterpart in the League Covenant; and a new paragraph 1 was added to Article 65 of the Court's Statute.[117] In addition, a new and more organic relationship between the Court and the world organization was established.[118]

What significance did the substitution of "any legal question" for "any dispute or question" have? Probably, very little indeed, the views of Judge Azevedo notwithstanding.[119] It may be recalled that in the drafting of Article

---

grounds for not rendering an opinion in that case. See separate opinion of Judge Winiarski, ICJ Reports, 1956, pp. 106–7; and dissenting opinion of Judge Cordova, *ibid.*, pp. 160–61.

[117] As noted above, this provision has frequently been adduced in support of the Court's discretionary right to refuse to render an opinion requested. See Chapter V.

[118] On the effect of this new relationship on the Court's view of its advisory function, see Chapter V. See also Leo Gross, "The International Court of Justice and the United Nations," *RC*, 121 (1967-II): 314.

[119] In several separate opinions, Judge Azevedo argued that it was no longer open to the Court, in its advisory capacity, to consider concrete "disputes," the "anomaly" of "advisory arbitration" having now been suppressed. The new formula in Article 96, in his view, called for the rendering only of "theoretical or abstract" opinions, as far removed as possible from any concrete situations of fact. See, especially, ICJ Reports, 1948, pp. 73–81; and 1950, pp. 79–88. See also Chapter V. There certainly is no support in the *travaux préparatoires* for this viewpoint. Rather, with the League experience in mind, the framers clearly laid great stress on the possible use of the Court's advisory function as an aid in the peaceful settlement of disputes. Moreover, the provisions of the Statute and Rules lead to the opposite conclusion. Thus, Article 68 of the new Statute is virtually identical to Article 68 of the old. Articles 82 and 83 of the Rules have been modified somewhat in wording, in line with the elimination of the phrase "any dispute or question" from the Charter. Thus, Article 82(1) of the Rules now reads: "It [the Court] shall also be guided by the provisions of these Rules which apply in contentious cases to the extent to which it recognizes them to be applicable; for this purpose it shall above all consider whether the request for the advisory opinion relates to a legal question actually pending between two or more States." Article 83 allows judges *ad hoc* if the opinion is requested "upon a legal question actually pending between two or more States." Judge Azevedo, true to his own views, objected to the provisions in Articles 82 and 83, both of which, in his opinion, "endeavour to maintain an obsolete system, represented by the dangerous distinction between a 'question' and a 'dispute.' " ICJ Reports, 1950, p. 85. The discussions leading up to the adoption of the 1946 Rules were never published.

Some of the modifications in wording introduced into Articles 82 and 83 of the Rules appeared minor at the time, but assumed some significance in the *Namibia* case, when the ICJ received its first application for a judge *ad hoc* in an advisory case. As observed earlier, the new phrase in Article 82, "for this purpose it shall above all consider . . ." was possibly more restrictive of the Court's discretion than its counterpart in the PCIJ Statute. See n. 73 above. Furthermore, the French version of "above all"–"*avant tout*"–might imply that a full preliminary procedure to determine the contentious or noncontentious nature of the request was necessary. See p. 277, n. 2, below. Finally, the fact that Article 83 (regarding the appointment of a judge *ad hoc*) spoke of an advisory opinion "requested *upon* a legal question actually pending between two or more States," unlike Article 82 (and the former Article 83), which referred to an

14 of the Covenant, the substitution was reversed. The term "any legal question" was suppressed in order to avoid the inference that the PCIJ was to be the general legal counsellor of the League organs.[120] *A contrario*, it might be argued that inclusion of the term in the Charter indicated the intention that the ICJ should play just such a role in relation to UN organs. If present, however, this intention would appear to have emerged more from the terms of Article 92 than from Article 96.

Nor has the use of the qualifying term "legal" before "question" effected any real limitation in the scope of the advisory function—though its inclusion may have been motivated by a desire to prevent *"Customs Union*-type" requests from being addressed to the Court.[121] By the same token, it is doubtful that the word "any" preceding the term "legal question" was intended to *broaden* significantly the range of questions which might be submitted to the Court for its advice.[122]

As for Article 96(2), in spite of the subsequent Assembly debate over whether general or *ad hoc* authorizations were intended,[123] the evidence in the *travaux préparatoires* unequivocally favors general authorizations. The United Kingdom, sponsor of the provision, clearly indicated that its purpose

---

opinion which *"relates"* to such a question, was understood by the ICJ to have narrowed the class of advisory cases in which a judge *ad hoc* might be appointed. ICJ Reports, 1971, p. 26.

[120]Miller, *Covenant*, 1: 391–92. See also p. 8 above.

[121]See, e.g., the statement of Mr. (as he then was) Fitzmaurice in the Washington Committee of Jurists, *UNCIO Documents*, 14: 204–5. See also Grant Gilmore, "The International Court of Justice," *Yale Law Review*, 55 (1946): 1054, 1064–65. Gilmore considers that the term "legal question" did limit the Court's advisory jurisdiction. But, clearly, the request and the opinion in the *Customs Union* case, for example, were never premised on the assumption that the PCIJ might give opinions on "nonlegal" or "political" questions. Rather, they were based on the supposition that the questions involved were, indeed, "legal." (See Chapter V.) In fact, it might plausibly be argued that the qualification "legal" in Article 96 is both unnecessary and meaningless. The Court, as a matter of its discretion, may refuse to give an opinion which it feels it should not give. And, given the absence of anything even remotely approaching a litmus test to differentiate the "legal" from the "political," the question whether or not a matter is "legal" is virtually translatable into the equivalent question: is the matter one which a Court should properly (i.e., as a matter of its discretion) deal with? It is therefore scarcely accidental that, as Rosenne points out, "the contentions that have been advanced against the rendering of an opinion on the ground that the question put to the Court was not a legal one can hardly be distinguished from the contentions that for reasons of judicial propriety the Court ought to exercise its discretion and refrain from giving the requested opinion." *Law and Practice*, 2: 703.

[122]It has been suggested that opinions may now relate to questions of fact, and perhaps to completely abstract or even hypothetical questions regarding future law. For a discussion of the Court's competence to deal with "abstract" and "factual" questions, see Chapter V.

[123]See *UN Repertory*, Art. 96, par. 191. The use of the plural "questions" in paragraph 2 (in contrast to the singular in paragraph 1) was cited in support of *ad hoc* authorizations.

was precisely to avoid the necessity of applying to either the General Assembly or the Security Council for each individual request.[124] And, before Committee IV/1 proceeded to vote on the final provision, it first defeated a Soviet proposal to substitute the words "in each case" for "at any time."[125] The evidence in the preparatory work is further corroborated by considerations of logic. Unless general authorizations were intended, the entire provision would be superfluous, for it would always be open to the two authorized organs to transmit, at their discretion, requests originating with outside agencies. The situation as it existed in the League period would, then, remain virtually unchanged. In fact, all authorizations have been general.

Authorizations under Article 96(2)[126]

In accordance with Article 96(2), the General Assembly has authorized the following to request advisory opinions: the Economic and Social Council;[127] the Trusteeship Council;[128] the Interim Committee of the General Assembly;[129] the Committee on Applications for Review of Administrative Tribunal Judgments;[130] all the specialized agencies (except the UPU);[131] and the IAEA.[132] In sum, the present number of bodies so authorized is seventeen.

[124] *UNCIO Documents*, 9: 161, 357-59; 13: 298-99. To quiet fears that the specialized agencies might abuse their right to request opinions by addressing political questions to the Court, it was pointed out that the Assembly might lay down conditions for the authorizations, and would, undoubtedly, consider the case of *each specialized agency* (note: not *each request*) on its merits. *Ibid.*, 9: 161.

[125] *Ibid.*, 13: 298-99. In the light of the drafting history, what is most surprising—indeed, incomprehensible—is that doubts concerning the meaning of the clause "at any time" were later raised at the San Francisco Conference itself (in the Coordination Commission), and that the discussion ended on an inconclusive note. *Ibid.*, 17: 372-73.

[126] For a convenient listing of the authorized bodies and some details regarding the authorizations, see Rosenne, *Law and Practice*, 2: app. 11 (pp. 917-19). For a discussion of this topic, see *ibid.*, pp. 87-90, 669-82; C. Wilfred Jenks, *The Prospects of International Adjudication* (Dobbs Ferry, N.Y.: Oceana, and London: Stevens, 1964), pp. 193-224 *passim*. See also the discussion of UN practice under Article 96(2) in *UN Repertory* and Supp. Nos. 1 and 2.

[127] GA Res. 89(I), 11 December 1946.

[128] GA Res. 171B(II), 14 November 1947. The Trusteeship Council had not requested authorization, a fact which led the Soviet delegation to attempt to postpone the authorization. *UN Repertory*, Art. 96, pars. 201-2.

[129] The initial authorization was contained in GA Res. 196(III), 3 December 1948, and was repeated in GA Res. 295(IV), 2 December 1949, wherein the Committee was established on a permanent basis. In deciding to authorize the Interim Committee, the Assembly overruled objections that the term "other organs" in Article 96(2) could not include a subsidiary organ of the Assembly. *UN Repertory*, Art. 96, pars. 203-7.

[130] The authorization was contained in the amended Article 11 of the UN Administrative Tribunal Statute, adopted by the General Assembly in Res. 957(X), 8 November 1955. Some representatives voiced doubts as to whether the Committee could qualify under Article 96(2) (which refers to questions arising within the scope of the requesting organ), when the Committee's *only* activity would be to request advisory opinions. *UN*

The terms of authorization are broadly as follows: the Economic and Social Council, the Trusteeship Council, and the Assembly's Interim Committee may request opinions on legal questions arising within the scope of their activities. So too may the specialized agencies,[131] except that questions concerning the mutual relationships of the agencies and the UN or other specialized agencies are specifically excluded from the scope of their authorizations and, correspondingly, are included in that of the Economic and Social Council. Specialized agencies are required to notify the Economic and Social Council of any requests made by them.

The liberal attitude of the Assembly with respect to authorizations was adopted in the face of considerable initial reserve on the matter. The more halting and cautious attitude was reflected in the early debates regarding the

---

Repertory, Supp. No. 1, Art. 96, par. 63. More serious reservations centered on the equality of the parties in the contemplated review procedure (see pp. 317–21 below).

For the interesting view that the authorization of the Committee might be viewed as an Assembly delegation of its own rights under Article 96(1) of the Charter, see Rosenne, *Law and Practice*, 2: 690.

[131]Provisions to authorize the specialized agencies were included in the draft relationship agreements, and authorizations were effected by the following General Assembly resolutions approving those agreements: 50(I), 14 December 1946 (ILO, UNESCO, FAO, and ICAO); 124(II), 15 November 1947 (IBRD, IMF, ITU, and WHO); 204(III), 18 November 1948 (IMCO); 531(VI), 20 December 1951 (WMO); 1116(XI), 20 February 1957 (IFC); and 1594(XV), 27 March 1961 (IDA).

[132]IAEA was authorized by GA Res. 1146(XII), 14 November 1957, to request advisory opinions "on legal questions arising within the scope of its activities other than questions concerning the relationship between the Agency and the United Nations or any specialized agency." GA Res. 1145(XII), of the same date, approved the draft relationship agreement between the UN and IAEA, but was not considered sufficient, because Article X had been purposely vague on the question of blanket authorization. By its terms, the UN was to "take the necessary action to enable the General Assembly or the Board of Governors of the Agency to seek an advisory opinion of the International Court of Justice." Serious doubts were entertained regarding the applicability of Article 96(2) to the IAEA, since the latter was neither a UN organ nor, technically, a specialized agency. (Unlike the specialized agencies, its agreement was not negotiated with ECOSOC, and its ties with the General Assembly are closer than those with ECOSOC.) Because of these doubts, the UN Secretary-General had recommended that the General Assembly pass on each request for an advisory opinion which might be made by the IAEA. UN Doc. A/3122, 20 April 1956, par. 15. Although reservations with respect to blanket authorization of the IAEA continued to be expressed (see, e.g., UN Doc. IAEA/CS/OR. 33, pp. 61–62; GAOR [XII], Plenary, 715th Mtg., 14 November 1957, pp. 440–42), the General Assembly unanimously approved the authorization. It apparently concurred with the views expressed at the time to the effect that the authorization was "within the spirit, if not actually within the letter," of Article 96(2), and that, in the final analysis, the Court itself would decide whether to accept a specific request addressed to it by the IAEA. See GAOR (XII), Plenary, 715th Mtg., 14 November 1957, p. 441. See also *UN Repertory*, Supp. No. 2, Art. 96, pars. 23–32; Rosenne, *Law and Practice*, 2: 680–82.

[133]The agreements with WHO, ITU, and WMO refer to questions within the scope of their "competence."

granting of blanket authorizations and the revocability of the authorizations thus granted,[134] as well as in the more restrictive terms originally contemplated for some relationship agreements.[135]

While on various occasions doubts were raised as to whether or not a proposed authorization could come under the terms of Article 96(2),[136] the authorizations were almost all granted in practice.[137]

[134]On the question of general, as opposed to *ad hoc*, authorizations, see pp. 34–35 above. See also *Report of the Preparatory Commission of the United Nations*, UN Doc. PC/20, 23 December 1945, p. 44. The assumption that any grant might be revoked was made by the Preparatory Commission and confirmed by the Sixth Committee in a resolution it adopted when the first agreements were under consideration. *UN Repertory*, Art. 96, par. 199. But cf. F. Blaine Sloan, "Advisory Jurisdiction of the International Court of Justice," *California Law Review*, 38 (1950): 834, to the effect that such revocation would constitute breach of an agreement by the UN and would give rise to the usual remedies for breach of treaty obligations. Were a request to be addressed to the Court by an agency following such an attempted revocation, it would be up to the Court itself to determine the effectiveness of the revocation. See also Jenks, *op. cit.*, p. 199, whose views are somewhat similar.

[135]The original draft agreement with UNESCO, as well as the drafts proposed for ICAO and FAO, would have given ECOSOC the power to veto individual requests and the General Assembly the power to override the ECOSOC veto and approve the request in question. (The possibility of making prior ECOSOC approval of each request a condition of authorization was earlier raised in the Preparatory Commission's report, cited above.) In the end, however, the more liberal formula, which had already been approved for the ILO, was adopted. It has since become the standard formula. *UN Repertory*, Art. 63, pars. 26–28, 43, 46–48, 54, 56, 172.

[136]With respect to the Interim Committee, the Committee on Applications for Review of Administrative Tribunal Judgments, and IAEA, see nn. 129, 130, and 132 above.

[137]However, with regard to the proposed Human Rights Committee, to be established under the Covenant on Civil and Political Rights, the Secretary-General adopted a restrictive interpretation of Article 96(2). Asked to report on how the Committee might be able to obtain advisory opinions, he concluded that it could not be directly empowered under Article 96(2), since it would be neither an "organ" nor a "specialized agency." Nor could its requests be transmitted to the Court in an automatic fashion by a duly authorized organ, since this would be tantamount to direct requests. An authorized organ might, however, take the Committee's recommendations into account, provided that that organ retained its discretion with respect to presenting and framing the question. UN Doc. E/1732, 26 June 1950. In accordance with the Secretary-General's opinion, it was decided at the time to include in the draft Covenant a provision merely empowering the Human Rights Committee to recommend to ECOSOC that the latter request an advisory opinion "on any legal question connected with a matter of which the Committee is seized." See UN Docs. E/1992, 24 May 1951, p. 79, and E/2573, April 1954, p. 71. (For criticism of the Secretary-General's interpretation as unduly restrictive, see Jenks, *op. cit.*, p. 197.) In the end, the entire draft provision was deleted by the General Assembly's Third Committee. Even the proposed indirect method of requesting advisory opinions was thought to entail a "strong element of compulsion," and was deemed particularly objectionable if (as was then contemplated) individuals were to be allowed the right of petition. It was feared that the Court would possess "a right to adjudicate on a complaint by an individual against his State of Nationality," and this "would be an unprecedented departure from the accepted rules of international law." UN Doc. A/6546, 13 December 1966, pp. 131–33.

It should be noted that, of all the principal UN organs, the Secretariat alone is not authorized to request advisory opinions.[138] In light of the fact that it is also the only organ not composed of states, its authorization, while it cannot be ruled out, would, as Rosenne points out, constitute a "radical . . . departure from what has hitherto been the fundamental postulate of all the Court's judicial activities."[139]

Provisions for "Binding" Opinions

A number of instruments now contain what might be described as "advisory compromissory clauses"—i.e., provisions for requesting advisory opinions in certain circumstances and for accepting the resultant opinions as binding.[140] Such clauses owe their existence to a confluence of factors: the

---

[138]Nor has the Secretariat ever officially requested such authorization, though on at least two occasions the possibility of such authorization for specific purposes was raised. In 1950, in his report regarding the proposed Human Rights Committee, the Secretary-General suggested that legal questions raised by that Committee might be referred, alternatively, to four UN organs—one of the four being the Secretariat itself—for transmission to the Court. UN Doc. E/1732, 26 June 1950, pars. 16, 19. Again, in 1955, the Secretary-General suggested that he might be the proper vehicle for bringing questions relating to certain UN Administrative Tribunal judgments before the Court for an advisory opinion. The suggestion was made in a working paper submitted to the special committee set up to study the question of establishing a procedure for judicial review of UN Administrative Tribunal judgments. UN Doc. A/2909, 10 June 1955, Annex II, par. 67.

[139]Rosenne considers that this departure would be "too radical." *Law and Practice*, 2: 673. But cf. Jenks, *op. cit.*, p. 195; and Sloan, *op. cit.*, p. 833.

While political control over requests and over treatment of the resultant opinion is obviously no guarantee of the opinion's effectuality (as will be seen below), the absence of any such control is, it is submitted, even more likely to result in exercises in futility.

[140]These include the following: the Convention on the Privileges and Immunities of the United Nations, 13 February 1946 (sec. 30); the Convention on the Privileges and Immunities of the Specialized Agencies, 21 November 1947 (sec. 32); the Headquarters Agreement of 26 June 1947 between the United States and the United Nations (sec. 21); Article 37(2) of the amended ILO Constitution; Article XII of the amended Statute of the ILO Administrative Tribunal; Article 11 of the amended Statute of the UN Administrative Tribunal; the Agreement of 14 April 1951 between ICAO and Canada regarding the Headquarters of ICAO (sec. 31); the Agreement of 18 June 1958 between the United Nations and Ethiopia regarding the Headquarters of the UN Economic Commission for Africa (sec. 21). For a list of further instruments, as well as the texts of the relevant provisions, see Chapter X of the ICJ *Yearbooks*. Several provisions are cited in Appendix 2 of the present volume. Not all specify that the Court's opinion will be "binding," though this would seem to be the general purport of all of the provisions. See Kelsen, *op. cit.*, pp. 486–87. In the drafting of Article 11 of the amended Statute of the UN Administrative Tribunal the term "binding" was avoided, though the envisaged opinions were apparently to have binding force. See *UN Repertory*, Supp. No. 1, Art. 96, pars. 78–86.

Cf., for the League period, Art. 12(2) of the unratified Convention for the Creation of an International Mortgage Credit Company, 12 May 1931, in Manley O. Hudson, *International Legislation*, 9 vols. (Washington, D.C.: Carnegie Endowment for International Peace, 1931–50), 5: 968–69; and Art. 5 of the abortive Geneva Protocol, LN,

decision at San Francisco to bar international organizations from appearing as parties before the Court; the proliferation of agreements to which international organizations are parties, and the resulting necessity to establish suitable procedures for arbitrating differences;[141] the corresponding increase in multilateral agreements which vitally affect the interests of international organizations, but for which traditional compromissory clauses are probably inadequate;[142] and the availability of the advisory procedure—to an even greater extent than was the case under the League—for use as an alternative route to the Court. In effect, Venezuela's unsuccessful drive at San Francisco to amend Article 34 of the Statute so as to include international organizations, and to set up the International Court as an administrative court of appeal, has been at least partially compensated for by the "advisory compromissory clauses" and by provisions for the review of administrative tribunal judgments. The word "partially" needs to be emphasized, however. The contemplated use of the advisory procedure is, at most, only "an artificial expedient,"[143] even for organs and agencies empowered to request advisory opinions.[144] Important differences between advisory and contentious proceedings remain.[145] Certain difficulties—some of which were considered by

---

Records of the 5th Ass., Plenary, 1924, p. 499. In both instances, provision was made for binding opinions.

[141] Such differences may arise between the international organization and states, or, alternatively, between the organization and private individuals (e.g., its own staff) or companies.

[142] The various conventions on Privileges and Immunities are examples. They are multilateral conventions between states, but in most disputes the interests of the organization will be those principally at stake. Cf. the advisory opinions given on ILO affairs during the League period despite the existence of a compromissory clause allowing adjudication in contentious procedure. And see the memorandum of the International Labor Office, Minutes of the 1929 Ctte. of Jurists, pp. 102–4. The suit which was filed in Court by India against Pakistan in August 1971 and which related to the competence of the ICAO Council is exceptional in this regard.

[143] Jenks, *op. cit.*, p. 219.

[144] Three of the organizations recognizing the jurisdiction of the ILO Administrative Tribunal are not themselves authorized to request advisory opinions. Moreover, of these organizations—the Secretariat of GATT, the European Organization for Nuclear Research, and the United International Bureaux for Intellectual Property—the last two have no official relationship with the UN whatever. All would be dependent on some authorized agency to request an opinion on their behalf, but whether the Court would consent to give an opinion—particularly within the framework of Article XII of the ILO Administrative Tribunal's Statute, and particularly with reference to the last two organizations—is questionable. See Rosenne, *Law and Practice*, 2: 687.

[145] Thus, as Rosenne points out, the interested states have much less control over the terms of submission of the question to the Court. Moreover, the obligation to accept an opinion as binding is probably "not so definite as the obligation to comply with a judgment contained in Article 94(1) of the Charter," nor does it "confer upon the opinion the quality of *res judicata* (unless it be subsequently embodied in an arbitral award), nor give it binding force within the terms of Article 59 of the Statute." *Ibid.*, pp. 683–85.

the Court in the *UNESCO* case[146] —are also inherent in the various schemes. Since only the request in the *UNESCO* case was made within the framework of the special advisory provisions considered in this section, the practical efficacy of such provisions has yet to be tested.

CONCLUSIONS

The advisory function was introduced in bare outline—and almost inadvertently—in Article 14 of the League Covenant. League organs were to be allowed access to the Court, not, however, as plaintiffs or defendants, but rather as clients requesting the legal advice of their counsellor. As such, the Court's replies could in no way bind these organs; much less could they bind the interested states, who were, technically, not involved in the proceedings at all. The advisory function clearly was not intended to be an alternative to compulsory jurisdiction. Yet neither would it necessarily be a simple lawyer-client affair. The fact that the *Court*, and not a mere committee of jurists, was to be the counsellor, and that the term "advisory opinion" was deliberately employed to imply a *judicial* function; the fact that the purpose of the advisory jurisdiction was to allow the League organs to clarify legal aspects of disputes brought before them for peaceful settlement, and that such disputes would necessarily entail parties with a stake in the Court's replies, parties whose views the Court might wish to ascertain—all militated against development of the advisory function as legal consultation pure and simple. Nonetheless, such development was not totally excluded by the terms of Article 14.

When the original Statute of the Court was being drafted in 1920, concern for safeguarding the Court's judicial nature led to a proposal by the Advisory Committee of Jurists which contemplated two types of procedures for advisory opinions, one for "disputes" and one for "questions." Requests relating to "disputes" were to be closely assimilated to contentious procedure, but, where "questions" were concerned, the Court, as such, was to be dissociated from the opinion. The two conceptions of the advisory function—as a "quasi-contentious" function, on the one hand, and as a "lawyer-client" function, on the other—were both present in this proposal, but each was assigned to a different type of request. Two species of advisory opinions would have

---

[146]These difficulties are particularly likely to arise in connection with the review of Administrative Tribunal judgments. Thus, the question of the equality of the parties, though it did not prevent the Court from giving an opinion in the *UNESCO* case, may conceivably present more difficulty in future cases. As will be seen in Chapter V, the Court's reasoning was confined to the facts of that case.

On the other hand, the Court's explicit affirmation that the attribution of binding force to an advisory opinion could not affect the Court's jurisdiction would appear to eliminate any potential difficulty on that account. See Chapter V.

resulted: one would have been truly advisory; the other, quasi-contentious. When the League Assembly considered this proposal, serious reservations were voiced, particularly with respect to the wisdom and feasibility of the proposed dual procedure for advisory opinions. These reservations, coupled with the desire not to bind the Court in an area where previous international experience was almost nonexistent (and whose future importance could not be foretold), led to the suppression of any reference to advisory opinions altogether in the original Statute.

The task of fashioning the advisory jurisdiction thus fell wholly into the lap of the Court itself. From the very outset, the Court clearly established the judicial character of the advisory function. In no case was the Court to be merely a private lawyer to its League client. Full publicity was to be given to the request and the opinion; notice of the request was to be given to states and international organizations; and all opinions were to be given after deliberation by the full Court. No distinction was made between "disputes" and "questions."

Thereafter, the Court moved progressively in its practice and subsequent revision of the Rules toward obliterating the line separating its advisory function from its contentious function until, in the end, where there were "in fact contending parties, the difference between contentious cases and advisory cases . . . [was] only nominal."[147] Not content to view the request as involving an exclusive relationship between itself and the requesting organ, the Court increasingly looked behind the façade to the real interests involved and permitted interested states and organizations to express their views.[148] Nonetheless, the theoretical nature of advisory opinions as matters which concerned solely the requesting organ and the Court was never totally displaced.[149] Until 1927, the Court refused to depart from the theory that all states were merely informants of the Court—though some might be more interested informants than others. Throughout the history of the PCIJ, a certain tension prevailed between the "lawyer-client" and "quasi-contentious" conceptions of the Court's advisory function.[150] The nature of the requests directed to the Court went far toward tipping the balance in favor of the "quasi-contentious" conception.[151]

[147]PCIJ, Ser. E, No. 4, p. 76.

[148]In the *Eastern Carelia* case, the Court probably went farthest in penetrating to the reality behind the request. See Chapter V.

[149]Thus, the Court considered itself bound by the limits of the question asked by the Council and would not consider, additionally, questions raised by one party (*Exchange of Greek and Turkish Populations* case, PCIJ, Ser. B, No. 10, p. 17), or even by both parties (*Caphandaris-Molloff Agreement* case, PCIJ, Ser. A/B, No. 45, p. 87).

[150]For further discussion of the two conceptions, see Chapter V.

[151]See Chapter II.

By the time the Court had ceased functioning, advisory practice had been largely codified in Articles 65–68 of the revised Statute and in Articles 82–85 of the Rules. But, in all the codifications, care was taken to preserve a large measure of latitude for the Court to adapt its advisory procedure to the requirements of each case. No enumeration of the articles applicable by analogy was ever sanctioned. Nor was any rigid dichotomy between procedure on "disputes" and that on "questions" ever established. While assimilation to contentious procedure was as complete as that envisaged in the 1920 draft scheme, procedure on "questions" also was characterized by a large measure of assimilation. The difference between the two procedures was more one of degree than one of kind. Even the 1927 addition to Article 71 of the Rules and the final proviso of Article 82 of the 1936 Rules—in which the Court came closest to establishing a dual procedure—did not serve to place opinions on "questions" beyond the judicial pale.[152] The principal distinguishing element was the opportunity to appoint judges *ad hoc* in "dispute" cases.

The code of advisory practice bequeathed by the Permanent Court to its successor was left virtually intact by the draftsmen at San Francisco, in framing the relevant provisions of the UN Charter and ICJ Statute, and by the new Court in framing its Rules. Reflecting, presumably, considerable satisfaction with the manner in which the PCIJ had developed its advisory function, concern centered mainly on extending the availability of the advisory jurisdiction to a wider range of organs and agencies.

Underlying the provisions adopted at San Francisco were conceptions clearly fashioned by League experience. Thus, the first paragraph of Article 96 of the Charter closely followed the third sentence in Article 14 of the Covenant in permitting the two major political organs of the world organization to consult the Court. The General Assembly was given the right to request advisory opinions, despite the fact that its League counterpart had never employed its right to petition the Court. In its role as coordinator of the organization's economic and social activities, the UN General Assembly, it was believed, would have more need of the Court's advice than did its predecessor. Nevertheless, the primary purpose to be served by the advisory function was the one envisaged for it at Paris in 1919 and effected in practice under the League—namely, to aid in the peaceful settlement of disputes. The elimination of the term "any dispute or question" was probably not signifi-

---

[152]Undoubtedly, the establishment of any hard and fast differentiation would have tended to weaken the authority of some of the Court's opinions. It might also have had significant implications for the UN period, when (as will be seen below) most requests did not relate to existing disputes between states.

☐ ARMS CONTROL AGREEMENTS: Designs for Verification
and Organization. David W. Wainhouse and Associates. 1968. 179 pages. $6.95

☐ UNCERTAIN MANDATE: Politics of the U.N. Congo
Operation. Ernest W. Lefever. 1967. 254 pages.
                                            $8.50

☐ PEACEFUL COEXISTENCE: International Law in the
Building of Communism. Bernard A. Ramundo. 1967.
262 pages. $8.50

☐ INTERNATIONAL PEACE OBSERVATION: A History and Fore-
cast. David W. Wainhouse and Associates. 1966.
681 pages. $15.00

☐ THE UNITED STATES IN A DISARMED WORLD: A Study of
the U.S. Outline for General and Complete Disarmament. Arnold Wolfers and Others. 1966. 256 pages
                            $8.50 cloth, $2.95 paper

To order any of these books, simply check the box to
the left and mail this form, with your check or money
order, to THE JOHNS HOPKINS UNIVERSITY PRESS, Baltimore, Maryland 21218.

Name_____

Street_____

City_____

State_____ Zip_____

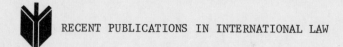 RECENT PUBLICATIONS IN INTERNATIONAL LAW

THE JOHNS HOPKINS UNIVERSITY PRESS   Baltimore, Maryland 21218

☐ UNITED NATIONS PEACEMAKING: The Conciliation
Commission for Palestine. David P. Forsythe.
1972. 208 pages. $10.00

☐ SOUTH WEST AFRICA AND THE UNITED NATIONS: An
International Mandate in Dispute. Solomon Slonim.
1972. 352 pages $13.50

☐ CIVIL STRIFE IN LATIN AMERICA: A Legal History of
U.S. Involvement. William Everett Kane. 1972.
240 pages. $10.00

☐ POWER AND LAW: American Dilemma in World Affairs.
Charles A. Barker, ed. 1971. 224 pages. $8.50

☐ THE SOVIET UNION AND THE LAW OF THE SEA. William
E. Butler. 1971. 272 pages. $12.00

☐ THE INTERNATIONAL LAW OF CIVIL WAR. Richard A.
Falk, ed. 1970. 471 pages. $15.00

☐ THE SOVIET UNION AND ARMS CONTROL: A Superpower
Dilemma. Roman Kolkowicz and Others. 1970. 212
pages. $9.00 cloth, $2.95 paper

☐ THE MERCHANT SHIPPING CODE OF THE USSR (1968).
Translated and edited by William E. Butler and John
B. Quigley, Jr. 1970 181 pages $9.00

☐ FORCE, ORDER, AND JUSTICE. Robert E. Osgood and
Robert W. Tucker. 1967. 384 pages.
                              $12.00 cloth, $2.95 paper

cant in this respect. Both the Statute and the Rules of Court retained provisions allowing for greater assimilation in dispute cases than in nondispute cases (although the term "dispute" was dropped).

The second paragraph of Article 96 of the Charter had no counterpart in the Covenant, but was nonetheless equally based on League experience. The League Council had frequently acted as a transmission belt for other international bodies—most notably, the ILO. In fact, Article 96(2) represented, in a very real sense, the culmination of the ILO's long campaign for direct access to the Court.

The authorizations actually granted under the terms of Article 96(2) have been quite numerous, and the terms of those authorizations quite liberal.

No really drastic changes were instituted at San Francisco. Individual states were denied direct recourse to the advisory procedure, even as they had been under the terms of the Permanent Court's Statute. Conversely, the contentious jurisdiction was not to be available to international organizations. Thus, the basic pre-existing scheme was retained: contentious jurisdiction for states; advisory jurisdiction for international organizations.[153] Subsequently, however, an attempt was made, by means of advisory compromissory clauses, to compensate in part for the exclusion of international organizations from access to the contentious jurisdiction.

One change introduced at San Francisco related to the official relationship between the Court and the new world organization rather than directly to the advisory jurisdiction. Under the terms of Article 92, the Court is now "the principal judicial organ of the United Nations"; and, when account is taken of Article 96(2), the Court may be deemed "the principal judicial organ" of the specialized agencies as well. The new status granted the Court was to affect, to some extent, the Court's view of its advisory function—particularly, its readiness to overcome and overlook difficulties in order to cooperate with other organs and agencies of the United Nations.

On balance, one could not have predicted, on the basis of the new provisions governing the advisory jurisdiction, any drastic change in the exercise of

[153] States may, however, receive declaratory judgments from the Court. See, e.g., PCIJ, Ser. A, No. 13, p. 20; and cf., esp., the pleadings and judgment in the *Northern Cameroons* case. The dividing line between a declaratory judgment and an advisory opinion is sometimes rather thin. (For a discussion of the nature of declaratory judgments, see Edwin M. Borchard, *Declaratory Judgments*, 2nd ed. [Cleveland: Banks-Baldwin, 1941].) Furthermore, submissions in contentious cases may be framed so as to elicit from the Court a nonexecutory judgment very close to an advisory opinion. This emerges from the *North Sea Continental Shelf* cases, in which the three states concerned asked the Court for guidance as to the applicable "principles and rules of international law," and subsequently settled their controversy on the basis of the judicial guidance received. See, in this connection, the remarks of Senator Javits in the General Assembly's Sixth Committee, UN Doc. A/C.6/SR.1211, 3 November 1970, p. 5.

the advisory function. If anything, more extensive use, corresponding to the new ease of access, might have been expected. UN practice, however, was to prove these expectations wrong. The purpose for which the advisory function was, in fact, used was different, and the plethora of authorizations contrasted markedly with the paucity of requests.

II
REQUESTS FOR ADVISORY OPINIONS: SOME GENERAL COMPARISONS

The most obvious contrast between the use of the advisory function in the two periods under consideration is the numerical one. Whereas the PCIJ was called upon to render twenty-seven advisory opinions,[1] the ICJ has, to date, been asked to give only fourteen.[2] When it is recalled that the present Court has already outlived its predecessor,[3] and that direct access to the advisory jurisdiction has been so greatly facilitated in the UN period, this numerical differential assumes added significance.[4]

The following table of the annual number of requests addressed to each Court is rather instructive:

[1] One Council request—that relating to the expulsion of the Oecumenical Patriarch—was later withdrawn. LNOJ, 1925, p. 855. A further request, involving the case of ex-officials of the Saar, was contemplated by a Council resolution of 14 December 1939, but was never filed in Court. *Ibid.*, pp. 502–3.

[2] Two of the fourteen opinions (the two phases of the *Peace Treaties* case) resulted from a single General Assembly request.

For a list of the advisory opinions in the two periods, the dates on which the resolutions requesting the opinions were voted, and the dates on which the opinions were delivered, see Appendix 5. Hereinafter, the PCIJ opinions will at times be cited by reference to the numbers preceding them in Appendix 5. (The numeration there follows the chronological order in which the opinions were delivered.)

[3] In reality, the ICJ has outlived its predecessor by close to a decade. For, while the PCIJ was not formally dissolved until 1946, its effective functioning ceased in 1940.

[4] The decline in the present Court's contentious business, while not of quite the same order of magnitude, is also noteworthy. For a comparison of the number of cases instituted before the two Courts, see Rosenne, *Law and Practice*, 2: Appendix 16, pp. 937–38. For the relevant judicial statistics after 1964, see the ICJ *Yearbooks*.

PCIJ[a]		ICJ	
Year	Number of Requests	Year	Number of Requests
1922	4	1946	0
1923	4	1947	1
1924	2	1948	1
1925	2	1949	3[b]
1926	2	1950	1
1927	1	1951	0
1928	1	1952	0
1929	0	1953	1
1930	2	1954	1
1931	6	1955	2[c]
1932	1	1956	0
1933	0	1957	0
1934	0	1958	0
1935	2	1959	1[d]
1936-1940	0	1960	0
		1961	1
		1962-1969	0
		1970	1[e]
		1971	0

[a]The requests relating to the expulsion of the Oecumenical Patriarch and the ex-officials of the Saar are not included in this list.

[b]One of the requests—that relating to the *Peace Treaties* case—was dealt with by the Court in two phases.

[c]One of the two requests was made by UNESCO.

[d]Request by IMCO.

[e]Request by the Security Council on the Namibia issue.

It can readily be seen that each Court had the greatest number of requests addressed to it during the early years of its existence; that in the last period of its life the Permanent Court had hardly any advisory business;[5] that since

[5]The years 1933 and 1935 are clearly watersheds—and hardly accidentally. The rise of Nazism and the breakdown of the world power balance could not leave the Court unaffected.

1955 only two requests have been made under Article 96(1) of the Charter; and that from 1961 to 1970 the advisory function was virtually relegated to limbo.

Turning now from the number of requests to the formal sources of those requests, another obvious difference between the two periods emerges. Whereas all the League requests proceeded from the League Council, all but one of the eleven requests made by the UN under Article 96(1) of the Charter emanated from the General Assembly.[6] In addition, under the terms of Article 96(2) of the Charter, UNESCO and IMCO each addressed a single request to the Court.

If we look beyond the formal source of League requests to either the real initiators of those requests or the real addressees of the resultant opinions, the picture presented is a rather more variegated one, for, in its recourse to the Court, the Council did not always act in the same capacity. It frequently served as the avenue of access to the Court for other international bodies and for states in dispute. Thus, in four cases, the Council merely transmitted questions formulated by the ILO Governing Body,[7] and, in an additional two cases, the requests, though originating with the Council, related to the competence of the ILO.[8] Requests were also made on behalf of the Mixed Commission for the Exchange of Greek and Turkish Populations[9] and the Greco-Bulgarian Mixed Commission.[10] In two instances the Council's action was prompted directly by agreements of the interested states.[11] Two cases related to the powers of the Conference of Ambassadors, and, in one of these, the

---

[6] The first and, to date, single occasion on which the Security Council employed its power to request advisory opinions was July 1970. Earlier, however, numerous proposals and suggestions for requesting opinions were presented in the Security Council. See Chapter IV for a discussion of these and other stillborn requests in the League and UN eras. (As will be seen, the League Assembly, though it never actually requested an opinion, had its share of abortive requests.)

[7] In Nos. 1 (*Netherlands Workers' Delegate*), 13 (*ILO and the Employer*), 18 (*Danzig and the ILO*), and 25 (*Employment of Women during the Night*).

[8] Nos. 2 (*ILO and Agricultural Labor*) and 3 (*ILO and Agricultural Production*). The Council acted upon the suggestion of France. Serious misgivings regarding the Council's action—particularly in relation to No. 3—were voiced by the ILO Director. LNOJ, 1922, pp. 527–28, 896–903. Upon receipt of both opinions, the Council merely forwarded them to the competent ILO authorities. *Ibid.*, p. 1173. This became the Council's standard practice in ILO cases.

[9] Nos. 10 (*Exchange of Greek and Turkish Populations*) and 16 (*Greco-Turkish Agreement*). The Mixed Commission's proposal to the Council in No. 10 was, in turn, prompted by an earlier suggestion of the League Council's Rapporteur. LNOJ, 1924, p. 1669.

[10] No. 17 (*Greco-Bulgarian Communities*).

[11] Nos. 4 (*Tunis-Morocco*) and 14 (*Danube Commission*). In the latter case, a written agreement, registered with the League Secretariat, was concluded between France, Italy, Great Britain, and Rumania. LNTS, 59: 237.

idea of recourse to the Court originated with the Conference itself.[12] Similarly, in one of the four cases arising out of Polish-Danzig differences, the suggestion of the High Commissioner at Danzig led the Council to apply to the Court.[13] (It will be observed that, except for the ILO, the international agencies enumerated—not excluding the Council itself—were involved in implementing and supervising the peace settlement.)

Paradoxically, and in contrast, the sources of requests in the UN period have been *less* varied. The authorizations extended under the terms of Article 96(2) of the Charter have remained largely unused. Ironically, the ILO, whose history with advisory opinions in the League period and whose long campaign for direct access to the advisory jurisdiction were so largely responsible for the insertion of Article 96(2) in the Charter, has never tasted the fruits of its victory.[14]

Apart from the single request made by the Security Council, all UN requests, as noted, were addressed to the court by the General Assembly. These, in turn, had their origins in the following main committees: three in the political committees;[15] three in the Fourth (Trusteeship) Committee;[16] two in the Fifth (Administrative and Budgetary) Committee;[17] and two in the Sixth (Legal) Committee.[18]

If we move now from the obvious statistical comparisons to the *kinds* of questions posed before each Court in its advisory capacity, the full measure of the difference in the employment of the advisory function in the two periods appears in even sharper focus.

---

[12] Nos. 8 (*Jaworzina*) and 9 (*Monastery of Saint-Naoum*). In the latter case, the Council's Rapporteur initiated the suggestion for requesting an opinion. However, once delivered, that opinion was merely communicated to the Conference. LNOJ, 1924, pp. 1369–72. Conversely, in No. 8, the Council continued to deal with the dispute even after delivery of the opinion. See Chapter VI.

[13] No. 23 (*Polish Nationals in Danzig*). The preceding opinion (*Polish War Vessels in Danzig*) was solicited at the Council Rapporteur's suggestion, but was not dealt with by the Council after delivery of the opinion. See Chapter VI.

[14] For suggestions as to why this might be so, see C. Wilfred Jenks, *The Prospects of International Adjudication* (Dobbs Ferry, N.Y.: Oceana; London: Stevens, 1964), pp. 206–8; and Herbert C. Merillat, ed., *Legal Advisors and International Organizations* (Dobbs Ferry, N.Y.: Oceana, 1966), pp. 10–11.

[15] The requests in the *Admission* case (First Committee), and in the *Competence* and *Peace Treaties* cases (Ad Hoc Political Committee).

[16] All three requests related to South West Africa. In the *South West Africa (Voting)* case, the idea of consulting the Court was first proposed by the Committee on South West Africa. A draft resolution to effect such a consultation was approved by the Fourth Committee, but was not voted on in Plenary. Subsequently, however, the Assembly reversed itself and adopted a resolution which, although originating in Plenary, was similar in substance to the earlier draft resolution of the Fourth Committee. See Chapter III, pp. 130–37.

[17] The requests in the *UN Administrative Tribunal* and *Expenses* cases.

[18] The requests in the *Reparation* and *Reservations* cases.

Apart from the ILO cases, the overwhelming majority of League requests were in a rather direct way related to the peaceful settlement of disputes between states.[19] Only four of the non-ILO cases are classified by Goodrich as belonging in the nondispute category,[20] but, even of these, three are recognized as borderline cases.[21] While all four related to the Council's performance of its "administrative" functions,[22] in only one case were there clearly no states that could be identified as "parties" to a dispute or to a potential dispute.[23]

The kinds of questions referred to the PCIJ for advisory opinions were, on the whole, not very different from those submitted to it under its contentious jurisdiction.[24] In its advisory, no less than in its contentious, capacity, the

[19] The term "dispute" is here used in the sense of a conflict of views and interests which has crystallized and become manifest outside the organizational confines, and in which two or more states have a particular and more immediate interest than does the membership of the organization at large. (Cf. the discussion of the term in the joint dissenting opinion of Judges Spender and Fitzmaurice, *South West Africa Cases* [Preliminary Objections], ICJ Reports, 1962, pp. 547-49.)

[20] The four are No. 6 (*German Settlers in Poland*), No. 7 (*Acquisition of Polish Nationality*), No. 26 (*Minority Schools in Albania*), and No. 27 (*Danzig Legislative Decrees*). Leland M. Goodrich, "The Nature of the Advisory Opinions of the Permanent Court of International Justice," *AJIL*, 32 (1938): 744-45.

[21] In Nos. 6, 7, and 26, "the alleged infringements of international obligations were capable of developing into actual disputes between States." Goodrich, *op. cit.*, p. 747. The interpretation of minorities provisions was at issue in all three cases, and, as noted by Julius Stone, "the idea of the framers of the minorities treaties was to make minorities questions a matter between the Council and the State concerned and avoid having two individual States ranged against each other." *International Guarantees of Minority Rights* (London: Oxford University Press, 1932), p. 136. Nevertheless, interstate disputes on the same subject often preceded, coexisted with, or followed Council treatment of the question. *Ibid.*, pp. 130 ff.

[22] Goodrich, *op. cit.*, p. 746.

[23] No. 27 (*Danzig Legislative Decrees*) involved the League guarantee of the Free City's constitution. The dispute in this case was an intra-Danzig one between the dominant National Socialist party, on the one hand, and three minority parties, on the other. In Nos. 6 and 7, although Germany did not appear as a party before the Council (the complaints having been brought by the German Minority League in Poland), the questions had earlier been the subject of direct Polish-German negotiations; Germany and Poland were represented before the Court; and, in No. 7, in the post-opinion phase, the matter was again taken up in direct German-Polish negotiations and resolved only by the conclusion of a German-Polish convention (see below). Moreover, in the League Council, the question in No. 7 was at one point referred to as a "dispute." LNOJ, 1923, p. 881. And cf. Stone, *op. cit.*, pp. 131-33. In No. 26, it was the Greek minority in Albania, not the Greek government, which petitioned the Council to consider the issue; Greece was not represented before the Council; and the Court apparently considered the question as one not related to an existing dispute. PCIJ, Ser. E, No. 11, p. 151; Ser. C., No. 76, p. 205. Nevertheless, Greece was the only state, besides Albania, represented before the Court. Cf. the recognition of Greece's special interest, in the post-opinion discussions. LNOJ, 1935, p. 627.

[24] See Goodrich, *op. cit.*, p. 755 and n. 92. In many cases, recourse to advisory procedure appeared as an alternative to the employment of contentious procedure. See Chapter III.

Court was called upon to adjudicate disputes arising out of the peace settlement.[25] Thus, requests for advisory opinions related to such matters as frontier disputes,[26] international waterways,[27] the special status of Danzig,[28] and problems connnected with minorities and the exchange of populations.[29] As noted above, the sources of most League requests were agencies charged with implementing and supervising the peace settlement. The Court's role was frequently that of final appellate jurisdiction in relation to these various agencies.[30]

Most of the questions which came before the Permanent Court had a rather "concrete" aspect—i.e., they generally arose out of specific factual situations and were framed in fairly specific terms.[31] Most involved the interpretation of treaty provisions. While several requests required judicial interpretation of Covenant provisions,[32] in no case was the Court asked to interpret such provisions in the abstract.[33] Requests relating to provisions of the ILO Constitution were, however, framed in more generalized and abstract terms.[34]

On almost every point enumerated above, the situation in the UN era presents elements of counterpoise and contrast. For here the advisory function was *not* used, save perhaps in one instance,[35] in relation to disputes

---

[25] The only non-ILO advisory opinion not related to the postwar settlement was No. 4.

[26] Nos. 8, 9, and 12.

[27] No. 14.

[28] Nos. 11, 15, 18, 22, 23, and 27.

[29] Nos. 5, 6, 7, 10, 16, 17, 19, 23, and 26.

[30] The Court's role was often that of court of appeal at third instance. Thus, e.g., in cases relating to Polish-Danzig relations, the route of the dispute led, several times, from High Commissioner to Council to Court.

[31] Some questions were more general in character, as, e.g., in No. 10, where the Court was asked to interpret the word *établis* in Article 2 of the Convention of Lausanne of 30 January 1923. Nevertheless, reference was made in the question to the discussions and arguments contained in the dossier submitted to the Court, and the Court took this reference as its cue for dealing with the question in a more concrete fashion. PCIJ, Ser. B, No. 10, p. 9. This tendency of the PCIJ to treat questions as "concrete" contrasted markedly with the tendency of the ICJ—particulary in its early years—to consider questions in the abstract. See Chapter V, pp. 307–12.

[32] E.g., Nos. 4, 5, 12, and 21.

[33] But, on a number of occasions, suggestions were made that this be done. See Chapter IV.

[34] The request in No. 3 was the most "abstract" in that it did not result from any disagreement between states on the point in question.

[35] In the *Peace Treaties* case, the ICJ affirmed the existence of "disputes" within the meaning of the provisions of the treaties in question. ICJ Reports, 1950, p. 77. But it may be doubted whether the states that brought the disputes before the UN did so for the purposes of "peaceful settlement." See Chapter III.

Classification of the South West Africa (Namibia) issue is much more problematical. It is to be viewed perhaps most realistically as a dispute between the world organization

brought before the organization for peaceful settlement; and it was only on that same solitary occasion that the Court was asked to interpret provisions of a peace treaty. The new requests, emanating from the General Assembly, bore a rather strong "organizational" stamp. The differences of opinion directly preceding the requests arose, became manifest, and crystallized within the organizational confines.[36] And the requests generally related to administrative difficulties facing the organization[37]—whether in connection with the admission of new states to membership,[38] UN staff matters,[39] the Secretary-

---

and an individual member state—a kind of dispute not represented in League requests. Until the 1960s, this was clearly the way the issue was generally viewed. In 1962, however, the ICJ, in assuming jurisdiction, affirmed the existence of an interstate dispute, separate and distinct from the dispute between the organization and South Africa. (This view was rejected by the dissenting judges, who saw the applicants as agents of the UN.) The 1966 judgment did not formally deny the existence of a dispute, although this was the thrust of the Court's reasoning. (Formally, the Court merely denied that applicants had any legal right or interest in the subject matter of their claims. On this point, see the dissenting opinion of Judge Gros, ICJ Reports, 1971, pp. 328–29.) After the General Assembly declared the mandate terminated (in Resolution 2145, 27 October 1966), the issue began to "spill over" into the direct interstate level (e.g., in relation to consular representation in South West Africa and the right of South Africa to represent the territory in the ITU). Basing itself particularly on post-1960 developments, South Africa argued in the *Namibia* case that the request related to a dispute. (South Africa's application for a judge *ad hoc*, as well as several of its arguments bearing on the Court's competence and on substantive issues in the case, was premised on the existence of a dispute. See *Namibia* case, ICJ Pleadings, 1971, 1: 42–47; *ibid.*, Verbatim Record, C.R. (H.C.) 71/1 (Rev.), 27 January 1971.) For its part, the Court denied that an interstate dispute, or even a UN versus South Africa dispute, was involved in the request. ICJ Reports, 1971, pp. 24–27. (Several of the individual judges, however, took issue with the Court's categorization of the request. See Chapter V.) In the proceedings, the Secretary-General and South Africa clearly emerged as quasi litigants.

It should be noted that the dearth of UN requests in the "dispute" category was certainly not due to any lack of proposals (in connection with specific disputes) that such requests be made. See Chapter IV.

[36] That these "organizational" differences were themselves generally rooted in political events and tensions originating outside the organization was to be expected. Quite obviously, the organization does not operate in a vacuum.

In the case of South West Africa (Namibia), what began as an "organizational" issue subsequently "spilled over" to the direct interstate level. See n. 35.

[37] Even the one "dispute" case—the *Peace Treaties* case—had somewhat of an "organizational" aspect in that the Secretary-General's function under the treaties also was implicated.

Due, perhaps, to the more markedly "organizational" nature of UN requests, the UN Secretary-General has assumed a far more active role in advisory proceedings than did his League counterpart. For a discussion of this new role, and a description of it as "an *amicus curiae* function," see Rosenne, *Law and Practice*, 2: 742–43. However, in the *Namibia* case, the Secretary-General fulfilled a role more closely akin to "quasi applicant" than to *amicus curiae*. (Cf. the dissenting opinion of Judge Gros for the view that, in the *Namibia* case, the *amicus curiae* function was assumed by France alone. ICJ Reports, 1971, p. 328.)

[38] The *Admission* and *Competence* cases.

[39] The *Reparation* and *UN Administrative Tribunal* cases. The *UNESCO* case related to a UNESCO staff matter.

General's function as depositary of treaties,[40] the organization's finances,[41] or the organization's role in regard to the administration of non-self-governing territories.[42] In most cases, the Court was called upon to interpret Charter provisions, and frequently the requests for such interpretation were framed in relatively abstract terms.[43] Whereas the bulk of the PCIJ's advisory work was comprised of the interpretation of treaties of a nonconstitutional nature, in the advisory work of its successor, general questions of international law[44] and of "international constitutional law" became predominant.[45] Generally speaking, the earlier blurring of the lines between the subject matter presented to the Court in its advisory and contentious capacities has given way, in the UN period, to a new and rather sharp differentiation.

Nothing perhaps better illustrates the contrast between the kinds of questions asked of the two Courts than a review of state participation in advisory proceedings.[46] In a total of twenty-seven PCIJ advisory cases, only twenty states participated, while, in fourteen ICJ cases, fifty-one states participated. Furthermore, in eighteen out of the twenty-one non-ILO League cases, no more than two states per case were represented before the Court;[47] and, in an additional two cases, only the directly interested states were represented.[48]

[40] The *Reservations* case.

[41] The *Expenses* case.

[42] The requests relating to South West Africa (Namibia).

[43] UN requests have had, on the whole, a more "abstract" and generalized character than those of the League. For its part, the Court has frequently preferred to deal with the request on an even higher level of abstraction than the strict terms of the Assembly resolution requesting the opinion might have required. This was especially true of the Court's early advisory pronouncements. See Chapter V, pp. 309-10.

[44] This is not to imply that the PCIJ did not have occasion to pronounce on general questions of international law. Quite apart from the principles of treaty interpretation and questions of treaty law—themselves part of general international law—the Court elucidated many other questions of wide import, questions relating to such matters as (to cite but a few): state succession (in Nos. 6 and 7); res judicata (in Nos. 8, 9, and 11); individuals as subjects of international law (in No. 15); and the relationship between municipal law and international law (in Nos. 6, 10, 15, 17, and 26). See also Lauterpacht, *International Court, passim*. But these pronouncements were incidental to the settlement of a dispute and were not the main questions presented for the Court's determination.

[45] On the other hand, while the PCIJ elucidated ILO "constitutional law" on five occasions, the ICJ has had to interpret the constitutive instrument of a specialized agency only in the *IMCO* case. (The Indian application for a judgment, filed in August 1971, involves the interpretation of the ICAO Constitution.)

[46] See Appendix 6.

[47] In three of the eighteen cases, only one state appeared. In Nos. 5 and 12, the second parties—Russia and Turkey, respectively—refused to appear (though Turkey did supply some information to the Court, and the Russian telegram in the *Eastern Carelia* case did touch on the merits of the dispute in that case). No. 27 (*Danzig Legislative Decrees*) was a "nondispute" case.

[48] In No. 14, France, Italy, Great Britain, and Rumania—the parties to the special agreement which led to the institution of advisory proceedings—were represented. In the

Participation in ICJ advisory proceedings has obviously been broader, with more states being represented in some manner in each case. However, whereas in the League period the participant states were usually represented in both written and oral proceedings,[49] in the UN period, only twenty-five states have ever participated in oral proceedings,[50] most states being content to limit their participation to rather brief written statements.[51] Quite obviously, the League cases partook of a bilateral or "plurilateral" nature, while the UN cases were more truly "multilateral": they were of wider, though less immediate, import to states. Or, in other words, the League cases generally related to "disputes," while the UN cases were "organizational."

In this context, it is also instructive to note the respective "clustering" in state participation during each period. The states appearing most frequently in advisory proceedings before the PCIJ were Poland (ten times); Danzig, Greece, and Great Britain (six times each); and Germany and France (five times each). The prominent position of Poland, Danzig, Greece, and Germany is attributable to the fact that disputes in which these states were involved were often adjudicated by the Court in its advisory capacity.[52] In the UN period, on the other hand, the three states leading all others in terms of participation in advisory proceedings were the United States (represented in all fourteen cases) and the United Kingdom and France (each represented in nine).[53] Quite apart from any more direct interests which these states may have had in particular cases[54] (especially those cases related to the Cold War), their extensive participation is probably traceable to their special status as great powers—a status which reflected itself in greater involvement in organizational affairs.[55]

Customs Union case, the five states most immediately concerned were represented. Only in No. 9 did a state not directly concerned (Greece) participate in the proceedings.

[49] In No. 11, no oral hearings were requested, and a second round of written statements was substituted.

[50] No oral proceedings were conducted in the *South West Africa (Voting)* and *UNESCO* cases. In the former, no state requested to be heard; in the latter, the Court decided (for reasons related to the equality of the parties, about which see Chapter V) to dispense with oral proceedings.

[51] Frequently, states merely set forth their conclusions or cited their previously stated positions. In addition, many statements (particularly those emanating from the Soviet bloc) threw up challenges to the Court's competence to render the opinion requested and did not touch on the merits of the questions raised.

[52] As for Great Britain and France, the high figures are partially the result of participation in ILO cases. (The former was represented in three ILO cases, the latter in two.)

[53] When oral participation alone is considered, the same three states predominate, but here the relevant figures are: the United Kingdom, 8; the United States, 6; and France, 5.

[54] Thus, e.g., the United States clearly had a rather immediate interest in the *UN Administrative Tribunal* and *UNESCO* cases, since the root causes in both were American internal security laws.

[55] The Soviet Union's position was shaped more by its general attitude of hostility toward the Court. Its "participation" generally consisted of voicing opposition to the

What were the real interests being arbitrated, directly or indirectly, by means of the advisory opinions of the two Courts? Due to the nature of League requests, the tensions to which they related were closer to the surface. Many of these tensions, as noted by Rosenne, were those "which in time played a major role in the course of events leading to the outbreak of the Second World War."[56] German-Polish differences (under which rubric Danzig-Polish differences may also be subsumed) were most prominent.[57] Germany was also involved in the "hottest" question ever posed to the Court, that of the Austro-German customs regime, an issue in which fears of German resurgence were laid bare. The very last advisory opinion of the PCIJ involved Germany too—this time in the form of Nazi ideology as reflected in certain Danzig legislative decrees.[58] Polish-Lithuanian, Polish-Czechoslovak, and Albanian-Yugoslav conflicts also engaged the Court's attention,[59] as did differences between Britain and France; Finland and Russia; Greece and Turkey; Britain and Turkey; Greece and Bulgaria; and Greece and Albania.[60] Geographically, all the non-ILO cases were, to all intents and purposes, European. Even in the cases of *Mosul* and *Tunis-Morocco*, which technically related to Asian and African affairs, the states principally concerned were the European states of Britain and France, and the partially European state of Turkey.

Turning now to the UN requests, the underlying conflicts were frequently once removed, as it were, from the issues presented to the Court. Cold War tensions undoubtedly underlay the requests in the *Admission, Competence, Peace Treaties,* and *Expenses* cases. The pressure of decolonization, which pitted the world community of states against South Africa, was reflected in the four advisory opinions on South West Africa (Namibia). Two of the requests relating to staff matters had their genesis in United States internal security legislation. The issue of flags of convenience was behind the request in the *IMCO* case.

While most of the UN requests have been "universal" and not geographically localized, in a number of respects the advisory work of the present

Court's giving the opinion requested. The only case in which a Soviet representative appeared in oral proceedings was the *Expenses* case—one in which the Soviet Union had a rather immediate interest. Czechoslovakia and Poland were each represented once in oral proceedings.

[56] *Law and Practice*, 1: 11.

[57] They were involved, in varying degrees, in Nos. 6, 7, 11, 15, 19, 22, and 23.

[58] PCIJ, Ser. A/B, No. 65. The controversial decrees were declared unconstitutional and were repealed at the time.

[59] Nos. 21, 8, and 9, respectively. In the last two, questions of sovereignty over disputed territory were involved.

[60] Respectively, Nos. 4; 5; 10 and 16; 12; 17 and 24; and 26. As noted above, many of the differences revolved around the problem of minorities and the cognate issue of the exchange of populations.

Court has been geographically broader than that of its predecessor:[61] four cases related to the question of South West Africa; the flags-of-convenience issue involved the interests of Panama and Liberia; the *Expenses* case related to peace-keeping forces in the Middle East and Africa; and the *Reparation* case arose mainly out of events occurring in Palestine. Perhaps more important, *participation* in advisory proceedings has been broader. The only "European" advisory case has been the *Peace Treaties* case, and here, too, a non-European power, the United States, appeared as a "party."

In sum, the advisory jurisdiction of the Court was employed neither to the same extent nor for the same purposes in the two periods. The "quasi-contentious" nature of the earlier advisory opinions gave way to the kind of advisory opinions which more nearly resemble those of national courts.[62] But in one important respect, in particular, even the new advisory opinions differ from the more typical "national" opinions. The fact that no dual procedure for "dispute" and "nondispute" cases was ever adopted, and that, as a result, the procedure for *all* advisory opinions remains a truly "judicial" procedure, lends even to the "new" opinions a measure of authoritativeness and definitiveness not normally possessed by "national" opinions, where judicial safeguards are generally absent.[63] Indeed, this very authoritativeness becomes an important consideration in the determination of whether or not, in a particular case, the Court's advisory jurisdiction is to be employed.

---

[61] Jenks, *op. cit.*, pp. 85–86.

[62] The latter usually relate to proposed administrative measures rather than to concrete disputes. On the nature of national advisory opinions, see Felix Frankfurter, "Advisory Opinions," *Encyclopedia of the Social Sciences*, 1: 475–78; Manley O. Hudson, "Advisory Opinions of National and International Courts," *Harvard Law Review*, 37 (1924): 970–1001.

[63] Nevertheless, although the Court's procedure gives states the *opportunity* for a full hearing, this does not mean that states will avail themselves of the opportunity to the extent which might, from the viewpoint of sound jurisprudence, be considered desirable. Thus, some ICJ opinions were given without the benefit of a real hearing of both sides on the issue simply because of the failure of one side to be represented before the Court. This was true of the 1955 and 1956 South West Africa opinions. Similarly, in the *Reparation* case, the organization's capacity to claim reparation for injuries suffered in the service of the UN was not "squarely challenged before the Court." See Lissitzyn, *International Court*, pp. 15–16.

Immediacy of concern is obviously one important determinant of state participation in advisory proceedings, and, to the extent that it is, inadequate pleadings in certain "organizational" cases is probably unavoidable. Moreover, even a state with an important interest in a case (as, e.g., South Africa in the 1955 and 1956 South West Africa opinions) may fail to be represented before the Court, for reasons of policy.

III
REQUESTS FOR ADVISORY OPINIONS: CASE STUDIES

What considerations have, in fact, determined whether and in what manner the Court's advisory jurisdiction would be invoked?

Quite obviously, recourse to the Court is not prompted by the desire for mere intellectual edification regarding difficult points of international law. "Litigation" (and this holds true for the advisory process as well), "is but a phase in the unfolding of a political drama."[1] Regardless of the "abstract" or "concrete" nature of the question posed before the Court, the decision to involve the Court springs from specific difficulties with which states are confronted—whether in their individual capacities or in their capacities as members of an international organization. But employment of the advisory jurisdiction generally appears to states as merely one of several alternative courses of action that might be taken at a particular juncture. The most likely alternative to requesting an opinion might well be resort to some other channel of law clarification, the adoption of an immediate "political" decision, or, in some instances, the acknowledgment by the organ concerned of its inability to affect the root problem altogether. What peculiar advantage, then, was expected to be derived from consultation of the Court? And why was the Court's advisory, rather than its contentious, jurisdiction turned to?

The answers to these questions do not usually appear on the surface. There is frequently little or no explicit indication of the factors motivating a particular request. The paucity of arguments for and against consulting the Court is most notable with respect to League requests, which were generally adopted unanimously[2] and without much public discussion, following a Rap-

---

[1] Rosenne, *Law and Practice*, 1: 2.

[2] Although the question of the vote required for requests remained unsettled throughout the life of the League (see Chapter IV, pp. 213–21), the Council hesitated to adopt requests in the absence of unanimity. Only in two cases (*Acquisition of Polish Nationality* and *Mosul*) was unanimity apparently not attained. See p. 219, n. 215, below.

porteur's recommendation.[3] In the UN era, on the other hand, all decisions to employ the advisory jurisdiction were, at least to some degree, contested.[4] (Given the majority system of voting and the role of "permanent opposition" to recourse to the Court which the Soviet bloc has assumed,[5] this is hardly surprising.) However, even extensive discussions do not always clearly reveal why the Court's advisory function was invoked in the particular circumstances. Indeed, not infrequently, the suggestion or proposal for requesting an opinion emerges as an unexplained "given" around which subsequent debates revolve but whose raison d'être remains, to some extent, shrouded in mystery. Thus, in any attempt to fathom the true motivation behind the decision to request an opinion, elements of conjecture are probably unavoidable. Nevertheless, important clues to the considerations prompting a request are to be found in such contextual elements as the following: the previous methods employed in an attempt to resolve the root problem; the manner in which the request was initiated and formulated; the alignment of states for and against recourse to the Court; and the debates on the substantive problem, on the principle of recourse to the Court, on the formulation of the request, and on the interim action to be taken pending receipt of the Court's opinion. A study, in this manner, of specific League and UN requests should highlight the principal considerations motivating requests in the two periods and should point up significant intereral similarities and differences.[6]

[3] The League Rapporteur functioned very much as a "behind-the-scenes" conciliator between the interested parties. He did not generally make public recommendations before a thorough private exploration of the attitudes of the states concerned had been made. In these circumstances, extensive public debate was often unnecessary.

[4] Even the General Assembly's request in the *Reparation* case, which was adopted unanimously in Plenary, was opposed to some extent in the Sixth Committee. The Security Council's request on Namibia was adopted with no negative votes, but with three abstentions. As in many other Security Council votes, the abstentions (especially of permanent members) indicated a measure of opposition. See, especially, the views of the United Kingdom on the formulation of the request (UN Doc. S/PV.1550, 29 July 1970, pp. 88–91), as well as the views of France, which voted *for* the request (*ibid.*, pp. 87–88).

[5] This is by no means to imply that opposition to requests stemmed solely from the Communist bloc. But, whereas most states are guided by their assessment of the particular situation, the Soviet bloc's hostility is additionally based on ideological grounds. The Soviet attitude in the Cuban question (about which see Chapter IV) was exceptional.

[6] Due to the large number of League cases, only twelve will be singled out for detailed study. Some are representative of a class of two or more cases. Thus, No. 1 was the first of six ILO cases; No. 6, the first of the "minorities" cases; No. 8, the first case involving the powers of the Conference of Ambassadors; No. 10, the first of two Greco-Turkish cases; No. 11, the first of the Danzig cases; and No. 17, the first of two Greco-Bulgarian cases. Nos. 4, 5, 12, 14, 20, and 21 are included because of the individual importance of each.

As for the UN period, all ten Assembly requests and the Security Council's request on the Namibia question will be discussed. In addition, the *IMCO* case—as representative of a specialized agency case—will be studied.

THE LEAGUE PERIOD

Nomination of the Netherlands Workers' Delegate to the Third Session of the International Labour Conference

The very first request for an advisory opinion addressed to the Permanent Court was one which the League Council transmitted on behalf of the ILO Governing Body and which involved interpretation of the ILO Constitution.[7] The Court was asked to answer the following question:

> Was the Workers' Delegate for the Netherlands at the Third Session of the International Labour Conference nominated in accordance with the provisions of paragraph 3 of Article 389 of the Treaty of Versailles?

It was in the following circumstances that the Court's advice was sought.

Whereas the Netherlands workers' delegates to the first two sessions of the International Labour Conference had been chosen from the largest Netherlands trade-union confederation, the delegate to the third session was appointed after consultation with three smaller confederations only (whose combined membership, however, exceeded that of the largest confederation). A letter of protest was thereupon addressed to the International Labour Office by the largest Netherlands trade-union confederation. Opposition to the Netherlands government's action was echoed by most of the principal workers' federations and by the International Federation of Trade Unions.[8]

The Conference's Credentials Committee, whose task it was to review these various protests, concluded unanimously that legal advice should be sought, since the protests raised a legal question involving the interpretation of Article 389 of the Versailles Treaty.[9] But, after soliciting the advice of two

---

[7] Of the five other requests related to the ILO, all but one (No. 25) entailed constitutional interpretation. The request in No. 25 involved interpretation of an ILO convention.

For a thorough study of the relations between the ILO and the Permanent Court, including an assessment of the Court's pronouncements in the ILO cases, see Georges Fischer, *Les Rapports entre l'Organisation Internationale du Travail et la Cour Permanente de Justice Internationale* (Paris: Pedone, 1946).

[8] These organizations saw in the Dutch action a threat to independent workers' representation at the Conference, for, once it be conceded that a government was not bound to obtain the agreement of the one largest trade-union organization in its country, the door might be opened to unfettered discretion or even arbitrary nominations on the part of governments. Cf. *ibid.*, pp. 296 ff.

[9] PCIJ, Ser. C, No. 1, pp. 381–82. Under paragraph 3 of Article 389, governments undertook to nominate the nongovernment delegates and advisers in agreement with the industrial organizations which were "most representative of employers or work-people." The main question at issue was whether this required the agreement of the one largest professional organization, or whether the collective agreement of a number of smaller organizations also was permissible.

jurists—the legal adviser of the Conference and the Director of the Legal Section of the League Secretariat—the Conference was faced with conflicting interpretations,[10] and it decided to request the opinion of yet a third jurist, M. Anzilotti. However, M. Anzilotti, having been informed that several delegations favored submission of the question to the PCIJ, felt constrained to refuse the desired opinion.[11] Under these circumstances, the Credentials Committee endorsed the suggestion for consulting the Court and recommended that the Conference invite the Governing Body to solicit the Court's opinion (via the intermediacy of the League Council) on "the interpretation of Article 389 of the Treaty of Versailles and . . . the rules which should be observed by the members of the International Labour Organisation, in order to comply with the terms of this Article in appointing non-Government Delegates and Advisers to the Sessions of the General Conference."[12] An authorized interpretation of the Article was considered essential, and the Court was deemed best qualified to give such an interpretation while guaranteeing to all three groups at the Conference impartiality and competence. As for the practical issue at hand—the seating of the Netherlands workers' delegate—the Committee recommended that that delegate be admitted on the condition that this action not be treated as a precedent.[13] These recommendations were adopted unanimously by the General Conference. Acting upon the Conference's recommendation, the Governing Body instructed the ILO Director to request the League Council to solicit the Court's opinion. Without much discussion, the League Council agreed to comply with the ILO request.[14]

[10]*Ibid.*, pp. 384-95. The former considered the Dutch action inconsistent with Article 389 (3); the latter deemed it consistent.

[11]*Ibid.*, pp. 396-98. At that time (November 1921), M. Anzilotti had already been elected to the bench of the Permanent Court.

[12]*Ibid.*, pp. 399-402.

[13]*Proceedings of the International Labour Conference*, 3rd Sess., 1: 515-22.

[14]LNOJ, 1922, pp. 528-29, 610-12. The Council, following the Rapporteur's suggestion, transmitted the question as framed in the letter of the ILO Director. Unlike the formulation of the question in the General Conference's resolution, which referred to the interpretation of Article 389 in the abstract, the new formulation appeared to ask the Court to pass on the legality of the Netherlands government's action. On this ground, Lord Balfour objected that, by complying with the ILO request, the Council would be interfering with the discretion of a League member. But, upon being assured by M. Thomas that the Netherlands government had consented to the ILO proposal, Lord Balfour withdrew his objection. *Ibid.*, p. 529. However, the Netherlands' consent had been to the more generalized version of the question contained in the Conference resolution—a point which was later brought out by the Netherlands government. In a note to the Secretary-General and in a memorial before the Court, that government criticized the new formulation as amounting to the submission of its actions, without its consent, to the Court's judgment. PCIJ, Ser. C, No. 1, pp. 424-28. The Court, in its interpretation of the question, was careful to point out that, since the Netherlands workers' delegate had already been seated, the "sole object" of the question was "to obtain an interpretation of the provisions of paragraph 3 of Article 389," the form of the question being intended solely "to fix clearly the state of facts to which the interpretation has applica-

Thus, in this instance, the Court's advisory function was resorted to for an authoritative interpretation of an article of the ILO Constitution when recourse to other legal channels had led to inconclusive results. In the circumstances, continued uncertainty was insufferable to the workers' delegates at the Conference. To them, it could only mean the undermining of a provision designed specifically to secure for workers the right of independent representation at the Conference and the sanctioning of subjective and arbitrary action by governments. The desire for an authoritative interpretation corresponded, then, to the need to allay the very real anxieties of the workers' delegates in this matter.[15]

Nationality Decrees Issued in Tunis and Morocco (French Zone) on 8 November 1921

In this case the League Council's function was again that of intermediary, but this time for two states in dispute, Britain and France. Advisory in form, the case essentially amounted to arbitration by the Court of a preliminary question—that of domestic jurisdiction.

The dispute to which the request related arose as a result of nationality decrees issued on 8 November 1921 in the French protectorates of Tunis and Morocco. These decrees would have had the effect of conferring French nationality (and, hence, such obligations as military service) on certain persons born in those protectorates and regarded by Britain as British nationals (mainly the Anglo-Maltese community). Britain strongly protested against these measures, and an extensive and futile diplomatic correspondence en-

---

tion." *Ibid.*, Ser. B, No. 1, p. 17. This interpretation, besides meeting the Netherlands' objections, accorded with the statements made throughout the pre-request stage, all of which indicated that the request was designed to obtain a general interpretation for the purposes of future guidance for the ILO and for governments. See, e.g., the ILO Director's Report to the Governing Body (*ibid.*, Ser. C, No. 1, pp. 415–18), and particularly the Director's remarks at the Council meeting (LNOJ, 1922, p. 529). For the view that the overly concrete formulation of the question prevented the Court from offering the ILO meaningful guidelines for the future, see Fischer, *op. cit.*, pp. 302 ff.

[15] See the explanation of the ILO Director, PCIJ, Ser. C, No. 1, pp. 415–18.

It is instructive that neither in this case nor in any other ILO case was invocation of the Court's compulsory jurisdiction contemplated. This was so, despite the theoretical availability of the compulsory jurisdiction under the terms of the ILO Constitution's compromissory clause (Article 423 of the Versailles Treaty). The fact that the questions at issue were "organizational" ones, generally involving disputes between different groups within the ILO (rather than interstate disputes), made the advisory jurisdiction a far more suitable avenue for the resolution of legal differences than was the contentious.

The International Labour Office at various times argued that Article 423 embraced the advisory jurisdiction as well as the contentious. See, e.g., Minutes of the 1929 Ctte. of Jurists, pp. 102–4. See also PCIJ, Ser. B, No. 18, pp. 8–9; Ser. C, No. 18-II, p. 148; and No. 60, p. 207. But cf. Hudson, *Permanent Court*, pp. 439–40. In general, see Fischer, *op. cit.*, chap. II.

sued, during the course of which British proposals to submit the dispute to the Court or to arbitration were rejected by France.[16]

When Britain announced its resolve to place the dispute before the League Council under Article 15(1) of the Covenant, France argued that in accordance with Article 15(8)—the domestic jurisdiction clause—the Council was incompetent to deal with it. However, when the Council met, both governments joined in requesting the Council to submit the preliminary question of domestic jurisdiction to the Court for an advisory opinion and agreed to attribute binding effect to the resultant opinion.[17] The Council's role was entirely passive. It merely approved the resolution in the terms presented by the British representative and concurred in by the representative of France.

Quite obviously, in this case the advisory procedure was employed merely as an alternative to contentious procedure. The procedure employed was, in fact, so close to contentious[18] that it is difficult to comprehend why France should have preferred this "advisory arbitration" to outright arbitration or adjudication of the preliminary point in question.[19]

German Settlers in Poland

Both this case and the *Acquisition of Polish Nationality* case related to the Polish Minorities Treaty of 28 June 1919 and the League Council's competence under that treaty. In both instances, reference to the Court was decided upon only after an alternative method of legal clarification—the employment of a committee of jurists—proved ineffective.[20]

[16] France deemed the Franco-British Arbitration Convention of 14 October 1903 (cited by Britain) inapplicable to the dispute on the grounds, *inter alia*, that the interests of a third state were involved and that nationality questions were too intimately bound up with the very constitution of a state to be considered "exclusively legal." PCIJ, Ser. C, No. 2, additional vol., pp. 178–84, 189–92.

[17] In the event that the Court rejected the French contention, the whole dispute was to be referred to "arbitration or judicial settlement under conditions to be agreed between the Governments." LNOJ, 1922, pp. 1206–7.

[18] The initiative to refer the matter to the Court, as well as the terms of reference, came from the parties; the opinion was accepted, in advance, as binding; the "documents likely to throw light upon the question" were furnished directly by the two states; and the parties presented cases and countercases (concluding with formal submissions) to the Court.

[19] Some of the earlier French arguments against arbitration—e.g., the implication of third parties' interests—may have been considered less applicable to "advisory arbitration." Possibly, too, France found this alternative more palatable and face-saving than outright reversal on the issue of arbitration.

[20] Although only the *German Settlers* case will be treated in detail here, the considerations prompting the requests in the two cases were very similar. The questions involved were considered jointly by the Council and would probably have been referred jointly to the Court, were negotiations on the question involved in the second case not then in progress. LNOJ, 1923, p. 396. When these negotiations proved abortive, the request contemplated earlier was made. *Ibid.*, pp. 933–35.

At issue in the *German Settlers* case was the consistency with Poland's obligations under the Minorities Treaty of measures taken by the Polish government to expel certain colonists of German origin (but of Polish nationality) who had been settled in formerly German territory in pursuance of Prussia's Germanization policy.[21]

The matter was first called to the League's attention by a telegram of 8 November 1921 from the German League for the Protection of the Rights of Minorities. League intervention was urgently requested on behalf of several thousand families of German origin who had been called upon to vacate their lands before 1 December 1921.[22] More than a year elapsed between the date of that telegram and the date on which the decision to request the Court's opinion was made—3 February 1923. During that period the Council's efforts were devoted first toward obtaining more information concerning the question and, subsequently, toward clarification of the legal issues through the employment of a committee of jurists. Simultaneously, during most of the period, Poland granted League requests for postponement of the execution of the expulsion measures. The possibility of requesting an advisory opinion was first broached in a Council resolution of 17 May 1922, adopted after receipt of a detailed report on the legal questions by a three-man committee of the Council.[23] But, before such a request could be contemplated, further study

[21] The expulsion measures were taken pursuant to a Polish law of 14 July 1920, under whose terms sales of, or changes in, landed property or real property rights effected after 11 November 1918 by the Prussian Treasury in favor of third persons were to be null and void. The law was directed against two classes of German settlers: (1) those holding *Rentengutsverträge* (contracts under which property was handed over in perpetuity on payment of a fixed rent) who, prior to 11 November 1918, had not obtained *Auflassung* (the transfer and consequent inscription in the land registry required to perfect the rights of ownership); and (2) those holding land under leases (*Pachtverträge*) contracted before 11 November 1918, for which *Rentengutsverträge* were substituted after that date. Poland's legal case was based on the view that, until *Auflassung*, the settlers' rights to the land had been inchoate and unenforceable at law; that, by granting *Auflassung* after the armistice date, Germany had violated the conditions of the armistice regarding nondiminution of state property during the armistice period; and that Poland was entitled to the property being held by the two abovementioned categories of settlers, by virtue of Article 256 of the Versailles Treaty (the provision vesting in Poland the right to all property and possessions situated in its territory which previously belonged to the German Empire or states). The contrary view was based, *inter alia*, on a different understanding of the character of the rights conferred by the *Pacht-* and *Rentengutsverträge* and of the nature of *Auflassung* under German civil law. In accordance with this view, Poland was interfering with the acquired rights of Polish nationals of German origin, in violation of the Minorities Treaty.

[22] PCIJ, Ser. C, No. 3, vol. III, p. 8. In August, the same question had been placed by Germany before the Conference of Ambassadors, but the latter's suggestions, both with respect to Polish-German negotiations and to possible arbitration, proved fruitless (Poland alone accepted the arbitration proposal); and, in February 1922, the Conference dissociated itself from the matter. *Ibid.*, pp. 368–71.

[23] LNOJ, 1922, pp. 555, 702–7. Preliminary consideration of minorities petitions by

of the legal questions raised in the committee's report was considered desirable, and, for that purpose, the Polish representative was invited to consider these questions further with the Secretary-General. By September 1922, copious documentation on the entire question was at the Council's disposal. The Council's Rapporteur then thought it preferable to have the legal questions clarified by a committee of jurists rather than by the Court, and a decision to this effect was taken. Dictating this choice were such factors as the accessibility of the jurists at the Council seat, the availability of rather full documentation and argumentation upon which to base legal conclusions, and the felt need for a speedy solution of the problem.[24]

However, after the committee of jurists gave its opinion,[25] a turning point in the Council's consideration of the problem was reached. Although Poland had agreed to submission of the question to the committee of jurists,[26] the Polish government now announced that it would not accept the committee's conclusions and that it would refuse to grant any further respite to the petitioners.[27] Moreover, for the first time, Poland challenged the Council's competence to consider the question altogether.[28] In this state of impasse, the earlier suggestion to request the Court's opinion appeared to present a possible way out, and the Rapporteur's recommendation to this effect was

<hr />

three-man committees of the Council was established Council procedure. For an excellent study of the League Council's treatment of minorities questions, see Julius Stone, *International Guarantees of Minority Rights* (London: Oxford University Press, 1932).

[24]*Ibid.*, pp. 1293–98; 1181–82. The committee was composed of three legal advisers to Council representatives and the head of the Legal Section of the Secretariat. It was asked to present its conclusions within seven days, if possible, and, in any case, before the end of the Council session. In fact, the committee's opinion was given within seventeen days. In the case of even "urgent" requests for advisory opinions, an interval of 2–2½ months between request and opinion had to be expected.

The same committee of jurists dealt also with the question involved in the *Acquistion of Polish Nationality* case.

For other reasons which may have dictated preference for a committee of jurists, see Stone, *op. cit.*, pp. 209–11. In his view, the purpose of the jurists' committee in this case was perhaps more to persuade than to clarify.

[25]For the text of the jurists' opinion, see PCIJ, Ser. C, No. 3, vol. III, pp. 281–85. The committee's conclusions were unfavorable to Poland's contentions—though somewhat less so than the Court's conclusions were to be. The Council, in a resolution of 30 September 1922, did not explicitly accept the committee's opinion, but asked the Polish representative to bring the opinion to his government's attention. LNOJ, 1922, pp. 1205, 1301.

[26]*Ibid.*, p. 1181. The Polish representative had, however, voiced some objections to submission of the question involved in No. 7 to the committee.

[27]Note of 7 December 1922, PCIJ, Ser. C, No. 3, vol. III, pp. 244–76. Expulsions had already been renewed. *Ibid.*, p. 276.

[28]Poland maintained that the question involved was not a minorities question within the meaning of the relevant provisions of the Minorities Treaty (*ibid.*, pp. 248–52, 272), and simultaneously challenged the Council's competence with respect to the interpretation of Article 4 of the treaty.

accepted. Both the preliminary question of the Council's competence and the substantive questions involved were referred to the Court.[29]

In explanation of his recommendation, the Rapporteur declared that, although the Council might, on the basis of the jurists' opinion and the Polish reply, take an immediate decision, it might be desirable to ask the PCIJ to examine the matter afresh, since the question involved was clearly of a legal nature and of great importance. But this explanation appears to miss the point. Poland's refusal to accept the jurists' opinion and its challenge to the Council's competence foredoomed any Council attempt to take a direct decision on the question. In contrast, the prospects for Polish acceptance of a judicial pronouncement on the matter and for a consequent break in the deadlock between the Council and Poland appeared more promising. Moreover, the delay involved in seeking the Court's opinion—one of the considerations which had prompted the earlier use of a committee of jurists—could not be decisive now, for Poland had, in any event, refused further respite to the colonists.[30]

It should be noted, however, that, in this case, an alternative method of securing a judicial pronouncement was available—one that would have led to a legally binding decision rather than to an advisory opinion. Under Article 12 of the Minorities Treaty, it was open to any Council member to invoke the Court's compulsory jurisdiction in respect of any difference of opinion between that member and Poland arising out of the provisions of the Minorities Treaty.[31] This proved not to be a practical alternative to the advisory jurisdiction in this case, since Germany, the only state that would presumably have had sufficient interest to be prepared to incur the bother and expense of instituting proceedings against Poland, was not then a Council member.[32]

[29]LNOJ, 1923, pp. 395–97, 232. The decision to request the opinion was made on 2 February 1923; the questions to be submitted were subsequently drafted by the Rapporteur and approved by the Council. *Ibid.*, p. 240. The recorded discussion was brief and centered on the question of whether the decision to request an opinion might be postponed, pending the outcome of Polish-German negotiations. At a later date the Council adopted a report confirming Poland's interpretation of one of the questions, and this report was forwarded to the Court. *Ibid.*, pp. 558, 637.

[30]See the Rapporteur's remark, *ibid.*, p. 396.

[31]For the text of the article, see PCIJ, Ser. B, No. 6, pp. 20–21.

Any attempt to bring the *German Settlers* case before the Court would probably have called forth a Polish challenge to the Court's jurisdiction on grounds similar to those on which Poland challenged the Council's competence. But, in light of the Court's eventual opinion in the *German Settlers* case, it must be assumed that the Court would, in fact, have confirmed its jurisdiction in a contentious case.

For the Court's view that the possibility of instituting contentious proceedings under Article 12 did not preclude the Council from requesting an advisory opinion on a minorities question, see *ibid.*, pp. 22–23. (Cf., to similar effect, the ICJ's pronouncement regarding the right of the UN General Assembly to request an opinion in the *Reservations* case, ICJ Reports, 1951, p. 20.)

[32]In a subsequent case (*Rights of Minorites in Upper Silesia*, PCIJ, Ser. A, No. 15), Germany–then a Council member–did, in fact, file application against Poland, alleging

Significantly, Germany and Poland alone were represented before the Court in the advisory proceedings.

Status of Eastern Carelia

The decision to involve the Court in this controversy was made by the Council at the urging of one of the disputants—Finland—and despite the Council's recognition of the probable ineffectuality of the expected opinion, in light of the attitude of the other disputant—the Soviet Union.

Finland's interest in the fate of her kinsmen in the Eastern Carelian Workers' Commune had its legal foundation in the agreement which terminated the Finno-Soviet war of 1917. In Articles 10 and 11 of the Treaty of Peace signed at Dorpat in October 1920, provision was made for the withdrawal of Finnish troops from two communes occupied during the hostilities; their reincorporation into Russia as part of "the autonomous territory of Eastern Carelia . . . which shall enjoy the national right of self-determination"; and the granting of certain enumerated special rights to the population of the two communes.[33] More detailed provisions regarding the nature and extent of Eastern Carelian autonomy were included in a Declaration made by the Russian delegation on the date of the treaty's signature and inserted in the procès-verbal of the treaty. It was around the nature of this Declaration that the crux of the controversy was to revolve. Finland maintained that the Declaration constituted an integral part of the treaty and contained executory obligations which were binding on Russia, but that Russia had failed to fulfill them. Russia, on the other hand, contended that the Declaration gave rise to no contractual obligations, since it was given solely for informational purposes and merely recorded an already existent state of affairs—namely, the establishment of the Workers' Commune of Eastern Carelia.[34] The question of Eastern Carelian autonomy was, in Russia's view, a purely internal matter.

Finnish protests alleging Russia's nonobservance of its obligations with respect to Eastern Carelian autonomy and self-determination were lodged very soon after the treaty came into force, but were brushed aside by Russia. Subsequently, during an attempted Eastern Carelian insurrection, Finland brought the issue before the League Council.[35] In a resolution of 14 January

---

infractions of certain provisions relating to minorities in the Convention concerning Upper Silesia.

[33] For the text of the two articles and the Declaration annexed to the treaty, see PCIJ, Ser. B, No. 5, pp. 16–22.

[34] There was some discrepancy between the authoritative Finnish, Swedish, and Russian texts, on the one hand, and the authoritative French translation, on the other. The first three employed the present rather than the future tense, apparently implying reference to a pre-existing state of affairs. See Verzijl, World Court, 1: 51; see also the Finnish memorandum in PCIJ, Ser. C, No. 3, vol. II, p. 68.

[35] Finnish letter of 26 November 1921, ibid., pp. 27–30. The insurrection ended in early 1922.

1922, the Council expressed its willingness to consider the question, "if the two parties concerned agree," and suggested that one of the Baltic states maintaining diplomatic relations with the Soviet government "might ascertain that Government's intention in that respect."[36] But an attempt by the Esthonian government to have the Soviet government, as a nonmember state, submit the matter to the Council under Article 17 of the Covenant met with Soviet refusal, on the grounds that the matter was purely domestic.[37] Nor was the Soviet government any more receptive either to Poland's offer of its good offices[38] or to Finland's subsequent proposal to have the dispute adjudicated before the PCIJ or arbitrated.[39]

This state of impasse having been reached, Finland adopted a new approach: it attempted, as a minimum, to obtain clarification of the legal merits of the disputants' positions. To this end, the Finnish government solicited the opinions of three eminent jurists,[40] both as to the substantive issues in dispute and as to whether the Eastern Carelia question might be placed before the PCIJ. The three were unanimous in upholding the Finnish view of Russia's obligations and also agreed that a Court opinion might be requested even in the absence of Russian consent.[41] Armed with this weighty advice, Finland, on 19 April 1923, presented to the Council the draft of a question it wished to have referred to the Court.[42] Two days later the Council approved, without any discussion, its Rapporteur's recommendation to request the Court's opinion on the question presented by Finland.[43]

In view of the hostile Soviet attitude throughout the controversy, what benefit could reasonably be expected from this newest *démarche*? The Coun-

---

[36] LNOJ, 1922, p. 108. The fact that most League members had not, at that time, recognized the Soviet government deterred the League from extending it a direct invitation, as envisaged in Article 17 of the Covenant.

[37] PCIJ, Ser. C, No. 3, vol. II, pp. 77–79.

[38] LNOJ, 1922, p. 105.

[39] The Finnish offer was made on 23 March 1922 and was ignored by the Soviet government. PCIJ, Ser. C, No. 3, vol. II, p. 63.

[40] De Visscher, Lie, and Berlin.

[41] PCIJ, Ser. C, No. 3, vol. II, pp. 137–62. De Visscher, however, entertained some serious reservations regarding any League or Court intervention. *Ibid.*, pp. 142–43.

[42] LNOJ, 1923, pp. 660–61. Earlier, Finland had indicated its intention in general terms. PCIJ, Ser. C, No. 3, vol. II, pp. 57–61; LNOJ, 1923, pp. 221–22. The unsuccessful outcome of renewed Finno-Soviet negotiations hardened Finland's resolve to seek a judicial pronouncement in the matter.

[43] Certain drafting changes were introduced by the Rapporteur, M. Salandra, but these did not alter the substance of the question posed. In its final form, the question was: "Do Articles 10 and 11 of the Treaty of Peace between Finland and Russia, signed at Dorpat on October 14th, 1920, and the Annexed Declaration of the Russian Delegation regarding the autonomy of Eastern Carelia, constitute engagements of an international character which place Russia under an obligation to Finland as to the carrying out of the provisions contained therein?"

cil apparently entertained few illusions in this respect and was also well aware of the peculiar legal difficulties which the absence of Soviet consent entailed. This can be readily deduced from a review of the report presented by M. Salandra, the Council's Rapporteur. The following excerpts from the report are illuminating and bear extensive quotation:

> From the legal point of view, the Council undoubtedly has the right to refer this question to the Court. According to Article 14 of the Covenant, there is no restriction limiting the Council's right to ask advisory opinions on any dispute or point which it desires to submit to the Court.
>
> There can scarcely be any doubt that the question is within the competence of the League of Nations. It is the duty of the League to help its Members, through its institutions, to maintain good relations with their neighbours and to facilitate the peaceful settlement of disputes. It might perhaps be objected that Soviet Russia, being neither a Member of the League of Nations nor a party to the Statute of the Permanent Court, would not be bound by the decision of that Court, even supposing that the Court pronounced in favour of the Finnish view. The Finnish Government must realise this situation, and it must not be encouraged to entertain any illusion in regard to the subsequent assistance which the League of Nations would be able to give it.
>
> Nevertheless, there may be a certain advantage in ... obtaining the opinion of the Court. This opinion would be of great assistance in clearing up the legal points which are the subject of the dispute between Finland and Soviet Russia. If the Court decides in favour of Soviet Russia, Finland will know that she has no right in international law to continue the discussion with Russia and that, if Russia refuses to continue the discussion, this refusal could no longer be interpreted as a hostile act. If the Court pronounced in favour of the Finnish view, it is not impossible that Soviet Russia may recognise the authority of an opinion expressed by the highest international legal tribunal composed, on principles of the most complete impartiality, of eminent jurists from the various quarters of the world.
>
> The opinion expressed by the International Court would thus increase the chances of reaching a satisfactory solution of the dispute concerning Eastern Carelia, although it must be clearly laid down that the League of Nations cannot incur any subsequent responsibility in the matter. As regards procedure, the fact that in this question Soviet Russia is one of the parties concerned requires special attention. Soviet Russia is not only not a Member of the League of Nations, but its Government has not yet been recognised *de jure* by the majority of the other Governments. It has also, on several occasions, shown its hostility to the League of Nations.
>
> Does this situation raise special difficulties as regards the procedure which the Council is invited to follow? We must repeat that the Council is not asked to consider the question of Eastern Carelia as a dispute in which Finland and Soviet Russia are "parties" in the legal sense of the word. In this procedure there will be no "parties" in the strict sense of the word,

and the Court may give a reply to the question raised by the Council without the countries concerned appearing officially as parties to the case. The whole proceedings may even be carried out in writing.

If necessary, it would appear that the reply to this question might be based entirely on the interpretation of the Treaty of Dorpat and on the general principles of international law. It is for the Court to decide if it thinks that it should ask for fuller information or for the opinion of experts regarding the Soviet Government's case. In these circumstances the special situation of the Soviet Government does not seem to raise any particular difficulties which would prevent a request for the Court's opinion on the question of Eastern Carelia.

It would clearly be a great advantage if the Court could obtain explanations from both sides in order that the States concerned might be on a footing of absolute equality. In asking the opinion of the Court the Council will no doubt press this point.[44]

Clearly, the Rapporteur was rather hard-pressed to justify the request in this case. The considerations for requesting the opinion appear rather less convincing than the obvious anxiety to dissociate the League from any further responsibility in a dispute in which the League's helplessness was apparent.[45]

Nor was Finland, whose desires the Council was so eager to meet, any less aware of the inability of any Court opinion to aid in the solution of the problem or to affect materially the lot of the Eastern Carelians.[46] It did seek, in various ways, to justify recourse to the Court. Thus it was argued, *inter alia*, that a judicial opinion "would constitute an authorized as well as an impartial report upon the dispute";[47] that it would assist in the pacification of national feeling; and that it might establish the basis for a renewal of the offer of good offices by certain states.[48] But the more important considerations underlying Finland's moves seemed to be its felt need, in the face of its utter inability to alleviate the plight of the Eastern Carelians, to appear to be taking some "action" and its desire to achieve at least a psychological victory by having the Court endorse its viewpoint while repudiating that of Russia.[49] Similar considerations prompted the League Council to accede to the Finnish

[44] LNOJ, 1923, p. 663.

[45] It was probably the Council Rapporteur's obvious eagerness to accede to Finland's wishes that accounted for some of the inconsistencies in his report, and possibly, too, for the view of the advisory function enunciated by him—a view repudiated by the Court in this case. See Chapter V.

[46] See LNOJ, 1923, p. 662; PCIJ, Ser. C, No. 3, vol. I, p. 132.

[47] PCIJ, Ser. C, No. 3, vol. II, p. 60.

[48] LNOJ, 1923, p. 222. For further arguments, see *ibid.*, pp. 661-62.

[49] After the unanimous opinion of the three foreign jurists, Finland fully expected to have its position judicially sanctioned as well.

request. The only alternative to this "action" on the part of Finland or the League would have been total inaction.

Perhaps it was the Court itself which best recognized the dual motivation behind the request—the attempt to get a kind of declaratory judgment regarding Russia's obligations without Russian consent and the desire to show that "something" was being done. As for the first, the Court refused to allow itself to be used in this manner.[50] The second was given judicial recognition in the following consoling paragraph in the Court's Reply: "The Court cannot regret that the question has been put, as all must now realize that the Council has spared no pains in exploring every avenue which might possibly lead to some solution with a view to settling a dispute between two nations."[51]

Delimitation of the Czechoslovak-Polish Frontier (Question of Jaworzina)

The referral of this acute frontier controversy to the Court bore many of the marks of a submission to arbitration (resembling, in this respect, the *Tunis-Morocco* case). Although it originated with the Conference of Ambassadors, the suggestion to request an opinion was endorsed by the parties, and both disputants recognized in advance the finality of the Court's pronouncement.

The dispute between Poland and Czechoslovakia over the frontier in the Jaworzina district (a rich ore area) of the territory of Spisz traced its origin to the foundation of the two states. Under an agreement of 10 July 1920, both governments entrusted to the Principal Allied and Associated Powers the allocation of three disputed regions on their common border.[52] Accordingly, the Conference of Ambassadors rendered a decision on 28 July 1920[53] and set up a Delimitation Commission to execute it. The effect and interpretation of this decision were the key issues in the controversy. Czechoslovakia maintained, while Poland denied, that that decision and a subsequent Conference decision of 2 December 1921[54] had provided a complete and final solution to the question of the Czechoslovak-Polish frontier, including the frontier in the Spisz district. After an attempt to fix a line by agreement between the parties failed, the Conference of Ambassadors was again faced with the boundary question. By that time, passions on both sides were considerably aroused. The

[50] See Chapter V.

[51] PCIJ, Ser. B, No. 5, p. 29.

[52] A plebiscite which, in accordance with an earlier decision of the Supreme Council, was to determine the disposition of these regions, was never held. For a more complete account of the facts in this case, see *ibid.*, No. 8, pp. 6-26.

[53] *Ibid.*, Ser. C, No. 4, pp. 128-36.

[54] *Ibid.*, p. 197.

subsequent Conference determination that the line in the Jaworzina sector remained undefined succeeded neither in removing the obstacles to final delimitation nor in calming public opinion.[55] Under these circumstances, the Conference of Ambassadors, in a letter of 18 August 1923, brought the matter before the Council under Article 11(2) of the Covenant, and requested the Council to recommend a solution regarding the delimitation of the frontier in the Jaworzina district. In the same letter, the Conference indicated that it would not object if judicial clarification were to be sought on the question of whether or not the disputed frontier had been finally determined by previous Conference decisions.[56]

When the matter was considered by the Council on 20 September 1923, it was clear that both parties considered the dispute to be essentially legal in nature and that both would consent to have the Court determine the legal question with finality.[57] There was some detectable hesitation on the part of the Polish representative and rather more enthusiasm on the part of the Czechoslovakian. The former emphasized the urgency of the issue and the possible delay involved in recourse to the Court. He also raised the possibility of submitting the issue to another law-clarifying agency—e.g., the legal experts at the League. On the other hand, the Czechoslovakian representative (on whom, perhaps, the lesson of the reception granted by Poland to the opinions of the Committee of Jurists in the *German Settlers* and *Acquisition of Polish Nationality* cases was not lost) emphasized the authoritativeness of a Court opinion—an authoritativeness which, in his view, was best calculated to lead to acceptance by the losing party. Presumably, there would be no loss of face and less difficulty with domestic public opinion where a Court pronouncement was involved.

Without any discussion of either the merits of the substantive question or the merits of reference to the Court, the Council adopted, on 27 September 1923, a resolution drawn up by its Rapporteur, in consultation with the two parties, requesting the Court's opinion on the Jaworzina question.[58]

The powers of virtual arbitration entrusted to the Court in this case were, in a sense, delegated arbitration powers. The parties had entrusted solution of their boundary difficulties to the Conference of Ambassadors; the latter, upon encountering difficulties and aroused passions which it felt unable to cope with, vested the Council with its decision-making powers; and the Coun-

---

[55]*Ibid.*, Ser. B, No. 8, pp. 16-17.

[56]LNOJ, 1923, p. 1472.

[57]*Ibid.*, pp. 1316-17, 1473-74.

[58]*Ibid.*, pp. 1332-33, 1474-76. After reciting the facts and setting forth, at length, the "cases" of the two governments, the Council asked whether the question of the delimitation of the Polish-Czechoslovak frontier was still open, and, if so, to what extent.

cil, taking its cue from the Conference's own suggestion and the desire of the parties, delegated its new powers of decision to the Court.[59] Arbitration by the Court, it was thought, was the one most likely to lead to acceptance by the parties and the respective public opinions.

Exchange of Greek and Turkish Populations

The Court's opinion was sought by the Council in this case on behalf of the Mixed Commission for the Exchange of Greek and Turkish Populations, with the purpose of clarifying an important provision of the Convention of Lausanne of 30 January 1923. Despite the fact that the Mixed Commission was endowed by the Convention with powers of decision with respect to all questions arising under the Convention, the Commission's interpretation, though reinforced by the opinion of its Legal Section, was not accepted by Turkey.

At issue was the interpretation of Article 2 of the Convention, which provided exemption from compulsory exchange for two classes of persons: Greeks "established" (*établis*) in Constantinople before a certain date and Moslems "established" in Western Thrace. More specifically, the controversy centered on the meaning of the term "established" in relation to the first of the two classes. While in the view of the Turkish members of the Mixed Commission the term "establishment" was to be equated with the legal term "domicile" (as applied in Turkish law), the Greek delegates maintained that that term related solely to a situation of fact. These divergent views having been manifested early in the controversy, the three neutral members of the Commission were then called upon to give their opinions. In their unanimous opinion of 4 September 1924, they upheld the Greek interpretation.[60] The Turkish delegation, however, refused to accept this interpretation and insisted that the question be referred to the Commission's Legal Section—a request with which the Commission reluctantly complied.[61] Its hopes for support

---

[59] The *Monastery of Saint-Naoum* case resembled the *Jaworzina* case in most respects: it, too, related to a question of frontiers; the route to the Court led from the Conference of Ambassadors (which here, too, had been entrusted with powers of decision) to the Council to the Court; upon a recommendation of its Rapporteur, the Council adopted the resolution requesting an opinion without any discussion; and the resolution was explicitly accepted by both parties. See LNOJ, 1924, pp. 1006-10. In this case, however, the proposal to request an opinion originated with the Council's Rapporteur rather than with the Conference. And, while the parties consented to the request, they did not explicitly accept, in advance, the finality of the Court's opinion.

[60] *Ibid.*, pp. 1674-76.

[61] *Ibid.*, pp. 1672-73. The Commission's consideration of the question was punctuated throughout by Turkish threats to resign from the Commission, actual resignations, and withdrawals of resignations. *Ibid.*, pp. 1678-79. See also Stephen P. Ladas, *The Exchange of Minorities: Bulgaria, Greece, and Turkey* (New York: Macmillan, 1932), pp. 402-5.

from this new quarter having been equally disappointed,[62] Turkey proceeded to take matters into its own hands and arrested some 4,500 persons (whom it considered exchangeable) for purposes of expulsion to Greece. With these arrests, the conflict entered an acute stage, and Greece appealed to the League Council to take up the matter.[63] By the time of the Council's consideration, an agreement between the two parties had eased the tension and put an end to the incidents,[64] but had left unresolved the basic difficulty—namely, the interpretation of Article 2 of the Lausanne Convention. After hearing representatives of both parties and the President of the Mixed Commission, the Council adopted a report by Viscount Ishii expressing the hope that a plenary meeting of the Commission might be convened as soon as possible in order to determine finally the disputed points in the interpretation of the Convention, and suggesting possible recourse to the Court ("one of whose special duties is to undertake the interpretation of treaties"), should the Commission members encounter "points of great legal difficulty, which they doubt whether they have sufficient juridical knowledge to interpret." It was then left to the Commission to choose one of two routes to the Court: the contentious, by which the two disputants would bring their disagreements directly before the Court; or the advisory, by which the Council would be petitioned to request an opinion.[65] The Commission, in fact, decided to take the second route, when it became clear that it could not resolve the issue on its own.[66] The Council complied with the Commission's desire by adopting a resolution on 13 December 1924 without discussion and with the consent of the two governments concerned.[67]

[62] See the Report of the President of the Legal Section, LNOJ, 1924, pp. 1676–78. The Turkish delegation's absence prevented the Commission from taking a final decision in Plenary. *Ibid.*, p. 1673.

[63] *Ibid.*, pp. 1678–79.

[64] *Ibid.*, pp. 1672–73. In fact, the agreement had been concluded on 21 October 1924, before the first Greek appeal to the Council, but some arrests continued to be made. *Ibid.*, p. 1665.

[65] *Ibid.*, pp. 1669–70.

[66] For the Mixed Commission's discussions, see PCIJ, Ser. C, No. 7-I, pp. 90–100. Use of the contentious jurisdiction apparently was not contemplated at all.

The Mixed Commission's decision was taken at its Seventy-seventh Plenary Meeting on 16 November 1924. Turkey gave assurances at that time that it would not, pending receipt of the Court's opinion, take any prejudicial measures against the persons whose status was in dispute. *Ibid.*, pp. 99–100.

[67] LNOJ, 1925, pp. 155, 283. Relying on the Ishii report, the Mixed Commission petitioned the Council a few years later to request another opinion—that in No. 16 (*Greco-Turkish Agreement*). The League's Secretary-General questioned the applicability of the Ishii report to the Commission's second request, and only after solicitation of the opinion of a committee of jurists and after assurances that Greece and Turkey consented to the Commission's action was the Commission's request inscribed in the Council's agenda. *Ibid.*, 1928, pp. 370, 403–4, 453–56. The necessity to appeal to the Court in

Notwithstanding the theoretical power of the Mixed Commission to settle finally all questions arising under the Lausanne Convention, Turkey's unwillingness, in practice, to abide by the interpretation favored by the majority of the Commission led that body to turn to the Court, in accordance with the League Council's suggestion. In so doing, the Commission obviously hoped to draw not only on the Court's greater "juridical knowledge" but, more importantly, on that tribunal's authority—an authority which, it was expected, might cause the Court's pronouncement to be more favorably received than were the earlier opinions of the Mixed Commission and its Legal Section.[68]

Polish Postal Service in Danzig

This case was the first of four in which Polish-Danzig disputes were arbitrated by means of PCIJ advisory opinions.[69] In requesting these opinions, the Council was, in effect, delegating to the Court its own powers as court of appeal in relation to Polish-Danzig differences—differences which were, in the first instance, to be resolved by the League's High Commissioner at Danzig.[70]

The subject of contention in this instance was the nature and extent of the postal service, which, under the terms of the relevant treaties,[71] Poland was entitled to establish in the port of Danzig. In particular, the question was raised as to whether the Polish postal service in the port of Danzig could, by right, be extended beyond the building assigned to it and whether it could be open to the public as well as to Polish authorities and officials. When on 5 January 1925 Poland—without previously consulting the Danzig Senate—set up mailboxes in the streets of Danzig bearing the Polish emblem, the controversy reached a boiling point, for here was manifest, in a most acute form, the clash between the Free City's sovereignty and Poland's right of access to the sea. The Free City immediately asked the High Commissioner for a decision on the matter, in accordance with Article 39 of the Treaty of Paris.[72] On 2

---

this case was due not only to Greco-Turkish differences of interpretation but to a divergence of views among the neutral members as well. PCIJ, Ser. C, No. 15-I, p. 132.

[68] On the general inability of the Commission to exercise the authority vested in it, see Ladas, *op. cit.*, pp. 497-500.

[69] The other three were: No. 15 (*Jurisdiction of the Danzig Courts*); No. 22 (*Polish War Vessels in Danzig*); and No. 23 (*Polish Nationals in Danzig*). Danzig's special status was involved in two additional cases: No. 18 (*Danzig and the ILO*)—one of the ILO cases—concerning the possibility of the Free City's membership in the ILO; and No. 27 (*Danzig Legislative Decrees*), which related to the League guarantee of the Free City's constitution.

[70] See PCIJ, Ser. B, No. 11, p. 26, for the Court's characterization of the High Commissioner's functions as "judicial."

[71] The governing treaties were the Treaty of Versailles, the Treaty of Paris of 1920, and the Warsaw Agreement of 1921.

[72] The article provided for the submission of Polish-Danzig differences to the decision of the High Commissioner; the right of the parties to appeal from that decision to the

February 1925 the High Commissioner held that the questions at issue had already been finally decided in Danzig's favor by the preceding High Commissioner. Poland appealed this decision to the Council.

After examining the question, the Council's Rapporteur recommended that an advisory opinion be requested because, as he said, the affair had "assumed a certain political importance," which necessitated that both parties "be given the fullest assurance that all aspects of the question will be thoroughly considered."[73] Poland appeared to have some misgivings regarding the proposed recourse to the Court, on the grounds that the treaty texts were clear and that it was only to the Council, not to the Court, that the parties had a right to appeal.[74] In reply to the latter point, the President noted that what was involved "was not an appeal by Poland or Danzig to the Permanent Court of International Justice but a point of great difficulty on which the Council desired to have the advice of the Court. It would be for the Court to call before it anyone whom it wished to hear before giving its opinion." Thereupon the Council adopted the resolution proposed by its Rapporteur.[75]

In fact, the Court *was* playing the role of court of appeal, in lieu of the Council itself. In this, as in the other Danzig cases,[76] the Court's advisory

---

League Council; and the right of the High Commissioner to submit controversial matters to the Council, should he deem this necessary.

[73] LNOJ, 1925, pp. 564-65 .

[74] *Ibid.*, pp. 471-72. Nevertheless, Poland did not seriously object to requesting an advisory opinion.

[75] *Ibid.*, p. 472. The Court was asked to pronounce itself on whether the matter was already res judicata, and, if the question was still open, on the substantive issue involved in the dispute.

[76] In No. 15 (*Jurisdiction of the Danzig Courts*), the Danzig Senate appealed to the Council against a decision of the High Commissioner. After consultation with the parties, the Rapporteur recommended referring the legal question to the Court—a course this time suggested by Poland, welcomed by the High Commissioner, and merely acquiesced in by Danzig. LNOJ, 1927, pp. 1418-23. The request in No. 22 was made at the High Commissioner's own suggestion, to forestall the inevitable appeal to the Council by the losing state; only if his decision were based on a "legal opinion of undisputable authority," would it, he believed, prove acceptable to both parties. *Ibid.*, 1931, pp. 1135-37. The dispute involving *Polish War Vessels in Danzig* was similarly placed before the Council directly by the High Commissioner. At that point, Danzig had refused to further extend the pre-existing provisional arrangement for Polish warships, and the deterioration in Polish-Danzig relations made the probability of a direct arrangement between the parties remote. Recognizing the legal complexity of the issues involved, the Council's Rapporteur concluded that judicial clarification would be preferable to direct Council scrutiny of the legal questions. *Ibid.*, pp. 2253-56.

In No. 27—a case involving the Council's role as guarantor of the Danzig Constitution—intra-Danzig differences were at issue. These were first placed before the High Commissioner, who, recognizing the importance of the questions raised (the constitutionality of certain Danzig legislative decrees affecting Danzig's penal law), placed them immediately before the Council. The Council's Rapporteur in turn recommended seeking the Court's advice, since the questions at issue were deemed "both difficult and important." *Ibid.*, 1935, pp. 1192-97, 1336-39.

function proved a useful and welcome supplement to the two official chan-nels of dispute settlement.[77] For, particularly with regard to questions pre-senting a mixed aspect of legal complexity and political importance, the Court was able to provide that combination of legal competence and high authority which best assured speedy disposition of the controversy.

Interpretation of Article 3, Paragraph 2, of the Treaty of Lausanne (Frontier between Turkey and Iraq) (Mosul Question)

This case was one of the more important ones to reach the Court. Like the *Jaworzina* and *Monastery of Saint-Naoum* cases, it related to a territorial dispute. But it is with the *Eastern Carelia* case that it has more often been bracketed. Indeed, the similarities between the two cases are not difficult to find: opposition by one of the disputants to the request for an advisory opinion; and the opposing state's nonmembership in the League. Neverthe-less, upon closer examination, important contrasts appear. Morever, the con-siderations underlying recourse to the Court seem to have been quite dif-ferent in the two instances.

The parties to the *Mosul* controversy were Great Britain (as mandatory for Iraq) and Turkey, and the subject in dispute was the disposition of the vast and valuable oil region of Mosul. By virtue of Article 3(2) of the Treaty of Lausanne, the Iraqi-Turkish frontier was to be settled by direct negotiation between the parties, and, failing agreement within five months, the dispute was to be referred to the League Council. After direct negotiations ended in deadlock, the British government on 6 August 1924 requested the Council to consider the matter.[78] Turkey agreed to Council discussion of the question and participated in Council proceedings. Early in those proceedings, a diver-gence of views regarding the role assigned to the Council in the dispute became manifest. Unlike the British representative, who spoke of Council arbitration, the Turkish representative referred only to the "impartial exami-nation" of the Council.[79] After discussions with the Council rapporteur, how-ever, this divergence apparently gave way to a pledge by both parties to accept in advance any Council decision.[80] The Council then decided to set up

---

[77]Numerically, the four Court opinions represented only a very small proportion of the decisions which the High Commissioner and League Council were called upon to make. For a good discussion of the history of Polish-Danzig differences between the wars and the League's role, see John Brown Mason, *The Danzig Dilemma: A Study in Peace-making by Compromise* (Stanford, Calif.: Stanford University Press, 1946). See also the discussion by J. A. van Hamel (League High Commissioner at Danzig from 1926 to 1929), "Danzig and the Polish Problem," *International Conciliation*, No. 288 (March, 1933).

[78]LNOJ, 1924, p. 1465.

[79]*Ibid.*, pp. 1319–20, 1337.

[80]To the Rapporteur's question whether the Turkish representative could, on behalf

a Commission of Inquiry to investigate local conditions and the sentiments of the local population in the Mosul territory.[81]

On 16 July 1925 the Commission presented its report, recommending two alternative solutions: (1) giving the entire territory to Iraq, provided Iraq continued under a mandatory regime for another twenty-five years; or (2) if the mandate were to be terminated, awarding the territory to Turkey.[82] Although the results of the Commission's investigations did not completely satisfy either of the parties, they were most painful to Turkey.

When the Council came to consider the Commission's report in September 1925, the Turkish representative not only challenged the Commission's conclusions, on the grounds that they were ultra vires, but also, in a reversal of the Turkish position of a year before, denied that the Council could exercise anything more than a mediatory role.[83] He firmly maintained that no binding decision could be taken without the consent of both parties. After an extended discussion on the substantive question of the frontier line, the Council appointed a subcommittee to examine the Commission's report and recommend "a practical and just solution."[84] But, in face of the uncertainty created by Turkey's new challenge to the Council's competence, the subcommittee recommended, instead, submission of the following two preliminary questions to the PCIJ for an advisory opinion:

1. What is the character of the decision to be taken by the Council in virtue of Article 3, paragraph 2, of the Treaty of Lausanne—is it an arbitral award, a recommendation, or a simple mediation?

2. Must the decision be unanimous or may it be taken by a majority?

May the representatives of the interested Parties take part in the vote?[85]

This proposal was strongly opposed by the Turkish representative, and, for different reasons, was greeted with less than enthusiasm by the British repre-

---

of his government, "now give an undertaking to accept the Council's recommendation," Fethy Bey, the Turkish representative, replied that "on this point there was no disagreement between his Government and the British Government." *Ibid.*, p. 1358. See also the statements of Lord Parmoor and Fethy Bey to the same effect. *Ibid.*, p. 1359. And see n. 81.

[81] The resolution setting up the Commission was adopted on 30 September 1924 and was accepted by both representatives. In the preamble, the following paragraph appears: "Having heard the statements of the representatives of the British and Turkish Governments, who undertook on behalf of their respective Governments to accept in advance the decision of the Council on the question referred to it." *Ibid.*, p. 1359.

[82] LN Doc. C.400.M.147.1925.VII.

[83] LNOJ, 1925, pp. 1317–27.

[84] *Ibid.*, pp. 1336–37. The President reminded the parties "that they had before the Council placed their cause solemnly in the hands of the League of Nations."

[85] *Ibid.*, p. 1377.

sentative. The latter objected most to the delay involved in this new move, and the concomitant prolongation of an unstable and dangerous situation. He also felt that the first of the proposed questions had already been settled by the Turkish statements of the previous year. Nonetheless, he was willing to go along with the proposed consultation of the Court, since it was desirable that any remaining doubts "should be completely and authoritatively cleared up" and that the Council "know exactly in what capacity and by what procedure" it was settling "this very important question." Furthermore, he recognized that the Court's opinion might provide valuable guidance for governments in the future.[86] The Turkish representative, on the other hand, was quite adamant in his opposition to submission of the questions to the Court. There was no necessity to request judicial advice, since the history of the drafting of Article 3(2) of the Lausanne Treaty clearly indicated that only the *good offices* of the Council were contemplated; and no Court opinion could affect or modify Turkish treaty rights. Moreover, the questions were essentially extremely political.[87] In effect, Turkey was putting the Council on notice that it would not accept any opinion unfavorable to its contentions. Nevertheless, the Council proceeded to adopt the subcommittee's proposal.[88]

Clearly, the opposition of Turkey to the request in this case was not to be equated with the Soviet attitude in the *Eastern Carelia* case. Nor were the Council's motives comparable in the two instances. Turkey, although a nonmember of the League, had recognized the Council's competence not only to consider the dispute but, at least on one occasion (in September 1924), to arbitrate it.[89] Only as the Council moved toward a final determination of the dispute in a manner unfavorable to Turkey did Turkey raise questions relating to the Council's competence. It was to remove all impediments to the final solution of the Mosul dispute and to assure that the Council was proceeding with scrupulous legality that the decision was made to have the Council's competence elucidated by the Court. Despite Turkey's opposition, there appeared to be *some* hope that Turkey would accept a Court opinion voluntarily. If not, the Council and the stronger state, Britain, would at least know that their actions conformed to the legal position as enunciated by the highest judicial tribunal.

[86]*Ibid.*, pp. 1378-79.

[87]*Ibid.*, pp. 1380-81.

[88]*Ibid.*, p. 1382. There is no mention of the vote by which the resolution was adopted, but, subsequently, during Council consideration of the Court's opinion, the Turkish representative stated that his government had voted against requesting the opinion. *Ibid.*, 1926, p. 122.

[89]Whether or not Turkey had earlier undertaken (by virtue of the Treaty of Lausanne) to accept Council arbitration was, of course, one of the questions before the Court.

In sum, the request in the *Mosul* case could be justified, as that in the *Eastern Carelia* case could not, as a measure likely to aid in the solution of the substantive problem in dispute.

Jurisdiction of the European Commission of the Danube between Galatz and Braila

The Council's role in this case, as in the *Tunis-Morocco* case, was strictly that of a transmission belt between the states in dispute and the Court. In the *Danube Commission* controversy, the four states involved—Great Britain, France, Italy, and Rumania—went so far as to embody their agreement to seek an advisory opinion in a formal instrument registered with the League Secretariat. But, in contrast to the *Tunis-Morocco* case, there was no advance agreement to accept the opinion as binding. Rather, the expedient of an "advisory compromis" was designed to avoid actual judicial settlement.

What the Court was asked to clarify was the extent of the European Danube Commission's powers in the Galatz-Braila sector of the Danube. This issue had not been resolved by the postwar instruments relative to the Danube (the Versailles Treaty and the Definitive Statute of the Danube). These, by simply stipulating that the prewar situation was to be re-established, had in turn generated divergent opinions regarding the nature of the status quo ante in the disputed sector.[90] Protracted efforts to reconcile the views of Rumania, the territorial sovereign, and those of other members of the Commission proved unavailing. After September 1924, the aid of the League's Advisory and Technical Committee for Communications and Transit was sought. A special committee appointed to examine the question submitted a report containing conclusions adverse to Rumania's contentions and a number of conciliation proposals.[91] The special committee's conclusions were endorsed by the Transit Committee. Simultaneously, it was suggested that negotiations be undertaken by the members of the European Danube Commission under the guidance of the special committee.[92] However, the only agreement to which the subsequent negotiations—begun in September 1925—gave rise was the aforementioned agreement to seek an advisory opinion.[93] That the Court's opinion would be considered purely "advisory" was made abundantly clear. Rumania emphasized the nonbinding nature of the projected opinion

[90] An interpretative protocol itself became the subject of dispute. PCIJ, Ser. B, No. 14, p. 12.

[91] *Ibid.*, Ser. C, No. 13-IV, vol. II, p. 535.

[92] *Ibid.*, pp. 804–5.

[93] The agreement was signed on 16 September 1926. LNOJ, 1927, p. 233; LNTS, 59: 237. A protocol signed on the same day stipulated that, if, within six months of the Court's opinion, the procedure of conciliation then in progress had led to no result, that procedure should be considered closed. PCIJ, Ser. C, No. 13-IV, vol. II, p. 812.

when signing the agreement and, again, before the League Council adopted the resolution requesting the opinion.[94]

It should be noted that in the *Danube Commission* case, recourse to the advisory jurisdiction constituted a compromise solution. Great Britain and the other states represented on the European Commission contended that the dispute was one which, under Article 376 of the Versailles Treaty, came within the Court's *compulsory* jurisdiction. Their acceptance of the advisory alternative was merely a concession to Rumania; it was an "exceptional case," which was not to "constitute a precedent for similar action in the future." Moreover, they fully reserved their right to submit the question subsequently for judgment, in order to obtain a decision enforceable against Rumania.[95] For Rumania, on the other hand, the course decided upon represented merely the lesser of two evils.[96]

Greco-Bulgarian "Communities"

The opinion of the Court in this case was solicited on behalf of the Greco-Bulgarian Mixed Emigration Commission,[97] to aid in resolving difficulties of interpretation which had plagued the Mixed Commission since its creation.

The provisions at the center of the prolonged and confused debate in the Mixed Commission were those concerning the property of "communities."[98] At issue were rather complex questions related to the definition of "communities" and the conditions under which a community's property was to be liquidated by the Mixed Commission.[99] For our purposes, it is important to

[94] LNOJ, 1927, p. 151.

[95] *Ibid.*; PCIJ, Ser. E, No. 4, p. 204.

[96] See PCIJ, Ser. B, No. 14, p. 21. Rumania refused to acknowledge the Court's jurisdiction altogether; but, since the other states "appeared to have made up their minds in any case to bring the dispute before the Court," Rumania consented, as a maximum, to submission of the question for an advisory opinion—which opinion was, however, to remain truly "advisory."

[97] The Commission was established under the terms of the Greco-Bulgarian Convention on Reciprocal Emigration, signed at Neuilly on 27 November 1919. Its powers were very wide. See Ladas, *op. cit.*, chap. 2.

[98] Articles 6 and 7 of the Convention. The provisions of Article 12, which related to emigrations predating the Convention, also were at issue. Although Article 12 referred only to "persons," that word had been broadly construed by the Commission to encompass communities as well.

[99] E.g., did "communities" need to have juridical personality under the local law, or was their existence a question of fact? Were administrative communes included within the term? When was a "community" to be considered as dissolved, making its real property subject to liquidation by the Mixed Commission? To whom were the proceeds of the liquidation to be paid? Were the "communities," as such, beneficiaries of the Convention, or was the distribution of their assets intended merely as an additional pecuniary advantage accruing to the individual emigrants? Were pre-Convention emi-

note merely that, over the years, the Mixed Commission's pronouncements on the subject had been less than consistent; that the views of the parties themselves had been changed and exchanged several times;[100] and that, finally, no agreement could be reached, despite an attempted clarification of the issues by reference to the Legal Section of the League Secretariat. The suggestion to have recourse to the Court arose out of the felt need of the Mixed Commission's neutral members to extricate themselves somehow from a virtual "maze";[101] and to do so in a manner which would at once definitively settle the problem and save the faces of all the parties (including, perhaps, that of the Commission itself).

The earlier consultation of the League Secretariat's Legal Section arose in the following circumstances. In response to a series of questions posed by the neutral members of the Mixed Commission in August 1926, the Bulgarian and Greek representatives (in November 1927) finally stated their definite positions on the points raised. The Commission then decided "to instruct its President to put to the Legal Section of the League of Nations, on behalf of the Mixed Commission, such questions as he might consider advisable."[102] Largely on the basis of the opinions thus obtained, the neutral members presented a memorandum on the question of "communities" which incorporated two interpretations of the disputed clauses.[103] Not unexpectedly, Greece and Bulgaria each opted for the interpretation which accorded with its own previously stated position, and the divergent viewpoints thus remained unreconciled.

It was in this state of deadlock that the President of the Mixed Commission first raised the suggestion that a Court opinion be sought.[104] For a long time his suggestion went unheeded. When, however, the Commission convened in early September 1929, both neutral members pressed for a reaction by the two governments on the question of recourse to the Court. The considerations put forward in favor of such recourse were rather interesting.

---

grants entitled to a share in the proceeds of the now-dissolved community's property? For a fuller discussion of the issues, see Ladas, *op. cit.*, pp. 87–90, 157–79; and Verzijl, *World Court*, 1: 197–203.

[100] The inconsistencies and shifts in the two parties' positions were attributable largely to the complexity of the issues and the consequent difficulty of calculating the practical advantages and disadvantages of each interpretation to the respective parties. See Ladas, *op. cit.*, pp. 158–62.

[101] Verzijl, *World Court*, 1: 199.

[102] PCIJ, Ser. B, No. 17, pp. 12–13.

[103] Ladas, *op. cit.*, pp. 163–66.

[104] The suggestion was contained in a letter to the two governments dated 15 September 1928; it was renewed in a letter of 31 July 1929. PCIJ, Ser. C, No. 18-I, pp. 405–7.

Undoubtedly, the Mixed Commission was fully competent to decide all questions definitively without a supportive judicial opinion; but any decision thus taken, independently, would most certainly engender strong objections, criticism, and generally undesirable reactions on the part of the losing party and its public opinion; this, in turn, would tend to make the losing party less cooperative and would jeopardize the further work of the Commission. On the other hand, a Commission decision based on the advisory opinion of the highest authority on legal matters would prove more acceptable to the losing party and its public opinion.[105]

At the following meetings it appeared that, while in principle both parties were agreed as to the desirability of consulting the Court, they differed as to the timing of such consultation. Bulgaria insisted that an opinion be sought only *after* a Commission decision on the subject of "communities" failed to give satisfaction to one of the parties. But the Greek representative, joined by the two neutral members, took strong exception to the idea of any such retrospective consultation, which, in their view, could not but bear the character of proceedings by the dissatisfied party *against* the Commission.[106]

Early in December 1929, the disagreement over timing was resolved, both parties having indicated their consent to prior consultation of the Court.[107] But then another debate ensued on the question of whether or not the Court might examine decisions *already taken* by the Commission, and, if so, how such a judicial examination might affect the Commission's competence.[108] Since, as noted earlier, the Commission had already taken many conflicting decisions on the question of "communities," any consultation would, willy-nilly, have a retrospective aspect, involving the passing of judgment on the correctness of the Commission's past actions. The neutral members appeared to be quite cognizant of this dilemma. On the one hand, by submitting its actions to the review of the Court, the Commission cast doubt upon the justice of its former decisions and faced possible embarrassment if (as actually happened) some of its views were later repudiated by the Court. On the other hand—and this consideration was determinative[109]—any restriction on the Court's freedom to examine the question in all its aspects would corre-

---

[105]*Ibid.*, pp. 582, 880.

[106]This course was deemed particularly objectionable because, under the Convention of Neuilly, the Commission's decisions were to be final. For his part, the Bulgarian representative argued, *inter alia*, that a prior Commission decision would have the effect of clarifying the question before the Court, and that an advisory opinion might prove altogether unnecessary. *Ibid.*, pp. 881–84, 886–88.

[107]*Ibid.*, pp. 408–9.

[108]*Ibid.*, pp. 899–900.

[109]On this point, the neutral members sided with Bulgaria against Greece. *Ibid.*

spondingly limit the usefulness of the resultant opinion. Furthermore, as pointed out by the President, the parties could not seriously object to the Commission's rectification of decisions found by the Court to have been based on erroneous conceptions.[110]

As for the text of the questions to be submitted to the Court, it proved impossible to secure agreement on a single set of questions, and the Mixed Commission finally decided to forward three sets of questions to the Council—one each from the Mixed Commission, Bulgaria, and Greece—for submission to the Court.[111] On 16 January 1930 the Council voted, without prior discussion, to make the desired request.[112]

It is instructive to note the difference between the nature of the earlier consultation of the League Secretariat's Legal Section and the subsequent consultation of the Court. The former had the character of a legal consultation, pure and simple, for the benefit of the neutral members of the Commission. For this reason, the questions posed were not crucial and could be left to the formulation of the President. The Commission clearly was not delegating any of its decision-making powers to another body, so there was no question of the Commission's competence being in any way affected by the consultation. Of quite a different stripe was the subsequent recourse to the Court. Here, to all intents and purposes, one decision-making body—the Court—was being substituted for another—the Mixed Commission.[113] The very purpose of requesting an opinion was to get a pronouncement which would finally settle the questions involved, not reopen debate on them. In many respects, reference to the Court for an advisory opinion was hardly distinguishable from submission of a case for judgment.[114] Hence, extended discussions were held regarding the timing of the request and the propriety of having the Court review the correctness of the Commission's past decisions. Hence, too, great importance was attached to the formulation of the questions submitted, and three questionnaires were submitted as testament to that importance.

[110]Nevertheless, a measure of concern over the effect that consultation of the Court might have on the Commission's competence was reflected in the letter of the Mixed Commission's President to the League's Secretary-General. See PCIJ, Ser. B, No. 17, p. 8.

[111]Ibid., Ser. C, No. 18-I, pp. 901–4.

[112]LNOJ, 1930, p. 109.

[113]This is so, notwithstanding the disclaimer contained in the note of the Mixed Commission's President to the Secretary-General (dated 19 December 1929). The President therein declared that "it is not the intention of the Commission in any way to invalidate the powers and jurisdiction assigned to it by the Convention of Neuilly." PCIJ, Ser. B, No. 17, p. 8.

[114]In accordance with the Commission President's advice, the two parties concluded their written statements with formal submissions. This advice was apparently based on a misconception regarding advisory procedure. See the Court's comment, ibid., p. 14.

Railway Traffic between Lithuania and Poland
(Railway Sector Landwarow-Kaisiadorys)

In common with the *Danube Commission* case, this case concerned an aspect of what might be called "international traffic law."[115] Here, however, the "political" aspect was more marked, for the controversy constituted merely one incident in the long-standing Lithuanian-Polish dispute, which dated from the Polish occupation of Vilna in 1920. Unlike the earlier case, too, this time the initiative for requesting the Court's advice came from the Council itself.

Even after the formal state of war between Lithuania and Poland ended in December 1927, a state of enmity persisted. One of the manifestations of this enmity was the absence of any direct railway communication between the two countries. In particular, as a form of pacific reprisal, Lithuania refused to restore the Landwarow-Kaisiadorys sector of the former Vilna-Libau railway line, which had remained in a state of disrepair since 1920, and which, of all the interrupted railway links, was the only one of appreciable economic importance to Poland. Council efforts to improve communications between the two countries, begun in December 1927, appeared hopelessly deadlocked at the end of 1930, when a report of the League's Transit Committee failed to meet with the acceptance of the parties.[116]

In its report,[117] the Transit Committee had determined that failure to remove obstacles to freedom of transit was incompatible with the parties' international obligations,[118] and had recommended, *inter alia*, the conclusion of agreements to re-establish continuous service on the Landwarow-Kaisiadorys railway. On the legal questions involved, the Committee had consulted a special legal subcommittee composed of distinguished jurists (two of whom were subsequently elected judges of the PCIJ). However, Lithuania in particular refused to accept either the Committee's recommendations or its view of Lithuania's legal obligations.[119]

---

[115]Verzijl, *World Court*, 1: 270.

[116]The report had been drawn up pursuant to a Council resolution of 14 December 1928. LNOJ, 1929, p. 44. Earlier efforts at direct negotiations between the parties, undertaken at Königsberg during the spring and fall of 1928, proved fruitless in regard to the question of railway communications. PCIJ, Ser. A/B, No. 42, pp. 112-13, 117.

[117]PCIJ, Ser. C, No. 54, p. 31.

[118]The specific provisions in question were Article 23(e) of the Covenant and Article 3 of Annex III of the Memel Convention. For the texts of the relevant provisions, see PCIJ, Ser. A/B, No. 42, pp. 117-20.

[119]Poland, for different reasons, also refused to accept the Committee's report. LNOJ, 1931, pp. 479-80.

Lithuania disputed the Committee's interpretation of the relevant provisions of the Covenant and Memel Convention, and also claimed the right to engage in "pacific reprisals" against Poland. *Ibid.*, pp. 480-82.

In these circumstances, the Council's Rapporteur raised the possibility of seeking judicial clarification as a means of breaking the deadlock.[120] If, after its deliberations on the matter, the Council found that doubts regarding the scope of international agreements were impeding progress, it might, he thought, "consider the advisability of obtaining a legal opinion on the points at issue which would be recognized by the States concerned as final."[121] In this connection, he drew the Council's attention to the compromissory clause of the Memel Convention, in accordance with which any one of the Principal Allied Powers was entitled to invoke the Court's compulsory jurisdiction in the matter.

When the Council met on 23 January 1931, the Lithuanian representative reaffirmed his government's stand on the legal questions and its unwillingness to accept the Transit Committee's recommendations.[122] At this point, the Council President (Mr. Henderson of Great Britain) proposed that the Rapporteur's suggestion to solicit judicial clarification be accepted. It was important to settle, "once and for all," a question which had for so long engaged the Council's attention. Manifestly, however, Council efforts had been brought to a standstill by Lithuania's contention that, in the existing circumstances, it was not legally obliged, under any international agreement, to comply with the Council's wishes. "The legal question having been clearly raised, it was . . . most desirable that the . . . Court . . . be requested to settle it." Although, as noted by the Rapporteur, a binding judgment could be obtained under the Memel Convention's compromissory clause—and Great Britain, among others, was entitled to invoke that clause—"it might perhaps be more consonant with the usual procedure if the Council were to seek a settlement by requesting the Permanent Court to give an advisory opinion."[123]

This proposal was supported by the German representative, who felt that the question called for very serious examination, and that the Transit Committee had not yet said the last word on the matter. The Chairman of the Transit Committee, who was present at the Council meeting, apparently resented the proposed appeal to the Court. He pointed to the meticulous inquiry which had been conducted on the legal and technical aspects of the question and to the eminence of the jurists whose services had been utilized.[124] Nevertheless, the Rapporteur and the Council accepted the President's proposal without further discussion; and, on the following day, the

[120]*Ibid.*, p. 482.

[121]I.e., in contrast to the legal opinion of the Transit Committee, which had not been so recognized.

[122]LNOJ, 1931, pp. 212-13.

[123]*Ibid.*, p. 214.

[124]*Ibid.*, pp. 214-15.

Council adopted a resolution, drafted by the Rapporteur, to request the Court's opinion in the matter of Lithuania's obligations with respect to the Landwarow-Kaisiadorys railway.[125]

In sum, judicial clarification was considered desirable in this instance because a dispute over the existence of legal obligations appeared to be impeding progress toward solution of the underlying problem. The Transit Committee's views, though based on the opinion of noted jurists, proved unacceptable to Lithuania. Once judicial clarification was deemed necessary, it appeared most logical to seek it by recourse to the advisory jurisdiction. Voluntary submission by compromis was unthinkable in light of the antagonistic relations between the two parties. The compulsory jurisdiction was a distinct possibility, but no state other than Poland (to whom it was *not* open to sue Lithuania) had any real interest in the matter—as witness the fact that no third state intervened in the subsequent proceedings before the Court.[126] Nor was an advisory opinion apparently considered too inferior a substitute for an actual judgment. The stated hope and expectation was that, as with so many other advisory opinions in the League period, the Court's pronouncement—despite its theoretically nonbinding character—would settle the problem with finality.

Customs Regime between Austria and Germany

Of all the cases the Court was called upon to deal with (whether in its advisory or contentious capacity), this case was certainly one of the most important, controversial, and difficult. In light of later charges that the question was too "political" for judicial consideration,[127] it is particularly instructive to review the circumstances in which the request for the Court's opinion was made.

A virtual European "storm" was created by the surprise announcement in March 1931 that Germany and Austria had signed a Protocol designed to institute a customs union between them. This move was seen in many Euro-

---

[125]*Ibid.*, p. 239. The question asked was: "Do the international engagements in force oblige Lithuania in the present circumstances, and if so in what manner, to take the necessary measures to open for traffic . . . the Landwarow-Kaisiadorys railway sector." The words "in the present circumstances" referred to Lithuania's claim to exercise pacific reprisals. However, the Court did not deem it necessary to enter into this question. See PCIJ, Ser. A/B, No. 42, pp. 113-14; but cf. the statement of Judge Anzilotti, *ibid.*, p. 123.

[126]The absence of third-party intervention was noted by the Court. PCIJ, Ser. A/B, No. 42, p. 118.

In the *Interpretation of the Statute of Memel* case, the compromissory clause of the Memel Convention *was* invoked by Great Britain, France, Italy, and Japan. *Ibid.*, Nos. 47 and 49. The case was unusual, however, in that Lithuania preferred contentious proceedings to advisory proceedings. See Chapter IV, p. 177.

[127]See p. 301 and n. 80 below.

pean capitals—most notably, Paris and Prague—as representing a grave challenge to the existing balance of power, for was not the projected move to economic unity merely a prelude to that political unity—Anschluss—which the Allied Powers took such great pains to prevent in 1919?[128] And could not this Anschluss then bring Germany close to realizing the hegemony over *Mitteleuropa* denied her by her defeat in the war? Moreover, the complete secrecy in which negotiation of the Protocol had been shrouded could hardly serve to assuage the apprehensions thus aroused.[129] Austro-German protestations regarding the nonpolitical character of the proposed scheme and its compatibility with the plan for European Union then under discussion proved entirely unconvincing to the vexed European statesmen.

How could this explosive situation, in which the first really serious threat to the status quo appeared to be presented, be disposed of? Since the fear of Anschluss was at the root of the hostility to the proposed customs union, it was perhaps natural for the states concerned to seek support for their stand in the treaty obligations designed specifically to preserve Austrian independence and to bar the dreaded political union. Such provisions were not hard to find. Article 88 of the Treaty of Saint-Germain stipulated:

> The independence of Austria is inalienable otherwise than with the consent of the Council of the League of Nations. Consequently, Austria undertakes in the absence of the consent of the said Council to abstain from any act which might directly or indirectly or by any means whatever compromise her independence, particularly, and until her admission to membership of the League of Nations, by participation in the affairs of another Power.

In addition, upon acceptance of League financial aid in 1922, the government of Austria, in a Protocol signed at Geneva on 4 October 1922, declared that it

> undertakes, in accordance with the terms of Article 88 of the Treaty of Saint-Germain, not to alienate its independence; it will abstain from any negotiations or from any economic or financial engagement calculated directly or indirectly to compromise this independence.
>
> This undertaking shall not prevent Austria from maintaining, subject to the provisions of the Treaty of Saint-Germain, her freedom in the matter of customs tariffs and commercial or financial agreements, and, in general, in all matters relating to her economic regime or her commercial relations, provided always that she shall not violate her economic independence by

---

[128] In Article 61 of the Weimar Constitution of 31 July 1919, provision had been made for the eventual joining of German Austria to the Reich. By Article 80 of the Treaty of Versailles and Article 88 of the Treaty of Saint-Germain, any such political union was strictly proscribed. The relevant provision in Article 61 of the Weimar Constitution was later declared by the German government to be null and void.

[129] See LNOJ, 1931, pp. 1071–80.

granting to any State a special regime or exclusive advantages calculated to threaten this independence.

Thus it was possible to lay the question before the Council, not primarily as a "political" matter "which threatens to disturb international peace or the good understanding between nations upon which peace depends,"[130] but as a "legal" question involving the interpretation of specific treaty provisions with which the Council was intimately concerned. It was in this latter, "tamer" form that the British government, in a letter of 10 April 1931, requested Council consideration of the issue of the proposed customs union.[131]

However, even this "legal" question would have embroiled the Council in a heated, and perhaps embarrassing, debate, had it decided to determine for itself the question of the compatibility of the proposed customs regime with Austria's obligations—as, under Article 88 of the Treaty of Saint-Germain, it was entitled, and indeed expected, to do. A French memorandum of 14 May 1931,[132] which entered into a lengthy polemic regarding the economic and political consequences of the proposed customs union, gave a foretaste of the kinds of considerations with which the Council would be forced to grapple were it to attempt to resolve the matter itself. When the Council met to consider the question on 18 May 1931, it was mercifully spared the necessity for action by a proposal of the British representative, Mr. Henderson, that the question be sent to the Court. Explaining the reason for his recommendation, Mr. Henderson stated:

> In my view, the issue raises important economic and even political ques-
> tions; but the aspect of the case with which we as a Council are concerned
> this morning is essentially one of a juridical nature; and it is therefore
> eminently one on which it would be desirable for the Council to request
> an advisory opinion from the Permanent Court of International Justice. To
> follow any other course would mean protracted discussion in this Council,
> and, of necessity, a careful examination of the legal instruments bearing
> upon the issue which has been raised, and, in the end, a possible failure to
> reach a conclusion.[133]

Simultaneously, he sought assurances that no further progress toward establishment of the proposed regime would be made in the interim.

---

[130] Article 11(2) of the League Covenant.

[131] The British letter referred to the doubts that had been expressed regarding the compatibility of the proposed regime with Austrian obligations under the Protocols and the fact that these Protocols had been negotiated under Council auspices. LNOJ, 1931, p. 1160. Austria and Germany took less umbrage at the submission of the "legal" aspects of the question to the Council.

[132] *Ibid.*, pp. 1163–72.

[133] *Ibid.*, p. 1068.

The British proposal was immediately accepted by all concerned, and the otherwise to be expected stridency of the debate was thereby avoided. No one questioned whether a "legal" question was actually involved. Everyone assumed that it was, and that the Court was the proper forum for its consideration.[134] As M. Briand expressed it at the following meeting, on 19 May 1931:

> In reality, nothing is simpler than the situation now before us. By means of Mr. Henderson's proposal, to which we have all agreed, we have defined our attitude on a point of law which formed, so to speak, the preliminary question. The point at issue was as follows. Some of us said: "You cannot conclude this Protocol because your international obligations prohibit you from doing so"; to which others replied: "No: we have established this Protocol in the exercise of our sovereign national rights, without in any way disregarding our treaty obligations." Which of the two arguments is right?
>
> Such was the problem before us, and naturally our thoughts turned towards that institution which gives the Council legal advice in difficult cases. The Permanent Court of International Justice, having before it the texts, will tell us what is the law.[135]

The assumption appeared to be that questions of treaty interpretation were, ipso facto, justiciable. If any doubts were entertained as to the propriety of seizing the Court with the task of interpreting the *particular* provisions at issue—involving as that did the necessity of defining such terms as "independence" and the "alienation of independence" and of predicting future probabilities—these were not manifested. The principal difference of opinion was over whether—as maintained by France, Czechoslovakia, Italy, and Yugoslavia—the "legal" question was merely a preliminary one, leaving the Council free subsequently to discuss the issue on a political basis;[136] or whether—as Germany and Austria contended—the legal question was the *sole* admissible basis for Council discussion of the issue.[137]

The British draft resolution, requesting the Court's opinion on the compatibility of the proposed customs regime with Article 88 of the Treaty of Saint-Germain and Protocol No. 1 of 4 October 1922, was adopted unanimously on 19 May 1931, and the Court was asked to deal with the question as a matter of urgency.[138]

---

[134] All recognized, however, that the Court would have to take some political and economic considerations into account in order to resolve the "legal" issue.

[135] LNOJ, 1931, p. 1079.

[136] *Ibid.*, pp. 1072–73, 1075–80.

[137] *Ibid.*, pp. 1074–75.

[138] *Ibid.*, p. 1080.

In comparison with most League requests, the present one was made with particularly great haste. The legal question did not emerge as one which was impeding progress toward the solution of the underlying problem; rather, it was raised as an afterthought, and appeared somewhat contrived and artificial. By raising this issue, the Council was able virtually to "dump" the entire problem into the Court's lap, thereby extricating itself from it, if only for the time being. The element of delay, so often a consideration *against* consulting the Court, here appeared to be the primary purpose of the reference. For their part, Germany and Austria, not yet in a position to ignore international concern, apparently preferred to argue their case before the Court rather than before the Council. They hoped and expected that the Court would settle the matter definitively in their favor.[139] France and its allies, while hoping that the matter might be conveniently disposed of by the Court, nevertheless reserved the right to resume consideration of the political and economic issues—avowedly the more important—subsequently.

In its desire to relieve itself of the burden of dealing with such an explosive and emotional dispute, the Council failed to consider whether it was not unfairly—from the standpoint of the Court's prestige—embroiling the Court in this superheated controversy.

THE U.N. PERIOD

Conditions of Admission of a State to Membership in the United Nations (Article 4 of the Charter)

The first request for an advisory opinion to be sent to the new Court heralded a new direction for the use of the advisory function. There was no exact parallel to it in the requests which had emanated from the League Council. Certainly it bore little resemblance to the more "typical" Council requests, even to those few of an "organizational" nature. For one thing, the "organizational" character of the *Admission* request was more pronounced— in origin, subject matter, and scope. The differences of opinion underlying the request arose entirely within the United Nations; they related to a purely "organizational" question—namely, the admission of new members—and the expected effects of the advisory opinion also were confined to the organizational arena.[140] Unlike most League requests, too, the questions posed to the

---

[139]*Ibid.*, pp. 1073–75.

[140]In contrast, the four non-ILO, "nondispute" League cases (Nos. 6, 7, 26, and 27) arose out of intrastate disputes; their subject matter was either minority questions (in the first three cases) or (in the last case) the constitutionality of legislative decrees; and the main effects of the opinions were external to the organization. Only Nos. 1 and 18—both

Court were couched in rather abstract terms.[141] And although the PCIJ had in some instances been required to interpret the Covenant in the course of its treatment of specific controversies, it had never been asked to interpret Covenant provisions in the abstract—as the ICJ was (at least on the surface)[142] here called upon to do with respect to Article 4(1) of the Charter.

In important respects, the present request was most akin to that in the *Eastern Carelia* case—notwithstanding the fact that the earlier case related to a "dispute" and that it involved a nonmember of the League. For, as in the *Eastern Carelia* case, the request was in reality directed against one state. (In fact, the same state was involved, but in the new world organization that state was not only a member; it was a most important member.) The projected opinion here too could have no real effect without the acquiescence of that state in the opinion; and, so far from acquiescing, that state opposed the request and indicated in advance its refusal to abide by any Court pronouncement. As in *Eastern Carelia*, the request was not calculated to solve the basic problem to which it related, but was instead directed at other, more propagandistic, purposes.

The proposal to request the Court's opinion arose in the context of the admission deadlock, which, in turn, was but the organizational manifestation of the bipolar division of the world into Eastern and Western blocs. Each bloc within the UN employed the weapon at its disposal for excluding members of the other: the West used the weapon of the majority; the East, that of the veto. Thus, the desire of the General Assembly majority to see such noncommunist states as Finland, Italy, Portugal, Ireland, Austria, and Transjordan admitted was thwarted by the Soviet veto in the Security Council; for its part, the Soviet Union could not muster sufficient support in either political organ for the admission of such communist states and protegés as Rumania, Bulgaria, Hungary, Albania, and Mongolia. The reasons adduced for opposition to the several candidacies were varied.[143] Some were broadly related to the criteria set forth in Article 4(1) of the Charter ("peace-loving," "able and willing to carry out" Charter obligations), but others clearly were not. Among

---

ILO cases—were more similar, in their purely "organizational" nature, to the *Admission* case.

[141] The preamble of the requesting resolution did contain references to the concrete circumstances to which the questions related, but the Court subsequently chose to ignore those references and to dwell solely on the "abstract form" of the question. See p. 309, n. 109, below.

[142] See n. 141.

[143] See Goodrich and Hambro, *Charter*, pp. 128–30; SCOR, 1st Yr., 2nd Ser., Supp. No. 4; *ibid.*, 2nd Yr., Spec. Supp. No. 3. Grounds for opposition included a state's neutrality in the past war; the absence of diplomatic relations between the objecting and applicant states; and, in the case of former enemy states, the absence of peace treaties.

the latter was the stand finally taken by the Soviet Union regarding the five former enemy states referred to in the Potsdam Agreement: Italy and Finland could be admitted only if Bulgaria, Hungary, and Rumania were admitted simultaneously.[144]

It was in these circumstances that Belgium put forward, in the General Assembly's First Committee, a draft resolution[145] to request the Court's opinion on the following question:

> Is a Member of the United Nations which is called upon, in virtue of Article 4 of the Charter, to pronounce itself by its vote, either in the Security Council or in the General Assembly, on the admission of a State to membership in the United Nations, juridically entitled to make its consent to the admission dependent on conditions not expressly provided by paragraph 1 of the said Article? In particular, can such a Member, while it recognizes the conditions set forth in that provision to be fulfilled by the State concerned, subject its affirmative vote to the additional condition that other States be admitted to membership in the United Nations together with that State?

That the proposed recourse to the Court was a predictably futile exercise was recognized even by many of the states supporting such recourse. Indeed, proponents of the Belgian draft resolution were rather hard-pressed to find any convincing arguments in its favor. Thus, the United Kingdom representative stated that, although the projected opinion would not solve the present difficulties, he would vote for requesting it, because, under Article 96 of the Charter, the Court could be consulted in cases of conflicting interpretations of Charter provisions.[146] The Greek representative cited as grounds for his support the desirability of more frequent use of the ICJ.[147]

Opposition to the request came mainly, but not exclusively, from the Soviet bloc. Among the considerations adduced for this stand were the alleged clarity of Article 4;[148] the predictable ineffectuality of the projected

---

[144] SCOR, 2nd Yr., 204th Mtg., 25 September 1947, pp. 2414–15. In 1946, the United States had itself proposed "package" admissions, but had since abandoned that position. *Ibid.*, 1st Yr., 54th Mtg., 28 August 1946, p. 42.

[145] UN Doc. A/C.1/242, 7 November 1947. For the Belgian explanation of this draft resolution, see GAOR (II), 1st Ctte., 98th Mtg., 7 November 1947, p. 342.

[146] GAOR (II), 1st Ctte., 101st Mtg., 8 November 1947, p. 378. Cf. the statements of Australia, *ibid.*, 99th Mtg., 7 November 1947, p. 351; and Plenary, 117th Mtg., 17 November 1947, pp. 1053–55.

[147] *Ibid.*, 1st Ctte., 101st Mtg., 8 November 1947, p. 382.

[148] See, e.g., the statements of Poland (*ibid.*, 99th Mtg., 7 November 1947, p. 345; and Plenary, 117th Mtg., 17 November 1947, p. 1046); the U.S.S.R. (*ibid.*, p. 1048); and China (*ibid.*, 1st Ctte., 101st Mtg., 8 November 1947, p. 372). However, the states differed as to what the "clear" or "obvious" meaning of Article 4 was.

opinion;[149] the "political" nature of the request;[150] and the illegality or impropriety of eliciting from the Court an abstract interpretation of the Charter.[151]

In the First Committee the Belgian draft resolution was adopted by a vote of 26 to 13, with 16 abstentions; and in Plenary, by a vote of 40 to 8, with 2 abstentions.[152]

The motivation behind the request was perhaps best summed up by the Argentine representative, who, in agreeing to vote for the request, declared that he did so "on the understanding that an effort is being made to clarify the conduct of certain Members rather than, properly speaking, to interpret the Charter."[153] The trouble was that the member whose action was to be clarified had put the Assembly on notice that it would not accept judicial clarification, and in these circumstances the clarification was bound to be pointless. Nor, upon closer scrutiny, was the West's expectation that it would obtain a propaganda coup wholly justified. The conditions stated in Article 4(1) of the Charter are so broad that, even if deemed exhaustive—as, in fact, the Court majority subsequently deemed them to be—no state would experience much difficulty in confining itself to the stated criteria in order to bar the admission of any applicant state.[154] Moreover, no state is obliged to explain its

[149]See, in particular, the remarks of the Polish representative, *ibid.*, 1st Ctte., 99th Mtg., 7 November 1947, pp. 345–47. He countered with a proposal that the permanent Council members confer together in an attempt to reach agreement.

[150]Many of the representatives who asserted the "political" and "nonjudicial" nature of the question were content to confine themselves to the assertion, without explanation. The U.S.S.R. representative argued, *inter alia*, that the question was "political" because the grounds evoked for refusing certain states admission had been "political" and because every state had an equal right to be guided by political motives. *Ibid.*, Plenary, 117th Mtg., 17 November 1947, pp. 1050–51. See also the statements of India (*ibid.*, 1st Ctte., 100th Mtg., 8 November 1947, p. 364) and Argentina (*ibid.*, p. 370).

The "political" versus the "legal" nature of the questions was more fully discussed in the pleadings and in the majority and individual opinions. See Chapter V.

[151]See, e.g., the statement of the U.S.S.R., GAOR (II), 1st Ctte., 99th Mtg., 7 November 1947, p. 360. In this instance, India and Argentina also shared, to varying extents, reservations regarding judicial interpretation of the Charter. *Ibid.*, 100th Mtg., 8 November 1947, pp. 364, 370; and Plenary, 118th Mtg., 17 November 1947, p. 1071. Nevertheless, Argentina voted for the request. On the question of the Court's competence to interpret the Charter, see Chapter V.

[152]The resolution requesting the Court's opinion became Resolution 113B (II), 17 November 1947.

In the pleadings, Yugoslavia pointed to the split vote in the Committee as evidence of profound hesitation on the part of the Assembly as to the "legal" nature of the question. *Admission* case, ICJ Pleadings, 1948, p. 88. Belgium, on the other hand, cited the large majority by which the proposal was finally adopted in Plenary. *Ibid.*, p. 91.

[153]GAOR (II), Plenary, 118th Mtg., 17 November 1947, p. 1071. The argument that the request was designed to obtain judicial censure of one Security Council member was among those subsequently cited in the pleadings and dissenting opinions as evidence of the "political" nature of the request.

[154]At least at one point in the pre-request debate, the Soviet delegate conceded the exhaustive nature of the requirements of Article 4(1), and stated that his government

vote, in any case. In effect, the whole matter boils down to a question of motives and good faith[155] —neither of which are subject to judicial control.[156] Far from supplying a guide to action, the projected opinion could, quite foreseeably, "provide a cloak for any kind of action."[157] In these circumstances, the wisdom of involving the Court in the admission imbroglio was doubly questionable.

Reparation for Injuries Suffered in the Service of the United Nations

The considerations which prompted the second Assembly request for an advisory opinion were of a vastly different nature from those which prompted the first. This time the argument was not over the "legal" nature of the questions, but rather over which method of legal clarification was best suited to resolve a problem which the Assembly members were at one in wishing to see resolved. Significantly, this was the only Assembly request adopted by a unanimous vote.[158]

It was in the following circumstances that the Court's opinion was sought.

Following a series of assassinations of UN personnel in Palestine, including that of Count Bernadotte (UN mediator for Palestine), the Secretary-General placed on the agenda of the Assembly's third session the question of reparation for injuries incurred in the service of the UN. In a memorandum on the subject, the Secretary-General raised certain questions of law, policy, and procedure.[159] The legal question posed was whether a state may be held responsible to the UN for injury to, or the death of, a UN agent. While the Secretary-General himself did not doubt the organization's capacity under international law to present claims against states, he nevertheless deemed it advisable, in view of the absence of legal precedents on the matter, to solicit the Assembly's decision before proceeding to the actual presentation of claims.

In the Assembly's Sixth (Legal) Committee, extensive discussion of the question thus posed ensued.[160] It was readily apparent that widely divergent views were held by Committee members—not so much with respect to the existence of the capacity in question as with respect to the extent and scope

merely doubted the "peace-loving" nature of the states concerned. *Ibid.*, 117th Mtg., 17 November 1947, p. 1048.

[155] This is true, regardless of whether one adopts the view of the Court majority that the question posed related solely to the statements made concerning the vote, or the view of the joint dissenting minority that it embraced actual motives as well. ICJ Reports, 1948, pp. 60, 82–83.

[156] Lissitzyn, *International Court*, p. 91.

[157] Lauterpacht, *International Court*, p. 150.

[158] In the Sixth Committee, however, the vote was 34 to 5, with 1 abstention.

[159] UN Doc. A/674, 7 October 1948.

[160] The question was discussed at Mtgs. 112–24, 19–26 November 1948.

of that capacity. Could the UN, for example, present claims for injuries sustained by itself, the victim, or both? How could any UN right be reconciled with the rights of the victim's national state? What if the victim's national state was itself the responsible state? To deal with the very complex questions raised, several draft resolutions and amendments were put forward. These fell into three categories, in each of which a different mode of action was proposed: (1) draft resolutions under which the Assembly itself would set forth the general principles regarding UN competence to claim reparations and would give immediate directives to the Secretary-General;[161] (2) a proposal to refer the matter to the ILC in order that a draft convention on reparations might be drawn up;[162] and (3) proposals to request the Court's opinion in the matter.[163]

Those representatives (among whom were the representatives of France, the Soviet Union, Egypt, New Zealand, and Uruguay) who favored the first alternative considered that the UN undoubtedly possessed the competence to claim reparations;[164] that there was, therefore, no necessity[165] —and, indeed, it might be positively pernicious[166] —to request an advisory opinion; and that the practical problem of how to obtain speedy and adequate compensation

[161] The main draft resolutions in this category were sponsored by Egypt (UN Doc. A/C.6/279 and corr. 1, 20 November 1948) and Uruguay (UN Doc. A/C.6/281, 20 November 1948). Amendments to the Egyptian proposal were presented by France and the U.S.S.R. (UN Docs. A/C.6/282 and 284, respectively).

[162] See the Syrian draft resolution, UN Doc. A/C.6/276, 19 November 1948; and cf. the French amendment, UN Doc. A/C.6/278, 20 November 1948.

[163] The original draft resolution was proposed by Belgium (UN Doc. A/C.6/275, 19 November 1948). Amendments were submitted by France (UN Doc. A/C.6/277); the United Kingdom (UN Docs. A/C.6/280 and 283); France and Iran, jointly (UN Doc. A/C.6/285); Venezuela (UN Doc. A/C.6/292); and Greece (UN Doc. A/C.6/293). The draft of the working group set up to formulate a final text was UN Doc. A/C.6/294, 25 November 1948.

[164] See, e.g., the statements of the U.S.S.R. (GAOR [III/1], 6th Ctte., 114th Mtg., 20 November 1948, pp. 543–44); France (ibid., p. 547; and 115th Mtg., 22 November 1948, p. 552); and Egypt (ibid., 117th Mtg., 23 November 1948, pp. 568, 575). There was apparently no agreement, however, as to whether the organization was confined to bringing suit in national courts, or as to the measure of compensation which might be claimed.

[165] See n. 164. The Soviet delegate, pointing out that the Sixth Committee was composed of eminent jurists representing the legal systems of the world, considered it false modesty to maintain that the Committee was not qualified to deal with the problem under discussion. GAOR (III/1), 6th Ctte., 115th Mtg., 22 November 1948, p. 558.

[166] In the opinion of the French representative, recourse to the Court entailed casting doubt on the UN's capacity to protect its agents and exposed the organization to the risk of losing some of its rights. GAOR (III/1), 6th Ctte., 114th Mtg., 20 November 1948, p. 547; and 115th Mtg., 22 November 1948, p. 552. The Soviet representative feared that the authority of both Assembly and Court would be undermined, in the event the Assembly disagreed with the Court's advice. Ibid., 115th Mtg., 22 November 1948, p. 558.

was the overriding one and could best be solved by immediate Assembly action.[167]

Contrariwise, advocates of the second approach (most notably, the representatives of Syria, Sweden, and Greece) assumed that *de lege lata*, the organization *lacked* the capacity in question.[168] Since, in their view, what was needed was the creation of new law, the ILC—the organ for codification and progressive development—rather than the ICJ—the organ limited to affirming the existing law—was the proper addressee of the legal difficulties with which the Committee was grappling. Furthermore, even if the organization's capacity were to be upheld by the Court, many practical problems would remain to be resolved by the Assembly itself.[169] And, unlike a convention, an advisory opinion, even with Assembly endorsement, would not bind member states.[170]

However, the majority of the Sixth Committee favored the third proposed course of action: requesting an advisory opinion of the ICJ. Many of these states did not themselves doubt the organization's right, under existing international law, to present international claims. Nevertheless, in view of the doubts of others, and, more important, in view of the widely divergent views expressed regarding the scope and exercise of the right, they considered judicial clarification desirable. Because of its authoritativeness, a Court opinion was best calculated to dissipate remaining doubts and to provide a solid legal foundation for the protection of UN personnel. Moreover, a long and indecisive doctrinal debate within the Sixth Committee—which, in any event, lacked the requisite time and authority to resolve the legal questions at issue— could thereby be avoided. As for reference to the ILC, it was pointed out that that body was already overburdened;[171] that the ICJ's opinion would be both more authoritative and more quickly forthcoming than the ILC's; and that it

[167]The real problem was said to be the practical question of how to harmonize the competence of the UN and that of the victim's national state. See the statement of France, *ibid.*, 114th Mtg., 20 November 1948, p. 547. See also the statements of Uruguay (*ibid.*, 115th Mtg., 22 November 1948, pp. 553–55); the U.S.S.R. (*ibid.*, 117th Mtg., 23 November 1948, p. 569); and New Zealand (*ibid.*, p. 573).

[168]See, e.g., *ibid.*, 112th Mtg., 19 November 1948, pp. 530–31; 115th Mtg., 22 November 1948, p. 557; 116th Mtg., 22 November 1948, p. 564; and 117th Mtg., 23 November 1948, p. 567.

[169]Statements of Syria and Greece, *ibid.*, 112th Mtg., 19 November 1948, pp. 528, 531–32. The Greek representative also argued that judicial recognition of the UN's right to protect its officials would necessitate the recognition of a corresponding right for every other international organization, including regional organizations. *Ibid.*, 114th Mtg., 20 November 1948, p. 546.

[170]Syria. *Ibid.*, 117th Mtg., 23 November 1948, p. 567.

[171]This was attested to by the Secretary-General's representative. *Ibid.*, 115th Mtg., 22 November 1948, p. 550. He noted that the ILC already had three important items on its 1949 agenda. On the other hand, the ICJ was an organ which should be consulted on legal questions, particularly in light of Resolution 171 (II), of 14 November 1947, which called for greater use of the Court.

would be possible and preferable to turn to the ILC *after* judicial elucidation of the existing law, for the ILC might then proceed to fill any gaps revealed by the Court.[172]

After deciding that the Committee itself could not immediately determine the legal question of whether the UN had the capacity at issue,[173] and, after rejecting a draft resolution giving immediate directives to the Secretary-General,[174] the Committee decided to set up a working group to prepare a combined draft resolution embodying the questions to be presented to the Court.[175]

The final text, as it emerged from the working group, and as it was approved in Committee[176] (by a vote of 34 to 5, with 1 abstention) and in Plenary[177] (unanimously), was as follows:

> *Whereas* the series of tragic events which have lately befallen agents of the United Nations engaged in the performance of their duties raises, with greater urgency than ever, the question of the arrangements to be made by the United Nations with a view to ensuring to its agents the fullest measure of protection in the future and ensuring that reparation be made for the injuries suffered; and
>
> *Whereas* it is highly desirable that the Secretary-General should be able to act without question as efficaciously as possible with a view to obtaining any reparation due; therefore[178]

[172] Among the states that spoke in favor of recourse to the Court were the United States, the United Kingdom, Belgium, Australia, the Netherlands, Iran, Brazil, Turkey, and Venezuela. See *ibid.*, Mtgs. 112-16, 19-22 November 1948 *passim*.

Because of the fullness of the ILC agenda and the possibility of subsequent reference to the ILC, most ILC advocates acquiesced in the proposed recourse to the Court. However, the Syrian representative would have preferred the preparation of a convention by the Sixth Committee to consultation of the Court, and he indicated that his country might later contest the Court's competence to give the opinion. *Ibid.*, 116th Mtg., 22 November 1948, p. 564; and 124th Mtg., 26 November 1948, p. 614.

[173] *Ibid.*, 118th Mtg., 23 November 1948, p. 584.

[174] *Ibid.*, 120th Mtg., 24 November 1948, p. 596. The draft resolution had been sponsored by Egypt and amended by other states. Most representatives felt that immediate action would be premature and would lack the necessary authority. *Ibid.*, pp. 596-99.

[175] *Ibid.*, 121st Mtg., 25 November 1948, p. 610. The working group was composed of states which had submitted draft resolutions and amendments on the matter.

[176] *Ibid.*, 124th Mtg., 26 November 1948, p. 618.

[177] *Ibid.*, Plenary, 169th Mtg., 3 December 1948, p. 690 (Resolution 258 [III]). It was adopted without discussion.

[178] The preamble was taken from a French-Iranian draft (UN Doc. A/C.6/285, 22 November 1948) and was inserted to indicate the Assembly's desires in the matter. See the Iranian statements, GAOR (III/1), 6th Ctte., 116th Mtg., 22 November 1948, p. 559; and 120th Mtg., 24 November 1948, p. 603. These considerata were also in line with the earlier expressed Iranian hope that "the Court would recognize the changes that had come about in international life and that it would take into account the necessity for an

The General Assembly

Decides to submit the following legal questions to the International Court of Justice for an advisory opinion:

I. In the event of an agent of the United Nations in the performance of his duties suffering injury in circumstances involving the responsibility of a State, has the United Nations, as an Organization, the capacity to bring an international claim against the responsible *de jure* or *de facto* government with a view to obtaining the reparation due in respect of the damage caused (a) to the United Nations, (b) to the victim or to persons entitled through him?[179]

II. In the event of an affirmative reply on point I (b), how is action by the United Nations to be reconciled with such rights as may be possessed by the State of which the victim is a national?[180]

Instructs the Secretary-General, after the Court has given its opinion, to prepare proposals in the light of that opinion, and to submit them to the General Assembly at its next regular session.[181]

The contrast between the conditions under which recourse to the Court was decided upon in the *Reparation* case and the corresponding conditions in the *Admission* case could hardly be more stark. In this case, the question was raised originally by the Secretary-General as a "legal" question. It was considered by the Assembly's Legal Committee, which in turn thought the matter complex enough and important enough to require clarification by some other body. The clarification desired was to be of an *authoritative* nature. While some states preferred reference to the ILC and others (including the Soviet Union) preferred direct Committee action, no serious protest (even by the Soviet Union) was lodged against the course finally decided upon. On the

---

interpretation of the existing law which would ensure the protection of United Nations officials." *Ibid.*, 113th Mtg., 20 November 1948, p. 542.

[179] Point (b) was not included in the original Belgian draft. In the Committee, differences of opinion emerged on this question. Some recognized injury to the organization as the sole basis for a claim; others recognized only injury to the victim; while still others admitted both bases.

The new wording accorded with a United Kingdom amendment (UN Doc. A/C.6/280, 20 November 1948).

[180] This question, too, did not appear in the original draft, but emerged in the course of Committee discussions as a rather crucial one. It appeared in the second United Kingdom draft (UN Doc. A/C.6/283, 22 November 1948).

[181] This paragraph (inspired by Syrian and Venezuelan proposals [UN Docs. A/C.6/276 and 292]) evoked a Soviet query as to whether the Assembly was undertaking to accept the Court's opinion in advance. GAOR (III/1), 6th Ctte., 124th Mtg., 26 November 1948, p. 614. Assurances were given that the opinion would in no way be binding, the purpose of this paragraph being merely to save time. While the Secretary-General was bound "to prepare proposals in the light of" the Court's opinion, the Assembly was entirely free to decide on any action it deemed fit. *Ibid.*, pp. 616–17.

goal of compensation for UN agents, all were agreed. Neither Cold War issues nor any important state interests were implicated. Whatever opinion the Court might give (even if it was not the one for which the Assembly, in the preamble of the request, indicated its preference), employment of the ILC remained an available alternative for securing the desired results.

In sum, reference to the Court in this case was part of a problem-solving approach; and the augury for acceptance of the resultant opinion was as bright as that in the *Admission* case was dim.

Interpretation of Peace Treaties with Bulgaria, Hungary, and Romania

This was the first and perhaps the only UN request which related to a "dispute" (in the terminology of the Covenant) or "a legal question actually pending between two or more States" (in the words of Article 82 of the ICJ Rules).[182] It was made in the face of the opposition of the most important disputants, who, additionally, were not then UN members. The similarities between the *Peace Treaties* case and the *Eastern Carelia* case are on the surface and have, in fact, been widely recognized. The Court itself took great pains to distinguish between the two cases.[183] For our present purposes, the most important common element to be noted—and the two cases shared this with the *Admission* case as well—was the obvious futility of the proposed recourse to the Court. Thus, in the instant case, the prospects that a judicial opinion would result in any alteration in the observance of human rights in the three satellite countries were, to say the least, bleak. Even in terms of the expected propaganda dividends, it is doubtful whether reference to the Court, particularly when weighed against the harm to which the Court's prestige might thus be exposed, was justified.

The question of the observance of human rights in two of the three states—Hungary and Bulgaria—was first discussed by the General Assembly during the second part of its third session.[184] Earlier, on 2 April 1949, the United States and the United Kingdom had addressed notes to the governments of Bulgaria, Hungary, and Rumania, alleging violations of the human

---

[182] The existence of a "dispute" was, in fact, one of the questions before the Court—a question upon which the Court pronounced itself affirmatively. In the *Namibia* case, the Court denied the existence of a dispute. See p. 50, n. 35; and Chapter V.

[183] See Chapter V.

[184] The question had been raised by Australia and Bolivia (UN Docs. A/820 and A/821, 16 and 19 March 1949). The objects of particular concern were the trials of church leaders in the two countries and, most notably, that of Cardinal Mindszenty in Hungary. Before the fourth Assembly session, Australia requested that the question of the observance of human rights in Rumania be added to the original item. UN Doc. A/948, 20 August 1949. The Soviet bloc consistently opposed Assembly consideration of the matter.

rights provisions of the respective Peace Treaties.[185] In its resolution,[186] the Assembly therefore confined itself primarily to awaiting the results of the steps taken by the signatories, while retaining the item on its agenda for the fourth session. By that session, all efforts at settling the human rights questions in accordance with the dispute-settlement procedures of the Peace Treaties had proven clearly abortive.[187] The three communist governments (joined by the Soviet Union) denied the substantive allegations presented, and rejected all diplomatic interventions as unwarranted interference in their domestic affairs and in their processes of justice. Similarly, they denied the existence of any dispute between them and the Allied Powers and refused to designate representatives to the treaty commissions provided for in the Peace Treaties.[188]

In these circumstances, it was quite obvious that any Assembly action would meet with an equally defiant response. The only benefit to be derived from continued consideration of the issue was in the area of propaganda and world public opinion. Presumably, it was this hoped-for benefit which prompted introduction in the Ad Hoc Political Committee of a draft resolution to request the Court's opinion on the applicability of the dispute-settlement procedures of the Peace Treaties.[189] Four questions were to be put to the Court. First, did disputes exist between the three governments, on the one hand, and certain Allied and Associated Powers, on the other, within the terms of the Treaties? Second, if disputes did exist, were the three governments obligated to appoint their representatives to the Treaty Commissions provided for in the Peace Treaties? The third and fourth questions were to be answered only in the event of an affirmative reply by the Court to the second and failure of the three governments concerned to comply with the Court's opinion. In that event, was the Secretary-General authorized to appoint the third members of the Commissions? And, if so, would such two-member commissions be competent to make definitive and binding decisions?

---

[185] For the texts of these notes, see *Peace Treaties* case, ICJ Pleadings, 1950, pp. 23–30, 72–77.

[186] Resolution 272 (III), 30 April 1949.

[187] For the relevant diplomatic exchanges, see ICJ Pleadings, 1950, pp. 30–69, 77–104.

[188] Under the terms of the compromissory clauses of the respective Peace Treaties, disputes not otherwise settled (either by direct negotiations or by the three Allied Heads of Mission) were to be referred, at the request of either party, to a commission composed of one representative of each party and a third member, selected by mutual agreement of the two parties. Upon failure of the two parties to agree within a month on the appointment of the third member, either party might petition the UN Secretary-General to make the appointment.

[189] UN Docs. A/AC.31/L.1, 4 October 1949, and A/AC.31/L.1/Rev.1, 7 October 1949. The draft resolution was sponsored jointly by Bolivia, Canada, and the United States.

The competence of the Assembly to make the proposed request, and, indeed, to consider the matter at all, was vigorously challenged by the Soviet bloc. Among the arguments put forward in support of its position were the following: (1) The right to interpret, or seek interpretation of, a treaty appertained exclusively to the parties. Without the consent of *all* the parties, the Assembly could not seek, and the Court could not render, an interpretation. (2) Moreover, since peace treaties were involved, the UN was clearly barred, by Article 107 of the Charter, from dealing with them. (3) The Peace Treaties contained their own dispute-settlement procedures, and these procedures had not yet been exhausted. Requesting the Court's opinion meant substituting the Court's advisory jurisdiction for the dispute-settlement procedures of the treaties. (4) The dispute-settlement procedures were applicable only when all three Allied and Associated Powers (including the Soviet Union) were in dispute with the defeated states. (5) The Assembly's discussions and the proposed request constituted intervention in the domestic affairs of the three governments. (6) The political rather than the legal elements were in this case decisive, inasmuch as the item had been introduced for essentially political reasons.[190]

Further grounds for opposition to the request included injury to the prestige of both the UN and the ICJ and the impairment of the latter's authority which, it was said, would result; the alleged clarity of the matter at issue; and the necessity to resist attempts to transform the ICJ into a mere branch of the American State Department or the British Foreign Office.[191]

In defense of the Assembly's competence to refer the proposed questions to the Court (at least questions 1 and 2), the following arguments were advanced. What was involved was not the substantive question of human rights (which would in no way be prejudged by either the request or the opinion), but the procedural question of the applicability of the treaties' dispute-settlement procedure. There could therefore be no question of interference with the domestic jurisdiction of states—since treaty observance ipso facto was not a domestic matter—or of by-passing the treaty procedure—since the object of the request was precisely to facilitate settlement through the use of the treaty procedure. By promoting respect for treaties and facilitating the use of treaty machinery for dispute settlement, the Assembly was not only

---

[190]Most of these arguments were repeated before the Court. See Chapter V.

[191]These various arguments were culled from those presented in GAOR (IV): Gen. Ctte., 65th Mtg., 21 September 1949, pp. 3–4; Ad Hoc Pol. Ctte., Mtgs. 7–15, 4–13 October 1949; Plenary, 224th Mtg., 22 September 1949, pp. 18–19; and 234th and 235th Mtgs., 21 and 22 October 1949, pp. 130–50. See, in particular, Ad Hoc Pol. Ctte.: 8th Mtg., 5 October 1949, pp. 32–34; 11th Mtg., 10 October 1949, pp. 42–43, 45–46; 12th Mtg., 11 October 1949, pp. 48–49; 13th Mtg., 12 October 1949, pp. 53–54; 14th Mtg., 12 October 1949, p. 60; and Plenary, 234th Mtg., 21 October 1949, pp. 134–35.

acting within its competence; it was discharging a positive duty, in the spirit of Article 33 of the Charter.[192]

As for the desirability of the proposed reference, it was argued, *inter alia*, that, although the procedure might appear dilatory, political action based on undoubted legal foundations would, in the end, be more efficacious in impressing on the three governments the propriety as well as the strength of the world's interest in their behavior; that the proposed recourse was the last resort open to the UN in the purely legal field; and that consultation of the Court would allow the rule of law to come to the rescue of the endangered freedoms.[193]

With respect to questions 3 and 4, however, more opposition was expressed. An Australian amendment to the joint draft resolution would, in fact, have substituted for the second phase of the advisory proceedings the establishment of an ad hoc committee to investigate the substantive human rights issues (regardless of whether the Court's answer to question 2 was affirmative or negative).[194] Against referring questions 3 and 4, it was argued, *inter alia*, that (1) these questions probably would not be answered affirmatively, and that, in any event, two-member commissions would present other difficulties;[195] (2) by sending these questions to the Court, the Assembly would be asking for the *revision* rather than the interpretation of treaties— and this it was not competent to do;[196] and (3) such an Assembly request might be construed as interference in the internal affairs of states through

---

[192]See GAOR (IV), Ad Hoc Pol. Ctte., 7th Mtg., 4 October 1949 (the United States, pp. 27–29; Bolivia, pp. 29–30; Canada, p. 31); 9th Mtg., 6 October 1949 (the United Kingdom, p. 36; Belgium, pp. 36–37; Sweden, p. 37; Brazil, p. 38; Norway, p. 39); 10th Mtg., 7 October 1949 (China, p. 41); 11th Mtg., 10 October 1949 (the Netherlands, p. 44); 13th Mtg., 12 October 1949 (the United Kingdom, p. 56).
The French representative, while conceding that the Assembly might not, as a general rule, seek an interpretation of a treaty, nevertheless deemed the treaties at issue exceptional because (1) they involved human rights—a matter which fell within the Assembly's competence under the terms of Article 55 of the Charter; (2) they themselves contemplated possible intervention by the General Assembly. *Ibid.*, 14th Mtg., 12 October 1949, p. 58; Plenary, 234th Mtg., 21 October 1949, p. 132. See also the statement of Belgium, *ibid.*, Ad Hoc Pol. Ctte., 9th Mtg., 6 October 1949, pp. 36–37.

[193]Statements of the United Kingdom (*ibid.*, 9th Mtg., 6 October 1949, p. 36); Lebanon (*ibid.*, 11th Mtg., 10 October 1949, p. 46); Peru (*ibid.*, 15th Mtg., 13 October 1949, p. 66); and France (*ibid.*, Plenary, 234th Mtg., 21 October 1949, p. 133).

[194]UN Doc. A/AC.31/L.2, 7 October 1949.

[195]Australia, GAOR (IV), Ad Hoc Pol. Ctte., 10th Mtg., 7 October 1949, p. 42. The United Kingdom representative, while favoring the reference of these questions, deemed a negative judicial response probable. *Ibid.*, Plenary, 234th Mtg., 21 October 1949, p. 144.

[196]France, *ibid.*, Ad Hoc Pol. Ctte., 14th Mtg., 12 October 1949, pp. 58–59; Plenary, 234th Mtg., 21 October 1949, p. 133.

unilateral interpretation of peace treaties, and a dangerous precedent would thereby be created.[197]

On the other hand, those who favored the reference of questions 3 and 4 considered it necessary to exhaust the treaty procedure before proceeding to any other steps.[198] It was also pointed out that settlement of these questions might have a bearing on the drafting of future treaties.[199]

After separate votes on each of the four questions,[200] the joint draft resolution as a whole was adopted by the Ad Hoc Political Committee by a vote of 41 to 5, with 9 abstentions,[201] and, in Plenary, by a vote of 47 to 5, with 7 abstentions.[202]

In sum, it may be said that there was little trace, even among the strongest supporters of recourse to the Court, of any hope for real improvement in the human rights situation in the three satellite states as a result of such recourse. Indeed, the necessity of including questions 3 and 4 was itself testament to the expectation that compliance by the three governments with the Court's opinion would not be forthcoming. Even more than in the *Admission* case, the subject of the *Peace Treaties* request exposed a raw nerve in the communist world, for, at root, the internal totalitarian regimes of the states concerned were here being questioned.[203]

Moreover, it was not clear that the West's propaganda position stood to be significantly enhanced by the projected advisory opinion. An affirmative answer on the first two questions would presumably make clear to the world that the three governments, on top of their violations of treaty obligations concerning human rights and fundamental freedoms, also violated their treaty commitments regarding dispute settlement. If, in addition, the Court were to reply affirmatively to questions 3 and 4 (and even some of the strongest supporters of the proposed reference deemed this unlikely), treaty commissions might then pronounce themselves on the substance of the disputes, thereby possibly placing the three governments in an even more embarrassing position. And, for their part, the Western states would be proving to the

---

[197]Peru, *ibid.*, Ad Hoc Pol. Ctte., 15th Mtg., p. 66; Plenary, 235th Mtg., p. 150. Cf. the statement of the Dominican Republic, *ibid.*, 234th Mtg., 21 October 1949, p. 139.

[198]See, e.g., *ibid.*, Ad Hoc Pol. Ctte., 15th Mtg., 13 October 1949, pp. 65–66.

[199]India, *ibid.*, 10th Mtg., 7 October 1949, p. 40.

[200]The votes for submitting questions 3 and 4 were somewhat lower.

[201]GAOR (IV), Ad Hoc Pol. Ctte., 15th Mtg., 13 October 1949, p. 66.

[202]*Ibid.*, Plenary, 235th Mtg., 22 October 1950, p. 150. The resolution was numbered 294 (IV).

[203]In the words of the Netherlands representative, "The accusations against Bulgaria, Hungary and Romania were not accidental phenomena, but the inevitable consequences of their political and social structure." *Ibid.*, Ad Hoc Pol. Ctte., 11th Mtg., 10 October 1949, p. 44.

world that they were exhausting, to the very limits, the legal measures which it was within their power to take. They would thus appear to be taking "action." But did the additional propaganda points justify saddling the Court with these questions and placing its prestige in jeopardy? Might not the Australian proposal to appoint a fact-finding committee[204] have yielded equal propaganda dividends while sparing the Court possible embarrassment? These questions do not appear to have seriously troubled the Assembly majority. The Soviet bloc alone protested—for obvious reasons—against the Court's being dragged into the Cold War propaganda struggle.

Competence of the General Assembly for the Admission of a State to the United Nations

This case constituted a kind of epilogue to the *Admission* case and effectively drew the curtain on attempts to have the ICJ alleviate the admission woes of the organization.[205] It marked the culmination of a long Argentine campaign to gain Assembly acceptance of an interpretation of Article 4(2) of the Charter which would have by-passed the veto roadblock. The Assembly, though itself unwilling to endorse the Argentine interpretation, was nevertheless prepared to allow Argentina its "day in Court."

To void the effects of the Soviet veto on the admission of new members, Argentina had long espoused a rather controversial interpretation of Article 4(2), the crux of which was that the word "recommendation" in that provision did not necessarily mean "favorable recommendation."[206] Thus, the Assembly (which alone had powers of decision) might as readily reject an *unfavorable* Security Council recommendation—and admit a state—as it might reject a *favorable* recommendation—and deny a state membership. Alternatively (and, in this alternative interpretation, Argentina was far less isolated), the veto might be skirted by deeming Article 27(3) inapplicable to admission questions and allowing the Assembly to consider as a *favorable* recommendation one which received the affirmative vote of any seven Council members.[207] The Assembly was entitled, Argentina argued, to interpret independently the results of the Security Council's voting.

During the initial stages of its campaign, Argentina did not seek to employ the Court. In fact, Argentina's representatives were among those who had

---

[204] See p. 101 above. The proposal had been introduced in the third session.

[205] For a subsequent proposal envisaging a further advisory opinion on the issue, see Chapter IV, p. 229.

[206] As the Argentine delegate explained at one point, "recommendation" no more implies "favorable recommendation" than "woman" implies "pretty woman." GAOR (II), Plenary, 118th Mtg., 17 November 1947, p. 1072.

[207] These two alternative approaches are more fully set forth in the Argentine Written Statement submitted to the Court. ICJ Pleadings, 1950, pp. 123-48.

earlier expressed doubts regarding the Court's competence to interpret the Charter.[208] During the fourth session, however, Argentina introduced in the Ad Hoc Political Committee a draft resolution, the purpose of which was to obtain judicial clarification of the meaning of Article 4(2).[209] Argentina's reversal was apparently due primarily to its recognition that , independently, the Assembly was not prepared to go along with the Argentine proposals,[210] and to a corresponding hope that the Court might yet salvage some of the Argentine doctrine.[211] For, while on the substantive question Argentina found itself opposed by the United States, the Soviet Union, all the permanent members of the Security Council, and a majority of the Assembly members as well, on the question of submission to the Court, it could count on a large "sympathy vote."

That this appellation for the vote to request the Court's opinion was not misplaced can be readily seen from a review of the debates in the Ad Hoc Political Committee.[212] There was an undeniably strong and persistent undercurrent of opinion to the effect that recourse to the Court was totally unnecessary in this case, since the terms of Article 4(2) were perfectly clear. Moreover, several of those who either supported or abstained on the Argentine proposal appeared rather hard-pressed to find solid grounds (i.e., grounds reasonably related to a solution of the admission deadlock) on which to justify their stands and fell back, openly or otherwise, on their sympathy with Argentina's motives. Thus, the Belgian representative stated that there

[208] See, e.g., the Argentine view in the pre-request phase of the *Admission* case. As late as the third session, the Argentine representative rejected a suggestion that the interpretation of Article 4(2) be referred to the Court, on the ground that the Court would probably consider itself incompetent to deal with it. GAOR (III/1), Ad Hoc Pol. Ctte., 11th Mtg., 24 November 1948, p. 122.

[209] UN Doc. A/AC.31/L.18, 31 October 1949.

[210] In the third session, for example, an Argentine draft resolution (UN Doc. A/AC.24/15, 23 November 1948) was withdrawn after it became apparent that it would be defeated. GAOR (III/1), Ad Hoc Pol. Ctte., 14th Mtg., 26 November 1948, p. 156.

[211] The Soviet delegate's observation that Argentina, having failed in a frontal attack, decided to renew its efforts in a more veiled form, was rather cogent. GAOR (IV), Plenary, 252nd Mtg., 22 November 1949, p. 326.

Cf. the Argentine statements, *ibid.*, Ad Hoc Pol. Ctte., 26th Mtg., 1 November 1949, pp. 125-26; and 28th Mtg., 3 November 1949, pp. 153-54. At the same time, the Argentine representative expressed willingness to acquiesce in an adverse judicial decision. Conceivably, even a negative judicial opinion would not have been too unwelcome, for it would have permitted the Argentine representative to retreat gracefully from the rather untenable position in which he had ensconced himself. In this connection, Argentina's subsequent failure to be represented in the oral proceedings before the Court is noteworthy—the more so since Argentina thus reversed its previously announced intention to appear. *Competence* case, ICJ Pleadings, 1950, pp. 191, 192. It is difficult to avoid the impression that the Argentine thesis was becoming too onerous even for its authors.

[212] See GAOR (IV), Ad Hoc Pol. Ctte., Mtgs. 25-29, 31 October-4 November 1949.

was no reason why Argentina should not receive the satisfaction it desired. Although, in Belgium's view, Article 4(2) was clear, the Belgian delegation also held, as a general principle, that "when a State faced with a juridical difficulty expressed the desire to submit the question to an impartial court," UN organs "should accede to this request."[213] The Bolivian representative explained that he would vote for the Argentine draft resolution in order to show appreciation of Argentina's motives and because more frequent recourse to the ICJ would strengthen that body's prestige and authority.[214] And, after offering a rather convincing reason for *not* consulting the Court (namely, the problem could be solved only by Charter amendment), the Haitian representative nevertheless declared that he would vote for the request "because the opinion of the Court would be of great documentary and historical value."[215]

Apart from the abovestated reasons, the themes most frequently echoed in support of the proposed request were the need to dispel finally the doubts which had arisen and persisted, and the suitability of the Court for dispelling those doubts.[216]

Opposition to requesting the Court's opinion—which was by no means confined to the Soviet bloc[217]—was based primarily on the clarity of the provision in question.[218] Other reasons cited included the obvious futility of the proposed request;[219] the "political" nature of the request;[220] and the

---

[213]*Ibid.*, 27th Mtg., 2 November 1949, p. 139. See also the explanation of the Canadian representative for his abstention. While doubting whether the ICJ could confirm the Argentine interpretation, he nevertheless "always recognized the right of any State [*sic*] to request an advisory opinion . . . on any legal question" concerning the interpretation of the Charter. *Ibid.*, 28th Mtg., 3 November 1949, p. 155.

[214]*Ibid.*

[215]*Ibid.*, 29th Mtg., 4 November 1949, p. 162.

[216]See, e.g., the statements of Lebanon (*ibid.*, 27th Mtg., 2 November 1949, p. 146), Belgium (*ibid.*, 28th Mtg., 3 November 1949, p. 153), the Philippines (*ibid.*, p. 157), and Colombia (*ibid.*, p. 158).

[217]But, while many of the non-Soviet states abstained in the vote, the Soviet bloc voted against.

[218]See, e.g., the statements of Poland (GAOR [IV], Ad Hoc Pol. Ctte., 27th Mtg., 2 November 1949, p. 147), the U.S.S.R. (*ibid.*, 28th Mtg., 3 November 1949, p. 150), and Australia (*ibid.*, p. 153).

[219]The ineffectiveness of the *Admission* opinion was pointed to in this connection. See, e.g., the statements of Sweden (*ibid.*, 27th Mtg., 2 November 1949, p. 143) and France (*ibid.*, 28th Mtg., 3 November 1949, p. 151).

[220]The request was considered "political" because it was inspired by political motives and because the Court's opinion would have political implications. See, e.g., the statements of Poland (*ibid.*, 26th Mtg., 1 November 1949, p. 123; and 27th Mtg., 2 November 1949, pp. 147–48), Czechoslovakia (*ibid.*, 26th Mtg., 1 November 1949, p. 129), Norway (*ibid.*, 27th Mtg., 2 November 1949, p. 137), and the U.S.S.R. (*ibid.*, 28th Mtg., 3 November 1949, p. 150).

deleterious effects on the Court's prestige of involving it in an embittered political controversy.[221] Doubts were also expressed regarding the Court's competence to pronounce itself, even in an advisory opinion, on the voting procedure of the Security Council.[222]

Notwithstanding this opposition, the Ad Hoc Committee and, subsequently, the Plenary voted by wide margins to request the Court's opinion.[223] The question which the Court was called upon to answer was:

> Can the admission of a State to membership in the United Nations, pursuant to Article 4, paragraph 2, of the Charter, be effected by a decision of the General Assembly when the Security Council has made no recommendation for admission by reason of the candidate failing to obtain the requisite majority or of the negative vote of a permanent member upon a resolution so to recommend?[224]

[221]*Ibid.*, 28th Mtg., 3 November 1949, pp. 147–48.

[222]*Ibid.*, pp. 149–50; and Plenary, 252nd Mtg., 22 November 1949, pp. 325–26.

[223]The vote was, respectively, 37 to 9, with 8 abstentions; and 42 to 9, with 6 abstentions. The resolution was numbered 296 J (IV).

[224]This question was not the one in the original Argentine draft resolution. That draft had centered on the interpretation and legal effect to be given to a particular document in the *travaux préparatoires* of the UN Charter which Argentina had often cited in support of its interpretation of Article 4(2). The draft was seriously criticized for its narrow and one-sided focus, and also for the lack of conciseness in the formulation of the questions. See, e.g., GAOR (IV), Ad Hoc Pol. Ctte., 26th Mtg., 1 November 1949, pp. 130, 133; 27th Mtg., 2 November 1949, pp. 141–42; 28th Mtg., 3 November 1949, pp. 157–58. A new text, formulated jointly by the representatives of Argentina and Belgium (the latter being the Committee's rapporteur), was later substituted, and, except for the introduction of a new preamble, it was the one eventually adopted. UN Doc. A/AC.31/L.20, 3 November 1949.

Insofar as the Assembly desired a judicial answer to all parts of the Argentine thesis, the formulation of the above question was defective. For, while it required a reply as to the contention that an *unfavorable* Council recommendation might yet lead to admission by the Assembly, it allowed the Court to avoid answering directly the question—avowedly the more important—whether, despite the veto, a recommendation might be considered by either the Security Council or the General Assembly as *favorable*. As framed, the question assumed the absence of a Security Council recommendation. (See ICJ Reports, 1950, p. 7. The Court's interpretation of the question accorded with that urged by the United States. *Competence* case, ICJ Pleadings, 1950, p. 110. On the other hand, the Argentine Written Statement revolved entirely around the question of the veto. *Ibid.*, pp. 123–48.) Indeed, certain states—most notably, Lebanon—recommended the inclusion of more specific questions related to the effect of the veto on the admission of new members. GAOR (IV), Ad Hoc Pol. Ctte., 27th Mtg., 2 November 1949, p. 146. Most, however, appeared satisfied that the question, as framed, encompassed all the important elements of the problem.

Despite its narrow circumspection of the question, the Court did, in an oblique reference at the end of the opinion, indicate that the Assembly, at least, could not reverse to *favorable* a recommendation which the Security Council had deemed *unfavorable*. But the Court did not find it necessary to enter into the thicket of the applicability of Article 27(3) of the Charter to the admission of new states. Had the question of the veto been put unequivocally to the Court, it is conceivable that the Court would have

In sum, the request in this case was, to a very great extent, one desired by a single state and acquiesced in by the majority of the Assembly. This acquiescence was forthcoming primarily because the motives of the sponsoring state, in wishing somehow to break the admission deadlock, were considered admirable. With this consent went the full expectation that the Court would reject the Argentine thesis, thereby putting an end to a futile debate.

International Status of South West Africa

The question of the international status of South West Africa was certainly one of the most important and complex issues to have been placed up until that time before either of the two world courts.[225] As is well known, the ICJ's 1950 opinion proved to be merely the prelude to a long succession of UN efforts, largely abortive, to establish a UN role in the territory.[226] During the course of these efforts, the Court was increasingly implicated, in both its advisory and contentious capacities. In terms of its ultimate effect on a solution of the root problem, the 1950 opinion shared the fate of such preceding opinions as those in the *Admission* and *Peace Treaties* cases. It would be a mistake, however, to conclude that in all three cases the Court's pronouncements were equally foredoomed at the outset. While the circumstances in which the *South West Africa* request was made were not entirely promising, they probably did not seem, at the time, quite as inauspicious as they may now appear in retrospect. There was some prospect, however meager, that a Court opinion might form the basis of a settlement mutually acceptable to South Africa and the international community.

The problem of South West Africa—a territory which, alone of all former League mandates, was neither converted into a trust territory nor granted its independence—had occupied the General Assembly's attention since its first session. What transpired during the first three sessions of Assembly consideration of the matter may be briefly stated.

South Africa had hoped to incorporate the territory into the Union and had, for this purpose, sought Assembly consent. For its part, the Assembly declined to accede to South Africa's request, urging instead—in three resolutions adopted in three consecutive sessions[227]—the conclusion of a trusteeship

---

considered itself incompetent to answer it. For it is by no means clear that the Assembly's authority to request advisory opinions extends to questions involving the voting procedure of a coordinate organ.

[225] See the oral statement of M. Kerno, *South West Africa (Status)* case, ICJ Pleadings, 1950, p. 160.

[226] For an account of UN efforts with respect to South West Africa, see Solomon Slonim, *South West Africa and the United Nations: An International Mandate in Dispute* (Baltimore, Md.: The Johns Hopkins Press, 1973).

[227] Resolutions 65 (I), 14 December 1946; 141 (II), 1 November 1947; and 227 (III), 26 November 1948.

agreement for the territory. South Africa's response, up until July 1949, was a mixture of defiance and compliance. While refusing adamantly to convert South West Africa into a trust territory, South Africa nevertheless abandoned its plans for incorporation. It also submitted a report (in 1947)[228] on its administration of the territory, and supplementary information (in 1948)[229] at the request of the Trusteeship Council.[230] The report was originally intended to be merely the first of many annual reports which South Africa stated would be submitted in accordance with Article 73(e) of the Charter. Furthermore, the Union government did not, at that point, deny the existence of the mandate as an institution. In fact, it spoke of continuing to administer the territory "in the spirit of the existing mandate."[231]

It should be noted that, although several suggestions were put forward[232] (at least one by the Union government itself)[233] to consult the Court on the specific question whether South Africa was legally obligated to conclude a trusteeship agreement for South West Africa, no such suggestion was ever translated into a formal proposal. In fact, the issue of South Africa's obligations was, at least formally, left unresolved. A majority of the Assembly membership undoubtedly affirmed the existence of such an obligation—some merely on "moral" grounds. But the doubts of many Western states on this point, coupled with the need to procure a two-thirds majority in Plenary, led to the omission of any categorical assertion of such an obligation in all three Assembly resolutions.

After the adoption by the Trusteeship Council of a rather censorious report on South African administration of the territory,[234] and after the Nationalist party took the reins of power within South Africa, the Union government's stand with regard to South West Africa became more adamant. In a letter of 11 July 1949,[235] the Union government announced its refusal to

---

[228] *Report by the Government of the Union of South Africa on the Administration of South West Africa for the Year 1946* (Pretoria: Government Printer, 1947).

[229] UN Doc. T/175, 31 May 1948.

[230] The report had been sent to the Trusteeship Council over the protests of South Africa and the objections of several other—mainly Western—states.

[231] UN Doc. A/334, 1 August 1947.

[232] See, e.g., GAOR (II), 4th Ctte., 31st Mtg., 25 September 1947, pp. 8–9 (suggestion of the Netherlands); *ibid.*, 38th Mtg., 7 October 1947, p. 52 (suggestion of Argentina).

[233] During the Assembly's first session, Field Marshal Smuts expressed the view that "the legal problem was one which would be finally resolved only by submission to the International Court of Justice as the competent authority to interpret the Charter." GAOR (I/2), 4th Ctte., Annex 21 (UN Doc. A/C.4/68), p. 286.

[234] *Ibid.* (III), Supp. No. 4 (UN Doc. A/603), pp. 42–45.

[235] UN Doc. A/929.

furnish any further reports[236] and transmitted (for purposes of information only) the text of a Union government act,[237] the effect of which was to bring about a form of closer association between the Union and the territory. Specific references to the mandate (contained in the original 1925 act) had been deleted. No longer, then, was the Union government's recalcitrance limited to its refusal to convert South West Africa into a trust territory. Now, that government was presenting the UN with a far more formidable challenge: the denial of the territory's international status and the total exclusion of the world organization from any role with respect to the territory, whether in terms of supervision of its administration or of consent to the modification of its status.

It was in these circumstances that the first formal proposals to consult the Court on the South West Africa issue were put forward. Up until that point, no state really desired judicial clarification of South Africa's obligations with respect to the territory. As long as there appeared to be some hope that a modus vivendi might be worked out with South Africa, the trusteeship issue bade fair—at least to many Western states—to become somewhat academic.[238] And the more militantly anti-colonial states had positively opposed requesting an advisory opinion, for fear that the Assembly's moral cause might thereby be adversely affected. Now, however, both groups of states altered their previous positions. To the Western states especially, the need for an authoritative determination of the status of South West Africa and of the Union's obligations with respect to the territory seemed urgent. The serious doubts they entertained regarding the complex legal issues involved could no longer be held in abeyance, nor could these doubts be resolved by Assembly majorities.[239] Only the Court, it was argued, could furnish the necessary authoritative legal basis upon which further progress depended. Moreover, the alternatives to consultation of the Court were either unacceptable or predictably futile. Acquiescence in South Africa's latest moves could not be sanctioned. But the formalistic reiteration of resolutions had already proven to be

[236] South Africa considered that its distinct understandings in submitting the earlier report and supplementary replies (namely, that they were being furnished voluntarily, for purposes of information only, and without any recognition of accountability to the UN in respect of the territory) had been violated, and that the very act of submitting a report had created misconceptions regarding the status of South West Africa and the Trusteeship Council's competence in respect of the territory. *Ibid.*

[237] *Ibid.* South Africa insisted that this closer form of association accorded with the spirit of the mandate.

[238] See the remarks of the Danish representative, *ibid.* (IV), Plenary, 269th Mtg., 6 December 1949, p. 529.

[239] See, especially, the remarks of the United Kingdom representative, *ibid.*, 4th Ctte., 135th Mtg., 24 November 1949, pp. 246–47.

counterproductive—both in terms of the South West Africa problem and in terms of UN prestige.

The foregoing line of reasoning represented the thinking primarily of the Western and Western-allied states.[240] Many of the more militantly anti-colonial states, both in Latin America and in Asia, were less enthusiastic over the projected consultation of the Court and, generally, over what they considered an excessively legal approach to a problem which was to them essentially political and moral.[241] If they conceded the necessity of requesting the Court's opinion, they did so less because of their own doubts than out of their recognition that, without the support of the "doubters," their own efforts would be jeopardized.[242] For, not only was it objectively necessary to obtain two-thirds votes for the adoption of resolutions, but, unless near-unanimity could be maintained on the question, the moral strength and effectiveness of their cause might appear considerably attenuated. Morever, unless the Western states' doubts were laid to rest, they might hesitate to exercise any pressure on the Union government to mend its ways.

Outside of the Soviet bloc, few states opposed, outright, recourse to the Court.[243] But, despite this general consensus on the question of principle, considerable differences of opinion arose with regard to such matters as the wording of the requesting resolution, the questions to be submitted to the Court, and the interim action of the Assembly pending receipt of the advisory opinion.

[240] See, e.g., the following statements: Thailand (*ibid.*, 128th Mtg., 18 November 1949, p. 208); Belgium (*ibid.*, 129th Mtg., 18 November 1949, p. 211); Norway (*ibid.*, p. 212); and the United Kingdom (*ibid.*, 135th Mtg., 24 November 1949, p. 252).

[241] See, e.g., the statements of Haiti and Mexico (*ibid.*, 139th Mtg., 28 November 1949, p. 268); China and Cuba (*ibid.*, 140th Mtg., 29 November 1949, pp. 277, 280); and Liberia (*ibid.*, Plenary, 269th Mtg., 6 December 1949, p. 532).

[242] Thus, the Guatemalan representative emphasized that "the Court was to be consulted simply in order to meet certain moral or legal scruples of some delegations." *Ibid.*, Plenary, 269th Mtg., 6 December 1949, p. 533.

[243] Opposition to such recourse was based on the following grounds, among others. There was no more reason for consulting the Court now than during the Assembly's first three sessions; the Union's obligations were perfectly clear, and the Assembly had all the necessary documents upon which to base a decision; in any event, the political and moral aspects of the question should take precedence over the juridical aspect; recourse to the Court would entail unnecessary delay; moreover, no useful purpose would be served by the opinion, since it would not be binding and since, despite the attempt to elicit from South Africa an assurance that it would comply with the Court's opinion (*ibid.*, 4th Ctte., 134th Mtg., 23 November 1949, p. 237; 136th Mtg., 25 November 1949, p. 252), no such assurance had been forthcoming. See *ibid.*, Mtgs. 128–40, 18–29 November 1949, *passim*. See, especially, the statements of the U.S.S.R. (*ibid.*, 135th Mtg., 24 November 1949, p. 242), Cuba (*ibid.*, 136th Mtg., 25 November 1949, p. 252; 139th Mtg., 28 November 1949, p. 271; and 140th Mtg., 29 November 1949, p. 280), Poland (*ibid.*, 135th Mtg., 24 November 1949, p. 249; and 139th Mtg., 28 November 1949, p. 271), Yugoslavia (*ibid.*, 140th Mtg., 29 November 1949, pp. 275–76), Guatemala (*ibid.*, p. 279), and Liberia (*ibid.*, p. 280).

Two rival draft resolutions—one sponsored by India,[244] the other sponsored jointly by Denmark, Norway, Syria, and Thailand[245]—were presented to the Fourth Committee, each envisaging consultation of the Court. Each contained an introductory general question concerning the status of South West Africa and the Union government's obligations with respect to the territory. But, while the joint draft resolution asked specifically about the applicability of Chapters XI (Non-Self-Governing Territories) and XII (the International Trusteeship System) to South West Africa, the Indian draft omitted reference to these chapters and focused instead on the question of where the competence to modify the territory's status resided. The two drafts were subsequently combined into a new proposal,[246] in which the questions to be put to the Court were formulated as follows:

What is the international status of the Territory of South-West Africa and what are the international obligations of the Union of South Africa arising therefrom, in particular

(a) Does the Union of South Africa continue to have international obligations under the Mandate for South-West Africa, and if so what are those obligations?

(b) Is the Union of South Africa under the obligation to negotiate and conclude a trusteeship agreement for placing the Territory of South-West Africa under the international Trusteeship System?

(c) In the event of a negative reply to the question under (b): Is South-West Africa a territory to which the provisions of Chapter XI of the Charter apply?

(d) Has the Union of South Africa the competence to modify the international status of the Territory of South-West Africa, or, in the event of a negative reply, where does competence rest to determine and modify the international status of the Territory?[247]

With respect to questions (b) and (c), considerable opposition developed in the Fourth Committee, particularly on the part of some Latin American and Asian states. To refer the question of trusteeship, they argued, would be

[244] UN Doc. A/C.4/L.55, 18 November 1949.

[245] UN Doc. A/C.4/L.54, 18 November 1949.

[246] UN Doc. A/C.4/L.64, 28 November 1949.

[247] The second operative paragraph contained an enumeration of the documents which the Secretary-General was to include in the dossier transmitted to the Court with the request. Normally, the composition of the dossier is left to the Secretary-General's discretion. Apparently, one of the reasons for this unusual provision was the desire to include in the record the testimony of the Reverend Michael Scott, whom the Fourth Committee had earlier granted a hearing. Mainly for this reason, the provision was vehemently opposed by South Africa. GAOR (IV), Plenary, 269th Mtg., 6 December 1949, p. 528. The provision may also have been intended to give the Court some indication of the Assembly's desires. *Ibid.*, 4th Ctte., 140th Mtg., 29 November 1949, p. 275.

tantamount to casting doubt on a matter which the Assembly—by several resolutions adopted by overwhelming majorities—had already definitely decided. As explained by the Philippine representative: "While the Assembly might settle controversial issues either by a vote of the Members or by a reference of the matter to the Court, the choice of one alternative should preclude the other, to avoid an opinion of the Court being rejected by the Assembly, or conversely to prevent the will of the Assembly being nullified by an opinion of the Court."[248] A negative judicial answer, it was feared, would serve merely to weaken further efforts to bring South West Africa under trusteeship and would tend to rigidify South Africa's stand.[249]

Submission of the question regarding the applicability of Chapter XI was even more objectionable to many delegates. "In view of the fact that every question contained within itself its own reply," even the implication that Chapter XI might be applicable to South West Africa was insufferable.[250] For Chapter XI related to colonies, not to mandates, and involved a far lower degree of international accountability than that which appertained to the mandate status. Furthermore, since the administering powers considered that they alone were competent to determine which territories were non-self-governing, the application of Chapter XI to South West Africa would leave the Union government free to decide whether or not to furnish information.[251]

---

[248] *Ibid.*, 4th Ctte., 128th Mtg., 18 November 1949, p. 207. Cf. the statements of Guatemala (*ibid.*, 140th Mtg., 29 November 1949, p. 273) and Mexico (*ibid.*, p. 277).

[249] Similar reasoning underlay two amendments to the draft resolution, both of which failed of adoption. One, a Philippine amendment, would have asked the Court, *inter alia*, to give its opinion "in the light of the letter and spirit of the mandate system and of Chapters XI and XII of the Charter, and without prejudice to previous resolutions of the General Assembly on the matter." *Ibid.*, 140th Mtg., 29 November 1949, p. 274. The Philippine delegate argued that, since, under Article 36 of the ICJ Statute, the Court's jurisdiction comprises *all cases* which the parties refer, the Court was free to decide moral questions as well. *Ibid.*, p. 278. Others, however, emphasized that the Court's competence was strictly confined to legal matters. *Ibid.*, pp. 266–77. The amendment was rejected by a vote of 7 for, 22 against, with 17 abstentions. *Ibid.*, p. 281. Another amendment, submitted by Guatemala, would have substituted for the four questions in the joint draft resolution the following very general question: "What are the obligations of the Union of South Africa with respect to the Territory of South-West Africa under the relevant provisions of the Treaty of Versailles, the Covenant of the League of Nations, the 1920 Mandate and the Charter of the United Nations?" The advantage of this text, as explained by the Guatemalan representative, was that it would not cast doubt on the legality of previous General Assembly resolutions. *Ibid.*, p. 273. On the other hand, many delegates protested that the question was too vague and that the ICJ would not be able to give a precise reply. It was also suggested that the Court might reject such a question as being too theoretical and too far removed from reality. *Ibid.*, pp. 274–80 *passim*. The amendment was defeated by a vote of 15 for, 18 against, with 13 abstentions. *Ibid.*, p. 281.

[250] Brazil, *ibid.*, p. 275.

[251] *Ibid.* Cf. the statement of Mexico, *ibid.*, p. 277. France, for different reasons (reasons probably related to the French position on Algeria), opposed the reference of

On the other hand, many Western states were anxious to have questions (b) and (c) of the draft resolution—more especially, the former—finally decided by the Court.[252] Only thus could the Assembly know on what legal basis it was proceeding. To allay the fears expressed regarding submission of question (b), the Indian representative pointed out that, since the ICJ was essentially a legal organ and the General Assembly essentially a political body, nothing could prevent the Assembly from again recommending conclusion of a trusteeship agreement, even in the event of a negative judicial reply to question (b).[253] Nevertheless, in committee, questions (b) and (c) were deleted.[254] In Plenary, however, question (b)—in a different form—was reinserted.[255] Thus, a compromise solution was reached: the applicability of Chapter XII, but not of Chapter XI, was to be passed upon by the Court.[256]

The decision to request the Court's opinion was not the only action on the South West Africa issue taken by the Assembly during its fourth session. Two other measures were adopted, despite protests—mainly from Western quarters—that they conflicted with the decision to consult the Court.

The first of these measures was the decision of the Fourth Committee to grant a hearing to the Reverend Michael Scott, as a representative of the indigenous population of South West Africa.[257] Those states objecting to this step argued that to grant such a hearing would be equivalent to prejudging the status of South West Africa—the very issue to be determined by the Court.[258]

---

this question. It feared the undesirable consequences which might ensue from having the Court define non-self-governing territories. *Ibid.*, p. 279.

[252] See, e.g., the statements of Belgium (*ibid.*, 129th Mtg., 18 November 1949, pp. 211–12) and the United Kingdom (*ibid.*, 135th Mtg., 24 November 1949, pp. 246–47).

[253] *Ibid.*, 140th Mtg., 29 November 1949, p. 277.

[254] *Ibid.*, pp. 281–82.

[255] *Ibid.*, Plenary, 269th Mtg., 6 December 1949, p. 537. The resolution as a whole was adopted by a vote of 40 to 7, with 4 abstentions, and was subsequently numbered 338 (IV).

The new formulation of the original question (b) was: "Are the provisions of Chapter XII of the Charter applicable and, if so, in what manner, to the Territory of South-West Africa?" The amendment to include this question was sponsored by seventeen delegations, among whom were some who had urged deletion of question (b) in committee. In introducing the amendment, the Danish representative emphasized the necessity of seizing the Court with all the relevant questions on which doubts had been raised so that the Assembly would subsequently have an authoritative opinion on all the legal aspects of the question. It would then be in a better position to solve the whole problem. *Ibid.*, p. 529.

[256] Nevertheless, the applicability of Chapter XI was argued before the Court. See the discussions of the United States and of Dr. Kerno, ICJ Pleadings, 1950, pp. 124–26, 223–24. The South African representative, Dr. Steyn, discussed the matter at the Court's express invitation. *Ibid.*, pp. 299–312. In the end, however, the Court deemed it unnecessary to pronounce upon the relevance of Chapter XI. ICJ Reports, 1950, p. 138.

[257] GAOR (IV), 4th Ctte., 137th Mtg., 25 November 1949, p. 258.

[258] See, e.g., the statements of South Africa, Belgium, Israel, the Dominican Republic, and Canada (*ibid.*, 132nd Mtg., 22 November 1949, pp. 226–29); France and the

But the majority of the Fourth Committee discounted these objections. It was argued that, since the South West Africa issue had moral and political aspects, as well as legal ones, it was logical to hear the opinions of the populations concerned on the nonjuridical aspects, in order that the Assembly might be fully informed.[259] Furthermore, pending receipt of the Court's opinion, the Committee was entitled to proceed on the basis of its own views of the status of the territory.[260]

The second contentious measure taken during this session was the adoption of a resolution[261] in which the Assembly, *inter alia*, reiterated all its previous resolutions calling for the territory to be placed under the trusteeship system; expressed regret at the Union government's withdrawal of its previous undertaking to submit reports on its administration of South West Africa; and invited the Union government to resume the submission of reports. Several Western representatives strongly objected to the adoption of this resolution, on the grounds that it was premature and that it tended to prejudge the Court's opinion.[262]

These objections were rather hotly contested by many Latin American and Asian representatives.[263] They denied that there was any inconsistency between requesting the Court's opinion and reaffirming the Assembly's previous resolutions. The Court's pronouncement was to be confined to the legal aspects of the question. But, to them, the political, moral, and humanitarian aspects were more fundamental, and the opinion of the majority of the Assembly on these more important aspects would be unaffected by any Court pronouncement. Failure to reaffirm previous resolutions might be interpreted

---

United Kingdom (*ibid.*, 133rd Mtg., 23 November 1949, pp. 230–31, 233); Australia and Norway (*ibid.*, 134th Mtg., 23 November 1949, pp. 238, 241).

[259] *Ibid.*, 132nd Mtg., 22 November 1949, pp. 228–29 (Liberia and Guatemala); 134th Mtg., 23 November 1949, p. 237 (China).

[260] India, *ibid.*, 134th Mtg., 23 November 1949, p. 237; cf. the statement of the Philippines, *ibid.*, 133rd Mtg., 23 November 1949, pp. 231–32.

[261] Resolution 337 (IV), 6 December 1949.

[262] Thus, the representative of Belgium argued that by asking the Court to determine the territory's legal status and South Africa's obligations, the Assembly was admitting its ignorance on these points, as well as its doubts regarding the extent of its own competence. But, contradictorily, by adopting the resolution in question, the Assembly was affirming its right to take decisions that would be binding on South Africa. GAOR (IV), Plenary, 269th Mtg., 6 December 1949, p. 533. Cf. the statements of the United Kingdom (*ibid.*, 4th Ctte., 135th Mtg., 24 November 1949, p. 246), the United States (*ibid.*, 139th Mtg., 28 November 1949, p. 268; and Plenary, 269th Mtg., 6 December 1949, pp. 533–34), South Africa (*ibid.*, p. 527), and Greece (*ibid.*, p. 530).

[263] See, especially, the statements of the following representatives: Guatemala (*ibid.*, 4th Ctte., 135th Mtg., 24 November 1949, p. 245; 139th Mtg., 28 November 1949, pp. 268, 270; and Plenary, 269th Mtg., 6 December 1949, p. 533); Mexico (*ibid.*, 4th Ctte., 136th Mtg., 25 November 1949, p. 252; and 139th Mtg., 28 November 1949, pp. 268, 270); Haiti (*ibid.*, p. 268); China (*ibid.*, p. 271); and India (*ibid.*, p. 269; and Plenary, 269th Mtg., 6 December 1949, p. 531).

as depriving those resolutions of their authority, or as a possible reversal, and, in either case, as a consequent moral victory for the Union government. Unless these resolutions were reaffirmed, reference to the Court would amount merely to a dilatory measure.[264] Furthermore, the Committee had to beware of "becoming hypnotized by legal procedure."[265]

This emphasis on the political aspects of the question in the Fourth Committee (of which the abovementioned resolution and the granting of a hearing to the Reverend Scott were a manifestation) provided South Africa with a not unconvincing argument for its refusal to acquiesce in the projected consultation of the Court. As the South African representative argued in Plenary, there was every indication that the Court's opinion might be treated as of minor consequence and that, even afterward, the problem would continue to be raised on political grounds.[266] What South Africa appeared to be objecting to was what it considered a certain imbalance and unfairness in the expectations—a sort of "heads-I-win-tails-you-lose" orientation on the part of the Assembly. South Africa was to be prepared to accept the Court's opinion, even if that opinion proved adverse to its own contentions, but the Assembly was to be prepared to accept only an opinion endorsing its views. Otherwise, the Assembly was to be free to treat the Court's opinion as irrelevant and to continue to pursue its goals on nonlegal grounds. (This may have been a rationalization on the part of South Africa, but it was not without some substance.)

It should be noted, however, that, while South Africa did not consent to the request and declined to undertake in advance to comply with the Court's opinion, it nowhere stated categorically that it would refuse to comply. Nor did it oppose reference to the Court, in principle. Rather, the South African representative confined himself to criticism of the *specific formulation* of the resolution requesting the opinion[267] and of the attitude of the Assembly majority. He also emphasized his government's belief in the rule of law. Thus, there remained some faint glimmer of hope that the Court's opinion might not go totally unheeded.[268]

---

[264]The fear that, unless a Court opinion were quickly forthcoming, the Assembly would be hamstrung in its further deliberations on South West Africa prompted Mexico to introduce an amendment to the requesting resolution. Under this amendment, the Court was to be asked to render its opinion before the fifth Assembly session, if possible; the amendment was adopted. *Ibid.*, 4th Ctte., 139th Mtg., 28 November 1949, p. 281.

[265]This caution was sounded by the Mexican representative. *Ibid.*, p. 268.

[266]*Ibid.*, Plenary, 269th Mtg., 6 December 1949, pp. 527–28.

[267]South Africa considered the formulation of the questions one-sided, and objected, in particular, to the documents enumerated in the second operative paragraph of the requesting resolution. *Ibid.*

[268]Thus, the South African attitude could not be likened entirely to that of the Soviet bloc in the *Admission* and *Peace Treaties* cases. For, unlike the Soviet bloc, South

In sum, the decision to seek judicial clarification of the status of South West Africa was made at a time when South African moves threatened to eliminate the last vestiges of international supervision over the administration of South West Africa. At this critical juncture, many Western states became convinced that their doubts regarding the territory's status and the Union government's obligations would have to be clarified by a higher legal authority than the Assembly if any progress was to be made. For, clearly, continued reiteration of Assembly resolutions, even if in stronger terms, was likely to prove as unavailing in the future as it had been in the past. On the other hand, by providing a more solid basis for Assembly recommendations, a Court opinion might conceivably lead to South African acceptance of those recommendations.

But, if for the Western states a major consideration prompting the request for an advisory opinion was the existence of genuine doubts as to the legal basis of UN action, for most Latin American and Asian states the primary consideration was their inability to ignore the doubts of the Western states. The difference in the motivation of the two groups was reflected in such matters as the wording of the request and the action of the Assembly pending receipt of the Court's opinion. Thus, the "doubting" group sought to have the Court clarify all the crucial legal questions which had been broached in Assembly discussions—including the applicability of Chapters XI and XII of the Charter to South West Africa—and were wary of taking any action which might prejudge the issues before the Court. On the other hand, the states which merely acquiesced were anxious to assert the primacy of the Assembly and the paramountcy of the politico-moral aspects of the question. They therefore sought to exclude from Court consideration such questions as the trusteeship issue—since this had already been the subject of several Assembly resolutions—and the applicability of Chapter XI—since this was a possibility they preferred not to contemplate. Similarly, they refused to allow the pending request and legal niceties to bar the Assembly from taking interim action deemed politically and morally necessary. The result of these conflicting motivations was a compromise: the question of South Africa's obliga-

---

Africa was not opposed, as a matter of principle, to consulting the Court. Indeed, on several occasions, it had itself—even in connection with the South West Africa issue—suggested such a recourse. Moreover, South Africa did not challenge the Court's competence to give the opinion. It did not do so in the Assembly, nor did it do so subsequently before the Court, where it was represented in both the written and oral proceedings. (This is in contrast to its stance in subsequent advisory proceedings. In the 1955 and 1956 cases, South Africa did not contest the Court's right to render the opinion nor the propriety of its doing so; but South Africa did not participate in the pleadings. In the 1971 *Namibia* case, its position was the reverse: it argued vigorously against the Court's complying with the request, but it took an active part in the pleadings.) Furthermore, even on the general South West Africa issue, South Africa's attitude probably was not yet as totally intractable in 1949–50 as it was later to become.

tion to conclude a trusteeship agreement was referred to the Court, the question of the relevance of Chapter XI was not, and the controversial interim measures were adopted.

Reservations to the Convention on the Prevention and Punishment of the Crime of Genocide

The request in this case bore many similarities to the earlier request in the *Reparation* case: the questions submitted to the Court were generally acknowledged to be legal questions; the request originated in the Sixth Committee; it related to an item raised by the Secretary-General; and the decision to consult the Court followed a debate over which agency—the Sixth Committee itself, the ILC, or the ICJ—was best suited to clarify the issues raised. But, unlike the earlier case, in which the Sixth Committee opted for reference to the ICJ over reference to the ILC, in the *Reservations* case a compromise was reached involving the submission of a general question to the ILC and of more specifically formulated questions to the ICJ. In contrast to the *Reparation* case, too, the competence of the Assembly to make the proposed request was challenged.[269]

The item "Reservations to Multilateral Conventions" was placed on the Assembly agenda for the fifth session by the Secretary-General[270] and referred by the Assembly to the Sixth Committee. In asking for Assembly consideration of the matter, the Secretary-General pointed first to the general problem with which he, as depositary of many conventions adopted by the Assembly or concluded under UN auspices, was faced; and second to particular difficulties connected with the Genocide Convention which had endowed the problem with "current importance." There was, he noted, no unanimity either as to the procedure to be followed by a depositary in obtaining the necessary consent to a reservation or as to the effect to be attributed to objections to reservations. With respect to the Genocide Convention, however, this state of uncertainty put the Secretary-General in a particularly difficult position. For, while the deposit of the twentieth instrument of ratification or accession (required to bring the Convention into force) was expected momentarily, a number of states had, upon ratification or accession, entered reservations to which other states had objected.[271] It was therefore important to determine as soon as possible whether or not the reserving states

---

[269] Also unlike the *Reparation* case, the *Reservations* case had Cold War overtones. For, as will be seen below, the Soviet Union and members of the Soviet bloc had a direct stake in the matter of reservations to the Genocide Convention.

[270] UN Doc. A/1372, 20 September 1950.

[271] Among the reserving states to whose reservations other states had objected were the Soviet Union—which had yet to ratify the Convention—and Bulgaria—which had already acceded, and whose status was, therefore, immediately in question.

were to be counted in the number required for entry into force of the Convention. After setting forth the UN Secretariat's practice with respect to reservations,[272] the Secretary-General sought the Assembly's "approval and advice" in the matter.

The Sixth Committee's discussions[273] on the problems thus raised by the Secretary-General are divisible into two phases. During the first, and more important, phase, the issue was still deemed urgent. However, with the announcement, on 16 October 1950, of the receipt of sufficient ratifications to bring the Genocide Convention into effect (irrespective of the theory used), the practical urgency of the question was removed.

During the first phase, two distinct (though, in the discussions, somewhat confused) questions had to be determined: (1) How was the general problem of reservations to be clarified? (2) How was the particular problem of the Genocide Convention to be resolved? With respect to the first question, it was quickly concluded by most representatives that the Committee itself could not determine it. The very complexity of the issues raised and the wide divergence of views held[274] were sufficient to convince the majority that clarification by some more qualified body was essential.[275] However, there was sharp disagreement over whether the ICJ or the ILC was the more appropriate organ of reference, with sentiment being stronger on behalf of the ILC.

Preference for the ILC was based on the following considerations, among others: (1) The ILC was already codifying the law of treaties, and it might be requested to give the question of reservations priority.[276] Moreover, should a Court opinion conflict with the solution eventually proposed by the ILC, the Assembly might be placed in an exceedingly difficult position.[277] (2) Since

---

[272] That practice involved the application of one version of the "unanimity rule." (The objections of mere signatories were not counted, and allowance was made for tacit consent.) UN Doc. A/1372, 20 September 1950, pars. 4–6.

[273] The Committee's discussions took place at its 217th–225th Meetings, 5–20 October 1950.

[274] These ranged from the "absolute sovereignty" position of the Soviet Union (under which a state, as a matter of its sovereignty, would enjoy the unfettered right to participate freely in conventions, while entering any reservations it deemed fit) through the middle position of the "Pan-American Union rule" to a position endorsing the unanimity rule or some variant thereof. Nor was any agreement reached concerning the identity of the states whose consent to reservations was necessary.

[275] Some states (including the United States) did express the view that the sole issue before the Assembly was the determination of the Secretary-General's functions as depositary—an issue which the Assembly was competent to decide itself. GAOR (V), 6th Ctte., 217th Mtg., 5 October 1950, p. 33. The majority, however, felt that important international law questions were implicated and that the Sixth Committee was not well suited to settle these more fundamental questions.

[276] China (ibid., 219th Mtg., 10 October 1950, p. 43), Mexico (ibid., 220th Mtg., 12 October 1950, p. 50), and Yugoslavia (ibid., 221st Mtg., 14 October 1950, p. 56).

[277] Mexico, ibid., 220th Mtg., 12 October 1950, p. 50.

the law on the question was insufficiently developed, the ICJ was likely merely to reflect the same divergencies as the Assembly itself. The ILC, on the other hand, was free to develop the law and fill in gaps. (3) Furthermore, any Court opinion would be insufficient, since the question involved primarily the development of appropriate procedures to suit a wide variety of conventions, not the application of law to a concrete case. This task required a thorough study and classification of treaties, and the taking into account of considerations of expediency and effectiveness as well as those of law.[278] (4) While the Assembly was always free to debate and, if necessary, to alter the results of an ILC study, the same could not be said with respect to a Court opinion, which, though technically nonbinding, would be both difficult and undesirable to alter in any way.[279]

In support of consulting the ICJ, on the other hand, it was argued, *inter alia*, as follows: (1) The question of reservations was a highly complex and controversial question in international law. It was the ICJ's function to settle controversial points of law and to state the existing law, when doubtful; the ILC was confined to codifying the acknowledged existing law. (2) Moreover, recourse to the Court was the more expeditious alternative in this case, since the ILC was greatly overburdened, and its report might not be forthcoming until two years hence. (3) While the ILC's work was founded exclusively on the research work of its own members, the Court rendered an opinion only after a full airing of the divergent views of governments.[280] (4) Since, under the Genocide Convention—which was principally involved—the question would probably be referred to the Court in the final instance, it would be preferable to refer it to the Court immediately.[281] (5) It was also desirable, as a general matter, that the Assembly avail itself of the ICJ's service to the greatest extent possible.[282]

The above ICJ versus ILC debate was largely a reflection of the divergence of views on the substantive questions involved. It is noteworthy, in this

[278] Israel (*ibid.*, 219th Mtg., 10 October 1950, p. 46), the United States (*ibid.*, p. 41), Chile (*ibid.*, 220th Mtg., 12 October 1950, p. 50), and Turkey (*ibid.*, 221st Mtg., 14 October 1950, p. 54).

[279] Turkey (*ibid.*, 221st Mtg., 14 October 1950, p. 54) and Venezuela (*ibid.*, 223rd Mtg., 16 October 1950, p. 71). Cf. the French statement to the effect that a Court opinion might be accepted or rejected, but not altered in any manner. *Ibid.*, 218th Mtg., 5 October 1950, p. 39.

[280] All of these arguments were urged by the United Kingdom, which was the first state to propose requesting the Court's opinion in the matter. *Ibid.*, 217th Mtg., 5 October 1950, p. 35; 222nd Mtg., 16 October 1950, pp. 64–65. Cf. the statements of France (*ibid.*, 218th Mtg., 5 October 1950, pp. 38–39), India (*ibid.*, p. 40), Canada (*ibid.*, 219th Mtg., 10 October 1950, p. 42), Iran (*ibid.*, pp. 44–45), and Belgium (*ibid.*, 220th Mtg., 12 October 1950, pp. 51–52).

[281] Greece, *ibid.*, 219th Mtg., 10 October 1950, p. 45.

[282] The United Kingdom, *ibid.*, 217th Mtg., 5 October 1950, p. 35.

respect, that many of the foremost advocates of a judicial solution to the problem (and, most notably, the United Kingdom) were also among the most persistent defenders of the unanimity rule. On the other hand, the pro-ILC group (and, most notably, the United States) generally favored a more flexible rule on reservations.[283] While the correlation of views was by no means absolute, it was far from negligible. Apparently, both groups proceeded on the assumption that the ICJ was more likely to uphold the unanimity rule.[284] Given the Court's high authority, its views, once stated, would be difficult to override. To proponents of a more flexible rule, this meant that the law might be frozen in an undesirable manner. In their eyes, reference to the ILC was a safer course, not only because the ILC could study the question from the standpoint of "progressive development" of the law, but also, and primarily, because the Assembly, by submitting the question to the ILC, would be retaining complete freedom—in fact as well as in law—to dispose of the resultant report as it saw fit.[285]

As for the questions to be submitted to the Court, these were framed in very general terms in the early drafts and did not refer specifically to the Genocide Convention. Thus, the United Kingdom draft—the first to be submitted—would have asked simply whether the Secretary-General's depositary practice was in conformity with international law.[286] The French draft would have had the Court determine the conditions governing the validity of reservations to multilateral conventions and the legal effects to be ascribed to any objections made to such reservations.[287] Similarly, a new five-power joint draft resolution,[288] while it broke down the more general questions into their component parts, did not relate to any specific convention or group of conventions.

Both the French draft and the abovementioned joint draft resolution were designed to have recourse to the Court solve not only the general question raised by the Secretary-General but also the then more urgent question regarding the Genocide Convention. To the latter end, both included clauses which would have instructed the Secretary-General to follow, in his deposi-

---

[283] In the post-opinion stage, the roles were reversed. The formerly pro-ICJ group became pro-ILC (as far as the general question of reservations was concerned); and the formerly pro-ILC group favored generalizing the Court's ruling.

[284] The assumption that the unanimity rule was part of the existing international law was shared by most writers. See the citations in Annex B of Brierly's Report on Reservations to Multilateral Conventions, UN Doc. A/CN.4/41, 6 April 1951, pp. 6–11.

[285] This point is most clearly highlighted in the remarks of the representatives of Turkey and Venezuela cited in n. 279.

[286] UN Doc. A/C.6/L.115, 4 October 1950.

[287] UN Doc. A/C.6/L.118, 5 October 1950.

[288] UN Doc. A/C.6/L.123, 13 October 1950. The sponsors were Egypt, France, Greece, Iran, and the United Kingdom.

tary practice, the procedure resulting from the Court's opinion. Thus, both drafts would have accepted that opinion in advance. In defense of this provision, the French representative noted that the Assembly would not reconvene until the fall of 1951, and that it was essential to authorize the Secretary-General to adopt a definite attitude before then. Furthermore, if the matter was a question of law, it was pointless to reopen debate after receipt of the opinion of a more qualified body.[289] The general feeling in the Assembly, however, was that no findings of either the ICJ or the ILC could be put into practice by the Secretary-General before a specific Assembly recommendation on the matter. Therefore, most other attempts to solve the immediate problem regarding the Genocide Convention focused on interim instructions to the Secretary-General pending legal clarification of the fundamental issues. But there was as little agreement over these short-term instructions as there was over the long-range question.[290] Moreover, certain states objected altogether to the giving of interim instructions.[291]

With the announcement that the problem of entry into force of the Genocide Convention had been solved, the previous urgency of the reservations issue was removed, and the discussions entered a second phase. It was no longer necessary to elaborate any interim procedure for the Secretary-General. Still unresolved, however, were the general question of reservations to multilateral conventions, and, with respect to the Genocide Convention, the status of those states whose reservations had been objected to by other states.[292] To settle these difficulties, a new joint draft resolution[293] was introduced to replace all previous proposals. Sponsored by thirteen states,[294] it represented an attempt to reconcile the views of those who had favored recourse to the ICJ and those who had favored reference to the ILC. The ICJ

[289]GAOR (V), 6th Ctte., 218th Mtg., 5 October 1950, p. 39; and 223rd Mtg., 16 October 1950, p. 70. The provision had been criticized by several representatives. See, e.g., the statements of Israel (ibid., 219th Mtg., 10 October 1950, p. 46), Belgium (ibid., 220th Mtg., 12 October 1950, p. 52), and South Africa (ibid., 223rd Mtg., 16 October 1950, p. 72).

[290]See UN Doc. A/1494, 10 November 1950, pars. 11-18.

[291]France and Greece feared that such temporary instructions might conflict with the Court's opinion and lead to undesirable and complex legal consequences. The Soviet Union, on the other hand, denied the Assembly's competence to give interim instructions, since these instructions, it maintained, would complement the text of the Genocide Convention and create new legal relations between the parties not envisaged by the Convention. GAOR (V), 6th Ctte., 218th Mtg., 5 October 1950, p. 39; 219th Mtg., 10 October 1950, p. 45; 222nd Mtg., 16 October 1950, pp. 59-63; 223rd Mtg., 16 October 1950, p. 70.

[292]In particular, Australia objected to certain reservations entered by the governments of Bulgaria and the Philippines.

[293]UN Doc. A/C.6/L.125, 18 October 1950.

[294]Belgium, Chile, Denmark, Egypt, France, Greece, Iran, the Netherlands, Norway, Sweden, the United Kingdom, the United States, and Uruguay.

was to pass on the legal effects of reservations to the Genocide Convention only,[295] while the ILC was to study the question of reservations, in its general aspects, "both from the point of view of codification and from that of the progressive development of international law."[296] In the interim, pending the outcome of these consultations and further Assembly action, the Secretary-General was to follow his previous procedure; but this was to be done "without prejudice to the legal effect of objections to reservations to conventions as it may be recommended by the General Assembly at its sixth session."[297]

Superficially, the compromise appeared to be a reasonable one: the Court would state the existing law with regard to one specific convention; the ILC would study the general question from the viewpoint of both the codification and the "progressive development" of the law. If one moved beyond the verbal level, however, it was not difficult to discern that, to a very great extent, the same question was being submitted to both organs. On what basis, for example, could the Genocide Convention be differentiated from many other legislative-type treaties concluded under UN auspices?[298] The possibility that the compromise formula would yield contradictory results did not

[295] The first two drafts—those of the United Kingdom and of France—had been criticized as too general and imprecise, and some representatives had suggested relating the questions to a specific convention or category of conventions. GAOR (V), 6th Ctte., 219th Mtg., 10 October 1950, pp. 43–45. The first joint draft resolution (A/C.6/L.123), though more precisely formulated, did not relate to specific conventions. A joint amendment (A/C.6/L.124, 16 October 1950) would have related those questions to the conventions mentioned in the Secretary-General's memorandum. The representative of Iran, agreeing that the questions should be drafted in more concrete terms, thought the request might even be confined to the specific reservations that had caused the most difficulty. GAOR (V), 6th Ctte., 223rd Mtg., 16 October 1950, p. 74. The fact that no specific reservations were alluded to, and that, to that extent, the questions submitted were "abstract," was later cited by the Court in answer to some of the objections raised to the Court's competence. See Chapter V.

[296] The ILC was asked to give the question of reservations priority in its codification of the law of treaties.

[297] Thus, the clause providing for advance acceptance of the Court's opinion—which had appeared in some earlier drafts—was now eliminated. Assembly action was to be required before either the ICJ opinion or the ILC report might be implemented.

[298] Indeed, the general significance of the questions in the request was subsequently stressed by the Secretary-General's representative and by some of the states appearing before the Court. See the statement of M. Kerno, *Reservations* case, ICJ Pleadings, 1951, pp. 306–7, 325; and cf. the citation of these remarks in the joint dissenting opinion, ICJ Reports, 1951, p. 31. The United Kingdom—one of the cosponsors of the compromise solution—considered that the Assembly had actually hoped to gain some *general* guidance as to Genocide-type conventions; it was therefore desirable and proper for the Court to frame its opinion in such a way as to have more general application. *Reservations* case, ICJ Pleadings, 1951, p. 366. See also the Written Statement of Israel, *ibid.*, p. 198; but cf. the statement of the French representative, who emphasized the narrow terms in which the request was drafted. *Ibid.*, pp. 419–20.

escape the notice of the members of the Sixth Committee. Several representatives opposed the proposed recourse to the Court for that very reason.[299]

Opposition to requesting the Court's opinion was voiced on other grounds as well—grounds which related both to the expediency of consulting the Court and to the Assembly's competence to make the proposed request. Thus, on practical grounds, it was argued that, since there were no longer any urgent questions at issue, and since the ILC would be dealing with the general question of reservations anyway, a Court opinion was now totally unnecessary.[300] Nor could the Court's opinion effectively resolve the remaining problems connected with the Genocide Convention, since, in any case, that opinion would not be binding.[301] As for the Assembly's competence to request the opinion, this was challenged by the Soviet Union, Poland, and the Philippines,[302] on the following grounds. Since this procedure for consulting the Court was not provided for in the Genocide Convention, the Assembly's request constituted an attempt to revise the Convention. Such a request would also oblige the Court to insert new clauses in the Convention—something which the Court was not competent to do.[303] A Court opinion would alter the sovereign rights of states; but, according to the *Eastern Carelia* principle, the Assembly may not request an opinion which might imply limi-

[299] They included the representatives of the Soviet Union, Cuba, Peru, Poland, and Costa Rica. GAOR (V), 6th Ctte., 224th Mtg., 18 October 1950, pp. 78–81. The United Kingdom representative countered with the argument that, since the Court's opinion would be merely advisory, even the expression of divergent views by the ICJ and ILC would not amount to a real conflict. *Ibid.*, p. 81.

[300] Statements of Cuba, Syria, and Ecuador (*ibid.*, pp. 78, 82–83), and of the Philippines (*ibid.*, 225th Mtg., 20 October 1950, p. 85).

[301] Statements of the Philippines (*ibid.*, p. 86) and Ecuador (*ibid.*, 224th Mtg., 18 October 1950, p. 83).

[302] Soviet opposition was in line with a general posture of hostility to recourse to the Court. Additionally, the Soviet Union had more specific reasons for opposing the *Reservations* request. First, as already noted, the status of the Soviet Union and other members of the Soviet bloc as parties to the Genocide Convention might be adversely affected by a Court opinion. (In the case of Bulgaria, that status might be immediately affected.) Second, the Soviet "absolute sovereignty" position was not likely to be endorsed by the Court.

The Philippine stand was determined solely by its position with respect to the Genocide Convention, its reservations having been objected to by Australia. While the Philippines later expressed willingness to submit its "dispute" with Australia to the Court under Article IX of the Genocide Convention (see *Reservations* case, ICJ Pleadings, 1951, p. 180), it opposed settlement via advisory procedure. Article IX, however, was probably inapplicable to the Australian-Philippine differences. See Chapter V.

[303] Arguments of the Soviet Union (GAOR [V], 6th Ctte., 222nd Mtg., 16 October 1950, p. 62; and 224th Mtg., 18 October 1950, p. 78) and Poland (*ibid.*, Plenary, 305th Mtg., 16 November 1950, p. 387).

tation of the sovereign rights of a state without that state's consent.[304] Furthermore, the right to interpret or seek interpretation of a treaty was reserved solely for the states which had signed or ratified the treaty.[305] Further arguments against the Assembly's competence to consult the Court were premised, contradictorily, on the existence and nonexistence of a dispute in this case. Thus, on the one hand, it was said that, since Article IX of the Genocide Convention (the compromissory clause) required the existence of a dispute, and since no such dispute existed in the instant case, no judicial clarification—even if only by means of advisory procedure—could be sought.[306] On the other hand, it was contended that questions relating to the Genocide Convention would involve not general and abstract questions but an actual dispute, which the ICJ could not consider unless the disputants themselves submitted it on the basis of questions they themselves formulated.[307]

Despite these objections, the new thirteen-power joint draft resolution was adopted by large majorities in the Committee and in Plenary.[308]

The problem referred to the Court in this case was acknowledged to be of a legal nature, necessitating, as it did, clarification of an important aspect of the law of treaties. It was also an organizational issue, since it concerned the instructions to be given by the Assembly to the Secretary-General in his capacity as depositary of many multilateral conventions concluded under UN auspices. The Sixth Committee might have determined the content of those instructions without any outside assistance. But, out of the recognition that important and complex legal questions were at issue, and that the membership of the Sixth Committee was both widely and deeply split on these questions, the Committee felt constrained to appeal to some other, more competent, law-clarifying agency. When it appeared that the Committee membership was also divided on the question of the suitable agency of reference—the majority preferring the ILC, but a strong minority favoring the

---

[304] Poland, *ibid.*, 6th Ctte., 224th Mtg., 18 October 1950, p. 80.

[305] Poland, *ibid.*, Plenary, 305th Mtg., 16 November 1950, p. 387.

[306] *Ibid.*, 6th Ctte., 224th Mtg., 18 October 1950, p. 78; and 225th Mtg., 20 October 1950, p. 86 (arguments of the Soviet Union and the Philippines).

[307] *Ibid.*, 222nd Mtg., 16 October 1950, p. 62; 225th Mtg., 20 October 1950, p. 86; and Plenary, 305th Mtg., 16 November 1950, pp. 387–88. The foregoing arguments were subsequently repeated, elaborated upon, and supplemented, before the Court. See Chapter V, p. 293 and n. 50; p. 306; and p. 310, n. 115.

[308] In the Committee, the votes in favor of requesting the Court's opinion, requesting the ILC study, and adopting the resolution as a whole were, respectively, 28 to 13, with 10 abstentions; 46 to 0, with 7 abstentions; and 36 to 7, with 9 abstentions. GAOR (V), 6th Ctte., 225th Mtg., p. 87. The corresponding figures for the Plenary were 40 to 10, with 7 abstentions; 48 to 2, with 8 abstentions; and 47 to 5, with 5 abstentions. *Ibid.*, Plenary, 305th Mtg., 16 November 1950, p. 385. It can readily be seen that sentiment for the ILC solution was stronger, and, in the Committee, considerably so. The resolution adopted was later numbered 478 (V).

ICJ—a compromise solution was arrived at, one which involved a kind of "division of labor" between the ILC and the Court. The possibility that the Assembly would later be confronted with contradictory conclusions apparently did not seriously disturb most of the Committee members.

Several members opposed the projected consultation of the Court, and some of these (including the Soviet Union) even denied the Assembly's competence to make the request. But this opposition, unlike that of the Soviet Union in the *Admission* case, did not foredoom the Court's opinion to ineffectuality. There was one essential difference between the two cases, though both were of an "organizational" nature. In the *Reservations* case, the Assembly, acting through a majority, had the ability not only to request the Court's opinion but also, if it so desired, to give that opinion effect.

Effect of Awards of Compensation Made by the United Nations Administrative Tribunal

The Court's opinion was sought in this case with regard to an important organizational issue: the relationship between the General Assembly and the UN Administrative Tribunal. More specifically, the Court was asked whether the Assembly had the right, on any grounds, to refuse to give effect to an award of compensation made by the Tribunal in favor of a UN staff member whose contract of service had been terminated without his assent, and, if so, on what principal grounds the Assembly could lawfully exercise such a right.[309] The abstractly worded questions thus submitted grew out of a concrete conflict of interests between, on the one hand, certain UN staff members of United States nationality, and, on the other, the United States government.[310] It was the interests of the latter which largely influenced the Assembly majority to turn to the Court—less, perhaps, for clarification than for support.

The context in which recourse to the Court was decided upon was the Fifth Committee's consideration, during its eighth session, of a request by the Secretary-General for supplementary estimates of some $179,420 for the fiscal year 1953.[311] This sum was required to cover awards of compensation made by the UN Administrative Tribunal in favor of eleven staff members of United States nationality who had been discharged following their refusal to answer questions put to them by a United States Senate subcommittee on internal security. The Advisory Committee on Administrative and Budgetary Questions concurred in the proposed appropriations. When, however, the

---

[309] GA Resolution 785A (VIII), 9 December 1953.

[310] In turn, the position of the United States government was related to internal pressures exerted by Congress on the administration.

[311] UN Doc. A/2534, 2 November 1953.

Fifth Committee began its discussions of the Secretary-General's request,[312] the United States representative launched a vehement attack on the validity of the Administrative Tribunal's awards and strongly opposed the appropriation of funds for the purpose of honoring those awards.[313] In support of his position, the United States representative cited the following considerations. (1) The Assembly clearly had the legal right and responsibility to review, and refuse to give effect to, Tribunal decisions.[314] (2) The Tribunal had misconstrued its role and exceeded its powers.[315] (3) Serious errors of law, fact, and judgment had been made, both in awarding the compensations, and in calculating the amount of the awards. At the same time, the United States representative alluded to the delicacy of the issue for his government internally, and to the fact that the United States would be compelled to pay the lion's share of the controversial awards.

For its views on the substantive matter before the Committee, the United States could find few "takers." Of the almost thirty Committee members who expressed an opinion, only seven endorsed the American view,[316] and some of these merely wanted the sums reduced. The overwhelming majority of the Committee membership considered the Assembly to be bound, legally and morally, to honor the Tribunal's awards. Any other course would, it was thought, violate the organization's contractual obligations and deal a serious blow to the morale of the staff and the prestige of the organization. At the same time, however, given the peculiar sensitivity of the United States in the matter and its position as the largest single contributor to the budget, there was an understandable reluctance on the part of many of the United States' allies to adopt outright a decision which might be branded as "anti-American." In the circumstances, it appeared desirable to find a formula which would permit the Assembly majority "to have its cake and eat it too"— namely, to honor the Tribunal's awards while shifting the onus of responsibility for this decision to another body. Such a formula was not hard to find. The United States had based its objections to the awards, *inter alia*, on a particular view of the legal relationship between the Administrative Tribunal and the Assembly. It had insisted on the nonfinality of the Tribunal's judg-

[312] The question was discussed at Meetings 420-23 and 425-27, 3-8 December 1953.

[313] GAOR (VIII), 5th Ctte., 420th Mtg., 3 December 1953, pp. 281-87.

[314] This right was predicated on the view that the Tribunal was not a judicial body, but only a subsidiary administrative organ; that since the Assembly had the power to alter the Tribunal's Statute or completely abolish the Tribunal, it could *a fortiori* review the Tribunal's decisions; and that the Assembly lacked the power to relinquish its appropriations power to a small group of four individuals.

[315] It was argued that the Tribunal had substituted its discretion for that of the Secretary-General, instead of confining itself to questions of arbitrariness or bad faith.

[316] Argentina, Australia, China, Cuba, the Dominican Republic, Liberia, and Turkey.

ments, vis-à-vis the Assembly. The Court might, then, be asked for its opinion on this question. If, as the Assembly majority fully expected, the Court upheld the finality of the awards, the Assembly's hands would be "tied," and it could no longer be accused of insensitivity to the American position in the matter.

Significantly, a three-power joint draft resolution to request the Court's opinion was sponsored by states allied to the United States.[317] Significantly, too, opposition to consulting the Court came mainly from two quarters: the stronger opposition (leading to negative votes on the three-power draft resolution) from the Soviet bloc; the weaker opposition (leading to abstentions) from those of the United States' allies who concurred in the American view on the substantive issues. The Soviet bloc's position is not difficult to understand. It was, first of all, in full accord with the bloc's general posture with respect to employment of the Court. Second, the Soviet Union obviously did not need to defer a decision on the substance out of consideration for American sensitivities. Far from it. In this particular case, it could not but relish the thought of the United States being forced to contribute to the payment of awards made on behalf of officials who had been discharged as part of the United States' internal anticommunist drive. On the other hand, if such States as Australia, China, and Turkey were less than enthusiastic over the proposed recourse to the Court, one explanation may lie in the fact that, since they shared the American views on the substantive issue, they did not, for that very reason, share with other American allies the necessity of shifting to the Court the responsibility for their decision.[318]

---

[317]UN Doc. A/C.5/L.263, 6 December 1953. The sponsors were the United Kingdom, Canada, and Colombia.

Most of the representatives emphasized that their support of, or acquiescence in, the request for a Court opinion was due only to the doubts which "others" entertained. See, e.g., the statements of Canada, the United Kingdom, and New Zealand (GAOR [VIII], 5th Ctte., 423rd Mtg., 5 December 1953, pp. 303–7); India and Belgium (*ibid.*, 425th Mtg., 7 December 1953, pp. 324–25); Pakistan (*ibid.*, 426th Mtg., 7 December 1953, p. 334); and Israel (*ibid.*, 427th Mtg., 8 December 1953, p. 339). Perhaps most revealing was the understanding placed by the Belgian representative on the vote to consult the Court—namely, "that the majority would favour honouring the Administrative Tribunal's awards, but would like its decision to be covered by an opinion of the International Court." *Ibid.*, 427th Mtg., 8 December 1953, p. 339.

[318]It is possible, too, that they shared the general anticipation that the Court would uphold the finality of the contested awards.

Opposition to the request also came from such states as Mexico, who tended to view the request as a futile delaying tactic.

Among the arguments adduced against the proposed recourse were the alleged clarity of the issues (though what was clear to, e.g., the United States and Turkey was the reverse of what was clear to the Soviet bloc); the nonlegal nature of the questions to be referred; and the delay in justice which employment of the advisory procedure would entail. See, e.g., GAOR (VIII), 5th Ctte., 425th Mtg., 7 December 1953, pp. 322–25; 426th Mtg., 7 December 1953, pp. 329, 334; and 427th Mtg., 8 December 1953, p. 339.

While a majority of the Assembly was prepared to see the Court consulted, two strains of thought emerged regarding the formulation of the questions which the Court should be asked to clarify. The first was represented in the three-power draft resolution and was the one eventually endorsed by the Assembly. The Court was to be asked to set forth the principal grounds, if any, upon which the Assembly might refuse to give effect to awards of compensation made by the Administrative Tribunal. This abstract and general formulation was designed to avoid turning the ICJ into a court of appeal to retry the individual cases decided by the Administrative Tribunal.[319] It followed, in this respect, the guidelines laid down by the Secretary-General.[320] The second trend of thought was reflected in a French amendment to the joint draft resolution,[321] in accordance with which the Court would have been requested to determine not only the grounds upon which the Assembly might refuse to give effect to a Tribunal award but also whether those grounds "apply to any of the decisions which have led to the request for the appropriations." The reasoning behind this amendment was later explained by its sponsor, as follows: It was desirable that the application to the specific cases of the general grounds which might be enunciated by the Court not provoke another debate in the Assembly. Rather, "the Court itself should be asked to make the practical deductions relevant to the cases in question from whatever principles it might have formulated."[322] In other words, if the "buck" was, indeed, to be passed to the Court, it should be passed in its entirety! The French amendment received strong support from the representatives of Belgium, New Zealand, Mexico, and Israel. The feeling among these representatives was that the French amendment would lend greater precision to the question and more usefulness to the consultation.[323] Without it, the entire question would, it was feared, be reopened at the Assembly's ninth session.[324] On the other hand, the United States objected that the French amendment completely altered the nature of the draft resolution, in that the Court itself would now determine the question of the payment of compensation.[325] The French amendment was not accepted by the Committee.[326]

[319] See the explanation of the United Kingdom representative, *ibid.*, 425th Mtg., 7 December 1953, p. 325.

[320] *Ibid.*, p. 320.

[321] UN Doc. A/C.5/L.267, 7 December 1953.

[322] GAOR (VIII), Plenary, 471st Mtg., 9 December 1953, p. 459.

[323] *Ibid.*, 5th Ctte., 427th Mtg., 8 December 1953, p. 339.

[324] See, especially, the remarks of the Mexican representative, *ibid.*, Plenary, 471st Mtg., 9 December 1953, p. 460. Due to the abstraction of the questions, he feared that any Court opinion would inevitably engender conflicting interpretations and protracted debates.

[325] *Ibid.*, 5th Ctte., 426th Mtg., 7 December 1953, p. 334.

[326] *Ibid.*, 427th Mtg., 8 December 1953, p. 337. The amendment was defeated by votes of 19 for, 28 against, with 6 abstentions; and 15 for, 22 against, with 17 abstentions.

Another French proposal, also defeated, was similarly designed to carry the motivation behind the request to its logical conclusion and to preclude renewed discussion of the awards at the following session. This proposal was embodied in an amendment to another draft resolution then under consideration by the Fifth Committee.[327] Under the terms of this French amendment,[328] the Assembly would authorize the Secretary-General to pay the contested awards from funds provided for unforeseen and extraordinary expenses "in the event of the Court's finding that the General Assembly is not entitled to refuse to give effect to the said awards." While recognizing that advisory opinions should not, as a general rule, be binding, the French representative nevertheless considered that, in this case, justice and humaneness required that the Secretary-General be in a position to pay the awards immediately.[329] The request for an advisory opinion was, in his view, "wholly justified only if that opinion, should it uphold the Tribunal's authority, was unanimously accepted, precluding the possibility of reconsidering the findings made and of prolonging the waiting period of the staff members involved for another year or more."[330] Several assumptions were implicit in the French proposal: (1) that the Assembly was, in reality, delegating its own decision-making powers to the Court; (2) that the Court's opinion would probably conform to the desires of the Assembly majority; and (3) that the opinion would be self-executory and would not require Assembly interpretation and application to the concrete cases.[331] It was on these very grounds that the amendment was objectionable to several states, and, most notably, to the United States. The latter's representative observed that, although the Court's opinion would provide an "authoritative answer" regarding the Assembly-Tribunal relationship, that opinion would only be advisory. True, the Assembly would take its decision in the light of the opinion; but it could base its decision on additional considerations as well. In any case, it was improper to anticipate the Court's decision.[332] As noted earlier, this French amendment also was defeated in Committee.[333]

[327]UN Doc. A/C.5/L.264, 6 December 1953.

[328]UN Doc. A/C.5/L.268/Rev.1, 8 December 1953.

[329]GAOR (VIII), 5th Ctte., 426th Mtg., 7 December 1953, pp. 331, 336.

[330]*Ibid.*, Plenary, 471st Mtg., 9 December 1953, p. 460.

[331]Unless the other French amendment—that related to the three-power draft resolution—were accepted, such an assumption was, to a degree, untenable.

[332]*Ibid.*, 5th Ctte., 426th Mtg., 7 December 1953, p. 334. The United Kingdom had earlier stated that consultation of the Court did not entail abdication by the Assembly of any of its powers. *Ibid.*, 423rd Mtg., 5 December 1953, p. 305.

[333]The controversial provision was rejected by a vote of 20 for, 28 against, with 9 abstentions. *Ibid.*, 427th Mtg., 8 December 1953, p. 338. The French and Mexican representatives had argued that the vote on the French amendment should precede that on the three-power draft, since the attitude of many states toward the latter would depend on the assurance that the Secretary-General would be authorized to pay the indemnities, should the Court determine that the awards were final. The Chairman,

The three-power draft resolution was adopted by wide margins in Committee and in Plenary.[334]

It is instructive to note the attitude which the United States, as the state most directly concerned, adopted in this case. It abstained in the vote to request the Court's opinion, in deference to the "sincere misgivings" expressed by several delegations regarding the Assembly's power to refuse to honor the awards in question. At the same time, it insisted on the nonbinding nature of the Court's opinion and the retention by the Assembly of full decision-making powers with respect to the awards. Nevertheless, even the United States recognized that the opinion would furnish the Assembly with an "authoritative answer regarding the relationship between the General Assembly and the Administrative Tribunal." Thus, the American attitude was far from hostile. The United States was, perhaps, not oblivious to the benefits which consultation of the Court might offer it, if only in the negative sense that the most likely alternative—an immediate Assembly decision to pay the disputed awards—would have been even less palatable. Moreover, a positive advantage was to be derived from the proposed recourse, even in the event that the American contentions were judicially repudiated. For, if the Court could, by its authoritative opinion, extricate the Assembly majority from an embarrassing position vis-à-vis the United States, it could simultaneously extricate the United States government (at least to a degree) from an embarrassing position vis-à-vis important elements in the American political arena. Acquiescence in the payment of the controversial awards after such payment was sanctioned by the highest judicial authority in the world could be more readily justified as a matter of upholding the rule of law.

Voting Procedure on Questions Relating to Reports and Petitions Concerning the Territory of South West Africa

The General Assembly in 1950 accepted the Court's advisory opinion on the status of South West Africa and proceeded to devise means of implementing it. In the course of these efforts, the Assembly twice found it necessary to approach the Court again—in each instance for an interpretation of the original opinion.

The purpose of the request in the *South West Africa (Voting)* case was no longer (even nominally) the hope of persuading South Africa to submit to UN

---

however, held that it would be illogical to decide on the action to be taken as a result of an advisory opinion not yet requested. *Ibid.*, 426th Mtg., 7 December 1953, pp. 335–36.

[334] The vote in Committee was 35 to 7, with 12 abstentions; in Plenary, 41 to 6, with 13 abstentions. The resolution thus adopted became Resolution 785A (VIII), 9 December 1953.

supervision of its administration of South West Africa. Such a hope appeared quite forlorn by 1954. Rather, consultation of the Court was directed exclusively at allaying the misgivings of an important minority in the Assembly whose continued cooperation in the Assembly deliberations on South West Africa was deemed essential.

The Assembly proceedings in the ninth session, which led ultimately to the request for an advisory opinion, followed a rather complicated and tortuous course. The question of consulting the Court was considered in two distinct stages,[335] in each of which the action taken in Plenary differed from that taken in Committee.

Failure to request the Court's opinion in the first stage came about in the following circumstances.

The proposal to consult the Court was first made by the Committee on South West Africa.[336] That Committee had been established by the Assembly in 1953 as a subsidiary organ with functions analogous to those of the former Permanent Mandates Commission, and had been charged with the task, *inter alia*, of drafting rules of procedure for the examination of reports and petitions concerning South West Africa.[337] In its report to the Assembly, the Committee drew up a series of six such special rules (A-F).[338] Of these, only special rule F gave rise to controversy in the Committee. In accordance with that rule, a two-thirds majority of the Assembly would suffice for the adoption of decisions on questions relating to reports and petitions concerning South West Africa. But, in 1950, the Court had declared that "the degree of supervision to be exercised by the Assembly should not . . . exceed that which applied under the Mandates System, and should conform as far as possible to the procedure followed . . . by the Council of the League of Nations," particularly in reference to "annual reports and petitions."[339] On this basis, South Africa argued that only the unanimity rule (involving a South African veto) could fulfill the judicial stipulation. (I.e., even on the assumption that the 1950 opinion was correct—an assumption that South Africa was unprepared to accept—rule F did not comply with that opinion.) On the

---

[335] The first stage encompassed Meetings 399–402, 4–7 October 1954, of the Fourth Committee, and the 494th Meeting, 11 October 1954, of the Plenary. Discussions in the second stage took place at the Fourth Committee's Meetings 409 and 424–27, 19 October and 8–10 November 1954, and at Plenary Meetings 500 and 501, 23 November 1954.

[336] Actually, the proposal originated with a working group of that Committee consisting of Mexico, Pakistan, and Norway.

[337] GA Resolution 749A (VIII), 28 November 1953.

[338] GAOR (IX), Supp. No. 14 (UN Doc. A/2666), Annexes III and IV.

[339] ICJ Reports, 1950, p. 138. Although this passage did not appear in the operative part of the opinion, it was generally viewed as an integral part of the opinion, not as a mere obiter dictum. Both the 1954 and 1955 requests involved interpretations of this passage—the former, explicitly; the latter, merely implicitly.

other hand, the majority of the Committee thought special rule F to be fully consonant with the 1950 pronouncement, since the Court was not unaware of the voting procedure laid down in the Charter and could not have intended to affect that voting procedure in any way. Nevertheless, in deference to the doubts expressed by some of the Western states, the Committee proposed the adoption of special rule F, "subject to the concurring vote of the Union of South Africa as the State most directly concerned." It further recommended that, in the absence of South African concurrence, the Court be requested to give an advisory opinion on the question of the conformity of special rule F with the 1950 advisory opinion.[340]

When the report of the Committee on South West Africa came before the Fourth Committee, there was considerable opposition to the conditional clause in relation to special rule F, on the grounds that it would grant veto power to a single state.[341] Furthermore, with respect to the necessity and desirability of consulting the Court, the views of the members were split three ways: (1) A minority (mainly from the Western states) entertained serious doubts regarding the legality of special rule F, and desired a Court opinion to resolve those doubts and ensure that the Committee remained within the limits of the 1950 opinion.[342] (2) A larger group acquiesced in the decision to consult the Court in deference to the position of the minority and for the sake of Committee unity. Members of this group were careful to affirm their own personal conviction that special rule F was fully justified.[343] (3) A third group entirely opposed, for various reasons, the projected recourse to the Court.[344]

---

[340] In the event that rule F were held inconsistent with the earlier opinion, the Court was to indicate what voting procedure should be applied by the Assembly.

[341] See, e.g., the statements of Uruguay (GAOR [IX], 4th Ctte., 401st Mtg., 6 October 1954, p. 26) and of Yugoslavia and Haiti (*ibid.*, 402nd Mtg., 7 October 1954, pp. 34–35).

[342] See, e.g., the statements of Denmark (*ibid.*, 399th Mtg., 4 October 1954, p. 17) and the United States (*ibid.*, 401st Mtg., 6 October 1954, p. 25).

[343] Among this group were such states as India, Mexico, and Syria, which had (with the United States and Norway) cosponsored the draft resolution to request the advisory opinion (UN Doc. A/C.4/L.334). See GAOR (IX), 4th Ctte., 399th Mtg., 4 October 1954, p. 15; 400th Mtg., 5 October 1954, pp. 20–21; and 402nd Mtg., 7 October 1954, p. 32.

[344] Both the composition of the group and its arguments were varied. Thus, the Soviet Union—which rejected the 1950 opinion for not having gone far enough—and South Africa—which rejected the same opinion for having gone too far—both deemed derivative proceedings based on the 1950 opinion pointless. GAOR (IX), 4th Ctte., 401st Mtg., 6 October 1954, p. 25; and 402nd Mtg., 7 October 1954, p. 37. (However, South Africa acknowledged the Assembly's right to request the advisory opinion.) Other considerations invoked against the proposed recourse to the Court were the delay involved in such a procedure (Yugoslavia, *ibid.*, p. 34); the Assembly's competence to determine independently the applicability of its voting procedure (Uruguay, *ibid.*, 401st Mtg., 6 October 1954, p. 27); and the obvious uselessness of the projected opinion in light of its

In the Committee vote, the conditional clause regarding special rule F was retained,[345] and the entire draft resolution incorporating the rules of procedure was adopted. (It became draft resolution A in the Fourth Committee's report.) The proposal for requesting an advisory opinion was similarly approved, and by a wide margin.[346] (It became draft resolution B in the Fourth Committee's report.)

In Plenary, however, opposition to giving South Africa a "veto" was renewed, and, in a separate vote, the clause subjecting special rule F to South African acceptance failed of adoption.[347] Draft resolution A was then adopted minus the qualifying clause. Following this vote, the Assembly President ruled that, in view of the unconditional acceptance of special rule F, there was no longer any necessity to put draft resolution B to the vote. The President's ruling was challenged but sustained.[348]

The matter of requesting the Court's opinion might have been buried and forgotten but for the threats of nonparticipation in the votes on the South West Africa issue and/or in the work of the Committee on South West Africa subsequently raised by several important states.

The first such threats were presented to the Fourth Committee at its 409th meeting, upon resumption of discussions on the report of the Committee on South West Africa. At that time, the United States representative declared that, in the absence of judicial clarification of the voting procedure question, his government would be unable to participate in any vote on substantive resolutions regarding South West Africa. And the Norwegian and Thai representatives announced their governments' withdrawal from the South West Africa Committee.[349] All expressed regret that the Assembly had not been given the opportunity to vote on draft resolution B, and cautioned that remaining doubts would plague future debates on South West Africa and deprive Assembly actions of the requisite moral force. In the face of these statements and actions, the Fourth Committee decided to appoint a subcommittee to review the whole situation.[350] That subcommittee recommended

nonbinding nature and in view of South Africa's attitude (Belgium and Israel, *ibid.*, pp. 24–26; and 402nd Mtg., 7 October 1954, pp. 36–37).

[345] The vote to retain the clause (in modified form) was 15 to 7, with 28 abstentions, a vote which presaged possible trouble in Plenary, where a two-thirds majority was required.

[346] The vote was 35 to 1, with 11 abstentions. GAOR (IX), 4th Ctte., 402nd Mtg., 7 October 1954, p. 36.

[347] The vote (13 to 8, with 29 abstentions) fell short of the required two-thirds majority. *Ibid.*, Plenary, 494th Mtg., 11 October 1954, p. 248.

[348] The vote to sustain was 30 to 8, with 13 abstentions. *Ibid.*, p. 250.

[349] *Ibid.*, 409th Mtg., 19 October 1954, pp. 77–79. For the text of the letters of resignation, sent earlier, see GAOR (IX), Annexes, a.i. 34, p. 12.

[350] In moving to form such a subcommittee, the Iraqi representative emphasized the dangers of a breach in Fourth Committee solidarity on the South West Africa issue. *Ibid.*, 4th Ctte., 409th Mtg., 19 October 1954, p. 79.

reopening the question of submitting special rule F to the Court and presented a draft resolution to effect such a submission.[351]

In the discussion of the subcommittee's proposals, again, as in the debate in the first stage, three divisions of opinion emerged which corresponded to the following three groups of states: the genuine "doubters"; the acquiescing but nondoubting states; and the opponents of reference to the Court. At this stage, however, an additional factor, not present earlier, had to be taken into account. The controversial voting procedure had already been adopted by the Assembly, so that any request for an opinion would now be retrospective and would raise the issue of propriety[352]—of setting up the Court as a kind of court of appeal against the decisions of the Assembly. As the argument was later elucidated by the Israeli representative in Plenary:

These advisory functions can be exercised by the Court *ante factum*, not *post factum* . . . [The Assembly may not request an opinion] after it has taken a decision because, if it does, it risks being told by a co-ordinative organ, not a superior organ, that its decision was wrong. I do not believe that the General Assembly can risk such an answer being given by the International Court of Justice, an answer which would, in fact, cancel what the General Assembly has done. This would elevate the International Court of Justice to an international constitutional court, which it is not and which it was not intended that it should be.[353]

Considerations of this sort led some of those who had in the earlier stage acquiesced in the request for an advisory opinion to oppose reopening the question of reference now. In an attempt to counter this argument, the proponents of reference maintained that the Assembly's prestige would be strengthened rather than weakened by consultation of the Court, and that it was far better to recognize an error at the outset than to wait a year and risk a worsening of the situation.[354] Nevertheless, the Fourth Committee decided, by a tie vote,[355] to reject the subcommittee's recommendation to reopen the question of consulting the Court.

[351]GAOR (IX), Annexes, a.i. 34, p. 10. The subcommittee cited in support of its recommendation the new situation which had developed and the statements by various delegations that their favorable votes for draft resolution A had been predicated on the expectation that draft resolution B would also be voted on. In light of these statements, it is somewhat difficult to understand why the President's ruling not to put draft resolution B to the vote was sustained by such a wide margin (30 to 8, with 13 abstentions).

[352]See, on this point, Rosenne, *Law and Practice*, 1: 78.

[353]GAOR (IX), Plenary, 500th Mtg., 23 November 1954, p. 318. See also *ibid.*, 4th Ctte., 425th Mtg., 8 November 1954, p. 192.

[354]See, e.g., the statements of New Zealand (*ibid.*, 4th Ctte., 409th Mtg., 19 October 1954, p. 79) and Iraq (*ibid.*, 425th Mtg., 8 November 1954, p. 194).

[355]The vote was 18 to 18, with 16 abstentions. *Ibid.*, 425th Mtg., 8 November 1954, p. 195.

This action prompted those representatives (including the United States representative) who had previously reserved their positions regarding participation in Assembly votes and/or in the machinery on South West Africa to reaffirm their stands. In addition, they were now joined by the representatives of Sweden, Iraq, Brazil, Mexico,[356] Pakistan, and Syria—all of whom either declared their governments' inability to serve on the Committee on South West Africa or reserved their governments' stand on the matter.[357]

In light of this new "tide of defections," the issue of requesting the Court's opinion was raised afresh—this time in Plenary—in the form of a Guatemalan-Lebanese joint draft resolution.[358] The sponsors emphasized that their "new"[359] proposal would strengthen the UN's position in negotiations with South Africa by ensuring the "direct and proper participation" of certain governments in such negotiations and by depriving South Africa of any justification for its present attitude.[360] The Lebanese representative appealed to all those who, like himself, did not entertain doubts regarding the legality of special rule F to support the new draft resolution, "in order that those of our colleagues who think otherwise may see the matter clearly."[361]

Despite objections voiced by some delegates,[362] and despite the reaffirmation by South Africa of its negative attitude toward the projected consultation,[363] the joint proposal was adopted.[364]

---

[356] Mexico's position is least understandable, for in Committee it expressed strong reservations with respect to a retrospective judicial consultation, and subsequently, in Plenary, it abstained on the resolution to request the Court's opinion. *Ibid.*, 424th Mtg., 19 October 1954, p. 189; and Plenary, 501st Mtg., 23 November 1954, p. 322.

[357] *Ibid.*, 4th Ctte., 426th Mtg., 9 November 1954, pp. 197–98; and 427th Mtg., 10 November 1954, p. 201. After the decision was taken in Plenary to request the Court's opinion, all but one of the reservations and resignations (that of Norway) were withdrawn. *Ibid.*, 462nd and 463rd Mtgs., 9 December 1954, pp. 430–33.

[358] UN Doc. A/L.178, 23 November 1954.

[359] The main difference between the new proposal and the former draft resolution B was the addition of a rather extensive preamble. However, the "newness" was emphasized in order to avoid application of Rule 83 of the Rules of Procedure, under which the reconsideration of a decision requires approval by a two-thirds vote. After extensive discussion, the Assembly determined (by a vote of 25 to 18, with 11 abstentions) that Article 83 was not applicable. GAOR (IX), Plenary, 500th Mtg., 23 November 1954, pp. 313–20.

[360] *Ibid.*, pp. 309–11.

[361] *Ibid.*, pp. 312–13. Cf., to the same effect, the statement of India, *ibid.*, 501st Mtg., 23 November 1954, pp. 322–23. The Lebanese representative pointed, too, to the benefits which the 1950 opinion had afforded. It had allowed the Assembly to escape deadlock, avoid long and wearisome discussions of the legal issues, and consolidate its legal position. Similar advantages would, he felt sure, accrue from the present consultation.

[362] See, especially, the arguments of Israel and the Philippines, *ibid.*, 501st Mtg., 23 November 1954, pp. 323, 325–26. The Philippines representative argued that the UN was placing itself in a position where it was apt to lose everything and gain nothing. The Israeli representative objected, *inter alia*, to two assumptions which he held to be im-

Following this vote, the question arose as to what effect the decision to request the Court's opinion should have on the interim action of the Assembly. The Assembly then had before it four draft resolutions recommended by the Fourth Committee: A and B, which dealt with two petitions concerning South West Africa; and C and D, which dealt, respectively, with the report of the Committee on South West Africa and the status of the territory. On a Thai motion, the assembly decided to defer the vote on draft resolutions A and B "until such time as it is seized of the advisory opinion of the International Court of Justice."[365] But a South African motion which would have postponed the vote on draft resolution C as well was rejected. Against the South African view that draft resolution C related to a report on South West Africa and that special rule F covered both reports and petitions, it was contended that draft resolution C related merely to a report of an Assembly main committee and that special rule F was therefore inapplicable.[366] While logic may have been on South Africa's side, the sentiment of the Assembly majority clearly was not.

To summarize, the request for an advisory opinion in the *South West Africa (Voting)* case was motivated neither by the hope that such an opinion might persuade South Africa to abandon its intransigent stand on South West Africa nor by any felt need of the Assembly majority for judicial clarification. Rather, it was the recognition of the doubts of an influential minority of states which prompted the proposal to request the Court's opinion. The Fourth Committee initially adopted, by a sizable majority, a resolution to consult the Court, but, through a peculiar set of circumstances, that resolution was never voted on in Plenary. The disputed voting procedure was adopted unconditionally. Subsequently, however, the doubts of certain states were translated into threats of nonparticipation in aspects of the Assembly's deliberations on South West Africa. These doubts could then be ignored only at the risk of seriously jeopardizing the moral force of Assembly actions—the

---

plicit in the proposed request: (1) that the Assembly was duty-bound to accept a Court opinion; and (2) that the 1950 opinion contained within itself an answer which needed only to be elaborated or interpreted.

[363] *Ibid.*, pp. 324–25.

[364] The vote was 25 to 11, with 21 abstentions. *Ibid.*, p. 326. It thus involved the highest number of abstentions ever registered, up to that time, with respect to a resolution requesting an advisory opinion. The vote also contrasted with the earlier vote in the Fourth Committee on draft resolution B (35 to 1, with 11 abstentions). Presumably, this shift reflected primarily the prevalent misgivings with respect to the "propriety" issue referred to above. The resolution requesting the Court's opinion was numbered 904 (IX).

[365] *Ibid.*, pp. 326–29. The motion was adopted by a vote of 27 to 18, with 8 abstentions.

[366] *Ibid.*, pp. 329–30. The vote on the South African motion was 4 for, 18 against, with 30 abstentions.

only force which they could be said to have, in any case. The proposal to consult the Court met with more resistance at this second stage, for the consultation was to be no longer a prospective, but a retrospective, one, entailing judicial consideration of a measure already adopted by the Assembly. Nevertheless, after a series of oscillations, the decision to approach the Court was finally made in Plenary.

Admissibility of Hearings of Petitioners by the Committee on South West Africa

In contrast to the complex maneuvers leading up to the previous request, the decision to consult the Court on the question of the admissibility of oral hearings of petitioners was reached in a rather straightforward manner. Unlike the earlier case, too, the Fourth Committee members were more evenly split on the substantive issue. (If anything, it was the "Western" view which commanded more support.) In fact, the very closeness of the division dictated the necessity for outside clarification. Here, too, however, clarification was designed solely for the use of the Assembly, for, again, there was no question of swaying South Africa.

The problem of the admissibility of oral hearings was brought to the Fourth Committee's attention at its tenth session by the Committee on South West Africa, after the latter had received several applications for such hearings. The difficulty lay in the fact that the Committee on South West Africa had been instructed by the Assembly, following the terms of the Court's 1950 pronouncement, to examine petitions "as far as possible in accordance with the procedure of the former Mandates System"; and that the Permanent Mandates Commission had never made any provision for granting oral hearings to petitioners, nor had it, in fact, ever granted such hearings. On these grounds, many states—and not only the "Western" states—deemed the grant of oral hearings inconsistent with the Court's 1950 opinion.[367] Proceeding on this belief, the delegations of Mexico, Pakistan, Syria, Thailand, and the United States introduced a draft resolution[368] whereby the Assembly would decide that the granting of oral hearings by the Committee on South West Africa would *not* be in accordance with mandates procedure, but that individual Committee members might accord private audiences to petitioners. This proposal met with firm opposition on the part of a significant minority of the Fourth Committee members, which, for a variety of reasons,[369] favored the

---

[367] See *ibid.* (X), 4th Ctte., 500th Mtg., 8 November 1955, pp. 180–82; and 502nd Mtg., 9 November 1955, pp. 189–91.

[368] UN Doc. A/C.4/L.413, 8 November 1955.

[369] Among these reasons were: (1) the necessity for such hearings as a result of South Africa's uncooperative attitude; (2) the undesirability of freezing the defective elements of the mandates system; (3) the compatibility of oral petitions with the 1950 opinion; and (4) the absence of any obligation to adhere strictly to the terms of the 1950

granting of oral hearings by the Committee on South West Africa. It quickly became apparent that neither view would muster a majority sufficient for adoption, and, under these circumstances, the previous proposal on the substantive issue was withdrawn[370] and replaced by a new joint draft resolution[371] (sponsored by Lebanon, Liberia, Mexico, and Thailand)[372] to request the Court's opinion on the matter in dispute.

On behalf of this course of action, it was argued that only thus could the deadlock in the Committee be broken; that the question, involving as it did an interpretation of an earlier Court opinion, was eminently suitable for submisssion to the Court; and that no one could take exception to this course, since the Court's views commanded universal respect.[373] Against consulting the Court it was maintained that the matter was merely a procedural, not a legal, issue; that the Assembly itself should lay down the policy of the Committee on South West Africa; that the Committee could not request an advisory opinion every time a disagreement arose; and that, indeed, to apply to the Court on every pretext indicated a lack of consideration for the Court.[374] It was also objected that the proposed recourse to the Court might lead to indefinite postponement of the question of requests for hearings, for the Court's opinion might, quite conceivably, be ambiguous and involve the Committee in a perennial circle of consultations and discussions.[375]

The new joint proposal was adopted in Committee by a vote of 23 to 5, with 21 abstentions; and in Plenary by a vote of 32 to 5, with 19 abstentions.[376]

Subsequent to the vote in Committee to request the Court's opinion, two questions arose relating to the interim effect to be attributed to the decision to consult the Court. The first involved a request by the Reverend Scott for a hearing by the Fourth Committee. On several previous occasions,

---

opinion. GAOR (X), 4th Ctte., 500th Mtg., 8 November 1955, p. 182 (Lebanon); 501st Mtg., 8 November 1955, pp. 185–87 (Liberia, the Philippines, and Yugoslavia); 502nd Mtg., 9 November 1955, p. 190 (Poland and Egypt); and 504th Mtg., 10 November 1955, pp. 198–200 (Liberia and Uruguay).

[370]*Ibid.*, 505th Mtg., 10 November 1955, p. 201.

[371] UN Doc. A/C.4/L.415 and Add. 1, 10 November 1955.

[372]The sponsors were evenly split on the substantive issue, the first two favoring, the latter two opposing, the grant of oral hearings.

[373]These arguments were presented by the sponsors, and by the representatives of the United States, Denmark, New Zealand, and the Dominican Republic. GAOR (X), 4th Ctte., 506th Mtg., 11 November 1955, pp. 203–6.

[374]See the arguments of Peru, Poland, Ecuador, Egypt, Uruguay, and Yugoslavia, *ibid.*, 505th Mtg., 10 November 1955, p. 201; and 506th Mtg., 11 November 1955, pp. 203–6.

[375]Argument of Haiti, *ibid.*, 506th Mtg., 11 November 1955, p. 204.

[376]*Ibid.*, Plenary, 550th Mtg., 3 December 1955, p. 399. The resolution was numbered 942 (X). The number of abstentions in the final vote, it will be noted, was only slightly lower than the corresponding number in the *South West Africa (Voting)* case.

such a request had been granted (despite vigorous opposition by certain representatives). It was now argued, however, that to grant the request at this time would conflict with the decision to request the Court's opinion in the matter of oral hearings. For, if it was impossible to determine the powers of the Committee on South West Africa in this regard, it was equally impossible to determine the powers of the Fourth Committee, which also was an organ of the Assembly.[377] The majority remained unconvinced by these arguments, however, contending instead that the projected Court opinion would relate solely to the competence of the Committee on South West Africa. Moreover, to deny Scott a hearing at this time was to cast doubt on the Assembly's previous actions.[378] By a vote of 29 to 11, with 10 abstentions, the Committee decided to grant the hearing requested.[379]

The second question related to a Liberian proposal[380] which provided for transmission of the statements of the Reverend Scott to the Committee on South West Africa. Again it was objected that the move was incompatible with the decision to request the Court's opinion and might, indeed, prejudge that opinion. By transmitting the records of the hearing to the Committee on South West Africa, it was argued, the Fourth Committee was making that Committee a party to the oral hearings it had granted and was, thereby, presenting the Court with a *fait accompli*.[381] Furthermore, if the Court were subsequently to rule that oral hearings were inadmissible, not only in the Committee on South West Africa, but in the UN as a whole, the General Assembly might find that it had instructed a subordinate body to report on a hearing which had been found to be illegal. Such actions would give South Africa a very good argument and would play directly into its hands.[382] In response to these objections, it was maintained that, upon its transmission to the Committee on South West Africa, the Reverend Scott's statement would cease to be an oral hearing and would become a written petition. Hence, there could be no opposition to the Committee's receiving it.[383]

The decision was taken to transmit the record of the hearing to the Committee on South West Africa.[384]

---

[377] Arguments of Israel and Australia, *ibid.*, 507th Mtg., 11 November 1955, pp. 209-11.

[378] Remarks of the representatives of Peru, Lebanon, Liberia, and the Soviet Union, *ibid.*

[379] *Ibid.*, p. 212.

[380] UN Doc. A/C.4/L.417, 14 November 1955.

[381] Argument of Australia, GAOR (X), 4th Ctte., 510th Mtg., 15 November 1955, pp. 227-28.

[382] Remarks of the representative of Denmark, *ibid.*, p. 228.

[383] Argument of Venezuela, *ibid.*

[384] The vote in Committee was 27 to 6, with 16 abstentions; and, in Plenary, 34 to 6, with 14 abstentions. *Ibid.*, 511th Mtg., 15 November 1955, p. 231; and Plenary, 550th Mtg., 3 December 1955, p. 399.

The Court was turned to in this case in the face of Assembly division on the issue of the admissibility of granting oral hearings to petitioners. In line with the precedent of the previous year, the Court seemed to be the appropriate organ for settling the issue. The profound hesitations that had racked the Assembly before making the *South West Africa (Voting)* request were, for several reasons, absent in the instant case. First, while the question of voting procedure—with the concomitant possibility of a South African "veto"—might have effectively paralyzed UN supervisory machinery, the same could not be said of the question of the admissibility of oral petitions. Written petitions continued to be available. Second, the issue of "propriety" was not involved in this case at all. And, finally, the "favorable" outcome of the previous consultation undoubtedly reinforced the willingness to consult the Court again.

Certain Expenses of the United Nations
(Article 17, Paragraph 2, of the Charter)

The issue presented to the Court in this case was one of the thorniest to come before the ICJ in its advisory capacity. As in the *Admission* case, the issue was an "organizational" one in which the two superpowers were pitted against each other.[385] The *Expenses* case, however, was both different and potentially more serious than the earlier case. For, behind the surface disagreement over the organization's finances, there lay a more basic "organizational" controversy regarding the role of the UN in peace-keeping. And the stridency of the latter controversy was aggravated by specific East-West conflicts of interest in relation to the two areas of UN peace-keeping operations, the Middle East and the Congo (and especially the latter). By comparison, the *Admission* controversy, which was limited both in origin and in possible effects to the organizational realm, appeared tame. There was another major difference between the two cases. While the Soviet Union objected to both requests and could hardly be expected, in either case, to acquiesce willingly in an opinion adverse to its contentions, in the instant case there lurked in the background the sanction of Article 19 of the Charter, which, theoretically, might be employed in an attempt to compel the Soviet Union to comply with a Court opinion.[386] In the event, the sanction proved to be very theoretical indeed, but it was so proved only after the issue of its use had brought the organization to the grave constitutional crisis which culminated in the famous nineteenth "nonsession."

The context in which the Court's opinion was sought in the *Expenses* case was the threatened insolvency of the UN which resulted from the failure of

---

[385] France, this time, was on the Soviet side.

[386] Did this fact perhaps have some bearing on the Soviet decision to participate, for the first time, in the oral proceedings before the Court?

many states (most notably, the Soviet Union and France) to contribute to the financing of one or both of the peace-keeping operations then in progress.[387] Since the creation of those operations, the members of the UN had been deeply divided over the proper method of financing them, as well as over the question of whether the Assembly's apportionment of the expenses of the operations created legally binding obligations for member states to contribute. No consensus on these issues had ever emerged.[388] In 1961, as part of an effort to solve the financial woes of the organization, the Assembly set up the Working Group of Fifteen on the Examination of the Administrative and Budgetary Procedures of the United Nations and charged this group with the task of studying methods of covering the cost of peace-keeping operations.[389] But, predictably, the differences between the members of the Working Group proved unbridgeable.[390] The only concrete recommendation to emerge from the Working Group's deliberations resulted from the endorsement by the majority of the Working Group membership of a Canadian proposal to seek ICJ advice with respect to "the legal nature of financial obligations arising out of peace-keeping operations." The precise formulation of the question was to be determined by the Assembly.[391] In the Fifth Committee, this recommendation of the Working Group was translated into a formal proposal,[392] the terms of which no longer related to expenditures for peace-keeping opera-

---

[387] The Soviet Union failed to contribute to either UNEF (the Middle East Emergency Force) or ONUC (the UN force in the Congo); France, merely to the latter.

The Soviet Union's nonpayment of UNEF expenses was based on the view that the Assembly had authority neither to establish the force nor to finance it. In the case of ONUC—which was set up by the Security Council and hence was unobjectionable on that score—Soviet opposition centered on the manner in which the Council's directives were implemented by the Secretary-General and on the fact that the expenses for the operation were again, as in UNEF, apportioned by the General Assembly.

On the UN financial crisis generally, see John G. Stoessinger *et al.*, *Financing the United Nations System* (Washington, D.C.: The Brookings Institution, 1964); Ruth B. Russell, "United Nations Financing and the 'Law of the Charter,'" *Columbia Journal of Transnational Law*, 5 (1966): 68–95; and H. G. Nicholas, "The United Nations in Crisis," *International Affairs*, 41 (1965): 441–50.

[388] The divergence of opinion was reflected in the many (29) resolutions adopted in relation to UNEF and ONUC. After perusing these resolutions, Verzijl very aptly concludes that the organization had landed itself in "an inextricable legal chaos." *World Court*, 2: 490.

[389] GA Resolution 1620 (XV), 21 April 1961.

[390] The extent of the differences is graphically revealed in the Report of the Working Group, UN Doc. A/4971, 15 November 1961, pars. 7–23 and Annex II.

[391] *Ibid.*, par. 25. In the Working Group, France supported reference to the Court in principle, but desired to have the Sixth Committee consulted on the exact formulation of the question. The issue of Sixth Committee consultation was raised again in the Fifth Committee and in Plenary.

[392] UN Doc. A/C.5/L.702 and Add. 1 and 2, 7 December 1961, sponsored jointly by Brazil, Cameroun, Canada, Denmark, Japan, the United Kingdom, the United States, Liberia, Pakistan, and Sweden.

tions in the abstract but concerned the particular expenditures already incurred for the UNEF and ONUC operations.[393] Moreover, the question no longer specifically mentioned the financial obligations of member states. Instead, the Court was asked merely whether the expenditures incurred "constitute 'expenses of the Organization' within the meaning of Article 17, paragraph 2, of the Charter."[394] After some debate, the proposal was adopted by the Fifth Committee,[395] and, later (after rejection of a significant French amendment), in Plenary.[396]

The debates in the Fifth Committee and in Plenary[397] reveal, on the one hand, some of the hopes and expectations pinned by certain states on the projected opinion and, on the other hand, the very real misgivings and apprehensions experienced by other states in regard to both the purpose of recourse to the Court and the formulation of the questions referred.

The joint draft resolution to request the Court's opinion was introduced in the Fifth Committee by the representative of Canada, one of the cosponsors of the proposal. Pointing first to the urgency of resolving the basic questions relating to the financing of peace-keeping operations, and, second, to the inability of the Fifth Committee itself to resolve these questions over a period of five years, he concluded that an advisory opinion from the Court offered the best prospect of a break in the deadlock. As for the terms of the draft resolution, these were, he said, purposely framed "in the least contentious terms possible." He hoped, therefore, that all representatives, regardless of their views on the substantive issues, would be able to endorse the "simple and straightforward" proposal before them.[398]

---

[393] Thus, the question now possessed a retrospective aspect which a general question on peace-keeping operations for future guidance might have avoided. On this ground, among others, Judge Basdevant considered that the Court should have declined to give the opinion requested. "Where," he said, "it would have been possible to obtain from an opinion requested of the Court collaboration in the present work of the United Nations, it has been sought to obtain from the Court only a retrospective evaluation of what was done up to the end of 1961." ICJ Reports, 1962, pp. 237-38.

[394] In the preamble, however, the Assembly recognized its need "for authoritative legal guidance as to obligations of Member States under the Charter of the United Nations in the matter of financing the United Nations operations in the Congo and in the Middle East." The Court discounted the importance of this preamble. *Ibid.*, pp. 157-58. Cf. the separate opinion of Judge Fitzmaurice, *ibid.*, p. 198; and see p. 324, n. 165, below.

[395] GAOR (XVI), 5th Ctte., 899th Mtg., 11 December 1961, p. 299.

[396] *Ibid.*, Plenary, 1086th Mtg., 20 December 1961, pp. 1153-54. The resolution was numbered 1731 (XVI).

[397] The debates took place at Meetings 897-99 of the Fifth Committee, 8-11 December 1961; and at the 1086th Plenary Meeting, 20 December 1961.

[398] GAOR (XVI), 5th Ctte., 897th Mtg., 8 December 1961, p. 289.

Speaking in support of this proposal, several representatives, mainly of the Western states, acknowledged that the financial problem facing the organization was esssentially political, and that judicial clarification of the legal aspects would be insufficient to resolve the larger problem. Nevertheless, they argued, removing the legal doubts might at least provide a way out of the impasse.[399] Moreover, the alternative was "to do nothing and await a miracle, while endlessly repeating the same legal arguments on both sides of the controversy as the United Nations each day comes nearer to bankruptcy."[400]

The representatives of Mexico and Brazil emphasized the nonpolitical character of the joint proposal, and cited as evidence the fact that they, despite their contention that peace-keeping costs did *not* fall under the terms of Article 17(2) of the Charter, nevertheless supported the proposed recourse to the Court. Far from prejudging the issue, the joint draft merely sought to clarify it. While the nonpayment of assessments might be a political issue, the question of consulting the Court was not.[401]

But any hopes for unanimous or near-unanimous support of the "nonpolitical," "simple and straightforward," proposal to solicit the Court's advice were, at the very outset of the discussions, dashed by the attitude of the Soviet Union. Its opposition was, in this case, based not only on its traditional posture whenever recourse to the Court was at issue but also on the recognition that the proposal constituted an attempt to exert pressure on the Soviet Union to bear the cost of political actions to which it objected.[402] Arguing against requesting an advisory opinion, the Soviet representative contended, first, that the issue was clearly settled by the Charter and that the projected consultation of the Court would be equivalent to undermining the essential principles which member states had accepted upon signing the Charter; second, that the problem was essentially political and was not separable into legal, financial, and political elements; and, finally, that there was no need to seek judicial advice, since the requisite financing could and should be arranged in accordance with Article 43 of the Charter. The Soviet representative further served notice on the Assembly that his government would

[399]*Ibid.*, 897th-899th Mtgs., 8-11 December 1961, pp. 289-300 *passim*.

[400]Remarks of the Japanese representative, *ibid.*, 898th Mtg., 8 December 1961, p. 297.

[401]*Ibid.*, 897th Mtg., 8 December 1961, p. 290; and 898th Mtg., 8 December 1961, p. 297. Cf. the statement of the Italian representative, who affirmed the "legal" nature of the question on the ground that any question of treaty interpretation was a purely legal matter. *Ibid.*, 898th Mtg., 8 December 1961, p. 297. This view is in line with the Court's own oft-repeated dictum, reiterated in the present case, that the interpretation of a treaty provision is "an essentially judicial task." ICJ Reports, 1962, p. 155. See also Chapter V.

[402]Moreover, the political actions at issue (especially those in the Congo) were seen by the Soviet Union as having been directed against her.

not consider itself bound by any Court decision, because the question was not within the Court's competence.[403]

The French attitude in the Committee was no more encouraging. Despite the fact that France had, in the Working Group, endorsed the recommendation to consult the Court,[404] the French representative now argued quite forcefully against such a course of action. The product of the consultation, he warned, could only be, at best, inconclusive, and, at worst, positively harmful, because: (1) the judges would find no guidance in the *travaux préparatoires;* (2) UN debates and practice revealed that contributions to peace-keeping expenditures had become, in the opinion of many member states, purely optional; (3) the national composition of the Court was not very different from that of the Working Group, and, although the judges are independent, they rarely adopt views contrary to those taken by their respective governments; (4) a number of dissenting opinions would probably be involved, thus weakening the value of any opinion; (5) recourse to the Court would probably aggravate the situation by rigidifying the attitudes of governments; and (6) the financial reforms which could have been initiated in the meantime would have been delayed a whole year.[405]

Given the opposition of these two major powers (and especially of the Soviet Union), many nonaligned states justly concluded that no practical benefit would ensue from the proposed recourse. Although Article 19 had not been mentioned by any of the draft resolution's sponsors, it was alluded to by other states and undoubtedly was in the minds of at least some of the sponsors. For, ultimately, it was recognized that the removal of the doubts of the genuinely "doubting" states could not remove the organization's deficits. Somehow, the major defaulters, whose opposition was, admittedly, based on "political" grounds, would have to be persuaded. And this "persuasion" might have to take the form of the threat or use of Article 19.[406] To this line of reasoning, the Ceylonese representative voiced far-sighted objection:

> The present *de facto* situation could be altered only through the co-operation of Member States and particularly of the great Powers. An affirmative answer by the Court would only tend to complicate a situation which was already sufficiently complex. Such an answer would be of little value if a great Power still refused to pay its share of the present peace-keeping

[403] GAOR (XVI), 5th Ctte., 897th Mtg., 8 December 1961, p. 289; 898th Mtg., 8 December 1961, p. 295; and Plenary, 1086th Mtg., 20 December 1961, pp. 1151–52. Cf. the Rumanian argument, *ibid.*, 5th Ctte., 897th Mtg., 8 December 1961, p. 290.

[404] As noted above, France had merely insisted that the Sixth Committee be consulted with respect to the drafting of the question.

[405] GAOR (XVI), 5th Ctte., 897th Mtg., 8 December 1961, p. 291.

[406] See, especially, the statement of Australia, *ibid.*, 899th Mtg., 11 December 1961, pp. 299–300.

operations, and he doubted that much advantage would be gained by depriving that Power of membership in the United Nations on the basis of the Court's opinion. Legality could be of little value if it could not ensure compliance. Therefore, a practical approach involving a recognition of both reality and legality appeared preferable.

Co-operation could not be achieved through compulsion . . . the attempt to refer the present issue to the International Court was futile and negative.[407]

Apart from the opposition, whether on practical or other grounds, to the entire idea of consulting the Court in the *Expenses* case, specific objections were also voiced with respect to the formulation of the question in the draft resolution. These objections were directed both to the substantive terms of the question and the procedure by which the question had been drafted. Thus, the Peruvian representative would have preferred a broader question relating to peace-keeping in general and requiring judicial consideration not only of Article 17 but of other relevant provisions (such as Articles 19, 43, 48, and 50) as well. And the representative of the United Arab Republic regretted the absence of any reference to the reasons which had led up to the peace-keeping operations.[408] To remedy these alleged drafting defects, both representatives, joined by the representative of Mexico, urged that the Sixth Committee be consulted with respect to the precise formulation of the question, in accordance with the procedure outlined in Resolution 684 (VII), of 6 November 1952, and incorporated in Annex II of the Rules of Procedure.[409] However, no formal proposal to this effect was put forward, and the joint draft resolution was adopted in its orginal form by the Committee.[410]

Subsequent to the vote, however, the French representative strongly criticized the Committee's failure to consult the Sixth Committee. Because of this failure, he asserted, the question did not accord with Article 65(2) of the Court's Statute, and the wording was too restrictive to give the Court full

---

[407]*Ibid.*, 898th Mtg., 8 December 1961, p. 296. Cf. the statements of India (*ibid.*, 897th Mtg., 8 December 1961, p. 289) and of Afghanistan and Indonesia (*ibid.*, 899th Mtg., 11 December 1961, p. 301).

[408]*Ibid.*, 897th Mtg., 8 December 1961, pp. 291–92. See also the statements of France, China, and Mexico after the vote in the Committee, *ibid.*, 899th Mtg., 11 December 1961, pp. 300–301.

In reply to these objections, the United States representative declared that the sponsors had not intended to confine the Court to the examination of Article 17, but, rather (as shown by the preamble), had expected the Court to consider all relevant Charter provisions. Moreover, any member state was free to submit its views to the Court. *Ibid.*, 897th Mtg., 8 December 1961, pp. 292–93.

[409]*Ibid.*, 897th Mtg., 8 December 1961, pp. 289–92.

[410]*Ibid.*, 399th Mtg., 11 December 1961, p. 299. The vote was 31 to 10, with 20 abstentions.

freedom to consider every aspect of the matter. In answering the question as framed, the Court could not "elucidate the question of the Assembly's own powers or lack of powers in financial matters"; nor could it consider such other provisions as Articles 10, 11, 12, 14, and 19, all of which were highly relevant to the problem confronting the Assembly.[411]

The French criticisms were renewed in Plenary, where they became the focus of a sharp debate. This time France introduced an amendment which would have considerably broadened the scope of the request.[412] Under its terms, the Court would have been asked to determine, first, the question whether the resolutions authorizing the UNEF and ONUC expenditures were "decided on in conformity with the Charter," and, only in the event of an affirmative answer, the further question whether the expenditures constituted "expenses of the Organization."[413]

Ostensibly, the amendment was designed to expand the scope of judicial inquiry and to enhance the effectiveness of the consultation.[414] It is difficult, however, to assume that this was the true French motivation. If it were, the appreciative response accorded the amendment by the Soviet representative,[415] no less than the vigorous attack launched by the sponsors of the original draft resolution, would appear incomprehensible.

The reception accorded the amendment by the sponsors is indicated in the following excerpts from the statements of the Canadian and United States representatives, respectively.

> The amendment before us attempts to broaden the question to a significant degree. ... [It] clearly calls into question every resolution which this body has passed on these two operations [UNEF and ONUC] over a period of five years. This is not the question which has raised difficulties over the years. Clearly, the majorities obtained on all these resolutions indicate that the membership of the United Nations is virtually unanimous on its prerogatives and responsibilities. It would therefore be invidious for this Assembly to go to the Court and call into question a large number of its own decisions taken over the years.[416]

---

[411] *Ibid.*, p. 300. See also the statements of Peru and Mexico, *ibid.* In reply, the Chairman pointed out that no formal proposal for referral to the Sixth Committee had been made, and that such referral was purely optional. *Ibid.*, p. 301.

[412] UN Doc. A/L. 378, 16 December 1961.

[413] As the Court later noted, the French amendment would have had the Court consider the validity only of the resolutions authorizing the expenditures, not of the basic resolutions establishing UNEF and ONUC. ICJ Reports, 1962, p. 156.

[414] See the French explanation, GAOR (XVI), Plenary, 1086th Mtg., 20 December 1961, pp. 1151, 1154.

[415] *Ibid.*, pp. 1151–52.

[416] *Ibid.*, pp. 1152–53.

It is illuminating to observe that in the debates in the Fifth Committee the proponent of the amendment opposed the whole idea [of recourse to the Court]. The purpose of an amendment urged in these circumstances requires extraordinary reasons to justify its acceptance. . . .

. . . This amendment, in accordance with French opposition to the very idea of seeking the Court's opinion, does not clarify the questions at issue. Rather, it would tend to confuse it.[417]

It is quite conceivable that the amendment was designed as a maneuver to defeat the draft resolution as a whole, for many states, fearful of the expanded role to be assigned to the Court in assessing the legality of General Assembly actions, might be expected to withdraw their original support of submission of the problem to the Court.[418]

The French amendment was defeated by a vote of 47 to 5, with 38 abstentions,[419] and the Fifth Committee's draft resolution was then adopted by a vote of 52 to 11, with 32 abstentions.[420]

In truth, it must be said that neither the decision to involve the Court in the *Expenses* case nor the formulation of the question posed bore the marks of much forethought. As even the sponsors of the draft resolution recognized, the basic problem was, after all, to fill the empty coffers of the organization. In what way, then, could a Court opinion contribute to a solution of this problem? Surely not by virtue of the "moral force" or "authoritativeness" of such an opinion. Experience with such earlier judicial pronouncements as those in the *Admission* and *Peace Treaties* cases must have proved to all—if such proof was necessary—how unamenable the Soviet Union was to that particular form of influence. (Nor, for that matter, was it realistic to expect the other major defaulter, France, to bow willingly to a Court opinion.) Undoubtedly, it was the theoretical availability of the Article 19 sanction which was expected to "persuade" the defaulters to mend their ways. But could the sanction realistically be used against a major power? And, if it could not, but was merely to be held in reserve as a threat, was it, then, a

[417]*Ibid.*, p. 1153. See also the statements of the United Kingdom and El Salvador, *ibid.*, pp. 1152, 1154.

[418]It is noteworthy that France continued to manifest, even in Plenary, its lack of enthusiasm and, indeed, its hostility, toward the entire idea of consulting the Court. *Ibid.*, p. 1154.

[419]*Ibid.*, p. 1153. The effect of the rejection of the French amendment later proved to be an issue of considerable contention, both in the pleadings before the Court and among the members of the Court themselves. See Chapter V.

[420]Only the Soviet bloc and France voted in opposition. The abstainers included a majority (but by no means all) of the nonaligned Afro-Asian states, as well as Belgium, South Africa, and Yugoslavia. Curiously, one of the sponsors of the draft resolution—Cameroun—abstained in the vote.

credible threat? Moreover, if the matter had eventually to be settled by negotiations, if it was to be settled at all, why involve the Court in such a controversial issue, with all the concomitant risk to the Court's prestige? If, indeed, these questions engaged the minds of those who supported recourse to the Court (as opposed to those who, like Ceylon, abstained), there is no indication of this on the record.

Legal Consequences for States of the Continued Presence of South Africa in Namibia (South West Africa) notwithstanding Security Council Resolution 276 (1970)

The request in the *Namibia*[421] case marked a renewal in the use of the advisory function after a period of desuetude which lasted from 1962 (the year in which the *Expenses* opinion was rendered) until 1970. Apart from this fact, the most novel aspect of the *Namibia* request was the identity of its addressor—the Security Council, which, in the near quarter-century of its existence had never before employed its power to solicit advisory opinions from the Court. Various considerations apparently prompted this first Council request, but among these the desire for judicial guidance in relation to disputed points of law did not figure prominently (if at all). Nor, evidently, was there any serious expectation that a judicial pronouncement would succeed in dispelling the doubts entertained by certain influential Council members on the issues in question. More blatantly, perhaps, than in any previous advisory case, the requesting organ anticipated a "correct" answer from the Court. Indeed, the Court was to be permitted to furnish such an answer in order thereby "to redeem its impaired image."[422] To a large extent, this case constituted a "test case" for the Court in its new composition[423] —an opportunity to remove the "taint" of 1966[424] and to realign the Court with the political organs of the UN on the Namibia (South West Africa) issue.

By the time the Security Council decided to seek an advisory opinion, its efforts to secure South African withdrawal from Namibia had clearly reached an impasse. After two years of consideration of the Namibia issue, the Security Council found itself in a situation little different from that of the General Assembly. In 1966, the Assembly had declared (in Resolution 2145)[425] that

---

[421] By GA Resolution 2372 (XXII), 12 June 1968, the territory of South West Africa was renamed "Namibia."

[422] Statement of Nepal, UN Doc. S/PV.1550, 29 July 1970, pp. 38–40.

[423] In the 1966 and 1969 elections to the Court, the representation of the Third World (and particularly of Africa) had been increased.

[424] In 1966, the Court, after having accepted jurisdiction in the *South West Africa* cases in 1962, ruled that Ethiopia and Liberia had no standing to receive a judgment on the merits. ICJ Reports, 1966, p. 6.

[425] 27 October 1966.

South Africa's mandate over South West Africa was terminated and that "henceforth South West Africa comes under the direct responsibility of the United Nations." Subsequently, the Assembly had established a United Nations Council for South West Africa[426] (later rechristened the United Nations Council for Namibia[427]) to administer the territory until independence. South Africa, however, denied the validity of the Assembly's resolutions and refused to cooperate with the Council for Namibia. The Assembly sought to elicit the assistance of the Security Council, but not until the issue of the Pretoria "terrorist trial" of South West Africans arose[428] did the latter organ become seized with the Namibia question.[429] During the course of 1968-69, the Council moved ever closer to endorsing the Assembly's actions. At first, it merely "took note of" General Assembly Resolution 2145[430] and took it "into account";[431] but later, in 1969 (in Resolution 264), it "recognized" the Assembly's termination of the mandate, considered that South Africa's continued presence in Namibia was illegal, and called on South Africa to withdraw its administration from the territory immediately.[432] In a second resolution adopted in 1969 (Resolution 269), the Security Council set a deadline of 4 October 1969 for South African withdrawal, and decided that, in the event of failure to comply, "it will meet immediately to determine upon effective measures in accordance with the appropriate provisions of the relevant Chapters of the Charter of the United Nations."[433]

At this point, then, the Council had moved one step beyond endorsing the Assembly's resolutions on Namibia; it had implicitly threatened to apply enforcement measures under Chapter VII of the Charter. This threat, however, was not too credible. Significantly, four Security Council members (France, the United Kingdom, the United States, and Finland) had abstained in the vote on Resolution 269, and, in doing so, had expressed strong reservations about the possible invocation of Chapter VII.[434] Thus, when in January

[426] GA Resolution 2248 (S-V), 19 May 1967.

[427] GA Resolution 2372 (XXII), 12 June 1968.

[428] See John Dugard, "South West Africa and the 'Terrorist Trial,'" *AJIL*, 64 (1970): 19.

[429] For a review of the manner in which the Security Council became involved in the Namibia issue, see Slonim, *op. cit.*, chap. XII.

[430] SC Resolution 245, 25 January 1968.

[431] SC Resolution 246, 14 March 1968.

[432] SC Resolution 264, 20 March 1969.

[433] SC Resolution 269, 12 August 1969. In this resolution, Article 25 of the Charter was invoked for the first time with respect to the Namibia issue.

[434] See UN Docs. S/PV.1494, 6 August 1969, pp. 6-7; S/PV.1495, 8 August 1969, pp. 16-20; and S/PV.1496, 11 August 1969, pp. 2-15. France and the United Kingdom had also abstained on the earlier 1969 resolution (264), for they had questioned the juridical basis of Assembly Resolution 2145. See UN Docs. S/PV.1464, 20 March 1969, pp. 46-52; and S/PV. 1465, 20 March 1969, pp. 31-41. Both states continued to express

1970 the Council resumed its consideration of the Namibia question, it found itself predictably lacking the necessary consensus to adopt the mandatory sanctions which the African states, in particular, desired. In these circumstances of internal deadlock, the Security Council adopted Resolution 276,[435] by which it decided to establish an *Ad Hoc* Sub-Committee to study "ways and means by which the relevant resolutions of the Council, including the present resolution, can be effectively implemented in accordance with the appropriate provisions of the Charter, in the light of the flagrant refusal of South Africa to withdraw from Namibia." In the same resolution, the Council declared "that the continued presence of the South African authorities in Namibia is illegal and that consequently all acts taken by the Government of South Africa on behalf of or concerning Namibia after the termination of the Mandate are illegal and invalid"; and all states, "particularly those which have economic and other interests in Namibia," were called upon to refrain from any dealings with the South African government that were inconsistent with the Council's declaration of illegality.

The principal recommendations to emerge from the *Ad Hoc* Sub-Committee entailed an enumeration of those "dealings" with South Africa—in the diplomatic, consular, and economic spheres, especially—which the Council might deem to be inconsistent with the illegality of South Africa's presence in Namibia.[436] (There was still no consensus to invoke Chapter VII of the Charter, however.) In addition, the Sub-Committee's report included a proposal to request of the ICJ an opinion on "the legal consequences for States of the continued presence of South Africa in Namibia notwithstanding resolution 276 (1970)."[437]

The latter suggestion resulted from a Finnish initiative in the *Ad Hoc* Sub-Committee.[438] In explaining the advantages of recourse to the Court, the Finnish representative emphasized at the outset that the basic decisions of the General Assembly and the Security Council on the termination of the mandate would not be called into question. These decisions were irrevocable, and, consequently, the presence of South Africa in Namibia after 1966 was illegal. The Court would be asked merely to "define in legal terms" the *consequences*

---

doubts in this regard throughout the pre-request phase of the Council's proceedings, and (as will be seen in Chapter VI) even after delivery of the Court's opinion.

[435] 30 January 1970.

[436] UN Doc. S/9863, 7 July 1970.

[437] *Ibid.*, p. 7 (Recommendation 5).

[438] The suggestion was first raised at the 3rd Meeting of the *Ad Hoc* Sub-Committee, and was elaborated on at the 12th Meeting. See UN Docs. S/AC.17/SR.3, 27 February 1970, p. 8; and S/AC.17/SR.12, 10 June 1970, pp. 2–6. See also UN Doc. S/AC.17/SR.17, 7 July 1970, p. 8. For a review of the relevant proceedings in the *Ad Hoc* Sub-Committee, see the Written Statement of the Secretary-General, *Namibia* case, ICJ Pleadings, 1971, 1: 196–99.

for other states of the illegality of South Africa's presence in Namibia. An advisory opinion

> would dispel doubts, *inter alia*, about questions relating to diplomatic or consular relations which might be construed to imply recognition of South Africa's authority over Namibia and the question of amending or revising bilateral and multilateral treaties between States and South Africa to the extent that they contained provisions applying to Namibia. In the event that such agreements and treaties did not contain explicit provisions regarding their application to Namibia, the question of their applicability to the Territory would have to be determined on the basis of the relevant provisions of international law.[439]

In addition, the Court's opinion could be expected to yield these further benefits: (1) It would help to define more precisely the rights of Namibians resident in the territory and abroad. (2) It would prove the inequality of South Africa's arbitrary and repressive apartheid legislation. (3) It would underline the fact that South Africa had forfeited its mandate because it had violated the terms of the mandate and had acted contrary to international law and contrary to the international status of the territory.

Obviously, there was one major inconsistency in the Finnish explanatory statement. What was to be the scope of the question placed before the Court? Was the Court, indeed, to take as its starting point the validity of the General Assembly and Security Council resolutions and confine itself to spelling out the legal consequences of those resolutions for states? If so, how would the opinion serve to establish that South Africa had been justifiably divested of its mandate? And in what context would the Court have occasion to pronounce itself on the inequality of apartheid?[440]

For its part, the United Kingdom made it clear that it "would be willing to go along with the proposal" to request an advisory opinion only if "the Court was not debarred from considering the issue as a whole, including the competence of the General Assembly to assign to the United Nations responsibility for the administration of South West Africa, the legal status of which is central to the whole issue."[441]

---

[439] UN Doc. S/AC.17/SR.12, 10 June 1970, p. 3. It is interesting to note, parenthetically, that in the *Namibia* opinion, the Court held that even treaty provisions explicitly applicable to Namibia were (with certain exceptions) not to be invoked or applied by states if they involved active intergovernmental cooperation between South Africa and the State concerned. Amendment or revision of the relevant treaties was not deemed necessary. ICJ Reports, 1971, p. 55.

[440] This inconsistency regarding the scope of the question continued to characterize Finland's position, both in the Security Council and, subsequently, in the pleadings before the Court. See p. 327, n. 175, below.

[441] UN Doc. S/9863, 7 July 1970, Annex IV, p. 4.

Several other states voiced misgivings over the entire idea of a judicial consultation. The Soviet Union, for example, considered it an ineffective delaying tactic, and expressed its distrust of the Court.[442] And the representative of Burundi questioned the practical value of the proposed recourse, since he doubted that states refusing to abide by Assembly resolutions would agree to accept the Court's opinion.[443]

When the Security Council reconvened, on 29 July 1970, to consider the recommendations of the *Ad Hoc* Sub-Committee, it had before it two draft resolutions. The first[444] (later adopted by the Security Council as Resolution 283) embodied the principal recommendations of the Sub-Committee. As explained by the Finnish representative, it contained "a comprehensive programme of action" designed to translate into practical terms the Council's declaration regarding the illegality of South Africa's presence in Namibia and to "increase international pressure on South Africa with regard to Namibia."[445] In a word, the Security Council was itself spelling out, and in great detail, what were "the legal consequences for States of the continued presence of South Africa in Namibia notwithstanding Security Council resolution 276 (1970)." Why, then, refer this same question to the Court, as the second draft resolution[446] proposed to do? Was not "the natural distribution of roles as between the principal judicial organ and the political organs of the United Nations . . . reversed" in this instance, as Judge Petrén later suggested? "Instead of asking the Court its opinion on a legal question in order to deduce the political consequences flowing from it," was not the Council doing the opposite?[447] Affirmative answers to these questions serve merely to underscore the fact that the primary consideration motivating the request was not the desire to elucidate disputed points of law and to dispel genuine legal doubts; the principal motives must be sought elsewhere. Intimations of what these might be abound in the record.

Thus, the Finnish representative, repeating the arguments presented in the *Ad Hoc* Sub-Committee,[448] declared: "It is important . . . to expose the false

[442] *Ibid.*, p. 7. The Soviet Union recalled the "shameful judgment" of 1966; cf. the doubts of Sierra Leone, UN Doc. S/AC.17/SR.14, 24 June 1970, p. 6.

[443] UN Doc. S/AC.17/SR.14, 24 June 1970, p. 5.

[444] UN Doc. S/9891. (Burundi, Finland, Nepal, Sierra Leone, and Zambia were the cosponsors.)

[445] UN Doc. S/PV.1550, 29 July 1970, p. 17.

[446] UN Doc. S/9892. Finland alone sponsored this draft resolution.

[447] ICJ Reports, 1971, p. 127. On these grounds, Judge Petrén concluded that the Court would have had a valid reason for refusing to give an opinion in this case, although he thought the Court ought to respond even to this "abnormal" request, "in view of the particular circumstances in which the question of Namibia has evolved and the confused situation which has resulted." *Ibid.*, pp. 127–28.

[448] See UN Doc. S/PV.1550, 29 July 1970, p. 18. The Finnish representative did not, however, mention the issue of treaty relations with South Africa concerning Namibia

front of legality which South African authorities attempt to present to the world. This would help the United Nations and the Governments of Member States to mobilize public opinion in their countries—especially in those countries which have the power to influence events in southern Africa in a decisive way."[449] In addition, he said, "a more general argument" suggested itself—namely, "the need to reactivate the International Court of Justice," whose present state was a matter of concern to Finland.

> An organ which is left unused is in danger of atrophy. The decline in the authority of the Court is damaging to the interests of the United Nations system as a whole and to the structure of international law. The request for an advisory opinion on a question of great interest to the international community would reactivate the Court at a particularly difficult time in its existence.[450]

However, the Afro-Asian states, in particular, were wary of a reactivation of the Court. True, the composition of the 1970 Court was different from that of the 1966 Court, but what guarantee was there against a "repeat performance"? Could the majority in the UN political organs be certain that this time it would find itself on "the winning side" in the judicial organ as well? The thought of suffering a repudiation of its views at the hands of the Court—even by means of a nonbinding advisory opinion—obviously was not relished. Judicial legitimization, not judicial repudiation, was the desideratum.

Despite their hesitations, the Afro-Asian states were willing to acquiesce in the Finnish proposal, subject, however, to several understandings. First, the Court was clearly being presented with a test and an opportunity. The following excerpts are illuminating:

> If . . . the draft resolution would provide an opportunity for the International Court to redeem its impaired image, my delegation will only be too glad to support it.[451]

> This question above everything else will give the Court a crucial opportunity to restore world public confidence in its very existence.[452]

> [T]he International Court of Justice, whose prestige was violated by the partiality of some of its members in 1966, would gain in prestige by

---

(one legal consequence, incidentally, which Security Council Resolution 283 did *not* detail). Nor did he mention the issue of apartheid.

[449]*Ibid.*

[450]*Ibid.*, pp. 19–20.

[451]Statement of Nepal, *ibid.*, pp. 38–40.

[452]Statement of Zambia, *ibid.*, pp. 54–55.

adopting a new attitude which would rehabilitate the Court and the United Nations as a whole. . . . Of course at the present stage it would be premature to prejudge or try to foresee with any degree of mathematical accuracy the turn that the deliberations of . . . [the] court might take. . . . [T]here is, however, always the hope that an impartial judgement, which would be in conformity with the interests of the Namibian people, would serve the two-fold purpose of rehabilitating the prestige of the International Court . . . and also harmonizing the position of the Court with the position taken by the General Assembly in putting an end to South Africa's Mandate over Namibia.[453]

The second understanding was that recourse to the Court would affect neither the nature of the Namibia issue—which was, and would remain, political—nor the interim action of the Security Council pending receipt of the Court's opinion. Moreover, the opinion would not affect the *subsequent* action of the Council either, except to the extent that the opinion might afford additional legal and moral support to the political actions of the Council. Thus, the Zambian representative (after wondering whether the formulation of the request was "specific enough to elicit a clear opinion from the Court which would be *politically acceptable*") stated that he would support recourse to the Court "on the clear understanding that Namibia is a political problem requiring a political solution and that this resolution does not in any way affect our desire to continue pressing for political action."[454] "Once the advisory opinion of the Court is given," the Syrian representative declared, "it will merely represent an element in forcing United Nations measures against the defiance of South Africa."[455]

The third, and perhaps most important, understanding was that the nature of the question presented to the Court would be strictly circumscribed. It would relate solely to the legal consequences of the Assembly and Council resolutions and would not in any way call into question the validity of those resolutions. The Court was not to serve as an organ of judicial review in relation to the actions of its coordinate organs.[456]

On the other hand, France and the United Kingdom thought that, in the absence of judicial review of the basic decision on revocation of the mandate—a decision whose validity both states still questioned—the consultation of the Court would be pointless. With the obvious intention of permitting the

---

[453] Statement of Burundi, *ibid.*, p. 71.

[454] *Ibid.*, p. 53; italics added.

[455] *Ibid.*, pp. 47–50. See also Burundi's statement that "the political decision with regard to the status of Namibia is irrevocable." *Ibid.*, pp. 71–75.

[456] See the statements of Nepal (*ibid.*, p. 37), Syria (*ibid.*, p. 47), and Burundi (*ibid.*, pp. 71–75). See also the statement of Colombia in the *Ad Hoc* Sub-Committee, UN Doc. S/AC.17/SR.12, 10 June 1970, pp. 5–6.

Court to consider, rather than requiring it to assume, the validity of the underlying resolutions, France proposed a separate vote on the phrase "notwithstanding Security Council resolution 276 (1970)."[457] By a vote of 11 to 0, with 4 abstentions (France, Poland, the Soviet Union, and the United Kingdom), the phrase was retained. The Finnish draft resolution as a whole was approved by a vote of 12 to 0, with 3 abstentions (Poland, the Soviet Union, and the United Kingdom).[458] Despite the rejection of its suggested deletion, France approved the resolution as a whole, on the assumption that, even as it stood, the request would allow the Court "to clarify the legal position as regards the legality of the revocation."[459] The opposite assumption was made by the United Kingdom representative, who abstained in the final vote. He regretted that the question was "constructed in such a fashion that the Court might feel itself inhibited from pronouncing on the more fundamental issues concerning the present status of South West Africa."[460]

The scope of the question contained in the request was subsequently a matter of considerable debate before, and within, the Court.[461] As noted earlier, the statements of Finland, the sponsor of the requesting resolution, were themselves contradictory in this respect. Most of the Council members did not express themselves verbally on the matter. Nonetheless, on the basis of the pre-request proceedings as a whole (and, most notably, the vote on the French motion to delete the "notwithstanding" clause), it seems clear that the majority of the Council deemed judicial review of the revocation decision either unnecessary or undesirable or both.[462]

It was quite foreseeable at the time the Security Council decided to seek judicial advice that that advice would have little or no effect on the situation in Namibia, or even on the Security Council's further deliberations in the matter. South Africa was known to oppose the request,[463] and it was not

[457] UN Doc. S/PV.1550, 29 July 1970, p. 76.

[458] *Ibid.*, p. 81. The resolution was numbered 284.

[459] *Ibid.*, p. 87.

[460] *Ibid.*, p. 91. The Soviet abstention was based on the belief that the request would be an ineffective, and, even worse, a harmful measure, since "it would create illusions concerning the possibility of a solution . . . by legal means." *Ibid.*, pp. 63-65.

[461] See Chapter V, pp. 327-28.

[462] Even if this was the unequivocal intention of the Council, it is not clear that the Court must allow that intention to fetter it in the exercise of its judicial function. See Chapter V.

[463] South Africa had not requested, and did not receive, an invitation to participate in the Council's deliberations on Namibia. Failure to be invited, South Africa later contended in the pleadings before the Court, constituted a violation of Article 32 of the Charter and resulted in a formally invalid request which the Court was not competent to

likely to be persuaded to evacuate Namibia by any advisory opinion.[464] Persuasion of South Africa by force—i.e., by enforcement measures—was a possibility, but it was highly improbable, given the impasse in the Security Council on the question of invoking Chapter VII of the Charter. Nor was that impasse expected to be affected by an advisory opinion. The critical doubts of such states as the United Kingdom, France, and the United States involved the political wisdom and expediency of sanctions, and these doubts could in no way be removed by a judicial pronouncement. (In any event, the Court was not being asked to advise on the applicability of Chapter VII, a matter which is solely within the Security Council's discretion.) Furthermore, to the extent that lingering doubts about the validity of the Assembly's revocation of the mandate *were* impeding progress, the apparent circumscription of the question to *exclude* any judicial review of the revocation did not augur well for the opinion's ability to sway doubting states.[465]

As for means of persuasion short of invoking Chapter VII, the Security Council, simultaneously with the request, had probably gone as far as it was prepared to in spelling out what it deemed to be the "legal consequences of the continued presence of South Africa in Namibia." And those states which did not choose to follow the Council's lead were not likely to change their stands as a result of an advisory opinion. As the representative of Nepal stated:

> My delegation would not be surprised if the advisory opinion of the Court in this matter does not spur the major trading partners and military collaborators of South Africa into any positive effective actions, because, if they have so long resisted world opinion and neutralized the thrust of all positive United Nations endeavours on the question of Namibia, it is too much to expect that they will change their minds on the basis of the Court's opinion, whose effect would only be advisory.[466]

In truth, it must be said that the Security Council probably expected that the Court's opinion would be almost, if not entirely, irrelevant to the Council's further handling of the Namibia question. The legal issues were not considered the troublesome ones. Significantly, and in contrast to earlier

---

entertain. However, the Court considered that, since the Namibia question had been handled by the Council as a "situation," not a "dispute," Article 32 was inapplicable. See Chapter V, pp. 285–86.

[464] Although South Africa later participated in the judicial proceedings, it challenged the Court's right to comply with the request and made it clear that it would view the opinion as strictly advisory. See Chapter V.

[465] In the end, the Court *did* address itself to the revocation question, but the principal "doubters"—France and the United Kingdom—found the Court's reasoning unpersuasive. See Chapter VI.

[466] UN Doc. S/PV.1550, 29 July 1970, pp. 38–40.

requests on the South West Africa issue, no state even bothered to question the consistency of the interim action taken (in this case, the adoption of Resolution 283) with the decision to seek judicial advice. The Court's opinion, it was thought, might be useful as a means of strengthening the Council's efforts and of adding to their further legitimization.[467] But from the record it would seem that judicial support was to be enlisted for the sake of the *Court*, more than for the sake of the Council. The Court's image had been tarnished in relation to the South West Africa issue, and the Court was now being permitted to redeem itself in relation to the same issue.[468] If the answer was the "correct" one, it might restore the confidence of the Third World in the Court. On the other hand, the Court was put on notice in advance that, if it disappointed the expectations that accompanied the Council request by staging a repeat of 1966, it would be ignored in this case and, by implication, must expect to be ignored by the political organs in the future and to continue to content itself with "judicial thumb twiddling."[469]

Constitution of the Maritime Safety Committee of the Inter-Governmental Maritime Consultative Organization

The second and (to date) last request to be addressed to the Court under the terms of Article 96(2) of the Charter was the one addressed by the IMCO Assembly on 19 January 1959. It was the only request in the UN period which related to the interpretation of a specialized agency's constitution.[470] The Court was required to pass, retrospectively, on the constitutionality of an act of the IMCO Assembly—namely, its election of the members of the Maritime Safety Committee. This organizational issue involved the thorny problem of "flags of convenience"; it also involved two states—Liberia and Panama—as quasi plaintiffs.[471] In fact, the decision to request the Court's opinion was taken mainly in deference to the wishes of Liberia.

---

[467] See, in this connection, the following remark by Judge Petrén: "It clearly emerges from the context in which the request for advisory opinion was decided that its purpose was above all to obtain from the Court a reply such that States would find themselves under obligation to bring to bear on South Africa pressure of an essentially economic character designed to secure its withdrawal from Namibia." ICJ Reports, 1971, p. 127.

[468] It may also have seemed "natural" to send a further aspect of the South West Africa issue to the Court, since the issue had become a "traditional" one for the Court. And, after all, the Court's previous *advisory* pronouncements had been favorable to the views of the UN majority.

[469] The term is borrowed from Inis L. Claude, "States and the World Court: The Politics of Neglect," *Virginia Journal of International Law*, 11 (1971): 344.

[470] In contrast, five League requests involved interpretation of the ILO Constitution.

[471] In a memorandum to the Assembly, the Liberian government specifically referred to Liberia and Panama as "plaintiffs" in the case. IMCO/A.1/Wkg. Paper 19, 19 January

The facts of the IMCO case may be briefly stated. Under the terms of Article 28(a) of the IMCO Convention, the Maritime Safety Committee was to consist of fourteen members elected by the Assembly from IMCO members having an important interest in maritime safety, "of which not less than eight shall be the largest ship-owning nations." In the very first elections to the Committee, held on 15 January 1959, Liberia and Panama were not elected, despite the fact that they were among the eight IMCO members possessing the largest registered tonnage.

A Liberian motion to request an advisory opinion was first made before the elections to the Maritime Safety Committee took place. According to this proposal, an interim Committee would have been appointed, pending receipt of the Court's opinion.[472] The election of a permanent Committee, the Liberian representative contended, would prejudge the issue and would raise a very complex legal problem in the event the Court subsequently found that the Committee had been illegally constituted.[473] Nevertheless, it was decided to proceed with the elections, and, as noted, both Panama and Liberia were excluded from participation in the Committee.[474] Immediately following the elections, Liberia introduced a formal draft resolution under which a decision would be taken, in principle, to have the legal issues which had arisen in connection with the interpretation of Article 28 referred to the Court for an advisory opinion. The task of formulating the questions to be submitted would be delegated to the Legal Committee, whose formulation would be subject to subsequent Assembly approval.[475]

Even among those who opposed Liberia's election, the consensus favored the proposed recourse to the Court. The Netherlands representative alone spoke out against recourse to the Court,[476] though even he indicated that he would merely abstain, in order not to stand in the way of Liberia's desire to obtain an authoritative opinion from the ICJ on a problem to which the Liberian delegation attached such importance.

1959. The proceedings before the Court in the *IMCO* case did, in fact, bear some aspects of contentious procedure.

[472] IMCO/A.1/SR.7, 14 January 1959, p. 13; and IMCO/A.1/SR.8, 15 January 1959, pp. 6-7.

[473] IMCO/A.1/SR.8, pp. 9-10. Cf. the statements of Honduras and Argentina, IMCO/A.1/SR.9, 15 January 1959, pp. 2-3.

[474] IMCO/A.1/SR.8, pp. 13, 18; and IMCO/A.1/SR.9, pp. 4-5.

[475] IMCO/A.1/SR.9, p. 6.

[476] It was regrettable, he thought, that, at this very early stage of IMCO's activities, the organization should have to declare itself unable to settle a problem. Moreover, the request was both unnecessary and inappropriate because (1) the elections were undoubtedly legal; (2) the means of settlement within IMCO had not yet been exhausted; and (3) important matters of shipping policy lay behind the legal questions involved. IMCO/A.1/SR.9, p. 6; and IMCO/A.1/SR.10, 16 January 1959, pp. 2-4.

However, if, in principle, consensus on reference to the Court was easily obtained, agreement on the terms of the request proved very difficult indeed. In fact, no unified text emerged from the Legal Committee, and it was only in Plenary that a compromise formula was finally reached. The crucial difference underlying the divergent formulations was that between having the Court pass on the validity of the election which had taken place—as desired by Liberia, the United States, and Canada—or of having the Court determine more abstract questions relating to the interpretation of Article 28 of the Convention, particularly as to the relationship between registered tonnage and the term "the largest ship-owning nations."[477] The difference was significant because, if the validity of the election were submitted, and, if (as actually happened) the Court were to declare that election invalid, the Assembly could not, practically speaking, retain the Committee as then constituted. On the other hand, the general questions formulated by France and the United Kingdom, particularly since they involved interpretation of only one term in Article 28 ("the largest ship-owning nations") and excluded reference to the other important criterion therein mentioned (nations "having an important interest in maritime safety"), would have preserved for the Assembly considerable freedom in the application of the resultant opinion to the specific circumstances.

On behalf of their preferred formulation and against that desired by the United States and Liberia, the representatives of France and the United Kingdom (joined by the representatives of the Netherlands and Norway) argued, first, that a question regarding the validity of the election would not constitute an "exact statement" as required by Article 65(2) of the ICJ Statute, and would not, moreover, lead the Court to deal with the essential issues. Second, they contended, a more abstract formulation, in which reference to specific states or events was omitted, would have more permanent value. Finally, they argued, the criterion of "important interest" was an issue for IMCO, not the Court, to determine.

The representatives of Liberia and the United States (joined by the representative of Canada) counterargued that the essential question was the validity of the election, and that, unless this question was squarely placed before the Court, the proposed consultation would be valueless. As for the issue of precision, they maintained that the simpler the question posed, the more precise the reply would be; that the Court did not expect the parties to perform the task of analysis reserved for the Court; and that, since the request would be accompanied by the relevant documents, the Court would be

[477] The latter course was the one urged by France and the United Kingdom. For the texts of the various drafts, see IMCO/A.1/LEG/Wkg. Papers 4, 7, 8, and 9. For the deliberations of the Legal Committee, see IMCO/A.1/LEG/SR.4-6, 16–19 January 1959.

able to discover for itself the more particular issues which divided the members. Furthermore, the term "exact statement" was not to be deemed synonymous with "detailed statement." The former term meant merely that the question should be "so framed that either a simple affirmative or a simple negative answer would dispose of the whole dispute between the parties."[478] In response to the argument that the formulation should be abstract and general and should not mention specific states, it was noted that anonymity was nowhere required—as evidenced by such ILO cases as the *Netherlands Workers' Delegate* and *Danzig and the ILO.* As for excluding certain phrases in Article 28 from the terms of the request, the Court, it was said, was competent to interpret Article 28 in its entirety.

Notwithstanding the endeavors of a Legal Committee working group to consolidate the various texts, a unified text did not emerge, and the diverse proposals were returned to the lap of the Assembly.[479] There a compromise solution was finally reached,[480] in accordance with which the Court was to be asked: "Is the Maritime Safety Committee of the Inter-Governmental Maritime Consultative Organization, which was elected on 15 January, constituted in accordance with the Convention for the Establishment of the Organization?[481]

CONCLUSIONS

From a review of the foregoing League and UN cases, it can be readily seen that the considerations prompting the use of the Court's advisory function in each period were almost as varied as the cases themselves. Such factors as the timing of specific proposals and the configuration of interests which converged to make each of the proposals acceptable do not lend themselves to easy generalizations. Nevertheless, certain discernible patterns emerge from

---

[478] This oversimplified definition is contained in a Liberian memorandum to the IMCO Assembly. IMCO/A.1/Wkg. Paper 19, 19 January 1959, p. 11.

[479] When the Assembly met, it had before it the memorandum of Liberia mentioned above. In that memorandum, Liberia pleaded for the adoption of those questions which Liberia and Panama, as the plaintiffs and the aggrieved states, considered "will fairly and fully place the dispute before the Court," since it was "elementary justice that a plaintiff should be entitled to define the basis on which he alleges that he has been injured." *Ibid.*, pp. 11–12.

[480] IMCO/A.1/SR.11, 19 January 1959. The resolution was adopted unanimously, but with one abstention (China).

[481] The Court later considered that the question, though cast in general terms, was directed to a particular case. As reformulated by the Court, the question asked whether the Assembly, "in not electing Liberia and Panama to the Maritime Safety Committee, exercised its electoral power in a manner in accordance with the provisions of Article 28(a) of the Convention" for the establishment of the organization. ICJ Reports, 1960, pp. 152–53.

the variegated array of cases surveyed, and these allow one to distinguish between the more "typical" League requests and the more "typical" UN requests.

The divergent patterns are perhaps best seen by focusing on the following questions:

1. Was the "legal" nature of the issue referred to the Court contested? Was the competence of the requesting organ to address the proposed question to the Court challenged on any other grounds?

2. Had resort to other law-clarifying channels preceded recourse to the Court? Would the use of some other "legal" channel have been a probable alternative to employment of the Court's advisory jurisdiction? In the absence of a Court opinion, was a solution of the basic problem by some other decision-making body possible—or likely? What peculiar benefit was a Court opinion expected to contribute, over and above that which other alternatives already tried or in contemplation could, or did, give?

3. Was involvement of the Court part of a truly problem-solving approach, or was the Court consulted with the full (or partial) realization that solution of the root problem would not thereby be aided? In this connection, was the Court's opinion solicited with the consent (or, at least, acquiescence) of the states in whose power it lay either to lend or to deny effectiveness to the resultant opinion? What were the prospects that the interested states would, in fact, bow even to an adverse judicial pronouncement?

4. Was the Court's opinion requested on the basis of the hope and expectation that a *particular* answer would be forthcoming?

5. With regard to the timing of the request, did consultation of the Court entail the danger that decisions already taken by a political organ might be declared invalid? Did the question of the interim action to be taken, pending receipt of the Court's opinion, present any great difficulty?

6. How was the proposal to request the Court's opinion initiated? Did protracted debate over the desirability of reference ensue? Did formulation of the request present great difficulty? How was that formulation arrived at?

With respect to the League period, the answers to the foregoing questions may be generalized as follows.

Very rarely was the "legal" nature of the questions to be referred to the Court in any way contested. On the contrary, the "legal" character of the questions was normally acknowledged implicitly by all concerned.[482] In most instances, the interpretation of treaty provisions was at issue, and treaty

---

[482]The most notable exception was Turkey's claim that the questions in the *Mosul* case were "essentially extremely political." LNOJ, 1925, p. 1381.

interpretation was generally deemed to be ipso facto "legal." By the same token, the competence of the League Council to address the proposed request to the Court was not normally challenged.[483]

Not infrequently, consultation of the Court bore the character of an appeal from the pronouncements of other law-clarifying agencies resorted to earlier.[484] These earlier pronouncements were sometimes conflicting and inconclusive,[485] sometimes ineffectual.[486] Moreover, in most cases (including those in which legal advice had already been sought), one of the possible—and in some instances probable—alternatives to requesting the Court's advisory opinion was recourse to some other channel of law clarification. Consultation of either committees of jurists or the Legal Section of the League Secretariat was an ever-available (and oft-used) alternative. Furthermore, in a significant number of cases, compromissory clauses involving the Court's compulsory jurisdiction might, theoretically, have been invoked.[487] Even in the absence of such compromissory clauses, voluntary use of the Court's contentious jurisdiction was often a logical alternative to employment of the advisory jurisdiction.[488]

It is also significant that, in numerous cases, the organ initiating the request for an advisory opinion possessed the legal right to adopt a binding decision, independently, in the matter which it selected to refer to the Court.[489]

---

[483] Russia, in the *Eastern Carelia* case, and Turkey, in the *Oecumenical Patriarch* case, implicitly denied the Council's competence to consult the Court. Each deemed the matter at issue to be within its domestic jurisdiction and refused to be represented before either Council or Court. PCIJ, Ser. B, No. 5, pp. 12–14; Ser. C, No. 9-II, p. 107; and Ser. E, No. 1, p. 238.

[484] The law-clarifying agencies involved were, alternatively, individual legal experts (as, e.g., in No. 1); special committees of jurists (as, e.g., in Nos. 6, 7, and 21); the Legal Section of the League Secretariat (e.g., in No. 17); or the Legal Section of another international body (e.g., in No. 16). In addition, in regard to Polish-Danzig differences, the High Commissioner at Danzig fulfilled a "judicial" role. In two instances (Nos. 11 and 15), the Court acted, in effect, as a court of appeal against his decisions.

[485] E.g., in the cases of the *Netherlands Workers' Delegate* and the *Greco-Bulgarian Communities*.

[486] See, e.g., the cases of *German Settlers in Poland*, *Exchange of Greek and Turkish Populations* and *Railway Traffic between Lithuania and Poland*, pp. 61–65, 71–73, and 83–85 above.

[487] E.g., in Nos. 6, 7, 14, 19, and 21. The ILO Constitution, too, contained a compromissory clause (Article 423 of the Treaty of Versailles) which allowed recourse to the Court's compulsory jurisdiction, but it was never used.

[488] This was particularly true in such cases as *Tunis-Morocco* and *Jaworzina*. In the *Exchange of Greek and Turkish Populations* case, the Council Rapporteur suggested use of the contentious or advisory jurisdiction, alternatively. LNOJ, 1924, pp. 1669–70.

[489] Thus, arbitral or quasi-arbitral powers belonged to the Conference of Ambassadors (in regard to Nos. 8 and 9); the Greco-Turkish Mixed Commission (Nos. 10 and 16); and the Greco-Bulgarian Mixed Commission (No. 17). Again, the ILO organs were em-

In discussing the considerations which prompted League requests, it is therefore necessary to account, on the one hand, for the preference for a Court opinion over either a direct decision by the requesting organ or a decision based on legal advice *less* authoritative than a judicial opinion; and, on the other hand, for the failure to seek a truly binding judgment by means of the Court's contentious jurisdiction.

As for the first point, the short answer is simply that the authoritativeness of a Court opinion was precisely the desideratum. A judicial pronouncement was expected, *inter alia*, to have a greater chance of acceptance by the opposing interests;[490] to allow the losing state more readily to overcome internal political opposition and to save face;[491] and to relieve and lessen the responsibility of the requesting organ vis-à-vis the losing interest.[492] It was also expected to provide a more solid legal foundation for any subsequent action taken. Above all, whether explicitly stated or not, what was involved in most references to the Court was the delegation of decision-making powers with regard to the particular issues referred. Such a delegation could not be effected by consulting, e.g., committees of jurists or the Legal Section of the League Secretariat.[493]

However, such a delegation *could*, in many instances, have been effected even more completely by recourse to the Court's *contentious* jurisdiction. Preference for the advisory jurisdiction over the contentious in these cases is attributable to several factors. (1) In the ILO cases, the availability of the Court's compulsory jurisdiction was very theoretical indeed. The issues referred to the Court were "organizational" ones, involving differences of opinion among the various component groups of the ILO rather than among states,[494] and, as such, not suitable for submission to the contentious jurisdiction.[495]

---

powered to take decisions by majority which would be binding on the membership. In Opinion No. 12 (*Mosul*), the binding nature of the Council's decision was the very question at issue. And, in connection with Danzig affairs and some minorities questions, the Council possessed final decision-making powers.

[490] Significantly, in several instances where nonjudicial legal advice was rejected by one of the parties, the Court's opinion was treated with greater respect (e.g., in Nos. 6, 7, 17, and 21).

[491] See, especially, the *Jaworzina* and *Greco-Bulgarian Communities* cases.

[492] See, e.g., the explanation of the neutral members in connection with the request in the *Greco-Bulgarian Communities* case, p. 81 above.

[493] As will be seen in the following chapter, the desire *not* to delegate decision-making powers was a prime consideration in many instances in which committees of jurists were preferred over employment of the Court's advisory jurisdiction.

[494] It is significant that, in No. 13, no government was represented before the Court.

[495] In light of the majority opinion in the 1966 *South West Africa* cases, it might be argued that, in the ILO cases, the compulsory jurisdiction was not only unsuitable but perhaps not really available at all. But cf. the views of Judge Jessup, ICJ Reports, 1966, p. 414.

(2) In several cases—especially the "minorities" cases—the states which had an interest in employing the available compromissory clauses lacked the right to do so, and the states which had the right lacked the interest.[496] (3) Advisory procedure to some extent removed the stigma of plaintiff and defendant from the interested states.[497] Technically, at least, the Council was requesting an opinion and the disputants were merely "informants" of the Court. (4) As an alternative to voluntary submission by compromis, the advisory procedure also had distinct advantages. Even where passions were too greatly aroused to allow for outright adjudication, recourse to the advisory function was often acceptable to the parties.[498] Furthermore, difficulties with regard to the formulation of the terms of a compromis were, to a large extent, avoided. (5) Although the Court's opinions generally came to be accepted by the interested parties very much as if they were binding judgments, the formally nonbinding nature of advisory opinions presumably made the advisory jurisdiction more palatable than the contentious in several instances.[499]

With the glaring exception of *Eastern Carelia* (and to a degree the *Customs Union* case), consultation of the Court was part of a truly problem-solving approach. The consent of the interested states was forthcoming in almost all instances;[500] and the prognosis for acceptance of the opinion and for the opinion's materially aiding in the solution of the root problem was generally favorable. In the *Eastern Carelia* case, the Council entertained few illusions that the basic problem—improving the lot of the Eastern Carelians—would in any way be affected by a Court opinion, but it proceeded, nevertheless, to address the request proposed by Finland to the Court. The considerations

[496] Thus, e.g., in the cases of *German Settlers in Poland* and *Acquisition of Polish Nationality*, Germany alone had any strong interest in suing Poland, but it lacked the power to do so. When, at a later date, Germany, as a Council member, did possess the right to sue in connection with minorities in Poland, it thrice attempted to employ the right. (See Judgment No. 12, 26 April 1928, PCIJ, Ser. A, No. 15; and Ser. A/B, Nos. 59 and 60. The last two applications were subsequently withdrawn.) See also the remarks of the British representative in the case of *Railway Traffic between Lithuania and Poland*, p. 84 above.

In the case of *Interpretation of the Statute of Memel* (PCIJ, Ser. A/B, No. 49), the Court's compulsory jurisdiction was resorted to only because Lithuania opposed the more "natural" procedure of seeking an advisory opinion. See Chapter IV.

[497] The stigma could also have been removed by the conclusion of a special agreement in place of the invocation of the Court's compulsory jurisdiction. But such voluntary submission was not always practicable. See points 4 and 5 in the text.

[498] This was true, e.g., in Nos. 8 and 21. In the former case, the parties were even able to agree in advance to accept the opinion as binding.

[499] In the *Danube Commission* case, Rumania consented to the request for an advisory opinion on the clear understanding that the opinion would be treated as purely advisory. Thus, preference for the advisory jurisdiction in that case was particularly understandable. Normally, however, the opinions were expected to (and did in fact) have a more decisive character.

[500] The exceptions were the *Eastern Carelia*, *Acquisition of Polish Nationality*, and *Mosul* cases.

which motivated this request were primarily in the realm of propaganda. The main alternative to requesting the Court's opinion was neither recourse to other legal channels nor political action; it was total inaction. Having been dealt a rebuff by the Court in the *Eastern Carelia* case, the Council apparently learned its lesson and did not again attempt to employ the advisory function primarily as a propaganda weapon.[501]

The *Customs Union* case was peculiar in that, although all the parties concerned consented to the request, the willingness of any of them to acquiesce in an adverse decision was open to serious doubt. Indeed, if the root problem was to be in any way solved or ameliorated by consultation of the Court, the benefit was expected to be derived not so much from the *product* of that consultation as from the very *act* of consultation—i.e., from the breathing spell which the Council thereby bought for itself.

In seeking the Court's opinion, the requesting organ did not generally desire or expect a *particular* ruling from the Court. Where the requests related to existing disputes between states, to have shown any preference for a particular pronouncement would, quite obviously, have meant favoring the contentions of one of the disputants over those of the other. But, even where the request was of an "organizational" nature, there was seldom any indication that a particular pronouncement was desired.[502] To the extent that such a desire did exist, it was not generally of such intensity as to expose the Court's opinion to the danger of nonacceptance by the requesting organ.

In the vast majority of League requests, the possibility that a Court opinion might "overrule" past decisions taken by the requesting organ did not loom large.[503] Nor did the question of the effect of the pending request on the interim action of states and organs generally pose a major problem.[504]

---

[501] As noted above, despite Turkish refusal to accede to the request in the *Mosul* case, involvement of the Court nevertheless had a problem-solving basis. In Opinion No. 7 (*Acquisition of Polish Nationality*), Poland's objection to the request was more procedural than substantive. It wished to have the Council consult Czechoslovakia, Rumania, and the Serb-Croat-Slovene state prior to making the actual request. LNOJ, 1923, p. 934. Poland was subsequently represented before the Court.

[502] However, in No. 13 (*ILO and the Personal Work of the Employer*), the ILO Governing Body, which decided to solicit the Court's opinion only at the urging of the employers' group and after considerable hesitation, made it clear in the resolution transmitted to the League Council that "the majority considers that the International Labour Organisation is competent in the matter to which the request refers." LNOJ, 1926, p. 596; cf. PCIJ, Ser. C, No. 12, pp. 127–36.

[503] The principal cases in which such a possibility did exist originated in international organs other than the Council itself. See, e.g., No. 10 (originating with the Greco-Turkish Mixed Commission); No. 13 (originating with the ILO); and, especially, No. 17 (originating with the Greco-Bulgarian Mixed Commission). In No. 1 (*Netherlands Workers' Delegate*), the decision to seat the delegate in question had already been taken; but this action was not intended to constitute a precedent.

[504] For a discussion of the question of interim action in connection with Nos. 11, 16, and 17, see, respectively, LNOJ, 1925, pp. 564–65; PCIJ, Ser. C, No. 15-I, pp. 134–36;

The manner in which proposals to request advisory opinions were initiated varied from case to case. Sometimes, the initiative came from states, individually or jointly;[505] at other times, the initiative came from various international bodies;[506] and, in many instances, the proposal originated with a Council Rapporteur or rapporteurial committee.[507]

The role of the Rapporteur—particularly in most of the cases in which the Council was not acting as a mere transmission belt for other international agencies or for states—was, in fact, crucial. Whether or not the suggestion to consult the Court actually originated with the Rapporteur,[508] his assessment of the appropriateness of such a consultation usually carried the most weight. Frequently, the Rapporteur's recommendation followed upon a private exploration with the interested states of the possibilities and terms of reference, and bore the endorsement of the interested states. In the Council, the recommendation generally was confirmed quickly, with little or no prior debate regarding the desirability of reference or the exact formulation of the request.[509]

In sum, the "typical" League request was sought on an avowedly "legal" question and as part of a truly problem-solving approach. The decision to consult the Court, as well as the terms of the consultation, were reached on the basis of a consensus which encompassed the most interested states; and the decision was reached without much fanfare, publicity, or serious public soul-searching.

Turning now to the UN period, one finds, at almost every point, elements of contrast.

---

and *ibid.*, No. 18-I, pp. 905 ff. See also the text of the Council resolution in connection with Opinion No. 24, LNOJ, 1931, p. 2261.

[505] E.g., in Nos. 2 and 3 (France); 4 and 20 (Britain); 5 (Finland); and 14 (France, Britain, Italy, and Rumania).

[506] The sources of proposals *within* these international bodies were, in turn, diverse. Thus, e.g., the four ILO requests originated, respectively, with members of the ILO Conference's Credentials Committee (No. 1); the employers' group in the Governing Body (No. 13); the International Labor Office (No. 18); and the British government (No. 25). The decision of the Greco-Turkish Mixed Commission to solicit the Court's opinion in No. 10 was made following a suggestion by the Council's Rapporteur.

[507] E.g., in Nos. 6, 7, 9, 11, 15, 19, 22, 24, 26, and 27.

[508] Thus, e.g., with respect to No. 15, the Rapporteur indicated that, in private conversation, the Polish representative had raised the suggestion to request an advisory opinion. LNOJ, 1927, pp. 1421–22.

[509] Difficulties in formulating the request did, however, arise in several of the cases which originated outside the League Council. Thus, in No. 1, the Netherlands government objected to the terms of the question as finally framed. In No. 16, disagreements over the terms of the question to be submitted to the Court led to the submission of a simplified text which the Court later determined did not meet the requirements of Article 72 of the Court's Rules. See PCIJ, Ser. B, No. 16, pp. 11–15. And the difficulties

Only rarely did the Assembly's competence to address the proposed request to the Court go unchallenged. The most recurrent basis for the challenge was the allegation that the question to be referred was not "legal"—or at least not "essentially" so—but was, rather, political, moral, or humanitarian.[510] Other grounds, frequently heard, related to the Assembly's supposed incompetence to request an authoritative interpretation of the Charter[511] or of treaties.[512] Additionally, in the *Peace Treaties* case, the domestic jurisdiction issue was raised.

Resort to other "legal" channels of clarification did not, as a rule, precede consultation of the Court—except that, in the two opinions which originated in the Assembly's Sixth Committee (*Reparation* and *Reservations*), that Committee recommended reference to the Court after its own deliberations revealed wide and deep cleavages on the substantive issues involved. Moreover, the probable alternative to recourse to the Court was not—again, with the exception of the *Reparation* and *Reservations* cases—the taking of other "legal" counsel. Nor was it the employment of the Court in its contentious capacity.[513] Rather, the most likely alternative was either immediate action by a political organ[514] or—very frequently—inaction.[515] Even where an immediate "political" decision was possible and probable, the resultant deci-

---

encountered by the Greco-Bulgarian Mixed Commission (in No. 17) led to the unusual decision to submit three separate sets of questions.

[510] Expectedly, the "legal" nature of the two requests which originated in the Assembly's Sixth (Legal) Committee remained undisputed. However, in the *Reservations* case, the Assembly's competence was challenged on other grounds.

In the *Namibia* case, the competence of the Security Council to request the opinion was not challenged before that body. South Africa (which did not participate in the Council's deliberations) later argued before the Court against the rendering of the opinion and cited, among other grounds, the "political background of the question." See Chapter V.

[511] E.g., in the *Admission* and *Competence* cases.

[512] See the *Peace Treaties* and *Reservations* cases.

[513] This was due, first of all, to the absence of available compromissory clauses for this purpose, and, second, to the distinctively "organizational" stamp of most UN requests. It is noteworthy, in this connection, that Article 7 of the South West Africa Mandate was invoked only as a last resort, in order to convert the operative part of the 1950 opinion into a binding judgment. All along, the matter had been dealt with as an "organizational" issue, involving a dispute between the UN and South Africa. The Court's 1966 judgment, in effect, confirmed the "organizational," "nondispute," nature of the question. See p. 50, n. 35.

As for the compromissory clause of the Genocide Convention, it probably was not suitable for the submission of the issues presented to the Court in the *Reservations* case. The applicability of the clause was subsequently discussed by individual states and by the Court itself. See Chapter V.

[514] E.g., in the *UN Administrative Tribunal, South West Africa (Voting), South West Africa (Committee), UNESCO,* and *IMCO* cases.

[515] E.g., in the *Admission, Competence, Peace Treaties,* and *Expenses* cases. In the *Namibia* case, political action (but of an ineffective nature) was taken simultaneously with the adoption of the request.

sion would, in many instances, have been nonbinding, and its efficacy, in relation to the root problem, doubtful.

Thus, in discussing the advantages expected to be derived from consultation of the Court in the UN period, the questions to be answered differ somewhat from the corresponding questions for the League period. (1) It is still necessary—though only with reference to a select few of the cases—to account for preference for a Court consultation over an immediate binding decision by a political organ or over a decision based on nonjudicial legal counsel. (2) It is necessary—to a much greater extent—to understand why a Court opinion was requested in lieu of inaction or ineffective action. (3) It is not at all necessary to account for employment of the Court's advisory, in preference to its contentious, jurisdiction.

As for the first point, the expected advantages closely paralleled those mentioned in connection with League requests. The authoritativeness of a Court opinion was expected to enhance the possibilities of acceptance of the final decision and to smooth the relationships between, on the one hand, the requesting organ and the losing state, and, on the other hand, the losing state and its own public opinion.[516]

Where, as in the majority of cases, the alternative to recourse to the Court was either inaction or ineffective action, different considerations came into play relating, *inter alia*, to: the necessity of dispelling the doubts of important states, for the sake of securing a two-thirds majority and/or of attaining unanimity of action; the felt need to consolidate the organization's moral and legal position; the attempt to exercise pressure on recalcitrant states; the desire to *appear* to be taking some action; the willingness to give satisfaction to a particular state's plea for judicial clarification; and the hope of scoring a propaganda victory, if nothing else.[517] The authoritativeness of a Court opinion was still the desideratum, but the Court's authority was used less for problem-solving than for propaganda and supportive purposes. The Eastern Carelia "syndrome," which was, in the League period, the exception, became, in the UN era, the norm.

This "syndrome" was reflected most in the area of consent. Requests were often pushed through in the face of the outright opposition of the states without whose cooperation implementation of the resultant opinion was unthinkable—or virtually so. Thus, if the root problem prompting the requests

---

[516] These considerations were most prominent in the *UN Administrative Tribunal* case.

[517] In varying measure, these considerations were involved in the *Admission, Competence, Peace Treaties,* and *Expenses* cases, as well as in the three *South West Africa* opinions of the 1950s and in the *Namibia* case. (In this last case, however, unique considerations, related to the need to rehabilitate the Court's image in the eyes of the Third World, were probably paramount.)

in the *Admission* and *Competence* cases was the admission deadlock, the Court's opinion could, predictably, do nothing to resolve the basic difficulty. Similarly, the human rights situation in Bulgaria, Hungary, and Rumania would, quite foreseeably, remain unaffected by any Court pronouncement. And, unless the drastic sanction of Article 19 was seriously contemplated, the *Expenses* opinion could not, in any significant measure, diminish the UN's financial woes. As far as the *South West Africa* opinions of the 1950s were concerned (especially the later two), South Africa's more tolerant attitude toward the Assembly's *requesting* the Court's opinions did not, in the least, indicate a greater willingness to bow to adverse pronouncements.[518] In a real sense, consent was totally absent throughout; and this lack of consent was made explicit in the case of the Security Council's *Namibia* request. Furthermore, in the *Namibia* case, several of the permanent Council members were unprepared to face up to the consequences of a confrontation with South Africa, regardless of what the Court's opinion might be.

The unwillingness of the state or states concerned to accept an unfavorable "verdict" was matched in many instances by a corresponding attitude on the part of the requesting organ. Employment of the Court's advisory function for propaganda and supportive purposes (as opposed to problem-solving and law-clarifying purposes) went hand in hand with the desire for a *particular* pronouncement and with the expectation that such a pronouncement would, indeed, be forthcoming. At times the wishes of the political organ in this regard were stated, or hinted at, in the resolution embodying the request.[519] On many occasions, equivocation over whether to consult the Court and wrangling over the formulation of the request were but reflections of the fear that the Court might render a "wrong" pronouncement, thereby hindering the political organ in the pursuit of its goals. As insurance against such judicial hindrance, the Assembly often demonstrated, in advance, a determination to pursue its designs by political means in the event the Court failed to give the hoped-for satisfaction.[520] (A similar determination on the part of the Security Council in the *Namibia* case was even more obvious.) Moreover, the interim action adopted pending receipt of the Court's opinion (especially with respect to the South West Africa issue) was not always consistent with a

[518] On the other hand, the willingness of the United States to acquiesce in recourse to the Court in the *UN Administrative Tribunal* case probably did reflect a corresponding readiness to accept an adverse verdict.

[519] See, e.g., the preamble of GA Resolution 258 (III) in the *Reparation* case; the second operative paragraph of GA Resolution 294 (IV) in the *Peace Treaties* case; the reiteration in GA Resolution 338 (IV) of previous resolutions calling on South Africa to place South West Africa under the trusteeship system; and the preamble of SC Resolution 284 (1970) in the *Namibia* case.

[520] See, e.g., the pre-request discussions in the *South West Africa (Status)* case, pp. 113–17 above.

true state of doubt regarding the legal questions involved or with a sincere desire for judicial clarification. Rather, the Assembly frequently (and the Council, in the *Namibia* case) appeared more intent on reasserting its own views than on learning what the Court's views were.

The desire for a *particular* pronouncement was heightened in those cases in which the legality of action already taken by the political organ was at issue. While, theoretically, the Court was merely a coordinate, and not a superior, organ, the Court's acknowledged superiority in legal questions meant that *some* risk of reversal of political decisions was inevitably entailed.[521] Much of the debate in connection with the *Expenses* case, the *South West Africa* opinions (especially *South West Africa [Voting]*[522]), and the *Namibia* request demonstrated the peculiar sensitivity of the UN political organs to anything which might imply that they were casting doubt on the legality of resolutions already adopted.[523]

The method by which proposals to consult the Court were initiated, formulated, and adopted contrasted strikingly with that which prevailed in the League period; and the new method was far less conducive to a problem-solving approach. The initiative in almost all cases came from individual states. Most often, the proposal was introduced during the course of protracted discussion of the substantive issue involved; and, invariably, the proposal generated a lengthy debate over the desirability of reference and formulation of the request. Competing draft resolutions were common. The view expressed by the Brazilian representative (in the discussions of the South West Africa issue) that "every question contained within itself its own reply" was universally shared by UN members. And since, as noted, so much emphasis was placed on securing the "correct" reply, the process of private and public bargaining which preceded the final formulation of requests is hardly surprising.[524]

---

[521] A similar risk was taken by the IMCO Assembly in the *IMCO* case. While that body evinced less sensitivity than the UN General Assembly and Security Council in this matter, a certain amount of reservation was reflected in the debates over formulation of the request.

[522] See, especially, the remarks of the Israeli representative, p. 134 above.

[523] This sensitivity was in even greater evidence in connection with "stillborn" requests in the UN period. See Chapter IV.

[524] Resolution 684 (VII), which sought to assure more professional drafting of requests, was never employed—though frequently invoked. See Chapter V.

The specialized agencies attempted more professional drafting. The *UNESCO* request was drafted by that organization's Secretariat following the Executive Council's approval of the reference in principle. At a subsequent meeting, the Council approved the final request. UNESCO, 42 EX/SR.14 and 25, 18 and 25 November 1955. In the *IMCO* case, a similar procedure was attempted. Approval of the reference in principle was to be followed by professional drafting—in this case, by the IMCO Assembly's Legal Committee. However, as noted above, the Committee failed to produce an agreed text; the final text was introduced and adopted in Plenary.

In sum, although the UN requests—far more than their League counterparts—represented a "mixed bag of goods," the over-all picture one gets is one which is dominated by the following features: frequent challenges to the "legal" nature of the request; the decisiveness of considerations unrelated to true problem-solving in prompting the request; adoption of the request in the face of the opposition of crucial states; the desire for, and expectation of, a particular Court pronouncement; and considerable debate, fretting, and equivocation over the desirability and terms of reference and over the effect of the request on past and interim political decisions.

One feature common to the League and UN eras was the expectation in most instances—despite some arguments to the contrary in pre-request discussions—that a certain crystallization, and perhaps even ossification, of the legal issues would result from a Court pronouncement and that the subsequent freedom of the requesting organ might be correspondingly restricted. As opposed to either consultation of other law-clarifying agencies or, *a fortiori*, direct political action, recourse to the Court's advisory function entailed a certain measure of delegation of decision-making powers to another body. And, unless this was desired, reluctance to solicit the Court's advice could be expected. It did not matter, in this respect, whether the request involved a UN-type "organizational" issue or a League-type "dispute" case. In either event, given the absence of a dual procedure for requests, the Court's opinion would partake of some authoritativeness and definitiveness.

The greater reluctance of the UN to refer matters to the Court—a reluctance reflected in the use, almost as much as in the nonuse, of the Court's advisory function—was directly related to the jealousy of UN organs with respect to their own decision-making powers. Even where the issue was avowedly "legal," as in the *Reparation* or the *Reservations* case, this jealousy was in evidence.[525] The desire to retain absolute freedom of movement grew proportionately to the "political" importance of the issue.

The equivalence which was established in both periods between requesting an advisory opinion and relinquishing, to some degree, powers of decision is pointed up with even greater clarity when one examines the many "stillborn" requests in the two eras.

[525] The debates in those cases over whether to have recourse to the ICJ or to the ILC related, to a great extent, to the desire to maintain freedom of decision. The desire to maintain such freedom was in turn related to a feared insufficiency in the law on the subjects involved.

IV

"STILLBORN" REQUESTS

No less instructive than the study of the requests actually addressed to the Court is the study of the many "stillborn" requests—suggestions and proposals that never materialized into actual requests—which punctuated the League and UN eras (particularly the latter). By focusing on the situations in which recourse to the Court's advisory function was deliberately excluded as inappropriate, it is possible to gain greater insight into the *limits* which the political organs of the two world organizations placed on their use of the advisory function.[1] It is also possible, in this manner, to discover important clues as to why the advisory function was not used differently, in extent or purpose.

The need to study the "nonuse" of the Court's advisory function is particularly obvious in the case of the UN. As even a cursory examination will reveal, the instances of "nonuse," at least in the early UN period, were significant numerically.[2] But, more important, a large proportion of the proposals and suggestions involved in that "nonuse" related to interstate disputes—the very category which had dominated League requests and which, it was fully anticipated at San Francisco, would dominate UN requests as well. Moreover, many of these same proposals and suggestions originated in the

[1] This study is limited to those "stillborn" requests which "died" in the fora of the Council or Assembly of the League, on the one hand, or of the UN General Assembly or Security Council, on the other. No attempt is made to deal with requests which may have been contemplated by any other organs or specialized agencies. (Three such instances are briefly noted on p. 221, n. 218.) For a discussion of the "nonuse" of the Court by organs and agencies authorized under the terms of Article 96(2) to request opinions, see Rosenne, *Law and Practice*, 2: 670–71, 678–80, and 688, n. 2; C. Wilfred Jenks, *The Prospects of International Adjudication* (Dobbs Ferry, N.Y.: Oceana, and London: Stevens, 1964), pp. 195, 205–6; and Herbert C. Merillat, ed., *Legal Advisors and International Organizations* (Dobbs Ferry, N.Y.: Oceana, 1966), pp. 10–11.

[2] See the general survey on pp. 221–32 below.

Security Council, an organ from which, until July 1970, no actual request emanated.

As for the League, the number of "stillborn" requests was smaller, but not necessarily less important. In its nonuse, as in its use, of the Court's advisory function, the League affords interesting contrasts with the UN.

A survey of the instances in which consultation of the Court was contemplated (with more or less seriousness) indicates in itself something of the frequency and kinds of suggestions put forward in both periods. But a fuller understanding of the considerations militating against employment of the advisory function requires closer attention to the more important cases of "nonuse"—namely, those in which formal proposals were put forward or with respect to which a more than perfunctory debate over recourse to the Court ensued. These cases will be examined in terms of: the contexts in which the proposals or suggestions were made; the ostensible motivation of the initiators of the proposals; the arguments put forward by proponents and opponents of recourse to the Court; and, where appropriate, the alternative courses of action pursued and the possible effect of the proposed reference on the particular problems involved.

THE LEAGUE PERIOD: A GENERAL SURVEY[3]

In connection with the cases outlined below, proposals or suggestions were put forward before either the League Council or the League Assembly[4]—more frequently the former—contemplating recourse to the Court's advisory function.[5]

[3]The following survey does not pretend to be exhaustive and, as noted above, does not deal with requests contemplated by organs other than the League Council or Assembly.

[4]In connection with the Polish-Lithuanian dispute (discussed in more detail on pp. 197–201), Lithuania presented its proposal before both organs, consecutively.

[5]In addition to the cases surveyed below, three instances in which passing references to the possibility of requesting advisory opinions were made might be noted.

1. In 1923, during Assembly consideration of an interpretative resolution regarding Article 10 of the Covenant, the Persian representative suggested that the proposed interpretation be referred to the Court for an advisory opinion. This suggestion was not, however, embodied in a formal proposal. LN, Records of the 4th Ass., Plenary, 1923, p. 81.

2. A committee of the Council which in 1935 dealt with the later petitions of the Prince of Pless conceded that under ordinary circumstances the committee would have considered referring certain aspects of the question to the Court for an advisory opinion. But, in the light of Germany's withdrawal of an application for judgment in the case, referral of the matter to the Court—even in its advisory capacity—would now be difficult. LNOJ, 1935, p. 149.

3. A vague suggestion that the Court be asked for an advisory opinion was made by M. Litvinoff of the Soviet Union in 1935, in connection with sanctions against Italy. (Recourse to the Court was mentioned as a possible way of establishing the doctrine that

1. At various times during the Council's treatment of the Hungarian optants dispute between Rumania and Hungary, the possibility of requesting an advisory opinion from the Court was debated.[6] The first such occasion was in April 1923, when the Council's Rapporteur recommended that an advisory opinion be requested in lieu of direct referral to the PCIJ by the parties. Subsequent suggestions—in 1923 and, at a later stage of the dispute, in 1927 and 1928—emanated from Hungary. Rumania, however, steadfastly refused to consider any form of Court involvement, and, as a result, the Council never acceded to Hungary's desires in this respect.

2. Lithuania's dissatisfaction with the Council's 1923 recommendations concerning the Vilna Territory led her to seek an advisory opinion with a view to having the legality and force of the disputed recommendations judicially tested. The Lithuanian proposal was formulated in generalized terms and would have required the interpretation of Covenant provisions in the abstract. After the proposal was rejected by the Council (in April 1923), it was laid before the Assembly, where it engendered a debate over the Assembly's competence to consider it. Ultimately, the proposal was withdrawn.

3. In September 1923, in the aftermath of the Corfu incident, the Council desired clarification of certain abstract questions relative to Covenant interpretation and to general international law. It was proposed that these questions be referred to the Court for its opinion, but, mainly in deference to Italian objections, the questions were submitted to a specially constituted committee of jurists instead.

4. Early in 1926, Greece proposed that the Council seek an advisory opinion on the question of the Maritza River. The task of delimiting the Thracian frontier had been entrusted by the Treaty of Lausanne to a mixed commission empowered to take binding decisions by majority vote. But, in the question of the Maritza, sharp Greco-Turkish differences arose. These differences involved conflicting interpretations of the relevant treaty provisions and divergent views as to the importance of a map appended to the treaty.[7] Initially, Greece sought joint reference of the dispute to the Permanent Court for judgment. However, when the Greek overture was spurned by

---

nonexecution of contracts as a result of the enforcement of sanctions was to be regarded as the result of force majeure.) *Ibid.*, Spec. Supp. No. 145 (1935), p. 106. This suggestion is of historical note, in view of the general Soviet hostility to employment of the Court.

[6] For a more detailed consideration of this case, as well as of cases 2, 3, 5, and 6 in this survey, see pp. 184–221 below.

[7] Greece cited the map as evidence that the Commission's competence was confined to delimitation of the eastern branch of the Maritza. Turkey, discounting the importance of the map, considered that according to the treaty texts it was for the Commission to discover (on the basis of topographical and hydrographical studies) which of the two branches was the principal branch, the median line of which would constitute the Greco-Turkish frontier. Each state cited the *travaux préparatoires* in favor of its viewpoint. LNOJ, 1926, pp. 511–16.

Turkey, Greece turned to the Council, asking that it request the Court "*to take a decision in the form of an advisory opinion* to be given to the Council."[8] The Court would have been asked to interpret the disputed provisions, to determine the authoritativeness of the annexed map, and thereby to define the sphere of the Delimitation Commission's competence. The Greek request for judicial clarification had the blessings of the Commission's chairman.[9]

For its part, Turkey disputed the right of the Council to deal with a question which had by treaty been placed in the hands of another body fully competent to take binding decisions. The "normal execution of a contractual clause consented to by both parties" could not be cause for invoking Article 11 of the Covenant;[10] and since the Council could not *deal* with the question, neither could it request an advisory opinion on it.

The preliminary question raised by Turkey was referred to a committee of jurists, and the latter upheld Turkey's contentions.[11] In turn, the committee's conclusions were adopted by the Council.

5. In June 1927, while the case of the cruiser *Salamis* was pending before the Greco-German Mixed Arbitral Tribunal, Greece requested from the Council an "official interpretation" of certain articles of the Treaty of Versailles connected with the case and suggested that a PCIJ advisory opinion might be useful for this purpose. A Committee of Three, appointed by the Council to consider the problem, recommended that the preliminary question of the Council's competence to accede to the Greek request be referred to the Court for an advisory opinion. However, this proposal encountered strong opposition on the part of several Council members who desired the Council to declare itself incompetent and who entertained misgivings regarding judicial determination of the Council's competence. As a result, consultation of a committee of jurists was substituted for the proposed recourse to the Court.

6. The nature of the vote required for requesting opinions was never officially resolved by the League, but proposals to have the Court itself consulted on the issue were put forward in the Assembly on two separate occasions—in 1928 and in 1935. (Earlier, at the 1926 Conference of Signa-

---

[8] *Ibid.*, pp. 511–13, 590; italics added.

[9] Since the matter was "so vital for both countries," the Chairman thought it would be "more agreeable and easier for the Commission if it felt sure that it might work in accordance with the spirit of the treaty as determined by the Court." Quoted in *ibid.*, p. 513.

[10] *Ibid.*, pp. 513–15, 590–91. Turkey recalled the Council's own resolution of 24 January 1924, under whose terms the Council must refuse to examine an application brought by one party only if the dispute had already been validly submitted to an arbitral or legal procedure of any kind.

[11] *Ibid.*, pp. 529–30. The Council might be seized with the matter under Article 11(2) of the Covenant only in the event that the Commission exhausted all the available sources without being able to reach a decision, or if the Commission flagrantly exceeded its powers.

tories, a similar proposal had been presented, in connection with the fifth United States Senate reservation.) In the face of opposition to judicial determination of the matter, the 1928 and 1935 proposals were amended to provide instead for Council study of the problem.

7. Although the Council never consulted the Court in connection with any aspect of the mandates system,[12] on at least one occasion a recommendation envisaging a Court opinion was put forward by the Permanent Mandates Commission and not acted on by the Council. Interestingly enough, the proposal related to South West Africa. At issue was the compatibility of a Union Nationality Act (insofar as it applied to South West Africa) with the principles of the mandate.[13] After a long discussion, the Mandates Commission resolved that, "having regard to the complexity of the problem in its legal aspect and its political importance . . . it was desirable to call the Council's attention to the fact that this question appeared to be one which might merit reference to the Permanent Court of International Justice."[14] The Council, however, did not favor this recommendation. When the Council's Rapporteur drew that body's attention to the above passage in the Commission's report, several objections to requesting the Court's opinion were raised by the German representative,[15] and these were concurred in by the Rapporteur and the Council.[16]

8. On two separate occasions, when alleged Lithuanian infractions of the Memel Convention were before the Council, the respective Council Rapporteurs suggested recourse to the Court's advisory procedure, but abandoned their suggestions in the face of Lithuanian opposition. In the second instance, curiously, contentious proceedings (instituted under the compromissory clause of the Memel Convention) were substituted.

The first suggestion, presented in January 1931, related to certain charges brought to the Council's attention by the German government in a letter of 20 September 1930.[17] Subsequent Lithuanian-German negotiations failed to

----

[12] In contrast, four advisory opinions in the UN period related to the South West Africa mandate. For an account of two potential requests related to the Palestine mandate, see Shabtai Rosenne, "The International Court at Fifty," *Israel Law Review*, 7 (1972): 176–77. One of these would-be requests involved the issue of the 1939 White Paper limiting Jewish immigration to Palestine.

[13] In accordance with the Nationality Act, all inhabitants of South West Africa who were British subjects would automatically become Union nationals unless they left the territory. See LN, PMC, Minutes, 16 Sess., 1929, pp. 128–31.

[14] *Ibid.*, pp. 202–3; see also pp. 128–31, 155.

[15] It was contended that the question had to be viewed not only in its purely legal aspect but also in its political and practical aspects; that the question affected the basis of the entire mandate system; and that the problem, as a whole, was not yet sufficiently clear to enable the Council to adopt a "purely judicial procedure." LNOJ, 1930, p. 73.

[16] *Ibid.*, pp. 73–74.

[17] *Ibid.*, pp. 1618–39. Lithuania objected to the inclusion of the item in the agenda and alluded to the possibility of requesting an advisory opinion on that point. *Ibid.*

resolve all the differences. In his report to the Council on 19 January 1931, the Rapporteur clearly indicated his belief that a PCIJ advisory opinion was the most appropriate means of settling two of the questions still outstanding, and he regretted Lithuania's refusal to consent to such a procedure.[18] One of the reasons offered by Lithuania for its refusal was rather significant. It feared that its consent would be tantamount to "indirectly recognising Germany's right to bring before the Court a dispute relating to the . . . [Memel] Convention."[19] In any event, no attempt was made to override the Lithuanian "veto," and, instead, direct negotiations between the Principal Allied Powers and Lithuania were undertaken.[20]

In February 1932, Germany presented further complaints against Lithuanian actions in Memel. Specifically, it was alleged that the removal and arrest of the President of the Memel Directorate was an infringement of the Memel Statute.[21] After careful study of the matter with the help of jurists, the Council Rapporteur concluded that judicial scrutiny of the complex questions of law and fact involved was advisable, and that the most logical route to the Court was a Council request for an advisory opinion. However, since Lithuania objected to such a request, and since an alternative route to the Court—the contentious route—was available in this case, the Rapporteur refrained from recommending that the Council request an opinion on the basis of a mere majority vote. Instead, he urged the Principal Allied Powers to bring the matter before the Court in contentious proceedings.[22] Lithuania, for its part, favored contentious proceedings over advisory proceedings in this case.[23] This reversal of a state's normal scale of preferences might, at first glance, appear strange, but it is explicable by reference to Lithuania's desire— alluded to in 1931—to exclude Germany, at all costs, as a "quasi plaintiff" in the case.[24]

Contentious proceedings (relating also to Lithuanian actions subsequent to the Council meeting) were subsequently instituted by application of the four Principal Allied Powers on 11 April 1932.[25]

---

p. 1516. Later, however, it reluctantly acquiesced in a committee of jurists' report upholding the Council's competence to consider the matter. *Ibid.*, pp. 1523–24.

[18] *Ibid.*, 1931, pp. 232, 236–37.

[19] *Ibid.*, p. 235. The right to invoke the compromissory clause was limited to the Principal Allied Powers who were members of the Council.

[20] *Ibid.*, pp. 1131–32.

[21] *Ibid.*, 1932, pp. 529–40.

[22] *Ibid.*, pp. 540–41.

[23] *Ibid.*, p. 546.

[24] There is little doubt that, in any advisory proceedings in the case, Lithuania and Germany would have appeared as the two "parties."

[25] In the Council, the British representative regretted Lithuania's refusal to consent to requesting an advisory opinion, "the natural method of obtaining an answer" to the legal questions involved. *Ibid.* Cf. the views of Judge Anzilotti in *Interpretation of the Statute*

9. On 30 July 1931, the Finnish government laid before the Council its dispute with Great Britain arising out of the latter's requisitioning of Finnish merchant vessels during the war. The Finnish action followed persistent British refusal to submit the dispute to arbitration.[26] Only the preliminary issue whether the Council should entertain the Finnish request ever engaged the Council's attention, and, in respect to this issue, the possibility of requesting an advisory opinion from the Court was twice raised.

When the matter was first discussed by the Council, in September 1931, Lord Cecil, the British representative, demurred on two grounds to Council consideration of the matter: (1) the "private law" nature of the dispute and (2) the failure of the Finnish shipowners to exhaust local remedies. While conceding the Council's competence to discuss the matter, he questioned the desirability of such a discussion.[27] A committee of three, appointed to study the question whether the Council should deal with the dispute, concluded that the Council was competent, by virtue of Article 11(2) of the Covenant, to take steps with a view to conciliation, but that it was expedient to first resolve two questions relating to the exhaustion of local remedies. It recommended that the parties themselves seek a solution to the two questions, after which, "if any point relating to these . . . questions still remains unsettled, the Council might ask the Permanent Court . . . for an advisory opinion."[28] To this last allusion, Lord Cecil vigorously protested, on the grounds that requesting the Court's opinion would be equivalent to achieving arbitration of an important aspect of the dispute "by a somewhat circuitous method."[29] In any case, the contemplated eventuality never arose, since both parties agreed, in May 1932, to submit the preliminary questions regarding exhaustion of local remedies to arbitration.[30]

The issue of local remedies was settled by the arbitrator in Finland's favor. Subsequent negotiations proved fruitless, however, and, in 1934, Finland

---

of the Memel Territory (Merits), Judgment of 11 August 1932, PCIJ, Ser. A/B, No. 49, pp. 349–50, to the effect that the applicant states were, in fact, requesting an "advisory opinion" (since they were asking questions rather than presenting claims), and that the Court, therefore, was not entitled to answer. In truth, the case bore many similarities to an advisory opinion. Thus, as the Court pointed out, several questions were formulated "purely *in abstracto*, without any reference to the facts of the dispute." *Ibid.*, p. 311. Furthermore, as noted by the Court, the intention of the four Allied Powers "was only to obtain an interpretation of the Statute which would serve as a guide for the future." *Ibid.*, p. 337.

[26]LNOJ, 1931, pp. 2201–8. The British government was not bound to have the matter adjudicated in any way. Past disputes had been excluded from Britain's acceptance of the Optional Clause.

[27]*Ibid.*, pp. 2077–81.

[28]*Ibid.*, 1932, pp. 506–7.

[29]*Ibid.*, pp. 507–8. The Rapporteur denied that a request for an advisory opinion was tantamount to arbitration. *Ibid.*, p. 509.

[30]*Ibid.*, p. 1197.

again placed its dispute with Britain before the Council. Again the Council was in a quandary as to whether it should accede to the Finnish request. This time, Britain's objections initially appeared to be directed against the Council's competence.[31] Proceeding on this understanding, the Rapporteur proposed that the Court be asked to clarify the issue of the Council's competence.[32] However, during the course of the Council's discussion of this proposal on 19 January 1935, it became evident that at the core of the difference lay questions of *expediency* rather than of competence. These, it was generally acknowledged, the Council had to determine on the basis of its own discretion, an advisory opinion being both inappropriate and irrelevant.[33] The Rapporteur therefore agreed to withdraw his proposal.[34] At a subsequent meeting, the British representative reluctantly agreed to have the preliminary question of whether the Council should deal with the matter submitted to a committee of three.[35] On the basis of that committee's report,[36] the Council decided, on 13 September 1935, not to proceed to a consideration of the substance of the Finno-British dispute.[37]

10. In the course of Council consideration of the petition of the Szeklers in Rumania,[38] a preliminary question regarding the receivability of the petition on the grounds of failure to exhaust local judicial remedies was raised by Rumania. The Rapporteur expressed the view that it would "have seemed proper, in principle, to ask the Permanent Court of International Justice for an advisory opinion."[39] This view was strongly concurred in by several representatives.[40] Nevertheless, practical considerations, especially the need for a

[31] *Ibid.*, 1934, pp. 1451–53.

[32] *Ibid.*, 1935, pp. 163–64. The Court would have been asked whether the Finnish application fell under the terms of Article 11(2) of the Covenant.

[33] See the remarks of Mr. Eden, *ibid.*, p. 169; and of the representatives of Chile, France, Portugal, and Italy, *ibid.*, pp. 172–74.

It was also objected that Article 11 was too "political" an article for judicial interpretation, since, by its very terms, it left the Council certain "discretionary powers."

[34] *Ibid.*, pp. 175–76. He confessed to having had qualms about asking the Court's opinion on the Council's competence.

[35] *Ibid.*, p. 181. In accepting the suggestion, Mr. Eden emphasized that the committee's "advisory opinion" would be merely "advisory."

[36] *Ibid.*, pp. 1160–61. The committee considered that, while the Council was competent to deal with the Finnish application, it was undesirable for it to do so, since the Council was confined to conciliation, and since such conciliation would, in this instance, be obviously inadequate.

[37] *Ibid.*, p. 1168.

[38] The petitioners, descendants of the former Szekler (Hungarian) Frontier Guard Regiment, alleged that property belonging to their community had been expropriated by Rumania without compensation; and that such action constituted discriminatory treatment in violation of the Rumanian Minorities Treaty. See *ibid.*, 1932, pp. 665 ff.

[39] *Ibid.*, p. 493.

[40] See the remarks of M. Colban (Norway) and Lord Cecil (the United Kingdom), *ibid.*; and cf. the remarks of the German representative, *ibid.*, p. 1239.

speedy solution of the problem, dictated the use of a committee of jurists instead. In its report, the committee confined itself to the narrow issue of minority petitions and studiously avoided entering into the general international law question regarding the exhaustion of local remedies. The broader question, it emphasized, could be resolved only by means of an advisory opinion of the PCIJ.[41]

11. In 1934, Switzerland asked the Council to request an advisory opinion on five international law questions related to claims of Swiss nationals for reparation for damage sustained during the war.[42] As explained by M. Motta, the Swiss representative in the Council, these war victims were entitled "to obtain, from an international judicial authority . . . at least an advisory opinion on the justice of their claims." M. Motta also suggested that "the Court might possibly be prepared, not merely to define the existing law, but to mark out the main lines of development of future law." Thus, by acceding to the Swiss request, the Council would at once be contributing to the settlement of disputes and promoting the definition, development, and progress of international law.[43]

Objections were raised to this course of action and, indeed, to any form of Council consideration of the Swiss application. It was protested that, since a PCIJ advisory opinion, "owing to the procedure of the Court itself and to the respect which its opinions very properly possessed, had in effect, if not in form, nearly all the consequences of a judgment," to give effect to the Swiss request would clearly be equivalent to "circumventing the voluntary character of Article 13 and the reservations made in connection with the acceptance of the Optional Clause."[44] Moreover, the matter was not sufficiently important to warrant the Council's assumption of jurisdiction.[45]

After studying the Swiss request, the Council's Rapporteur concluded that the Court should not be consulted on this occasion, since the Court would be required "to mark out the main lines of development of future law," and that was a legislative, rather than a judicial, task.[46] The Rapporteur's conclusions

---

[41] *Ibid.*, pp. 1421–24. The committee reached a negative decision regarding the Rumanian objection. For its part, the Council decided to pursue a "practical" solution of the problem and did not deem it necessary to adopt the committee's conclusions. *Ibid.*, pp. 1238–40, 1738–45.

[42] *Ibid.*, 1934, pp. 1478–1510. The claims were against Germany, France, Italy, and the United Kingdom. Such compensation as had been paid was, in the Swiss view, inadequate.

[43] *Ibid.*, pp. 1437–38.

[44] *Ibid.*, p. 1439. Cf. the statement of M. Barthou that "it was useless to try and make a somewhat tenuous distinction between a legal opinion of the Permanent Court and an arbitral award." *Ibid.*, p. 1448. M. Motta had emphasized the nonbinding nature of advisory opinions. *Ibid.*, p. 1447.

[45] *Ibid.*, pp. 1439–46 *passim*.

[46] *Ibid.*, 1935, pp. 127–28. He also thought that the claims against each of the four

were endorsed.[47] Subsequently, the Swiss application was withdrawn from the agenda.[48]

12. A joint five-power draft resolution, introduced at the 1934 special Assembly session, would have had the Assembly request an advisory opinion on the territorial dispute involved in the Chaco conflict.[49] The forwarding of the request to the Court was to be contingent upon the refusal of either disputant to accept (by a certain date) the substantive recommendations adopted by the Assembly under Article 15 of the Covenant.[50] The sponsors reasoned that, if "one of the parties adopts an attitude precluding the legal examination of the dispute, it will still be desirable and essential for the Members of the League ... to form an opinion as to which of the States ... entered the territory of the other, thus violating Article 10 of the Covenant." Since the problem was "of the greatest importance to the League itself, it would seem natural for the Assembly to apply to the ... Court ... for an advisory opinion."[51]

The Assembly did not, in fact, adopt this "conditional request" for an advisory opinion. Instead, on 24 November 1934 it accepted a substitute proposal, inspired by the General Committee, under the terms of which the Assembly, in effect, "delegated" to the Advisory Committee set up to follow the dispute the power to request an opinion in the event the Committee deemed such a request "justifiable and opportune."[52] No such request was ever made.

13. During the Council's consideration of the Iraqi-Iranian frontier dispute, Mr. Eden, the British representative, suggested that, since at the core of the dispute lay "an irreconcilable difference of opinion on what is funda-

---

states had to be considered separately and could not be subsumed under the same general legal rule.

M. Motta conceded that no advisory opinion could be requested on a question of future law or even on a question of equity, but he now denied that either of these was involved in the Swiss request.

[47] Ibid., p. 189.

[48] The question of whether or not the Council could deal with the question of the Swiss claims was submitted to the same committee of three to which the question of the Finnish claims was referred. The committee's conclusions were similar in both cases. Ibid., pp. 621, 625–26.

[49] Ibid., Spec. Supp. No. 132 (1934), p. 26. The draft was sponsored by Denmark, Norway, Spain, Sweden, and Switzerland.

[50] Acceptance of the report would have led to arbitration of the territorial dispute.

[51] LNOJ, Spec. Supp. No. 132 (1934), p. 26.

[52] Ibid., pp. 32, 51. The Secretary-General was authorized to submit the Committee's request to the Court "on behalf of the Assembly." Both "the terms of the question and the date of the request" were left to the Committee's determination. For the view that this Assembly action constituted an ultra vires delegation of power, see Manley O. Hudson, "Two Problems of Approach to the Permanent Court of International Justice," AJIL, 29 (1935): 636–43.

mentally a purely legal issue" (namely, the validity of certain documents forming the basis of the then-existing frontier), the most appropriate course was to request an advisory opinion on the matter.[53] The Iraqi representative was prepared to agree to this suggestion, but the Iranian representative considered such a course premature and also pointed to the exclusion of "disputes relating to the territorial status" of Iran from his government's acceptance of the Optional Clause.[54]

The issue was subsequently withdrawn from the agenda by Iraq, in view of pending negotiations between the parties.

14. When the German government repudiated the Locarno Treaty, it justified its actions by reference to the Franco-Soviet pact. In March 1936, during Council consideration of the German actions, several governments invited Germany to lay its claim before the PCIJ in contentious proceedings.[55] The representative of Chile suggested that the matter might be submitted for an advisory opinion.[56] Neither of these suggestions was acted upon, and on 19 March 1936 the Council itself determined unanimously (with Chile abstaining) that Germany had, in fact, violated the Locarno Treaty.[57]

15. The withdrawal of several Latin American states from the League gave rise to certain legal and financial difficulties. In 1937, the Assembly's First Committee briefly considered the possibility of soliciting the Court's advice on the legal questions involved. In particular, the Court would have been requested to interpret Article 1(3) of the Covenant in relation to states which, at the time of their resignation, were still in default on their payments to the League.[58] However, several considerations prompted the Committee members to refrain from actually recommending recourse to the Court.

---

[53] LNOJ, 1935, p. 123.

[54] Ibid., pp. 190–91.

[55] Ibid., 1936, pp. 313, 349.

[56] Ibid., p. 324.

[57] Ibid., p. 340.

[58] Article 1(3) makes a state's withdrawal conditional upon its having previously fulfilled all of its obligations under the Covenant. Could, then, a defaulting state, such as Paraguay, withdraw, or must it remain a member? This question was among several referred by the Fourth Committee to the First Committee for its consideration. LN, Records of the 18th Ass., 1st Ctte., 1937, p. 31. The Swedish representative suggested that the questions might be clarified by means of a PCIJ advisory opinion. Ibid., p. 32. However, a subcommittee appointed to study the questions thought this course was unnecessary, and proceeded to give its own answers to the substantive questions involved. These, on the whole, met with Committee approval. But the subcommittee's conclusion that Paraguay was no longer a member (though it remained obligated to pay its debt) displeased Bolivia, which, because of the Chaco conflict, was anxious to keep Paraguay bound by Covenant obligations. Ibid., p. 38. In view of the Bolivian stand, the Venezuelan representative renewed the earlier Swedish suggestion for requesting an advisory opinion. Ibid., p. 40.

Among these considerations were: uncertainty regarding the Court's competence to interpret Covenant provisions; persisting doubts as to the nature of the vote required for requests, coupled with the belief that, in this case, unanimity would be unattainable; and the conviction that a practical, rather than a legal, solution was called for.[59]

A compromise formula, whereby *no* answer would be given regarding the most controversial question, was suggested by the First Committee's chairman and concurred in by the Committee.[60]

In two instances, the Council's attempts to implement advisory opinions already rendered gave rise to suggestions envisaging further consultation of the Court.

1. Following the Council's adoption of the advisory opinion in the *Acquisition of Polish Nationality* case, German-Polish negotiations were entered into, under the presidency of the Council's Rapporteur. But in the course of these negotiations new difficulties in interpretation of the provisions of the Polish Minorities Treaty arose. Finding each of the disputants firmly convinced of the correctness of its view and strongly resistant to compromise solutions, the Rapporteur entertained the thought of recommending a further request for an advisory opinion. The German delegation greeted this possibility with approval and offered to accept, in advance, any Court opinion. However, the Polish delegation opposed, on the grounds that further delay would be involved and that a negotiated solution was preferable.[61] The Rapporteur agreed that negotiations might be continued, though he saw little prospect of agreement in the absence of prior judicial settlement of the chief legal points of difference.[62]

The matters in dispute were eventually settled by a Polish-German convention.[63]

2. Practical application of the Court's advisory opinion in the *Polish Postal Service in Danzig* case depended (as the Court itself recognized) on the delimitation of the port of Danzig for the purposes of postal service. In June

[59] See the remarks of MM. Hambro and Politis, *ibid.*, pp. 40–41.

[60] The question of Paraguay's loss of membership was left open, but the Assembly was to remain free to make any purely financial arrangement with Paraguay that it deemed appropriate. *Ibid.*, p. 41.

[61] *Ibid.*, 1924, pp. 723–25. The fact that Poland had in both previous advisory opinions fared rather badly may have had some influence on the Polish attitude.

[62] *Ibid.*, p. 725. The argument regarding delay was apparently decisive. *Ibid.*, p. 543. The Council's proposal called for the continuation of negotiations under the auspices of a third party, who would act initially as mediator and subsequently, if necessary, as arbitrator.

[63] *Ibid.*, p. 1309; LNTS, 32: 331 ff.

1925, this task was given over to a committee of experts.[64] Neither party objected to this procedure at the time, but, when in September 1925 the committee's delimitation was placed before the Council for its acceptance, Danzig demurred. Displeased with what it viewed as too broad a delimitation, and professing to find a contradiction between the committee's opinion and the Court's guidelines, Danzig now recommended that the Court itself be asked to delimit the port, by means of either an advisory opinion or, preferably, a judgment.[65] The Council refused to entertain this proposal because it considered it both ill-timed[66] and purposeless.[67] Rather, it proceeded to endorse the committee's determination.

THE LEAGUE PERIOD: CASE STUDIES

Quite obviously, not all the proposals and suggestions surveyed above were put forward with equal seriousness. Both the intensity of interest in obtaining the Court's opinion and the extent to which such interest was shared by more than the state or states initiating the proposal varied considerably. So, too, did the amount of debate surrounding each proposal. The five cases treated below would appear, in one or more of the above respects, to merit more particular and detailed attention.

The Hungarian Optants

During the course of the Council's handling of this complex and protracted Hungaro-Rumanian dispute[68] (it was placed on the Council's agenda in April 1923 and not withdrawn until May 1930) the possibility of requesting an advisory opinion of the PCIJ was debated several times. Hungary's desire for an advisory opinion was but part of an over-all campaign to see the matter settled by a third party on the basis of existing international law (which Hungary assumed would be on its side). By the same token, Rumania's refusal to agree to a Court opinion must be seen in the context of

---

[64] LNOJ, 1925, p. 1887.

[65] *Ibid.*, pp. 1374–75.

[66] As noted by the Polish representative, the proper time for such a recommendation would have been *prior* to reference of the issue to the experts' committee. *Ibid.*, pp. 1375–76.

[67] *Ibid.*, pp. 1376–77.

[68] For a detailed account of the dispute from 1923 to 1927, see Mrs. Edgar Dugdale, *The Hungaro-Rumanian Dispute: the Optants' Case before the League* (London: Association for International Understanding, 1928); and Francis Deák, *The Hungarian-Rumanian Land Dispute* (New York: Columbia University Press, 1928). For an account of developments between 1927 and 1929, see Muriel Currey, *The Hungaro-Rumanian Dispute: the Optants' Case before the League, Part II* (London: Information Service on International Affairs, 1929).

that state's unwillingness to have its "vital interests" exposed to a possible adverse decision.

At the root of the dispute was the Rumanian agrarian reform legislation of 1921, in accordance with which all landed estates belonging to absentee landlords (of whatever nationality, including Rumanian) might be expropriated and redistributed to peasants.[69] Hungary claimed that these measures, as applied to the land of Hungarian optants, violated the provision of the Treaty of Trianon[70] which allowed inhabitants of newly acquired Rumanian territory to opt for Hungarian nationality while retaining their immovable property in Rumania. For its part, Rumania insisted that there was no incompatibility between the agrarian measures and the treaty: those measures were of *general* applicability, and Hungary was entitled only to equality of rights, not to privilege.

After the failure of direct negotiations, Hungary requested that the League Council deal with the matter under Article 11(2) of the Covenant.[71] This the Council proceeded to do in April, and again in July, of 1923. After hearing the explanations of both parties on 20 April 1923, M. Adatci, the Council Rapporteur, determined that "the essential point at issue was the interpretation of the Treaties."[72] Accordingly, he recommended that the dispute be referred to the PCIJ by the parties themselves, and that a compromis be concluded on the basis of a preliminary draft which he had already prepared, in anticipation.[73] This suggestion was heartily endorsed by the Hungarian representative. Clearly, he said, the matter was purely legal and thus eminently suitable for judicial determination. Should Rumania refuse to agree to such adjudication, this would be "a striking admission in the eyes of the whole world that Roumania fears justice and the light of truth."[74] In Rumanian eyes, however, the matter was far from being purely "legal"; it involved the "vital interests" of the Rumanian state and, as such, could not, under any circumstances, be placed at the mercy of a third party. The vehemence and depth of Rumanian feeling, as expressed both at that time and in the later course of the dispute, are revealed in the following excerpts.

[69] The compensation paid amounted to a very small percentage of the actual market value of the land.

[70] Article 63.

[71] In accordance with this provision, it is the friendly right of each League member "to bring to the attention of the Assembly or of the Council any circumstance whatever affecting international relations which threatens to disturb international peace or the good understanding between nations upon which peace depends." The Hungarian request is contained in LNOJ, 1923, pp. 729–35.

[72]*Ibid.*, pp. 573–77.

[73]*Ibid.*, pp. 604–5.

[74]*Ibid.*, pp. 605–6.

Is this a simple question of text? No, Gentlemen. The Hungarian demand puts before you the political and social transformation of a nation. . . .

Is this the kind of question which you would wish to see submitted to arbitration? To accept this solution would be to submit to arbitration not merely a problem but a veritable page of history. . . .

We are dealing with a State which represents millions of peasants, which is a collective body composed of millions of small individual interests of proprietors and taxpayers. You propose that an arbitrator should be allowed to decide that what the peasant possesses to-day he does not possess definitely. . . .

You would propose that this statute, embodying an equilibrium at which we arrived by previous agreement, should appear to-day in the eyes of the country as no longer possessing a final character.[75]

The Roumanian peasants . . . know only one thing. Starved of land for centuries, they have at length received it. They have only one fear—that they should lose it. . . . It is . . . before all, a political problem which Roumania has laid before you. My government . . . cannot take the responsibility of internal order . . . if the agrarian laws are not the steel wall against which will be shattered all attempts to jeopardise the results obtained by these laws, which are themselves the result of . . . long struggles, of compromises of class and of party.[76]

Hungary says, "I offer you arbitration. . . . Why do you not avail yourself of it?"

Really, gentlemen, do you sincerely believe that, if we were both on a footing of equality in this matter, I should not have given an affirmative answer long ago? But what is the question for Hungarian optants and for Hungary, and what is it for us?

For Hungary it is a question of money. Hungary has everything to gain and nothing to lose.

For Roumania it involves the whole of her social economy. . . .

If the optants lose, they retain their *status quo*; if they win, they improve their position. If Roumania wins, she keeps her *status quo*, with every chance of trouble in the meantime. If she loses, it means disorder.[77]

In the face of Rumanian opposition to a Court judgment, M. Adatci then proposed, as an alternative, that an advisory opinion be sought from the Court, "it being understood that the Council's freedom of decision would be

[75]*Ibid.*, pp. 607.
[76]*Ibid.*, 1927, p. 1391.
[77]*Ibid.*, p. 1394.

in no way limited."[78] Again, the Hungarian representative hastened to agree and, anticipating Rumanian resistance, declared that a majority vote would suffice, since requesting a Court opinion was a matter of procedure. Expectedly, the Rumanian representative rejected the new proposal. To his previous objections based on the "political" importance of the question, he now added an argument based on the Rapporteur's own assertion of the nonbinding nature of an advisory opinion.

> After receiving a technical opinion, you will be better informed legally, but peace demands that the question should not be kept open. . . .
> With final arbitration, the question would, at least, be closed; but in the case of an advisory opinion all the disadvantages . . . still exist; and, moreover, you would, in a few months, be in exactly the same position as you are to-day. . . .
> Do not, in the name of justice, make a demand the result of which might be permanent unrest.[79]

The Council was unwilling to override these objections by proceeding, on the basis of a majority vote, to request an advisory opinion. Thus it was that M. Adatci's second proposal also failed.

After much difficulty, the Council agreed to request M. Adatci to act as mediator between the parties and expressed the hope that the two governments would "direct their best efforts towards the attainment of an agreed solution."[80]

This hope was disappointed. Negotiations did take place in Brussels in May 1923, under the mediation of M. Adatci, and some measure of formal agreement resulted.[81] But the Hungarian government repudiated the acts of its representative in Brussels, and, when the Council resumed consideration of the matter in July 1923, it was largely occupied with explanations and arguments about the failure of the agreement.[82]

Denying any obligatory force to the Brussels agreement, the Hungarian representative now pressed for adoption of M. Adatci's original proposals to involve the Court, whether in its contentious or its advisory capacity. True, when Hungary had submitted its initial request for Council consideration of the optants issue, it had envisaged a direct Council ruling on the question. By now, however, it had come to realize that its best hopes lay with some sort of

[78]*Ibid.*, 1923, p. 608.

[79]*Ibid.*, p. 609.

[80]*Ibid.*, p. 611.

[81]*Ibid.*, pp. 1011-14. No agreement was reached on the principal issue: compensation.

[82]*Ibid.*, pp. 886-902.

judicial determination of the matter, and this realization was henceforth to guide its actions in the controversy. Rumania was as persistent in its refusal to submit to any form of arbitration "the whole social structure of Roumania."[83]

For its part, the Council was not inclined, at this new juncture in the dispute, to heed the Hungarian pleas. "What has to be found," M. Adatci now concluded, "is not an abstract legal solution ... but a practical solution which will give as full a measure of satisfaction as can be obtained with a view to a peaceful settlement."[84] Such a practical solution had appeared within grasp in Brussels, only to be subsequently torpedoed by Hungary; in these circumstances, the Council could see little justice in foisting upon Rumania an unwanted legal solution to the problem.[85]

Frustrated in its efforts to resolve the dispute, the Council contented itself with a rather noncommittal resolution which expressed the hope that both parties would "do their utmost to prevent the question of Hungarian optants from becoming a disturbing influence in their mutual relations" and exhorted the parties to exercise good will.[86]

The Council was not again called upon to deal with the problem until early 1927. Now, grafted onto the original issue of the expropriated landlords were further questions involving the competence of the League Council in relation to arbitral tribunals.

Having failed to obtain satisfaction from the League Council, Hungary attempted to obtain an arbitral award on the question by other means. Under the terms of Article 250 of the Treaty of Trianon, the property of Hungarian nationals in newly won Rumanian territory was to be exempt from measures of liquidation to which ex-enemy nationals in Allied countries were generally subject; and, under Article 239, claims involving such measures of liquidation might be compulsorily adjudicated by a Ruma..o-Hungarian Mixed Arbitral Tribunal. To this tribunal, then, the Hungarian optants began to bring their claims for restitution. Rumania, even more fearful of an arbitral decision on the

---

[83]*Ibid.*, p. 895.

[84]*Ibid.*, p. 1011.

[85]See, especially, the statements of Lord Robert Cecil (Britain) and M. Branting (Sweden), *ibid.*, pp. 904–5. Lord Cecil expressed the view that the consent of the disputants was, in theory, dispensable, since a request for an opinion was "a reference by the Council itself to the Court, independently of the parties to the dispute." However, in view of "what had taken place in Brussels," he did not deem it proper for the Council to consult the Court in this case. (It might be noted, in passing, that the formalistic view of the advisory function adopted by Lord Cecil in this instance is quite at variance with the view subsequently expressed by him in the case of the Finnish claims against Britain, when he contended that a request for an opinion without British consent would be tantamount to arbitration "by a somewhat circuitous method." However, the Court's pronouncement in the *Eastern Carelia* case and nine years of League experience with the advisory function intervened between the two statements.)

[86]LNOJ, 1923, p. 907.

question of its agrarian reform than it had been of a PCIJ determination, contested the Tribunal's jurisdiction. When, early in 1927, the Tribunal assumed jurisdiction, Rumania, instead of arguing on the merits, withdrew its arbitrator from the Tribunal. Simultaneously, it requested the opportunity to explain its actions before the League Council and based this request on Article 11(2) of the Covenant. Thus, in March 1927, the problem was again placed in the lap of the Council.

Before the Council, the Rumanian representative argued, first, that the Tribunal had exceeded its jurisdiction;[87] second, that the matter had been previously settled by the Brussels agreement; and, finally, that the question at issue was, in any case, not an ordinary judicial question, but one which involved the social and political reformation of an entire nation. Rumania could not, he declared, "accept the luxury of a further legal duel."[88]

It was precisely such a legal duel which Hungary insisted on. The Hungarian representative appealed to the League Council not to destroy the system of arbitration set up by the treaties. The matter of the Tribunal's competence was already res judicata, and the Council, an essentially political organ, ought not to act as a court of appeal and set itself above the international magistrature. In place of Rumania's request that the Council deal with the matter as a political issue, the Hungarian representative presented alternative counterproposals, each of which would have returned the issue to the legal arena. Under the first, Rumania's accusation regarding the Tribunal's abuse of power would have been tested by the PCIJ on the basis of a special agreement concluded between the parties. The second would have had the Council appoint (in virtue of Article 239 of the Treaty of Trianon) two deputy arbitrators to the Arbitral Tribunal, to fill the vacancy created by Rumania's actions.[89] Under either proposal, Rumania would have been compelled to submit to arbitration on the basis of existing treaty obligations, and, therefore, both suggestions were opposed by Rumania.[90]

Recognizing the complicated nature which the question had now assumed,[91] the Council appointed a committee of three[92] to deal with the Rumanian and Hungarian demands.

[87]Rumania maintained that the Tribunal was competent only with respect to war measures applied to ex-enemy property, as such, and not with respect to general social justice measures applied indiscriminately to nationals as well as to foreigners.

[88]LNOJ, 1927, pp. 350-64.

[89]Ibid., pp. 364-70.

[90]Ibid., p. 371. The Rumanian representative recalled the Council's 1923 decision not to refer the question to the PCIJ, in view of the Brussels agreement.

[91]As noted by the President, the question now involved the issue of "the competence of arbitral tribunals in relation to national and international laws on the subject." Ibid., p. 372.

[92]The committee consisted of Sir Austen Chamberlain (the rapporteur), Viscount Ishii (Japan), and M. Villegas (Chile).

In its primary objective—conciliation between the parties[93]—the committee reported failure.[94] Hungary's renewed offer to submit the question of the Arbitral Tribunal's jurisdiction to the PCIJ was rejected by Rumania, while Rumania's formulas proved equally unacceptable to Hungary. In these circumstances, the committee decided to undertake, with the assistance of "eminent legal authorities," an independent examination of the extent of the Arbitral Tribunal's jurisdiction. This examination resulted in the enunciation of three principles—generally reflecting the Rumanian view of the Tribunal's jurisdiction—which the committee considered obligatory of acceptance by both disputants.[95] The committee recommended that the Council endorse these principles, request both parties to comply with them, and invite Rumania to reinstate its arbitrator on the Tribunal. Furthermore, contemplating possible refusals by either or both parties, the committee proposed alternative "sanctions"[96] to induce compliance with the committee's recommendations. (1) If Hungary refused to comply, the Council "would not be justified in appointing two deputy members in accordance with Article 239 of the Treaty of Trianon." (2) Rumanian refusal would entitle the Council to take "appropriate measures to ensure in any case the satisfactory working of the Tribunal." (3) Refusal by both parties would relieve the Council of its duties under Article 11 of the Covenant.

The committee's report met with predictable responses on the part of the two disputants. Rumania, whose substantive views had been vindicated in the report, agreed to accept the renewal of arbitration on the basis of the three principles, which would become "law for the parties."[97] But, for Hungary, acceptance of the three principles meant the addition of new conditions to, and the placing in jeopardy of, its existing international rights. The Hungarian representative therefore forcefully opposed adoption of the committee's report. He objected to the attempt by the Council, on the basis of the opinion of "anonymous jurists," to determine anew the matter of the Tribunal's competence—a matter which was already res judicata. Such an attempt

[93]The committee refused to view the matter solely in the legal terms of Article 239, as demanded by Hungary. Appointment of the two deputy arbitrators, the committee members maintained, would not finally solve a dispute submitted successively to three international authorities. Moreover, the Council's intervention had first been requested by Rumania and had been based on the "political" provision of Article 11 of the Covenant.

[94]For the committee's report, see LNOJ, 1927, pp. 1379–83.

[95]The application of general agrarian reform schemes to Hungarian nationals, as long as these involved no inequality as between Hungarians and Rumanians, would be excluded from the Tribunal's competence.

[96]The appellation was later employed by the Hungarian representative and those Council members who joined him in opposing these suggestions.

[97]LNOJ, 1927, p. 1401.

represented a dangerous tendency to confuse political and judicial powers. Clearly, the PCIJ, and not the Council, was the competent authority for treaty interpretation. Consequently, the Hungarian representative renewed his earlier proposal that Hungary and Rumania jointly submit to the Court the issue of the Arbitral Tribunal's competence. In addition, he proposed that the Council ask the PCIJ for an advisory opinion as to whether the three principles enunciated by the committee have "in whole or in part, and if so, in which part, been rendered obligatory on Roumania and Hungary by the acceptance of the Treaty of Trianon."[98]

Sir Austen Chamberlain, the Rapporteur, strongly defended the committee's report against the Hungarian representative's attack. Reference to the PCIJ, he noted, was impracticable because of Rumania's opposition to this course and because of the great delay it would entail. The committee had therefore sought the advice of the "highest" legal authorities available on the spot, and it was on the basis of the unanimous opinion of those jurists that the three principles had been formulated. Thus, there was every justification for "exacting acceptance by both parties."[99]

As for other Council members, they were somewhat divided in their views. Most apparently endorsed the committee's recommendations in their entirety and agreed that the three principles correctly expressed the obligations arising out of the Treaty of Trianon. Four,[100] however, entertained serious reservations regarding the Council's power to compel acceptance of the three principles. At most, they were prepared to regard the committee's report as a basis for further negotiations between the parties. To go any further would amount to substitution by the Council of its own views for those of the arbitrator, and such a move would require the support of a PCIJ advisory opinion. These members therefore insisted on the deletion of the "sanctions" from the committee's proposals and expressed sympathy, in principle, with the Hungarian representative's desire for judicial clarification of the issue.[101]

To accommodate their views, the Council agreed to delete the objectionable provisions, and the resolution was thus adopted[102] in a much weaker form: it merely provided a starting point for the resumption of direct negotiations. A renewed plea (before the final vote) by the Hungarian representative for an immediate request for an advisory opinion fell on deaf ears. The

---

[98]*Ibid.*, pp. 1383–89.

[99]*Ibid.*, p. 1396.

[100]MM. Stresemann (Germany), Loudon (the Netherlands), Scialoja (Italy), and Urrutia (Colombia).

[101]LNOJ, 1927, pp. 1397–98, 1403, 1411–12.

[102]*Ibid.*, pp. 1413–14. Both parties abstained. The Hungarian representative was particularly fearful that his acceptance of the resolution might imply that the three principles had become new law binding on the parties.

responses to this plea ranged from the visible annoyance of the Rapporteur at what he viewed as but another manifestation of the intransigent "no concession" Hungarian attitude,[103] to the mere questioning of the opportuneness of the Hungarian proposal. In the latter category was the explanation of the German representative. Though he himself had advocated possible recourse to the Court, he nevertheless deemed it a "psychological error" for the Council to give the impression, at this stage, that it doubted the success of its own proposals.[104]

Such hopes for success as may have been entertained were quickly frustrated. Hungary refused to enter into negotiations on the basis of the three principles; Rumania was unprepared to negotiate on any other basis. Thus, in March 1928, when the Council resumed consideration of the problem, the deadlock between the parties remained unbroken.

The Hungarian representative then renewed all three of his previous alternative proposals for resolving the dispute: (1) appointment of deputy arbitrators by the Council; (2) submitting for PCIJ judgment the question whether the Arbitral Tribunal had exceeded its competence; or (3) requesting the Court's opinion on the legal validity of the three principles contained in the Council's September 1927 resolution. The last alternative, he recalled, had earlier met with a sympathetic response on the part of many Council members. Moreover, in view of the Council's hesitation regarding the first proposal, and Rumania's refusal to agree to the second proposal, requesting the Court's opinion offered perhaps the best prospect of finally resolving the dispute. For, if that opinion were unfavorable to Hungary's contentions, Hungary would nevertheless accept the consequences in full; and if it were favorable, the Council might proceed, with quiet conscience, to appoint the deputy arbitrators in accordance with the peace treaty. Again, as on previous occasions, the Hungarian representative appealed to the Council not to confuse its political power with judicial power and not to set itself up as a "superarbitrator."[105]

The Rumanian representative opposed all three Hungarian proposals and, in particular, presented a lengthy exposé of his objections to requesting the Court's advisory opinion.[106] He prefaced this exposé with an affirmation of Rumania's absolute freedom to reject adjudication by the Court.

---

[103] "The Council is not," he insisted, "a mere court of law; it is a court of equity. It is . . . not merely entitled but bound to take due account of those large issues upon which . . . in the last resort, the peace of the world depends." *Ibid.*, p. 1407.

[104] *Ibid.*, p. 1410.

[105] *Ibid.*, 1928, pp. 410, 414–21.

[106] *Ibid.*, pp. 424–25.

If I were obliged to go to the Court at The Hague, I would, of course, accept that obligation. Let Roumania perish but let her signature be honoured! If, however, I am not obliged to go to the Court, I am bound freely to consider . . . the political necessities of the situation. Being free in law, I must needs act in the interests of my country.

His specific objections to soliciting the Court's advice were the following.

1. The question was not a purely legal question.

The expropriation of a house, of a factory, or of an estate, is a legal question. The expropriation of six million hectares carried out in accordance with the dire necessities which arose in 1917 and 1919, with a view to the safeguarding of private ownership, the expropriation of the entire landowning class of the country, and the conferring of the property rights in the soil on the whole of the agricultural class . . . is not a purely legal question.

2. The purpose of an advisory opinion is to enlighten the Council, but that opinion is not binding.[107] Nor is the Council bound to seek its enlightenment from the Court. It may prefer to employ a committee of jurists, as it did in the present case. Were the Council to seek the Court's opinion now, it would be asking the Court to pass not merely on the Rumano-Hungarian dispute but also on the decisions of the committee of three. The result would be that "no one would again agree to act as Rapporteur, or to act as a legal adviser to the League, if his opinion were liable to be revised by another body."

3. The Council had already (in 1923) refused the Hungarian request for an opinion.

4. The Council was fully competent to deal with the question, since both parties submitted it under Article 11, and since, in 1923, Hungary itself had asked the Council "to declare the law as though it were a court of justice."

5. The proposal would entail considerable loss of time, and the matter had already dragged on for too long.

6. The proposal would, in effect, amount to compulsory arbitration.

It is essential that the provisions of the Covenant should not be evaded by means of the procedure of an advisory opinion. Such a procedure would render international justice compulsory, whereas it exists only subject to the consent of the parties. We are all aware of the moral value attaching to

[107]But cf. Reason No. 6, which is premised precisely on the assumption that an advisory opinion is very nearly binding.

an opinion of the Court, and that it is somewhat difficult not to defer to such an opinion.

To buttress this argument, the Rumanian representative quoted from the report of the judicial committee, which in 1927 recommended the appointment of judges *ad hoc* in certain advisory cases.[108] In conclusion, he declared:

> In face of the constant practice of the Council and this interpretation of the Court itself, I am obliged to say that, if the Covenant leaves me the right to refuse arbitration except with my own consent, you cannot by a side-track oblige me to go to arbitration by means of an advisory opinion, in view of the fact that the Court itself declares that, in its view, an opinion amounts to the same thing as a decision.

As for Hungary's opposition to the Council's assumption of "judicial" power, the Rumanian representative responded that there was no separation of powers in the international sphere, and that the Council combined, in some measure, all three powers—legislative, executive, and judicial.

As Rapporteur, Sir Austen Chamberlain now proposed a new solution, subject to acceptance by the parties: the Council would name two new members—nationals of states that were neutral in the war—to the Mixed Arbitral Tribunal; Rumania's membership would be restored; and to the new tribunal of five members would be submitted the claims filed under Article 250 of the Treaty of Trianon.[109]

The Hungarian representative gladly approved this proposal, for it coincided with his desire for a resumption of negotiations without any strings attached. But the Rumanian representative balked. He could accept the proposal only if the two new deputy judges were to be bound by the three principles contained in the September 1927 resolution, whereby claims under the agrarian law as such were declared to be outside the Tribunal's competence. Unless the judges were so bound, the proposal would amount to "arbitration pure and simple . . . equivalent to arbitration at The Hague," though offering, "perhaps, less guarantees."[110]

The resolution adopted at the March 1928 Council session did not meet Rumania's desires. While its previous recommendations had "value," the Council clearly did not wish to tie the hands of the arbitrators in any way. At the same time, Hungary's desires were not entirely fulfilled either, since the appointment of the two neutral arbitrators was conditional upon the approval of both disputants to resume the arbitration—and the approval of Rumania was not forthcoming.

[108] See Chapter I.
[109] LNOJ, 1928, pp. 426–27.
[110] *Ibid.*, pp. 436–40.

Thus, in June 1928, when the Council continued its discussion of the problem, the matter was no nearer solution than it had ever been. Hungary had opposed the Council's September 1927 solution; in turn, Rumania had rejected the March 1928 proposal. In these circumstances, the Rapporteur suggested that, since the Council "declined to enforce what was described as a sanction on the refusal of Hungary to accept the earlier proposal," it was not "proper to proceed to sanctions against Roumania for her later refusal." The resolution now proposed by the Rapporteur and concurred in unanimously by the Council (but with the Hungarian representative abstaining) merely called upon both parties "to bring this long dispute to a close by reciprocal concessions."[111] To the Hungarian representative's insistence that efforts at conciliation had proven futile and that the Council was therefore obliged to adhere strictly to the terms of Article 239 and appoint deputy arbitrators, the Rapporteur replied:

> The purpose of arbitration is not to arbitrate for the sake of arbitrating but to settle a dispute, and, in every case, a direct arrangement between the parties is better than an arbitral award; moreover, there are occasions when real peace can only be brought into the minds of men whose interests and sentiment are in conflict, if the decision ultimately taken as the result of mutual concessions is freely accepted and is not imposed by external authority.[112]

Nevertheless, the Hungarian representative declared in advance his intention (in the event of failure of the negotiations) to renew both his application for the reconstitution of the Tribunal and (if the Council maintained its doubts regarding the Tribunal's competence) his proposal to request the Court's opinion.[113]

At this point, the President declared the question of the Hungarian optants closed as far as the Council was concerned. He also professed to see, shining on the horizon, "a light of peace and conciliation."[114]

It was not until almost two years later that that "light" finally emerged from the "horizon" into full view. Despite the President's declaration that the matter was closed, the Council was again called upon several times to take up the matter during the course of tortuous Rumano-Hungarian negotiations.[115] Finally, on 28 April 1930 the two parties signed an agreement, and the issue of the Hungarian optants was at last withdrawn from the Council agenda.

[111] *Ibid.*, p. 934.
[112] *Ibid.*, p. 937.
[113] *Ibid.*, pp. 938–40.
[114] *Ibid.*, p. 940.
[115] For the development of the problem until June 1929, see Currey, *op. cit.*, pp. 26–33. For subsequent Council discussions on the matter, see LNOJ, 1929, pp. 1673–74; and 1930, pp. 85–86, 498.

After reviewing the various proposals to request the Court's advisory opinion in the context in which they were raised, one can readily discern the considerations which prompted both the proposals and their rejection.

For Hungary, the attempt to get a Court opinion represented only one facet of an over-all drive to get the dispute settled by a judicial tribunal on the basis of existing law. It was part of a "package" of alternative legal solutions which Hungary would offer, particularly at those junctures in the dispute at which its legal rights appeared to be most endangered—whether because of a later-regretted negotiated compromise (as in the Brussels agreement) or because of a Council attempt to set down "new" law to guide the Arbitral Tribunal. Within the "package," the idea of recourse to the Court's advisory jurisdiction constituted, as it were, a "second line of attack," the "first line" comprising proposals which would have led to a binding arbitral decision or Court judgment. Hungary fell back on proposals to request a Court opinion because the route to her preferred goals was blocked, on the one hand, by the refusal of Rumania to have the dispute arbitrated or adjudicated, and, on the other hand, by the refusal of the Council to compel such arbitration.

Rumania's steadfast opposition to requesting the Court's opinion was again merely a manifestation of its opposition to any species of judicial or arbitral determination (on the basis of the existing law) of a matter viewed by that state as too "vital" to be exposed to a possibly unfavorable decision by a third party. Rumania favored either conciliation, in which the ultimate decision would remain in its hands, or arbitration on the basis of the law laid down by the Council in September 1927, which in effect predetermined the issue in Rumania's favor.

The Council early concluded that the matter could not be approached on a strictly legal basis and that a negotiated solution was preferable. Throughout, it walked a tightrope between Rumanian and Hungarian demands (which were, most of the time, in the nature of "the irresistible force" versus "the immovable object"). Its role remained strictly mediatory. On the one hand, it refused to ignore Rumania's political interests, by foisting upon it such "legal" solutions as an arbitral award, a Court judgment, or a Court opinion. On the other hand, it was reluctant to ignore what Hungary viewed as its own "legal rights" by forcing it to accept the Council's version of what those rights were (even though the Council's version had the sanction of "eminent legal authorities").

On the whole, there was more sympathy in the Council for Rumania's position in the dispute. This sympathy was to a great extent based on the feeling that there was an imbalance of interests in this case: that, for Hungary, the issue was a matter of money and principle, while, for Rumania, it involved the very social fabric of the nation. In these circumstances, the corollary belief that Hungary should insist less on the rigor of the law and adopt a more compromising attitude was perhaps natural. Hence, too, opposition arose to strictly "legal" solutions, including recourse to the Court's advisory jurisdiction.

Given the imbalance in the interests in dispute and Rumania's strong opposition to requesting the Court's opinion, the decision not to approach the Court in this case was probably a wise one. Had a Court opinion been in Rumania's favor, Hungary quite probably (as she herself insisted) would have accepted it. (Indeed, in realistic terms, what other alternative was open to her?) In the face of Rumania's attitude, however, it was not reasonable to expect that government to abide by an adverse opinion. Far from solving the problem, such an opinion might have made final settlement more difficult by rigidifying Hungary's stand and thereby drawing the parties yet farther apart.

As noted, the problem was, in the end, settled by direct negotiations, and the hopes which the Council pinned on this avenue eventually bore fruit.

The Polish-Lithuanian Dispute

At one point in the Vilna dispute, Lithuania sought, by means of successive appeals to the League Council and Assembly, to obtain a Court opinion. The Lithuanian proposal was interesting in a number of respects. First, it was aimed at getting a judicial ruling on the validity and effect of action already taken by the Council; second, the questions contained therein were formulated in terms which called for the interpretation of certain Covenant provisions in the abstract; and, finally, presentation of the proposal to the Assembly, following its rejection by the Council, was most unusual, and raised complex questions regarding the Assembly's competence.

The circumstances in which Lithuania presented its initial proposal to consult the Court were as follows.

By early 1923, Council efforts to settle the fate of the Vilna Territory by means of mutual agreement between the parties had reached an impasse. A proposed plebiscite was never held, and direct negotiations under the chairmanship of the Belgian member of the Council, M. Hymans, proved equally abortive. Consequently, on 3 February 1923, the Council recommended the provisional apportionment between Lithuania and Poland of the administration of Vilna's neutral zone. The Lithuanian representative strongly objected, and even threatened hostile action if Poland proceeded to administer the part of the territory apportioned to it. Nevertheless, the Council adopted the recommendation "unanimously" (the Lithuanian representative opposing).[116] Following the vote, the Council President declared that,

---

[116] LNOJ, 1923, p. 239.

as the recommendation had been unanimously accepted, paragraph 6 of Article 15 of the Covenant[117] was applicable; consequently, if Lithuania opposed by force the execution of the measures provided for, Article 16[118] would come into play. If Lithuania resorted to war, she would be deemed to have committed an act of war against all other Members of the League.[119]

This attempt to attribute imperative force to the Council's recommendation aggravated Lithuania's sense of grievance. Its objections to the Council's actions were now twofold. First, it denied altogether the Council's competence to partition the neutral zone, since that matter had never been expressly submitted to it by the parties. The zone, having been established by agreement of the parties, could be modified only in the same way. Second, it rejected the applicability of Articles 15(6) and 16 of the Covenant to the Council's recommendation.

Shortly after adoption of the resolution in question, the Lithuanian representative requested that the Council submit to the Court for an advisory opinion "two points relating to the interpretation of the Covenant." These points represented Lithuania's translation into abstract form of its very concrete objections to the Council's actions.

> 1. Has the Council ... the right, when a dispute is submitted to it under paragraph 1 of Article 15 of the Covenant, to address to the Parties, with regard to incidental questions which have not been expressly submitted to it, recommendations having the force of the Council reports referred to in paragraphs 4, 6 and 7 of the same article?
>
> 2. If the recommendations of a report by the Council ... have been adopted in the circumstances in the sixth paragraph of Article 16 [sic] of the Covenant ... and have been accepted by one of the Parties, are such recommendations binding upon the other Party, if it does not accept them? And, secondly, if, within the period fixed by Article 12 of the Covenant, it goes to war with the Party which accepts the report, is it liable to the penalties laid down in Article 16?[120]

The Council took up the Lithuanian proposal on 21 April 1923, only to reject it very quickly. This rejection followed an eloquent plea by the Council's Rapporteur, M. Hymans, against acceding to the Lithuanian request.

---

[117]"If a report by the Council is unanimously agreed to by the Members thereof other than the Representatives of one or more of the parties to the dispute, the Members of the League agree that they will not go to war with any party to the dispute which complies with the recommendations of the report."

[118]The "sanctions" article.

[119]LNOJ, 1923, p. 239; cf. the mitigation of these remarks, *ibid.*, p. 240.

[120]*Ibid.*, pp. 667–70.

Briefly, M. Hymans' arguments were: (1) Submission to the Court of the questions proposed by Lithuania would be equivalent to having the PCIJ pass on the validity of a Council decision. Such a course of action was objectionable from the constitutional viewpoint and from the viewpoint of the harmonious working of League institutions. (2) The Council decision to which the Lithuanian proposal referred was only a provisional decision, since it was replaced by the decision of the Conference of Ambassadors of 15 March 1923 tracing Poland's frontiers. Thus, the question now "had no practical interest" and was "purely academic." Surely the Council need not open a legal debate before the Court merely "to further legal science and legal theory." (3) In any case, the Council undoubtedly acted within the scope of the Covenant. Hence, a judicial opinion was unnecessary.[121]

To these arguments M. Hanotaux, the French representative, added one of his own. He considered that the Court was not competent to interpret the Covenant, this competence having been specifically denied it when the Covenant was being drafted.[122]

The Lithuanian representative countered by arguing, first, that the matter was not theoretical for Lithuania, since she did not recognize the Conference of Ambassadors' decision; second, that Article 14 did not refer only to "practical" questions; and, finally, that the question of the Court's competence might well be left for the Court itself to determine.[123]

These arguments, however, went unheeded. The Council agreed with M. Hymans' conclusions; and Lithuania at once requested that her proposal be placed on the agenda of the next Assembly session.

Before passing on to the Assembly debates, a word should be said regarding the primary considerations prompting the Council's rejection of the Lithuanian proposal, since these have been widely misconstrued. The Council's action has frequently been cited in support of the proposition that the Council doubted the competence of the Court to interpret Covenant provisions in the abstract.[124] This interpretation places too much emphasis on the reason offered by M. Hanotaux (which apparently played a rather minor role), and not enough on the more determinative arguments put forward by the Rapporteur. Whereas M. Hanotaux based his opposition on the abstract

---

[121] *Ibid.*, pp. 585–86.

[122] *Ibid.*, p. 586. M. Hanotaux recalled the rejection of M. Larnaude's proposal at Paris in 1919, and the reasons which had been adduced by Lord Cecil and M. Orlando for such a rejection. See p. 7, n. 8, above.

[123] LNOJ, 1923, p. 586.

[124] See, e.g., the statement of M. Lachs in the *Admission* case, ICJ Pleadings, 1948, p. 110.

formulation of the question—the Court's competence to interpret the Covenant in the course of its treatment of a concrete case was never seriously disputed—M. Hymans' objections were directed at the specific factual situation, which the abstract formulation merely masked. M. Hymans realized that Lithuania's purpose was to get a judicial ruling on the validity and binding force of the Council's decision of 3 February 1923, and, in his view, such a ruling was neither necessary, proper, nor of any practical value. The Council members apparently agreed.

When the Lithuanian proposal came before the Assembly in September 1923, that body had first to grapple with a preliminary question relating to its competence: Since the matter had already been closed in the Council by the formal adoption of a report, could it now be reopened before the Assembly? This question was submitted to the Assembly's First (Legal) Committee. That committee proceeded to deal with it in terms of the particular circumstances surrounding the Lithuanian proposal and concluded that the Assembly possessed the theoretical right to request a Court opinion on the Council's competence. Nevertheless, it specifically reserved its opinion regarding other legal and expediential objections to requesting the Court's opinion in this case.[125]

Considerable debate, in which questions of competence and expediency were sometimes confused, preceded the Committee's adoption of its conclusions. There was general agreement that requesting the Court's opinion would be inadvisable, for it would create practical difficulties in Assembly-Council relations, particularly if the Court's view differed from the Council's.[126] But some representatives went even further and considered the Assembly *incompetent* to address the proposed request to the Court. In this category were the statements of the French and Belgian representatives.[127] The remarks of the latter were particularly significant. Analogizing from the case of states, he concluded that matters affecting the "vital interests and honour" of the Council could not be submitted to adjudication without its consent. The Assembly could not appeal, a posteriori, to a judicial organ and thereby expose the Council to the "risk of an adverse verdict which would definitely ruin its authority." Against this position it was argued that, since in questions of law the Court was a higher authority than either Council or Assembly, the Court could give a legal opinion on the question whether the Council had exceeded its powers;[128] that judicial control, far from injuring the Council's

[125] LN, Records of the 4th Ass., Plenary, 1923, pp. 366–67.
[126] See the remarks of M. Politis, *ibid.*, 1st Ctte., 1923, pp. 19, 22.
[127] *Ibid.*, pp. 19–21.
[128] M. Scialoja (Italy), *ibid.*, p. 20.

prestige, would rather assure more complete confidence in the League; and that an Assembly appeal to the Court was a way of checking possible Council autocracy and illegality.[129]

Nevertheless, as noted, these arguments were largely theoretical, since almost all the Committee members entertained serious misgivings regarding the wisdom of acceding to the Lithuanian request. At the suggestion of M. Rolin, the Committee specifically reserved its opinion with regard to several matters—among them, the clarity of the questions formulated by Lithuania and the existence of sufficient doubt to warrant an approach to the Court.[130]

In fact, the Assembly was never called upon to determine these last issues. Lithuania first proposed postponing discussion of the matter until the following (Fifth) Assembly session,[131] but, at that session, requested withdrawal of the item from the agenda.[132]

The issue which originally prompted Lithuania's desire for an advisory opinion—the division of the neutral zone—became, along with so many other events connected with the Vilna dispute, a matter of accomplished fact, which Lithuania could do nothing to reverse. Nor could a Court opinion have altered the situation, in any tangible manner, in Lithuania's favor. At most, Lithuania might have received the psychological satisfaction of seeing itself vindicated by the Court. From the Council's viewpoint, on the other hand, the proposed recourse was both futile and possibly dangerous, for the Council faced the risk of a judicial overruling of its decisions. As for the Assembly, the propriety of its challenging the legality of Council decisions was open to even more serious question. In these circumstances, it was hardly surprising that neither League organ acceded to Lithuania's desires.

Interpretation of Certain Articles of the Covenant and Other Questions of International Law (Corfu Aftermath)

The Corfu dispute left in its wake many unresolved questions relating to Covenant interpretation and general international law. At the time of the dispute, the Council had passed over many of these crucial questions in

[129]M. Politis (Greece), *ibid.*, pp. 21–22; see also the remarks of MM. Sidzikauskas (Lithuania) and Alvarez (Chile), *ibid.*, pp. 22–23.

[130]*Ibid.*, pp. 21, 24. It also reserved its position regarding the vote required for addressing the request to the Court.

[131]*Ibid.*, Plenary, 1923, p. 368.

[132]LN, Records of the 5th Ass., 6th Ctte., 1924, p. 9. The action followed the Sixth (Political) Committee's decision not to include Lithuanian and Polish representatives in the subcommittee appointed to report on the question. Lithuania obviously recognized that it was not likely to get its way in the Assembly, any more than it had in the Council.

silence, to the great consternation of an aroused world public opinion.[133] Particularly disturbing had been the Council's failure to judge the validity of the Italian contention that the bombardment and occupation of Corfu did not constitute an "act of war," in violation of Article 12 of the Covenant, but was merely a necessary measure to secure Greek compliance with Italy's just demands.

Now, in the immediate aftermath of Corfu, the Council members generally agreed that the controversial questions raised could no longer be ignored; these questions would have to be clarified, lest in future disputes they were to plague the Council again.[134] Most of the Council members would have preferred to see the PCIJ charged with the task of clarification. But, mainly in deference to Italian objections to requesting an advisory opinion, the task was given instead to a specially constituted committee of jurists.

The question of consulting the Court was first broached by Lord Robert Cecil in a proposal submitted to the Council on 22 September 1923. After outlining three problems which, in his view, required elucidation, he recommended that the Council decide, in principle, to submit these problems to the PCIJ, subject to the formulation of precise questions by a committee of jurists.[135] The three problems related to: (1) the powers and duties of the League under Articles 12 and 15 of the Covenant; (2) the legality of measures of coercion employed by one state against another (e.g., the occupation of territory); and (3) a state's responsibility for certain crimes committed on its territory.

Already at this stage, M. Salandra, the Italian representative, voiced reservations regarding the Court's competence to consider the subjects raised. Furthermore, to protect Italy from any pronouncement which might imply censure or approval of her actions, M. Salandra insisted that the second of Lord Cecil's points be generalized to include all "measures of coercion" (including commercial blockade and other forms of reprisals), not merely the occupation of territory.[136] The misgivings thus expressed regarding the addressee of the questions and the substance of the questions were related. Both were manifestations of the desire to avoid adjudication of the legality of Italian actions. Italy sought to ensure that the answers which would be forth-

---

[133] For a brief account of the Council's handling of the Corfu dispute, see T. P. Conwell-Evans, *The League Council in Action* (London: Oxford University Press, 1929), pp. 73-81.

[134] LNOJ, 1923, p. 1317. Such clarification was also intended to allay the anxieties of world public opinion. *Ibid.*, p. 1331.

[135] *Ibid.*, p. 1320.

[136] M. Salandra also objected to the third point, on the ground that it might prejudge an issue which Greece and Italy might submit to the PCIJ for judgment. *Ibid.*, pp. 1320-21.

coming would be "abstract" enough, and that they would also be "advisory" enough. It is primarily in this light that much of the later discussion must be viewed.

To accommodate M. Salandra's initial objections, the Council consented to reserve its decision regarding which organ to consult until after it had received precisely formulated questions. It also agreed that Lord Cecil's second point might be framed in more general terms.[137]

When the Council resumed its consideration of the matter, it had before it the following five questions drafted by a committee of jurists.

1. Is the Council, when seized, at the instance of a Member of the League of Nations, of a dispute submitted, in accordance with the terms of Article 15 of the Covenant, by such Member as "likely to lead to a rupture," bound, either at the request of the other party or on its own authority, and before enquiring into any other point, to decide whether in fact such description is well founded?

2. Is the Council, when seized of a dispute, in accordance with Article 15, paragraph 1, of the Covenant, at the instance of a Member of the League of Nations, bound, either at the request of a party or on its own authority, to suspend its enquiry into the dispute when, with the consent of the parties, the settlement of the dispute is being sought through some other channel?

3. Is an objection founded on Article 15, paragraph 8, of the Covenant the only objection based on the merits of the dispute on which the competence of the Council to make an enquiry can be challenged?

4. Are measures of coercion which are not meant to constitute acts of war consistent with the terms of Articles 12 to 15 of the Covenant when they are taken by one Member of the League . . . against another Member . . . without prior recourse to the procedure laid down in these articles?

5. In what circumstances and to what extent is the responsibility of a State involved by the commission of a political crime on its territory?[138]

As can readily be seen, all the questions were formulated in very abstract terms. The first three related to the Council's competence; the first four involved interpretation of Covenant provisions in the abstract; and the fifth involved a general question of international law. Despite its generalized form, the fourth question was, understandably, the most sensitive for Italy, and the one it least wished to see referred to the Court.

The decision to send all five questions to a committee of jurists followed a rather protracted debate over the appropriate addressee of the questions. In

---

[137] *Ibid.*, pp. 1321, 1324–25.
[138] *Ibid.*, p. 1328.

this debate, several points connected with the advisory function were raised. Was the PCIJ competent to give an opinion on questions framed in abstract terms? In particular, could the Court be asked to interpret Covenant provisions in the abstract? Could and should questions relating to the Council's competence be submitted to the Court? Were some or all of the five questions too "political," or otherwise unsuitable, for judicial determination? And would a Court opinion be truly advisory, or would it, rather, unduly tie the Council's hands?

These interconnected points were alluded to in M. Salandra's remarks, and his answers—supported in most instances by two of his colleagues, MM. Hanotaux of France and de Mello Franco of Brazil—were, briefly, the following.

1. The Court was not competent to pronounce itself on abstract questions of principle. In accordance with Article 36 of its Statute, it could deal only with concrete disputes referred to it and with matters specially provided for in treaties. Nor was there any *precedent* for submitting abstract questions to the Court.[139]

2. Moreover, the questions under consideration were not only abstract questions; they entailed interpretation of Covenant provisions in the abstract. The Court's answers might, therefore, constitute authentic interpretations of the Covenant. But the power to give such authentic interpretations was intimately bound up with the power to amend the Covenant. Both powers were vested solely in the sovereignty of the member states of the League and were not within a Court's competence.[140]

3. Particularly with respect to questions 3 and 4, judicial interpretation could not be countenanced. The "constitutional" question of the Council's competence (question 3) and the question how far the Covenant had "diminished the sovereignty" of member states (question 4) were not purely legal; they had "grave political" implications and consequently had to be reserved for Council consideration.[141]

---

[139] *Ibid.*, pp. 1330–31. After being reminded by M. Branting (Sweden) of the abstract questions referred to the Court in connection with the ILO's competence in agricultural matters, M. Salandra discounted the analogy because of the greater importance of the present questions. *Ibid.*, pp. 1331–32, 1339–40; cf. the statements of MM. Hanotaux and de Mello Franco, *ibid.*, p. 1332.

[140] *Ibid.*, pp. 1330–32, 1339–40; see also the statements of MM. Hanotaux and de Mello Franco, *ibid.*, pp. 1332, 1338, 1343. Cf. the controversy regarding the ICJ's power to interpret the Charter which raged during the early UN period (Chapter V).

[141] LNOJ, 1923, pp. 1331, 1340, 1342. Question 5 was objected to on different grounds. The matter was one which, in accordance with a Conference of Ambassadors' decision, might come before the Court in a concrete contentious case. If the Court were asked to pass on the question first in the abstract, it would subsequently be placed in an impossible position.

But would the Court's answers amount to an "authentic" interpretation? Would not the Council retain its prerogatives and freedom to determine for itself the "grave political" issues involved, even after receiving the Court's opinion? Was not an advisory opinion merely "advisory"? To these questions M. Salandra replied: "Theoretically, of course, we are entitled to have a different opinion from that of the Permanent Court, but in practice, after the latter had given its opinion, we should to some extent have lost our independence."[142] The same could not be said with respect to the opinion of a committee of jurists. That opinion would indeed "have only an advisory character."[143]

M. Salandra's views were not generally shared by the Council members. The term "any dispute *or question*," employed in Article 14 of the Covenant, was considered sufficiently broad to embrace the questions under consideration, despite their abstract nature and despite their subject matter.[144] Furthermore, it was argued, the Court itself was the best judge of its own competence.[145] Nor could most Council members subscribe to M. Salandra's fears regarding the binding force of an advisory opinion. In their reactions, they were, perhaps, not entirely consistent. On the one hand, they insisted that the Court's advisory opinion would be precisely that—advisory. It would in no way limit the freedom of the Council or the full sovereignty and independence of each state.[146] On the other hand, it was also argued that, in the wake of a Court opinion, a degree of limitation was desirable rather than objectionable.[147]

In point of fact, it was quite clear that the majority wanted precisely what M. Salandra feared—namely, an *authoritative* opinion which would dispel doubts and calm public opinion. In the words of Mr. Wood:

> The Council should take into account the considerable anxiety regarding this matter which was felt by public opinion in all parts of the world. . . . if the Council were to endeavour to meet and allay that anxiety,

[142] *Ibid.*, p. 1339.

[143] *Ibid.*, p. 1342.

[144] See the arguments of M. Branting and Mr. Wood, *ibid.*, p. 1331. See also the remarks of the Chinese and Japanese representatives (*ibid.*, p. 1344) to the effect that the Court was competent to answer any question addressed to it by the Council or the Assembly.

[145] *Ibid.*, p. 1331.

[146] See the statements of Lord Cecil (*ibid.*, pp. 1338, 1340, 1341) and Viscount Ishii (*ibid.*, p. 1345).

[147] To M. Salandra's argument that it would be difficult to maintain an opinion different from the Court's, Lord Cecil replied that, if a government disagrees with the Court's opinion as to that government's obligations, it *should* be more difficult for it to say so. *Ibid.*, p. 1340.

it could only be done by securing the most authoritative pronouncement—a pronouncement carrying the greatest weight—that it was within the power of the Council to seek.[148]

Recognition that the opinion of an ad hoc body of jurists would be less authoritative was universal. What lay at the heart of the controversy was not a difference in perception, but only a difference in goals.

As for the alleged "political" nature of the questions, it was argued that the interpretation of treaties was ipso facto legal;[149] that the Court's opinion would be taken into account only insofar as it dealt with the legal questions;[150] and that, since the Italo-Greek dispute was already settled, the questions were now purely legal.[151]

Notwithstanding the views thus expressed, there was some readiness to agree to a compromise: the submission of questions 4[152] and 5[153] to a committee of jurists, provided M. Salandra would consent to having the Court consulted on the first three questions (concerning the Council's competence). However, M. Salandra was willing to see only questions 1 and 2 referred to the Court. Although, like question 3, they related to the Council's competence, they, at least, were confined to the area of "procedure."[154] Thus, the snag in the compromise was question 3. On this M. Salandra remained adamant. Instead of either voting to request the Court's opinion on the basis of less than unanimity (a course which no one apparently contemplated) or sending only the first two questions to the Court (a course considered unworthy of the Council), it was finally decided to refer all five questions to a committee of jurists.[155]

---

[148] *Ibid.*, p. 1331; but cf. *ibid.*, pp. 1338, 1340–42.

[149] Lord Cecil, *ibid.*, p. 1340; M. Branting, *ibid.*, p. 1330.

[150] Lord Cecil, *ibid.*, p. 1342.

[151] Viscount Ishii, *ibid.*, pp. 1344–45.

[152] Thus, M. Hymans (Belgium) agreed that question 4 had a "definitely political character." *Ibid.*, p. 1332. Lord Cecil, for his part, at one point conceded doubts regarding the suitability of this question for judicial determination, since the writing of a virtual essay might be required. A well-selected body of jurists might be able to give an opinion as valuable as the Court's. *Ibid.*, p. 1339.

[153] *Ibid.*, pp. 1331, 1339.

[154] *Ibid.*, pp. 1332, 1340.

[155] *Ibid.*, pp. 1345–1352. Lord Cecil reasoned that the Council might still, after receipt of the jurists' opinion, submit any remaining points of difference to the Court. However, M. Salandra immediately reserved his position regarding any future consultation of the Court. *Ibid.*, p. 1345. M. Branting subsequently made a last-ditch attempt to have the questions referred to the Court, but was dissuaded from pressing his proposal. *Ibid.*, pp. 1349–50. Nevertheless, he and others persisted in the view that the Council had erred in foregoing the opportunity to obtain a Court opinion. See LN, Records of the 4th Ass., Plenary, 1923, pp. 138–42. They were reinforced in their view when the committee of jurists' replies were received, for the reply on the fourth question was studiously vague. LNOJ, 1924, pp. 525–26.

It would be incorrect to deduce from this case the conclusion that the Council, as a whole, opposed sending abstract questions, or even abstract questions related to Covenant interpretation, to the Court. The view that the Court was not competent to decide such questions was upheld by only three members of the Council—MM. Salandra, Hanotaux, and de Mello Franco.[156] As for the remaining members, they were originally desirous of having all the questions submitted to the Court, and they considered the Court fully competent to give the projected opinion. The compromise solution proffered was intended to meet Italy's wishes, and its failure to be accepted (over the issue of question 3) led to the abandonment of efforts to get a Court opinion on any of the five questions. Thus, for most Council members, the final decision was purely a tactical one and did not in any way reflect their views regarding the Court's competence.

The long debate over a committee of jurists versus the PCIJ is, however, more illuminating in another respect. It demonstrates vividly the character which a Court advisory opinion had come to assume in practice as early as 1923. The real issue behind the debate was: What force and effect should the product of the projected consultation have? Should it have the force of an authoritative statement of the law, which the Council would likely accept unquestioningly? Or should it rather bear the character of guidelines, providing merely a starting point for Council debate? In brief, should it be a quasi-decision of a Court, or a consultation of lawyers, pure and simple? Italy did not hesitate in selecting its preferred alternative. The greater the freedom retained by the Council and the less the weight of the legal pronouncement, the smaller the risk of any meaningful censure of Italian actions during the Corfu incident.[157]

The Cruiser Salamis

Two separate suggestions contemplating recourse to the Court's advisory procedure were put forward in connection with this case. The first originated with Greece and would have elicited a Court pronouncement on the substance of a matter then before an arbitral tribunal. The second—incorporated in a formal proposal—was presented by a Council committee of three, and would have confined the scope of the consultation to the preliminary aspect of the Council's competence vis-à-vis that of the arbitral tribunal in question.

Only the second was seriously considered, and it ran into considerable opposition in the Council. As a result, consultation of a committee of jurists was substituted for the proposed reference to the Court.

[156] The latter two were nevertheless willing, at various points, to have the questions submitted to the Court. LNOJ, 1923, pp. 1323, 1342.

[157] The fact that, subsequently, Italy had little difficulty in accepting the reply of the committee of jurists on the very sensitive fourth question was directly related to the vagueness of that reply. See *ibid.*, 1924, p. 524.

The facts which gave rise to the discussion in the Council were the following.

The Greek government had applied to the Greco-German Mixed Arbitral Tribunal for a decision canceling a prewar contract signed with a German company for the construction of the cruiser *Salamis*. While that arbitration was pending before the Tribunal, the Greek government requested of the League Council "an official interpretation of Articles 190 and 192 of the Treaty of Versailles[158] by any means at the Council's disposal, such as a request to the Permanent Court of International Justice for an advisory opinion."[159]

However, before the Council could decide whether to comply with the Greek request for an "official interpretation," a preliminary question had to be resolved: Was the Council, in fact, competent to give such an interpretation? On this question, the Greek and German representatives took opposing positions. Dr. Von Schubert, the German representative, argued that the dispute was purely a private law matter between a private German company, on the one hand, and Greece, in its capacity as a private party, on the other. The question of treaty interpretation, which was merely incidental to the private law dispute, could not alter the essential nature of the controversy. Consequently, the Tribunal alone was competent to deal with the matter, in all its aspects, and it was not for the Council to impair the Tribunal's authority.[160]

In opposition to this view, M. Politis, the Greek representative, maintained that the interpretation of the two provisions of the Versailles Treaty constituted merely a preliminary question connected with the private case before the Tribunal. Moreover, the Conference of Ambassadors, to whose powers of investigation and control the League Council had succeeded, had been generally acknowledged as competent to give an "official interpretation" of the texts in question.

At the same time, M. Politis also explained the bases for his government's suggestion that a PCIJ advisory opinion be requested.The suggestion, he said, accorded with previous Council practice in cases where outside international authorities were faced with difficulties in treaty interpretation. Consultation of the Court had provided for those authorities a welcome lessening of their own responsibilities and had strengthened the legal foundation of their final awards. In the *Salamis* case, too, Greek public opinion would more readily accept the Tribunal's decision as authoritative if that decision were based on a prior "official interpretation" by the Court.[161]

---

[158] Greece wished to know whether the clauses in the two articles which prohibited the construction and export of warships or naval materials by Germany applied to the case of the *Salamis*, which was contracted for before the war.

[159] LNOJ, 1927, pp. 1338–39. The request was dated 24 June 1927.

[160] *Ibid.*, p. 1150; see also the German memorandum, *ibid.*, p. 1339.

[161] *Ibid.*, pp. 1144–50. M. Politis recognized that his suggestion ran counter to the normal Council procedure of awaiting a direct request from the international authority

A committee of three,[162] appointed by the Council to study the Greek application, found itself unable to resolve the preliminary question of the Council's competence to accede to the Greek request for an official interpretation of the specified Versailles Treaty provisions. The committee therefore recommended that that question be referred to the Court for an advisory opinion.[163]

As explained by the members of the committee, the reasoning behind their recommendation was, briefly, the following.[164]

Admittedly, the Council had the right to determine its own competence. Admittedly, too, the dispute was, money-wise and otherwise, a minor one. However, implicated in the dispute were grave questions of principle which were important to all Versailles signatories.[165] Yet, the Council could not pronounce itself on these grave questions without first clarifying the preliminary issue of its competence to deal with the substantive questions. And, without judicial assistance, this complex preliminary issue would be most difficult to resolve. The Council would either be prevented from making any progress or be led to take a hasty decision which it would regret. A Court opinion, on the other hand, would permit the adoption of a decision more fully satisfying to the conscience of Council members in their capacity as "jurists and statesmen."

The committee's recommendations evoked strong criticism on the part of several Council members. Most of the latter objected to Council assumption of competence in the *Salamis* case, since, in their view, this would amount to interference with a pending private law arbitration. Moreover, all of these representatives insisted that the Council was the sole judge of its own competence.[166]

---

concerned before soliciting the Court's opinion, but he considered that the *Salamis* case warranted dispensing with such a precautionary measure because (1) the parties before the Tribunal and the Council were not identical; and (2) Greece considered the Tribunal totally incompetent with respect to the issue before the Council.

[162] M. Urrutia, the Rapporteur, had requested that two Council members assist him in studying the problem, and MM. Adatci and Scialoja had been appointed for this purpose. *Ibid.*, pp. 1150–51.

[163] *Ibid.*, pp. 1457–58.

[164] *Ibid.*, pp. 1457–73 *passim*.

[165] Thus, a Tribunal decision allowing exportation of the *Salamis* might clash with the rights of other Versailles signatories to have Article 192 of that treaty respected. *Ibid.*, p. 1464.

[166] See the statements of Herr Stresemann (Germany), *ibid.*, p. 1458; M. Loudon (the Netherlands), *ibid.*, p. 1460; the Earl of Onslow (Great Britain), *ibid.*, p. 1463; and Count Clauzel (France), *ibid.*, p. 1468.

While these representatives objected both to Council assumption of competence and to the proposed consultation of the Court, M. Titulesco objected only to the latter. *Ibid.*, p. 1467. His somewhat exceptional stand is fully comprehensible in light of the Rumanian position in the Hungarian optants issue, which was under Council consideration during this same period. Rumania, it will be recalled, desired the Council to set aside

Thus, Herr Stresemann feared that, unless the Council declared itself incompetent, it would establish a dangerous precedent and find itself overwhelmed in the future with relatively unimportant matters. As for requesting the Court's opinion: "If we ask the Hague to give us an opinion on the question whether we are in order in asking it to give an opinion,[167] an impression of very great uncertainty will certainly be given."[168]

M. Loudon, too, considered the Council incompetent,[169] and wondered "what would happen to arbitration if one of the parties, as soon as it foresaw an unfavourable judgment, could, against the desire of its opponents, approach the Council and ask for a verdict which, in actual fact, would set aside the process of arbitration."[170] He was also opposed to asking the Court's opinion on the question of the Council's competence. Such a step might "diminish the prestige of the Council and create the impression that it is incapable of settling such questions on its own authority."[171]

M. Politis and the members of the committee of three considered these misgivings regarding judicial determination of the Council's competence misplaced. If the Council was free to judge its own competence, it was equally free to doubt it.[172] Moreover, the power of ultimate decision remained in Council hands, since the Court's opinion would be purely advisory.[173] In referring the proposed question to the Court, the Council would, in fact, merely be following its own precedents.[174] The dignity of the Council would not be diminished in any way by the proposed reference.

It was quite evident that a unanimous vote on requesting the Court's opinion would be unattainable. But the Council was also divided over the

---

the results of the arbitration in question and to decide the matter independently, without a Court opinion.

[167] This is a reference to M. Politis' original suggestion for requesting an opinion on the question of substance involved.

[168] LNOJ, 1927, p. 1458.

[169] The Council, he argued, had no general competence to interpret the Versailles Treaty unless the matter were brought under Articles 11 and 15 of the Covenant. But the present case involved only a matter of civil law. Moreover, Greece had not claimed that the Tribunal had exceeded its competence.

[170] LNOJ, 1927, p. 1460. See also the statements of the British and French representatives, ibid., pp. 1463, 1468. They considered applicable the reply which the 1923 committee of jurists (appointed in the aftermath of Corfu) had given to the second question referred to it—namely, that the Council must refuse, on the request of one party only, to consider a matter placed before some other authority with the consent of both parties and regularly proceeded with by that authority. M. Politis challenged the applicability of that reply to the Salamis case. Ibid., p. 1469.

[171] See also the statement of M. Titulesco, ibid., p. 1467.

[172] Ibid., p. 1459.

[173] Ibid., pp. 1464, 1472–73.

[174] M. Scialoja cited the Mosul case; M. Politis noted the German Settlers in Poland case. Ibid., pp. 1464, 1470.

question whether a majority vote would suffice in this case. As noted above, the members of the committee of three sought to emphasize the nonbinding nature of the Court's opinions.[175] In addition, M. Scialoja argued that in the present case there was even less reason for insisting on unanimity: "The opinion which we ask is one act of . . . procedure and we are always free not to accept that opinion and thus to remain masters of the situation. Further, the matter is one of an act of procedure in regard to a question of procedure, for questions of competence belong to the category of the larger questions of procedure."[176]

This view of the nature of advisory opinions and of the vote required was most vigorously opposed by M. Titulesco, the Rumanian representative.[177] First, "an advisory opinion is not an act of procedure. By asking for an advisory opinion, the Council in actual fact ceases to deal with the question and substitutes for itself the Permanent Court in the matter of the decision." Second, the Court's prestige necessitated acceptance of its opinions. But such acceptance, which required unanimity in the Council, would hardly be forthcoming if the request were made by a mere majority vote. And, finally, even if, under ordinary circumstances, the *Salamis* case might be deemed exceptional, the effect of Council action on possible United States accession to the PCIJ Statute had to be reckoned with. Were the Council now to reverse its constant practice of demanding unanimity, the present "provisional" American abstention might well become final.

This last argument appears to have carried some weight with the Council. Even the members of the committee of three concurred in the general feeling that the moment was not opportune for determining the question of the vote required for requests.

Thus, the road to the Court was blocked; and the Council was deadlocked between, on the one hand, those who favored Council discussion of the Greek request, but wished prior judicial clarification of the Council's competence, and, on the other hand, those who sought an immediate Council decision against dealing with the Greek request.[178] In these circumstances, the President (M. Villegas of Chile) proposed a compromise, which proved acceptable to both groups. A committee of jurists, consisting of the legal advisers of all the Council members, would study the legal aspects of the question and

---

[175] While insisting on the Council's theoretical right not to accept the Court's opinion, M. Scialoja conceded that the Council did not normally avail itself of that right. *Ibid.*, p. 1464. It is instructive to compare the Italian attitude on the binding nature of advisory opinions and on the vote required for requests in the *Salamis* case with that adopted by Italy in the aftermath of Corfu.

[176] LNOJ, 1927, p. 1473.

[177] *Ibid.*, p. 1474. Rumania's insistence on unanimity was probably related to her desire to avoid an advisory opinion in the Hungarian optants question.

[178] M. Titulesco, as noted above, fell into neither category.

particularly the question of competence, and would report to the Council in December.[179]

In December, the Council had before it a unanimous report by the committee of jurists on the question of the Council's competence.[180] Rejecting the Greek contentions on the issue, the committee concluded:

> In view of the importance of the principle that the Council should not take any action which could be misinterpreted as an encroachment on the sphere of an international tribunal which has been duly seized of a question, it would be courteous for the Council to address a communication to the Mixed Arbitral Tribunal informing the Tribunal that, if it should judge it to be desirable that an interpretation of Article 192 (and 190, if that article is considered relevant) should be obtained by way of an advisory opinion by the Permanent Court of International Justice and should address a communication to the Council to that effect, the Council would defer to such a desire.

This conclusion was said to accord with the Council's usual procedure when soliciting opinions affecting the functions of other international authorities.[181]

The report of the committee of jurists was approved by the Council and was concurred in by M. Politis.[182] Thus, in this case, consultation of a committee of jurists proved to be fully as effective as recourse to the Court might have been.

The decision not to consult the Court on the issue of the Council's competence must be seen primarily in the context of the reluctance of many Council members to interfere with a pending arbitration. Strongly opposed to any Council consideration of the Greek request, these members could see no point in carrying the matter any further by an appeal to the Court. Coupled with the conviction that such an appeal was pointless was the feeling that it was improper and demeaning to have the Council's competence determined by an outside body. But, in view of the fact that in several other instances the Council had not hesitated to refer questions relating to its competence to the Court, it would appear that the first consideration—the pointlessness of the request—was the more determinative. The possibility that the Council might

---

[179] LNOJ, 1927, pp. 1474-75.

[180] *Ibid.*, 1928, pp. 179-80.

[181] As noted above, M. Politis had acknowledged that this was the normal Council practice, but had deemed the *Salamis* case exceptional.

[182] LNOJ, 1928, p. 181.

override these objections by voting, on the basis of a mere majority, to request the Court's opinion was not seriously contemplated. At that stage, the Council was not prepared to settle the thorny issue of the vote required to request advisory opinions. Consultation of a committee of jurists proved an acceptable alternative to proponents and opponents of recourse to the Court. For the first group, it provided the consolation of seeing the matter of competence clarified by some legally expert body, while, for the second group, it represented retention by the Council of its freedom to judge its own competence. Clearly implicit in the discussions was the view that to request a Court opinion was equivalent to *delegating* to an outside body the task of judging the Council's competence.

The Vote Required for Requesting Advisory Opinions

The question of the vote required for requesting advisory opinions occupied the League, in varying degrees, throughout its history.[183] As was seen earlier, the prevailing uncertainty regarding this question was a factor in some of the decisions to substitute recourse to committees of jurists for recourse to the Court.[184] Moreover, at certain junctures—most notably, when the question of American accession to the PCIJ Statute was under consideration[185]—the problem became particularly acute.

On at least three separate occasions, the possibility of having the Court itself clarify the nature of the vote required for requests was broached, only to be rejected in every instance. A proposal to this effect was first put forward outside the League framework, at the 1926 Conference of Signatories, during the deliberations on the troublesome second part of the fifth United States Senate reservation. The suggestion was renewed in the League Assembly in 1928 and again in 1935 by League members who were disturbed by the decline in the Court's advisory business and the corresponding pen-

---

[183] The history of League consideration of the matter is reviewed in detail in Series E of the PCIJ publications under the heading "Procedure for Voting upon Requests for Opinions." See, especially, PCIJ, Ser. E, No. 12, pp. 117-27; and No. 16, pp. 62-64. See also Salo Engel, *Art. 5 und Art. 14 Satz 3 der Völkerbundsatzung* (Annemasse, France: Rosnoblet, 1936); Hudson, *Permanent Court*, pp. 488-94; Cromwell A. Riches, *The Unanimity Rule and the League of Nations* (Baltimore: The Johns Hopkins Press, 1933), pp. 69-90, 192-93; Albert E. Kane, "The Unanimity Rule as Applied to Requests for Advisory Opinions from the World Court," *China Law Review*, 6 (1933): 185-212.

[184] E.g., in the aftermath of Corfu and in the *Salamis* case. In both cases, however, the Council might well have refrained from consulting the Court, even had a majority vote been deemed theoretically sufficient for this purpose.

[185] For a review of the protracted and unrewarding efforts to induce the United States to accede to the PCIJ Statute, see Denna Frank Fleming, *The United States and the World Court* (New York: Doubleday, Doran & Co., 1945); and Hudson, *Permanent Court*, chap. XI.

chant for employing committees of jurists. For various reasons, however, the majority of the League membership preferred to let the issue of the vote required for requests ride, unresolved.

As noted, the suggestion to request the Court's advisory opinion in the matter first arose in connection with the second part of the fifth United States Senate reservation.[186] Only this clause caused the 1926 Conference of Signatories any real difficulty, for it was based on an assumption which the Conference was unprepared to concede—namely, that unanimity was necessary for all requests. In the course of the debates on the means to overcome this one apparently major obstacle to the hoped-for American accession, M. Rolin of Belgium proposed soliciting (by means of a Council request) the Court's own view on the issue of the vote required.[187] He fully expected that the United States government would accept the Court's "authoritative" opinion. Several other participants concurred in this recommendation, on the grounds, *inter alia*, that, while a slow evolution of League practice was preferable, the American reservation precluded such a luxury. But, unlike M. Rolin, they emphasized that a Court opinion would in no way prejudge the final decision of the League organs.[188] The majority of the Conference, however, considered judicial clarification of the issue inopportune, and agreed, in this respect, with Sir Cecil Hurst. The latter had argued that a Court opinion would inevitably serve to crystallize the matter and that the issue was not yet ripe for such crystallization.[189] Furthermore, a Court opinion upholding the sufficiency of a majority vote would merely serve to alienate the United States utterly.[190] The Conference therefore reserved its opinion on the vote required for requests and contented itself with offering the United States a position of equality with the members of the Council and the Assembly.[191]

---

[186] The relevant part of the reservation read as follows: "nor shall it [the Court], without the consent of the United States, entertain any request for an advisory opinion touching any dispute or question in which the United States has or claims an interest." The original draft of this clause would have been quite innocuous. It provided that "the United States shall be in no manner bound by any advisory opinion of the Permanent Court of International Justice not rendered pursuant to a request in which it, the United States, shall expressly join." See Minutes of the 1926 Conf. of Signatories, p. 30.

[187] *Ibid.*, p. 23.

[188] See the remarks of MM. Pilotti (Italy), Dinichert (Switzerland), and Erich (Finland), *ibid.*, pp. 25–26, 39–40, 42.

[189] *Ibid.*, p. 24. For other arguments adduced against recourse to the Court, see the remarks of MM. Fromageot (France), Osusky (Czechoslovakia), and Negulesco (Rumania), *ibid.*, pp. 27, 43.

[190] M. Rolin apparently considered this last consideration the key to the failure of his proposal. LN, Records of the 9th Ass., 1st Ctte., 1928, p. 49.

[191] The United States reservation was understood to refer to three categories of requests: (1) those related to disputes in which the United States was a party; (2) those related to disputes in which the United States merely "claims an interest"; and (3) those

At the ninth Assembly session, the possibility of requesting an advisory opinion on the question was again raised. A formal draft resolution was introduced by the Swiss delegation in the following terms.

The Assembly recommends the Council to consider whether it would not be desirable to submit to the Permanent Court of International Justice, for an advisory opinion, the question whether the Council or the Assembly can, by a simple majority, request an advisory opinion under Article 14 of the Covenant of the League of Nations.[192]

Underlying this proposal was the belief that "more frequent, more confident, and more courageous" recourse to the Court's advisory function was being hampered by the uncertainty regarding the vote required for requests; that a solution of that question would enlarge the possibility of "finding legal solutions for political problems and inter-State disputes"; that the question should be finally settled before a fixed "jurisprudence" developed; and that the Court was best qualified to decide a question relating to interpretation of the Covenant.[193]

When the proposal came to be considered by the First (Constitutional and Legal) Committee, it encountered rather stiff opposition. The objections put forward fell into two main categories, those related to expediency and those related to principle. On the practical side, it was argued that the empirical method by which the League had gradually developed its own "jurisprudence" was more appropriate than clarification by the Court; that the League's political organs had to be guided by the circumstances of each particular case and not hamstrung by rigid rules; and that the issue of American accession made a Court opinion as inopportune now as it had been in 1926.[194] It was further contended that, if, for political reasons, the Council or Assembly were later to find itself at variance with the Court's opinion, the

---

involving "questions" in which the United States "has or claims an interest." The *Eastern Carelia* precedent was thought sufficient to provide satisfaction with respect to the first category. But, as regards the other two categories, the Conference could merely agree to offer the United States a position of equality with the members of the Council or the Assembly. As for the American assumption that unanimity was required for requests, the Conference stated that "it is . . . impossible to say with certainty whether in some cases, or possibly in all cases, a decision by a majority is not sufficient." Minutes of the 1926 Conf. of Signatories, p. 79.

[192] LN, Records of the 9th Ass., Plenary, 1928, p. 65. It is noteworthy that a direct Assembly request was not contemplated. The Council's interest in the problem was obviously thought to be paramount.

[193] Remarks of MM. Motta and Bruckhardt, *ibid.*, pp. 64–65; *ibid.*, 1st Ctte., 1928, pp. 41–42.

[194] See the remarks of MM. Fromageot (France), Ito (Japan), Politis (Greece), and Sir Cecil Hurst, *ibid.*, 1st Ctte., 1928, pp. 41, 45–47.

prestige of the Court would suffer.[195] The second class of objections was directed against Court interpretation of the Covenant in the abstract. Several of the arguments presented in connection with the Corfu aftermath and the Lithuanian request for an advisory opinion were now repeated. Thus, it was again contended that the Court could deal only with concrete cases, not with abstract questions; and that judicial interpretation of Covenant provisions in the abstract was particularly objectionable, because it was the equivalent of either "authentic" interpretation or amendment, both of which were reserved for Covenant signatories.[196] It was further maintained that to request an advisory opinion with respect to the competence of the Council and the Assembly would amount to depriving those organs of their powers.[197]

Counterarguments to the various objections raised were presented by the representatives of Norway, Belgium, and Sweden.[198] The Court's prestige, they contended, would not suffer from nonacceptance of an advisory opinion, since such an opinion had, in any case, no legally binding force. Moreover, the Court would readily find ways and means of replying without lessening its authority. As for American accession, the continuing uncertainty had not served to bring the United States into the Court. There was therefore no justification for perpetuating that uncertainty. By revealing once again the wide divergence of views on the issue,[199] the present discussions merely served to accentuate the need for an appeal to the Court's high authority. Even if the Court ruled a majority vote sufficient, the Council would certainly, in particular cases, take the objections of the protesting minority into account.

The majority of the Committee, however, would clearly have rejected the allusion in the Swiss proposal to possible consultation of the Court.[200] In

---

[195] Remarks of MM. Scialoja and Ito, *ibid.*, pp. 44–45.

[196] See *ibid.*, pp. 44, 47, 49–50. Again, reference was made to the rejection of M. Larnaude's amendment in 1919.

[197] *Ibid.*, p. 50.

[198] *Ibid.*, pp. 46, 49, 57.

[199] Some states favored a majority vote for all requests; others favored a unanimous vote in all cases; and the greatest number thought that the required vote depended on circumstances. However, the distinguishing critieria proposed were almost as numerous as the proposals (e.g., the "procedural" versus the "substantive" nature of the matter referred; opinions entailing "political" consequences versus those without such consequences). Further differences arose in relation to the necessity of securing the consent of the states most directly concerned. See *ibid.*, pp. 40–50. Cf. LNOJ, 1937, pp. 170–86, where the observations of governments are set forth.

[200] See the remarks of M. Linburg (the Netherlands), LN, Records of the 9th Ass., 1st Ctte., 1928, p. 51. Action on the original Swiss proposal entailed yet another difficulty. What vote would be necessary in order for the Council to address the suggested request to the Court? Would a majority vote suffice for the adoption of a request intended to discover whether a majority vote would suffice for the adoption of requests generally? Apparently, the Swiss representative himself, while approving the majority

recognition of this fact, the Swiss delegation amended its proposal to provide merely for Council study of the question whether a majority vote sufficed for requesting an opinion.[201] In this form, it was adopted by the Assembly on 24 September 1928.[202] For its part, the Council proposed that the Council members "study the subject individually," in order that an "exchange of views" might later ensue.[203]

By 1935, however, no such exchange of views had taken place.[204] At the Assembly's sixteenth session, therefore, a new proposal (sponsored jointly by Belgium, Norway, the Netherlands, Sweden, and Switzerland) revived the issue of Council study of the question of the vote required for requests and, like the original 1928 Swiss proposal, contemplated possible recourse to the Court for elucidation of the problem.[205] The reasons which prompted this proposal were clearly set forth in the consideranda of the draft resolution and in the statements of the sponsoring delegations. Thus, in the preamble, it was stated:

... whereas the desired study has not ... been undertaken and the situation is still undefined;

And whereas the result has been to retard the activities of the Permanent Court of International Justice;

And whereas it is essential to the legal security of Members of the League that, even in the case of disputes submitted to the Council, the

---

principle for most requests, admitted the necessity of a unanimous vote in the case of a request involving an abstract interpretation of the Covenant. *Ibid.*, p. 42. But, clearly, even if a majority vote had been attainable in the Assembly, the achievement of unanimity in the Council on the actual request was a vain hope.

[201] *Ibid.*, p. 53.

[202] *Ibid.*, Plenary, 1928, p. 139.

[203] LNOJ, 1929, p. 10.

[204] The issue of the vote required had, however, been broached again on several occasions. In the 1929 Committee of Jurists the matter was discussed only incidentally. No suggestion to have the Court clarify the nature of the vote required for requests was made on that occasion. As in 1926, the matter was left open, with interest focusing rather on practical arrangements to be worked out with the United States. In 1930, a special committee set up to consider amendments to the League Covenant in order to "bring it into harmony with the Pact of Paris" recommended the addition of a provision to Article 15 of the Covenant, under the terms of which a majority vote would have sufficed to request the Court's opinion in certain cases. The proposal was linked to one attributing binding force to unanimous recommendations of the Council. Since the latter was not retained, the former was thought to have lost its raison d'être and was therefore deleted by the Eleventh Assembly. LN Doc. C.160.M.69.1930.V, pp. 62–76, 122; LN, Records of the 11th Ass., 1st Ctte., 1930, p. 166. An intention to raise the question of the vote required was expressed in the course of the Council's discussion of the Swiss reparations issue. LNOJ, 1935, pp. 142–43.

[205] The Assembly would express its desire that, "should the Council be unable to arrive at a decision ... the question itself may be submitted to the Court for an opinion." LN, Records of the 16th Ass., Plenary, 1935, p. 76.

points of law involved should be enquired into by the legal authority qualified to do so, with the safeguards afforded to the parties by the customary procedure of the Court.

In the Assembly's First Committee, M. Rolin of Belgium further expanded on this theme. He deplored the decline in the Court's advisory business which had set in, particularly since 1933, and the corresponding tendency to refer questions to committees of jurists, which sit "*in camera*, no opportunity being given for the parties to be heard." In his opinion, both developments were attributable to continuing uncertainty regarding the nature of the vote required. In brief, the question was a "burning" one which urgently called for Court clarification.[206]

Again, as in 1926 and 1928, objections were raised to involving the Court in the problem. The same arguments were reiterated.[207] In addition, many representatives disputed the urgency of resolving the question and rejected the implied criticism of the Council's employment of committees of jurists.[208] Proponents of recourse to the Court again insisted that the Council would retain its complete freedom of appreciation with respect to particular cases, even in the event the Court upheld the majority rule.[209] But these arguments did not serve to sway opponents of judicial clarification of the issue. The vote in the Committee on that part of the joint draft resolution which recommended possible consultation of the Court was 11 to 11. The Committee was apparently evenly divided between those who, dissatisfied with the fixed practice of requiring unanimity for all requests, sought a more flexible rule, and those who were rather content with the prevailing "jurisprudence."

The upshot of the debate in the Committee was the adoption of only the first part of the joint draft resolution, in modified form.[210] The Assembly merely expressed its desire that "the Council will examine the question in what circumstances and subject to what conditions an advisory opinion may be requested under Article 14 of the Covenant." Two important modifica-

---

[206] *Ibid.*, 1st Ctte., 1935, pp. 44–46. M. Rolin further expressed the hope that, in the event the Council did not refer the question to the Court, "certain Governments would lay the matter before the Permanent Court" in contentious procedure. However, it is not clear how a matter of this kind could possibly have been brought as a contentious case.

[207] *Ibid.*, pp. 51–62 *passim*. One of the voices questioning the Court's competence to interpret the Covenant was a voice newly added to the League chorus, that of the Soviet Union. *Ibid.*, p. 53. Thus, when in the early UN period the Soviet Union denied the ICJ's competence to interpret the UN Charter, it was acting true to its "tradition."

[208] See, especially, the remarks of Sir William Malkin (Great Britain) and M. Sobolewski (Poland), *ibid.*, pp. 54, 58.

[209] *Ibid.*, pp. 47, 56.

[210] *Ibid.*, pp. 69, 72. It was adopted by the Plenary on 28 September 1935. *Ibid.*, Plenary, 1935, p. 95.

tions were introduced in the preamble. In place of the original categorical assertion that uncertainty regarding the vote required had resulted in retardation of the Court's activities, the new preamble merely stated that such uncertainty "*may* have contributed to" diminishing the Court's activity. Furthermore, the absolute preference for use of the Court's advisory function and the implied criticism of the use of committees of jurists did not find their way into the final resolution.[211]

Upon receipt of the Assembly's resolution, the Council invited the members of the League to express their views on the problem,[212] and some seventeen governments responded.[213] The Council was then faced with a bewildering array of viewpoints on the matter, and some members doubted whether the divergence revealed was really bridgeable at all. Nevertheless, on 26 January 1937 the matter was referred by the Council to a special committee set up to study the application of the principles of the Covenant.[214] In that committee the matter, in effect, died.

In the absence of judicial clarification of the nature of the vote required for requests, the Council had developed a rather fixed practice of soliciting the Court's opinion only on the basis of a unanimous vote.[215] As noted earlier, the drive to get a Court opinion on the issue was initiated and supported by states that wished to see a more flexible rule than absolute unanimity adopted; it was resisted by states that found the existing practice satisfactory. The division over recourse to the Court was but a reflection of the

---

[211] The following paragraph was substituted for the original in the preamble:

Considering that it is desirable for the security of the legal rights of the Members of the League . . . that, in cases where it appears indispensable for the accomplishment of the task of the Council or the Assembly that advice should be obtained on some point of law, such advice *should, as a general rule,* be requested from the Permanent Court of International Justice [italics added].

Recourse to the Court was no longer deemed "essential," only somewhat preferable to the employment of committees of jurists.

[212] LNOJ, 1936, pp. 117-18.

[213] *Ibid.*, 1937, pp. 170-83, 186, 664.

[214] *Ibid.*, p. 108.

[215] The two apparent exceptions to the rule were the requests in the *Acquistion of Polish Nationality* and *Mosul* cases. In the first, the Council may have proceeded on the basis of a mere majority vote. See LNOJ, 1923, p. 1934; and Julius Stone, *International Guarantees of Minority Rights* (London: Oxford University Press, 1932), pp. 193, 214. In the second, the unanimity attained may have excluded the vote of the parties. Cf. LNOJ, 1925, pp. 1380-82; and 1926, p. 122.

In two additional cases (*Eastern Carelia* and *Expulsion of the Oecumenical Patriarch*) the Council adopted the requests unanimously, but in the absence of, respectively, Russia and Turkey. (The request in the latter case was subsequently withdrawn. LNOJ, 1925, pp. 488, 854-55, 895.)

division over the nature of the vote required for requests. Quite obviously, those who favored a more liberal rule had nothing to lose, and everything to gain, from consulting the Court. At worst, a Court opinion would merely confirm the existing practice; at best, it would sanction a majority vote, at least for some categories of cases. For those who were content with the existing jurisprudence, the stakes were manifestly reversed.

To a great extent, the effort to obtain judicial clarification of the issue was misconceived. It was based on an assumption which was not entirely warranted and an objection which was not wholly justified. The assumption was that uncertainty regarding the nature of the vote required was a primary cause in the decline in the Court's business. But what of the earlier years, when business hummed despite the prevailing uncertainty, and despite the unanimity requirement? Should not the search for primary causes have led elsewhere? And was there not an element of unreality in the expectation that the Court's business would be susceptible to such easy stimulation—particularly in the year 1935?

Admittedly, in the case of some of the "stillborn" requests surveyed above, the impossibility of procuring a unanimous sustaining vote was manifest. It does not follow, however, that, given the sufficiency of a majority vote for requests, all (or even any) of the "stillborn" requests would necessarily have become actual requests.

But, even granting the truth of the assumption, was the objection to which it gave rise justified? The objection was directed at what had become a kind of modus operandi for the Council when it was faced with legal difficulties. Where unanimity was attainable, the Court was often appealed to; where it was not, recourse was frequently had to committees of jurists. This setup was, in fact, rather commendable, for it allowed "legal" clarification of questions while, at the same time, preserving the Court's judicial character and prestige.

Indeed, what benefits could have accrued to the Council from a Court advisory opinion on the vote required for requests? Had the Court upheld the unanimity vote, the existing practice would merely have been reinforced. On the other hand, a pronouncement favoring a vote by majority or by qualified unanimity (i.e., minus the parties) might merely have hastened the appearance of one of the UN phenomena: a relatively large crop of ineffectual opinions.[216]

In any case, the fact is that the majority of the Council members preferred to leave matters as they were. Undoubtedly, the desire not to alienate

---

[216] That this might be the result of abandoning the unanimity requirement for requests was frequently stressed in League discussions. See, e.g., the remarks of M. Titulesco in the *Salamis* case, LNOJ, 1927, p. 1474; Sir Cecil Hurst, LN, Records of the

the United States was one of the factors which accounted for this preference. More important, however, was the satisfaction felt by the majority with the Council's modus operandi, outlined above.

As in some previous cases, objections were raised—and in even stronger terms—to involving the Court in an abstract interpretation of Covenant provisions. But, again, these must be seen in context—in this case, the context of a desire either to maintain the unanimity rule for requests, or, at least, to allow the Council a free hand in the matter. Thus, what was opposed was not so much judicial interpretation of Covenant provisions in the abstract as it was judicial interpretation of the *particular* provisions then at issue. [217]

THE U.N. PERIOD: A GENERAL SURVEY

The following survey indicates, in brief, the cases in connection with which proposals and suggestions to request the Court's advisory opinion were put forward in the General Assembly and the Security Council. [218] In some cases, formal draft resolutions were submitted, voted on, and rejected; in

---

9th Ass., 1st Ctte., 1928, p. 45; and M. Politis, LN, Records of the 16th Ass., 1st Ctte., 1935, p. 59. On the reception of advisory opinions, see Chapter VI.

[217] See, e.g., the remarks of M. Egoriev (the U.S.S.R.), LN, Records of the 16th Ass., 1st Ctte., 1935, p. 53.

[218] As for the organs and agencies authorized under Article 96(2) (not treated in this survey), three instances of nonuse—involving, respectively, ECOSOC, the Trusteeship Council, and UNESCO—may be noted in passing:

1. In 1947, ECOSOC considered the possibility of requesting an advisory opinion on the survival of prewar minorities treaties and declarations, but decided to refer the matter to the UN Secretariat, instead. See ECOSOCOR (VI), Supp. No. 1, par. 37; and UN Docs. E/CN.4/52, 6 December 1947, pp. 18–19; and E/AC.7/SR.34, 23 February 1948, pp. 2–4.

2. An Indian proposal introduced in a committee of the Trusteeship Council in 1954 would have had the Council recommend that the General Assembly request an opinion on the legality of the use of a trust territory "for purposes which result in the destruction or disappearance of a part of the Territory itself and have very adverse effects on the health of the population" (i.e., of nuclear tests). The proposal was not adopted by the committee. TCOR (XIV), Annexes, a.i. 5, pp. 63, 67 (UN Doc. T/L.498, 12 July 1954).

3. At its seventieth session, the UNESCO Executive Board voted to exclude Portugal from participation in UNESCO-sponsored conferences, pending the results of "a study *in situ* of the present state of education" in Portugal's African territories. UNESCO, 70/EX/Decisions, 14, 4 June 1965. In a letter of 30 June 1965 to the Director-General, Portugal contested the legality of this decision and proposed that an ICJ advisory opinion be sought in this matter. (UNESCO, 14C/34, Annex 1). The Portuguese request was placed on the agenda of the fourteenth session of the General Conference. After extensive and stormy discussions (see UNESCO, 14C/LEG/SR.9–15, 18–20), the Conference's Legal Committee adopted a draft resolution to refer the matter to the ICJ for an advisory opinion. But the General Conference did not consider this draft resolution in Plenary, and instead voted to confirm the disputed Executive Board action and to reject the Portuguese request for judicial clarification. Resolution 20, of 28 November 1966, UNESCO, Records of the General Conf., 14th Sess., Resolutions, p. 106.

others, formal proposals were made but not voted on; and, in still others, suggestions were made without ever being translated into formal proposals.[219]

1. In connection with the first election of judges to the ICJ in 1946, some difficulty was encountered, both in the General Assembly and in the Security Council, over interpretation of the word "meeting" in Articles 11 and 12 of the ICJ Statute.[220] In the Security Council, on a United Kingdom motion, it was agreed that the Security Council propose to the General Assembly that both, as separate bodies, or the General Assembly alone, ask the Court for an advisory opinion on the matter, for the purpose of future elections.[221] A similar proposal was put forward in the General Assembly by France and the United Kingdom.[222] At that time, however, the General Committee refused to recommend inclusion of this proposal in the Assembly's agenda.[223]

During the second part of the first session, the question was referred to the Assembly's Sixth Committee for its consideration. That Committee unanimously adopted a rule of procedure on the question at issue and recommended that no action be taken, at that stage, to request the Court's opinion.[224] The rule of procedure met with the acceptance of the Assembly[225] and the Security Council,[226] and, consequently, an advisory opinion was no longer deemed necessary.

2. When the General Assembly had to consider, in early 1946, the question of the expiration date of the terms of the members of the Council, France suggested in the General Committee that the Court be asked for an advisory opinion regarding the compatibility with the Charter of a special rule of procedure formerly adopted by the Assembly.[227] In Plenary, France referred to its earlier suggestion but did not pursue the matter further.[228]

[219] In addition, passing references to the possibility of requesting advisory opinions were made in connection with the following cases: (1) the Corfu Channel case; (2) the legality of establishing the Interim Committee; (3) nationalization of the Suez Canal; and (4) the status of the German-speaking element in Bolzano. See, respectively, the Australian statement (SCOR, 2nd Yr., 111th Mtg., 24 February 1947, p. 364), the United Kingdom statement (GAOR [II], 1st Ctte., 97th Mtg., 6 November 1947, pp. 335-36); the Belgian statement (SCOR, 11th Yr., 737th Mtg., 8 October 1956, p. 26), and the Jordanian statement (GAOR [XV], Spec. Pol. Ctte., 182nd Mtg., 25 October 1960, pp. 35-36). Most of the discussions in the last case revolved around referring the dispute to the Court in its contentious capacity.

[220] There was some doubt as to whether the term meant a single balloting or a series of ballotings.

[221] SCOR, 1st Yr., 1st Ser., 9th Mtg., 6 February 1946, p. 160.

[222] GAOR (I/1), Plenary, 25th Mtg., 6 February 1946, p. 346.

[223] Ibid., General Ctte., 17th Mtg., 14 February 1946, p. 28.

[224] GAOR (I/2), 6th Ctte., 17th Mtg., 11 November 1946, p. 81.

[225] Ibid., Plenary, 49th Mtg., 19 November 1946, p. 986.

[226] SCOR, 2nd Yr., 138th Mtg., 4 June 1947, p. 952.

[227] GAOR (I/1), General Ctte., Mtgs. 14 and 15, 11 February 1946, pp. 24, 26.

[228] Ibid., Plenary, 31st Mtg., 13 February 1946, p. 463. The matter is now governed by Rule 140 of the Assembly's Rules of Procedure.

3. In 1946, in the course of Security Council discussion of the Spanish question, the United Kingdom representative suggested that the entire juridical question be submitted to the Court for clarification by means of an advisory opinion.[229] At that point, the Council was considering a recommendation by the special subcommittee it had created to study the situation in Spain. The subcommittee, finding that the Franco government constituted only a "potential," not an actual, threat to international peace, concluded that the matter could be dealt with only under Chapter VI of the Charter. At the same time, it suggested that the Council transmit to the Assembly the evidence and reports of the subcommittee, together with the recommendation that, unless the Franco regime were withdrawn and other conditions of political freedom were satisfied, the Assembly recommend the severance of diplomatic relations with the regime.[230] The United Kingdom representative entertained "grave doubts" as to the validity of the subcommittee's reasoning and the power of the UN to recommend the severance of diplomatic relations in the absence of a clear menace to international peace and security. Nevertheless, he did not submit a formal proposal to request an advisory opinion on the question, and he voted in favor of the subcommittee's recommendations.[231]

4. In 1946, during the Security Council's consideration of Jordan's application for admission to the UN, the Netherlands representative suggested that two general questions raised in the course of the discussions might usefully be referred to the Court for an advisory opinion.[232] The first was whether a state was entitled to oppose the admission of a state which fulfills the Charter requirements for admission;[233] the second, whether the abstention of a permanent Council member in the vote could bar a state's admission.[234] However, the Netherlands representative did not attempt to translate his suggestion into a formal proposal, partly out of the recognition that such a proposal would, in any case, meet with a Soviet veto.

5. In connection with the Assembly's handling of the treatment of Indians in South Africa[235] during the second part of the first session, a number of formal proposals were submitted both in the Joint First and Sixth Committee and in Plenary, which would have referred aspects of the dispute to the

[229]SCOR, 1st Yr., 1st Ser., 46th Mtg., 17 June 1946, pp. 344-49.

[230]UN Doc. S/75, 1 June 1946.

[231]The subcommittee's recommendations were defeated in any case, because the Soviet Union (for reasons unrelated to the British objections) opposed them.

[232]SCOR, 1st Yr., 2nd Ser., 56th Mtg., 29 August 1946, pp. 95-96. The points had been raised earlier by Australia and China, respectively.

[233]Cf. the request in the *Admission* case.

[234]Cf. the subsequent Iraqi proposal to request an advisory opinion on the effect of the United Kingdom's abstention on the admission of Israel. See p. 256 below.

[235]For a more detailed account of this case and the next two cases in this survey, see pp. 233-59 below.

Court. The only proposal put to a vote was one presented by the South African representative in Plenary, in accordance with which the Court would have been asked to clarify the Assembly's competence to deal with the Indian complaint. Further suggestions that the question of competence be sent to the Court for an advisory opinion were made during subsequent sessions, but none were translated into formal proposals.

6. In 1947, during the Security Council's handling of the Indonesian question, Belgium formally submitted a proposal under the terms of which the Council would have requested an advisory opinion on its competence to deal with the Indonesian issue, in light of the Netherlands' invocation of Article 2(7) of the Charter. This proposal was rejected.

7. The Palestine issue gave rise to more proposals and suggestions for requesting the Court's opinion than any other single issue. In the period 1947–52, such proposals and suggestions were put forward on no fewer than seven occasions. Some of the proposals were presented in the Security Council; others, in the General Assembly. Five of the proposals were voted on and rejected.

8. In 1948, during the course of Assembly discussion of Soviet violations "of fundamental human rights, traditional diplomatic practices and other principles of the Charter,"[236] Australia presented a draft resolution which would have referred to the Court one aspect of the Chilean complaint— namely, Soviet violation of traditional diplomatic practices.[237] However, the draft resolution evoked little support.[238] Although some doubts were apparently entertained regarding the legal points raised in the Australian draft,[239] a

[236] Chile alleged that the Soviet Union, by preventing Soviet wives of foreign nationals from joining their husbands abroad, was violating fundamental human rights and other principles of the Charter. Additionally, by refusing an exit visa to the daughter-in-law of the former Chilean ambassador to Moscow, it was violating traditional diplomatic practices. Letter of 27 May 1948 to the Secretary-General, UN Doc. A/560, 16 June 1948.

[237] The questions to be referred to the Court were:

1. To what degree do the privileges and immunities granted to the head of a foreign mission in accordance with diplomatic practices traditionally established by international law extend to his family and to his establishment?

2. In particular, is the action of a State in preventing one of its nationals, who is the wife of a member of a foreign diplomatic mission or of a member of his family or of his establishment, from leaving its territory with her husband, or in order to join her husband, a breach of international law?

UN Doc. A/C.6/316, 6 December 1948.

[238] France, the United Kingdom, and the United States were among its opponents. On the other hand, Chile supported the Australian proposal, obviously seeing in it an opportunity of getting its dispute with the Soviet Union adjudicated by the Court. A Chilean offer to submit the dispute directly to either the Permanent Court of Arbitration or the ICJ had been rejected by the Soviet Union. See GAOR (III), 6th Ctte., 135th Mtg., 3 December 1948, p. 728; and 139th Mtg., 7 December 1948, p. 779.

[239] Thus, while in the original Chilean proposal presented to the Sixth Committee the Soviet government's violation of "diplomatic practices traditionally consecrated by inter-

Court opinion was thought to be unnecessary—since, in any case, violations of human rights and of diplomatic usage and international courtesy constituted sufficient grounds for Assembly action in the instant case—and of doubtful utility—since the Soviet attitude could hardly be expected to change because of a Court pronouncement.[240]

The Australian draft resolution was put to a vote in the Sixth Committee and rejected.[241]

9. In 1949, Pakistan suggested that the question of the Security Council's competence to deal with the Hyderabad question be referred to the Court for an advisory opinion. Council discussion of the question had resumed, even though a cablegram had been received from the Nizam of Hyderabad withdrawing the original complaint. The Indian representative argued that Hyderabad was not a state under international law and therefore was not competent to bring any question before the Council. Pakistan maintained the opposite view, and thereupon declared that, if there were any remaining doubts as to the Council's competence, the Court should be asked to elucidate the matter.[242] However, no formal proposal to this effect was made.

10. In 1950, during the Security Council's consideration of the complaint of armed invasion of Taiwan, an Ecuadorian draft resolution inviting the representative of the People's Republic of China to participate in the Security Council's discussions on the question was declared adopted, despite the negative vote of the Chinese representative. The Chinese representative stated that a nonprocedural question was involved, whereupon the President put the question of the procedural nature of the Ecuadorian proposal to a vote. China alone voted against regarding the Ecuadorian draft as procedural. The President then ruled the proposal to regard the Ecuadorian draft as procedural adopted. On the other hand, the Chinese representative maintained that he had completed the double-veto procedure and that, consequently, the original

national law" was said to be "fully established" (UN Doc. A/C.6/296, 25 November 1948), the amendments presented to this draft avoided any categorical assertion that "international law" had been violated. Under the terms of a United Kingdom amendment (UN Doc. A/C.6/311, 1 December 1948), the expression "international usage and courtesy" would have been substituted for "international law." The resolution finally adopted was based on a French-Uruguayan amendment (UN Doc. A/C.6/319, 7 December 1948), which similarly skirted the legal issue by declaring that the Soviet action was "contrary to courtesy, to diplomatic practice, and to the principle of reciprocity."

[240]See the statements of the United Kingdom (GAOR [III], 6th Ctte., 135th Mtg., 3 December 1948, p. 733; and 137th Mtg., 6 December 1948, p. 752); the United States (ibid., p. 756); and Greece (ibid., 138th Mtg., 7 December 1948, p. 766).

Opposition to the Australian proposal was also based on (1) the assertion (put forward by Egypt and concurred in by France and Syria) that the Court could not deal with specific cases, but only with general questions of principle; and (2) the belief that reference to the Court would cast doubt on the resolution (see n. 239) already adopted. GAOR (III), 6th Ctte., 139th Mtg., 7 December 1948, pp. 779–80.

[241]Ibid., p. 781. The vote was 9 for, 13 against, with 12 abstentions.

[242]SCOR, 4th Yr., 426th Mtg., 24 May 1949, p. 28.

Ecuadorian draft resolution could no longer be considered adopted. He contended that the President's ruling was arbitrary and ultra vires, and he submitted a proposal which would have requested a Court opinion on China's right to employ the double veto in this case. No vote was taken on this proposal.[243]

11. In 1951, the Security Council was confronted with the problem of what action to take in view of the refusal of Iran to comply with the provisional measures indicated by the Court in the *Anglo-Iranian Oil Company* case. Two objections to Council discussion of the British complaint were raised. The first concerned the applicability of Article 2(7); the second, the applicability of Article 94(2) of the Charter to provisional measures. Ecuador suggested that the Court itself might be asked to elucidate the second question, in an advisory opinion. This suggestion was not, however, submitted as a formal proposal.[244]

12. During the Assembly's tenth session, Belgium introduced a formal proposal in Plenary which would have had the Assembly request an advisory opinion on the juridical validity of the procedure proposed by the Fifth Committee for the review of Administrative Tribunal judgments.[245] In particular, the Court would have been asked whether the contemplated review procedure was "compatible with the pertinent Articles of the Charter and with the contractual obligations assumed by the . . . Organization toward its officials."[246]

In the course of earlier discussions of the review procedure, doubts had been expressed as to whether the projected screening committee could, under Article 96(2), be authorized to request advisory opinions;[247] whether it was in conformity with the Charter and the Court's Statute to confer upon the

---

[243] The President interpreted the Chinese remarks as a challenge to his ruling, whereupon, over China's protest, he put the challenge to his ruling to a vote. No vote to overrule having been cast (the vote to overrule was 0 for, 0 against, with 0 abstentions!), the President considered that his ruling stood. China had not participated in the vote, which it considered illegal. *Ibid.*, 5th Yr., 507th Mtg., 29 September 1950, pp. 1 - 8.

[244] *Ibid.*, 6th Yr., 562nd Mtg., 17 October 1951, pp. 8 - 9. At its 565th meeting, on 19 October 1951, the Council decided to suspend further consideration of the item, pending the Court's ruling on its own competence in the matter. It has justly been pointed out that this Council decision was almost equivalent to requesting an advisory opinion on the question of domestic jurisdiction. Leland M. Goodrich and Anne P. Simons, *The United Nations and the Maintenance of International Peace and Security* (Washington, D.C.: The Brookings Institution, 1955), p. 166.

[245] The procedure was recommended in the aftermath of the Court's opinion in the *UN Administrative Tribunal* case, and was incorporated in the amended Article 11 of the UN Administrative Tribunal Statute. See *UN Repertory*, Supp. No. 1, Art. 96, pars. 15 - 26, 55 - 86; see also Chapter I (p. 35, n. 130) and Chapter V (p. 321, n. 153).

[246] UN Doc. A/L.199, 7 November 1955.

[247] See p. 35, n. 130.

Court reviewing functions as between the organization and individuals; and whether the review procedure (despite safeguards incorporated in the proposal) did not entail an unavoidable inequality between the parties—i.e., between the organization and its staff members.[248]

The Belgian proposal was opposed on the grounds that it was ill-timed—having been raised in Plenary rather than in Committee—and that the Court, when faced with a concrete case, would have the opportunity of ruling on the issues raised in the Belgian proposal.[249]

The Assembly proceeded to defeat the Belgian draft resolution[250] and to adopt the Fifth Committee's proposal.[251]

13. In 1957, the Swedish representative suggested that the Security Council refer certain legal questions relating to the Kashmir problem to the Court for an advisory opinion.[252] At the request of India, the Swedish representative later formulated a series of questions concerning the status of Kashmir and its accession to India which, he thought, might profitably be submitted to the Court.[253] He did not, however, present a formal proposal, and he agreed that, in the meantime, a political solution might best be pursued. Neither India nor Pakistan expressly rejected the suggestion, but they indicated that, in their view, the dispute was more "political" than "legal" in nature, and that reference to the Court might delay settlement and endanger peace.[254]

14. The question of the voting majority required in the Assembly on matters concerning non-self-governing territories was debated in the Fourth Committee at the Assembly's twelfth session, in 1957. Six states,[255] dissatisfied with the former Assembly practice of determining the vote required for each case ad hoc, introduced a draft resolution which, in its revised form, would have had the Assembly address the following questions to the Court:

1. Which is the voting majority that is applicable to resolutions of the General Assembly on matters concerning Non-Self-Governing Territories? . . .

[248] See GAOR (IX), 5th Ctte., Mtgs. 474-80, 3-9 December 1954, *passim*; UN Docs. A/2909, 10 June 1955, and A/3016, 5 November 1955; GAOR (X), 5th Ctte., Mtgs. 493-99, 17-25 October 1955, *passim*.

[249] GAOR (X), Plenary, 540th and 541st Mtgs., 8 November 1955, pp. 278-84.

[250] The vote to reject was 31 to 15, with 13 abstentions. *Ibid.*, 541st Mtg., 8 November 1955, p. 288.

[251] *Ibid.*, p. 291. The resolution adopted was 957 (X).

[252] SCOR, 12th Yr., 769th Mtg., 15 February 1957, p. 9; and 798th Mtg., 29 October 1957, p. 10.

[253] *Ibid.*, 801st Mtg., 13 November 1957, p. 34.

[254] *Ibid.*, p. 36; and 802nd Mtg., 15 November 1957, p. 14.

[255] Costa Rica, Greece, Iraq, Mexico, Morocco, and Yugoslavia.

2. Considering that matters concerning Non-Self-Governing Territories are not included in the questions listed in Article 18(2), would it be in accordance with the Charter to submit a resolution on Non-Self-Governing Territories to a two-thirds vote if an additional category to that effect has not been established beforehand for the Non-Self-Governing Territories in the terms of Article 18(3)?[256]

The sponsors of the draft resolution considered that the conflicting interpretations and vacillations which had marked past Assembly decisions in the matter indicated a need for an "authoritative" interpretation by a "better-qualified" body.[257] On the other hand, opponents of the draft resolution contended that an advisory opinion was both unnecessary and ill-advised, for the following reasons. (1) The Charter provisions were clear. (2) The proposed questions were not "legal," but were "political" or "procedural"; consequently, they were entirely within the Assembly's competence. (3) It was undesirable for the Assembly to relinquish its complete freedom to determine each case in accordance with circumstances. (4) Besides rigidifying a matter which ought to remain flexible, a Court opinion might have the effect of making illegal many of the Assembly's past decisions on the issue. (5) Furthermore, the proposed questions (especially the second) were important to the entire Assembly, not merely to the Fourth Committee.[258]

Responding to a Colombian suggestion,[259] the sponsors agreed to amend their draft resolution and to refer the proposed questions to the Sixth Committee instead.[260] However, the Assembly completed its deliberations on the subject of non-self-governing territories before the Sixth Committee could reply to the Fourth Committee's queries; and, in the circumstances, the Sixth Committee deemed it inopportune to give the desired replies.[261]

At the next Assembly session, in 1958, a five-power draft resolution proposing reference to the Court of the questions left unanswered at the twelfth

---

[256] GAOR (XII), Annexes, a.i. 35, p. 29 (UN Doc. A/C.4/L.497/Rev.1).

[257] See GAOR (XII), 4th Ctte., 675th Mtg., 22 October 1957, p. 117; 679th and 680th Mtgs., 24 October 1957, pp. 153, 156; and 681st Mtg., 25 October 1957, p. 160.

[258] See the views expressed by Colombia, Brazil, Portugal, Ecuador, the United Kingdom, the Dominican Republic, Pakistan, and Venezuela, ibid., Mtgs. 679–81, 24–25 October 1957, pp. 152–61.

[259] UN Doc. A/C.4/L.499, 24 October 1957.

[260] GAOR (XII), 4th Ctte., 680th Mtg., 24 October 1957, p. 157.

Many of the opponents of reference to the Court also objected to submission of the questions to the Sixth Committee; but others, like Pakistan, reasoned that, since the Sixth Committee (unlike the Court) was part of the Assembly, reference to it would not derogate from the authority of either the Fourth Committee or the Assembly. Ibid., 680th and 681st Mtgs., 24–25 October 1957, pp. 157, 160–63.

[261] UN Doc. A/C.6/L.417, 2 December 1957.

session was introduced directly in Plenary.[262] Opponents of such reference added to their previous grounds for opposition additional objections based on the *timing* of the new proposal,[263] and a New Zealand motion not to consider the proposal further at that session was adopted.[264]

15. In 1957, Argentina suggested that the question of the Assembly's competence to deal with the question of apartheid in South Africa be referred to the Court for an advisory opinion.[265] The suggestion was not, however, translated into a formal proposal.[266]

16. In March 1962 the Security Council rejected a Cuban proposal which would have had the Council address a series of seven questions—all related to the legality of the 1962 Punta del Este resolutions of the OAS—to the Court for an advisory opinion.[267]

Requests for advisory opinions were also contemplated in connection with two issues which had previously engaged the Court's attention: (1) the admission of new members; and (2) South West Africa.

1. Because of the wording of the request in the *Competence* case, the Court was able to avoid pronouncing upon the effect of the veto on Security Council recommendations for admission and to confine its opinion strictly to an interpretation of Article 4(2) of the Charter.[268] A proposal submitted to the First Committee in 1952 by five Central American states would have solicited a Court opinion on the issue previously avoided—namely, the application of Article 27(3) to admissions questions.[269] Later, the sponsors agreed to have consideration of their proposal deferred until the next (seventh) Assembly session.[270] At that session, four of the original sponsors abandoned the idea of seeking a Court opinion and substituted a resolution under which the Assembly would attempt to resolve the admission problem itself.[271]

---

[262] UN Doc. A/L.259 and Add. 1, 12 December 1958. The sponsors were Ghana, Iraq, Liberia, Mexico, and Morocco.

[263] It was said that the proposal had been "sprung" on the Assembly at the eleventh hour and that the deliberation which was its due would not, therefore, be forthcoming. Reference was made, in this regard, to Resolution 684 (VII). GAOR (XIII), Plenary, 790th Mtg., 13 December 1958, pp. 590–93.

[264] *Ibid.*, pp. 590, 595. The vote was 55 to 2, with 21 abstentions.

[265] GAOR (XII), Spec. Pol. Ctte., 54th Mtg., 29 October 1957, pp. 60–61.

[266] At the next session, Argentina apparently had a change of heart. See *ibid.*, 86th Mtg., 10 October 1958, pp. 8–9.

[267] For a fuller consideration of this case, see pp. 259–66 below.

[268] See p. 106 and n. 224 above, and p. 322 below.

[269] UN Doc. A/C.1/708, 24 January 1952.

[270] UN Doc. A/C.1/716, 29 January 1952.

[271] GAOR (VII), Ad Hoc Pol. Ctte., 42nd Mtg., 12 December 1952, p. 255. The Assembly subsequently adopted Resolution 620A (VII), 21 December 1952, in accordance with which a special committee was set up to study the admission question.

2. In connection with the South West Africa issue, the possibility of further consultation of the Court was broached on several occasions, including the following.

a. A passage in the 1955 report of the Committee on South West Africa appeared to infer that a further advisory opinion (regarding, in this case, the legal aspects of South West African representation in the Union Parliament) might be in order.[272] The passage was so interpreted by the South African representative.[273]

b. In the Committee's 1956 report, a suggestion to this effect was explicitly stated. Recourse to the Court's advisory function was recommended as one of two alternative methods of elucidating the question at issue.[274]

Instead of adopting either of the Committee's recommended solutions, the Assembly, at its eleventh session, requested the Committee on South West Africa to study the question of what legal action was open to the UN or its members to ensure that South Africa fulfilled its obligations under the mandate.[275]

c. In 1957, the Committee submitted a special report on the question of the legal action which might be taken with respect to South West Africa.[276] Mention was made of the possibility of requesting additional advisory opinions relating not only to aspects of UN supervisory procedure but also to the compatibility of specific administrative acts of the mandatory with the obligations assumed under the mandate. At the same time, citing the *Eastern Carelia* precedent, the Committee cautioned against assuming that the Court would necessarily agree to render the opinion asked.[277]

In Resolution 1142B (XII), of 25 October 1957,[278] the Assembly requested the Committee to:

> consider further the question of securing from the . . . Court . . . advisory opinions in regard to the administration of . . . South West Africa, and to make recommendations . . . concerning acts of the administration on which a reference to the Court may usefully be made as to their compati-

[272] GAOR (X), Supp. No. 12 (UN Doc. A/2913), Annex II, par. 33.

[273] *Ibid.*, 4th Ctte., 491st Mtg., 31 October 1955, p. 135. During a subsequent meeting, the Reverend Scott suggested that an advisory opinion be sought. *Ibid.*, 508th Mtg., 15 November 1955, p. 215.

[274] *Ibid.* (XI), Supp. No. 12 (UN Doc. A/3151), Annex II, par. 21. The second alternative was reference to a Joint Fourth and Sixth Committee.

[275] GA Resolution 1060 (XI), 26 February 1957.

[276] GAOR (XII), Supp. No. 12A (UN Doc. A/3625).

[277] *Ibid.*, pars. 16–20. Most of the report was devoted to the study of legal action open to individual states.

[278] In Part A of the same resolution, the attention of member states was drawn to the possibility of instituting contentious proceedings.

bility or otherwise with Article 22 of the Covenant . . . , the Mandate for South West Africa and the Charter of the United Nations.

d. In compliance with this request, the Committee submitted a special report to the Assembly's thirteenth session.[279] Individual acts of administration, related either to the international status of the territory or to the material and moral well-being of the inhabitants, were listed,[280] as an indication of the kinds of subjects upon which advisory opinions might be sought. The Committee refrained, however, from explicitly endorsing further recourse to the Court's advisory function, and appeared, rather, to advise caution in this respect.[281]

e. Further consideration of the question of legal action having been deferred to the fourteenth session,[282] the Committee on South West Africa decided to set up a subcommittee to study the question. That subcommittee drafted (for illustrative purposes and in order to supplement the previous reports) a series of questions which might be submitted to the Court for an advisory opinion.[283] But the main thrust of the discussions in the subcommittee, the Committee on South West Africa, and the Assembly, was toward invocation of the Court's compulsory jurisdiction.[284] The resolution adopted at that session drew the attention of member states to the possibility of instituting contentious proceedings under Article 7 of the mandate.[285]

f. While contentious proceedings instituted by Ethiopia and Liberia and based on the *existence* of the mandate were still pending before the Court, the representative of Mexico suggested that the Court be asked for an advisory opinion regarding the Assembly's right to *revoke* the mandate.[286] The

[279] GAOR (XIII), Supp. No. 12 (UN Doc. A/3906), Part II.

[280] In the first category were such questions as representation of the territory in the Union Parliament; in the second, apartheid, racially discriminatory legislation, etc.

[281] The Committee cited two main aspects which merited Assembly consideration: (1) whether it was "useful" to refer to the Court "for further review matters on which the judgment of the Assembly has already been exercised, and, moreover, exercised under an authority which the Court, in the advisory opinions already given . . . has recognized as belonging to the Assembly"; and (2) whether the Assembly wished "to embark upon the advisory opinion procedure concurrently with the other and different courses of action" which it was pursuing in the matter. GAOR (XIII), Supp. No. 12 (UN Doc. A/3906), Part II, pars. 42–45.

[282] GA Resolution 1247 (XIII), 30 October 1958.

[283] UN Doc. A/AC.73/2, 31 August 1959, pp. 7–10; see also Annex III of the report.

[284] But cf. the remarks of the Philippine representative to the effect that the Assembly ought not to take precipitate action, but should, rather, confine itself to more "moderate" steps, such as seeking advisory opinions. GAOR (XIV), 4th Ctte., 919th Mtg., 21 October 1959, p. 195.

[285] GA Resolution 1361 (XIV), 17 November 1959.

[286] GAOR (XVII), 4th Ctte., 1376th Mtg., 8 November 1962, pp. 303–4.

Mexican representative argued that there was no inconsistency between his suggestion and the contentious proceedings. The latter could result, at most, in Security Council action to ensure *fulfillment* of the mandate; but Assembly action to *terminate* the mandate required the "endorsement" of a further Court opinion, so that the Assembly might not be accused of an "abuse of power."[287]

Several representatives expressed sympathy, in principle, with the suggestion that an advisory opinion be sought before attempts were made to revoke the mandate.[288] At the same time, the anomaly of addressing such a request at that particular juncture was noted.[289] The Mexican representative agreed not to pursue his suggestion further in the meantime.[290]

g. After the protracted proceedings before the Court reached their startling and (for the Assembly) disappointing denouement in 1966, the Assembly was not generally in a mood to contemplate further recourse to the Court with favor. Nevertheless, some suggestions were heard for referring to the Court in its advisory capacity the questions left unanswered by the Court in its contentious capacity.[291] None of these, however, were presented as anything more than passing suggestions.

THE U.N. PERIOD: CASE STUDIES

Only in six of the cases just surveyed were formal proposals voted on and rejected. Of these six, four were related to important disputes which came before the organization for the purpose of pacific settlement—namely, the

[287] *Ibid.* Mexico argued that, by accepting, in Resolution 449 (V), the Court's original 1950 opinion, the Assembly had incorporated the requirement of South African consent to modification of the mandate status into the UN's "constitutional law." Alteration of that law could be accomplished only by the procedure through which the law had been created—namely, solicitation of an advisory opinion, followed by Assembly confirmation of the opinion. *Ibid.*, 1387th Mtg., 16 November 1962, pp. 389–91.

[288] See, e.g., the remarks of Argentina (*ibid.*, 1378th Mtg., 9 November 1962, p. 314), the United States (*ibid.*, 1382nd Mtg., 13 November 1962, p. 352), Colombia (*ibid.*, 1383rd Mtg., 14 November 1962, p. 359), and Canada (*ibid.*, 1387th Mtg., 16 November 1962, p. 387). But cf. the views of Ghana (*ibid.*, 1382nd Mtg., 13 November 1962, p. 348) and Afghanistan (*ibid.*, 1386th Mtg., 15 November 1962, p. 379).

[289] See the remarks of the Chinese representative, *ibid.*, 1386th Mtg., 15 November 1962, p. 386.

[290] *Ibid.*, 1387th Mtg., 16 November 1962, p. 389.

[291] See, especially, the suggestion of the Japanese representative, *ibid.* (XXI), Plenary, 1419th Mtg., 27 September 1966, p. 15. Among the legal points which he desired to have the Court clarify was the compatibility of apartheid with the provisions of the mandate and Article 73 of the Charter. Vaguer allusions are to be found in the remarks of the representatives of Ireland (*ibid.*, 1427th Mtg., 3 October 1966, p. 5), Brazil (*ibid.*, p. 14), Italy (*ibid.*, 1431st Mtg., 5 October 1966, p. 18), and Canada (*ibid.*, 1433rd Mtg., 7 October 1966, p. 5). These suggestions may have represented an attempt—albeit feeble and ill-timed—to rehabilitate the Court in the eyes of the Africans.

treatment of Indians in South Africa, the Indonesian question, the Palestine question, and the Cuban complaint. All, except the first, were handled (either separately, or jointly with the General Assembly) by the Security Council. And, in all of these cases, the proposals for consulting the Court generated considerable debate. It thus seems appropriate to single out these cases for more detailed consideration.

Treatment of Indians in South Africa

This issue—one of the UN "perennials"[292]—was first discussed by the General Assembly in 1946, during the second part of its first session. At that time, various formal proposals were put forward which would have referred to the Court questions related to the dispute—most particularly, the question of the Assembly's competence to deal with the matter. None of these proposals was adopted. The Assembly assumed competence, in the absence of a judicial determination, and continued to deal with the matter in increasingly "political" terms.

The item was first inscribed in the Assembly's agenda at the request of India[293] and over the objections of South Africa.[294] It was then referred to a Joint First and Sixth Committee.[295]

In the Joint Committee, much of the discussion centered on the question of the Assembly's competence.[296]

The Indian position was clearly stated at the outset. Discriminatory legislation enacted by the Union government against Indians—most recently, the 1946 Asiatic Land Tenure and Indian Representation Act, which resulted in the complete segregation of Indians commercially and residentially—constituted a unilateral repudiation by South Africa of its international obligations under the Capetown Agreement of 1927[297] and under the UN Charter. Moreover, it created a situation "likely to impair . . . friendly relations" between

---

[292] The question was discussed at every session of the General Assembly except the fourth. Since 1962, the issue has been merged with the general problem of apartheid in South Africa.

[293] UN Doc. A/149, 22 June 1946.

[294] GAOR (I/2), Gen. Ctte., 19th Mtg., 24 October 1946, pp. 69–73; and Plenary, 46th Mtg., 31 October 1946, p. 924.

[295] This decision represented a compromise between those who, like the United Kingdom, regarded the matter as essentially "legal" and those who, like India and the Soviet Union, considered the matter "political." *Ibid.*, Gen. Ctte., 19th Mtg., 24 October 1946, pp. 70–73. Significantly, after the Assembly's first session, the matter was considered by political committees exclusively.

[296] The Committee's discussions were completed in six meetings, lasting from 21 to 30 November 1946.

[297] The agreement was reaffirmed by a joint South African–Indian communiqué of 1932.

the two states concerned.[298] Article 2(7)—the domestic jurisdiction clause—was inapplicable for the following reasons. (1) The 1927 Capetown Agreement was ratified by the South African and Indian legislatures and gave rise to true international obligations. (2) Questions involving violation of the UN Charter's human rights provisions were not "domestic." (3) Likewise, a situation which impaired friendly relations between two UN member states could not be considered domestic. (4) Furthermore, India's intervention on behalf of the particular group of Union nationals in question was based on moral and political obligations (derived from the Indian government's responsibility for the initial Indian immigration to South Africa), and this intervention had, in fact, always been recognized by South Africa in the past.[299]

What India desired the Assembly to do was set forth in a draft resolution submitted by it to the Committee.[300] Under its terms, the Assembly would declare that the Union government's action violated Charter principles and impaired friendly relations between the two member states; would recommend that the Union government revise its general policy and its legislative and administrative measures affecting Asiatics in South Africa so as to bring them into conformity with the principles and purposes of the Charter; and would request the Union government to report at the next session of the General Assembly on the measures taken.

In his rejoinder, the South African representative focused on the question of the Assembly's competence.[301] He argued that, since South African nationals were concerned, the matter was purely "domestic"; and that India had no right to impair friendly relations or endanger the maintenance of international peace and security merely because it disapproved of the manner in which the domestic affairs of another state were being conducted. As for treaty obligations, these did, indeed, constitute an exception to the domestic jurisdiction principle, but the Capetown Agreement was *not* an instrument which gave rise to treaty obligations.[302] Nor did the Charter's human rights provisions derogate in any way from the domestic nature of the question, since these provisions did not create any *specific* obligations for member states, but, rather, left for the future the precise formulation of the human rights to be protected. Furthermore, the Charter spoke only of "funda-

---

[298] India had already given notice of termination of a trade agreement and had recalled its High Commissioner from South Africa.

[299] GAOR (I/2), Joint 1st and 6th Ctte., 1st Mtg., 21 November 1946, pp. 1-3; and 2nd Mtg., 25 November 1946, pp. 8-11.

[300] UN Doc. A/C.1 and 6/3, 20 November 1946.

[301] GAOR (I/2), Joint 1st and 6th Ctte., 1st Mtg., 21 November 1946, pp. 3-4.

[302] South Africa pointed to the fact that the Agreement had not been registered with the League Secretariat. *Ibid.*, 2nd Mtg., 25 November 1946, p. 19.

mental" rights and freedoms, and these were in no way implicated in the present case.[303]

The South African representative therefore challenged the Assembly's competence to adopt any recommendation on the matter.[304] Since the case would "form a precedent," South Africa formally proposed that the ICJ be asked for an advisory opinion on whether the matter before the Assembly was essentially within South Africa's domestic jurisdiction.[305]

Four other draft resolutions contemplating recourse to the Court also were introduced. (1) A Swedish proposal, like the South African draft, would have limited the consultation to the question of competence.[306] (2) A United Kingdom proposal would have had the Court determine aspects of the *substance* of the Indian complaint—namely, whether South Africa had "neglected to observe any, (and, if so, which) international obligation in regard to the treatment of Asiatics."[307] (3) A draft resolution introduced by Colombia incorporated a series of abstract questions regarding the obligation of UN Members to conform their international legislation to the human rights provisions of the Charter and the Assembly's competence with respect to racially discriminatory legislation.[308] (4) A joint United Kingdom-United States-Swedish draft was confined to the question of the Assembly's competence.[309]

On the other hand, a French-Mexican amendment[310] to the Indian proposal would have retained the matter in the Assembly, while adopting a more conciliatory and moderate tone than the original proposal. Under its terms, the Assembly would (1) state that, because of the treatment of Indians in South Africa, relations between two member states had been impaired and

---

[303] Equality of *fundamental* freedoms in a multiracial society required, in the South African view, a measure of discrimination in respect of *nonfundamental* rights. *Ibid.*, p. 21.

[304] However, he did not object to Assembly *discussion* of the matter. In subsequent sessions, South Africa's position hardened to the point where even discussion was deemed "intervention" within the meaning of Article 2(7).

[305] UN Doc. A/C.1 and 6/8, 23 November 1946.

[306] UN Doc. A/C.1 and 6/10, 26 November 1946.

[307] UN Doc. A/C.1 and 6/15, 27 November 1946.

[308] UN Doc. A/C.1 and 6/14, 27 November 1946.

[309] UN Doc. A/C.1 and 6/20, 28 November 1946. The preamble of the resolution (taken from the United Kingdom draft) stated that, "since the jurisdiction of the United Nations to deal with the matter is denied and since the questions involved are consequently of a legal as well as of a factual nature, a decision based on authoritatively declared juridical foundations is the one most likely to promote realization of . . . [the] purposes of the Charter . . . as well as to secure a lasting and mutually acceptable solution of the complaints which have been made." The Court would have been asked whether the subject of the Indian application was, under Article 2(7), essentially within the Union's domestic jurisdiction.

[310] UN Doc. A/C.1 and 6/12, 26 November 1946.

were likely to be further impaired unless a satisfactory settlement was reached; (2) express the opinion that the treatment of Indians in the Union "should be in conformity with the international obligations under the agreements concluded between the two Governments, and the relevant provisions of the Charter"; and (3) request the two governments to report to the next session of the Assembly. Implicitly, the Indian view of the Assembly's competence would therefore be endorsed.

In the discussions of the various draft resolutions, it became apparent that the Committee members were divided over both the issue of the Assembly's competence and the advisability of recourse to the Court.

A majority clearly favored the assumption of competence by the Assembly and opposed any recourse to the Court on this matter. These representatives emphasized the "political," "moral," and "humanitarian" aspects of the Indian complaint, all of which they deemed far more important than the legal aspects. For them, the substantive issue was a very emotional one, involving, as it did, the sensitive question of racial discrimination; and, for this reason, they evinced impatience with what they viewed as misplaced legalism on the part of other Committee members. Thus, the Guatemalan representative wondered whether the UN members could "be indifferent to the fate of the hundreds of thousands of human beings who were appealing to them."[311] And the Mexican representative queried whether all of the Charter's human rights provisions were to "be ignored on the strength of a possible legalistic interpretation of Article 2, paragraph 7."[312] In the view of this group of representatives, a Court opinion was to be feared rather than welcomed. For, conceivably, the Court might render an unduly restrictive interpretation of the Assembly's competence, thereby hamstringing the UN in its subsequent deliberations in this case, and perhaps in respect of future cases as well.[313] Objections were also voiced to the delay which recourse to the Court would entail.[314] Moreover, these same representatives could not see any *necessity* for requesting the Court's opinion and accepting all the concomitant dangers. First, the Assembly's competence was (for reasons similar to those invoked

[311] GAOR (I/2), Joint 1st and 6th Ctte., 1st Mtg., 21 November 1946, p. 7.

[312] *Ibid.*, 3rd Mtg., 26 November 1946, p. 23. For other statements asserting the "political" nature of the question, see, e.g., *ibid.*, 2nd Mtg., pp. 16–17 (France); and 3rd Mtg., 26 November 1946, pp. 24, 28–29 (Venezuela and the U.S.S.R.). In the French view, the "political" element derived mainly from the deterioration in interstate relations which the dispute had engendered.

[313] See, e.g., the statements of Mexico (*ibid.*, 3rd Mtg., 26 November 1946, p. 23) and China (*ibid.*, 5th Mtg., 28 November 1946, p. 38). The view was also expressed that Article 2(7) was not suitable for judicial determination, since the word "essentially" implied a question of degree. *Ibid.*, 2nd Mtg., 25 November 1946, pp. 10–11.

[314] *Ibid.*, 5th Mtg., 28 November 1946, pp. 38, 45.

by India) indisputable. Second, the Sixth Committee, which included many eminent jurists, was itself fully qualified to determine the Assembly's competence without outside help.[315]

Opposition to involving the Court in the matter was further based, at least ostensibly, on concern for safeguarding the Court's prestige by shielding it from embroilment in "political" controversies.[316]

On the other hand, a vociferous and numerically significant minority favored reference of the question of competence to the Court.[317] Members of this group differed from the majority on almost every point. To them, the legal aspect of the problem was basic, and it was both unfair and impractical either to ignore the legal aspect or to have a nonjudicial organ determine it perfunctorily. It was unfair because South Africa had a right to know the extent of the Assembly's jurisdiction before seeing its government's policies condemned. It was impractical because a judicial solution would be more readily acceptable to the Union government than a purely political one.[318] Indeed, so far from resolving the prevailing doubts and aiding the Indian cause, a narrowly political solution might tend merely to exacerbate matters.[319]

Furthermore, while conceding the majority's contention that the decision in the present case would set a precedent, these representatives deduced from this fact an opposite conclusion—namely, that a Court opinion was all the more warranted. Whereas the Assembly was equipped to give only a hasty and perfunctory interpretation, the Court was in a position to study all elements of the case with patience and impartiality.[320]

As for the Court's prestige, the proposed reference was more likely to enhance it than to injure it, because the Court would be exercising an impor-

---

[315] *Ibid.*, pp. 38, 40.

[316] See the statements of China, Yugoslavia, and India, *ibid.*, pp. 38, 40; and 6th Mtg., 30 November 1946, p. 48. The Chinese representative also feared that a less than unanimous opinion by the Court on an issue of such great importance might seriously impair the Court's prestige.

[317] Representatives of the following states were included in this group: Argentina, Belgium, Brazil, Canada, Costa Rica, Ecuador, El Salvador, the Netherlands, New Zealand, Norway, Peru, Sweden, Turkey, the United Kingdom, and the United States. For their arguments, see *ibid.*, Mtgs. 1–5, 21–28 November 1946, *passim*.

[318] The South African representative himself maintained that a Court opinion would have more influence on his government than an Assembly decision. *Ibid.*, 5th Mtg., 28 November 1946, p. 44.

[319] The United Kingdom representative argued that such a course "would antagonize certain European elements and weaken the liberal elements in South Africa." *Ibid.*, 4th Mtg., 27 November 1946, p. 36.

[320] The Belgian representative cited, approvingly, the League Council's decision to refer the question of its competence in the Aaland Islands dispute to a committee of jurists. *Ibid.*, p. 32.

tant role, rather analogous to that exercised by the national judiciary in some federal systems of government.[321]

Members of this group also regarded fear of the Court's opinion as unjustified. The Assembly would in no way be relinquishing its powers of final decision. A Court opinion would merely serve to reinforce eventual Assembly action.

Before the Committee proceeded to a vote, South Africa indicated its support of the joint United Kingdom-United States-Swedish draft, while India, for its part, withdrew its own proposal in favor of the joint French-Mexican amendment.[322] The last was adopted (by a rather close vote),[323] and none of the other drafts were put to a vote.[324]

Since the Committee had not had an opportunity to vote on the joint three-power draft, South Africa resubmitted it in Plenary, in the form of an amendment to the draft resolution proposed by the Joint Committee.

Arguing in favor of the amendment's adoption, the South African representative stated that the vote in the Committee had been indecisive, and that a matter of such vital importance should be decided by the Assembly itself. South Africa, he declared, clearly had a right to have its international obligations determined by a court of justice, and not by a "mere political forum."[325]

The United States representative strongly supported South Africa's contention. By adopting the French-Mexican draft, he said, the Committee had assumed the existence of international obligations on the part of the Union and the "nondomestic" nature of the Indian complaint. But these assumptions involved disputed issues of international law which the Assembly was obligated to submit to the Court for its determination. While the Committee discussed the legal aspects of the question, it tended to emphasize the *political* character of the alleged discrimination. The best possible way of removing the legal controversy from the "contending winds of political adjudication" was by means of recourse to the Court.[326] Furthermore, he continued, this

---

[321] See the remarks of Canada, *ibid.*, 2nd Mtg., 25 November 1946, pp. 11–12.

[322] *Ibid.*, 5th Mtg., 28 November 1946, p. 43; and 6th Mtg., 30 November 1946, p. 47.

[323] The vote was 24 to 19, with 6 abstentions. *Ibid.*, 6th Mtg., 30 November 1946, p. 51.

[324] Several representatives considered that the question of competence should have been given priority in the vote, but this view was not accepted by the Chairman. *Ibid.*, p. 50.

[325] GAOR (I/2), Plenary, 50th Mtg., 7 December 1946, pp. 1007–10.

[326] "This is not to involve the Court in political controversy," the United States representative maintained. "On the contrary, it is to remove the legal problem from the political debate."

was the method contemplated by the Charter, which, in Article 92, established the Court as the principal judicial organ of the UN.[327]

In the ensuing discussions, many of the arguments expressed in the Joint Committee were repeated. This time, however, opponents of recourse to the Court devoted less time to legal argumentation and emphasized, instead (to an even greater degree), the moral and ethical issues at stake and the organization's duty to uphold the principles of human rights and fundamental freedoms for all, without discrimination. In the opinion of these representatives, adoption of the South African amendment would amount to an evasion of the moral issue involved and might harm the organization's prestige.[328] Even if the question had legal aspects, its *predominant* element was clearly "political."[329]

On the other hand, supporters of the proposed reference to the Court insisted that the politico-legal method was preferable to the purely political one, which purports to deal with legal questions, such as the question of competence, by a majority decision in a political organ;[330] that denial of South Africa's appeal for an authoritative legal decision would do great harm to the organization; and that a juridical solution would be more acceptable to the parties and, consequently, in the long run, more beneficial to the Indian cause than a mere majority decision in a political forum.[331]

The Assembly rejected the South African amendment and proceeded to adopt the Committee's draft resolution.[332]

---

[327]GAOR (I/2), Plenary, 50th Mtg., 7 December 1946, pp. 1010–14. The United States representative would have preferred to see the proposed question confined to the "narrower" issue of the existence of international obligations rather than have it encompass the broader issue of "domestic jurisdiction." However, in the Joint Committee, the United States had cosponsored a resolution incorporating the "broader" question.

[328]See, e.g., the views of Panama, the Philippines, and Uruguay, *ibid.*, 51st Mtg., 8 December 1946, pp. 1026–31.

On the legal issues, it was argued, *inter alia*, that (1) the Committee's resolution was unobjectionable, since Charter obligations were undoubtedly involved and since the resolution amounted to nothing more than an offer of good offices (China, *ibid.*, 50th Mtg., 7 December 1946, pp. 1019–23); and that (2) Assembly recommendations did not constitute "intervention" within the meaning of Article 2(7) (Mexico, *ibid.*, 51st Mtg., 8 December 1946, pp. 1023–26).

[329]Egypt, *ibid.*, 51st Mtg., 8 December 1946, pp. 1037–38.

[330]Belgium, *ibid.*, pp. 1032–33.

[331]The United Kingdom, *ibid.*, pp. 1033–37. To this last argument, the Indian representative retorted that South Africa might flout an adverse ICJ ruling as readily as an Assembly resolution. *Ibid.*, 52nd Mtg., 8 December 1946, p. 1045. The fate of the Court's *South West Africa (Status)* opinion tends to bear out the Indian assessment.

[332]The vote on the former was 21 for, 31 against, with 2 abstentions; and on the latter, 32 for, 15 against, with 7 abstentions. *Ibid.*, 52nd Mtg., 8 December 1946, p. 1061. Before the vote, the question of the majority required for adoption of the

The subsequent history of this problem in the United Nations has been a long and none too rewarding one—with annual debates culminating in annual, fruitless resolutions. Until 1962, when the question was merged with the general issue of apartheid in South Africa,[333] the Assembly's efforts were directed primarily at bringing about negotiations between the interested states.[334] Various approaches, ranging from a simple call for direct negotiations to the designation of mediating bodies to assist in the negotiations, were attempted. All were equally abortive.[335] A faint glimmer of hope for a negotiated settlement appeared when, in February 1950, the parties reached a preliminary agreement on a conference agenda. But this glimmer dimmed when India withdrew from the proposed conference on the grounds that South Africa was then considering new discriminatory legislation—namely, the Group Areas Act. And all hope was extinguished by South Africa's subsequent defiant attitude in the case. It repeatedly refused to heed Assembly pleas that it suspend implementation of the disputed legislation.[336] It also persistently declined to negotiate on the basis of Assembly resolutions. Since South Africa denied the Assembly's jurisdiction, it viewed the resolutions as unconstitutional, and it feared that consenting to negotiations would prejudice its "juridical position."[337]

Although the Assembly refused, in 1946, to refer the question of its competence to the Court, it certainly did not thus dispose of the issue.

Committee draft and the South African amendment was raised and thoroughly debated. It was decided, by a separate vote (29 for, 24 against, with 1 abstention), that the Committee draft would require a two-thirds majority. The President then ruled that the South African amendment also could not be adopted without receiving a two-thirds majority, but he clearly indicated that this ruling would not constitute a precedent. *Ibid.*, pp. 1048–61.

[333] Earlier proposals to combine the two questions were resisted on the grounds that the treatment of Indians question had an additional, and hence, stronger, legal basis than the broader apartheid issue. For, apart from the general human rights provisions of the Charter, specific bilateral international agreements and bilateral relations were implicated. See, e.g., *ibid.* (XII), Spec. Pol. Ctte., 59th Mtg., 4 November 1957, pp. 81–82.

[334] After 1946, Pakistan joined India as a complainant state.

[335] For a history of UN treatment of the problem, see the annual UN yearbooks. In 1952, a Good Offices Commission was set up; in 1954, at the Assembly's request, the Secretary-General designated a special ambassador; and, in later years, the individual member states of the UN were urged to use their good offices. South Africa declined to cooperate with any of these would-be mediators.

[336] See GA Resolutions 395 (V), 2 December 1950; 511 (VI), 12 January 1952; 615 (VII), 5 December 1952; and 719 (VIII), 11 November 1953.

[337] See, e.g., South Africa's explanation to the Secretary-General for its refusal to cooperate with his special ambassador. UN Doc. A/3001/Add.1, 14 November 1955. But, even after the Assembly—in Resolution 1302 (XIII), 10 December 1958—specified that negotiations would be "without prejudice to the position taken by the Union of South Africa regarding its juridical stand on the issue," South Africa evinced no greater willingness to enter into negotiations.

Rather, discussion of the competence issue became a regular feature of the debates. As might be expected, South Africa continued to raise the question at every opportunity—in the General Committee, where it steadfastly objected to inclusion of the item in the agenda; in the political committees to which the item was assigned; and in Plenary. Moreover, South Africa's attitude on the question, far from becoming more pliant and acquiescent with time, progressively hardened. Whereas, during the Assembly's first session, South Africa did not object to *discussion* of the Indian complaint, in later years, inscription of the item on the agenda was considered, in itself, "intervention." In the beginning, South Africa touched on some of the substantive issues of the complaint; later, it limited its statements to the issue of competence; and, still later (from 1955 on), it refused altogether to participate in Assembly deliberations on the matter.

Doubts regarding the Assembly's competence in this case were not confined to South Africa, however. At least until 1960, they were shared, in varying degrees, by a considerable number of states.[338] Some members of this group—a "hard core" of "doubters," as it were—tended to question, along with South Africa, the Assembly's right to adopt any recommendations in the matter.[339] Others—a "middle-of-the-road" group—did not experience the strong reservations of the "hard core" group, but were nevertheless uncertain as to the *extent* of the Assembly's competence.[340] This uncertainty led members of the second group to oppose certain features of proposed or actual resolutions—e.g., references to specific South African legislative or administrative acts; imposition of a specific method of settlement; and language which might appear too condemnatory. These states seemed frequently to be caught between two unpleasant alternatives: on the one hand, appearing to condone South Africa's racial policies, and, on the other, supporting resolutions of doubtful constitutionality and efficacy. It is in terms of this dilemma that

[338] At least thirty states expressed reservations, at one time or another, regarding the Assembly's competence to "intervene" in this case.

[339] Included in this group were the following: Australia, Belgium, Canada, the Dominican Republic, Finland, France (from the third session on), Luxembourg, the Netherlands, New Zealand, Portugal, Spain, Turkey, and the United Kingdom. These states generally abstained on the substantive resolutions. However, several voted for some of the milder resolutions (e.g., those in the third, tenth, eleventh, and thirteenth sessions). Some states were in this group only during part of the period—e.g., Argentina, Colombia, Greece, Italy, and Venezuela.

[340] In this group were Brazil, China, Denmark, Norway, Peru, Sweden, and (to a certain extent), the United States. All these states (except China) supported reference to the Court in the first session. Their votes in subsequent sessions were determined by their evaluation of the specific resolutions under consideration. The United States, despite its initial strong support for consulting the Court, modified its enthusiasm for this course once it became clear that the Assembly would continue to assume competence.

the original enthusiasm of these states for reference to the Court is best explained. For a Court opinion might readily have served a dual purpose: clarification of the extent of the Assembly's competence and removal from the Assembly members of some of the onus of decision-making in this highly emotion-charged issue. Similar considerations may have prompted the further suggestions for requesting an advisory opinion which were put forward, separately, by two members of this group, Sweden and Brazil.[341]

Both groups of "doubters"—"hard-core" and "middle-of-the-road"—were, however, in the minority. An ever-increasing majority of the Assembly (consisting of the Soviet bloc, the Afro-Asian bloc, and most Latin American states) entertained no doubts on the issue of competence whatever. The moral issue was to them the overriding one, and they became progressively more impatient with the repeated injection of the competence issue into the debates. To the legal arguments earlier presented in favor of competence, they now added the further argument that rejection of the South African proposal in the first session, combined with the continued assumption of competence by the Assembly, foreclosed, for all time, any reconsideration of the issue of competence in this case.

The division of the Assembly on the question of competence persisted until 1960. That year marked a decisive turning point with respect to the question of racial conflict in South Africa. In the face of the Sharpeville incidents, on the one hand, and the proliferation of newly independent African states in the Assembly, on the other, South Africa found itself increasingly abandoned by its erstwhile allies. The latter found it difficult to maintain their opposition to Assembly measures on the basis of what came to appear more and more, even to them, as a trivial technicality. South Africa's isolation was henceforth far more complete.

Had an advisory opinion in fact been requested at the first session, what effect might it have had on the subsequent development of the problem in the UN?

If the Court's opinion had been adverse to South Africa's contentions, is it reasonable to assume that South Africa's attitude would have been significantly different from what it was? In light of the reception accorded to the Court's opinion in the *South West Africa (Status)* case, the answer must be:

---

[341] For the Swedish suggestion, see GAOR (VI), Ad Hoc Pol. Ctte., 30th Mtg., 3 January 1952, p. 163. For the Brazilian suggestion, see *ibid.* (VIII), Ad Hoc Pol. Ctte., 19th Mtg., 26 October 1953, pp. 92–93. At the particular junctures when these suggestions were put forward, it appeared especially difficult to steer a middle course, since the resolutions under consideration referred to internal South African legislation, and seemed to raise the question of competence in a more acute form.

probably not.[342] The main effect of this hypothetical Court opinion would presumably have been to sway the group of states sharing South Africa's doubts regarding the Assembly's competence, thereby hastening the day of South Africa's isolation in this matter. But, if South Africa's post-1960 isolation has not led to a solution of the problem, would a pre-1960 isolation have been more effective in this regard? Again, the answer must be: probably not.

Now, assuming the contrary—that the Court would have pronounced the Assembly incompetent either to discuss or to make recommendations in this case—would the Assembly majority have accepted such an opinion? Judging from the mood of the Assembly, even at the very first session, one must conclude that the Assembly would have been extremely reluctant to accept such a limitation of its competence and to relinquish its "moral" right to consider the Indian complaint. On the other hand, South Africa's position would certainly have hardened—but hardly much more than it did in any case.

If, as is believed, a Court opinion would probably have been ineffectual (and perhaps totally ignored), then it is indeed better, particularly from the standpoint of the Court's prestige, that the Court was not implicated at all, and that the Assembly continued to set its own precedents in the matter.[343]

The Indonesian Question

In 1947, in the course of the Security Council's consideration of the Indonesian question,[344] Belgium proposed that the Court be asked for an advisory opinion on the Council's competence to deal with the question, in

---

[342] In 1953, India cited South Africa's attitude in respect to the 1950 case as grounds for opposing the Brazilian suggestion that an advisory opinion be requested. On the same occasion, the South African representative indicated that his government would not feel obliged to accept a Court opinion, which was, in any case, only advisory. *Ibid.* (VIII), Ad Hoc Pol. Ctte., 20th Mtg., 27 October 1953, pp. 101-2; and 21st Mtg., 28 October 1953, p. 104.

[343] From the viewpoint of the development of a sound jurisprudence with respect to the interpretation of Article 2(7), failure to request the Court's opinion in this case—as also in the Indonesian case—may have been unfortunate. (At San Francisco, it will be recalled, a proposal to have disputes regarding the application of Article 2[7] adjudicated compulsorily by the Court failed of adoption. But judicial interpretation by means of an advisory opinion was not thereby precluded. See pp. 30-31 above.) On the other hand, since the UN has increasingly ignored any fetters implied in Article 2(7), and has increasingly relegated that clause to virtual limbo, any broad judicial interpretation of the clause probably would not have met with general acceptance.

[344] For the UN's handling of the Indonesia case, see J. Foster Collins, "The United Nations and Indonesia," *International Conciliation*, No. 459 (March 1950); Alastair M. Taylor, *Indonesian Independence and the United Nations* (Ithaca, N. Y.: Cornell University Press, 1960); S. Windass, "Indonesia and the UN: Legalism, Politics and Law," *International Relations*, 3, No. 8 (November 1969): 578-98.

view of the Netherlands government's invocation of Article 2(7) of the Charter. The background to this Belgian proposal was as follows.

When, in late June 1947, the Security Council discussed the question of hostilities between the Netherlands and the Republic of Indonesia,[345] the Netherlands government argued that, since it was sovereign in the area, the question was essentially within its domestic jurisdiction. At that time, however, the issue of competence was, to a degree, skirted by the adoption of a resolution which called on the parties to declare a cease-fire and to settle their dispute by arbitration or other peaceful means, but which omitted any reference to Articles 39 and 40 of the Charter.[346] The Netherlands agreed to this resolution, while reserving its position on the question of the Council's competence.

Discussion of the Council's competence, thus held in abeyance, was reopened when, in the face of the continuation of hostilities, the Council met later in August to consider further measures in the case.

An Australian draft resolution which would have had a Security Council commission report on implementation of the cease-fire met with objections from the Netherlands, on the grounds that such a resolution implied that the Security Council had jurisdiction. The Netherlands representative counterproposed that the career consuls in Batavia be asked to report on the situation instead.[347]

In the ensuing discussions and the presentation of proposals and counterproposals, some representatives (those of Australia, Colombia, Poland, Syria, and the Soviet Union) insisted on a more active role for the Security Council in the matter; others (the representatives of Belgium, France, and the United Kingdom) doubted the competence of the Council to undertake any action, but were willing to acquiesce in resolutions which did not impose any particu-

---

[345] Australia and India separately drew the Council's attention to the matter. UN Docs. S/447 and S/449, 30 July 1947. Australia invoked Article 39 of the Charter; India, Article 35(1).

[346] An Australian draft resolution would have had the Security Council expressly invoke Articles 39 and 40 and call on the parties to arbitrate their dispute in accordance with the Linggadjati Agreement. UN Doc. S/454, 31 July 1947. The final resolution was based on a United States amendment designed to evade the competence issue by nonspecification of the grounds for Security Council action and by nonimposition of a particular method of dispute settlement. SCOR, 2nd Yr., 173rd Mtg., 1 August 1947. Belgium, France, and the United Kingdom abstained because of their feeling that, even in the amended form, the resolution prejudged the jurisdictional issue and implied that Article 2(7) did not apply.

[347] SCOR, 2nd Yr., 181st Mtg., 12 August 1947, pp. 2012–13. A Polish amendment to the Australian proposal would have gone even further in attempting to impose a method of settlement on the parties. Under its terms, a second Security Council commission would have acted as mediator and arbitrator between the parties. See UN Docs. S/488 and S/488/Add. 1, 12 and 15 August 1947.

lar settlement and which minimized the role of the Security Council. Still others (Brazil, China, and, most notably, the United States) tried to steer a middle course and took the lead in proposing and supporting resolutions which were least objectionable to the Netherlands from a jurisdictional point of view, which did not attempt to impose a particular method of peaceful settlement on the parties, and which provided for the least amount of intervention by the Security Council. They hoped thereby to avoid debate on the issue of jurisdiction.

Thus, China moved an amendment[348] to the Australian draft resolution which would have gone along with the Netherlands suggestion that a consular report be forwarded to the Security Council. This proposal was supported by the United States, but was opposed by Australia and India.

Subsequently, a compromise joint Australian-Chinese draft resolution was introduced.[349] This draft, which was later adopted by the Council, provided that the career consuls who represented members of the Security Council in Batavia report to the Council on the situation following the cease-fire resolution.

On the long-term problem of peaceful settlement of the dispute, Australia introduced a further draft resolution, under the terms of which the parties would be requested to submit all matters in dispute to arbitration by a commission composed of two members selected by the respective parties and a third member selected by the Security Council. [350] For its part, the United States attempted to avoid further debate on the issue of competence by presenting a substitute proposal which provided for a good offices, rather than an arbitral, commission, and by leaving selection of the third member to the first two members rather than to the Security Council.[351] This substitute proposal was opposed by the Soviet Union, Poland, and the Republic of Indonesia, on the grounds that it attempted to by-pass the Security Council in seeking a settlement of the issue.

Belgium, on the other hand, objected to the new Australian draft resolution, on the grounds that it would have attempted to impose a particular method of settlement on the parties and would have given the Security Council a more active part in the settlement of the dispute.[352] To prevent adoption of this proposal, Belgium at that point formally submitted a draft resolution in accordance with which the Court would be asked for an advisory opinion

[348] UN Doc. S/488/Add.2, 19 August 1947.

[349] UN Doc. S/513, 22 August 1947.

[350] SCOR, 2nd Yr., 193rd Mtg., 22 August 1947, p. 2174 (UN Doc. S/512).

[351] *Ibid.*, p. 2179 (UN Doc. S/514).

[352] The same objections were directed against the Polish amendment to the first Australian draft resolution.

on the Security Council's competence to deal with the Indonesian question in light of the Netherlands' invocation of Article 2(7) of the Charter.[353]

The Belgian proposal was supported by France, the United States, and the United Kingdom. Explaining his approval of the proposal, the United States representative said that he himself did not doubt the Council's competence to consider the matter or to issue cease-fire orders, but that he did doubt its competence to impose a particular method of settlement in a case of this type. However, out of courtesy to those representatives who seriously questioned the Council's competence even to consider the matter, he supported reference of the entire jurisdictional issue to the Court.[354] The representatives of France and the United Kingdom urged adoption of the proposal and denied that reference to the Court would, as some representatives claimed, in any way prevent or delay action on resolutions which had already been adopted. Moreover, besides aiding the Council in the present case, a Court opinion would help build up a body of precedents in the interpretation of the disputed domestic jurisdiction clause.[355]

Most of the Council members, however, expressed opposition to the proposed recourse to the Court. They argued, *inter alia*, that the question of competence was "political," not "legal";[356] that, even if legal considerations were involved, these were purely of secondary importance—the question of jurisdiction being, in fact, merely a "swamp" in which to sink the substance of the Indonesian question;[357] that to deal with the matter on a purely legal basis was to disregard the implications of the problem for world security and the high moral principles which were at stake;[358] and that the opinion of the Court might place the Security Council in a straitjacket and cast doubt on its previous decision in the matter.[359]

The Belgian proposal did not muster more than four affirmative votes, and was rejected.[360] Three substantive resolutions were adopted: the Australian-Chinese proposal (which provided for a report by the career consuls in Batavia); the United States proposal on the long-term problem (which established a Good Offices Committee); and a Polish draft resolution which called on the parties to adhere strictly to the earlier cease-fire resolution.[361]

[353] SCOR, 2nd Yr., 194th Mtg., 25 August 1947, p. 2193 (UN Doc. S/517).

[354] *Ibid.*, 195th Mtg., 26 August 1947, p. 2222.

[355] *Ibid.*, pp. 2214–15, 2218–19.

[356] Poland, *ibid.*, p. 2222.

[357] U.S.S.R., *ibid.*, 194th Mtg., 25 August 1947, pp. 2207, 2210–11.

[358] Australia and India, *ibid.*, 195th Mtg., 26 August 1947, pp. 2215–17, 2219–20.

[359] China, *ibid.*, pp. 2217–18.

[360] *Ibid.*, p. 2224.

[361] Resolutions of 25 and 26 August 1947 (UN Doc. S/525).

All three resolutions met with the approval of the Netherlands government, although that government maintained its position regarding the Council's competence.[362]

During the Council's later consideration of the problem, the question of competence was raised whenever an attempt was made to go beyond the offer of good offices and the call for a cease-fire.[363] In the words of one writer, "the problem of jurisdiction haunted the Council for the next two years and considerably hampered its freedom of action."[364]

However, notwithstanding its persistent objections regarding the Council's competence, the Netherlands government often cooperated with the Council and adhered to many of the Council's resolutions.[365] Final settlement of the Indonesian problem was facilitated by the Good Offices Committee (and later by the United Nations Commission for Indonesia).[366]

In this case, as in so many others, it is difficult to assess the effect that reference to the Court of the question of competence might have had on the eventual solution of the underlying problem. It may be argued that, if the Council members were intent on pursuing the matter, regardless of the opinion the Court might render (and there is some indication that this was, indeed, the attitude of the majority of the Council members), then the course actually pursued (i.e., implicit assumption of competence) was better, both for the Court and for the eventual solution of the problem. A certain measure of caution and compromise was observed by the Security Council in its adoption of resolutions on the problem, probably due to uncertainty with respect to the extent of its jurisdiction and the desire to secure the cooperation of the Netherlands. On the other hand, a Court opinion which upheld or denied the Council's competence might have served to make either or both of the parties more intransigent in their respective stands.

[362] UN Doc. S/537, 3 September 1947.

[363] Thus, the Netherlands, supported by France and Belgium, opposed attempts to change the nature, competence, or procedure of the Good Offices Committee. See, e.g., the discussions in SCOR, 4th Yr., 406th Mtg., 28 January 1949. In fact, the resolution of that date marked a turning point in the Security Council's handling of the Indonesian question. Henceforth, the "good offices" policy was abandoned "in favour of extensive UN intervention in the whole military and political situation in favour of the Republican Government." Windass, *op. cit.*, p. 580.

[364] Collins, *op. cit.*, p. 127; cf. Taylor, *op. cit.*, chap. XI.

[365] The amenability of the Netherlands government to Council initiatives owed much to pressures exerted by the United States government. Throughout the conflict, the latter's role was pivotal. Windass, *op. cit.*, pp. 578 ff.

[366] See *UN Yearbook*, 1947–48, pp. 362–87, and 1948–49, pp. 212–37, for detailed accounts of the subsequent development of the case in the UN.

It should be noted that the present controversy was a particularly strident one, involving the actual outbreak of violence. In these circumstances, the prevalent feeling in the Council that an extralegal "political" approach was called for was perfectly understandable.

The Palestine Question

In the period 1947–52, numerous proposals and suggestions for requesting advisory opinions from the Court were put forward in connection with the Palestine question[367] (and, subsequently, in connection with the Arab-Israeli conflict). These cannot be understood unless they are examined in the contexts in which they were presented and in terms of the courses of action then under consideration.

The first of these proposals were presented at the General Assembly's second session, during discussions of the report of UNSCOP.[368] That report[369] contained a majority plan (which proposed the partition of Palestine into Arab and Jewish states, an international regime for Jerusalem, and an economic union linking the three) and a minority plan (which envisaged an independent federal state with Jerusalem as its capital), neither of which met with the approval of the Arab states and the Arab High Committee. The Arab position was that, with the termination of the mandate, Palestine should become an independent unitary state controlled by the Arab majority; and that the UN was not competent to determine the constitutional organization of Palestine, since this would amount to interference in an internal matter of an independent nation.

Three Arab states—Iraq, Egypt, and Syria—introduced in the Ad Hoc Committee on Palestine separate draft resolutions[370] which would have referred to the Court various questions relating to the Assembly's competence. The Iraqi draft would have had the Assembly ask whether or not Palestine was included in the area to which British World War I pledges (promising independence to the Arabs) applied.[371] The Egyptian draft, on the other hand, focused more directly on the issue of competence. It would have referred to the Court the

---

[367] On the treatment of the Palestine question in the UN, see L. Larry Leonard, "The United Nations and Palestine," *International Conciliation*, No. 454 (October 1949); J. C. Hurewitz, *The Struggle for Palestine* (New York: Norton, 1950), chaps. XXI–XXIII and Epilogue; Carnegie Endowment for International Peace, *Israel and the United Nations: Report of a Study Group Set up by the Hebrew University of Jerusalem*, National Studies on International Organization (New York: Manhattan Publishing Co., 1956).

[368] United Nations Special Committee on Palestine, established by the 1947 special Assembly session.

[369] GAOR (II), Supp. No. 11 (UN Doc. A/364).

[370] UN Docs. A/AC.14/21, 14 October 1947; A/AC.14/24, 16 October 1947; and A/AC.14/25, 16 October 1947.

[371] It was argued that these pledges, having preceded the Balfour Declaration and the Palestine mandate, rendered certain provisions of the two latter documents invalid. See,

question of the Assembly's right to recommend either of the two proposed plans and the right of member states to implement such plans without the consent of the Palestinian population. The Syrian draft contained a series of questions dealing with the following matters: the consistency of the Palestine mandate with the League Covenant and with the right of self-determination; the consistency of a forcible plan of partition with the objectives of the mandate, the principles of the Charter, and the ultimate fate of the mandated territories referred to in Chapter XII of the Charter; and the competence of the Assembly to execute forcibly the partition plan.

The Arab states insisted that the legal questions raised in the above draft resolutions had to be determined before any action could be taken on the UNSCOP plans. Syria proposed the establishment of a subcommittee of jurists to deal with the legal aspects of the problem and with the question of the Assembly's competence.[372] However, the general feeling was that the competence issue could not be decided in the absence of specific proposals to which the question of competence could be related.[373]

It was decided to set up two subcommittees and a conciliation group. Subcommittee One would draw up a detailed plan based on the proposals of the UNSCOP majority. Subcommittee Two would draw up a detailed plan in accordance with Arab proposals for establishing an independent unitary state in Palestine. And the conciliation group would try to bring the parties together. In point of fact, Subcommittee Two also dealt with the legal issues raised by the Arab states.

The report of Subcommittee Two[374] contained in its conclusions three draft resolutions, one of which would have referred to the Court for an advisory opinion a series of eight questions (very comprehensive in scope) which encompassed most of the legal arguments presented by the Arabs: the inherent right of the indigenous Palestinian population to determine its future constitution and government; the inclusion of Palestine within the area of World War I British pledges of Arab independence; the consistency of the Balfour Declaration with the earlier British pledges; the validity of the Balfour Declaration and its binding force for the indigenous Palestinian population; the consistency of the provisions of the mandate which related to the creation of a Jewish National Home with the League Covenant (particularly, Article 22) and with other provisions of the mandate; the lapse of the mandate with the dissolution of the League, and the duty of the mandatory

---

e.g., GAOR (II), Ad Hoc Ctte. on the Palestinian Question, 12th Mtg., 13 October 1947, p. 74.

[372]*Ibid.*, 19th Mtg., 21 October 1947, p. 129.

[373]See the views of the Chairman (*ibid.*, p. 128) and the United States representative (*ibid.*, p. 135).

[374]UN Doc. A/AC.14/32 and Add. 1, 11 November 1947.

power to hand over power to a government representative of the indigenous population; the consistency of forcible partition with the objectives of the League Covenant and the provisions of the mandate; the competence of the UN to recommend either of the UNSCOP plans or any plan of trusteeship without the consent of the Palestinian population; and (question 8) the competence of the UN to enforce, or to recommend the enforcement of, any proposal concerning the future government of Palestine, particularly any plan of partition adopted without the consent of the Palestinian population.

During debate in the Ad Hoc Committee, the following views were expressed by those who upheld the Assembly's competence in the matter and denied either the necessity or the desirability of referring the question of competence to the Court. (1) The Assembly's competence was based on its broad powers of recommendation under Articles 10 and 14 of the Charter and, since Palestine was not yet a sovereign state, on Chapters XI and XII of the Charter as well.[375] (2) The Palestine question should not be examined from an exclusively legal standpoint.[376] (3) Doubts now being expressed concerning the Assembly's competence were based on *political* not legal grounds.[377] (4) In other cases, the Arab states opposed reference to the Court on the grounds that the questions involved were political. Yet, it could not be denied that the Palestine question was essentially political.[378]

On the other hand, the Arab states and other supporters of the draft resolution argued as follows. (1) The plan for partition proposed by Subcommittee One had no juridical basis, since the Assembly could only make recommendations, not impose a solution.[379] (2) Chapters XI and XII of the Charter were both inapplicable—the first because, with termination of the mandate, Palestine would have ceased to be a non-self-governing territory; the second because trusteeship was intended to be only a temporary status.[380] (3) Before taking such far-reaching decisions as were here involved, the Assembly ought to examine carefully the legal basis of its actions; and recourse to the Court was the best means of obtaining the necessary clarification. Such a referral would not be a negative solution, since active attempts at conciliation could continue simultaneously.[381]

Before the draft resolutions were voted on, the French representative requested that a separate vote be taken on question 8. The other questions, he

[375] Poland, GAOR (II), Ad Hoc Ctte. on Palestine, 27th Mtg., 22 November 1947, pp. 160–61.

[376] The Dominican Republic, *ibid.*, 29th Mtg., 22 November 1947, p. 180.

[377] The U.S.S.R., *ibid.*, 30th Mtg., 24 November 1947, p. 184.

[378] Guatemala, *ibid.*, p. 187.

[379] Egypt (*ibid.*, pp. 185–87), Pakistan (*ibid.*, p. 189), and Lebanon (*ibid.*, 31st Mtg., 24 November 1947, p. 194–95).

[380] Pakistan, *ibid.*, 30th Mtg., 24 November 1947, p. 189.

[381] Colombia, *ibid.*, 32nd Mtg., 24 November 1947, pp. 201–2.

considered, were of a political, or "philosophical," rather than a legal, nature. However, he entertained some doubts concerning the eighth question—namely, the competence of the Assembly to enforce, or to recommend the enforcement of, the partition plan.[382]

The draft resolution was defeated.[383] On question 8, however, the vote was very close: 20 in favor, 21 against, with 13 abstentions.

The Committee then proceeded to adopt, with some revisions, the draft resolution recommended by Subcommittee One, which embodied, in substance, the UNSCOP majority plan.[384] This resolution was endorsed by the Plenary on 29 November 1947 and became Resolution 181 (II). Under its provisions, a Palestine Commission was established to implement the partition plan. Furthermore, the Security Council was requested to (1) take the necessary measures to implement the plan; (2) consider whether the situation in Palestine constituted a threat to the peace; and (3) determine as a threat to the peace within the terms of Article 39 of the Charter any attempt to alter by force the settlement envisaged by the Assembly's resolution.

On 16 February 1948, the Palestine Commission reported that, in the absence of adequate armed assistance, it would be unable to maintain law and order after termination of the mandate.[385] Accordingly, the Security Council had to consider what measures it should take to implement the Assembly's recommendations. The general opinion in the Council during its discussions in February, March, and April was that the Council lacked the power to enforce a settlement, since Chapter VII was as yet inapplicable. The United States led other representatives in maintaining this view.[386] Retreating from its strong pro-partition stand, the United States recommended on March 19 that action on partition be suspended and that a special session of the Assembly be called to consider the establishment of a temporary trusteeship over Palestine, without prejudice to the character of an eventual political settlement.[387] In its April 1948 resolutions, the Security Council concentrated on appeals for a truce and abandoned all efforts to implement the partition plan.

Since it appeared that the partition plan was being relegated to limbo, the Arab states did not deem it necessary during these months to put forward proposals for referring any aspect of the Palestine question to the Court.

---

[382] *Ibid.*, pp. 202–3.

[383] The vote was 18 for, 25 against, with 11 abstentions. *Ibid.*, p. 203.

[384] *Ibid.*, 34th Mtg., 25 November 1947, pp. 222–23.

[385] UN Doc. A/AC.21/9, 16 February 1948.

[386] SCOR, 3rd Yr., 253rd Mtg., 24 February 1948, pp. 264–69. Only the Soviet Union insisted on implementation of the November 29 resolution.

[387] *Ibid.*, 271st Mtg., 19 March 1948, pp. 167–68.

However, with the proclamation of the Jewish state and the intervention of the Arab states in Palestine, discussions of the Palestine problem in the Security Council entered a new phase. The question of the applicability of Chapter VII was now raised with full force. At the Security Council's May 15 meeting, the representative of the Jewish Agency urged that action be taken under Chapter VII to stop Arab aggression.[388] For their part, the Arab states claimed that their military action did not constitute aggression, but was, rather, assistance to an independent Palestine in suppressing a rebellious minority. As such, it was an internal matter, which precluded action under Chapter VII. Syria suggested that Council examination of the status of Palestine precede any move under Chapter VII.[389]

The United States (which, after granting de facto recognition to Israel, had once more shifted its position) now proposed that Article 39 of the Charter be expressly invoked.[390] However, other delegates, led by the United Kingdom, preferred to keep the problem within the framework of Chapter VI, mainly to avoid difficulties with regard to the questions of the juridical status of Palestine, the definition of an act of aggression, and the degree of binding force Assembly recommendations can have.[391] As long as action was confined to Chapter VI,[392] the Arab states did not formally press for a consideration of the legal status of Palestine.

In its resolution of 29 May 1948, the Security Council called on all parties to observe a four-week truce and threatened to invoke Chapter VII if the terms of the resolution were rejected or repudiated. These proposals were accepted by both parties.

On July 7, the Security Council appealed to both parties for a prolongation of the truce. This proposal was accepted by Israel but was rejected by the Arab states. In these circumstances, the Security Council members (including, this time, the United Kingdom)[393] were prepared to expressly invoke Article 39 and to take action under Chapter VII.[394] At this point, Syria introduced a draft resolution which would have referred to the Court for an advisory opinion the question of the legal status of Palestine after termination of the mandate.[395] The Syrian representative argued that it had never been proven that the problem was international, and that no action could be taken

[388] *Ibid.*, 292nd Mtg., 15 May 1948, pp. 4–7.

[389] *Ibid.*, pp. 16 ff.

[390] *Ibid.*, 293rd Mtg., 17 May 1948, p. 2.

[391] See the statement of the United Kingdom, *ibid.*, 296th Mtg., 19 May 1948, pp. 2–6.

[392] The resolution of 22 May 1948 did not mention Article 39.

[393] *Ibid.*, 334th Mtg., 13 July 1948, pp. 54–56.

[394] The United States submitted a draft resolution to this effect. *Ibid.*, pp. 40–41.

[395] *Ibid.*, pp. 52–53.

under Chapter VII unless this was judicially determined. He proposed that a subcommittee of three be created to draft the questions to be submitted to the Court, and he assured the Council that, if the Court "gave justice in reply to such questions as may be prepared . . . the Arabs would submit to it and yield very meekly and humbly."[396]

Discussion of the Syrian draft resolution continued even after the substantive draft resolution to which Syria objected was adopted.[397] The propriety of making the Court a kind of court of appeal against the Security Council's decisions and the possible hindrance which reference to the Court might work upon the implementation of previous decisions thus became issues of prime importance in the debates.

The Syrian draft resolution was supported by Argentina, Belgium, China, Colombia, and the United Kingdom.[398] Representatives of these states argued that all peaceful means should be pursued; that the Security Council had no right to refuse a party that asked for judicial clarification; that an ICJ opinion would greatly eliminate the opposition of the Arabs; and that, while negotiations might continue without an advisory opinion, the application of sanctions under Chapter VII required a firm legal basis.

Against submission to the Court it was argued that the question was "too complex" and "too political" to be settled by "judges bound only by law";[399] the proposed reference might affect the implementation of previous resolutions adopted and delay a genuine political solution;[400] the International Court could not be regarded as a court of appeal from the decisions of the Assembly and the Council;[401] if the legal question were to be reopened now, negotiations for a peaceful settlement would be hindered, and doubts and uncertainties would be introduced into the mediator's work;[402] the proposed reference would prolong instability and uncertainty in Palestine.[403]

Against the Syrian draft resolution, the Israeli representative put forward a particularly detailed argument in which he questioned the necessity and pro-

---

[396] Ibid., p. 53.

[397] UN Doc. S/902, 15 July 1948. Under the terms of this resolution, the Council ordered all governments and authorities concerned to desist from further military action, and declared that failure to comply would be deemed a breach of the peace within the meaning of Article 39, such as would necessitate immediate Council action.

[398] See SCOR, 3rd Yr., 335th Mtg., 14 July 1948, pp. 4–5 (Belgium); ibid., p. 13 (Egypt); ibid., 336th Mtg., 14 July 1948, pp. 25–26 (Colombia); ibid., 339th Mtg., 27 July 1948, pp. 2 ff. (Syria).

[399] France, ibid., 336th Mtg., 14 July 1948, p. 24.

[400] The U.S.S.R., ibid., 338th Mtg., 15 July 1948, p. 67.

[401] The Ukrainian S.S.R., ibid., p. 68.

[402] Canada (ibid., 339th Mtg., 27 July 1948, p. 12) and the United States (ibid., p. 14).

[403] The U.S.S.R., ibid., p. 17.

priety of asking the Court's opinion in the present case, as well as the motives behind the unwonted enthusiasm of the Arab states for juridical solutions. Among the specific points presented were the following. The prestige of the Court could not be aided by submitting questions in a casual or automatic spirit. Chapter VII had already been applied, and it was not proper to appeal to the Court against action already taken by a principal UN organ. The existence of a state was a question of fact, not of law, to be determined by the criterion of effectiveness, not of legitimacy. Even if the criterion of legitimacy were the determining factor, Israel was the only state with a "legitimate birth certificate." In any case, the question of a state's existence was unrelated to the determination of an act of aggression. Reference to the Court might do practical harm by encouraging aggression. Above all, the Palestine problem was "the most uniquely political problem of all questions in international history," and its submission to the Court would involve that body "in one of the most intractible problems of political relations."[404]

A Colombian amendment making the request provisional on its not delaying or impairing "the normal process of mediation" was accepted by Syria. Nevertheless, the Syrian proposal failed of adoption.[405]

During the course of the General Assembly's consideration, at its third session, of the mediator's progress report, Syria again put forward a draft resolution which would have referred to the Court the question of the competence of the Assembly to partition Palestine and to create a sovereign Jewish state against the wishes of the majority. The resolution would also have referred to the Court the question of the international status of Palestine after termination of the mandate.[406] The mediator's report accepted partition as an established fact, but the Arab states still contested its legal validity. Syria claimed that the General Assembly had no power to delimit the frontiers of any state without its consent, and that the resolution of 29 November 1947 was a mistake which could still be corrected.[407]

In support of the Syrian resolution it was argued that, on previous occasions, the United Nations had come very close to accepting resolutions for reference of legal aspects of the Palestine question to the International Court, a fact which showed that many delegates doubted the legal basis of the

[404] *Ibid.*, 340th Mtg., 27 July 1948, pp. 27-32.

[405] There were six votes in favor (Argentina, Belgium, China, Colombia, Syria, and the United Kingdom), one against (the Ukrainian S.S.R.) and four abstentions (Canada, France, the Soviet Union, and the United States). *Ibid.*, p. 34.

[406] UN Doc. A/C.1/405, 30 November 1948.

[407] GAOR (III/1), 1st Ctte., 219th Mtg., 1 December 1948, pp. 833-35.

action taken by the Assembly. Moreover, from a practical viewpoint, efforts at mediation and conciliation were more likely to be accepted if the parties knew the limits of their rights.[408]

The draft resolution was voted on and rejected by a tie vote.[409] Subsequently, the Assembly adopted a resolution on 11 December 1948 which established a Conciliation Commission to assist the parties in achieving a final settlement of all questions, particularly those relating to the Arab refugees. The resolution accepted as its premise the reality of partition and the existence of the state of Israel.

When the question of Israel's admission was first discussed in the Security Council, Syria introduced a draft resolution[410] which, besides reiterating former questions with regard to the international status of Palestine and the competence of the General Assembly to partition Palestine, would also ask two questions based on the more recent developments—namely, whether the Assembly's partition resolution created a right for the Jews to proclaim a separate state at the termination of the mandate; and whether the Security Council would be acting in conformity with the UN Charter if it recommended the admission of Israel.

The Syrian representative cited the votes on previous Arab proposals regarding reference to the Court as evidence of a large measure of doubt on the part of a majority of the UN members. Now that this new phase of the problem had arisen (Israel's application for admission), submission to the Court was all the more obligatory. The question of delay was not involved, for three and a half months remained until the next Assembly session.

In opposition, it was argued that the admission of Israel could not be considered exclusively from a legal point of view and could not be separated from the entire Palestine question.[411] Furthermore, there was no need to consult the Court, since the status of Palestine was defined by Assembly resolution, and there were full legal and political grounds for recommending the state of Israel for membership in the United Nations.[412]

The Syrian draft resolution was not adopted, the vote being two in favor (Belgium and Syria) and nine abstentions.[413] The application of Israel was also rejected at this meeting.

[408] Egypt, *ibid.*, 228th Mtg., 4 December 1948, p. 932.
[409] 21 to 21, with 4 abstentions.
[410] SCOR, 3rd Yr., 385th Mtg., 17 December 1948, pp. 9–11 (UN Doc. S/1125).
[411] France, *ibid.*, p. 16.
[412] The U.S.S.R., *ibid.*, 386th Mtg., 17 December 1948, pp. 31–32.
[413] *Ibid.*, pp. 36–37.

Israel reapplied for admission in 1949, and on 3 March 1949 the Security Council recommended its admission (with the United Kingdom abstaining in the vote). Although Argentina and Egypt maintained that the resolution was not adopted, since it lacked the affirmative vote of the United Kingdom, they did not formally challenge the President's ruling.[414]

However, when the question was considered by the Assembly, the Arab states, besides arguing on the merits, also raised the question of the validity of the Security Council's recommendation, in light of the United Kingdom's abstention. In the Ad Hoc Political Committee, and again in Plenary, Iraq suggested that the Court be asked for an advisory opinion on the validity of the Council's recommendation.[415] A formal proposal was, in fact, introduced in the Committee, only to be withdrawn later.[416] The feeling of the Assembly majority was that UN practice on this matter was clear,[417] and the admission of Israel was subsequently approved.[418]

In 1951, the Security Council considered the Israeli complaint regarding restrictions on passage through the Suez Canal. Egypt insisted that France, Turkey, the Netherlands, the United Kingdom, and the United States were parties to the dispute and should abstain from voting on the draft resolution under consideration.[419] Subsequently, Egypt submitted a draft resolution which would have had the Council ask for an advisory opinion on whether the abovementioned states were, indeed, obliged to abstain.[420] At a later meeting, however, the proposal was withdrawn, in recognition of the fact that, in any case, it would have failed to receive the majority required for adoption.[421]

---

[414] SCOR, 4th Yr., 414th Mtg., 4 March 1949, pp. 14–15.

[415] GAOR (III/2), Ad Hoc Pol. Ctte., 42nd Mtg., 3 May 1949, pp. 183–84; and Plenary, 207th Mtg., 11 May 1949, p. 310.

[416] Ibid., Ad Hoc Pol. Ctte., 42nd Mtg., 3 May 1949, p. 188.

[417] See ibid., 42nd–44th Mtgs., 3–4 May 1949; and Plenary, 207th Mtg., 11 May 1949. Cf., to the same effect, the Court's view in the Namibia case, when it upheld the validity of Council resolutions adopted in the face of voluntary abstentions by permanent Council members. ICJ Reports, 1971, p. 22.

[418] GAOR (III/2), Plenary, 207th Mtg., 11 May 1949, pp. 330–31.

[419] A joint French-United States-United Kingdom draft resolution would have had the Council call on Egypt to terminate its restrictions on shipping through the Canal. For the Egyptian statement, see SCOR, 6th Yr., 553rd Mtg., 16 August 1951.

[420] Ibid., 555th Mtg., 27 August 1951, p. 16 (UN Doc. S/2313).

[421] For this reason, Egypt (not itself a member of the Council) concluded that sponsorship of its draft resolution by a Council member "would serve no practical purpose." Ibid., 556th Mtg., 29 August 1951, p. 5.

A further attempt to get an aspect of the Palestine question to the Court was made by Syria in 1952, at the General Assembly's seventh session. At issue was the question of the Arab refugees. Following adoption of the Assembly's 11 December 1948 resolution, the Arabs began to demand strict adherence to the letter of that resolution, particularly with regard to the repatriation of Arab refugees. Israel, on the other hand, insisted on inclusion of the refugee problem in general negotiations for a peace settlement and maintained that the terms of the Assembly resolution could be modified by direct agreement of the parties, on the basis of the de facto situation.

In 1952, an eight-power draft resolution was introduced in which previous resolutions were not referred to and in which the parties were to be called upon to negotiate directly with respect to all outstanding problems (i.e., the refugee problem as well).[422]

At this point Syria presented a draft resolution to refer to the Court for an advisory opinion a series of questions on the rights of Arab refugees.[423] Syria claimed that the eight-power draft resolution sought to impose on one party decisions which imperiled rights established and confirmed by the General Assembly. Israel and the Arab states could not negotiate with respect to the rights of the Arab refugees, which were purely private rights. The eight-power draft thus raised legal questions of the highest importance, questions which should be referred to the Court for clarification.[424]

France, the Soviet Union, and Yugoslavia spoke against the proposed reference, claiming mainly that the question was essentially political and that, from a practical viewpoint, recourse to the Court would not aid the fate of the Arab refugees.[425]

The Syrian draft resolution was rejected.[426] No resolution was adopted at that Assembly session.

When the various draft resolutions proposing recourse to the Court are viewed in the contexts in which they were put forward, a certain pattern emerges. At various stages of UN consideration of the Palestine problem, the Arab states—and particularly Syria[427]—sought to prevent action felt to be

[422] UN Doc. A/AC.61/L.23/Rev.1–4, 25 November 1952.

[423] UN Doc. A/AC.61/L.33, 10 December 1952. The questions related to the refugees' right to repatriation and the right of states of which the refugees were not nationals to negotiate on their behalf.

[424] GAOR (VII), Ad Hoc Pol. Ctte., 38th Mtg., 10 December 1952, pp. 227–28.

[425] Ibid., p. 237.

[426] The vote was 13 for, 23 against, with 19 abstentions. Ibid.

[427] Syria's prominence in this matter may be partially attributable to the fact that

inimical to Arab interests; and presentation of the draft resolutions in question bore the character of maneuvers in tight situations.[428]

Thus, in the Assembly's second session, when it appeared that the UNSCOP partition plan would be adopted, the Arab states hoped to have action suspended while the legal questions raised were being referred to the Court.

In the Security Council, no formal proposals to involve the Court were made until the Council seriously contemplated taking action under Chapter VII.

In the Assembly's third session, when it was about to adopt further resolutions based on the acceptance of partition, Syria again proposed that certain legal aspects of the problem be referred to the Court.

The next stage was reached when the Security Council considered the admission of Israel to UN membership. Once again, Syria was not slow to propose a judicial solution to the problem. Questions previously debated, as well as questions relating to the new phase which had arisen, were to be referred to the Court.

When Israel's application successfully passed the Security Council and reached the Assembly, a new strategy was adopted. The question to be referred was no longer the substantive issue of Israel's right to existence; it was the more technical point of the validity of the Council's recommendation of admission.

In 1951, when the question of the restrictions Egypt had imposed on Israeli shipping was considered, Egypt attempted to prevent the adoption of any resolution on the question by insisting that five of the Security Council members were parties to the dispute and should therefore abstain. When it appeared that this point of view would not be accepted by the interested states, Egypt proposed referring the procedural question of compulsory abstention to the Court, but later withdrew this proposal, since, in any event, it could not be adopted without the support of the states concerned.

In the seventh Assembly session, a resolution under consideration might have had the effect of allowing the refugee problem to become an object of direct negotiations. Syria then proposed referring the substantive issue of the Arab refugees to the Court in order to prevent adoption of the resolution.

In none of the cases were the proposals adopted. In many instances, however, they were supported by a large number of representatives. For some, this support reflected a generally pro-Arab stand; others may have had serious doubts concerning the Assembly's competence; and still others may have

---

Faris Bey El-Khoury, Syria's UN representative at the time, was also a member of the International Law Commission.

[428] The Arab stance in the Palestine issue contrasted starkly with a generally negative attitude toward recourse to the Court adopted on other occasions.

been motivated by a desire to free the Assembly, if only temporarily, from a burdensome problem.

It is difficult to see how the Palestine problem could have been solved effectively by referring to the Court the questions proposed. The problem was clearly one of the most emotional and volatile which the UN was called upon to deal with. Reference to the Court probably would not have aided either the Court's prestige or the solution of the vexed problem. Quite obviously, none of the parties would have accepted an opinion inimical to their interests. In the light of subsequent developments, it is not reasonable to assume that the Arab states would have accepted any opinion which validated the existence of the state of Israel. On the other hand, had a Court opinion implied a denial or limitation of Israel's right to exist, it is inconceivable that that state would willingly have accepted recommendations for its own demise or for radical limitation of its sovereignty.

Furthermore, the International Court (and, indeed, this applies to courts in municipal systems of law as well) is probably not an effective organ for dealing with the outbreak of violence.

The Cuban Question

This case is unique in the annals of the United Nations to date. Here was the unusual spectacle of a communist state—Cuba—with the support and sponsorship of the Soviet Union itself, pressing the Security Council to request an advisory opinion from the Court (and, moreover, to request that opinion on a category of questions which the Soviet Union had always denied the Court's competence to answer—namely, the abstract interpretation of Charter provisions) while the traditional proponents of greater use of the Court's advisory function—the United States and its allies—were placed on the defensive.

The circumstances in which this peculiar array of forces developed were the following.

At the 1962 Punta del Este meeting of the OAS, several anti-Cuban resolutions were adopted, in accordance with which, *inter alia*, Cuba was excluded from participation in the inter-American system, and certain categories of trade with Cuba were suspended.[429] These measures, Cuba maintained, constituted enforcement action, in violation of Article 53 of the UN Charter, which required prior Security Council authorization of any such action by a regional agency. Furthermore, Cuba argued, the OAS measures contravened the purposes and principles of the UN Charter[430] and certain provisions of

---

[429] See UN Doc. S/5075, 3 February 1962.

[430] Cuba claimed that its exclusion was based solely on its social system and that such exclusion violated, *inter alia*, the principles underlying Articles 2(7) and 4 of the Charter.

the OAS Charter and the Rio Treaty. Cuba's arguments were translated into a series of seven—decidedly loaded—questions[431] which Cuba sought to have the Security Council refer to the Court for an advisory opinion. At Cuba's request, the Council met to consider whether or not to solicit the Court's opinion in this case.[432]

The Council's debates were long[433] and, not surprisingly, acrimonious.

At the very outset, the Cuban representative sought to place the United States and its allies on the defensive. After setting forth the substance of the Cuban complaint, he called upon the Security Council to refer to the Court the "specific legal questions" submitted by Cuba. Clearly the organ of greatest authority, the Court should be asked its opinion in order that the principles of international law might prevail. Failure to agree to this course of action could be due only to fear of an adverse verdict, fear based on a lack of faith in the legality of the Punta del Este resolutions. For its part, Cuba, confident that international law was on its side, would welcome a Court decision.[434]

Taking up the cudgels on behalf of Cuba, the Soviet representative added further reasons for referring the proposed questions to the Court. The Court was obviously the organ most competent to give an impartial and objective reply on the legal points raised; and, unless "some improper pressure" were put on the Court, it could do so in the shortest possible time. Such an

---

[431] UN Docs. S/5086 and S/5095, 8 and 19 March 1962. Questions 3 and 6, in particular, called for interpretation of the Charter in the abstract.

3. Can the expression "enforcement action" in Article 53 of the United Nations Charter be considered to include the measures provided for in Article 41 of the United Nations Charter? Is the list of these measures in Article 41 exhaustive?

6. Is one of the main principles of the United Nations Charter that membership in the United Nations is open to States which meet the requirements of Article 4 of the Charter, irrespective of their systems?

That the purpose of these and the other relatively "abstract" questions was to get a reply regarding a specific set of facts was indicated by the terms of the final question of the series:

7. In the light of the replies to the foregoing questions are, or are not, the resolutions adopted at Punta del Este . . . relating to the expulsion of a State member of the regional agency because of its social system and the taking of other enforcement action against it, without the authorization of the Security Council, consistent with the provisions of the United Nations Charter, the Charter of the Organization of American States and the Treaty of Rio?

[432] This is the only instance in which the Security Council was specially convened for the purpose of deciding whether or not to request an advisory opinion. Normally, as was seen, proposals for requesting opinions arise in connection with issues already under discussion.

It might be noted that Cuba had been thwarted in its earlier effort to get a Security Council consideration of the Punta del Este resolutions. See SCOR, 17th Yr., 991st Mtg., 27 February 1962.

[433] The matter was discussed at meetings 992–98, 14–23 March 1962 (ibid.).

[434] Ibid., 992nd Mtg., 14 March 1962, pp. 2–28.

objective reply would make it impossible for the United States and its allies "to continue to use the smoke-screen behind which they are now making political, economic and military preparations for a new attack on Cuba."[435]

The majority of the Council members, however, viewed the Cuban move as a thinly veiled attempt to introduce the Soviet veto into the activities of regional agencies. These members based their opposition to requesting an advisory opinion in this case on three principal grounds: (1) the clarity of the issues raised in the Cuban proposal and the consequent pointlessness of reference to the Court; (2) the "political" nature of the request; and (3) the impropriety of seeking an opinion regarding OAS decisions.

As for the first ground, it was argued that the measures complained of were undoubtedly within the exclusive jurisdiction of the OAS. Clearly, a regional agency had the exclusive right to determine its own membership. Moreover, the economic measures adopted were not in the nature of "enforcement measures"—that term (as the Council had already determined in connection with the Dominican Republic question)[436] being reserved for action solely within the Security Council's competence (i.e., the use of armed force).[437]

The second theme, that the Cuban proposal was "political" both in "content and intent," was played upon—with certain variations—by several representatives.

Thus, the United States representative noted that "the representative of Cuba has, regrettably, not presented his request for a judicial opinion in a very judicial manner." The "tone and substance" of the Cuban speech proved that "a political dispute" between Cuba and representatives of the Western Hemisphere was involved. "The Cuban letter is camouflaged with legalisms, but the issues it raises are 100 per cent political."[438] Particularly suspect were the Cuban and Soviet *motives* in presenting the proposal. In fact, these motives, above all, branded the Cuban proposal as political.

> The United States Government has repeatedly made clear that it favours increased recourse to the International Court of Justice. But it does not favour use of the Court for cold war political purposes foreign to the Charter and the Statute of the Court. It is significant, in this connexion,

[435] *Ibid.*, 993rd Mtg., 15 March 1962, pp. 2–13.

[436] See *ibid.*, 15th Yr., Mtgs. 893–95, 8–9 September 1960. But cf. Inis L. Claude, Jr., "The OAS, the UN, and the United States," *International Conciliation*, No. 547 (March 1964): 48–53, to the effect that the "Dominican precedent" was by no means as unequivocal as it was later construed to be.

[437] See, e.g., the remarks of the representatives of the United States (SCOR, 17th Yr., 993rd Mtg., 15 March 1962, pp. 15–24), the United Kingdom (*ibid.*, 995th Mtg., 20 March 1962, pp. 4–6), China (*ibid.*, pp. 6–9), Ireland (*ibid.*, 996th Mtg., 21 March 1962, pp. 12–13), and Venezuela (*ibid.*, 997th Mtg., 22 March 1962, pp. 1–7).

[438] *Ibid.*, 993rd Mtg., 15 March 1962, p. 14.

that the Soviet representative, whose Government is consistently hostile to the use of the Court for the settlement of genuine legal disputes between States and has deprecated the Court's advisory jurisdiction, should so enthusiastically favour submission to the Court of the rhetorical and self-serving questions which have been conjured up by the Cuban representative.[439]

In America's judgment, the purpose of the Soviet and Cuban action was to attack the autonomy of regional agencies by imposing upon them a Soviet veto. In the process, the Court was to be dragged into the Cold War and into "the jungle of Communist propaganda."[440]

Similar views were expressed by the representatives of the United Kingdom, France, and Ireland.

For the United Kingdom representative, evidence of the "political" motivation behind the Cuban request was to be found in the patently "political" character of the last question (to which the others led up);[441] in the "history of Cuban complaints in the past"; and in the "general character and tone" of the Cuban and Soviet speeches in the instant case. The proposed questions had not been "inspired merely by a thirst for legal knowledge"; they were but "political questions disguised in a legal form."[442]

The French representative thought that the Cuban proposal was merely "a device—rather a tendentious one . . . —to raise the essentially political question of the present relations between Cuba and the rest of the Western hemisphere"; and that the Cuban government was attempting, "behind a screen of legality, to inveigle the . . . Court . . . into giving an opinion on questions whose legal nature cannot be separated from their political aspect."[443]

Perhaps most incisive were the comments of the Irish representative. Differences of interpretation regarding Article 53 and other issues were not "purely juridical," because they entailed a "basic conflict of political opinion as to the scope of the role which the Security Council—and the veto power of its permanent members—is entitled to play in relation to the operation of regional organizations. . . . such a conflict of opinion cannot be satisfactorily resolved by an advisory opinion of the Court. It must be settled by agreement—primarily by agreement between the major powers."[444]

Finally, as far as the third ground was concerned—namely, the impropriety of referring the legality of OAS decisions to the Court—particular objection

---

[439] *Ibid.*, p. 24.

[440] *Ibid.*, 994th Mtg., 16 March 1962, p. 7.

[441] For the text of that question, see n. 431 of this chapter.

[442] SCOR, 17th Yr., 995th Mtg., 20 March 1962, pp. 2–4.

[443] *Ibid.*, pp. 10–12.

[444] *Ibid.*, 996th Mtg., 21 March 1962, pp. 12–13.

was raised to those questions which involved interpretation of the OAS Charter. By referring such questions, it was argued, the Security Council would "be unwarrantably invading the autonomy which the Organization of American States is justifiably entitled to enjoy," for the Council would be constituting itself "a court of review in respect of the Organization's interpretation of its own Charter."[445]

In response to the foregoing objections, the Cuban and Soviet representatives in effect raided the arsenal from which the Western states had traditionally drawn their arguments in favor of greater recourse to the Court's advisory function. Posing as champions of the rule of law and of the authority of the Court, they pleaded for the right of a member state to get a clear and final ruling from a competent judicial forum; for applying international law even in respect of political problems;[446] and for upholding the effectiveness of treaties.[447]

The Cuban representative addressed himself at some length to the main objection raised—namely, that his government's proposal was "political."

First, he argued, the Court itself should be allowed to rule on the "judicial" nature of the questions.[448] Second, acceptance of the argument that the Cuban questions were political "would render Article 96 of the . . . Charter virtually inoperative: a State concerned in a case would only have to assert that political questions were involved for the . . . Court . . . to be precluded from giving an opinion." In the present case, Cuba's legal questions were "being withheld from the Court by politicians, using political arguments, on the pretext that such questions have a concealed political purpose." In any event, however, the motivation behind the request was irrelevant.

We seem to have heard some member of the Council object to the questions we raised on the ground that they are not "purely legal" and are not prompted by a desire for "legal knowledge," as if the reasons motivating a State in requesting an advisory opinion also had to be legal and as if the International Court of Justice, that modern academy of international law, existed solely to dispel the scientific doubts of those who bring before it legal questions which are "chemically pure"; as if every one of us, every time we came to this Council or engaged in any activity in this house, were not doing so in response to political necessity. If the questions put to the

---

[445] Ibid., p. 11; cf. 994th Mtg., 16 March 1962, pp. 14–15.

[446] To deny the applicability of law to political problems, M. Morozov, the Soviet representative, argued, "would be tantamount to admitting that anarchy, chaos and arbitrary action reigned in the United Nations." Ibid., 998th Mtg., 23 March 1962, p. 8.

[447] See ibid., 994th Mtg., 16 March 1962, pp. 1–5; 997th Mtg., 22 March 1962, pp. 7–16; and 998th Mtg., 23 March 1962, pp. 1–12.

[448] Ibid., 994th Mtg., 16 March 1962, p. 4; see also the remarks of the Soviet representative, ibid., 998th Mtg., 23 March 1962, pp. 1–8.

Court are framed in legal terms, objectively legal terms, that should be sufficient, and we should refrain from any consideration of their motivation.[449]

The true reason for opposition to the Cuban proposals, the Cuban representative repeatedly emphasized, was fear of an adverse verdict:

> If the United States representative is so sure of the rightness of his position, why is he against requesting the . . . Court . . . for an opinion? And if not . . . of what value is his statement that his Government favours increased recourse to the Court?[450]

> Why should we not let the Court answer the legal issues we raise? Is it because we have doubts about the Court? Or do we not want an advisory opinion because the legal arguments are on the side of a small Member State in the war which another powerful Member State has launched against it?[451]

Clearly, Cuba was playing its propaganda advantage to the hilt.

Outside of the Soviet bloc, the Cuban proposal found its only real support in Ghana.[452] The Ghanaian representative conceded that some of the Cuban questions were either "political" or not relevant to the main juridical issue involved. The key issue, as far as he was concerned, was whether the Punta del Este resolutions did, in fact, constitute "enforcement action" within the meaning of Article 53 of the UN Charter (question 3 of the Cuban proposal). On this point, doctrine was divided, and, despite the so-called Dominican precedent, reasonable doubt remained among Council members. The existence of these doubts constituted the strongest argument in favor of the Cuban request.

> For, if juridical proprieties were to be abandoned in the formulation and execution of such important political decisions as those complained of, the very principles of international law and the basis of the Charter would be undermined; and those who would suffer most from such a

---

[449] *Ibid.*, 997th Mtg., 22 March 1962, p. 12.

[450] *Ibid.*, 994th Mtg., 16 March 1962, p. 2.

[451] *Ibid.*, 997th Mtg., 22 March 1962, p. 12.

[452] The U.A.R., which might normally have been expected to lend more enthusiastic support to the Cuban proposal, was apparently caught up in a dilemma because of the implications of the Cuban request for regional organizations generally—including, therefore, the Arab League. Particularly objectionable to the U.A.R. was the Cuban theory that the regional agency should be a "microcosm" of the UN without the right to exclude members at will. *Ibid.*, 996th Mtg., 21 March 1962, pp. 7–9. The U.A.R. voted for referring question 3 of the Cuban request to the Court, but it abstained on the other questions.

development would be the small, weak States, whose only recourse is the rule of international law.

The Ghanaian representative therefore appealed to the Security Council to grant the request which Cuba, "as an aggrieved party," had presented. Although "bedevilled with political arguments," that request was—at least insofar as the interpretation of "enforcement action" was concerned—a "specific legal request" which merited the Council's endorsement.[453]

On Ghana's motion, a separate vote was taken on question 3.[454] That paragraph was defeated by a vote of 7 to 4.[455] The remainder of the Cuban draft was defeated by an even wider margin.[456]

Quite obviously, Cuba and the Soviet Union were well aware, in advance, that the Cuban proposal would not muster the support necessary for soliciting the Court's opinion. What, then, prompted the Cuban move? Apparently, it was the propaganda dividend which was expected to accrue to the Soviet bloc from placing the United States and its allies in the uncomfortable position of having to deny a Soviet bloc member what on other occasions the West had considered to be a state's prerogative—namely, to have a judicial, and not merely a political, forum determine its rights. The West was to be embarrassed into conceding, at least implicitly, that it feared an advisory opinion; that it perhaps doubted the legality of the OAS actions.

As for the Western states, they were, indeed, anxious to avoid judicial interpretation of Article 53 of the Charter, for they were well aware of the risk which such a course entailed.[457] It was precisely because of the Cold War that that article had been evaded (even with respect to the use of armed force);[458] and the West was not now going to allow the Soviet Union and

[453] SCOR, 17th Yr., 996th Mtg., 21 March 1962, pp. 13–19.

[454] Ibid., 998th Mtg., 23 March 1962, pp. 16–17. Cuba agreed to this motion. Ibid., p. 21.

[455] Voting in favor were Ghana, Rumania, the Soviet Union, and the U.A.R.

[456] The vote was 2 for, 7 against, with 1 abstention. (The U.A.R. abstained, and Ghana did not participate in the vote. After the vote on question 3, the Soviet and Cuban representatives, for obvious reasons, did not wish to have the remainder of the proposal voted on. The President's ruling to put the rest of the draft to a vote was upheld by a vote of 7 to 2, with 2 abstentions (the U.A.R. and Ghana).

[457] See, on this point, Claude, op. cit., p. 59. Although the West had made its interpretation prevail in the Security Council, it "could have no assurance that the Court would similarly place general political considerations above textual analysis of the Charter."

[458] The Western regional organizations had generally invoked Article 51 for this purpose; their Eastern counterparts had employed the exception contained in Article 53 itself (namely, measures directed against a former enemy state).

Cuba to refoist upon the Western regional organizations the shackles of the veto, from which those organizations had, in effect, extricated themselves.

Neither side, in fact, was about to accept an adverse judicial determination of the underlying question of regional autonomy versus Security Council control.[459] Despite Cuban talk of a "clear and final ruling" by the Court, had such a ruling been unfavorable to Cuba's contentions, a Soviet veto would undoubtedly have prevented Council acceptance of the Court's opinion. On the other hand, had the Cuban arguments been upheld, the opinion, regardless of the formal reception accorded it by the Council, would probably have remained ineffectual in practice.

CONCLUSIONS

As the foregoing study has shown, League and UN organs did not lack opportunities to use the Court's advisory function more extensively or to use it for purposes other than those for which it was employed. Why, then, were the opportunities presented not, in fact, seized? What limits were placed on the use of the advisory function, and why were they placed?

The considerations which prompted the *rejection* of proposals and suggestions for requesting advisory opinions were quite as multifarious as those which prompted the *adoption* of requests.[460] Nevertheless, here, too, distinctive League and UN patterns are discernible. Indeed, upon closer inspection,

---

[459] See the remarks of the Irish representative, p. 262 above.

[460] As in the case of actual requests, the contextual aspects of the proposals for recourse to the Court—particularly such matters as the timing of the proposals and the array of states pro and con—are all-important but are difficult to generalize.

For illustrative purposes, the following examples of the importance of the timing factor may be recalled. In the Hungarian optants case, the first proposal for requesting a Court opinion, put forward by the Rapporteur, had a greater chance of acceptance than did the second proposal, which originated with Hungary and followed that government's repudiation of an earlier agreement at Brussels. And, again, in that same case, after the Council recommended the renewal of negotiations on the basis of certain postulates, even those who favored, in principle, requesting the Court's opinion deemed it a "psychological error" for the Council to give the impression, at that stage, that it doubted the success of its own proposals. In the matter of delimiting the port of Danzig, the suggestion by Danzig that the Court itself be charged with the task of delimitation was put forward at the end of the Council's deliberations on the matter and, largely for this reason, it was rejected. During the UN period, the timing of such draft resolutions as the Belgian proposal regarding the legality of the review procedure for Administrative Tribunal judgments and the 1958 five-power draft regarding the question of the vote on non-self-governing territories was an important factor in the rejection of those proposals.

The abovementioned Belgian proposal is also a good illustration of the significance of the particular configuration of interests involved. For, here, the legal doubts of a relatively unimportant state clashed with the positive interest of an important state (the United States) in securing immediate action. The key question in most decisions to have recourse to the Court is not "Do legal doubts (in the abstract) exist?" but, rather, "Whose doubts are involved?" and, further, "Are those doubts ignorable?"

these patterns prove to be merely the counterparts of the patterns of actual requests. (The two sets of patterns taken together provide a more complete understanding of the employment of the advisory function.)

To discover what these divergent patterns were, it is useful (as in the case of actual requests) to concentrate on several more particular questions, relating, this time, to the proposals and suggestions which *failed* of adoption.

1. How was the proposal or suggestion for requesting an advisory opinion initiated, and what was the apparent purpose of the initiator? (In particular, was the proposal or suggestion put forward as part of a problem-solving approach? Was it motivated by a sincere desire to remove legal doubts? Did it represent an attempt to get a dispute arbitrated by means of advisory procedure, against the wishes of one of the disputants? Did it bear the character of a maneuver intended to delay or prevent action deemed undesirable? Was its purpose to remove from the political organ concerned the onus of decision-making? Was it designed to score a propaganda or psychological victory?) In this connection, was the proposal put forward with the knowledge that it would not be accepted?

2. What considerations carried the most weight in defeating proposals or in nipping them in the bud? Would adoption of the proposal have involved the danger that the previous actions of a political organ would be judicially overruled?

3. What were the attitudes of states toward employment of the advisory jurisdiction, and was there any consistency in these attitudes?

4. What alternative to the advisory procedure was actually pursued ("political" action, "legal" action, or no action)?

5. Did the absence of judicial clarification in any way hinder the further course of the political organ's treatment of the problem to which the proposed consultation related?

6. What effect would a Court opinion have had on the solution of the root problem? Would it have been likely to remove a major obstacle to settlement of the difficulty? Would it, rather, have been irrelevant? Or, even worse, might it, by rigidifying previously flexible positions, have been positively harmful?

Most frequently, in both periods, the unsuccessful attempts to consult the Court were launched by individual states. In the UN period, this was, of course, to be expected, since most proposals—of whatever sort—are initiated by states. In the League period, however, where the Rapporteur's initiative played such a determinative role in the adoption of actual requests, the absence of such initiative in relation to many "stillborn" requests is significant. It immediately raises a suspicion of unilateralism—namely, that one party to a dispute may have been attempting to employ the advisory procedure as a weapon against the other party without the latter's consent. In several instances, this suspicion was, indeed, borne out.[461] On the other hand, a number of the proposals put forward by individual states related to organizational questions and bore a very different character.[462] Moreover, a significant number of proposals *were* presented by Rapporteurs and Rapporteurial committees.[463] The proposals in the last two categories—those initiated by states in regard to organizational issues and those initiated by Rapporteurs or Rapporteurial committees in regard to all issues—were more clearly aimed at true problem-solving. Whether the prime motivation was a sincere desire to remove legal doubts or the hope of relieving the political organ concerned of the onus of decision-making, the expectation was that a Court opinion would, indeed, help to resolve the basic difficulty. There apparently was no foreknowledge—at least insofar as concerns the formal proposals in these two categories—that the recommendation to have recourse to the Court would be rejected. In contrast, some of the proposals presented by states and involving existing disputes were put forward despite advance recognition that they would probably fail of acceptance. These may have represented tactical maneuvers to prevent distasteful action from being taken[464] or attempts to score at least psychological victories.[465]

Passing to the "stillborn" requests of the UN period, one finds the problem-solving approach receding farther into the background. Many more proposals and suggestions were put forward in a rather casual spirit and without any expectation that they would be accepted. Even when such an expectation

---

[461] Cf., e.g., Hungary's proposals in the Hungarian optants case; Greece's suggestion in the *Salamis* case; the Swiss proposal in relation to reparations for war damages; and Danzig's proposal to have the Court delimit the port of Danzig.

In addition, some states, acting as third parties, sought to obtain adjudication of disputes by means of advisory procedure, despite the absence of consent on the part of one or both of the disputants. Cf., e.g., the proposal in the Chaco dispute and the suggestions presented in connection with the Locarno Treaty and the Iraqi-Iranian dispute, pp. 181–82 above.

[462] E.g., the proposals raised in connection with Corfu; the vote required for requests; and the implications of withdrawal from League membership.

[463] E.g., the initial proposal in the Hungarian optants case; the proposals in the *Salamis* and Finnish ships cases to have the Court determine the question of competence; and the suggestions of the respective rapporteurs in connection with German minorities in Poland and the Memel question. The recommendation of the Permanent Mandates Commission in the matter of South West Africa might be included in the same category.

[464] Some of the Hungarian proposals in the Hungarian optants case appear to have been of this nature.

[465] Such a consideration may have underlain Lithuania's proposals in the matter of the Vilna Territory.

did exist, there was rarely a corresponding prospect that a judicial pronounce-ment would resolve, or even ameliorate, the root problem involved. This was so, first, because the desire for recourse to the Court was generally unilateral, with one of the disputants being obviously unprepared to accept a Court opinion inimical to its interests;[466] and, second, because even those states which pressed most for recourse did not themselves, in many instances, seriously contemplate acquiescing in a judicial opinion adverse to their own views.[467] Far more frequently than in the League period, proposals bore the character of tactical maneuvers in tight situations, maneuvers designed not so much to elicit judicial clarification as to prevent, or, at least, postpone, action deemed detrimental to the sponsoring states' interests. At other times—most notably, in the Cuban question—proposals were put forward primarily in the hope of reaping expected propaganda dividends, if only from the discussions surrounding the proposal. Very few proposals were prompted by a genuine desire for judicial clarification of complex legal issues and/or by the expecta-tion that a judicial pronouncement would, indeed, be more effective than other means in resolving the basic difficulty involved.[468]

What considerations weighed most heavily in the decisions not to employ the Court's advisory jurisdiction?

In the League period, the foremost consideration involved the matter of consent. Although (as noted above) the question of the vote required for requests remained controversial throughout, the League organs were reluctant

---

[466] Thus, e.g., the Australian draft resolution in connection with the Soviet refusal to grant exit visas, if accepted, might have resulted in an adjudication—by circuitous means—of the Soviet-Chilean disagreement in that case; but Soviet compliance (assuming the Court's opinion were unfavorable to the Soviet stand) probably would not have been forthcoming.

[467] This was probably true of most of the Arab proposals in connection with the Palestine issue; and of the South African proposal in regard to the treatment of Indians in South Africa. In the League period, by contrast, states such as Hungary in the Hungarian optants case, or Switzerland in the Swiss reparations case, were prepared to accept even an unfavorable judicial verdict.

[468] In this category are some of the proposals and suggestions involving such organiza-tional matters as the interpretation of Articles 11 and 12 of the ICJ Statute; the question of the terms of office of Council members; and the legality of the UN Administrative Tribunal review procedure.

It should be noted that the motives of nonsponsoring states which supported refer-ence to the Court at times diverged somewhat from those of the sponsors. In several instances "supporting" states were more sincere in their desire for judicial guidance than were the sponsors. (At least part of the not inconsiderable support for referring certain aspects of the Palestine issue to the Court and for consulting the Court on the Assem-bly's competence in the matter of the treatment of Indians in South Africa is attribut-able to this motive.) And, not infrequently, there came into play an anxiety to see the political organ concerned disburdened, if only temporarily, of a vexed problem.

to address requests to the Court on the basis of a less-than-unanimous vote.[469] However, even more important than unanimity was the insistence upon securing the consent of the interested states. Regardless of the theoretically nonbinding nature of advisory opinions, in practice, advisory procedure was viewed as little less than "quasi arbitration."[470] This was most evident in cases related to actual "disputes." But, even in regard to such nondispute issues as that involved in the Corfu aftermath, the Council was unwilling to override the wishes of the state principally concerned.

The feeling that a Court opinion was unnecessary or that it would be of no practical value was determinative in several instances.[471] Reluctance to relinquish decision-making powers to another body—so prominent a feature of the UN period—was manifest at various times during the League period as well.[472] And, like the UN organs, the League Council sometimes evinced jealousy regarding its right to be the sole judge of its competence.[473] Moreover, the Council was not particularly anxious—in the one case where the issue was most forcefully presented[474]—to have the Court judge the validity of the Council's past actions.

The argument that recourse to the Court would unduly delay the solution of a pending difficulty was often invoked, with some effectiveness, in both periods.[475]

---

[469] This tendency to require unanimity worked to the disadvantage of the Assembly, where unanimity was more difficult to attain.

[470] Cf., especially, the views of M. Titulesco, in the Hungarian optants question; of M. Salandra, in the Corfu aftermath; and of Lord Cecil, in the matter of the Finnish ships, pp. 193–94, 178, and 205 above.

[471] E.g., in the cases of the *Salamis*, the Lithuanian request, the Finnish ships, Swiss reparations, and delimitation of the port of Danzig.

[472] E.g., in the matter of the vote required for requests and in the *Salamis* case.

[473] This was especially evident in the *Salamis* case. However, the jealousy in that case must be seen in the context of the Council's general unwillingness to interfere with pending arbitration. Furthermore, unlike the UN organs, the League Council was jealous of its right *not* to assume competence.

It should also be recalled that the League Council did, on several occasions, refer to the Court questions related to its competence. (See Opinion Nos. 6 and 7, pp. 61–65 above; and cf. the Council's request for an advisory opinion from a committee of jurists in the Aaland Islands case. LN, *Procès-Verbal* of the 7th Sess. of the Council, 9–12 July 1920, pp. 24–25.)

[474] The Lithuanian request with respect to division of the Vilna Territory.

[475] This argument, however, may not have been justified in most cases. The League Council frequently requested the Court to deal with questions as a matter of urgency, and the Court complied with the Council's wishes. As for the UN period, Article 82(2) of the ICJ Rules enables the Court to accelerate its procedure, if necessary. For the time lag between passage of the resolution requesting the Court's opinion and the rendering of the Court's opinion, see Appendix 5. It may be noted that, in the *Namibia* case, the Court (undoubtedly sensitive to recent criticism over long delays in judicial proceedings before the ICJ) refused to grant the full time extension requested by South Africa for presentation of its Written Statement. ICJ Reports, 1971, p. 18.

While questions involving interpretation of the Covenant in the abstract were never referred to the PCIJ, and while arguments denying the competence of the Court in this area were frequently heard, in every instance, other, overriding considerations were responsible for the decision not to send such questions to the Court.[476] Nevertheless, by the end of the League era, the very fact that no such questions had ever been referred reinforced the earlier doubts and uncertainty regarding the Court's competence to render abstract interpretations.[477]

Turning to the UN period, certain arguments which for the League organs played a relatively minor role in preventing recourse to the Court became for the UN organs overriding and dominant considerations.

Thus, the argument that the issue was basically "political"[478] or "moral" became a stock argument in the UN representatives' "repertoire" whenever recourse to the Court was contemplated. That reluctance to refer questions of competence to the Court, already adumbrated in certain League cases, was transformed, in the UN period, into an unwritten law which barred such questions—particularly as they related to Article 2(7) of the Charter—from ever being submitted to the Court.[479] Suggestions that Article 2(7) be judicially clarified were raised in connection with either decolonization or racial issues[480] —matters about which the majority in the UN held strong views. This majority, therefore, considered that it had a stake in avoiding adverse judicial pronouncements which might only place the organization in a straitjacket and make it more difficult to take the action which the majority was determined to take in any event.[481]

---

[476] See the discussions of the Polish-Lithuanian dispute, the Corfu aftermath, and the nature of the vote required for requests, pp. 197–201, 201–7, and 213–21 above.

[477] This was one of the considerations which prompted the Assembly to refrain from requesting a Court interpretation of Article 1(3) of the Covenant in connection with the withdrawal of certain states from League membership. See pp. 182–83 above.

[478] This was often in the nature of an assertion, with no explanation being offered as to what it was that made the matter "political." At times, the request was said to be "politically motivated"—i.e., not motivated by the desire for legal edification. (See the discussion of the Cuban and Palestine questions, pp. 248–59 and 259–66 above.) Most frequently, the matter was deemed too emotional or volatile for judicial consideration and/or for effective solution by means of judicial pronouncements.

In the League period, the "political" nature of the issue was urged most forcefully in the Hungarian optants case. The argument was heard in respect of other cases as well (see, especially, the Corfu issue).

[479] The terminology of Article 2(7), in contrast to its Covenant counterpart, foreshadowed a more "political" approach to the matter.

[480] Cf. the cases of Indonesia, the treatment of Indians in South Africa, and apartheid.

[481] Not much attention was ever paid to a passage in the 1950 report of the Interim Committee, which, on the handling of questions of competence in the General Assembly, stated:

> The essentially political character of the General Assembly inclines it to decide its competence for itself or more often to assume competence without an express deci-

The idea that the Court should not be used as a court of appeal against the decisions of political organs also took particularly strong root in the UN period.[482] Frequently, decisions on the substantive issues had been taken prior to discussion of the suggestion for requesting the Court's opinion, and the political organ concerned was unwilling to see those decisions exposed to the risk of judicial overruling; nor did it wish even to imply that it was casting doubt on the validity of its own decisions. Moreover, in some cases, it was feared that recourse to the Court might affect the implementation of previous decisions and delay solution of the underlying problem.

The reluctance to relinquish any measure of decision-making power to another organ was not limited to those issues which were deemed "political." Even in respect to matters of a more avowedly legal character, UN organs feared any crystallization and consequent restriction of their absolute freedom to set their own precedents, on a pragmatic basis.

What attitude did individual states adopt toward employment of the advisory jurisdiction?

In neither period were the states' attitudes marked by any striking measure of consistency. While a state might establish a "long-range" or "strategic" view as to the desirability of greater use of the Court's advisory function, where its own interests dictated support for, or opposition to, particular proposals, the "strategic" view invariably gave way to the "tactical" or "short-range" view. Thus, in the League period, a state might well argue for the sufficiency of a majority vote in a case in which it was not concerned, while insisting on unanimity where its own interests were at stake. Or, again, in one instance a state might emphasize the theoretically nonbinding nature of advisory opinions, and, in the other, stress the binding character which opinions had come to assume in practice.[483] In some cases, of course, the "short-range" and "long-range" views tended to coincide; and certain states—possibly be-

---

sion. On the other hand, where opinions among Members differ on the interpretation of the Charter and legal doubts as to the Assembly's competence are strongly and sincerely held, the force of a recommendation by the Assembly will be weakened if it is made without an affirmative decision upon the question of competence, preferably with the assistance of the International Court of Justice in cases where it is practicable.

GAOR (V), Supp. No. 14, p. 26.

[482] Cf., to the same effect, Chapter III.

[483] Cf., e.g., the Italian views in the Corfu aftermath and in the *Salamis* case.

Even in the same case, and in support of the same position, a state may invoke both the "binding" and "nonbinding" nature of advisory opinions. See, e.g., the Rumanian arguments in the Hungarian optants case, pp. 187 and 193–94 above.

cause of their particular experiences with the use or attempted use of the advisory function—came to display more consistency in their arguments.[484]

The inconsistency in states' attitudes was, if anything, heightened in the UN period. Although, in "strategic" terms, attitudes toward the submission of questions to the Court ranged from the West's favorable, through most Afro-Asian states' lukewarm, to the Soviet bloc's hostile, on any given matter positions were reversed, modified, and intermingled. Thus, it has not been too unusual for the West to find itself on the defensive—most notably, in the Cuban case, but in other cases as well.[485] And the role of advocate of more extensive employment of the advisory function has been assumed not only by Arab states[486] and Soviet-oriented African states[487] but even by the Soviet Union itself.[488] Arguments for and against recourse to the Court are not difficult to find. There is, as it were, a ready-made "repertoire" from which states may, and do, select at will, without any regard to consistency. Thus, for example, a state may in one instance argue against making a political organ subordinate to the Court in constitutional matters and, in another, similar case, urge use of the Court as the most suitable body for the interpretation of constitutional provisions. One issue may be branded "political," while another, apparently indistinguishable, issue is labeled "legal." The right of a state not to have a mere "political" forum determine its rights may be asserted in one case and denied in another.[489] What is "clear" in one case is not clear in the next. These examples could be multiplied ad infinitum. The fact is—and this fact is made abundantly clear by the case studies of actual and "stillborn" requests—that the position of states is determined primarily by an assessment of how reference to the Court will affect their interests in a

---

[484] Thus, Turkey, Rumania, and Poland insisted on the unanimity requirement for all requests (see, e.g., the views of Rumania in the *Salamis* case, p. 211 above; and the observations of Poland and Turkey, LNOJ, 1937, pp. 175–80, 183). Significantly, both Turkey and Rumania fairly frequently found themselves having to oppose submitting to the Court aspects of disputes to which they were parties; Poland found itself perennially on the losing end in opinions actually rendered.

On the other hand, Belgium, and the Scandinavian states, who generally were not involved in either actual or prospective requests, tended to favor a majority requirement for requests. Finland, possibly because of its experience in the *Eastern Carelia* case, also supported the sufficiency of a majority vote.

[485] E.g., on the Palestine issue and on the question of voting on the non-self-governing territories.

[486] In support of their proposals on the Palestine question, they frequently cited the need for greater use of the advisory function.

[487] See, in particular, the position of Ghana on the issues of Cuba and voting on matters related to non-self-governing territories.

[488] See the Soviet arguments in the Cuban case, p. 263 and n. 446 above.

[489] Cf., for example, the position of states in the matter of the treatment of Indians in South Africa with their positions on the Cuban request.

particular case. Positions of principle are always subject to modification under "particular circumstances."[490]

What alternatives were, in fact, adopted, in lieu of requesting the Court's opinion?

During the League period, use of a totally "political" alternative was rare. More often than not, some other channel of law clarification was resorted to. Frequently, that channel was an ad hoc committee of jurists. As noted earlier, the Court had declined to establish a dual procedure for advisory cases. It had insisted on safeguarding its judicial character in *all* advisory cases, refusing to act at *any* time as a mere committee of jurists. As a result, all advisory opinions were imbued with a certain authoritativeness. But that very fact meant that the need for *less* authoritative advice had to be satisfied outside the judicial confines. Thus, the League Council established, as it were, its own dual procedure. Where it wished authoritative advice; where it desired final settlement of an issue; where it was willing, in effect, to delegate its decision-making powers to the Court; and where unanimity in favor of consulting the Court was attainable—requesting an advisory opinion often appeared as the normal and natural course of action. On the other hand, where the Council wanted a truly "advisory" opinion; where it wished to retain absolute freedom in its decision-making; and/or where unanimity clearly was not forthcoming—committees of jurists were often employed as an alternative.[491]

However, notwithstanding the League's normal preference for "legal" solutions, where—as in the Hungarian optants case—a political approach was deemed more conducive to dispute settlement, the League did not insist on pursuing the available "legal" alternatives. Given Rumania's attitude in the Hungarian optants case, it was felt that only a negotiated solution could realistically dispose of the basic problem.

Finally, in some instances, the alternative to asking the Court's opinion was not to take any action at all.[492]

[490] The case of Belgium is especially instructive. In the early UN years, Belgium was one of the most consistent advocates of greater use of the Court. Yet, in the *Expenses* case, when its own interests were involved, it did an about-face.

[491] See, especially, the discussion of the Corfu aftermath and the *Salamis* case, pp. 201–7 and 207–13 above. The advice of anonymous jurists also was taken at one point in the Hungarian optants controversy. Cf. the Finnish claims and Swiss reparations cases. In the Memel case, failure to secure Lithuania's consent to request an advisory opinion led to the institution of contentious proceedings. But, as already noted, this case was unusual.

[492] See, especially, the Lithuanian request, pp. 197–201 above.

In the UN period, the tables were reversed. Rarely were other "legal" channels resorted to as an alternative to consulting the Court.[493] Most commonly, direct action by a political organ ensued. And in some instances, no action was taken.[494]

In most instances—especially in the League period—the absence of judicial clarification apparently did not seriously hamper the political organs concerned in their subsequent handling of the issues to which the proposed recourse to the Court related. In the League period, use of alternative legal channels proved generally effective. In the case of the Hungarian optants, hopes for a negotiated settlement were eventually rewarded. On the other hand, in the UN period, failure to determine the limits of the UN organs' competence may have hindered, in some measure, the subsequent handling of such issues as Palestine, Indonesia, and the treatment of Indians in South Africa.[495]

But, had the Court in fact been consulted, would the resultant opinions necessarily have been beneficial? Or would they have been irrelevant or even harmful? To answer this question is to enter the realm of speculation, but in some instances, at least, the results of the hypothetical consultation are not difficult to imagine. The subsequent fate of such actual requests as those made in the *Peace Treaties* and *South West Africa (Status)* cases is rather significant in this regard. Quite probably, by their "deaths," many of the more important "stillborn" requests of the UN era were spared the kind of humiliating life which was the lot of some of the actual requests. Particularly where consent to the request on the part of all disputants was not forthcoming, where the root problems were particularly explosive and volatile, or where the political organ concerned had resolved to assume competence in any event, involvement of the Court would likely have been unrewarding, both from the standpoint of the requesting organ and from that of the Court. On the other hand, some of the avowedly "legal" questions of both periods—and, as noted, there

---

[493] The interpretation of Articles 11 and 12 of the ICJ Statute and the question of voting on non-self-governing territories were both sent to the Assembly's Sixth Committee.

In 1956–57, Secretary-General Hammarskjöld suggested the possibility of soliciting an ICJ advisory opinion on questions relating to the status of the Gulf of Aqaba and the right of innocent passage through the Straits of Tiran. In this instance, the 1958 Geneva Conference on the Law of the Sea was used as a law-clarifying alternative to the Court. Rosenne, "The International Court at Fifty," pp. 178–79.

[494] E.g., in the Cuban case.

[495] See the text discussion of these cases, as well as Leonard, *op. cit.*; Collins, *op. cit.*; and Taylor, *op. cit.*

were more of these in the League period—might, with benefit, have been determined by the Court.

In sum, the picture which emerges from a study of the many "stillborn" requests in the League and UN eras is one which corroborates and strengthens that already received from the study of actual requests. The peculiar character which a Court opinion came to assume in practice, in both periods; the more "legal" approach of the League, in contrast to the more "political" approach of its successor; and the greater reluctance of UN organs to cede any of their decision-making powers (even in regard to "legal" questions)—all are highlighted by nonuse of the advisory function, even more, perhaps, than by its use.

Beyond completing our understanding of *how* the advisory function was used and not used in the two eras, the composite picture of actual and "stillborn" requests also points up the two areas which, more than any others, hold the key to an understanding of *why* the advisory function was employed so differently in the two periods. The two questions which appear to require further investigation are: (1) Why were more issues deemed "political" in the UN period? and (2) Why, even in respect of "legal" questions, were UN organs reluctant to accept any restriction? The answers to these two questions must be sought, on the one hand, from the general framework of international relations, and, on the other, from the attitudes of states toward international law. These will be discussed further at the conclusion of this study. But first, for a better comprehension of the *totality* of the advisory process, it is necessary to devote some attention to the handling of the request by the Court, and to the treatment of the resultant opinion by the requesting organ.

V

THE COURT'S VIEW
OF ITS
ADVISORY FUNCTION

Quite obviously, what is involved in any consultation of the Court is a situation of interaction *par excellence*. Requests are addressed not to a dis-embodied dispenser of "authoritative legal pronouncements" but to an estab-lished institution operating within the framework of particular legal provi-sions[1] and of particular precedents based on an interpretation of those provisions. When a request is sent to the Court, it is accompanied by the expectation—largely based on the past practice of the Court—that the Court will dispose of its advisory function in a certain manner. On the other hand, the Court does not operate in a political vacuum. It responds to a specific request submitted to it under specific circumstances (of which the Court is aware even when, as in the early UN period, the question is framed and/or treated *in abstracto*). Thus, the use of the advisory function made by political organs is both reflected in, and influenced by, the Court's view of that func-tion.

The Court's view of its advisory function emerges perhaps most clearly from those cases in which some challenge was presented to the rendering of the opinion. The challenge may have raised the issue of judicial competence or judicial propriety or both; it may have been considered—alternatively or jointly—by individual states represented before the Court; by the Court itself (sometimes *proprio motu*); and by individual judges, in separate or dissenting opinions. Not unexpectedly (in view of the UN system of majority voting), almost all the challenges were made in the UN period,[2] and most of these emanated from the Soviet bloc.

---

[1] On the governing legal texts, see Chapter I.

[2] Objections to the rendering of an advisory opinion were raised in connection with seven of the thirteen requests (*Admission, Competence, Peace Treaties, Reservations, UNESCO, Expenses,* and *Namibia*). Only in the *UNESCO* case, however, did the ICJ take

277

Beyond this, the Court's view emerges, in a sense, from every advisory opinion rendered. The Court's interpretation of the question, and the manner in which it handles the request generally, determines, in no small measure, the kind of guidance offered to the political organ concerned.

Before discussing the specific grounds upon which refusal to render opinions was urged, it is necessary to consider the general question of the Court's right not to give an opinion requested of it, as well as the limits of the

---

a separate vote on the question whether to comply with the request. (The Court's vote [9 to 4] was recorded in the *dispositif* of the opinion.) In addition, in the *Namibia* case, the Court unanimously decided that "it was not proper . . . to entertain" certain South African objections (those relating to "political pressure to which the Court, according to . . . South Africa, had been or might be subjected"); and the President announced this decision at the opening of the oral hearings. *Namibia* case, ICJ Pleadings, 1971, Verbatim Record, C.R. 71/1, 8 February 1971, pp. 10–11; ICJ Reports, 1971, pp. 20 and 23.

In no case did the ICJ employ a preliminary objection procedure on the issue of compliance with the request, though this course was urged upon it by Czechoslovakia in the *Peace Treaties* case (*Peace Treaties* case, ICJ Pleadings, 1950, p. 204; cf. the criticism of Rosenne, *Law and Practice*, 2: 726–29) and by South Africa in the *Namibia* case (*Namibia* case, ICJ Pleadings, 1971, 2: 659–63). (It may be noted that, in the *Eastern Carelia* case, the Finnish representative was invited by the PCIJ to discuss the preliminary issue of the Court's competence to comply with the request. PCIJ, Ser. B, No. 5, p. 12.)

In contrast to preliminary objections, preliminary *questions* relating to the possibility of appointing judges *ad hoc* in advisory cases were given separate consideration by both Courts—by the PCIJ in the *Customs Union* and *Danzig Legislative Decrees* cases (see PCIJ, Ser. A/B, No. 41, pp. 88–91; Ser. C, No. 53, pp. 201–9; Ser A/B, No. 65, pp. 69–71; and Ser. C, No. 77, pp. 171–79), and by the ICJ in the *Namibia* case (see *Namibia* case, ICJ Pleadings, 1971, Verbatim Record, C.R. (H.C.) 71/1 (Rev.), 27 January 1971; ICJ Reports, 1971, pp. 19 and 24–27). However, the ICJ's treatment of the South African application for a judge *ad hoc* differed in two major ways from its predecessor's handling of similar applications. First, the hearing on the preliminary question was held *in camera*. (Only after the Court rejected the application was the record of the hearing made public. ICJ Reports, 1971, p. 19.) Second, the order refusing South Africa a judge *ad hoc* was not accompanied by a statement of reasons. (Only in the advisory opinion were those reasons revealed.) For the view that the Court's treatment of the judge *ad hoc* issue in the *Namibia* case was merely "*prima facie*" and not truly "preliminary," see the dissenting opinion of Judge Gros, *ibid.*, pp. 325–26. According to Judge Gros, the Court violated the provision in Article 82 of the Rules requiring it to determine "above all" (in French: "*avant tout*") whether "a legal question actually pending between two or more States" was involved in the case. Cf., however, the Court's defense of its action; its emphasis on the "relatively unschematic context of advisory proceedings"; and its denial that any "rigid sequence" was intended by the words "*avant tout.*" *Ibid.*, pp. 25–26. It should be noted that in the *Namibia* case (unlike the *Danzig Legislative Decrees* case) determination of the "contentious" or "noncontentious" nature of the request for the purposes of the judge *ad hoc* issue had implications for more substantive issues in the case as well (as, e.g., the competence of the Court and the formal validity of Security Council resolutions). See n. 14 below. Further questions relating to the composition of the Court in the *Namibia* case (involving South Africa's objections to the participation of three judges in the proceedings) were decided by the Court without hearing any oral argument. ICJ Reports, 1971, pp. 18–19.

Court's discretion in this respect. Each of the following grounds for non-compliance with a request will then be discussed: the incompetence of the requesting organ to address the request to the Court; the formal invalidity of the requesting resolution; the absence of consent on the part of a state immediately concerned; the "political" nature of the question posed; the incompetence of the Court to interpret Charter provisions; the exclusive right of the parties to a treaty to give or seek an authentic interpretation of that treaty; the availability of a contentious procedure for resolving the question embodied in the request; the "abstract" nature of the question; the involvement of too great a "factual" element in the case; the binding force attributed to the Court's opinion; and the absence of equality between the parties.

Finally, brief attention will be paid to the importance of judicial interpretation of the request and of the manner in which the Court handled particular requests.

Throughout, elements of continuity and contrast in the views of the two Courts will be highlighted.

COMPLIANCE WITH REQUESTS–THE COURT'S DISCRETION

Apart from specific provisions which implied that the Court possessed the discretionary right to refuse, in appropriate circumstances, to give an advisory opinion, this right was posited, from the very outset, on certain general considerations of principle–e.g., the Court's duty to safeguard its fundamental purpose of deciding disputes between states,[3] and the necessity of maintaining its independence of the League's political organs.[4]

The provisions which in the early League period were held to imply judicial discretion with respect to the rendering of advisory opinions were Article 14 of the League Covenant and Article 74 of the 1922 and 1926 Rules of Court.[5] No express provision on the matter was inserted in the original Rules,

---

[3] This was one of the considerations which led Judge Moore, in his 1922 memorandum to the Court, to argue against any unconditional obligation to render advisory opinions upon request. PCIJ, Ser. D, No. 2, p. 383.

[4] As Judge Anzilotti subsequently stated: "It is, indeed, difficult to see how the Court's independence . . . could be safeguarded, if it were in the power of the Assembly or the Council to oblige the Court to answer any question which they might see fit to submit to it." *Ibid.*, Ser. A/B, No. 65, p. 61. Cf. the national practice with respect to advisory opinions cited by Felix Frankfurter, "Advisory Opinions," *Encyclopedia of the Social Sciences*, 1: 477. Even where the duty of giving advisory opinions is well established, judges may normally pass on the reasonableness of the demand made upon them and refuse to give an opinion.

[5] See the discussion of Judge Moore's memorandum, p. 00 and n. 40 above; but cf. PCIJ, Ser. D, No. 2 (3rd Add.), p. 788. As noted in Chapter I, when Article 65 of the Rules was amended in 1931, the clause in Article 74 which implied the existence of judicial discretion not to render particular opinions was automatically deleted.

despite the suggestion that this be done.[6] Nevertheless, by its action in the *Eastern Carelia* case (the only case in which either Court refused to render an opinion), the PCIJ clearly demonstrated that it entertained no doubts as to its right to withhold opinions in appropriate circumstances. When, subsequently, Article 68 of the amended Statute was adopted, the Court's right and obligation to review its own competence in advisory, as well as in contentious, cases became even more firmly established.[7]

In the UN period, the permissive nature of the new Article 65(1) has been frequently cited in support of the proposition that the Court has "the power to examine whether the circumstances of the case are of such a character as should lead it to decline to answer the Request."[8]

The discretion which the Court is thus held to possess is theoretically distinct from, and supplementary to, the Court's power to determine its own jurisdiction. Even if the Court has jurisdiction, considerations of "propriety" may dictate that it refuse to give an opinion.[9] In practice, however, considerations of competence and propriety are often intermingled.

On what grounds can this discretion be invoked? Is the discretion unlimited?

The principal ground is the Court's felt need to protect its "judicial character."[10] There is clearly no consensus, however, as to which circumstances

---

[6] Under the proposed provision, the Court would have reserved "the right to refrain from replying to questions put to it which require an advisory opinion on a theoretical case." PCIJ, Ser. D, No. 2, p. 308.

[7] See the Report of the Registrar of the Court of June 1933, *ibid.* (3rd Add.), p. 837.

[8] ICJ Reports, 1950, p. 72. Cf. *ibid.*, 1951, p. 19; 1956, p. 86; 1962, p. 155; and 1971, p. 27. As noted above, the French text of the new Article 65(1) of the Statute (unlike the French text of Article 14 of the Covenant) is equally permissive (*"peut donner"*). See *ibid.*, 1948, pp. 94-95; and 1956, p. 112.

[9] See, e.g., the Court's statement in the *Expenses* case, *ibid.*, 1962, p. 155. Considerations of "propriety" were held applicable to contentious cases as well. See the pronouncement of the Court in the *Northern Cameroons* case, *ibid.*, 1963, pp. 29-31. See, especially, the separate opinion of Judge Fitzmaurice, *ibid.*, pp. 100 ff. For a discussion of the issue of propriety, see Rosenne, *Law and Practice*, 2: 708 ff.

In the statements of states before the Court, as in the invididual opinions of judges, it is not always clear whether the view that the Court should refrain from giving an opinion is based on grounds of incompetence or of impropriety. In the *UNESCO* case, however, three judges (Winiarski, Klaestad, and Zafrulla Khan) clearly invoked the issue of propriety. Judge Cordova alone considered the Court incompetent in that case. ICJ Reports, 1956, pp. 109-15; 155-68. The clearest differentiation between the two categories of objections was undoubtedly that presented by South Africa in the *Namibia* case. See *Namibia* case, ICJ Pleadings, 1971, 1: 398-424 (on the Court's competence) and 425-50 (on the Court's discretion). In its opinion, the Court maintained the differentiation. See ICJ Reports, 1971, pp. 21-23 (on competence) and pp. 23-27 (on propriety).

[10] Thus, in the *Eastern Carelia* case, the PCIJ stated that the Court could not "depart from the essential rules guiding their activity as a Court." PCIJ, Ser. B, No. 5, p. 29. In the *Northern Cameroons* case, the ICJ cited the Court's obligation to be the "guardian"

would justify a Court determination that its judicial character is, in fact, being exposed to threat.[11] Even such basic considerations as the inequality of the parties or the insufficiency of the facts remain, in the particular case, a matter for subjective appreciation. Thus, theoretically at least, the Court's discretion is almost unlimited.[12]

In practice, however, the ICJ has never once—despite repeated affirmations of its discretionary right to decline to give an opinion—exercised that right. Instead, it has developed a countervailing doctrine, in which the rendering of advisory opinions is proclaimed to be an obligation which should not, except for "compelling reasons," be refused. This obligation, in turn, is derived primarily from the Court's duty, as "an organ of the United Nations," to participate in the activities of the organization and its agencies.[13]

The Court's discretion in advisory matters is not limited to the question of *whether* to comply with a request. It also embraces questions of advisory procedure. As already noted (in Chapter I), a large measure of flexibility was always retained in respect of advisory procedure. Even Article 68 of the amended PCIJ Statute and Article 82 of the 1936 Rules—both of which were incorporated, in only slightly modified form, in the ICJ Statute and Rules—did not seriously restrict the Court's discretion in this regard. The Court remains free to determine just how much assimilation to contentious procedure is necessary or desirable in a particular case.[14]

---

of its "judicial integrity" and to "safeguard the judicial function." ICJ Reports, 1963, pp. 29, 38.

[11] See pp. 282–321 for the specific grounds which have been invoked in this connection—particularly, the discussion of "political" questions.

In the *Danzig and the ILO* case, Judge Anzilotti suggested that the Court should have refused to comply with a request "based on a hypothesis which is legally unsound." PCIJ, Ser. B, No. 18, pp. 18–20. Similarly, in the *Namibia* case, several judges considered that the Court would have violated its "judicial function" had it traced the "legal consequences" of resolutions whose legal validity was merely assumed, for the Court thereby would have "run the risk of rendering an opinion based on a false premise." Separate opinion of Judge Onyeama, ICJ Reports, 1971, pp. 143–44. See also the separate opinions of Judge Petrén, *ibid.*, p. 131; and Judge Dillard, *ibid.*, p. 151; as well as the dissenting opinions of Judge Fitzmaurice, *ibid.*, pp. 301–4; and Judge Gros, *ibid.*, p. 331. Had the Security Council unequivocally expressed an intention to fetter the Court in its examination of the legal premises, in the view of Judges Onyeama and Fitzmaurice, the Court would have been entitled to decline to render an opinion. *Ibid.*, pp. 144–45 and 303. See, further, the discussion of the scope of the question in the *Namibia* case, pp. 326–28 below.

[12] Refusal to consider the request or rejection of the request without supportive reasoning might, however, involve an "abuse of right."

[13] ICJ Reports, 1950, p. 71; 1951, p. 19; 1956, p. 86; 1962, p. 155; and 1971, p. 27.

[14] Cf., in this respect, the views of the Court in the *Peace Treaties* case against those of Judges Winiarski and Zoričić. The Court emphasized the "large amount of discretion"

OBJECTIONS TO THE RENDERING OF ADVISORY OPINIONS

Incompetence of the Requesting Organ

A finding that the requesting organ lacked the competence to address a particular request to the Court was deemed—by both Courts—to constitute a bar to the Court's complying with that request. This conclusion emerges from the PCIJ's pronouncement in the *Eastern Carelia* case—in which the Council's alleged lack of jurisdiction was the principal ground for denial of an opinion—and from the ICJ's reasoning in the *Peace Treaties* and *Reservations* cases—in which objections based on the General Assembly's incompetence were shown to be inapplicable rather than being dismissed out of hand.

---

it possessed in the matter of applying contentious procedure by analogy. ICJ Reports, 1950, p. 72. On the other hand, Judges Winiarski and Zoričić deemed the Court's discretion to be more restricted. If the Court considers that the matter is "actually pending between two or more States," it *must* apply the relevant provisions relating to contentious procedure. *Ibid.*, pp. 91, 100. (See Rosenne, *Law and Practice*, 2: 712–13, 727, to the effect that the Court failed to determine in this case whether, and to what extent, contentious procedure should be followed.)

In the *Namibia* case, the question of the limits of the Court's discretion arose in a different context. If the Court considers that Articles 82 and 83 of the Rules are inapplicable because no "legal question actually pending between two or more States" is involved, can the Court nevertheless apply contentious procedure, on the basis of a "residual discretion" embodied in Article 68 of the Statute? The Court's conclusion on this point (though somewhat ambiguous) appears to be negative. ICJ Reports, 1971, pp. 26–27. On the other hand, the two dissenting judges (Fitzmaurice and Gros), joined in this respect by three of the judges in the majority (Petrén, Onyeama, and Dillard), affirmed the existence of such a "residual discretion." *Ibid.*, pp. 128–29 (Petrén), 139–41 (Onyeama), 152–53 (Dillard), 309–13 (Fitzmaurice), and 330 (Gros). In the words of Judge Fitzmaurice: "The object of the Rule [Rule 83] was *not* to specify the only class of case in which the Court could so act [i.e., allow the appointment of a judge *ad hoc*], but to indicate the *one* class in which it *must* do so." *Ibid.*, p. 310; italics in the original. The issue of residual discretion was particularly important in the *Namibia* case because a finding of "legal pendency" (i.e., of the applicability of Articles 82 and 83 of the Rules) for the purposes of appointing a judge *ad hoc* might prejudice some of the substantive issues in the case (including the formal validity of several Security Council resolutions and the competence of the Court to render the opinion). Premising the appointment of a judge *ad hoc* on the "residual discretion" of Article 68 of the Statute, rather than on Articles 82 and 83 of the Rules, offered a way out of this dilemma. Of the five judges who favored South Africa's application for a judge *ad hoc*, only Judges Onyeama and Dillard based themselves exclusively on Article 68 of the Statute. Significantly, since their view did *not* prejudice the substantive questions in the case, they alone felt able to append to the Order of 29 January 1971 (denying South Africa's application) the reasons for their dissent. The other judges (as, indeed, the Court itself) did not disclose the reasons for their stands on the judge *ad hoc* question until the time of delivery of the opinion. See, on this point, the explanations of Judges Dillard and Gros, *ibid.*, pp. 152 and 325.

It would seem that the Court's interpretation of the discretion permitted it by Article 68 was too restricted and that failure to apply quasicontentious procedure in this case was misconceived. Cf. the views of Judge Fitzmaurice, *ibid.*, p. 313. In any event, having denied South Africa's application for a judge *ad hoc*, the Court appeared intent on avoiding any procedure that might imply recognition of South Africa as a "quasi liti-

The League Council's incompetence to recommend any solution in a case in which a nonconsenting nonmember of the League was involved constituted for the PCIJ the major obstacle to compliance with the request in the *Eastern Carelia* case.

> As Russia is not a Member of the League . . . the case is one under Article 17 of the Covenant. . . . This rule . . . only accepts and applies . . . a fundamental principle of international law, namely, the principle of the independence of States. . . . [N]o State can, without its consent, be compelled to submit its disputes with other States either to mediation or to arbitration, or to any other kind of pacific settlement. Such consent can be given once and for all in the form of an obligation freely undertaken, but it can, on the contrary, also be given in a special case apart from any existing obligation. The first alternative applies to the Members of the League who, having accepted the Covenant, are under the obligation resulting from the provisions of this pact dealing with the pacific settlement of international disputes. As concerns States not members of the League, the situation is quite different; they are not bound by the Covenant. The submission, therefore, of a dispute between them and a Member of the League for solution according to the methods provided for in the Covenant, could take place only by virtue of their consent. Such consent, however, has never been given by Russia. On the contrary, Russia has, on several occasions, clearly declared that it accepts no intervention by the League of Nations in the dispute with Finland. The refusals which Russia had already opposed to the steps suggested by the Council have been renewed upon the receipt by it of the notification of the request for an advisory opinion. The Court finds it impossible to give its opinion on a dispute of this kind.[15]

Other reasons for the refusal to render an opinion—especially the Court's inability to establish the facts in Russia's absence—were merely supportive, secondary reasons.[16]

---

gant" rather than as a mere *"informateur"* before the Court. (E.g., the alphabetical order of hearing states [other than Finland, the sponsor of the request in the Security Council] was maintained; and South Africa was not permitted to present its plebiscite proposal out of the regular order. *Namibia* case, ICJ Pleadings, 1971, Verbatim Record, C.R. 71/1, 8 February 1971, pp. 9–10.) Nevertheless, in the oral proceedings, the Secretary-General and South Africa clearly emerged as the main protagonists, with the former acting as quasi Applicant and the latter as quasi Respondent. And, as Judge Fitzmaurice later noted, "the Court found itself obliged in practice, and in a manner virtually unprecedented in previous advisory proceedings, to conduct the oral hearing as if a litigation were in progress." ICJ Reports, 1971, p. 313, n. 16.

[15] PCIJ, Ser. B, No. 5, pp. 27–28. Thus, the Court appears to have considered the application of Article 17 of the Covenant to be contrary to international law in certain instances. See, on this point, Verzijl, *World Court*, 1: 52; and Lauterpacht, *International Court*, p. 356, n. 50.

[16] Most discussions of the *Eastern Carelia* case, however, appear to have overlooked the major reason proffered by the Court. See p. 288, n. 36, and p. 289, n. 39, below.

In the *Peace Treaties* case, the ICJ's competence to deliver an opinion was challenged on the grounds, *inter alia*, that the Assembly, in addressing the request to the Court, had acted ultra vires, in contravention of Article 2(7) of the Charter.[17] To this objection the Court responded by noting that the purpose of the request was limited "to obtaining . . . certain clarifications of a legal nature regarding the applicability of the procedure for the settlement of disputes" contained in the Peace Treaties. "The interpretation of the terms of a treaty for this purpose could not be considered as a question essentially within the domestic jurisdiction of a State. It is a question of international law which, by its very nature, lies within the competence of the Court."[18] True, in adopting the requesting resolution, the Assembly was interested in the treaty procedures only as part of its treatment of the wider human rights issue, but, as to that, "for the purposes of the present Opinion,[19] it suffices to note that the General Assembly justified the adoption of its Resolution" by reference to Article 55 of the Charter.[20]

Again, in the *Reservations* case, the Court found it necessary to answer an objection to its competence which was based on the alleged incompetence of the General Assembly to request the opinion.[21]

In both cases, the clear implication was that, had the Assembly indeed acted ultra vires, the Court would have considered itself debarred from giving an opinion. Given, however, the ICJ doctrine regarding its duty to render opinions in the absence of "compelling" countervailing reasons and the very broad jurisdiction granted the General Assembly and the Security Council under the Charter, the Court might be expected to conclude, in most cases, that the request was, in fact, intra vires the political organs.[22]

[17]*Peace Treaties* case, ICJ Pleadings, 1950, pp. 196–204 and 210–12 *passim*. In addition, Article 2(7) was said to restrict the Court's power directly, the Court itself being a UN organ bound by Charter provisions.

[18]ICJ Reports, 1950, pp. 70–71. These considerations were also deemed sufficient to dispose of the objection that the Court, too, was bound by Article 2(7).

[19]No general interpretation of Article 2(7) and its bearing on human rights issues was attempted. Nor did the Court consider whether the exercise of the Court's advisory jurisdiction constituted "intervention" within the terms of Article 2(7) of the Charter. See Lauterpacht, *International Court*, p. 272; F. Blaine Sloan, "Advisory Jurisdiction of the International Court of Justice," *California Law Review*, 27 (1950): 844–45.

[20]ICJ Reports, 1950, p. 71. The Court thus demonstrated reluctance to delve too deeply into the requesting organ's competence to deal with the root issue. In this respect, the present Court may present a contrast with the former.

[21]In this case the Assembly's request was said to "constitute an inadmissible interference" in the interpretation of the Genocide Convention, since only states that are parties to the Convention "are entitled to interpret it or to seek an interpretation of it." The Court considered the Assembly's right to solicit the Court's advice unassailable. ICJ Reports, 1951, pp. 19–20. See the discussion of the Court's right to interpret treaties, pp. 305–7 below.

[22]The exception might be a case in which competence was explicitly reserved to another organ. See Rosenne, *Law and Practice*, 2: pp. 713–15. The question of compe-

Formal Invalidity of the Requesting Resolution

On only one occasion was a challenge to the Court's competence to render an opinion premised on the allegation that the requesting resolution was formally invalid. In the *Namibia* case, South Africa contended, first, that the requirements of Article 27(3) of the Charter were not complied with, since two permanent Council members (the United Kingdom and the Soviet Union) abstained in the vote on Security Council Resolution 284, whereas decisions on nonprocedural questions require the "*concurring* votes" of all the permanent Council members;[23] and, second, that, by failing to invite South Africa to participate in the discussions preceding adoption of Resolution 284, the Security Council violated the terms of Article 32 of the Charter.[24] In addition, South Africa raised the question whether the Security Council was properly constituted at all times, given the nonrepresentation of the People's Republic of China.[25]

Before addressing itself to the specific South African objections, the Court entered this prefatory remark:

---

tence is more likely to arise in the case of organs authorized under Article 96(2) of the Charter. *Ibid.*, p. 715.

Cf. the individual opinion of Judge Anzilotti in the case of *Danzig and the ILO*, PCIJ, Ser. B, No. 18, p. 20, in which the view is expressed that, since admission to the ILO was exclusively a consequence of admission to the League, and, since, moreover, the latter function was exclusively within the Assembly's competence, only the Assembly was entitled to request an opinion on the matter.

In the *Admission* case, Yugoslavia argued before the ICJ that the Assembly, in asking for an opinion regarding Security Council procedure, had overstepped the limits of its competence. *Admission* case, ICJ Pleadings, 1948, p. 90. However, this question was not discussed by the Court.

[23] *Namibia* case, ICJ Pleadings, 1971, 1: 398–99, and 403–21. South Africa attempted to prove the nonprocedural nature of the requesting resolution. *Ibid.*, pp. 418–21. The issue of the vote required for Security Council requests is not explicitly governed by any Charter text; and the Court did not find it necessary to pronounce itself on this question, since, in any case, it considered that the voluntary abstention of a permanent member did not prevent the adoption of nonprocedural resolutions. ICJ Reports, 1971, p. 22. However, cf. the questions of Judges Jiménez de Aréchaga and Morozov to the United States representative (*Namibia* case, ICJ Pleadings, 1971, Verbatim Record, C.R. 71/19, 9 March 1971, p. 27; and C.R. 71/20, 10 March 1971, pp. 6–7), which were designed to elicit clarification on the applicability of the veto to requests for advisory opinions.

[24] *Namibia* case, ICJ Pleadings, 1971, 1: 421–24. Under the terms of Article 32, "any Member of the United Nations which is not a member of the Security Council . . . if it is a party to a dispute under consideration by the Security Council, shall be invited to participate, without vote, in the discussion relating to the dispute." The "Article 32 issue" was used by South Africa to contest the validity of Resolution 284, as well as of some of the substantive Council resolutions involved in the case.

[25] *Ibid.*, pp. 400–403. South Africa was more circumspect in presenting this argument—and understandably so, given South Africa's own recognition of the Nationalist Chinese regime.

A further ground for challenging the Court's competence in the *Namibia* case was the alleged need for too extensive a factual enquiry in the case. See pp. 313–16 below.

A resolution of a properly constituted organ of the United Nations which is passed in accordance with that organ's rules of procedure, and is declared by its President to have been so passed, must be presumed to have been validly adopted. However, since in this instance the objections made concern the competence of the Court, the Court will proceed to examine them.[26]

The Court then set about rebutting the first two South African arguments, as well as the additional argument (not presented by South Africa with respect to the requesting resolution) that the provision for mandatory abstention of Council members who are parties to a dispute should have applied.[27] (The Chinese representation issue was ignored by the Court.)[28] In brief, the Court upheld as valid the practice of adopting Security Council resolutions despite the abstention of one or more permanent members;[29] and considered Article 32 and the mandatory abstention provided for in Article 27(3) inapplicable, since the Namibia question was placed on the Security Council agenda as a "situation," rather than as a "dispute," and no state (including South Africa) protested that appellation.[30]

From the Court's handling of South Africa's objections it may be deduced that, while the requesting resolution will normally be presumed to be formally valid,[31] the presumption of validity remains for the Court a rebuttable presumption. This is so because objections directed against the validity of the request cast doubt upon the Court's competence to render an opinion. And, as a coordinate and judicial organ, the Court obviously considers itself free to establish independently the bases of its competence.

---

[26] ICJ Reports, 1971, p. 22.

[27] The Court appears to have assumed, erroneously, that the "mandatory abstention" argument was raised by South Africa with respect to Resolution 284. *Ibid.* In fact, however, the argument related solely to other Security Council resolutions (including, especially, Resolution 276, mentioned in the request). On the other hand, the issue of voluntary abstention by permanent Council members related to these substantive resolutions as well as to the requesting resolution. See *Namibia* case, ICJ Pleadings, 1971, 1: 424

[28] The issue was considered by Judge Padilla Nervo in his separate opinion. ICJ Reports, 1971, p. 117.

[29] *Ibid.*, p. 22. In this manner the Court pronounced itself on an issue which it was twice proposed should be sent to the Court for an advisory opinion. See pp. 223 and 256 above.

[30] ICJ Reports, 1971, pp. 22–23. The Court also seemed to base itself on the notion of estoppel. "Having failed to raise the question at the appropriate time in the proper forum, it is not open to it [South Africa] to raise it before the Court at this stage." *Ibid.*, p. 23.

[31] Although the Court referred only to UN organs, its reasoning would apply as well to agencies authorized under Article 96(2) to request advisory opinions.

Absence of Consent

In the issue of consent, the ever-present tension between the "lawyer-client" and the "quasicontentious" concepts of the advisory function[32] comes most to the fore. Indeed, it is mainly in terms of this tension that the Court's pronouncements on the matter become more comprehensible.

The Court's jurisdiction in contentious cases is based on the consent of states. But what of advisory cases relating to disputes between states? Should absence of consent on the part of one or more disputant states prevent the Court from rendering to its "client," the requesting organ, the elucidation it desires? This question confronted the PCIJ in the *Eastern Carelia* and *Mosul* cases, and the ICJ in the *Peace Treaties, Reservations,* and *Namibia* cases, respectively.[33]

Much of the subsequent discussion of the Court's reply in the *Eastern Carelia* case has been based on a misconstruction of its true import. The Court's pronouncement has frequently been cited in support of the general proposition that the consent of disputant states—at least where the request touches on the merits of an existing dispute—is a prerequisite for the Court's rendering an advisory opinion. However, upon closer inspection of the Court's statements in the *Eastern Carelia* case itself, and upon comparing those statements with the Court's action in the *Mosul* case, the "*Eastern Carelia* principle" is seen to stand for a much narrower proposition.

As already noted, the Court's refusal to give an opinion in connection with the Finno-Soviet dispute was grounded in the alleged incompetence of the Council to deal with the dispute without Russia's prior consent. That the Court had no intention of broaching the general problem of consent was stated unequivocally in the following passage.

> There has been some discussion as to whether questions for an advisory opinion, if they relate to matters which form the subject of a pending dispute between nations, should be put to the Court without the consent of the parties. *It is unnecessary in the present case to deal with this topic.*[34]

If consent was crucial in this case, it was because the *particular circumstances* of the *Eastern Carelia* case made it difficult for the Court to view the

---

[32] See Chapter I.

[33] In the *Reservations* case, neither the Court nor most of the states represented before it viewed the request as one relating to an existing dispute. The Philippines, however, considered itself a party to a dispute before the Court. Similarly, in the *Namibia* case, the Court denied South Africa's contention that the request related to an interstate dispute. (But the contention was accepted by several judges. See n. 58 below.)

[34] PCIJ, Ser. B, No. 5, p. 27; italics added.

question before it as a "lawyer-client" affair. Given Soviet objections to the Court's rendering of an opinion, the Court could proceed only if it found that its "client"–the League Council–possessed some independent grounds which entitled it to a reply in this case. But the Court was hard-pressed to find such grounds. To the contrary, the Council's interest in the case had been neither sanctioned nor tolerated by the Soviet Union at any point. As a nonmember of the League, Russia could not be said to have accepted, in advance, the Council's interest in the pacific settlement of disputes to which it was a party. Nor was any recognition of the Council's right to intervene extended *ad hoc* (as per Article 17 of the Covenant). Nor again–and this is significant, though not mentioned explicitly by the Court–was the Council given any role to perform in connection with the Treaty of Dorpat, the text around which the Finno-Soviet dispute revolved. In these circumstances, the request could be represented as little else than an attempt to get the dispute between Finland and Russia adjudicated without the latter's consent. In a word, it could be viewed solely as a "quasicontentious" case, and not at all as a "client-lawyer" consultation.

Apart from this principal ground for denying the Council the guidance it sought, "other cogent reasons" also were cited–namely, the difficulty of elucidating the facts without Russian testimony.[35] In other words, even if the Court agreed to grant its "client" the desired advice, that advice would not, in view of Russian noncooperation, be well-grounded.

Under these conditions, the Court felt compelled to refrain from pronouncing on the dispute, even in an advisory opinion. It summarized its views in the following, oft-quoted passage.

The question put to the Court is not one of abstract law, but concerns directly the main point of the controversy between Finland and Russia,[36]

---

[35] As noted above (Chapter III), the key issue was whether the Declaration annexed to the Treaty of Dorpat was intended to be a contractual arrangement giving rise to executory obligations or a statement of existing fact given for purposes of information only. Since this key issue involved the question of the intention of the parties, Russian testimony was deemed crucial. PCIJ, Ser. B, No. 5, pp. 25–29.

The Court also raised the general question as to whether the Court might, in advisory proceedings, ascertain questions of fact. See the discussion on factual questions, pp. 312–16 below.

[36] The clear implication of this passage is that a question framed in a more "abstract" form, and not related so specifically to the Finno-Soviet dispute, might have been accorded different treatment. Thus, many of the subsequent arguments in the *Peace Treaties* case–including those of the Court itself–which sought to distinguish that case from the *Eastern Carelia* case on the basis of the "preliminary" nature of the questions in the *Peace Treaties* case (see, e.g., the statement of Mr. Fitzmaurice, *Peace Treaties* case, ICJ Pleadings, 1950, p. 307; and ICJ Reports, 1950, p. 72) were misconceived. The crucial distinction for the PCIJ in the *Eastern Carelia* case was not a "preliminary-merits," but a "concrete-abstract," one. In fact, the question in the *Eastern Carelia* case

and can only be decided by an investigation into the facts underlying the case. Answering the question would be substantially equivalent to deciding the dispute between the parties. The Court, being a Court of Justice, cannot, even in giving advisory opinions, depart from the essential rules guiding their activity as a Court.[37]

Despite the sweeping language of this summarizing statement and subsequent attempts to construe the "Eastern Carelia principle" as embracing the question of consent in general,[38] the Court's reasoning clearly points to the conclusion that the principle was confined to nonmembers of the League, who, moreover, had never accepted the Council's competence for the purposes of a particular dispute.[39] This conclusion is borne out by the Court's apparently contrasting action in the *Mosul* case.

The latter case shared certain surface similarities with the earlier, *Eastern Carelia*, case—namely, nonmembership in the League of one of the disputants involved and that disputant's failure to agree to, or be represented in, the proceedings before the Court.[40] In this instance, however, the Council was in

---

also was "preliminary." The issue before the Court was whether international obligations *existed*, not whether the Soviet Union had *violated* those obligations. Indeed, Finland specifically urged that the Court view the question "as a preliminary question relating to the nature of the dispute by analogy to Article 15, par. 8 of the Covenant." PCIJ, Ser. B, No. 5, pp. 26–27. But, for the Court, the question of the existence of executory obligations on the part of the Soviet Union constituted a new dispute, and to adjudicate upon it was to adjudicate "the main point" of this *new* controversy. This point was better understood by some of the individual judges in the *Peace Treaties* case. See n. 48 below.

[37] PCIJ, Ser. B, No. 5, pp. 28–29.

[38] See, e.g., the letter from Secretary Stimson to the Chairman of the U.S. Senate Foreign Relations Committee, *ibid.*, Ser. E, No. 8, pp. 124–28. The dissenting judges in the *Peace Treaties* case and Judge Azevedo (who on the question of the Court's compliance with the request was also in dissent) understood the principle similarly. ICJ Reports, 1950, pp. 79 ff., 89 ff., 98 ff., 105 ff.; cf. the Written Statement of the Philippines in the *Reservations* case, ICJ Pleadings, 1951, pp. 295–96.

[39] This was the way the principle was understood by several delegates at the 1926 Conference of Signatories. See, e.g., Minutes of the 1926 Conf. of Signatories, pp. 37, 43–44. The Committee of the Court, which studied the question of advisory opinions prior to the 1936 revision of the Rules, was most explicit on this point. PCIJ, Ser. D, No. 2 (3rd Add.), pp. 796–97. See, especially, the draft Rules, which incorporated the Court's jurisprudence in the *Eastern Carelia* and *Mosul* cases. See also LN, Records of the 9th Ass., 1928, 1st Ctte., pp. 51–52; and Records of the 16th Ass., 1935, 1st Ctte., p. 45. It was also argued that member states, having accepted Article 14 of the Covenant, were bound to acquiesce in the Council's right to receive judicial advice. A similar view has been expressed with regard to the effect of accepting Article 96 of the Charter. See p. 294 and n. 56 below.

[40] Turkey's attitude toward the Court's proceedings was, however, by no means as hostile as that of Russia in the earlier case. Turkey deemed the questions before the Court to be "of a distinctly political character," such as could not "form the subject of a legal interpretation," but it stopped short of challenging outright the Court's competence to give an opinion. Furthermore, its nonrepresentation before the Court was based

a strong position to argue in support of an independent right to obtain its "lawyer's" advice. For, not only had Turkey, by treaty, expressly granted the Council a role in its dispute with Great Britain;[41] it had all along participated in Council proceedings and at one stage had even explicitly consented to accept the Council's decision in advance. The Council's request for judicial advice came at a very late stage in the proceedings; and it involved not the question of *whether* the Council had competence to take a decision—this was generally conceded—but rather the question what character the decision should have and by what vote it should be taken. In these circumstances, the Court apparently felt that its "client's" claim to the judicial clarification it sought was unassailable; and that, in the face of this claim, the "quasicontentious" aspects assumed only minor significance.[42]

The *Peace Treaties* case before the ICJ fell somewhere between the *Eastern Carelia* and *Mosul* cases, but was probably closer in character to the former. Again, states that were not members of the world organization were the "quasi defendants." Again they challenged the Court's jurisdiction to give the opinion requested. And, as in the *Eastern Carelia* case (and unlike the *Mosul* case), objections had been raised earlier to the requesting organ's competence to deal with the root issue (in this case, the observance of human rights in the three satellite states). Nonetheless, the General Assembly was not totally without an independent need for "enlightenment" in this case. In particular, the UN Secretary-General's role in appointing the third members of the envisaged treaty commissions gave the organization a very direct interest in knowing how properly to proceed. However, it was not this very direct interest which determined the Court to render an opinion in the *Peace Treaties* case.[43] It was, rather, the Assembly's general need to ascertain what its future course of action in the question should be. The reasoning of the Court,

---

not on general hostility toward the Court—in fact, it professed to having the "greatest esteem and respect" for the Court—but rather on the sufficiency of the Turkish explanations before the Council. PCIJ, Ser. B, No. 12, pp. 8–9. Moreover, Turkey cooperated with the Court by furnishing documents related to the question and by replying to certain questions presented to it.

[41] The relevant provision was Article 3(2) of the Treaty of Lausanne. See the discussion of the *Mosul* case in Chapter III, pp. 75–78.

[42] Turkey's position in the case did not even receive judicial mention. As for the secondary consideration cited for denying an opinion in *Eastern Carelia* (namely, the difficulty of determining the facts in the absence of one of the disputants), this may have appeared less crucial in this case since, as noted, Turkey did supply information and reply to certain questions.

[43] The Secretary-General's role was not even mentioned by the Court in the first phase, though it had been alluded to in the preamble of the resolution requesting the Court's opinion, and though the United States and the United Kingdom made reference to that role in their oral statements. *Peace Treaties* case, ICJ Pleadings, 1950, pp. 281, 311.

following mainly the line of argument urged upon it by the United States and the United Kingdom, ran as follows.

The Court's opinion is merely "advisory" and is given to the organization for *its* enlightenment (i.e., it is a "lawyer-client" affair). Hence, no state, member or nonmember of the UN, can prevent the giving of such an opinion. Moreover, "the reply of the Court, itself an 'organ of the United Nations', represents its participation in the activities of the Organization, and, in principle, should not be refused." Nevertheless, since the Court is also the "principal *judicial* organ," it must examine whether its judicial character bars it from giving the opinion in this case. For this purpose the case must be distinguished from the *Eastern Carelia* case, which it appears to resemble.

In the opinion of the Court, the circumstances of the present case are profoundly different from those which were before the Permanent Court of International Justice in the Eastern Carelia case ... when that Court declined to give an Opinion because it found that the question put to it was directly related to the main point of a dispute actually pending between two States, so that answering the question would be substantially equivalent to deciding the dispute between the parties, and that at the same time it raised a question of fact which could not be elucidated without hearing both parties.

... [T]he present Request ... is solely concerned with the applicability to certain disputes of the procedure for settlement instituted by the Peace Treaties, and it is justifiable to conclude that it in no way touches the merits of those disputes. Furthermore, the settlement of these disputes is entrusted solely to the Commissions provided for by the Peace Treaties. Consequently, it is for these Commissions to decide upon any objections which may be raised to their jurisdiction in respect of any of these disputes, and the present Opinion in no way prejudges the decisions that may be taken on those objections. It follows that the legal position of the parties to these disputes cannot be in any way compromised by the answers that the Court may give to the Questions put to it.[44]

---

[44] ICJ Reports, 1950, pp. 71–72. The Court did not specifically state that no inquiry into the facts was required in this case, though this argument was presented by the United States and the United Kingdom (*Peace Treaties* case, ICJ Pleadings, 1950, p. 281–82, 309–10) and may have been implied by the Court. Cf., on this point, the dissenting opinion of Judge Winiarski, ICJ Reports, 1950, p. 95.

More significantly, by confining itself to demonstrating the inapplicability of the *Eastern Carelia* case to the facts of the *Peace Treaties* case, the Court may have deliberately avoided another line of argument presented by the two Western states and directed toward excluding the *Eastern Carelia* case altogether as a governing precedent for the ICJ. In particular, these states had cited the new organic relationship between the Court and the UN; the more expanded role of the UN vis-à-vis nonmember states (as evidenced by such Charter provisions as Articles 2[6], 10, 11, 14, 32, 35, and 55, and as pointed

In conclusion, the Court again emphasized the "lawyer-client" nature of the request.

In the present case the Court is dealing with a Request for an Opinion, the sole object of which is to enlighten the General Assembly as to the opportunities which the procedure contained in the Peace Treaties may afford for putting an end to a situation which has been presented to it.[45] That being the object of the Request, the Court finds in the opposition to it made by Bulgaria, Hungary and Romania no reason why it should abstain from replying to the Request.[46]

In opposition to the Court's view on the matter of consent, individual judges emphasized the "nonadvisory" character which advisory opinions had come to assume in practice;[47] the substantive, "nonpreliminary" nature of the dispute at issue;[48] and the "quasicontentious," as against the "lawyer-client," aspect of the opinion.[49]

---

up by the Court's pronouncement in the *Reparation* case); specific mention, in Article 36 of the ICJ Statute, of the UN Charter as an independent source of jurisdiction for the Court; and the broad language of Article 96 of the Charter and of the new Article 65(1) of the Court's Statute. *Peace Treaties* case, ICJ Pleadings, 1950, pp. 274–76, 305–6, 312. Some of these arguments were, to an extent, implicit in the Court's statements.

The dissenting opinions emphasized the continuity between the advisory function of the two Courts. ICJ Reports, 1950, pp. 91, 100, 109–10.

[45] Thus, the Court implicitly recognized that the Assembly was competent to deal with human rights issues, even in respect of nonmember states of the UN. Cf. p. 284 above.

[46] ICJ Reports, 1950, p. 72.

[47] In the words of Judge Winiarski, "States see their rights, their political interests and sometimes their moral position affected by an opinion of the Court, and their disputes are in fact settled by the answer which is given to a question relating to them." *Ibid.*, p. 92. According to Judge Zoričić, "in practice, an advisory opinion . . . in regard to a dispute between States is nothing else than an unenforceable judgment." *Ibid.*, p. 101; see also pp. 80–81, 91–92, 101–2. Judge Azevedo deemed particularly objectionable the attempt (by means of automatic institution of the second phase, in the event the three states remained recalcitrant) "to attribute material effects" to the Court's opinion. In his view, the opinion was thereby endowed with "an enforceability *sui generis* somewhat in the nature of an interdict or a writ." *Ibid.*, pp. 86–87.

[48] The earlier dispute regarding human rights was said to have given way to a later dispute regarding applicability of the Peace Treaties' dispute-settlement procedures. *Ibid.*, pp. 93–94 (Judge Winiarski), and, esp., pp. 99–100 (Judge Zoričić). Judge Azevedo conceded that the present question was "preliminary" in relation to the main dispute; nevertheless, it constituted a "pivotal point" in the case–even as did the "preliminary" question in the *Eastern Carelia* case. *Ibid.*, pp. 87–88.

[49] The following excerpts are instructive. "I cannot agree that the advisory functions of the Court are exercised between the Court on the one hand and the Assembly, the Security Council and other authorized organs on the other. . . . [T]he Opinion is given to the organ from which the Request emanated, but is addressed to the parties, to the Organization, and to public opinion" (Judge Winiarski, *ibid.*, p. 97). "[A] request for an opinion cannot be regarded as giving rise solely to a relation between the Court and the

Whereas the applicability of the "Eastern Carelia principle" to the *Peace Treaties* case was a matter for serious debate, the same could not be said in respect of the Philippines' invocation of that principle in the *Reservations* case.[50] Clearly, the interest of the "client"—the General Assembly—was incontrovertible and paramount here. As the Court stated:

> The object of this request for an Opinion is to guide the United Nations in respect of its own action. It is indeed beyond dispute that the General Assembly, which drafted and adopted the Genocide Convention, and the Secretary-General, who is the depositary of the instruments of ratification and accession, have an interest in knowing the legal effects of reservations to that Convention and more particularly the legal effects of objections to such reservations.[51]

Moreover, it should be noted that the contention that the request related to an existing dispute was not generally acknowledged. Rather, the Court and most of the states represented before it emphasized the "abstract" nature of the question.[52] Beyond this—even admitting some relationship between the request and an existing dispute—since the parties to the "dispute" were all UN members, the "Eastern Carelia principle" was, again, inapplicable. It is significant that there was no dissent regarding the Court's competence to give an opinion in this case.[53]

The "Eastern Carelia principle" was invoked once more in the *Namibia* case, and once more it was deemed inapplicable by the Court. South Africa argued that, since the questions before the Court bore directly on an interstate dispute, the Court should, as a matter of its discretion, refuse to entertain the request. South Africa's participation in the proceedings, it was em-

---

international organ which asks for the Opinion, but . . . on the contrary, in addition to that relation, other relations may be established first, between the Court and the parties, and, again, between the parties themselves" (Judge Zoričić, *ibid.*, p. 101).

[50] The Philippines contended that answering the questions raised "would be substantially equivalent to deciding the dispute" pending between itself and Australia. (Australia had objected to a Philippine reservation to the Genocide Convention, and had declined to view the Philippine ratification as valid.) The "dispute," the Philippines argued, could come before the Court only by means of a joint submission under the Convention's compromissory clause. *Reservations* case, ICJ Pleadings, 1951, pp. 295–97; cf. the Rumanian objection, *ibid.*, p. 291.

[51] ICJ Reports, 1951, p. 19.

[52] *Ibid.*, p. 21. See also, e.g., the Written Statement of Israel, *Reservations* case, ICJ Pleadings, 1951, pp. 198–99.

[53] Other objections to the Court's rendering an opinion were also raised. See pp. 305–7 below.

phasized, was not to be construed as consent to the Court's acceding to the request.[54]

In denying the relevance of the *Eastern Carelia* precedent, the Court argued as follows:[55] First, at the time of the *Eastern Carelia* case, the Soviet Union was not a member of the League; in contrast, South Africa is a UN member and "is bound by Article 96 of the Charter, which empowers the Security Council to request advisory opinions on any legal question."[56] Second, the Soviet Union did not appear before the PCIJ, whereas South Africa participated in the *Namibia* proceedings, "and, while raising specific objections against the competence of the Court, . . . addressed itself to the merits of the questions."[57] Third, the Court denied the "quasicontentious" character of the *Namibia* case and emphasized the "client-lawyer" aspect.

> It is not the purpose of the request to obtain the assistance of the Court in the exercise of the Security Council's functions relating to the peaceful settlement of a dispute pending before it between two or more States. The request is put forward by a United Nations organ with reference to its own decisions and it seeks legal advice from the Court on the consequences and implications of these decisions. This objective is stressed by the preamble to the resolution requesting the opinion, in which the Security Council has

[54]*Namibia* case, ICJ Pleadings, 1971, 1: 442–47; Verbatim Record, C.R. 71/7, 19 February 1971, pp. 37–42.
It might be noted that, in the *South West Africa (Voting)* and *South West Africa (Committee)* cases, South Africa's position was the reverse of the one it adopted in the *Namibia* case. It was not represented before the Court, but it did not object to the Assembly's seeking judicial advice or to the Court's extending that advice. For its part, the Court made no mention of South African nonparticipation. The issues were obviously considered organizational ones, and, moreover, South African testimony was deemed dispensable.

[55]Again, as in the *Peace Treaties* case, the Court set about *distinguishing* the case before it from the *Eastern Carelia* case, and once more did not explicitly "buy" the argument that the new "organic link" between the Court and the United Nations made the "Eastern Carelia principle" obsolete. For the presentation of the "organic link" argument in the *Namibia* proceedings, see, e.g., the statement of the representative of the Secretary-General, *Namibia* case, ICJ Pleadings, 1971, Verbatim Record, C.R. 71/1, 8 February 1971, p. 24. The argument was endorsed by Judge de Castro, ICJ Reports, 1971, p. 172. For the presentation of the argument in the *Peace Treaties* case, see p. 291, n. 44, above.

[56]ICJ Reports, 1971, p. 23. See, to the same effect, the Oral Statement of the United States, *Namibia* case, ICJ Pleadings, 1971, Verbatim Record, C.R. 71/19, 9 March 1971, p. 13; and cf. the Oral Statement of Finland, *ibid.*, C.R. 71/2, 9 February 1971, p. 15. The Court's views regarding the effect of accepting Article 96 of the Charter coincide with those expressed earlier by many writers. See, e.g., Lauterpacht, *International Court*, pp. 357–58; and Sloan, *op. cit.*, pp. 847 and 859.

[57]ICJ Reports, 1971, pp. 23–24; see also the separate opinion of Judge Dillard, *ibid.*, p. 156. Does the Court's reasoning suggest that South Africa, from its standpoint, would have been better advised to confine itself to a statement of objections to the Court's competence (as did Bulgaria, Hungary, and Rumania in the *Peace Treaties* case)?

stated "that an advisory opinion from the International Court of Justice would be useful for the Security Council in its further consideration of the question of Namibia and in furtherance of the objectives the Council is seeking."[58]

The Court concluded that no "compelling reasons" prevented it from acceding to the request in the *Namibia* case. "Moreover," the Court said, "by replying to the request it [the Court] would not only 'remain faithful to the requirements of its judicial character' ..., but also discharge its functions as 'the principal judicial organ of the United Nations.' "[59]

Neither for the PCIJ nor for the ICJ did absence of consent on the part of a disputant state and/or failure to appear before the Court constitute an absolute bar to the rendering of an advisory opinion. The important question for both was: Did the requesting organ—the "client"—possess an independent claim which entitled it to obtain its "lawyer's" advice? Where the dispute involved member states of the organization or states which had recognized the organization's right to deal with the dispute on an *ad hoc* basis, such an independent claim on the part of the organization was held to have been consented to in advance. The problem arises, then, primarily with respect to disputes involving nonmember states. Because of its organic relationship to the UN and its theory regarding its duty to participate in the activities of the organization, the ICJ will probably continue its tendency to view requests as

[58]*Ibid.*, p. 24. "The object of this request," the Court said, quoting from the *Reservations* case, "is to guide the United Nations in respect of its own action." *Ibid.* The Court insisted that the request involved neither an interstate dispute nor even a UN versus South Africa dispute. The existence of "radically divergent views" between South Africa and the UN on the legal issues before the Court "does not convert the present case into a dispute." The case was no different from the three previous advisory cases on South West Africa. *Ibid.* See also the separate opinion of Judge de Castro, *ibid.*, p. 177. For criticism of the Court's finding as representing "a purely formal view of the facts of the case which does not, ... correspond to realities," see the dissenting opinion of Judge Gros, *ibid.*, p. 326. See also the separate opinion of Judge Petrén, *ibid.*, pp. 128–30; and the dissenting opinion of Judge Fitzmaurice, *ibid.*, pp. 313–16. Judge Dillard recognized the existence of a dispute between the UN and South Africa. *Ibid.*, p. 155.

The "noncontentious" nature of the request was cited by the Court for its preliminary (unexplained at the time) decision to deny South Africa a judge *ad hoc*. For the Court's attempt to answer the charge that, by its rejection of the South African application, it prematurely prejudged the substantive issue of the existence of a dispute, see *ibid.*, pp. 24–27. But cf. the views of Judge Fitzmaurice, *ibid.*, p. 316; and Judge Gros, *ibid.*, pp. 325–30.

It is perhaps worthy of note that, in contrast to the *Peace Treaties* case, the Court, in discounting the relevance of *Eastern Carelia*, did not emphasize the *advisory* nature of the opinion. But cf. the separate opinion of Judge de Castro, *ibid.*, p. 172.

[59]*Ibid.*, p. 27.

"client-lawyer" matters and to overlook the request's "quasicontentious" aspects, even when nonmember states are the disputants. The burden of proof will fall on those who try to prove that insufficient client interest exists. Nevertheless, it is probably not entirely correct to conclude, as many writers have, that the *Eastern Carelia* case "can no longer be regarded as a precedent of authority."[60] Certainly, as a precedent, its sphere of application has been greatly diminished, but it has not yet been totally eliminated.[61]

"Political" Questions

The ICJ's jurisdiction is explicitly limited—as the PCIJ's jurisdiction was not—to the rendering of opinions on "legal" questions. Yet, it was never assumed that the PCIJ might concern itself with "political" or "nonlegal" questions. Admittedly, introduction of the term "legal" owed much to the dissatisfaction to which the request and opinion in the *Customs Union* case subsequently gave rise.[62] But, clearly, the difficulty in that case was not the absence of the term "legal." It was, rather, the basis for differentiating the "legal" from the "political";[63] and this latter difficulty has not, by any means, been eliminated by the new terminology. If anything, the term "legal" has merely provided a convenient peg on which to hang various objections to the Court's exercise of its advisory jurisdiction. At the same time, the true grounds for opposition have frequently remained somewhat obscure.

To understand how the Court has dealt with challenges to the "legal" nature of the questions before it, it is necessary to go beyond the mere

[60] Lauterpacht, *International Court*, p. 249; and Sloan, *op. cit.*, pp. 847, 859. Cf. Edvard Hambro, "The Authority of the Advisory Opinions of the International Court of Justice," *ICLQ*, 3 (1954): 13.

[61] It remains applicable to a case which involves a nonconsenting nonmember state and which the Court is willing to view as "quasicontentious." For an interesting view on the authority of *Eastern Carelia*, see Leo Gross, "The International Court of Justice and the United Nations," *RC*, 121 (1967-II): 369-70. And see *ibid.*, pp. 359-70, for a penetrating comparison between the *Eastern Carelia* and *Peace Treaties* cases.

[62] See, e.g., the statement of Mr. (now Judge) Fitzmaurice at the 1945 Washington Committee of Jurists, *UNCIO Documents*, 14: 204-5.

[63] Attempts to "define" the terms "legal" and "political" inevitably wind up in nothing more than tautological and circuitous utterances. The following example—which could be multiplied indefinitely—will suffice. " '*Political*' as opposed to 'legal' as used in Articles 36 and 65 of the Court's Statute, can only refer to situations where some sort of political judgment is involved which is not capable of legal determination." D. W. Greig, "The Advisory Jurisdiction of the International Court and the Settlement of Disputes between States," *ICLQ*, 15 (1966): 331, n. 17. Introduction of the synonymous terms "justiciable" and "nonjusticiable" is scarcely more illuminating.

For a good attempt to winnow out the diverse ways in which the term "political," or "nonjusticiable," has been used in practice, see Rosalyn Higgins, "Policy Considerations and the International Judicial Process," *ibid.*, 17(1968): 58-84. Cf. Ian Brownlie, "The Justiciability of Disputes and Issues in International Relations," *BYIL*, 42 (1967): 123-43, where the question is dealt with from the standpoints of both municipal and international law.

assertion that a particular question was or was not "legal" and to discover the more specific grounds which were deemed to make judicial consideration inappropriate.

Arguments regarding the "nonlegal" nature of the issue before the Court have not generally been based on the *non liquet* ground, as such; the Court has not had occasion, in its advisory opinions, to pronounce itself on this question.

However, even granting that there *is* an applicable legal norm, will that norm provide a definitive solution to the basic problem? It may be perfectly clear that an important state in whose power it lies to deny effect to the Court's pronouncement will be unwilling to accept an adverse "legal" verdict. That state may consider that its vital interests are at stake and that the law must be amended, if necessary, to secure those interests. The requesting organ itself may be similarly unwilling to bow to an opinion which does not endorse its own views. In such cases, should the Court deem the question "political" and decline to give an opinion? Should it concern itself with the effect which possible or probable nonacceptance of its opinion will have on its prestige? Neither Court has ever formally taken such considerations into account, though there have been suggestions that each do so;[64] and, in the *Eastern Carelia* case, these considerations may not have been far from the minds of the judges.

In a similar vein, it has been argued that the Court should steer clear of any really "hot" or "emotional" issues which might tend to drag it into the "political" arena. Likewise, the "political" motivation of the request—the desire to employ a Court opinion as a weapon in a "political" disagreement with other states—has been urged upon the Court as grounds for denying an opinion.[65]

A particularly interesting variation on these arguments was presented by South Africa in the *Namibia* case. The gist of South Africa's contentions was that the question posed by the Security Council had "a political background

---

[64] Thus, Judge Yovanovitch would have left the PCIJ the option of refusing to render an opinion which was not likely to be followed in practice. PCIJ, Ser. D, No. 2 (Add.), p. 291. On similar grounds, some critics of the Court's pronouncement in the *Customs Union* case would have preferred to see the Court withhold that opinion. See, e.g., Philip Marshall Brown, "The Anschluss and the Permanent Court of International Justice," *AJIL*, 25 (1931): 511–12; and cf. the oral statement of Dr. (now Judge) Lachs in the *Admission* case, ICJ Pleadings, 1948, p. 106.

In the *Northern Cameroons* case, the ICJ took into account the fact that no compliance whatever was possible. ICJ Reports, 1963, p. 37. But this is quite different from considering the *willingness* of the parties to comply. Cf., on this point, Rosenne, *Law and Practice*, 1: 310, n. 1.

[65] See n. 74 below.

in which the Court itself has become embroiled to an extent rendering it impossible for the Court to exercise its judicial function properly."[66] Specifically, South Africa pointed to such factors as the "abuse and villification" which had been heaped upon the 1966 *South West Africa* judgment, the Court, and individual members of it;[67] the subjection of the Court to a kind of "court-packing" scheme in the triennial elections held in the wake of the 1966 judgment;[68] and the extent to which the Security Council's request was designed merely to test the Court in its changed composition and to give it an opportunity to "redeem its impaired image." After citing the statements of several representatives, in which the "political" nature of the Namibia question was emphasized,[69] South Africa concluded:

> The representatives concerned made it abundantly clear that in their opinion the problem of South West Africa was a political one to be solved by political means, and that any judicial decision in conflict with what they regard as the proper political solution would be unacceptable to them.
>
> On the other hand, should any opinion which the Court might decide to give be unfavourable to South Africa, it is inevitable that there will exist in the minds of reasonable men doubt as to whether the Court did not bow to political pressure and as to whether justice was in fact done.[70]

"The Court itself," South Africa urged, "has become so involved in the political disputes which have led to the present proceedings that . . . the Court as such should in effect 'recuse' itself by refusing to give the requested opinion."[71]

The Court, however, refused to "recuse" itself in this manner. Moreover, it took the unusual step of announcing at the opening of the oral hearings its

[66] *Namibia* case, ICJ Pleadings, 1971, 1: 425. For the arguments on the political nature of the request, see *ibid.*, pp. 425–42.

[67] *Ibid.*, pp. 427 ff. South Africa also cited the refusal of the General Assembly's Fifth Committee to approve supplementary appropriations requested by the Court for the financial year 1966. *Ibid.*, p. 433.

[68] *Ibid.*, pp. 433–37. South Africa alleged that the majority sought to ensure that the political views of the five new judges would coincide with its own.

[69] *Ibid.*, pp. 441–42. See Chapter III, pp. 153–54, for excerpts from those statements.

[70] *Namibia* case, ICJ Pleadings, 1971, 1: 442.

[71] *Ibid.*, p. 439. South Africa also requested that three members of the Court—President Zafrulla Khan and Judges Padilla Nervo and Morozov—be recused from sitting in the case because they had "become identified with their countries' political campaign against South Africa concerning its administration of South West Africa." *Ibid.*, p. 441. For South Africa's arguments, see *ibid.*, pp. 437–40. The Court, by three orders dated 26 January 1971, rejected South Africa's objections. See ICJ Reports, 1971, pp. 18–19. For criticism of the Court's decisions, see the separate opinions of Judges Petrén and Onyeama, *ibid.*, pp. 130 and 138–39; and the dissenting opinions of Judges Fitzmaurice and Gros, *ibid.*, pp. 309, 317, and 323–24.

unanimous decision "that it was not proper for it to entertain" the South
African observations which requested the Court to disqualify itself "because
of political pressure to which the Court, according to . . . South Africa had
been or might be subjected." The observations in question, the Court said,
bore

> on the very nature of the Court as the principal judicial organ of the
> United Nations, an organ which, in that capacity, acts only on the basis of
> the law, independently of all outside influence or interventions whatso-
> ever, in the exercise of the judicial function entrusted to it alone by the
> Charter and its Statute. A court functioning as a court of law can act in no
> other way.[72]

Although the decision with respect to the argument of "political pressure"
was unanimous, individual judges of the Court clearly harbored some grave
misgivings regarding the prominent "political background" and motivation of
the request in the *Namibia* case.[73]

Objections regarding "political" motivation and "political" consequences
were not new to the ICJ in the *Namibia* case. In connection with its very first

[72]*Namibia* case, ICJ Pleadings, 1971, Verbatim Record, C.R. 71/1, 8 February 1971,
pp. 10-11, and ICJ Reports, 1971, p. 23.

[73] The following excerpts bear quotation:

Judge Petrén: "[I] t clearly emerges from the context in which the request for advisory opinion was decided that its purpose was above all to obtain from the Court
a reply such that States would find themselves under obligation to bring to bear on
South Africa pressure of an essentially economic character designed to secure its withdrawal from Namibia. The natural distribution of roles as between the principal judicial
organ and the political organs of the United Nations was thereby reversed. Instead of
asking the Court its opinion on a legal question in order to deduce the political consequences flowing from it, the Security Council did the opposite. . . . [T] he request for
advisory opinion lies outside the normal framework of the Court's advisory function. . . . The Court would therefore have had a valid reason for declining to accede to
the request." ICJ Reports, 1971, pp. 127-28.

Judge Fitzmaurice: "[T] he political background of a question would only justify a
refusal to answer where this background loomed so large as to impart a political character to the question also. In spite of doubts as to whether something of the kind has not
occurred in the present case, the legal character of the questions themselves remains."
Ibid., p. 308. "The present case might well be regarded as being at the least a borderline
one, for the political nature of the background is unusually prominent." *Ibid.*, p. 308,
n. 9.

See also the dissenting opinion of Judge Gros, *ibid.*, p. 328. And cf. the insistence by
Judge Onyeama that the Court "is in no way obliged or concerned to render a judgment
or opinion which would be 'politically acceptable.' " *Ibid.*, p. 143. (The words "politically acceptable" had been used by the Zambian representative in the pre-request proceedings. See *ibid.*, p. 142; and Chapter III, p. 154, above.) The "political" nature of the
request was also bound up with the issue of the scope of the question posed by the
Security Council. See the discussion on pp. 327-28 below.

advisory opinion—the *Admission* opinion—arguments of this kind were voiced.[74] In that case, the "political" nature of the request was premised on these further grounds as well: that the Court would be required to pass judgment on the *specific* actions of states;[75] that, conversely, the "abstract" nature of the question made it unsuitable for judicial treatment;[76] that questions involving interpretation of the Charter in the abstract were not "legal";[77] and that the "discretionary" power of a political organ was not a matter for judicial determination.[78]

In the following passage, the Court sought to dispose of most of the objections that had been raised:

> [T] he question . . . is and can only be a purely legal one. To determine the meaning of a treaty provision—to determine, as in this case, the character (exhaustive or otherwise) of the conditions stated therein—is a problem of interpretation and consequently a legal question. . . .

---

[74] See, e.g., the arguments of Yugoslavia, *Admission* case, ICJ Pleadings, 1948, pp. 84 and 87; and the dissenting opinions of Judges Zoričić and Krylov, ICJ Reports, 1948, pp. 95, 107-8. See also the Czechoslovakian statement in the *Competence* case, ICJ Pleadings, 1950, pp. 108-9. And cf. the dissenting opinion of Judge Koretsky in the *Expenses* case, ICJ Reports, 1962, p. 254.

[75] It was argued that, despite the abstract formulation of the question, the specific actions and arguments of certain Security Council members were on trial. Support for this view was drawn from the preamble of the Assembly's resolution wherein Security Council meetings dealing with the admission of particular states were cited. See *Admission* case, ICJ Pleadings, 1950, p. 106. See also the dissenting opinions of Judges Zoričić and Krylov, both of whom discussed the concrete cases from which the request arose. ICJ Reports, 1948, pp. 94 ff., 107 ff.

In connection with the proposal to request the Court's opinion on the matter of Soviet exit visas, Egypt argued that the Court could not deal with specific cases, but only with general questions of principle. GAOR (III), 6th Ctte., 139th Mtg., 7 December 1948, pp. 779-80.

[76] The judicial function was said to be confined to dealing with concrete issues. On this point, see p. 310 and n. 115 below.

[77] For discussion of this objection, see pp. 303-5 below.

[78] See the statements of Yugoslavia, Poland, and Czechoslovakia in the *Admission* case, ICJ Pleadings, 1948, pp. 82-83, 109, 116. But cf. the arguments of France and Belgium to the effect that determining the limits of a discretionary power is itself a legal question. *Ibid.*, pp. 60, 96. The Court implicitly endorsed these views. See ICJ Reports, 1948, pp. 60-61.

In their joint dissent, Judges Basdevant, Winiarski, McNair, and Read deemed the second question in the request "political" because the Court was being asked to "assess the validity" of a "particular political consideration" upon which a member might rely. *Ibid.*, pp. 92-93. However, the substantive views of these judges might as readily have been translated into the following statement: The discretion of states in respect of the admission of new members does not "legally" exclude such considerations as might be involved in certain cases of collective admissions—the only "legal" limitation on that discretion being the limitation of "good faith." In this alternative formulation, both question and answer remain "legal."

... The Court cannot attribute a political character to a request which, framed in abstract terms, invites it to undertake an essentially judicial task, the interpretation of a treaty provision. It is not concerned with the motives which may have inspired this request, nor with the considerations which, in the concrete cases submitted for examination to the Security Council, formed the subject of the exchange of views which took place in that body. It is the duty of the Court to envisage the question submitted to it only in the abstract form which has been given to it; nothing which is said in the present opinion refers, either directly or indirectly, to concrete cases or to particular circumstances.[79]

Repeatedly thereafter, the ICJ evinced a willingness to consider questions involving treaty interpretation (including Charter interpretation) as ipso facto "legal," and to leave aside as irrelevant the circumstances leading up to the request or the probable consequences of the opinion. The Court did not indicate in any way that it might differentiate between various types of treaty provisions. Yet, in the *Customs Union* case, the *type* of treaty provision involved (perhaps more than anything) had branded the request as "political" in the eyes of its critics. For, in order to determine whether Austrian "independence" was being "alienated," and, even more, whether any acts were being undertaken which might "directly or *indirectly* or by any means whatever *compromise*" Austrian independence, the Court was called upon to speculate on future probabilities in the sphere of economic and political relationships. Much of the sharp debate to which the *Customs Union* opinion gave rise revolved, in essence, around divergent views as to whether this kind of speculation could be encompassed within the "judicial function."[80]

---

[79] ICJ Reports, 1948, p. 61. The Court also answered objections regarding its right to respond to "abstract" questions and to interpret Charter provisions. See pp. 303–5, 310–11, below.

In the *Competence, Peace Treaties,* and *Expenses* cases, the Court again affirmed that questions of treaty interpretation (including Charter interpretation) were "legal." ICJ Reports, 1950, pp. 6–7, 70–71; and 1962, pp. 155–56.

In the *Expenses* case, the Court determined that it was dealing with a "*concrete* legal question," indicating, thereby, that a question need not necessarily be "abstract" to be "legal." The Court's insistence on the "abstract" nature of the questions in the *Admission* and other cases must be seen in the context of the need to overcome the more serious objection that the Court would (if it dealt with the matter in more concrete terms) be censuring the acts of particular states. See pp. 309–10 below.

[80] Within the Court itself, it was Judge Anzilotti who, in his individual opinion, faced the question most squarely.

... The question amounts to asking whether, in view on the one hand of the respective positions of Austria and Germany, and in view, on the other hand, of the consequences which the Customs Union would have on Austria's economic life, it can reasonably be foreseen that a dangerous situation would ensue for the independence of Austria.

In any event, neither Court has ever expressly declared that a particular provision, either because of its ambiguity or because it involved elements of "subjective appreciation," was more suitable for interpretation by statesmen than by judges and should therefore be retransferred from the judicial forum to the political forum.[81] Nor does the ICJ's new doctrine of its duty to cooperate with other UN organs by rendering opinions on request make it any more likely that a treaty provision—no matter how ambiguous—will be declared inappropriate for judicial interpretation. Moreover, if the past his-

---

> We are therefore definitely concerned with a particular instance . . . which derives all its importance from the fact that we are dealing with the relations between Germany and Austria. It is quite probable that a similar customs union, or even a closer union between Austria and Czechoslovakia, would not have raised the slightest difficulty. It is not Austria's right to enter into customs unions in general with which we are concerned. . . .
>
> Everything points to the fact that the answer depends on considerations which are for the most part, if not entirely, of a political and economic kind. It may therefore be asked whether the Council really wished to obtain the Court's opinion on this aspect of the question and whether the Court ought to deal with it. . . .
>
> . . . the Court must either refuse to give the opinion asked for, or it must give it on the question as a whole.

PCIJ, Ser. A/B, No. 41, pp. 68–69.

The Court's inadequately reasoned opinion would appear to have been based, implicitly, on reasoning similar to Judge Anzilotti's.

The joint dissenting minority, on the other hand, professed to be excluding any speculation on future facts and future probabilities and to be confining itself to the material presented to the Court. In fact, however, while the minority placed more emphasis on the formalistic interpretation of provisions than did the majority, its opinion was, to no mean extent, based on an appreciation of the facts which differed from that of the majority. *Ibid.*, pp. 74–87.

The literature on the "political" nature of the *Customs Union* case is voluminous. The following represents but a small sampling: Brown, *op. cit.*, pp. 508–12; Edwin M. Borchard, "The Customs Union Advisory Opinion," *AJIL*, 25(1931): 711–16; J. L. Brierly, "The Advisory Opinion of the Permanent Court on the Customs Regime between Germany and Austria," *Zeitschrift für ausländisches öffentliches Recht und Völkerrecht*, 3 (1932): 68–75; Philip C. Jessup, "The Customs Union Advisory Opinion," *AJIL*, 26 (1932): 105–10; Robert E. Mathews, "Judicial Attitudes in the Customs Union Case," *Michigan Law Review*, 30 (1932): 699–708; Manley O. Hudson, "The World Court and the Austro-German Customs Regime," *American Bar Association Journal*, 17 (1931): 791–93; Alexander P. Fachiri, "The Austro-German Customs Union Case," *BYIL*, 13 (1932): 68–75; John W. Davis, "The World Court Settles the Question," *Atlantic Monthly*, 149 (January 1932): 119–30; C. A. W. Manning, "The Permanent Court and the Customs Union," *New York University Law Review*, 9 (1932): 339–43; Grant Gilmore, "The International Court of Justice," *Yale Law Review*, 55 (1946): 1049–66.

[81] However, individual judges have not hesitated to assert such a view. Thus, in the *South West Africa* cases (Preliminary Objections), Judges Spender and Fitzmaurice considered that interpretation of Article 2 of the South West Africa mandate (requiring South Africa "to promote to its utmost the material and moral well-being and the social progress of the inhabitants of the territory") involved subjective "appreciation" rather than "objective determination," and was therefore more suitable for resolution by a political organ. ICJ Reports, 1962, pp. 466–67. A similar opinion was expressed by

tory of the ICJ is any indication, the Court will make every attempt to overcome all other objections to the "legal" nature of questions before it, and will continue to ignore both the "political" motivation of the request, and the possible "political" consequences of the opinion.

Interpretation of the Charter

As already noted, the PCIJ was never asked to interpret Covenant provisions in the abstract. Moreover, throughout the League period, a distinct measure of uncertainty as to whether the Court was, indeed, competent to render such abstract interpretations persisted.[82] The very fact that no requests in this category were ever made tended to reinforce the earlier uncertainty in the matter.[83]

At San Francisco, a Belgian proposal to establish the Court as the official organ of Charter interpretation was defeated. It was understood that each organ would interpret the Charter in the course of its day-to-day operations; that, in the presence of divergent interpretations, various methods, including recourse to the Court's advisory or contentious jurisdiction, might be employed; that interpretations not generally accepted would lack binding force; and that, in order "to establish an authoritative interpretation as a precedent for the future, it may be necessary to embody the interpretation in an amendment to the Charter."[84]

During the early UN period, the Court's competence to render abstract interpretations of the Charter was frequently debated. In the General Assembly, the occasions for such debate were, *inter alia*, the pre-request phases of the *Admission* and *Competence* cases and the proceedings leading up to the adoption of Resolution 171A(II).[85] While opposition to Charter interpreta-

---

Judge Spender in regard to a provision in the trusteeship agreement for the Northern Cameroons. *Ibid.*, 1963, pp. 77–78. (Cf. the dissenting opinion of Judge Tanaka in the *South West Africa* cases [Second Phase], *ibid.*, 1966, pp. 279–84.) For the view that considerations of the same sort may have underlain the 1966 *South West Africa* judgment, see Solomon Slonim, *South West Africa and the United Nations: An International Mandate in Dispute* (Baltimore, Md.: The Johns Hopkins Press, 1973), chap. XII.

[82] See the discussions of the Polish-Lithuanian dispute, the Corfu aftermath, and the nature of the vote required for requests, in Chapter IV.

[83] The earlier uncertainty was in large measure based on rejection of M. Larnaude's proposal at Paris. See Chapter I.

[84] These understandings were contained in the report of Committee IV/2. *UNCIO Documents*, 13: 709–10. See Chapter I.

[85] In this resolution, the General Assembly recommended that UN organs and specialized agencies make greater use of the ICJ in connection with "difficult and important points of law," including "points of law relating to the interpretation of the Charter" or of the specialized agencies' constitutions. Polish amendments, introduced in the Sixth Committee and in Plenary, would have deleted reference to Charter interpretation. For the relevant discussions, see GAOR (II), 6th Ctte., 52nd Mtg., 22 October 1947,

tion by the Court came primarily from members of the Soviet bloc, it was not, at first, confined to these states.[86]

The challenges raised in the Assembly were repeated before the Court in the *Admission* and *Competence* cases. Among the principal arguments presented to the Court—all of them by Soviet bloc countries—were the following. (1) League practice with respect to Covenant interpretation should be followed.[87] (2) The defeat of the Belgian proposal at San Francisco and the absence of any provision for judicial interpretation in the Charter barred the Court from exercising an interpretative function in relation to Charter provisions.[88] (3) The power to interpret the Charter is reserved to the UN's political organs.[89] (4) Not even the General Assembly possesses the right to interpret the Charter, for that right appertains exclusively to the individual member states. Consequently, the Assembly cannot delegate, and the Court cannot exercise, the power to interpret the Charter.[90] (5) Under Article 36 of its Statute, the Court is confined to the interpretation of *treaties*. But the Charter, far from being an ordinary treaty, is a constitutional document whose interpretation is a "political" matter.[91] (6) The Court's function is to apply the law in concrete cases. On the other hand, the rendering of abstract interpretations of the Charter is a legislative and quasiconstitutional power. As Committee IV/2 at San Francisco clearly indicated, "authoritative interpretation could only be accomplished by means of Charter amendment."[92]

In opposition to these views it was maintained that only "authentic interpretation" was reserved for member states; that the possibility of employing the Court for Charter interpretation was envisaged in the report of Committee IV/2 at San Francisco; that defeat of the Belgian proposal only eliminated the Court as the exclusive organ of Charter interpretation;[93] and that the vast

---

pp. 96–99; *ibid.*, Plenary, 113th Mtg., 14 November 1947, pp. 859–94 *passim*; and UN Docs. A/459, 11 November 1947, and A/474, 13 November 1947.

[86] See, e.g., the views of India and Argentina in the pre-request phase of the *Admission* case, GAOR (II), 1st Ctte., 100th Mtg., 8 November 1947, pp. 364, 370.

[87] See the oral statement of Poland in the *Admission* case, ICJ Pleadings, 1948, pp. 110–11; and the dissenting opinion of Judge Krylov, ICJ Reports, 1948, p. 108. The Court's competence to render the opinion requested was not doubted, but the propriety of its doing so was.

[88] *Admission* case, ICJ Pleadings, 1948, pp. 29, 88; *Competence* case, *ibid.*, 1950, pp. 100–105.

[89] *Competence* case, *ibid.*, 1950, pp. 100–105.

[90] *Admission* case, *ibid.*, 1948, p. 89.

[91] *Ibid.*, pp. 89–90; and *Competence* case, *ibid.*, 1950, pp. 100–105.

[92] *Admission* case, *ibid.*, 1948, pp. 89–90; ICJ Reports, 1948, pp. 108–9. See the discussion of "abstract" questions, pp. 307–12 below.

[93] *Admission* case, ICJ Pleadings, 1948, pp. 62–63, 92–94 (oral statements of France and Belgium). However, the line between "authentic" interpretation and the avowedly "authoritative" interpretation of the Court is a rather thin one. While one organ's inter-

majority of the General Assembly, by voting in favor of Resolution 171 (II) and of requesting the Court's opinion in the *Admission* case, unequivocally indicated its views in the matter.[94]

The Court, for its part, answered all objections with simple syllogistic reasoning. The Court may interpret treaties. The Charter is a multilateral treaty. Hence, the Court may interpret the Charter. In the Court's own words,

> Nowhere is any provision to be found forbidding the Court, "the principal judicial organ of the United Nations," to exercise in regard to Article 4 of the Charter, a multilateral treaty, an interpretative function which falls within the normal exercise of its judicial powers.[95]

Implicit in this argument was the view, first, that interpretation of the Charter was not really different from interpretation of other treaties; and, second, that, even if it were different, the Court's status as "principal judicial organ of the United Nations" would nevertheless entitle it to exercise an interpretative function.

In later years, objections to the Court's interpreting the Charter became muted. Even in the *Admission* case, the Soviet judge did not go so far as to endorse his government's view that the Court was *incompetent* to interpret the Charter. He merely considered that, as a matter of its discretion, the Court ought not to do so.[96] In the *Competence* case, the Soviet objection found no echo at all among the learned judges. And in the *Expenses* case, the Soviet Union failed to throw up its customary challenge.[97] The Soviet about-face on the question became more complete, when, in the Cuban case, it pressed for acceptance of a resolution which would have elicited from the Court abstract interpretations of Article 53 and other provisions of the Charter.[98]

Interpretation of Treaties

Among the grounds cited in opposition to the court's exercise of its advisory function in the *Peace Treaties* and *Reservations* cases were the con-

---

pretation cannot bind another organ, in practice, attribution of a certain superiority in matters of treaty interpretation to the Court is only natural. It is thus not surprising that both proponents and opponents of Court interpretation drew support for their respective views from the Report of Committee IV/2 at San Francisco.

[94] *Ibid.*, pp. 92–94.

[95] ICJ Reports, 1948, p. 61.

[96] *Ibid.*, pp. 108–9.

[97] The Court nevertheless reaffirmed its competence to interpret the Charter in that case. *Ibid.*, 1962, pp. 155–56.

[98] See Chapter IV.

tentions that (1) the power to interpret, or to seek interpretation of, the treaties at issue appertained exclusively to states that were parties to the treaties; and (2) that, since the treaties contained their own dispute-settlement procedures, the Court was barred from rendering the advisory opinions requested.[99]

In both cases, the Court affirmed the Assembly's independent right to solicit judicial interpretation. In the *Peace Treaties* case, the Court said that "no State . . . can prevent the giving of an Advisory Opinion which the United Nations considers to be desirable in order to obtain enlightenment as to the course of action it should take."[100] The Court was even more explicit in the *Reservations* case.

[I]t has been contended that the request for an opinion would constitute an inadmissible interference by the General Assembly and by States hitherto strangers to the Convention in the interpretation of that Convention, as only States which are parties to the Convention are entitled to interpret it or to seek an interpretation of it. It must be pointed out in this connection that, not only did the General Assembly take the initiative in respect of the Genocide Convention, draw up its terms and open it for signature and accession by States, but that express provisions of the Convention . . . associate the General Assembly with the life of the Convention; and finally, that the General Assembly actually associated itself with it by endeavouring to secure the adoption of the Convention by as great a number of States as possible. In these circumstances, there can be no doubt that the precise determination of the conditions for participation in the Convention constitutes a permanent interest of direct concern to the United Nations which has not disappeared with the entry into force of the Convention. Moreover, the power of the General Assembly to request an Advisory Opinion from the Court in no way impairs the inherent right of States parties to the Convention in the matter of its interpretation. This right is independent of the General Assembly's power and is exercisable in a parallel direction.[101]

[99] See the *Peace Treaties* case, ICJ Pleadings, 1950, pp. 196–99 (Bulgarian telegram); *Reservations* case, *ibid.*, 1951, pp. 283–85, 295–98; and cf. *ibid.*, pp. 198–200, 359–63.

As to the applicability of Article IX of the Genocide Convention, the same inconsistency noted in the pre-request discussions was reflected in the pleadings before the Court as well. Thus, the Philippines argued that an Australian-Philippine dispute existed, and that this dispute could come before the Court only by means of voluntary submission by the disputants. On the other hand, Poland based its argument on the nonexistence of a dispute. The conditions specified in Article IX were said to have worked a limitation on the Court's *advisory*, as well as on its contentious, jurisdiction.

[100] ICJ Reports, 1950, p. 71. This remark was made in connection with the general question of consent. But cf. the dissenting opinion of Judge Winiarski, in which the fact that the Court was specifically excluded from any role in relation to the Peace Treaties is pointed up. *Ibid.*, pp. 94, 96.

[101] *Ibid.*, 1951, pp. 19–20.

In both cases, too, the Court emphatically denied that its exercise of advisory jurisdiction would in any way take the place of the dispute-settlement procedures of the treaties. Thus, in the *Peace Treaties* case,

> So far from placing an obstacle in the way of the latter procedure [i.e., the Peace Treaties' dispute-settlement procedure], the object of this Request is to facilitate it by seeking information for the General Assembly as to its applicability to the circumstances of the present case.[102]

And, in the *Reservations* case, the Court answered in the following manner the objections based on the availability of the Court's contentious jurisdiction under Article IX of the Genocide Convention.

> The existence of a procedure for the settlement of disputes, such as that provided by Article IX, does not in itself exclude the Court's advisory jurisdiction, for Article 96 of the Charter confers upon the General Assembly and the Security Council in general terms the right to request . . . an Advisory Opinion "on any legal question."[103] Further, Article IX, before it can be applied, presupposes the status of "contracting parties"; consequently, it cannot be invoked against a request for an Opinion the very object of which is to determine, in relation to reservations and objections thereto, the conditions in which a State can become a party.[104]

It can readily be seen that, whereas the Court's second consideration applies exclusively to the *Reservations* case, the first reason is of more general applicability.

In sum, the Court's pronouncements on the issues of treaty interpretation and the existence of a dispute-settlement procedure reinforce the impression that the Court will not lightly assume that the Assembly lacks sufficient interest to warrant receiving the Court's advice.

"Abstract" Questions

Should the Court adhere closely to the facts which gave rise to the request for an advisory opinion, or should it prefer to deal with the request in more abstract terms? May the Court deal with questions having an "abstract" character, and, in this regard, is there a limit beyond which questions may be deemed too "abstract" for judicial consideration? Further, do the views of the two Courts contrast in any way in respect of these issues?

---

[102] *Ibid.*, 1950, p. 71.

[103] The PCIJ expressed a similar view in the case of *German Settlers in Poland*. PCIJ, Ser. B, No. 6, pp. 22–23.

[104] ICJ Reports, 1951, p. 20. Cf. the more elaborate argument of the United Kingdom to the same effect, *Reservations* case, ICJ Pleadings, 1951, pp. 362–63.

Within the League, doubts were voiced, at various times, regarding the Court's competence to pronounce itself on "abstract" questions. Such competence, some thought, would partake more of a "policy-making" function than of a "judicial" one.[105] Moreover, if the question dealt with in the abstract were subsequently submitted in connection with a concrete case, the Court's decision might, it was feared, be unfairly prejudiced.[106]

In fact, the majority of League requests (including almost all of the non-ILO requests) bore a rather "concrete" aspect. The Court was most frequently asked to declare the law in relation to specific sets of facts. To be sure, some of the ILO requests were formulated in abstract terms. For its part, however, the Court imparted even to these requests an element of "concreteness," by tracing, and taking account of, the specific circumstances in which the decisions to solicit the Court's advice were made.[107]

The PCIJ had no occasion to defend its power to answer "abstract" questions in advisory cases. In two contentious cases, however, the Court ex-

[105] See, especially, the views of M. Salandra in the Corfu aftermath, Chapter IV. But cf. the views of M. Branting to the effect that the term *"any* dispute *or question"* was broad enough to encompass the questions then at issue. LNOJ, 1923, pp. 1330–31. See also the discussion of the Polish-Lithuanian dispute, the nature of the vote required for requests, and the questions relating to withdrawal from League membership, pp. 197–201, 213–21, and 182–83 above.

[106] See, e.g., LNOJ, 1923, p. 1550, in connection with the Corfu aftermath.

[107] See, e.g., the Court's recital of the facts in No. 2 (*ILO and Agricultural Labor*), PCIJ, Ser. B, No. 2, pp. 14–21. (The Court's discussion of the substantive question is preceded by the statement: "On the facts thus set forth, the Court gives the following opinion.") Only in No. 3 (*ILO and Agricultural Production*) was the familiar narration of the pre-request events missing. But that case was, indeed, the most "abstract" request presented to either Court, in that the ILO denied ever claiming the competence in question, and there apparently was no real difference of opinion on the matter before the Court.

In the *Exchange of Greek and Turkish Populations* case, the request was somewhat abstract, in that the Court was asked to interpret the term *"établis"* in Article 2 of the Lausanne Convention of 30 January 1923. However, the allusion in the request to the "discussions" and "arguments" contained in the dossier submitted to the Court provided the Court with its cue for dealing with the question in a more concrete fashion. PCIJ, Ser. B, No. 10, p. 9.

In one case, the PCIJ reversed its tendency to "concretize the abstract," and instead "abstractified the concrete." The question in No. 1 (*Netherlands Workers' Delegate*) was, in its terms, very specific, relating, as it did, to a situation which had arisen. Yet, the object of the question was said by the Court to be "to obtain an interpretation of the provisions of paragraph 3 of Article 389," the specific facts having been recited "solely in order to fix clearly the state of facts to which the interpretation has application." PCIJ, Ser. B, No. 1, p. 17. The Court's apparent reversal must be understood in the context of the particular case, and, especially, of a particular objection raised by the Netherlands. The Netherlands delegate had, in fact, been seated, so that the aspect of *future* guidance was the paramount purpose of the request (see Chapter III). Furthermore, the Netherlands government objected that the request, as framed, amounted to submission of its actions to judicial scrutiny without its consent. PCIJ, Ser. C, No. 1, pp. 424–28. Even in this case, however, the Court adhered very closely to the facts.

pressed a willingness to comply with the desire of states for abstract interpretations of treaty provisions.[108]

As has already been seen, in the UN period there was a tendency—particularly marked in the early years—to formulate requests in more abstract terms. Correspondingly, the ICJ tended to "abstractify" its treatment of requests—to an even greater extent than the actual terms of the requests might have warranted.[109]

The Court's early inclination to treat requests in an abstract manner must, in turn, be seen in light of the specific contexts in which the requests were made. In most instances, "abstractification" permitted the Court to overcome, to its satisfaction, some of the more serious objections to its rendering an opinion. Thus, in the *Admission* case, by abstracting the request, on the one hand, from "the motives which may have inspired" it, and, on the other, from "the concrete cases submitted for examination to the Security Council," the Court felt able to affirm the nonpolitical character of the request. Again, in the *Reservations* case, only by dealing with the question abstractly—and not in relation to any specific reservations or objections—could the Court refute the Philippine contention that it was, in effect, deciding a dispute by means of advisory procedure. Clearly, then, even when the Court

---

[108]In the case of *German Interests in Polish Upper Silesia*, the Court stated, in answer to an objection based on the abstract character of one of the questions: "There seems to be no reason why States should not be able to ask the Court to give an abstract interpretation of a treaty; rather would it appear that this is one of the most important functions which it can fulfil." PCIJ, Ser. A, No. 7, pp. 18–19.

In the case of *Interpretation of the Statute of Memel*, the Court expressed some displeasure over the abstract formulation of the first three questions in Applicants' submissions. These questions, apart from being formulated *in abstracto*, were said to "go beyond the facts out of which the dispute has arisen and . . . beyond the questions of law or fact on which the Parties to the dispute had differed in opinion before the initiation of these proceedings." The Applicants should, the Court thought, have questioned the legality of the particular acts in question, "leaving the Court to enunciate in its decision the principles on which that decision was based." Nevertheless, the Court proceeded to answer the questions posed. *Ibid.*, Ser. A/B, No. 49, pp. 311–12; cf. the dissenting opinion of Judge Anzilotti, *ibid.*, pp. 349 ff.

[109]Thus, references in the preambles of some requesting resolutions to the concrete circumstances leading up to the requests were ignored by the Court. In the *Admission* case, for example, the Assembly referred to the "exchange of views" which had taken place in the Security Council, but the Court preferred to be guided exclusively by "the abstract form" in which the question was stated. ICJ Reports, 1948, p. 61; cf. the separate opinion of Judge Azevedo, *ibid.*, p. 75. But see the dissenting opinions of Judge Zoričić, *ibid.*, p. 96; and Judge Krylov, *ibid.*, p. 107. In the *Competence* case, an allusion to discussions in the *Ad Hoc* Political Committee was overlooked without comment.

Even in questions recognized by the Court as not being abstract, the ICJ did not generally follow its predecessor's practice of reciting the relevant facts of the pre-request stage. The *UNESCO* and *IMCO* cases—and, to a degree, the *South West Africa (Committee)* and *Namibia* cases—are exceptional in this respect.

deals with a request in an abstract manner, frequently an awareness of the concrete circumstances leads it to do so.[110]

A certain reversal in the pattern of treating requests as "abstract" set in during the Court's second decade. Thus, the Court's opinion in the *South West Africa (Committee)* case bore a less abstract aspect than the *South West Africa (Voting)* opinion of the previous year.[111] In the *Expenses* case, the Court emphasized that the request related to "a concrete legal question."[112] Above all, the Court did not extend its "abstract question" doctrine to the two requests made under Article 96(2). Both requests were framed in concrete terms; in both cases the Court recited the facts of the case; and, in the *IMCO* case, in reinterpreting the question posed, the Court "concretized" it still further.[113] In view of the terms of Article 96(2), a more "abstract" handling of requests in this category is not anticipated for the future.[114]

At various times, objections were directed against the ICJ's responding to abstract questions,[115] but the Court dismissed these without much ado.

It has also been contended that the Court should not deal with a question couched in abstract terms. That is a mere affirmation devoid of any justification. According to Article 96 of the Charter and Article 65 of

---

[110] Cf. the PCIJ's insistence on the abstract nature of the request in opinion No. 1.

[111] See, on this point, Rosenne, *Law and Practice*, 2: 721–22.

[112] ICJ Reports, 1962, p. 156. And cf. the "concrete" handling of the *Namibia* case. *Ibid.*, 1971, pp. 27 ff.

[113] See *ibid.*, 1960, pp. 152–53. The Court considered that the question, "cast though it is in general form, is directed to a particular case," and it therefore reformulated the question to ask whether the nonelection of Liberia and Panama to the Maritime Safety Committee violated the terms of the IMCO Convention. In the pre-request stage, there was some debate as to whether specific states should be mentioned. The United States representative insisted that anonymity was not required. See IMCO, A.1/LEG/SR.4, 16 January 1959; and Chapter III above.

[114] See, in this connection, Rosenne, *Law and Practice*, 2: 707–8.

[115] Yugoslavia, in its Written Statement in the *Admission* case, argued that the limitation mentioned in Article 96(2) ("arising within the scope of their activities") is implicit in Article 96(1) as well, and restricts the subject matter of requests to "concrete" questions; that abstract interpretations have a quasiconstitutional, rather than a judicial, character; and that the very elimination of the Court's own jurisprudence as a positive source of international law indicated that the Court could not render abstract interpretations. *Admission* case, ICJ Pleadings, 1948, pp. 89–90. Cf. the dissenting opinion of Judge Krylov, ICJ Reports, 1948, pp. 108–9; and the statement of Judge Zoričić, *ibid.*, p. 96.

In the *Reservations* case, the Philippines argued that the request, to the extent that it was framed in "hypothetical," "general," or "theoretical" terms, was beyond the Court's purview. *Reservations* case, ICJ Pleadings, 1951, pp. 297–98.

the Statute, the Court may give an advisory opinion on any legal question, abstract or otherwise.[116]

Notwithstanding the Court's willingness to answer "abstract" questions and its tendency to deal with requests before it in the abstract, it is not clear that the Court would agree to answer a completely hypothetical question,[117] a question regarding future law,[118] or an obviously "moot" question.[119] No matter how abstract either the requests or the opinions have been in the past, the Court has always been aware of the concrete circumstances out of which each request sprang;[120] and, to the extent that these circumstances were taken into account, even implicitly, the resultant opinions gained more meaning. Furthermore, in all past cases, the opinions had a sphere of applicability, and one which was not too difficult to discern.

Theoretically, of course, the term "any legal question" might be considered broad enough to embrace even "moot" or purely academic questions. However, the more important question is: Would the Court, as a matter of propriety, choose to answer such questions? The evidence in the *Northern Cameroons* case points to a possibly negative conclusion. For, in that case, the Court, in refusing to entertain a claim which it deemed purposeless, "moot," and incapable of effective application, based its refusal on general considerations related to the need to "safeguard the judicial function."[121] But this

[116] ICJ Reports, 1948, p. 61. The Court did not find it necessary to answer the Philippine objection on this matter in the *Reservations* case.

[117] In 1922, a Committee of the PCIJ recommended that the Court include in its Rules a provision reserving for itself "the right to refrain from replying to questions . . . which require an advisory opinion on a theoretical case." PCIJ, Ser. D, No. 2, p. 308.

[118] In the case of the Swiss reparations (see Chapter IV) the Rapporteur argued that the Court could not be asked to define future law, because this was a legislative, not a judicial, function.

[119] The *Customs Union* opinion was "moot" by the time it was delivered—Germany and Austria having renounced, two days earlier, their plans to institute the proposed customs union. But this fact was not communicated to the Court, and the Court did not officially take cognizance of it.

[120] A dossier of documents is always submitted to the Court, and, additionally, it has been the UN Secretary-General's practice to review the facts leading up to the Assembly's request.

The General Assembly has on several occasions insisted on an element of concreteness in requests for advisory opinions. Thus, in connection with Resolution 171A (II) on greater use of the Court's advisory function, the Sixth Committee emphasized that requests should not be made on abstract, hypothetical questions that were likely to arise in the future, but rather on questions arising from concrete cases. GAOR (II), Plenary, Annex 18, p. 1560 (1947). Similarly, in the pre-request phase of the *Reservations* case, the Sixth Committee insisted that reference be made to a particular convention, in order to lend an element of concreteness to an otherwise abstract question.

[121] ICJ Reports, 1963, pp. 34–38; cf. the separate opinion of Judge Fitzmaurice, *ibid.*, pp. 97–108.

need is as applicable to advisory cases as it is to contentious cases; it constitutes the very essence of the judicial discretion sanctified in Article 65(1) of
the ICJ Statute.[122]

From a practical viewpoint it is clear that, beyond a certain point, there is
an inverse relationship between the degree of abstraction of the opinion and
the usefulness of the opinion.[123] As noted by Judge Zoričić in the *Admission*
case: "In human life all activity is based on concrete considerations of fact.
To attempt to judge ... acts in the abstract would be ... to work in a
vacuum, and to misunderstand the meaning of real life."[124]

"Factual" Questions

May the Court ascertain questions of "fact" in advisory proceedings?
Undoubtedly, hardly any "legal" question can be regarded as "pure," in the
sense that no admixture of factual elements is present. And, as Rosenne has
pointed out, both the PCIJ and the ICJ, in their advisory capacity, "regularly
made simple findings of fact, established on the basis of the documentation
submitted to the Court."[125] But what if the "factual" element in the case is
more prominent, or, indeed, if it is predominant? What if any finding on the
law must be preceded by findings on controverted "primary" facts? The
possibility of even extensive factual inquiries—involving, e.g., the testimony
of witnesses or experts—was clearly envisaged for contentious proceedings.[126]

---

[122] Cf. Judge Fitzmaurice's view in the *Namibia* case, to the effect that, unless the
validity of termination of the mandate were examined by the Court, the case would be
(like the *Northern Cameroons* case) a hypothetical one falling outside the judicial function. *Ibid.*, 1971, p. 302.

[123] See, on this point, Lissitzyn, *International Court*, p. 30; Shabtai Rosenne, "The
Court and the Judicial Process," *IO*, 19 (1965): 524; Sloan, *op. cit.*, p. 841. As noted by
Lissitzyn, requests too far removed from concrete circumstances are likely to result in
the inadequate presentation of views to the Court, thus depriving the Court of "the
benefit of a quasi-contentious proceeding."

[124] ICJ Reports, 1948, p. 96. Both he and Judge Krylov discussed the specific cases
of nonadmission which had given rise to the request in the *Admission* case.

On the other hand, Judge Azevedo would have gone even further than the Court in
the tendency to treat requests in the abstract. In his view, substitution of the term "any
legal question" in Article 96 of the Charter for the former "any dispute or question"
denoted a desire that the Court deal, in its advisory capacity, purely with abstract cases,
and not at all with concrete disputes. See his separate opinions in the *Admission* and
Peace Treaties cases, *ibid.*, pp. 73 ff.; and 1950, pp. 79 ff. As noted above (Chapter I),
there is no support for this view in the *travaux préparatoires*.

[125] Rosenne, *Law and Practice*, 2: 701.

[126] See, e.g., Article 36(2) of the PCIJ and ICJ Statutes, in which legal disputes to
which the compulsory jurisdiction may extend include those concerning "the existence
of any fact which, if established, would constitute a breach of an international obliga-

But can the same be said for the advisory jurisdiction? Do questions that are "essentially factual" fall within the compass of "legal questions" (in the terminology of Article 96 of the Charter)? And, even if they do, are advisory proceedings appropriate for the purpose of conducting wide-ranging factual investigations? The relevant pronouncements of the PCIJ and ICJ offer some answers—albeit somewhat ambiguous—to these questions.

In the *Eastern Carelia* case, the PCIJ (after explaining the primary reason for refusing to render an advisory opinion) cited "other cogent reasons" for its refusal. These reasons related to the difficulty of establishing disputed facts in the absence of Russian testimony. In this connection, the Court went on to state: "The Court does not say that there is an absolute rule that the request for an advisory opinion may not involve some enquiry as to the facts, but, under ordinary circumstances, it is certainly expedient that the facts upon which the opinion of the Court is desired should not be in controversy, and it should not be left to the Court itself to ascertain what they are."[127]

In the *Danube Commission* case, the Court evinced reluctance to undertake an independent investigation into the facts. A special committee set up by the League had made findings of fact, but Rumania had refused to accept them. The Court held that it was not "proper to make new investigations and enquiries"; it was necessary to "accept the findings of the Committee on issues of fact unless in the records submitted to the Court there is evidence to refute them."[128]

The first frontal challenge to the Court's entertaining "factual" issues in advisory proceedings was made before the ICJ in the *Namibia* case. South Africa presented two alternative arguments,[129] and—for the contingency that neither would be accepted—it offered a unique set of proposals.

Underlying the question posed by the Security Council, South Africa argued, were unresolved factual issues which "do not fall within a small or confined ambit." The General Assembly resolution (2145) terminating the mandate—the basic resolution from which all further Assembly and Council resolutions flowed—was premised on South Africa's failure to promote the moral and material well-being of the indigenous population. This issue lay at the heart of the *South West Africa* litigation of the 1960s; it was then, and remained thereafter, an essentially factual question. "The Court will not be in a position to give the requested advisory opinion unless it also makes findings

---

tion"; and Article 54 of the 1936 PCIJ Rules of Court and of the 1946 ICJ Rules, relative to the testimony of witnesses and experts and the production of evidence.

[127]PCIJ, Ser. B, No. 5, p. 28; and cf. *ibid.*, Ser. D, No. 2 (Add.), pp. 290–91.

[128]*Ibid.*, Ser. B, No. 14, p. 46.

[129]For the South African arguments, see *Namibia* case, ICJ Pleadings, 1971, 1: 447–50; Verbatim Record, C.R. 71/7, 19 February 1971, pp. 41–47.

on controverted and controversial factual issues of such proportions that the present question, in ultimate analysis, cannot be regarded as a purely legal one."[130] The first contention, then, was that the Court was *incompetent* to render an opinion in this case, because the question posed was "factual" rather than "legal."

Alternatively, South Africa argued that the advisory process was inappropriate for making findings as to disputed "primary" facts, and that the Court, as a matter of its *discretion*, should refuse to render an opinion.[131]

Anticipating that neither argument would be accepted, South Africa requested permission to adduce voluminous factual evidence regarding the promotion of well-being in South West Africa;[132] and it also proposed the holding of a plebiscite in South West Africa, a plebiscite to be jointly supervised by South Africa and the Court. In accordance with the latter proposal, the population of the territory would state its preference as between continued South African administration and administration by the UN. The object of the plebiscite was solely to elucidate the facts for the purposes of the *Namibia* proceedings.[133]

Both of South Africa's arguments and both of its proposals were premised on a single assumption: that the Court could not furnish an answer to the request unless it first established "controverted primary facts which do not fall within a limited compass and which are not capable of easy and speedy ascertainment."[134] This assumption the Court denied. Perhaps intentionally avoiding the thicket of "factual" issues of which South Africa spoke, the Court justified the Assembly's revocation of the mandate primarily on the basis of the readily ascertainable and *uncontroverted* fact of South Africa's failure to submit reports and transmit petitions relating to South West Africa.[135] For this and other reasons,[136] South Africa's proposals were re-

---

[130]*Namibia* case, ICJ Pleadings, 1: 449–50.

[131]*Ibid.*, pp. 448–49. In this connection, South Africa also pointed to several "practical difficulties" which were peculiar to advisory proceedings and which stemmed from the absence of parties and from the absence of an onus upon the parties to assist the Court to establish the facts. *Ibid.*; and Verbatim Record, C.R. 71/7, 19 February 1971, pp. 42–43.

[132]See *ibid.*, Verbatim Record, C.R. 71/17, 5 March 1971, pp. 47 ff.; and C.R. 71/23, 17 March 1971, pp. 6 ff. and esp. pp. 51–53.

[133]The suggestion was raised in letters of 27 January and 6 February 1971, sent to the Court prior to the opening of the oral hearings, and it was further elaborated and explained during the course of the proceedings. See *Namibia* case, ICJ Pleadings, 1971, 2:668–69, 673–76; Verbatim Record, C.R. 71/6, 16 February 1971, pp. 46–54. South Africa recognized the unusual nature of the suggestion but considered that it fell within the ambit of Article 68 of the Statute. *Ibid.*, p. 49.

[134]*Ibid.*, Verbatim Record, C.R. 71/7, 19 February 1971, p. 42.

[135]See ICJ Reports, 1971, pp. 47 and 50. (But cf. the criticism of Judge Fitzmaurice that South Africa was under no legal obligation to submit to UN supervision, since the

jected.[137] Strictly speaking, therefore, it was unnecessary to answer South Africa's objections regarding the competence of the Court to deal with extensive factual issues. Nevertheless, the Court declared:

> In the view of the Court, the contingency that there may be factual issues underlying the question posed does not alter its character as a "legal question" as envisaged in Article 96 of the Charter. The reference in this provision to legal questions cannot be interpreted as opposing legal to factual issues. Normally, to enable a court to pronounce on legal questions, it must be acquainted with, take into account and, if necessary, make findings as to the relevant factual issues. The limitation of the powers of the Court contended for by . . . South Africa has no basis in the Charter or the Statute.[138]

From the relevant PCIJ and ICJ pronouncements on the issue of "factual" questions in advisory cases, the following conclusions may be deduced. First, it is certainly preferable and more "expedient" for the basic facts in the case to be uncontroverted or ascertainable with relative ease from the documentation. Second, the term "legal question" does not exclude factual questions,

---

so-called obligation had only been established in an advisory opinion. *Ibid.*, pp. 121–22. In other words, even if the *fact* was uncontroverted, the legal deduction flowing from it was *not*.)

Several other ways of extricating the Court from the "factual" thicket were offered in the pleadings, but were either ignored or de-emphasized by the Court. Thus, the Court did not take up the suggestion by the representatives of the Secretary-General, Viet Nam, and the United States that the Court need not, or ought not, to establish the facts, since these had already been established by the competent authorities. See *Namibia* case, ICJ Pleadings, 1971, Verbatim Record, C.R. 71/1, 8 February 1971, pp. 26–27; C.R. 71/11, 25 February 1971, p. 10; and C.R. 71/19, 9 March 1971, p. 20. (This had been one of the principal arguments offered by Applicants in the *South West Africa* litigation of the 1960s. Slonim, *op. cit.*, chap. X.) The argument that many of the facts of apartheid were common knowledge (see, e.g., the Oral Statement of Finland, *Namibia* case, ICJ Pleadings, 1971, Verbatim Record, C.R. 71/2, 9 February 1971, pp. 16–17) was only secondary with the Court. See ICJ Reports, 1971, pp. 56–57. Cf. Judge Ammoun's criticism of the Court for having chosen "the easy way out" and having overlooked "the gravest violations." *Ibid.*, pp. 80–81.

[136] Other reasons included the obvious inconsistency between apartheid legislation and Charter obligations, and (as for the plebiscite proposal) South Africa's illegal presence in the territory. ICJ Reports, 1971, pp. 57–58.

[137] The Court deferred its answers to South Africa's requests until after the end of the oral hearings, and on 17 March 1971 notified South Africa of its rejection of both requests. *Ibid.*, p. 21. For criticism of the Court's refusal to allow further factual evidence, see the dissenting opinion of Judge Fitzmaurice, *ibid.*, pp. 222–23. In Judge Fitzmaurice's view, the Court, by refusing to allow the seating of a judge *ad hoc*, precluded itself at an early stage from going into any question of fact (since the elucidation of disputed facts requires quasicontentious procedure). *Ibid.*, p. 316.

[138] *Ibid.*, p. 27.

and the Court is, therefore, presumably *competent* to make even extensive factual inquiries. Third, there is still room for the Court, in the exercise of its *discretion*, to refuse to answer questions requiring far-reaching factual investigations.[139] Whether the Court will exercise its discretion will depend on the particular circumstances of each case. Given the desire to cooperate with other organs of the UN, the Court may be expected to strain every effort to ferret out an uncontroverted factual basis so as to be able to comply with the request.

Binding Force of the Opinion

Must the Court be satisfied that its opinion will, at least formally, be nonbinding, before it consents to comply with a request?

This question never engaged the attention of the PCIJ—though, on two occasions,[140] the Court's opinion was explicitly accepted by the parties as binding, in advance.

Advance acceptance in the League period was, however, extended strictly on an *ad hoc* basis. General provisions for binding opinions were almost totally absent. As was seen earlier, such provisions are a phenomenon of the UN era.

It was within the framework of one such provision—Article XII of the ILO Administrative Tribunal Statute—that the request in the *UNESCO* case arose. And, in that case, the ICJ was quite explicit in affirming that advance acceptance of an opinion as binding could not, as such, affect its jurisdiction:

> Under Article XII of the Statute of the Administrative Tribunal, the Opinion thus requested will be "binding". Such effect of the Opinion goes beyond the scope attributed by the Charter and by the Statute of the Court to an Advisory Opinion. However, the provision in question is nothing but a rule of conduct for the Executive Board, a rule determining the action to be taken by it on the Opinion of the Court. It in no wise affects the way in which the Court functions; that continues to be determined by its Statute and its Rules. Nor does it affect the reasoning by which the Court forms its Opinion or the content of the Opinion itself. Accordingly, the fact that the Opinion of the Court is accepted as binding provides no reason why the Request for an Opinion should not be complied with.[141]

---

[139] In the *Namibia* case, after all, the Court emphasized the absence of any need for such an inquiry.

[140] In the *Tunis-Morocco* and *Jaworzina* cases.

[141] ICJ Reports, 1956, p. 84. But cf. the separate opinions of Judges Winiarski and Klaestad and the dissenting opinion of Judge Cordova. The attribution of binding force to the opinion did not, in the view of the first two, affect the Court's competence. It did, however, provide further proof of the appellate nature of the request (Judge Winiarski, *ibid.*, p. 107) and lead to a particularly close assimilation to contentious cases (Judge

The Court's reasoning would appear broad enough to dispose of any objections which might arise on this score in the future.[142]

On the other hand, the Court experienced far more difficulty with another question raised in the same case—namely, the equality of the parties. And its pronouncement on that subject has not necessarily eliminated potential trouble in the future.

Equality between the Parties

While, theoretically, advisory proceedings give rise solely to a "lawyer-client" relationship, in fact, many other interests are usually implicated. Normally, these interests appertain to states and international organizations which, in accordance with the Court's Statute and Rules, are granted the opportunity to argue their cases before the Court in written and oral proceedings. Where, however, the interests of individuals are being adjudicated by means of advisory procedure, the problem of equality between the contending parties arises. The problem was presented in an acute form in the *UNESCO* case—a case in which the ICJ acted, in effect, as a court of appeal between UNESCO and certain of its staff members.[143] Moreover, given the

---

Klaestad, *ibid.*, p. 112). For Judge Cordova, on the other hand, this attribution of binding force to the opinion transformed the case from an advisory one to a contentious one, thereby affecting the Court's *competence*, and not only its discretion. *Ibid.*, pp. 161–64.

Most writers have agreed with the Court's view on this matter. See, e.g., Manley O. Hudson, "The Effect of Advisory Opinions of the World Court," *AJIL*, 42 (1948): 630–32; Edvard Hambro, "Some Observations on the Compulsory Jurisdiction of the International Court of Justice," *BYIL*, 25 (1948): 155–57; Hans Kelsen, *The Law of the United Nations* (London: Stevens, 1950), pp. 485–87; C. Wilfred Jenks, *The Prospects of International Adjudication* (London: Stevens, 1964), p. 141; D. Negulesco, "L'évolution de la procédure des avis consultatifs de la Cour Permanente de Justice Internationale," *RC*, 57 (1936-III): 84.

[142] But cf. Rosenne, *Law and Practice*, 2: 683.

[143] The *UN Administrative Tribunal* case did not present the problem to the same extent. Although, as in the *UNESCO* case, the finality of Administrative Tribunal judgments in favor of staff members was in question, there were important differences between the two cases. In the earlier case, the Court was merely to determine, in the abstract, preliminary questions regarding the binding nature of the UN Administrative Tribunal's judgments and the grounds, if any, upon which the General Assembly might refuse to give effect to the Tribunal's awards of compensation. The Court was not required, in any way, to retry the specific cases before the Tribunal. Moreover, upon receipt of the Court's opinion, the Assembly was theoretically free to make its own determination as to whether or not to honor the Tribunal's awards. In contrast, the *UNESCO* case required the Court to determine whether the ILO Tribunal was justified in confirming its jurisdiction in *specific* cases; and the Court's pronouncement was to be legally determinative of the issue. These proceedings bore a more immediate appellate character.

In the *UN Administrative Tribunal* case, the Court barred representatives of the staff members concerned from presenting written or oral statements, or from receiving copies of the written statements filed in the case. The Court assimilated the staff members

provisions of Article XII of the ILO Administrative Tribunal Statute and the amended Article 11 of the UN Administrative Tribunal Statute,[144] more—and perhaps more serious—difficulties may be anticipated in the future.

The problem was one with which the League and the PCIJ were not unfamiliar.

Thus, the *Danzig Legislative Decrees* case involved an intra-Danzig dispute in which the parties—the Danzig government, on the one hand, and the three minority parties that had brought the matter to the League Council's attention, on the other—were not equally represented before the Court.[145] The original petition of the minority parties was forwarded to the Court with the request. Subsequently, the Court invited the petitioners to submit an explanatory memorandum, and two additional documents were filed. In the oral proceedings, however, Danzig alone was represented. No invitation was extended to the petitioners, who, it was thought, were precluded by the Court's Rules from appearing.[146] This inequality between the parties was one of the grounds which led Judge Anzilotti to oppose the rendering of an opinion in the case.[147] The Court, however, made no mention of this point.

Perhaps in part because of this precedent, the League Council's resolution of 14 December 1939, which requested the Court's opinion in the matter of ex-officials of the Saar, contained elaborate provisions to ensure absolute equality between the Secretary-General and the officials. The exchange of memoranda (including, at the discretion of the officials, a second round of memoranda) was to precede submission of the request to the Court. Furthermore, the League renounced the exercise of the right to present written and oral statements (in accordance with Article 66 of the Statute), "if the same possibility cannot be given to the petitioners, since it does not wish to have greater opportunities of furnishing information to the Court than the petitioners themselves."[148]

---

concerned to "members of the public." See *UN Administrative Tribunal* case, ICJ Pleadings, 1954, pp. 389–90, 394, 397, 409–11. For criticism of the Court's stand as unduly conservative and restrictive, see Rosenne, *Law and Practice*, 2: 737–39.

[144] See Appendix 2.

[145] In a letter to the Court's Registrar, the League Secretariat's Political Section revealed that, before proposing recourse to the Court, the Council's Rapporteur had been "anxious to know whether the Court's procedure limited it to seeking information from the Government of the Free City and excluded it from also seeking information from the parties or persons who petitioned against the two decrees." To the Rapporteur's query, the Secretariat replied that "it understood the Court could seek information from any quarter it chose and could, therefore, call for evidence from the petitioners." On this understanding, the Rapporteur proceeded to recommend consultation of the Court. PCIJ, Ser. C, No. 77, pp. 248–49.

[146] *Ibid.*, Ser. E, No. 14, p. 161; and Ser. D, No. 2 (3rd Add.), pp. 701–2.

[147] *Ibid.*, Ser. A/B, No. 65, pp. 64–66.

[148] LNOJ, 1939, pp. 502–3. The request was never sent to the Court.

In contrast, the provisions made by UNESCO to ensure equality between itself and its staff members in the *UNESCO* case were much less elaborate. The organization's Legal Adviser merely envisaged transmission to the Court of written memoranda submitted by the staff members.[149] For its part, the Court went further. It decided to dispense with oral hearings and to accept supplementary written memoranda. Even so, serious opposition to the Court's complying with the request was voiced by certain members of the Court. These members questioned the propriety of utilizing the advisory procedure in an appellate case between an international organization and its officials.[150] They objected, too, to the necessity of altering the normal course of advisory proceedings. Moreover, they could not agree that the expedients adopted accomplished in fact their intended goal of removing all inequality between the parties.[151]

In the face of this opposition, the Court appeared somewhat hard-pressed to defend its decision to comply with the request.[152] It recognized, first, that Article XII of the ILO Administrative Tribunal Statute, under whose rubric the request for an opinion was made, constituted an attempt to circumvent Article 34(1) of the Statute; and, second, that the advisory proceedings involved a twofold inequality between UNESCO and its officials—one relating to the "origin" of the proceedings, the other to their "progress."

As to the first inequality (namely, the fact that, under Article XII, the legal remedy used was available exclusively to the UNESCO Executive Board), this was held not to constitute "an inequality before the Court." "It

---

[149] UNESCO, 42 EX/SR.25, 25 November 1955, pp. 269–71.

[150] This was the only ICJ advisory case in which a separate vote was taken on whether or not to comply with the request. The vote to comply was 9 to 4, with Judges Winiarski, Klaestad, Zafrulla Khan, and Cordova presumably voting against. The first three clearly indicated that their opposition was based on grounds of propriety. ICJ Reports, 1956, pp. 104–15. Judge Cordova, however, went much further. In his view, the Court was incompetent *ratione personae* and *ratione materiae* to play the role of court of appeal between an organization and its officials, since only *states* may appear in a contentious capacity, and since the Court could apply only international law, not "international administrative law." *Ibid.*, pp. 155–68.

[151] Among the factors deemed significant in this regard were: the availability of the legal remedy to only one party to the dispute; the dependence of one party on its opponent to forward its case to the Court; and the absence of oral hearings solely because of the need to remedy inequality between the parties. *Ibid.*, pp. 104–15. In addition, Judge Zafrulla Khan pointed up the dilemma with which the Court would have been faced had any state or organization availed itself of its right, under Article 66(2) of the Statute, to request an oral hearing. *Ibid.*, pp. 114–15.

Similar reservations were expressed in the General Assembly in the course of the drafting of the amended Article 11 of the UN Administrative Tribunal Statute. See UN Docs. A/2909, 10 June 1955; A/C.5/634, 14 October 1955; A/C.5/635, 17 October 1955; and A/3016, 5 November 1955. See also *UN Repertory*, Supp. No. 1, Art. 96, pars. 68–70.

[152] ICJ Reports, 1956, pp. 84–86.

is antecedent to the examination of the question by the Court. It does not affect the manner in which the Court undertakes that examination." Furthermore, the fact that the officials had been successful before the Tribunal made the inequality in this case "somewhat nominal." On "the facts of the present case," then (the Court studiously avoided expressing an opinion on the legal merits of Article XII as a whole), the inequality in the origin of the proceedings was not deemed crucial.

Potentially more serious was the inequality in "the actual procedure before the Court"; but this inequality was overcome to the Court's satisfaction by the expedients outlined above. Nevertheless, the Court was careful to emphasize the *ad hoc* nature of the procedure followed.

> The Court is not bound for the future by any consent which it gave or decisions which it made with regard to the procedure thus adopted. In the present case, the procedure which has been adopted has not given rise to any objection on the part of those concerned. . . . The principle of equality of the parties follows from the requirements of good administration of justice. These requirements have not been impaired in the present case by the circumstance that the written statement on behalf of the officials was submitted through Unesco. Finally, although no oral proceedings were held, the Court is satisfied that adequate information has been made available to it.

The Court's concluding comments on the matter of complying with the request are, however, of potentially wider import.

> In view of this there would appear to be no compelling reason why the Court should not lend its assistance in the solution of a problem confronting a specialized agency of the United Nations authorized to ask for an Advisory Opinion of the Court. Notwithstanding the permissive character of Article 65 of the Statute . . . only compelling reasons could cause the Court to adopt in this matter a negative attitude which would imperil the working of the régime established . . . for the judicial protection of officials. Any seeming or nominal absence of equality ought not to be allowed to obscure or to defeat that primary object.

What, then, of future cases which might come before the Court under the framework of Article XII of the ILO Administrative Tribunal Statute or Article 11 of the amended UN Administrative Tribunal Statute?[153] The

---

[153] The latter article contains provisions for enhancing the equality of staff members. Thus, the initiative for activating the review procedure appertains to the staff member as well; and the transmission of the staff member's views to the Court is mandatory. States are also recommended not to make oral statements. (Cf., however, the observations of Judge Zafrulla Khan in the *UNESCO* case; and the views of the UN Staff Council, UN Doc. A/C.5/634, 14 October 1955.)

Court's reasoning in the *UNESCO* case points to the following conclusions. Whether or not the Court would agree to comply with a request would depend, first, on its ability to adopt appropriate procedures for overcoming the more serious manifestations of inequality;[154] second, on the absence of any objection to the procedure adopted on the part of the individuals concerned; and, finally, on the Court's satisfaction that it was being furnished with adequate information. Given the Court's felt duty to cooperate with UN organs and agencies, barring compelling countervailing reasons, the Court might be expected to make every attempt to devise appropriate procedures and to overlook any residual inequality of a "nominal" sort.

THE COURT'S HANDLING OF REQUESTS

The amount of guidance which the requesting organ actually derives from the Court's opinion is the end product of a number of factors, among the most important of which are the drafting of the request, the Court's interpretation of the request, and the reasoning upon which the Court's reply is based.

As for the drafting of the request, this is quite obviously the responsibility of the requesting organ, and, to judge from the number of times both Courts have had to reinterpret questions before them,[155] it is a responsibility which in

---

In one respect, however, Article 11 may raise the problem of equality in a more acute form, because it includes, as an additional ground for appealing to the Court, the Tribunal's error on a question of law relating to the Charter. In other words, the Court may be asked to review the *merits* of Tribunal judgments and not merely to examine its *jurisdiction*. See, on this point, Leo Gross, "Participation of Individuals in Advisory Proceedings before the International Court of Justice," *AJIL*, 52 (1958): 16–40. In Gross's opinion, the *UNESCO* case might have been viewed as a strictly intraorganizational dispute involving the respective spheres of two organs' competence; but a future case involving the additional ground contained in Article 11 could not possibly be viewed in this manner.

Judge Cordova, in his dissenting opinion in the *UNESCO* case, concluded that the Court would be incompetent to hear cases under either of the two articles. *Ibid.*, pp. 155–68. None of the other judges broached the question of Article 11.

In this connection, it might be noted that, in adopting Article 11, the Assembly fully expected that the Court itself would be the "guardian of due process," and that, if the Court considered one of the parties to be at a disadvantage, it would refuse to give an opinion. UN Doc. A/3016, 5 November 1955, par. 19; GAOR (X), 5th Ctte., 496th Mtg., 19 October 1955, p. 53.

[154] However, should the Court continue to dispense with hearings in cases of this kind, "it might come very close to erecting into a principle what cannot but appear to be a truncated procedure." Gross, "Participation of Individuals," p. 31. Cf. the views of Jenks to the effect that the elimination of oral proceedings may not be a *sine qua non* for equality between the parties. *Op. cit.*, pp. 141–44.

[155] In the following cases the Court felt constrained either to define or to reinterpret the question posed: *ILO and Agricultural Production* (PCIJ, Ser. B, Nos. 2 and 3, p. 59); *Tunis-Morocco* (*ibid.*, No. 4, pp. 21–22); *Eastern Carelia* (*ibid.*, No. 5, pp. 24–27); *ILO and the Personal Work of the Employer* (*ibid.*, No. 13, pp. 12–14); *Jurisdiction of the*

neither period has been too well fulfilled. Many of the UN requests, especially, have borne the marks of hasty drafting and of imprecision. Resolution 684 (VII), designed to remedy this defect, has remained totally unused, though it has frequently been invoked.[156]

Yet, it would be a mistake to place all the blame for the Court's failure to render hoped-for guidance on the doorstep of the requesting organ. In the first place, the Court's definition of a question frequently appears to be related to the Court's own desire to limit the scope of the request, so as to avoid passing upon certain issues. Thus, if in the *Competence* case the Court excluded from the scope of the request the one question deemed by the Assembly to be most crucial (namely, whether the veto was applicable to recommendations for admission in the Security Council), defective drafting may have been only partly responsible.[157] The Court may have been anxious to avoid involving itself in such a thorny issue as the Security Council's voting procedure—particularly since the request emanated from the Assembly, not from the Council.[158] And, in the *UN Administrative Tribunal* case, the limita-

---

Danzig Courts (ibid., No. 15, pp. 13–15); *Greco-Turkish Agreement (ibid.*, No. 16, pp. 14–16); *Danzig and the ILO (ibid.*, No. 18, pp. 9–10); *Polish War Vessels in Danzig (ibid.*, Ser. A/B, No. 43, p. 140); *Polish Nationals in Danzig (ibid.*, No. 44, pp. 19–20); *Admission* (ICJ Reports, 1948, pp. 60–61); *Reparation (ibid.*, 1949, p. 177); *Competence (ibid.*, 1950, p. 7); *Peace Treaties (ibid.*, pp. 75–76); *UN Administrative Tribunal (ibid.*, 1954, pp. 50–51); *South West Africa (Voting) (ibid.*, 1955, p. 72); *South West Africa (Committee) (ibid.*, 1956, pp. 25–26); *IMCO (ibid.*, 1960, pp. 152–53); *Expenses (ibid.*, 1962, pp. 156–58). It will be observed that the majority of UN requests have been redefined or reinterpreted. However, in some of the cases cited above (e.g., the *Reparation* case), the Court's definition of the question involved merely a clarification of the phraseology employed, not a modification in the meaning of the question posed.

[156] See, e.g., in respect of the request in the *South West Africa (Voting)* case, GAOR (IX), 4th Ctte., 400th Mtg., 5 October 1954, p. 21; 401st Mtg., 6 October 1954, pp. 24–26; Plenary, 494th Mtg., 11 October 1954, p. 247; and 501st Mtg., 23 November 1954, p. 323. In respect of the *Expenses* request, see *ibid.* (XVI), 5th Ctte., 897th Mtg., 8 December 1961, pp. 289–91; 899th Mtg., 11 December 1961, pp. 300–301; and Plenary, 1086th Mtg., 20 December 1961, p. 1151.

Drafting assistance by the Sixth Committee does not, of course, guarantee that the request will not require redefinition by the Court, as witness the fate of the Sixth Committee's own request in the *Reparation* case. The history of the *UNESCO* request is also noteworthy in this connection. For, despite the professional drafting of the request by the UNESCO Secretariat, the Court refused to answer two of the questions posed, on the grounds that they fell outside the framework of Article XII of the ILO Administrative Tribunal's Statute. ICJ Reports, 1956, pp. 98–100. Interestingly enough, similar objections to the inclusion of the two questions had been voiced earlier in the UNESCO Executive Board. However, in defense of the Secretariat's draft, it had been argued that the "client" ought to accept his "lawyer's" formulation. UNESCO, 42 EX/SR.25, 25 November 1955, pp. 262–68.

[157] Recommendations that would have resulted in the adoption of more specific questions related to the veto were not heeded by the Assembly. See Chapter III.

[158] As noted above (Chapter III), the Court might have refused to comply with a request in which the question of the veto had been stated unequivocally. It might

tion read into the question by the Court probably was not warranted by the terms of the request.[159]

Moreover, it is by no means clear the the Court must consider itself shackled by defective drafting. In the words of Judge Lauterpacht:

> The previous practice of the Court supplies authority for the proposition that the Court enjoys considerable latitude in construing the question put to it or in formulating its answer in such a manner as to make its advisory function effective and useful. . . .
>
> Undoubtedly it is desirable that the request for an Advisory Opinion should not, through excess of brevity, make it necessary for the Court to go outside the question as formulated. . . . However, the absence of the requisite degree of precision or elaboration in the wording of the request does not absolve the Court of the duty to give an effective and accurate answer in conformity with the true purpose of its advisory function.[160]

On several occasions, the PCIJ went beyond the terms of the question as posed, in order to discover, and provide an answer for, the crucial issues in dispute.[161] Thus, in the *Jaworzina* case, although the terms of the request were limited to the frontier in the Spisz region, the Court felt obliged to express an opinion on the Polish case and to consider the question of other parts of the frontier as well.[162] And, in the *Greco-Turkish Agreement* case,

---

conceivably have deemed the Assembly incompetent to request an opinion regarding the voting procedure of a coordinate organ.

The Court's interpretation of the question conformed with that advocated by the United States and conflicted with that of Argentina, the original sponsor of the draft resolution to request the Court's opinion in the matter. *Competence* case, ICJ Pleadings, 1950, pp. 110, 123-48. Cf. the dissenting opinion of Judge Azevedo, who criticized the Court for omitting "the most important part of the question" submitted to it. ICJ Reports, 1950, pp. 22 ff.

[159] The Court reinterpreted the question to ask "whether the General Assembly is legally entitled to refuse to give effect to an award of compensation made by the Administrative Tribunal, properly constituted *and acting within the limits of its statutory competence*" (italics added). The Court thereby explained away the words "on any grounds" in the Assembly's question. ICJ Reports, 1954, pp. 50-51. (One of the United States' arguments, however, had been that the Tribunal had not, in fact, acted within the limits of its competence.) As noted by Verzijl, "it may be doubted whether the root of the difficulty lay in a defective drafting of the request or in the general tendency of the Court to confine its examination of a case within the narrowest possible limits." *World Court*, 2: 180. The Court appears subsequently to have reconsidered, however briefly, the validity of its own interpretation. ICJ Reports, 1954, p. 55.

[160] ICJ Reports, 1956, pp. 37-38.

[161] But cf. Judge Anzilotti's understanding of the Court's task in the case of *Railway Traffic between Lithuania and Poland* with that of the Court, PCIJ, Ser. A/B, No. 42, pp. 108-23. Implicitly, Judge Anzilotti criticized the Court for adhering too strictly to the terms of the request and failing, thereby, to come to grips with the essential problem before the League Council.

[162] *Ibid.*, Ser. B, No. 8, p. 50.

while holding that the request did not state exactly the question upon which the opinion was being sought, the Court itself undertook to formulate an "exact statement of the question."[163] Again, the Court's reinterpretation of the request in the case of *Danzig and the ILO* apparently coincided with the ILO Governing Body's desires.[164] In line with its tendency to view requests in the abstract, however, the ICJ has been far more restrained in going beyond the terms of the questions as drafted.[165]

No less important than the Court's interpretation of the question is the Court's formulation of the answer. Failure to elaborate an answer adequately

---

[163] *Ibid.*, No. 16, p. 14. The Court warned, however, that it might not always be possible to undertake such a reformulation. Neither Court, it should be noted, ever refused to comply with a request on the grounds that it did not contain an "exact statement of the question," as required by Article 65 of the Statute (and prior to 1936, by Article 72[2] of the Rules). However, this course was urged upon the Court in the *Expenses* case. See the dissenting opinion of Judge Basdevant, ICJ Reports, 1962, pp. 235–38.

[164] The ILO did not wish to have the larger question of the relationship between League and ILO membership prejudged by a Court opinion. PCIJ, Ser. C, No. 18-II, pp. 145–46, 193. While acknowledging that ILO membership may be dependent on membership in the League, the Court preferred to leave this question to one side and to concentrate, instead, on the compatibility of Danzig's status with the rights and duties of ILO membership. *Ibid.*, Ser. B, No. 18, pp. 9–10. This approach was criticized by Judge Anzilotti, who thought that the Court should have refused to give an opinion on the basis of "a hypothesis which is legally unsound." *Ibid.*, pp. 18 ff. As noted by Verzijl, the Court "consciously narrowed its field of vision by putting on exactly the same juridical blinkers as the League of Nations Council itself." *World Court*, 1: 208–9.

[165] Moreover, the ICJ has not paid much attention to the preambles of the resolutions embodying the requests for the purpose of discovering the Assembly's true intentions. When a preamble appeared to conflict with the Court's interpretation of a question, it was usually explained away. Thus, in the *Admission* case, as noted above, a clause in the preamble which referred to "the exchange of views which had taken place" in the Security Council with respect to the admission of particular states was "not understood as an invitation to the Court to say whether the views thus referred to are well founded or otherwise." The "abstract form" in which the question was stated was said to preclude such an interpretation. ICJ Reports, 1948, pp. 60–61. In the preamble to the request in the *Expenses* case, the Assembly recognized its need "for authoritative legal guidance as to obligations of Member States under the Charter of the United Nations in the matter of financing the United Nations operations in the Congo and the Middle East." Nevertheless, in its interpretation of the question, the Court confined its task to a determination of whether the expenditures at issue could be identified as "expenses of the Organization," and excluded the necessity of passing on two further questions related to the financial obligations of member states—namely, the matter of apportionment by the Assembly and the meaning of the phrase—"shall be borne by the Members." The Court understood the preamble to be merely indicative of the Assembly's expectation (an expectation apparently concurred in by the Court) that the necessary guidance in relation to members' obligations would follow from the Court's opinion on the primary question contained in the request. *Ibid.*, 1962, pp. 157–58. (The Court's intention to define the terms of the request narrowly was reflected in the deliberate change of the title of the case from "Financial Obligations of Members of the United Nations" to "Certain Expenses of the United Nations." *Ibid.*, p. 198.) However, cf. the views of

or summariness in the statement of reasons may deprive the opinion of its meaningfulness or usefulness. Such PCIJ pronouncements as those in the *Greco-Bulgarian Communities* and *Danzig and the ILO* cases have been criticized on these grounds.[166] And the ICJ's reply to one of the more vexing questions posed in the *Reparation* case—namely, how UN action may be reconciled with the claims of the victim's national state—was more in the nature of a *pia vota* than a guide to action.[167] The *South West Africa (Voting)* opinion was wanting in a different respect. The Court, by its excessively narrow and formalistic reasoning, failed to address itself to the crux of UN-South African differences over the question of voting procedure—differences which were in turn related to the more basic issue of organizational succession.[168] Subsequently, however, in the *South West Africa (Committee)* case,[169] and, more particularly, in the *Expenses* case, the Court adopted what has been aptly described as "a less timorous attitude to the fundamental problems of the Organization of which it is the principal judicial organ."[170] The *Namibia* case represented a slight—but, in the last analysis, insignificant—reversion to a more "timorous" stance.

Judge Fitzmaurice to the effect that the Court construed the question too narrowly; that an "expenditure" might be an "expense" without creating an obligation for member states to contribute; and that, failing clarification of the issue of financial obligation, the identification of the expenditures in question as "expenses of the Organization" was pointless. *Ibid.*

On occasion, the ICJ has invoked preambular material in support of a particular interpretation, as, e.g., in the *Peace Treaties* case (ICJ Reports, 1950, p. 76) and in the *UN Administrative Tribunal* case (*ibid.*, 1954, p. 50). Cf. the *Namibia* case (*ibid.*, 1971, p. 24).

In the Vienna Convention on the Law of Treaties, the preamble is deemed part of the text of a treaty for purposes of interpretation (Article 31). But whether a parallel can be drawn in this respect from the interpretation of treaties to the interpretation of UN resolutions is, of course, questionable.

[166] See, e.g., Lauterpacht, *International Court*, p. 43; and Verzijl, *World Court*, 1: 202 ff. Cf. Judge Huber's view of the judicial task in the *Danzig and the ILO* case, PCIJ, Ser. B, No. 18, pp. 28 ff.

[167] See Verzijl, *World Court*, 2: 44. The Court stated that "there is no rule of law which assigns priority to the one or to the other, or which compels either the State or the Organization to refrain from bringing an international claim." Nevertheless, the Court saw "no reason why the parties concerned should not find solutions inspired by goodwill and common sense." Although the bases of the two claims are different, "that does not mean that the defendant State can be compelled to pay the reparation due . . . twice over." The Court had "no doubt that in due course a practice will be developed." ICJ Reports, 1949, pp. 185–86.

[168] See, e.g., the discussions of Verzijl, *World Court*, 2: 218–29; Rosenne, *Law and Practice*, 2: 722–24; and Shabtai Rosenne, "Sir Hersch Lauterpacht's Concept of the Task of the International Judge," *AJIL*, 55 (1961): 825–62 *passim.*

[169] But cf., even in this case, the approaches of the Court, on the one hand, and Judge Lauterpacht, on the other.

[170] Rosenne, "The Court and the Judicial Process," p. 524.

In this connection, it is relevant to note that in both the *Expenses* and *Namibia* cases, the issue of "the scope of the question" entailed the problem of reconciling judicial independence, on the one hand, with the absence of any power of judicial review of the acts of UN political organs, on the other. In both cases, the pre-request history (which, in each instance, involved rejection of a French amendment which would have unequivocally permitted judicial review) seemed to point to a desire to restrict the Court's freedom to pass on the validity of the underlying resolutions in question.[171] The Court in each instance opted for freedom to consider all relevant legal data. In the *Expenses* case, it did so boldly; in the *Namibia* case, hesitatingly.

In the *Expenses* case, several governments and members of the Court argued that the Court ought not (as a matter of propriety), or need not, examine the validity of the resolutions authorizing UNEF and ONUC expenditures.[172] But the Court was unwilling to accept any such restriction and declared:

> The rejection of the French amendment does not constitute a directive to the Court to exclude from its consideration the question whether certain expenditures were "decided on in conformity with the Charter", if the Court finds such consideration appropriate. It is not to be assumed that the General Assembly would thus seek to fetter or hamper the Court in the discharge of its judicial functions; the Court must have full liberty to consider all relevant data available to it in forming an opinion on a question posed to it for an advisory opinion. Nor can the Court agree that the rejection of the French amendment has any bearing upon the question whether the General Assembly sought to preclude the Court from interpreting Article 17 in the light of other articles of the Charter. . . . If any deduction is to be made from the debates on this point, the opposite conclusion would be drawn from the clear statements of sponsoring delegations that they took it for granted the Court would consider the Charter as a whole.[173]

The Court then proceeded to examine the validity of the underlying resolutions, and, in doing so, it interpreted Charter provisions other than Article 17 as well.

---

[171] For the pre-request histories of these cases, see Chapter III, pp. 140–48 and 148–57.

[172] See, e.g., the Written Statements of the Netherlands and the United States, *Expenses* case, ICJ Pleadings, 1962, pp. 167–70, 203–4; and the Oral Statements of the United Kingdom, Norway, Australia, Ireland, and the United States, *ibid.*, pp. 336, 352, 384, 387–89, 416. Cf. the declaration of Judge Spiropoulos, ICJ Reports, 1962, pp. 180–81, and the separate opinions of Judges Spender and Morelli, *ibid.*, pp. 182 ff., 216 ff.

[173] ICJ Reports, 1962, p. 157.

The issue of "the scope of the question" was more serious in the *Namibia* case, and this probably accounted for the Court's more cautious stance. The idea of calling into question the validity of the resolution terminating South Africa's mandate was clearly anathema to many states in the Security Council; and it was on the understanding that that resolution was irrevocable, and unreviewable by the Court, that these states had consented to the request. Taken as a whole, the pre-request history pointed to an expectation that the Court would, and could, trace the legal consequences of resolutions whose validity it would assume rather than examine.[174] Nevertheless, many states participating in the pleadings discussed the validity of mandate revocation (some, even while protesting that it was not necessary or proper to do so);[175] and South Africa argued forcefully against assuming any intention by the Security Council to fetter the Court in the exercise of its judicial function.[176] For its part, the Court examined the basic resolution (2145) terminating the mandate, but it did so in an apologetic spirit. "Undoubtedly," the Court said, it "does not possess powers of judicial review or appeal in respect of the decisions taken by the United Nations organs concerned." Furthermore, "the question of the validity or conformity with the Charter of General Assembly resolution 2145 (XXI) or of related Security Council resolutions does not form the subject of the request for advisory opinion." "However," the Court continued, "in the exercise of its judicial function and since objections have been advanced the Court, in the course of its reasoning, will consider these objections before determining any legal consequences arising from those resolutions."[177]

Some of the judges would have preferred a far more emphatic statement by the Court on the matter.[178] In their view, the judicial function and the

---

[174]See, e.g., the Written Statements of the Secretary-General (*Namibia* case, ICJ Pleadings, 1971, 1: 75–77) and the United States (*ibid.*, pp. 852–54).

[175] See, e.g., the Written Statements of Finland (*ibid.*, pp. 370–72) and India (*ibid.*, pp. 830–42); and cf. the separate opinion of Judge Padilla Nervo, ICJ Reports, 1971, pp. 101 ff. (It may be noted that Finland, the sponsor of the requesting resolution was equally inconsistent in the pre-request stage. See Chapter III, p. 151.) In the course of the oral proceedings, the representative of the Secretary-General retreated from his earlier stance, in which he had rigidly insisted on attributing a narrow scope to the question. See *Namibia* case, ICJ Pleadings, 1971, Verbatim Record, C.R. 71/1, 8 February 1971, p. 19; and C.R. 71/18, 8 March 1971, p. 21.

[176]*Namibia* case, ICJ Pleadings, 1971, Verbatim Record, C.R. 71/7, 19 February 1971, pp. 14 ff.; and C.R. 71/15, 3 March 1971, p. 14. Furthermore, South Africa contended, had the Security Council indeed attempted to fetter the Court, the Court would have had to ignore the attempt or decline to give the opinion. *Ibid.*, C.R. 71/7, 19 February 1971, p. 33.

[177]ICJ Reports, 1971, p. 45.

[178] See the separate opinions of Judges Petrén, *ibid.*, pp. 129 and 131; Onyeama, *ibid.*, pp. 141–45; and Dillard, *ibid.*, pp. 151–52. See also the dissenting opinions of

principle of judicial independence were clearly incompatible with the acceptance of legal blinkers imposed by the requesting organ. The Court could not risk giving an opinion based on a false premise. And it could not assume (unless the contrary evidence were unequivocal)[179] that there was any intention on the part of the Security Council to fetter the Court so drastically in its judicial task. However, had such an intention been proven, the Court would have been entitled to refuse to give an opinion.[180]

CONCLUSIONS

In the manner in which the two Courts have viewed the advisory function, there are significant elements of both continuity and change.

Neither Court has felt itself to be under an absolute obligation to render opinions requested of it. Rather, each has underscored, in varying ways, its discretion as to whether, and in what manner, to comply with requests. The incompetence of the requesting organ was acknowledged by both to be grounds for refusing an opinion. And, for both Courts, lack of consent on the part of an interested state might, under suitable circumstances, warrant denial of the advice sought. Again, the two Courts showed some similarity in their attitudes[181] toward such matters as: the definition of "legal" questions (questions of treaty interpretation were deemed by both to be ipso facto legal); the possibility of answering "abstract" questions; the desirability of avoiding an extensive independent judicial inquiry into controverted facts; the irrelevance to the Court of the binding nature of the opinion; the right to invoke the advisory procedure even where other dispute-settlement procedures were provided for by treaty; the effect of "nominal" inequality between the parties on the Court's right to render an opinion; and the Court's right to restate and reinterpret the request.

The elements of change are to be found not in any abrupt reversals of previous practice but rather in subtle shifts of emphasis. Based on its new

---

Judges Fitzmaurice, *ibid.*, pp. 301–4; and Gros, *ibid.*, p. 331. But cf. the separate opinion of Judge de Castro, *ibid.*, pp. 180–82.

[179] For the opposite view—namely, that the burden of proof falls on those affirming, not on those negating, an intention to permit judicial review—see the Oral Statement of Pakistan, *Namibia* case, ICJ Pleadings, 1971, Verbatim Record, C.R. 71/5, 15 February 1971, pp. 32–36.

[180] This conclusion emerges most clearly from the separate opinion of Judge Onyeama, ICJ Reports, 1971, pp. 144–45; and the dissenting opinion of Judge Fitzmaurice, *ibid.*, p. 303. The latter considered that the Court's right to refuse to render an opinion entailed, *a fortiori*, the right to undertake a preliminary examination of the assumptions underlying the request.

[181] The attitude of the PCIJ is often derived more by implication than from express pronouncements.

organic relationship with the world organization, the ICJ has enunciated a new doctrine regarding its duty to cooperate with UN organs and agencies, barring compelling countervailing reasons. Hand in hand with this doctrine, and largely on the basis of it, has come a greater willingness to view a request for an opinion as a purely "client-lawyer" consultation, and to ignore or isolate any "quasicontentious" aspects which might be involved. Hence, the ICJ has tended to view questions in the "abstract." Hence, too, the burden of proof was shifted to those who would deny the "client" sufficient claim or right to its "lawyer's" advice—whether because of, e.g., lack of consent, the "political" nature of the question, the "factual" issues involved, or the availability of a contentious procedure embodied in a treaty.

The effect of this new emphasis on the "client-lawyer" nature of a request for an opinion has been to re-erect, to a large extent, the "wall" between the contentious and advisory functions which, in the era of the PCIJ, was almost, if not entirely, crumbling.[182] True, the building of this "wall" did not originate with the Court. The kinds of questions submitted to the ICJ have been more "organizational"—and hence more "client-lawyer" in nature—than those in the League period. But the Court's attitude has nevertheless had much to do with reinforcing the "wall" between the two functions.

The implications of the Court's new attitude for the requesting organs are particularly significant. If, for the Court, objections based on the "political" nature of the request or on the absence of consent to the request on the part of an interested state are not crucial, the same should not be true for the requesting organs. More than ever, it is their responsibility to shield the Court from inappropriate requests—i.e., requests which are likely neither to resolve the root problems out of which they emerged nor to enhance the Court's prestige. In this respect, past experience with the reception of advisory opinions can provide perhaps the best guide for future action.

---

[182] The building of such a "wall" was precisely what Judge Azevedo so ardently advocated. See ICJ Reports, 1950, p. 88.

For a most provocative and illuminating analysis of the "wall" between the ICJ's advisory and contentious functions, see Gross, "The International Court of Justice and the United Nations," *passim*. It is Gross's contention that the new "organic connection" between the Court and the world organization has resulted in a kind of schizophrenic Court, which acts as an "organ of international law" in its contentious capacity and as an "organ of United Nations law" in its advisory capacity.

VI
THE RECEPTION OF
ADVISORY OPINIONS

Once the advisory opinion is rendered, it is returned to the political arena whence it was solicited, and, primarily in this arena, its ultimate fate is determined. But, in a larger sense, the opinion's fate—in most instances, at least—is predetermined by the conditions existing in the pre-request stage, and the post-opinion events serve merely to seal and confirm that fate. One would expect, therefore, that the differences between the League and UN eras, so marked in the pre-request phase,[1] would be reflected as well in the action taken on the opinions rendered. This expectation is, in fact, fulfilled. At the same time, one would expect to find significant points of identity between the two eras; and this expectation, too, is realized.

To discover what these points of similarity and difference are, it is useful to consider, more particularly, such matters as the following: the reception accorded the opinion by the organ from which the request emanated; the discussions, if any, which preceded that reception; the attitude of the states upon whom implementation of the opinion in fact depended; the predictability of those states' responses on the basis of their pre-request stances; and the effectiveness of the opinion in solving the root problem to which it related.

Apart from highlighting intereral similarities and differences, a study of the reception of advisory opinions by organs and states should permit us to draw certain conclusions as to the binding force of advisory opinions in practice.

THE LEAGUE PERIOD

How were the Court's opinions treated by the organs which solicited them?[2]

[1] See Chapter III.

[2] On the reception of advisory opinions in the League period, see Hudson, *Permanent Court*, pp. 513–22; Leland M. Goodrich, "The Nature of the Advisory Opinions of the Permanent Court of International Justice," *AJIL*, 32 (1938): 747–53.

Formally, of course, all requests emanated from the League Council. But, in those cases in which the Council acted merely as a transmission belt for other international bodies which had been denied direct access to the Court,[3] the Council, upon receipt of the Court's opinion, again served merely as a transmission belt—this time in the reverse direction.[4] In these cases, then, it is the action of the other international bodies concerned that has to be considered.

Furthermore, several of the opinions solicited by the Council for its own use did not call for any Council action. Among these were Nos. 4,[5] 15,[6] 20,[7] 21,[8] and 24.[9]

The Court's refusal to render an opinion in the *Eastern Carelia* case was in a category of its own. Strictly speaking, the reply did not call for any Council action. But, since the Court had, in effect, denied the Council's competence

---

[3] In Nos. 1, 13, 18, and 25, the Council transmitted requests on behalf of the ILO; in Nos. 10 and 16, on behalf of the Greco-Turkish Mixed Commission; and, in No. 17, on behalf of the Greco-Bulgarian Mixed Commission. In No. 14, the Council was formally acting on behalf of the League's Transit Committee, but that Committee was merely a transmission belt between the four governments concerned and the Council. Nos. 2 and 3 were exceptional, in that they originated with the Council, although they related to ILO affairs. In the post-opinion phase, however, they were, like the more "regular" ILO opinions, immediately forwarded to the Director of the ILO.

[4] At times, the Council "took note" of the opinion thus forwarded. Additionally, in No. 10, the Council expressed its conviction "that the Mixed Commission would attribute to this Opinion the same high value and authority which the Council always gave to the opinions of the Permanent Court of International Justice." LNOJ, 1925, pp. 441–42.

[5] This case bore the character of an "advisory arbitration" on a preliminary point. The Council's role throughout was strictly secondary. The two governments had agreed that, if the British view were upheld by the Court, the merits of the dispute would be submitted either to arbitration or to judicial settlement. Immediately following delivery of the Court's opinion, the French agent asked the Court to take note of his government's proposal that the merits of the dispute now be submitted to the Court for adjudication. Subsequently, the dispute was settled by an exchange of notes between the two governments. PCIJ, Ser. E, No. 1, pp. 198–99. The Council took no action whatever on the opinion.

[6] Shortly before delivery of the Court's opinion, Poland and Danzig agreed to accept that opinion in advance and to request the Council not to place the question involved on its agenda. (The agreement was formalized after the Court's opinion was rendered.) Although the Council did place the item on its agenda, it confined itself to taking note of the opinion and of the Polish-Danzig Agreement. LNOJ, 1928, p. 433.

[7] Two days prior to delivery of the opinion, Austria and Germany announced their intention not to pursue the Customs Union project. The Council, therefore, merely took note of the opinion and expressed its thanks to the Court. *Ibid.*, 1931, pp. 2185–90, 2069–70.

[8] Since the Court had upheld Lithuania's contention that it was under no obligation to open for traffic the railway sector in question, the Council contented itself with merely taking note of the opinion. *Ibid.*, 1932, pp. 480–81. Both governments concurred in this decision.

[9] In view of Greece and Bulgaria's conclusion of the Athens Agreement of 11 November 1931 regarding execution of the Caphandaris-Molloff Agreement, the Council simply

to address the request to the Court,[10] the Council felt put upon to justify its own actions. Under the terms of the original draft resolution proposed by M. Salandra, Council Rapporteur on the question, the Council would have noted the Court's opinion, thanked the Court for "the care it has taken in the consideration of this matter," and entered the following reservation of its powers:

> Whilst noting the view of the Court that an advisory opinion concerning this question would have involved an investigation into facts for which certain conditions were lacking, the Council feels sure that the opinion expressed by the Court in connection with the procedure described in Article 17 of the Covenant cannot exclude the possibility of resort by the Council to any action, including a request for an advisory opinion from the Court, on a matter in which a State non-member of the League and unwilling to give information is involved, if the circumstances should make such action necessary to enable the Council to fulfill its functions under the Covenant of the League in the interests of peace.[11]

Some members of the Council, however, while agreeing with the substantive views expressed in the reservation, wished to see the reservation transferred from the resolution to the body of the report, in order, as they explained, to avoid the "unfortunate" impression that the Council "was trying to remonstrate with the Court."[12] This transfer was readily acquiesced in by the Rapporteur and the Council.[13] Thus, despite obvious annoyance at the Court's action, the Council eschewed a frontal challenge to the authoritativeness of the Court's pronouncement.[14]

In all other cases, the Council's recommendations were invariably based on full acceptance of the Court's opinion—regardless of whether or not the opinion was formally "adopted."[15]

---

took note of the Court's opinion and congratulated the two governments on conclusion of the Athens Agreement. *Ibid.*, pp. 1185-87.

[10] See Chapter V, pp. 282-83.

[11] LNOJ, 1923, p. 1336. The Court's reply had been strongly criticized by Finland in a memorandum submitted to the Council. *Ibid.*, pp. 1497-1501.

[12] See the remarks of Lord Robert Cecil and M. Branting, *ibid.*, pp. 1336-37.

[13] M. Salandra affirmed that he had never intended "to contradict the findings of the Court." *Ibid.*, p. 1337.

[14] Subsequently, the "Eastern Carelia principle" met with rather widespread approval. See, e.g., the citation of the principle by a committee of jurists charged with advising the League Council as to whether it might entertain a request by the Greco-Turkish Mixed Commission to solicit the Court's advice. *Ibid.*, 1928, pp. 403-4.

[15] In several cases the Council "adopted" the opinion (e.g., in Nos. 7, 8, 11, 12, 22, and 27). However, it is not clear in all instances what the effect of such "adoption" was. See, on this point, Hudson, *Permanent Court*, p. 515, n. 96.

Thus, in No. 6, the Council noted the Court's opinion and invited Poland to inform the Council of the measures it proposed to take in order to settle the question of the German colonists.[16] Later, dissatisfied with Poland's proposals, the Council requested the submission of new proposals, while affirming its view that "the question of the German Settlers in Poland can only be settled on the basis of the Advisory Opinion" of the Court, "with which the Council is in agreement."[17] With the assistance of a Council committee and a committee-appointed expert, a negotiated settlement which met with Council approval was finally concluded.[18]

The Council's action in the companion case to No. 6—the *Acquisition of Polish Nationality* case—was no less unequivocal. It "adopted" the Court's opinion, while offering its good offices in the practical application of the Polish nationality clauses and, if necessary, in the Polish-German negotiations on the subject.[19] After rather tortuous negotiations and the rendering of an arbitral award, a Polish-German convention was concluded which embodied, with some qualifications, the Court's interpretation of Article 4 of the Polish Minorities Treaty.[20]

Again, the Council's recommendations in the other two "minorities" cases—Nos. 19 and 26—were firmly grounded in the Court's pronouncements.[21]

---

[16]LNOJ, 1923, p. 1489. The Court had held that the question was within the Council's competence, and that Poland's position "was not in conformity with its international obligations."

For a thorough discussion of the post-request history of this case, see Julius Stone, *International Guarantees of Minority Rights* (London: Oxford University Press, 1932), pp. 212–22, 227–28.

[17]LNOJ, 1924, p. 359.

[18]By the time the settlement was reached, Poland had accomplished its primary goal of expelling the majority of the colonists from the land, in defiance of the judicially enunciated legal position. Stone, *op. cit.*, p. 221. The final settlement did not provide full compensation for the settlers illegally expelled from their properties. Nevertheless, as noted by Goodrich, "it was based on full acceptance on points of law of the opinion of the Court." *Op. cit.*, p. 748, n. 53.

[19]LNOJ, 1923, pp. 1333–35, 1489–90. The Polish representative abstained in the vote.

In the light of Article 12 of the Polish Minorities Treaty, "adoption" of the opinion in this instance may have had more than formal significance. Hudson, *Permanent Court*, p. 515, n. 96. Cf. Stone, *op. cit.*, p. 214, and the remarks of Lord Cecil in LNOJ, 1923, p. 1333.

[20]LNOJ, 1924, pp. 351, 405–6, 543, 722–25, 1309; LNTS, 32: 337.

[21]In No. 19, the Council considered that the sixty children to whom the Court's opinion related "should be transferred immediately to the minority schools to which their admission had been requested." These conclusions were concurred in by the Polish representative, who, at a subsequent meeting, informed the Council that the Polish government had complied with the opinion and had already notified the parents of the children of their admission to the minority schools. LNOJ, 1931, pp. 1151, 2263.

The two opinions which related to the powers of the Conference of Ambassadors were dealt with as follows. In No. 8, the Court's opinion was adopted by the Council and "accepted in its entirety" by Poland and Czechoslovakia.[22] The Council further considered that previous proposals submitted by the Delimitation Commission did not accord with a 1920 Conference of Ambassadors decision—a decision declared by the Court to be definitive—and the Commission was therefore invited to submit "fresh proposals in conformity with the opinion of the Court." These "fresh proposals" were later approved by the Council, and, shortly thereafter, the disputed frontier was finally settled.[23] In No. 9, the Council considered that the Court's opinion "gives the answer" to the question posed by the Conference of Ambassadors, and it therefore decided to communicate the opinion to that body for its use.[24] A frontier line was subsequently fixed by the Conference in accordance with the Court's opinion.[25]

The Court's pronouncements in respect of Polish-Danzig relations and intra-Danzig differences also met with full acceptance by the Council. The Council adopted the Court's opinion in No. 11 and took practical steps to implement it.[26] In No. 15, as noted, the opinion was accepted in advance by the parties, and no Council action was necessary. The Council adopted the Court's opinion in No. 22, ordered the opinion communicated to the High Commissioner at Danzig, and expressed the view that, since the legal points in dispute had "now been elucidated by the opinion," it was up to both parties to settle the practical questions directly between themselves.[27] This the parties proceeded to do.[28] In No. 23, the Council merely communicated the

---

In No. 26, the Council continued to deal with the question of minority schools in Albania until it was satisfied that Albanian measures corresponded, in all respects, with the Court's guidelines. *Ibid.*, 1935, pp. 626-27, 1185-86, 1290-91; *ibid.*, 1936, pp. 115-17, 263-65, 560-61, 741-43.

[22]*Ibid.*, 1924, pp. 345-48, 356-58, 364, 398-99. The two parties differed, however, in their understanding of the purport of some of the Court's statements.

[23]*Ibid.*, pp. 520-21, 627-29, 828; PCIJ, Ser. E, No. 1, pp. 219-20.

[24]LNOJ, 1924, pp. 1369-72.

[25]PCIJ, Ser. E, No. 1, p. 225. The disputed monastery was at first allocated to Albania. Later, however, the Conference reversed its decision and allocated the monastery to Yugoslavia, after the latter had invoked "new facts" previously unknown to the Court. *Ibid.*, No. 2, pp. 137-38.

[26]LNOJ, 1925, pp. 882-87, 1371-77. The Court itself had recognized that practical application of the opinion would depend on the delimitation of the port of Danzig for postal purposes. A committee of four experts was charged by the Council with the task of delimitation, and its recommendations were later endorsed by the Council.

[27]LNOJ, 1932, pp. 488-89.

[28]*Ibid.*, pp. 142-45. PCIJ, Ser. E, No. 8, p. 231; and No. 9, p. 117. Under the auspices of the High Commissioner, a protocol was signed on 13 August 1932 which defined the conditions that were to govern the access of Polish warships to Danzig waters. The Court had denied that Poland could claim any such rights as a matter of law.

opinion to the High Commissioner.[29] The parties themselves subsequently signed an agreement which incorporated the Court's conclusions with respect to the treatment of Polish nationals in Danzig.[30] And, finally, in No. 27, the Council "adopted" the Court's opinion and noted with satisfaction that the Danzig Senate had already taken steps to amend the decrees that had been declared unconstitutional by the Court.[31]

In the *Mosul* case, the Council adopted the Court's opinion unanimously (excluding the vote of the parties). In so doing, the Council overruled a Turkish objection that failure to count the Turkish vote implied prior acceptance of the opinion by the Council.[32] The Turkish representative further contended that, without his concurring vote, "the opinion in question will have only the character of a legal consultation of a theoretical character without any practical bearing on the issue." In the face of Council acceptance of the opinion, Turkey withdrew from further Council deliberations. Nevertheless, the Council proceeded with the arbitration, and, in its decisions of 16 December 1925 and 11 March 1926, fixed the "Brussels line" as the definitive Iraqi-Turkish frontier.[33] This frontier line, with slight modifications, was subsequently incorporated in the treaty of 5 June 1926 concluded between Great Britain, Iraq, and Turkey.[34]

In sum, as noted by Goodrich, "opinions relating to matters that have been before the Council for action have been uniformly accepted and have provided the legal basis for the action taken where the matter has not been withdrawn from the consideration of the Council by the action of the interested parties."[35]

The action of the ILO on opinions related to it was, if anything, even more unequivocal than the Council's. Thus, the ILO Director, reporting to the fourth session of the International Labour Conference, emphasized the practical consequences of Opinion No. 1 and set forth certain indications, derived

[29] LNOJ, 1932, pp. 522-23.

[30] *Ibid.*, p. 2282; and 1933, pp. 1157-61, 1330-33, 1541-42. PCIJ, Ser. E, No. 9, p. 118; and No. 10, pp. 99-105.

[31] LNOJ, 1936, pp. 122-25. Notice of the amendment of the decrees was forwarded subsequently. *Ibid.*, pp. 511-16.

[32] *Ibid.*, 1926, pp. 120-29. The Court had ruled that the Council's decision under Article 3(2) of the Treaty of Lausanne was binding on the parties, and that that decision must be based on a unanimous vote (excluding the vote of the parties).

The President defended the Council's voting procedure by noting that, since the question of adopting an advisory opinion was a procedural one, even a majority vote should, theoretically, suffice.

[33] *Ibid.*, pp. 187-93, 502-3.

[34] LNTS, 64: 379. No mention was made, however, of the Council decision.

[35] *Op. cit.*, p. 748.

from the Court's reasoning, to guide governments in selecting their workers' delegates.[36] In the same report, the Director stated that Opinion Nos. 2 and 3 had confirmed the ILO's previously held position, and that the ILO would proceed with the task it had undertaken.[37] The draft convention which gave rise to the request for the Court's opinion in No. 13 entered into force some years later.[38] In conformity with Opinion No. 18, Danzig was excluded from ILO membership.[39] And, finally, the revision of the Convention concerning the Employment of Women during the Night was based on acceptance of the Court's interpretation (in Opinion No. 25) of the original convention.[40]

In contrast to the ILO, neither the Mixed Commission for the Exchange of Greek and Turkish Populations nor the Greco-Bulgarian Mixed Emigration Commission could boast of unquestioned compliance with the Court's opinions. Yet, in none of the three cases involved was there any evidence of lack of respect for the Court. In each case, circumstances, rather than will, prevented the Commission concerned from giving full effect to the Court's pronouncement. In Nos. 10 and 16, direct Greco-Turkish negotiations made the Court's opinions largely irrelevant.[41] On the other hand, in No. 17, the somewhat oracular nature of the Court's statements complicated the Greco-Bulgar-

[36] PCIJ, Ser. E, No. 1, p. 188.

[37] *Ibid.*, p. 193.

[38] Hudson, *International Legislation*, 3: 1620; LNOJ, 1933, p. 112. The convention related to night work in bakeries, and included in its sphere of application proprietors as well as workers. The Court held that the ILO might propose labor legislation which, in order to protect certain classes of workers, also regulates incidentally the work of the employer.

[39] PCIJ, Ser. E, No. 7, p. 260; *The International Labour Organisation: The First Decade* (London: G. Allen, for the International Labour Office, 1931), p. 47.

[40] Doubts as to the need for revising the original convention were responsible for the invocation of the advisory procedure. PCIJ, Ser. C, pp. 54–160 *passim*. Once these doubts were removed, revision of the convention so as to exclude women in managerial or supervisory positions proceeded apace. See ILO, Minutes of the Governing Body, 61st Sess., pp. 19, 81–84; 62nd Sess., pp. 148–51; 63rd Sess., pp. 256–62; and 64th Sess., pp. 330–33. See also International Labour Conference, 18th Sess., 1934, pp. 190–96, 318–19, 650, 652.

[41] The definition of the term "*établis*"—the subject of Opinion No. 10—was encompassed in wide-ranging negotiations already under way at the time of delivery of the Court's opinion. The definition adopted did not exactly correspond with the Court's opinion, but, as noted by Stephen Ladas, the matter was no longer viewed as a legal question "but as a political question subject to solution by concession and compromise." *The Exchange of Minorities: Bulgaria, Greece, and Turkey* (New York: Macmillan, 1932), p. 408. See also PCIJ, Ser. C, No. 15-I, pp. 78, 82, 101–2; and LNTS, 68: 11 and 108: 233.

As for Opinion No. 16, negotiations for the final solution of all pending questions had earlier begun at Angora, and the Court's opinion therefore "did not serve any practical purpose." Ladas, *op. cit.*, p. 539.

ian Commission's task of applying the opinion.[42] Nevertheless, in this last case, the opinion formed the basis of the final solution.[43]

It is a noteworthy fact that the decisions to implement the Court's opinions were generally taken with little fanfare and after little or no discussion. That the Court's opinion was determinative of the legal issues was normally in the nature of a "given"; it was, to a remarkable degree, placed beyond debate.[44] Such discussion of the Court's opinions as did occur, generally revolved around the issue of *interpretation* or *application* of opinions.[45]

Noteworthy, too, is the fact that, with but few exceptions, the Court's opinions met with favorable responses on the part of states. In some instances, compliance (or the offer of compliance) with the Court's pronouncement was spontaneous;[46] in other cases, agreement to accept the Court's opinion was indicated by means of express statements made before the Council;[47] and, in still other cases, such agreement was implicit either in a state's acceptance of the Council's report on the opinion[48] or in a state's subsequent action.[49]

[42] It was not surprising, therefore, that the Greek and Bulgarian representatives interpreted principal passages of the opinion differently. PCIJ, Ser. E, No. 8, p. 213; cf. Lauterpacht, *International Court*, p. 43 and n. 13.

[43] The neutral members of the Commission were left to find a practical solution, "taking the Court's opinion as a basis, and adopting the same generous methods as had been employed by the Commission in regulating the liquidation of private property." See PCIJ, Ser. E, No. 8, pp. 213-14, for the terms of the Commission's decisions.

[44] The attitudes of Turkey and Rumania in Nos. 12 and 14, respectively, constituted the main exceptions to this rule. The immediate post-opinion stance of Poland in the *German Settlers in Poland* case was also rather negative.

Significantly, Finland's challenge to the authoritativeness of the Court's views in the *Eastern Carelia* case was partly based on the contention that the Court's "reply" was not a true "opinion." LNOJ, 1923, p. 1497.

[45] See, e.g., the conflicting views of the Polish and Czechoslovakian representatives in connection with the *Jaworzina* opinion, *ibid.*, 1924, pp. 345-48, 356-58, 364; Polish-Danzig differences over delimitation of the port of Danzig in the implementation of Opinion No. 11, *ibid.*, 1925, pp. 1374-77; and Greco-Bulgarian interpretations of Opinion Nos. 17 and 24, PCIJ, Ser. E, No. 8, p. 213; and LNOJ, 1932, pp. 1185-87.

[46] E. g., in Nos. 4, 8, 15, 19, and 27. In No. 26, the Albanian delegate to the Council indicated to the Council Rapporteur that his government had decided "to adopt new provisions corresponding to the present situation." Despite the vagueness of the statement, it was understood by Council members to mean that Albania intended to adopt measures in conformity with the Court's opinion. LNOJ, 1935, pp. 626-27.

[47] See, e.g., the statements of the Greek and Turkish representatives, in which they associated themselves with the Council Rapporteur's conviction that the Mixed Commission would attribute great value and authority to Opinion No. 10 (*ibid.*, 1925, pp. 441-42); Poland's statements regarding Opinion Nos. 11 (*ibid.*, p. 885) and 21 (*ibid.*, 1932, p. 481); and Danzig's statement concerning Opinion No. 22 (*ibid.*, p. 489).

Turkey's attitude toward the Court's opinion in the *Mosul* case and Rumania's attitude toward the *Danube Commission* opinion constituted the major exceptions to the foregoing.[50] In the first case, Turkey refused to consider itself bound by the Court's opinion.[51] Nevertheless, the outcome of the dispute was not seriously affected by this refusal.[52] In the second case, delivery of the Court's opinion did little to abate the continuing controversy over the subject of the opinion—namely, the Danube Commission's jurisdiction over the Galatz-Braila sector. Rumania refused to acquiesce in the opinion, and was able to cite, in support of its attitude, a pre-request reservation in which it had insisted on the nonbinding character of the Court's opinion.[53] The three opposing governments apparently respected Rumania's position and did not insist on strict compliance with the opinion. Instead, they resumed negotiations on the subject, and, after a lapse of several years, a modus vivendi was finally reached.[54]

With the possible exception of Opinion No. 14, then, no opinion of the Court remained totally unimplemented because of the recalcitrance of one of the states directly concerned.[55] And, even in the case of No. 14, since the other states did not insist on their legal rights, it might not be appropriate to

[48] Thus, in No. 9, Yugoslavia apparently concurred reluctantly in the Council's report. *Ibid.*, 1924, pp. 1371–72. See also No. 11, *ibid.*, 1925, p. 884; No. 16, *ibid.*, 1928, p. 1487; No. 17, *ibid.*, 1930, pp. 1300–1301; and No. 24, *ibid.*, 1932, p. 1187.

[49] The attitude adopted by Poland during initial Council consideration of Opinion Nos. 6 and 7 contrasted with its ultimate acceptance of solutions based largely on the Court's pronouncements. In No. 6, the Polish representative agreed to bring the Council's report to his government's attention, but refused to commit his government to acceptance of the opinion. The Polish government remained critical of the opinion. See LNOJ, 1923, p. 1333; and 1924, p. 359. See also Stone, *op. cit.*, pp. 212–22. In No. 7, the Polish representative abstained in the vote on the Council resolution "adopting" the opinion. LNOJ, 1923, pp. 1334–35. During subsequent negotiations, however, the Polish delegation "admitted in principle the legal thesis expressed" in the Court's opinion. *Ibid.*, 1924, p. 723. As already noted, the final solutions adopted in both cases were based, in broad outline, on the Court's opinions.

[50] Finland's negative attitude toward the Court's reply in the *Eastern Carelia* case was of little practical consequence, since that reply did not call for any action. Poland's obdurate stance in No. 6 was not persisted in throughout.

[51] In opposition to the Court's views, the Turkish representative cited the "advisory opinion" of Professor Gidel. LNOJ, 1926, pp. 124–25.

[52] The fact that British forces were in de facto control of the Mosul Territory undoubtedly had much to do with Turkey's willingness to accept an unfavorable frontier line.

[53] LNOJ, 1928, pp. 339–400. For the earlier statement, see *ibid.*, 1927, p. 151.

[54] See PCIJ, Ser. E, No. 5, pp. 223–26; No. 7, pp. 241–44; No. 9, pp. 115–17; and No. 10, p. 91.

[55] Initial Polish recalcitrance following the opinion in No. 6 led to the continuation of expulsion measures declared illegal by the Court. Only after Poland had succeeded in effecting about two-thirds of the projected expulsions did it moderate its attitude in the matter. Cf. Stone, *op. cit.*, pp. 212–22.

speak of "recalcitrance." Such cases of nonimplementation as did exist were due primarily to freely negotiated compromise solutions. But, then, as the Court itself recognized, states are always "free to dispose of their rights."[56] In the one case in which the danger that a Court opinion would be defied loomed largest—the *Eastern Carelia* case—that danger was effectively averted by the Court's refusal to render an opinion.[57]

The attitudes of states toward the Court's opinions were, in almost all cases, predictable on the basis of those states' pre-request postures. Thus, the negative attitudes of Turkey toward Opinion No. 12 and of Rumania toward Opinion No. 14 accorded with pre-request statements made by these states. In the majority of cases, as already noted in connection with the considerations which prompted requests,[58] the Court's advice was sought with the consent of the most interested states; and, in turn, this consent was accompanied by an apparent willingness to accept the Court's opinion as definitive. In two cases, of course, this willingness was expressed in the form of an advance agreement to accept the Court's opinion as binding. But, even in other cases, there were strong grounds for expecting that compliance would, in fact, be forthcoming.

Connected with this expectation was the corresponding expectation that the Court's opinion would aid in solving the root problem to which the request related. With the notable exception of those cases in which action of the parties made the opinion irrelevant, this expectation was usually confirmed. Thus, elimination of the preliminary difficulty in the *Tunis-Morocco* case permitted quick settlement of the basic dispute. And, in the *German Settlers in Poland* and *Acquisition of Polish Nationality* cases, negotiated solutions were facilitated, at least to a degree, by the Court's clarification of the Council's competence and of the substantive issues involved.[59] Efforts at delimiting the Polish-Czechoslovak frontier, which had reached a dangerous impasse prior to consultation of the Court, were brought to a successful conclusion shortly after delivery of the Court's opinion in the *Jaworzina* case. Following the Court's opinion in the *Monastery of Saint-Naoum* case, the

[56] PCIJ, Ser. A/B, No. 46, p. 153.

[57] And, in No. 20, Austro-German renunciation of the plan for the proposed customs union eliminated what might otherwise have been a serious controversy over acceptance of the Court's opinion.

[58] See Chapter III.

[59] On the other hand, Stone considers that the Council's attempt to use the Court's opinion as a tool of persuasion failed in essence. Only after the Polish government had altered the status quo in its own favor—and contrary to the Court's pronouncement—did it become amenable to a negotiated solution of the problem. *Op. cit.*, pp. 212-22, 266. Nevertheless, it is conceivable that, in the absence of a judicial opinion, Poland might have persisted in its obduracy by effecting all the projected expulsions and by refusing to pay even the measure of compensation for expellees that was finally agreed upon.

Conference of Ambassadors was able to settle the frontier issue involved in that case.[60] The question of *Polish Postal Service in Danzig*, one of the most heated of the Polish-Danzig controversies, was amicably settled on the basis of the Court's opinion. The other three Polish-Danzig disputes which came before the Court were similarly resolved in the wake of clarification of the legal issues hindering settlement.

The effect of the Court's opinion in the *Mosul* case is somewhat more difficult to assess. Although Turkey refused to accept the Court's opinion, that opinion strengthened the Council in its efforts to put an end to the dispute. And, eventually, as noted above, the Council's decision was consecrated in an agreement between the parties. (Given Britain's favorable power position, however, such an agreement might well have come about even in the absence of a Court opinion. Hence, it is possible that the Court's opinion was irrelevant in this case.)

The advisory opinion in the *Greco-Bulgarian Communities* case undoubtedly helped, in some measure, to resolve the fundamental issues in dispute, though the nature of the Court's opinion limited its usefulness to some extent. The children whose applications for admission to German minority schools had given rise to the request for the Court's opinion in the case of *German Minority Schools in Upper Silesia* were admitted to the schools of their choice shortly after delivery of the Court's opinion.[61] In the case of *Railway Traffic between Lithuania and Poland*, on the other hand, the Court's opinion left matters pretty much as they were. The problem of railway traffic between the two countries was not resolved until Poland took matters into its own hands. In the *Caphandaris-Molloff Agreement* case, the Court's opinion to the effect that there was no dispute between Greece and Bulgaria within the meaning of Article 8 of the Agreement also left the previous situation unchanged. But, in this case, the parties themselves had earlier agreed to solve their dispute amicably. In the case of *Minority Schools in Albania*, repeal of the controversial provisions in the Albanian Constitution in accordance with the Court's guidelines effectively removed the grievances out of which the petition to the Council had arisen. And the Court's determination that certain Danzig legislative decrees conflicted with the Danzig Constitution led—if only temporarily—to the repeal of the controversial decrees. As for the ILO, the Court's opinions apparently facilitated solution of the problems which gave rise to the six requests related to that organization's competence and activities.[62]

[60] As noted above, the Conference later reversed itself, because of fresh evidence presented by Yugoslavia.

[61] LNOJ, 1931, p. 2263. See also Julius Stone, *Regional Guarantees of Minority Rights* (New York: Macmillan, 1933), pp. 178–80.

[62] However, for a more critical evaluation of some of the Court's jurisprudence in relation to the ILO, see Georges Fischer, *Les rapports entre l'organisation internationale*

In brief, during the League period the relationship between a Court opinion and the root problem to which the opinion related was as follows: in most cases, the opinion was helpful; in a few, it was irrelevant; but in none was it harmful.

THE U.N. PERIOD

Far more complex and variegated is the pattern of post-opinion action in the UN era. Acceptance of the Court's opinion by the requesting organ continued to be the norm. But, while such acceptance, in the League period, was usually followed (and occasionally, preceded) by speedy compliance with the opinion on the part of the states concerned, this was frequently not the case in the UN period. Where the requesting organ had the ability to effectively implement the opinion by majority vote, or where the acquiescence of the states most directly concerned was forthcoming, the League pattern of short and fruitful post-opinion histories was repeated. In this category might be included the *Reparation, Reservations, UN Administrative Tribunal, UNESCO,* and *IMCO* cases. The Court's opinions in the *South West Africa (Voting)* and *South West Africa (Committee)* cases were also implemented by the requesting organs, but these cases must be viewed as merely incidental to the main *South West Africa (Status)* opinion, which remained without effect. In some cases, again as in the League period, the negative character of the Court's opinion precluded the necessity of further action. This was true of the opinions in the *Competence* and *Peace Treaties* (Second Phase) cases. Finally, in several cases—namely, the *Admission, Peace Treaties* (First Phase), *South West Africa (Status)*, and *Expenses* cases—the obdurate attitude adopted by certain states effectively sabotaged attempts to implement the Court's opinions. (And, while it is perhaps too early to judge the final effects of the opinion in the *Namibia* case, that opinion might tentatively be included in the last category.)

As already noted, the Court's opinions were favorably received by the organs that requested them. In no case did a requesting organ refuse to accept and act upon the judicial advice rendered—though, in some instances, initial insistence on absolute compliance with the Court's opinion was followed by subsequent tactical retreats. These conclusions emerge more clearly from a review of the actions taken by the General Assembly, the Security Council, UNESCO, and IMCO upon receipt of advisory opinions.

---

du travail et la Cour Permanente de Justice Internationale (Paris: Pedone, 1946), chap. VIII.

In the *Admission* case, the Court had concluded that the conditions laid down in Article 4(1) of the Charter were exhaustive, and that, therefore, in explaining its vote on the admission of an applicant state, a member state might not invoke extraneous considerations such as the demand for simultaneous admission of other states. On the basis of this opinion, at the first part of its third session, the Assembly adopted a number of resolutions. In Resolution 197A (III), after citing the Court's conclusions, the Assembly recommended that "each member of the Security Council and of the General Assembly, in exercising its vote on the admission of new Members, should act in accordance with" the Court's opinion. In Resolution 197B (III), "having noted" the Court's advisory opinion and "the general sentiment in favour of the universality of the United Nations," the Assembly asked the Security Council to reconsider certain pending applications. And in Resolutions 197C-H (III), after determining that certain states had fulfilled the requirements laid down in Article 4(1) of the Charter, the Assembly requested the Security Council to reconsider the applications of those states, in light of the Assembly's determination and the Court's advisory opinion.[63]

These resolutions, as well as subsequent resolutions which made reference to the 1948 opinion,[64] had no effect on the Soviet Union's position,[65] and the admission deadlock continued unabated until the conclusion of the 1955 package deal—a solution which was certainly inconsistent with the Court's pronouncement. In the eyes of the UN membership, the overriding goal of universality apparently justified this retreat from a position of strict legality.[66]

---

[63] GAOR (III/1), Plenary, 177th Mtg., 8 December 1948, p. 797. The states mentioned in the resolutions were Portugal, Transjordan, Italy, Finland, Ireland, and Austria. In Resolution 197 (I), which concerned Ceylon's application, a Burmese amendment to delete reference to the advisory opinion was accepted. UN Doc. A/AC.24/32, 1 December 1948; UN Doc. A/771, 6 December 1948; and GAOR (III/1), Plenary, 175th Mtg., 8 December 1948.

For the discussions that preceded adoption of the abovementioned resolutions, see pp. 356-58.

[64] See, e.g., Resolutions 506 (VI), 1 February 1952; and 620 (VII), 21 December 1952.

[65] Even among those who voted for the Assembly resolutions, there was widespread recognition that a practical solution to the problem would require agreement between the permanent members of the Security Council. See, e.g., GAOR (III/1), Ad Hoc Pol. Ctte., 8th and 9th Mtgs., 23 November 1948, pp. 87, 90-92 (statements of Chile, India, Greece, and Pakistan). A similar recognition was prevalent in the pre-request phase. See Chapter III.

[66] The words of Judge Krylov in his dissenting opinion in the *Admission* case were, in this respect, prophetic: "In the present case, it may be asked whether the political organs of the United Nations, acting under conditions which cannot even be foreseen at the present time, might not one day depart from the precepts of the Court's opinion." ICJ Reports, 1948, p. 109.

Following the Court's opinion in the *Reparation* case, the Assembly, "having regard to" that opinion, authorized the Secretary-General,

> in accordance with his proposals, to bring an international claim against the Government of a State, Member or non-member of the United Nations, alleged to be responsible, with a view to obtaining the reparation due in respect of the damage caused to the United Nations and in respect of the damage caused to the victim or to persons entitled through him and, if necessary, to submit to arbitration, under appropriate procedures, such claims as cannot be settled by negotiation.

It also authorized him "to take steps to negotiate in each particular case the agreements necessary to reconcile action by the United Nations with such rights as may be possessed by the State of which the victim is a national."[67]

Although the Court's opinion was not explicitly "accepted,"[68] the action which was authorized followed closely the terms of the Court's opinion.[69]

In the *Competence* case, the Court merely confirmed the validity of the organization's past practice in the matter of admissions. The opinion did not call for any action, and, indeed, it was not even mentioned in the Assembly resolution adopted in the wake of the Court's opinion.[70]

Following the Court's opinions in the two phases of the *Peace Treaties* case, the Assembly took note of the two opinions and condemned the willful refusal of the three governments concerned to fulfill their obligation under the Peace Treaties, "which obligation has been confirmed by the International Court of Justice." UN members, and, particularly, parties to the Peace Treaties involved, were invited to submit evidence in relation to the question to the Secretary-General for transmittal to member states of the UN.[71] The three governments persisted in their refusal to nominate representatives to the treaty commissions. This fact notwithstanding, all three governments were admitted to membership in the UN in 1955.[72]

[67]Resolution 365 (IV), 1 December 1949.

[68]A proposal that the Assembly "accept the advisory opinion of the Court as an authoritative expression of international law on the questions considered" was not adopted. See pp. 358–61 below.

[69]Subsequently, the Secretary-General pursued several claims to successful conclusions. See p. 364 below.

[70]Resolution 495 (V), 4 December 1950. For Assembly discussion of the Court's opinion, see GAOR (V), Plenary, 318th Mtg., 4 December 1950, pp. 565–86 *passim*.

[71]Resolution 385 (V), 3 November 1950.

[72]For criticism of the Assembly's action, see Shabtai Rosenne, "On the Non-Use of the Advisory Competence of the International Court of Justice," *BYIL*, 39 (1963): 42; *idem*, "The Court and the Judicial Process," *IO*, 19 (1965): 531.

To implement the Court's 1950 *South West Africa (Status)* opinion,[73] the General Assembly attempted various alternative approaches—all equally vain.[74]

In the immediate aftermath of the opinion, the Assembly adopted Resolution 449A (V), in accordance with which it "accepted" the opinion; urged the South African government "to take the necessary steps to give effect to the opinion . . . including the transmission of reports . . . and of petitions"; and proceeded to establish an *ad hoc* committee with a dual function—(1) "to confer with the Union of South Africa concerning the procedural measures necessary for implementing the advisory opinion," and (2), "as an interim measure, . . . to examine the report on the administration of the Territory . . . covering the period since the last report, as well as petitions and any other matters relating to the Territory that may be submitted to the Secretary-General, and to submit a report thereon to the . . . General Assembly."[75]

---

[73] The Court held, *inter alia*, that the mandate status of South West Africa persisted and that that status could be modified only by South Africa "acting with the consent of the United Nations"; that the obligation to submit to international supervision over the territory—including the obligation to render reports and transmit petitions—continued, and that the supervisory functions were to be exercised by the UN; and that Chapter XII of the Charter did not impose on South Africa a legal obligation to place the territory under the trusteeship system. ICJ Reports, 1950, pp. 143–44.

[74] The action taken by the Assembly year by year is summarized in the UN yearbooks. See also Solomon Slonim, *South West Africa and the United Nations: An International Mandate in Dispute* (Baltimore, Md.: The Johns Hopkins Press, 1973), chaps. VI–VIII and XII.

[75] This resolution emerged as a compromise between two rival approaches reflected in rival draft resolutions. (1) A proposal sponsored by the United States *et al.* (UN Doc. A/C.4/L.124, 30 November 1950) would have had the UN negotiate with South Africa on the implementation of the opinion. Such negotiations were deemed necessary in order to avoid foisting on South Africa, without her consent, obligations more onerous than those prevalent under the League, and in order to make South African cooperation in any scheme of implementation more probable. GAOR (V), 4th Ctte., Mtgs. 190–98, 29 November–5 December 1950, *passim*. (2) Proposals sponsored by the more militantly anticolonial bloc would have had the Assembly immediately establish an organ (counterpart of the Permanent Mandates Commission) to examine reports and petitions. Negotiations with South Africa, it was said, would be predictably fruitless and possibly harmful, since the substance of South African obligations stood to be negotiated away. See UN Docs. A/C.4/L.116/Rev. 1 and A/C.4/L.121. See also, e.g., GAOR (V), 4th Ctte., 194th Mtg., 2 December 1950, pp. 346–48; and 196th Mtg., 4 December 1950, p. 362. While the second approach was endorsed in the Fourth Committee, the necessity of obtaining a two-thirds majority in Plenary led to adoption of a compromise solution.

In the final resolution, as noted above, the Court's opinion was "accepted." This, too, represented a compromise between the United States *et al.* draft, which would have had the Assembly "accept and endorse" the opinion, and the other drafts, under which the opinion would merely have been noted. Initial unwillingness to explicitly "accept" the opinion may have reflected dissatisfaction with the Court's conclusions on the trusteeship issue.

On that issue, a further resolution was adopted—reiterated annually for many years—which called upon South Africa to place South West Africa under the trusteeship system

By the eighth session, it was clear that negotiations between South Africa and the *Ad Hoc* Committee were hopelessly deadlocked.[76] South Africa was unwilling to negotiate on the basis of full acceptance of the Court's opinion,[77] and the *Ad Hoc* Committee, supported by the Assembly, was unwilling to negotiate on any other basis.[78] South Africa also refused to submit any reports or transmit any petitions relating to the territory. Under these circumstances, the Assembly set about attempting to implement the 1950 opinion without South African cooperation. For this purpose, a new organ—the Committee on South West Africa—was established, to assume, on behalf of the UN, the role that the Permanent Mandates Commission had assumed for the League. The Committee was charged, *inter alia*, with examining reports, petitions, and "such information and documentation as may be available in respect of the Territory of South West Africa"; and with preparing, "for the consideration of the General Assembly, a procedure for the examination of reports and petitions which should conform as far as possible to the procedure followed in this respect by the Assembly, the Council and the Permanent Mandates Commission of the League of Nations."[79] The consistency with the 1950 opinion of one of the special rules of procedure thus devised

---

(Resolution 449B [V], 13 December 1950). Proponents of this resolution cited the Court's statement that "the normal way of modifying the international status of the Territory would be to place it under the Trusteeship System," and emphasized South Africa's political and moral obligations in this regard. See, e.g., the views of Brazil (GAOR [V], 4th Ctte., 190th Mtg., 29 November 1950, pp. 315–16; and 197th Mtg., 5 December 1950, pp. 370–71) and the statement of India (*ibid.*, 191st Mtg., 30 November 1950, pp. 320–21). On the other hand, opponents of the resolution thought it both purposeless and harmful to repeat a long-standing invitation which South Africa had spurned in the past and intended to spurn in the future, particularly after the Court had confirmed South Africa's legal right to act in this manner. See, e.g., the statements of Peru, *ibid.*, 194th Mtg., 2 December 1950, p. 345; and Belgium, Canada, the United States, and the United Kingdom, *ibid.*, 197th Mtg., 5 December 1950, pp. 371–72.

[76] The *Ad Hoc* Committee was reconstituted by Resolution 570A (VI), 21 January 1952, by which the Assembly reaffirmed the necessity of implementing the Court's opinion fully. During the seventh session, the Assembly postponed further consideration of the South West Africa question, pending the outcome of the negotiations.

[77] South Africa contended that any form of UN supervision would automatically impose on it greater obligations than had prevailed under the League mandate. At most, it was prepared to reassume some of its former obligations by negotiating a new agreement with France, the United States, and the United Kingdom (the remaining Principal Allied and Associated Powers of World War I). The UN's role would be confined to authorizing the initial negotiations and confirming the final agreement. Slonim, *op. cit.*, chap. VI.

[78] The Committee's counterproposals involved the institution of UN counterparts to the League Council and Permanent Mandates Commission. *Ibid.*

[79] Resolution 749A (VIII), 28 November 1953. The Committee was also authorized to continue negotiations with the South African government concerning the implementation of the 1950 opinion, but this task was by now distinctly secondary. South Africa immediately declined to enter into any negotiations.

by the Committee—special rule F—subsequently formed the subject of a further request for an advisory opinion. The Court was also consulted in connection with a difficulty which arose a year later in the matter of the admissibility of oral hearings by the Committee on South West Africa.[80] Both of the Court's opinions accorded with the desires of the UN majority, and both were readily "accepted and endorsed" by the Assembly.[81]

However, none of the Court's opinions, or the Assembly resolutions implementing them, was bringing the UN any closer to the goal of establishing effective supervisory authority with respect to South Africa's administration of South West Africa. While the reports of the Committee on South West Africa and the resolutions of the Assembly grew ever more critical of South African administration, the South African government grew ever more intransigent in its refusal to submit to any measure of international accountability in respect of the territory. Recognition of this fact prompted the Assembly to search for new courses of action. In particular, the Assembly requested the Committee on South West Africa to study the question what legal action was open to UN organs, UN members, or former League members, "acting either individually or jointly to ensure that the Union of South Africa fulfils the obligations assumed by it under the Mandate."[82] In the reports and resolutions that followed, the possibility of further advisory opinions was contemplated,[83] but the main thrust of Assembly thinking in the matter was toward the invocation of the Court's compulsory jurisdiction. In this manner, it was hoped, the Court's 1950 pronouncement would be given "teeth"; it would be transformed into an enforceable judgment. The institution of contentious proceedings was encouraged in two Assembly resolutions.[84] Following the

[80] See Chapter III.

[81] Resolutions 934 (X), 3 December 1955; and 1047 (XI), 23 January 1957. In the latter resolution, the Assembly also authorized the Committee on South West Africa to grant hearings to petitioners. A Swedish amendment (UN Doc. A/C.4/L.44), which would have specified that the Committee, in granting hearings, take into account "the prerequisites laid down in the advisory opinion," was not adopted. (The Court had interpreted the question to relate to persons who had already submitted written petitions. ICJ Reports, 1956, p. 25.) Several representatives stated, however, that they would consider the Court's qualification to be implicitly incorporated in the Assembly's resolution. See, e.g., the statements of the United Kingdom, the United States, and Sweden, GAOR (XI), 4th Ctte., 569th Mtg., 7 December 1956, p. 101.

[82] Resolution 1060 (XI), 26 November 1957.

[83] See Chapter IV, pp. 230–31.

[84] In Resolution 1142A (XII), 25 October 1957, the Assembly drew the attention of member states "to the failure of . . . South Africa to render annual reports to the United Nations and to the legal action provided for in Article 7 of the Mandate read with Article 37 of the Statute of the International Court of Justice." (Cf. the operative part of the South West Africa [Status] opinion, ICJ Reports, 1950, p. 143.) In Resolution 1361 (XIV), 17 November 1959, the attention of member states was drawn to the conclusions of the special report submitted by the Committee on South West Africa on the question of instituting contentious proceedings against South Africa.

failure of a further, last-ditch attempt by the UN to reach a negotiated solution with South Africa,[85] contentious proceedings were, in fact, instituted by Ethiopia and Liberia, in November 1960. This action was commended by the Assembly.[86]

During the course of the protracted proceedings before the Court, the Assembly continued to deal with the South West Africa issue[87] on the basis of the existence of the mandate,[88] although the Assembly was, on occasion, urged to divest South Africa of the mandate.[89] Following the Court's unexpected refusal in 1966 to render a judgment on the merits of the *South West Africa* cases, however, the Assembly, in Resolution 2145 (XXI), of 27 October 1966, declared the mandate terminated and decided that "henceforth South West Africa comes under the direct responsibility of the United Nations."[90] Thereby the Assembly formally abandoned the goal of imple-

[85] A Good Offices Committee was established in 1957 to discuss with the Union government "a basis for an agreement which would continue to accord to the Territory of South West Africa an international status." A partition proposal contemplated by the Committee was rejected by the full Assembly. See GAOR (XIII), Annexes, a.i. 39, pp. 2–10 (UN Doc. A/3900); and 4th Ctte., Mtgs. 756–63, 10–16 October 1958, pp. 57–97. The 1959 discussions were totally unproductive. *Ibid.* (XIV), Annexes, a.i. 38, pp. 1–5 (UN Doc. A/4224).

[86] See Resolution 1565 (XV), 18 December 1960.

[87] On the basis of the sub judice principle, South Africa repeatedly objected to Assembly consideration of the South West Africa question. See, e.g., GAOR (XV/1), 4th Ctte., 1049th Mtg., 14 November 1960, pp. 296–97. However, the Assembly majority considered the principle inapplicable. See, e.g., the arguments of India, *ibid.* (XV/2), 4th Ctte., 1110th Mtg., 21 March 1961, pp. 61–62. Cf. Rosenne, *Law and Practice*, 1: 84 ff.

[88] Nevertheless, the Assembly was moving away from strict compliance with the 1950 opinion. Thus, e.g., Resolutions 1568 (XV), 18 December 1960, and 1596 (XV), 7 April 1961, which invited the Committee on South West Africa to conduct an on-site investigation of the territory and to do so even without South African cooperation, were not easily reconcilable with the continuation of the mandate status. See, in this connection, the statements of Ireland (GAOR [XV/1], 4th Ctte., 1073rd Mtg., 5 December 1960, p. 437) and the United Kingdom (*ibid.*, 1076th Mtg., 6 December 1960, p. 460).

[89] Thus, an African-sponsored draft resolution introduced at the fifteenth session would have, *inter alia*, entrusted the administration of South West Africa to a special administrative commission, which would have been charged with leading South West Africa to self-government and independence. UN Doc. A/C.4/L.653, 24 November 1960. The incompatibility between the pending legal action (premised as it was on the *continuance* of the mandate) and the proposed draft was pointed up by several delegates. See, e.g., the statement of the Bolivian representative, GAOR (XV/1), 1064th Mtg., 25 November 1960, p. 381.

[90] The compatibility of this action with acceptance of the 1950 advisory opinion was apparently not seriously questioned. As will be recalled, the Court, in 1950, had ruled that "the competence to determine and modify the international status of the Territory rests with the Union of South Africa acting with the consent of the United Nations." ICJ Reports, 1950, p. 144. A Mexican suggestion (see p. 231 above) to ask the Court for an advisory opinion on the Assembly's right to revoke the mandate was based on the assumption that such revocation was contrary to the 1950 opinion—an opinion accepted by the Assembly in Resolution 449A (V)—and therefore required judicial sanction.

menting the 1950 opinion and instead set its sights on attaining immediate independence for the territory (which in 1968 the Assembly renamed "Namibia").[91] To attain this new goal, the Assembly sought to elicit the cooperation of the Security Council, and since 1968 the Council has been actively involved in the Namibia issue. In the course of this involvement the Security Council had occasion to turn to the Court in 1970 and to receive an opinion which, in effect, redefined the status of Namibia after the Assembly's revocation of the mandate.[92]

The reception accorded the Court's opinion in the *Reservations* case is particularly interesting in light of the peculiar difficulties surrounding compliance with that opinion. As will be recalled, the same question, in essence, had been submitted simultaneously to the ILC and to the Court—although, by its terms, the question submitted to the Court had been limited to the Genocide Convention.[93] The pre-request apprehensions of several delegates that the Assembly might thus be faced with conflicting pronouncements were fully substantiated. In its 1951 Report, the ILC rejected for general application, and impliedly criticized, the Court's "compatibility" rule.[94] Moreover, the Court itself was deeply divided on the issue, the most incisive criticism of the Court's criterion having been presented in a joint dissenting opinion.[95] In turn, much of this criticism was echoed rather resoundingly in the Sixth Committee chambers.[96] Nevertheless, out of a recognition of the respect due the Court, most of the sharpest opponents of the "compatibility" rule agreed to see the opinion applied in relation to the one convention to which it was,

---

GAOR (XVII), 4th Ctte., 1376th Mtg., 8 November 1962, pp. 303–4; and 1387th Mtg., 16th November 1962, pp. 389–91.

Whether, quite apart from the 1950 opinion, the Assembly's determination that South Africa had consistently violated the mandate entitled that body to revoke the mandate is, of course, a separate question—one that the Court subsequently grappled with in the *Namibia* case.

For pre-1970 discussions of the legality and legal effect of the Assembly's action, see John Dugard, "The Revocation of the Mandate for South West Africa," AJIL, 62 (1968); 78–97; and Milton Katz, *The Relevance of International Adjudication* (Cambridge, Mass.: Harvard University Press, 1968), pp. 113–24.

[91] GA Resolution 2372 (XXII), 12 June 1968.

[92] For discussion of the pre-request history of the *Namibia* case, see pp. 148–57 above. For the reception of the opinion, see pp. 352–54 below.

[93] See Chapter III.

[94] *ILC Yearbook*, 1951, 2: 238 (Report, par. 24). The grounds for criticism were similar to those expressed in the joint dissenting opinion in the *Reservations* case. See n. 95.

[95] ICJ Reports, 1951, pp. 31–48; see, esp., pp. 42–48. The newness, difficulty of application, and subjectivity of the rule, as well as the lack of finality or certainty in the results, were all deprecated.

[96] See GAOR (VI), 6th Ctte., Mtgs. 264–78, 5 December 1951–5 January 1952.

ostensibly, confined—namely, the Genocide Convention.[97] It was with respect to *generalization* of the Court's ruling to other conventions that widely divergent views were expressed in the Committee.[98]

The resolution finally adopted—Resolution 598 (VI), of 12 January 1958—did not, however, limit application of the Court's rule to the Genocide Convention; it went far toward extending the rule—though in its objective variant[99]—to future conventions concluded under UN auspices. After noting the Court's opinion and the ILC report, and, after recommending that, in future conventions, consideration be given to the insertion of provisions on reservations, the Assembly proceeded with the following recommendation and directives.

2. *Recommends* to all States that they be guided in regard to the Convention on the Prevention and Punishment of the Crime of Genocide by the advisory opinion of the International Court of Justice of 28 May 1951;

3. *Requests* the Secretary-General:

a. In relation to reservations to the Convention on the Prevention and Punishment of the Crime of Genocide, to conform his practice to the advisory opinion of the Court of 28 May 1951;

b. In respect of future conventions concluded under the auspices of the United Nations of which he is the depositary:

i. To continue to act as depositary in connexion with the deposit of documents containing reservations or objections, without passing upon the legal effect of such documents; and

ii. To communicate the text of such documents relating to reservations or objections to all States concerned, leaving it to each State to draw legal consequences from such communications.

With time, support for generalizing the Court's ruling increased. The expansion of the international community and the corresponding need for more international legislation in the form of treaties militated against strict

---

[97]See, e.g., the statements of France (*ibid.*, 265th Mtg., 7 December 1951, p. 77), the United Kingdom (*ibid.*, 267th Mtg., 10 December 1951, pp. 86–88), the Netherlands (*ibid.*, 271st Mtg., 14 December 1951, p. 109), and Brazil (*ibid.*, pp. 113–14).

[98]These views were reflected in the discussions and in the bewildering array of draft resolutions and amendments presented. See "Report of the Sixth Committee," GAOR (VI), Annexes, a.i. 49, pp. 8–11 (UN Doc. A/2047).

[99]In its objective variant, the rule boils down essentially to the Pan-American Union rule for reservations. As noted by Sir Gerald Fitzmaurice, in the absence of an objective tribunal to apply the proposed standard, all "mixed theories," whatever their exact nature, must lead to the Pan-American rule. "Reservations to Multilateral Conventions," *ICLQ*, 2 (1953): 1–26. See also "First Report on the Law of Treaties by Sir Humphrey Waldock" (UN Doc. A/CN.4/144, 26 March 1962), *ILC Yearbook*, 1962, 2: 65–66.

conformity with the unanimity rule. Universality of participation in a convention appeared more important than the absolute integrity of the convention. The question of the propriety of the Secretary-General's handling of the Indian "reservation" to the IMCO Convention[100] gave rise to a further Assembly resolution, under whose terms the Assembly extended its previous directive to the Secretary-General to *all* conventions concluded under UN auspices—i.e., even to those concluded prior to 12 January 1952 (provided, of course, that no contrary provisions were contained in the convention).[101] It is significant, too, that the ILC subsequently reversed itself on the question of reservations and endorsed the Court's rule—in its objective variant—for general application.[102] The suggested rule was ultimately sanctified in the reservations provisions of the Vienna Convention on the Law of Treaties.[103]

Following the Court's pronouncement in the *UN Administrative Tribunal* case, the Assembly adopted Resolution 888 (IX) on 17 December 1954, in accordance with which the Assembly (1) decided to "take note of" the Court's opinion;[104] (2) adopted, in principle, judicial review of Administrative Tribunal judgments and set up a special committee to study the question; and (3) established a special indemnity fund to pay the awards of compensation made by the Administrative Tribunal. The United States joined other states in "taking note of" the opinion and in agreeing to pay the controversial awards.[105]

---

[100] See UN Doc. A/4188, 17 August 1959, in which the matter was brought to the Assembly's attention by India, and UN Doc. A/4235, 6 October 1959, in which the Secretary-General defended his action as being, *inter alia*, fully in accord with GA Resolution 598 (VI).

[101] GA Resolution 1452B (XIV), 7 December 1959. Part A dealt specifically with the IMCO Convention.

For a summary of the Sixth Committee's discussions, see UN Doc. A/4311, 1 December 1959.

[102] See Articles 18-21 of the 1962 draft on the Law of Treaties, *ILC Yearbook*, 1962, 2: 175 ff.; and Articles 16-19 of the 1966 draft, *ibid.*, 1966, 2: 202 ff. The "compatibility" rule was thought to be impracticable for determining the status of a reserving state. Nevertheless, the Court's criterion was said to "express a valuable concept to be taken into account both by States formulating a reservation and by States deciding whether or not to consent to a reservation." "First Report on the Law of Treaties by Sir Humphrey Waldock," *ibid.*, 1962, 2: 65-66.

[103] See Articles 19-21. UN Doc. A/CONF.39/27, 23 May 1969.

[104] This part of the resolution was adopted unanimously. GAOR (IX), 5th Ctte., 479th Mtg., 9 December 1954, p. 305; and Plenary, 515th Mtg., 17 December 1954, p. 549.

[105] The United States was, in fact, a cosponsor of the final resolution. However, it was United States insistence which led to payment of the awards out of a special indemnity fund rather than out of the regular budget. This insistence was prompted by a United States congressional resolution which declared that no part of the funds appropriated by the Congress should be used for paying the controversial awards. The resolution was approved by the House of Representatives on 10 August 1954 and by the Senate on

In Resolution 1854A (XVII), of 19 December 1962, the Assembly "accepted" the opinion of the Court "on the question submitted to it" in the *Expenses* case. The resolution was adopted by an overwhelming majority[106] after the defeat of a Jordanian amendment which would simply have "taken note of" the opinion.[107] In this instance, the significance was more than semantic, since the issue of the Article 19 sanction lurked in the background. It was generally acknowledged that "acceptance," as opposed to "taking note of," the opinion implied incorporation of the Court's ruling into the "law recognized by the United Nations." And such incorporation entailed, as a logical corollary, the employment of Article 19 in appropriate circumstances.[108] Yet, among the supporters of "acceptance" were some who, even at that date, did not wish to face the logical implications of their vote. Thus, the representative of India stated:

> The dignity of the Court should be maintained and its advisory opinion merited the respect which had never previously been denied to its advisory opinions. . . . The advisory opinion did not mean that Article 19 of the Charter would come automatically into operation or even that it had any relevance to an Assembly decision to accept the opinion. The advisory opinion merely established the legal position on a specific issue; no action automatically flowed from it. Considerations that were not legal might be equally valid and must influence the Assembly in determining its ultimate course of action.[109]

---

20 August 1954. U.S. *Congressional Record*, Vol. 100, Part 11, p. 13949; and Part 12, p. 15486.

It was largely United States insistence, too, which led to the establishment of a review procedure for UN Administrative Tribunal judgments. Neither the Secretary-General nor the UN staff felt any need for the review procedure. UN Doc. A/C.5/635, 17 October 1955.

[106] The vote in the Fifth Committee was 75 to 17, with 14 abstentions; in Plenary, it was 76 to 17, with 8 abstentions. GAOR (XVII), 5th Ctte., 973rd Mtg., 12 December 1962, p. 350; and Plenary, 1199th Mtg., 19 December 1962, p. 1199.

[107] See UN Doc. A/C.5/L.766, 11 December 1962; and GAOR (XVII), 5th Ctte., 973rd Mtg., 12 December 1962, p. 349. The vote to reject was 61 to 28, with 14 abstentions.

[108] See the discussions that preceded adoption of the resolution, pp. 361–64 below.

[109] GAOR (XVII), 5th Ctte., 972nd Mtg., 12 December 1962, p. 342. Cf. the statement of Afghanistan, *ibid.*, Plenary, 1199th Mtg., 19 December 1962, p. 1198.

Many of those who voted for acceptance may have been influenced by the Secretary-General's statement at the outset of the discussions, in which he expressed the hope

> that the Fifth Committee . . . will follow the time-honoured tradition whereby each principal organ of the United Nations respects and upholds the views, resolutions and decisions of other principal organs in their respective fields of competence. Not to do so in the present case would be not only a departure from the tradition relating to all the past precedents concerning advisory opinions of the Court, but also a blow at the authority and standing of both the Court and the Assembly in a matter vital to the future of the United Nations.

The Assembly's "ultimate course of action" was, indeed, determined by "considerations that were not legal." Already at the seventeenth session, and, in fact, in the resolution in which the Court's opinion was accepted, a retreat to the pre-opinion position was indicated.[110] That retreat was completed when, following the famous nineteenth "nonsession," the danger that the organization itself might be wrecked on the shoals of legal consistency loomed large. Under these circumstances, the price of legal consistency was universally acknowledged to be too high.[111]

In the wake of the *Namibia* opinion, the Security Council adopted Resolution 301, on 20 October 1971. Having received the judicial imprimatur for its previous actions on Namibia, the Security Council unhesitatingly reaffirmed these and recommended further measures based on the Court's opinion (concerning, in particular, treaty relations involving Namibia).[112] The formula which the Council employed with respect to the Court's opinion is curious. The Council "took note with appreciation" of the advisory opinion and "agreed with" the operative part (paragraph 133) of the opinion, which it proceeded to quote in full.[113] This formula resulted from a three-way split in

---

UN Doc. A/C.5/952, 3 December 1962. The negative factor that those who favored merely "taking note of" the opinion were also those who deprecated the authority of the Court's opinion in the *Expenses* case undoubtedly exercised an influence as well. See, e.g., the remarks of the Greek representative, GAOR (XVII), 5th Ctte., 972nd Mtg., 12 December 1962, p. 345.

[110] See Resolution 1854B (XVII), in which the Working Group of Fifteen was re-established with an enlarged membership. Although in one of the preambular paragraphs the Assembly declared that it was "taking into account" the Court's advisory opinion, the resolution "largely signifies a return to the *status quo* which prevailed prior to the request addressed to the Court." Leo Gross, "Expenses of the United Nations for Peace-Keeping Operations: The Advisory Opinion of the International Court of Justice," *IO*, 17 (1963): 27, n. 75. No reference was made, either in this or in succeeding resolutions, to Article 17(2) of the Charter.

[111] See Ruth B. Russell, "United Nations Financing and 'The Law of the Charter,' " *Columbia Journal of Transnational Law*, 5 (1966): 68-95; Robert O. Keohane, "Political Influence in the General Assembly," *International Conciliation*, No. 557 (March 1966): 45-64.

The end of the "Article 19 crisis" was signified by a United States statement of 16 August 1965 in the Committee of Thirty-three. The United States therein declared that, "without prejudice to the position that Article 19 is applicable, the United States recognizes, as it simply must, that the General Assembly is not prepared to apply Article 19 in the present situation and that the consensus of the membership is that the Assembly should proceed normally. We will not seek to frustrate that consensus, since it is not in the world interest to have the work of the General Assembly immobilized in these troubled days." UN Doc. A/AC.121/PV.15, 16 August 1965, pp. 8-10.

[112] See operative paragraphs 11 and 14 of the resolution. The issue of treaty relations had been left unregulated by Resolution 283, 29 July 1970.

[113] The operative part of the opinion reads as follows:

(1) that, the continued presence of South Africa in Namibia being illegal, South Africa is under obligation to withdraw its administration from Namibia immediately and thus put an end to its occupation of the Territory;

the Council. Some members (most notably, the African states) accepted the opinion's conclusions and its legal premises;[114] others (including the United States, Italy, Japan, and Belgium) accepted the conclusions but not the premises;[115] and still others (France and the United Kingdom) accepted neither the conclusions nor the premises.[116] (In its interpretation of Articles 24 and 25 of the Charter, the Court had attributed binding force to the relevant Security Council resolutions, even though they had not been adopted under Chapter VII of the Charter. This part of the Court's reasoning was particularly objectionable to many Council members.) The first group of states would have wished to "endorse" the entire opinion, but could not receive the support of the second group, which was willing to "endorse" only the operative part of the opinion, and certainly not of the third group, which was unprepared to countenance the "endorsement" of any part of the opinion. In fact, France indicated that, if the term "endorse" were used even with respect to the operative part, it would have to veto the resolution, not merely abstain in the vote.[117] In the end, the Council "agreed with," rather than "endorsed," the operative part of the opinion.[118] As an indication of its

---

(2) that States Members of the United Nations are under obligation to recognize the illegality of South Africa's presence in Namibia and the invalidity of its acts on behalf of or concerning Namibia, and to refrain from any acts and in particular any dealings with the Government of South Africa implying recognition of the legality of, or lending support or assistance to, such presence and administration;

(3) that it is incumbent upon States which are not Members of the United Nations to give assistance, within the scope of subparagraph (2) above, in the action which has been taken by the United Nations with regard to Namibia.

ICJ Reports, 1971, p. 58.

[114] See, e.g., the statements of Sudan (UN Doc. S/PV.1587, 30 September 1971, p. 33), Liberia (UN Doc. S/PV.1594, 14 October 1971, pp. 14–18), and Somalia (UN Doc. S/PV.1597, 19 October 1971, p. 6). Several African states spoke of the opinion as if it had been a binding judgment. See, e.g., the statement of Burundi, UN Doc. S/PV.1585, 27 September 1971, pp. 23–27.

[115] See the statements of Japan (UN Doc. S/PV.1589, 6 October 1971, pp. 39–40), Italy (*ibid.*, p. 47, and UN Doc. S/PV.1595, 15 October 1971, pp. 82–85), Belgium (UN Doc. S/PV.1594, 14 October 1971, pp. 19–21), and the United States (UN Doc. S/PV.1598, 20 October 1971, p. 11).

[116] See the statements of France (UN Doc. S/PV.1588, 5 October 1971, pp. 11–15) and the United Kingdom (UN Doc. S/PV.1589, 6 October 1971, pp. 23–33). The views of these states bore a remarkable resemblance to the dissenting opinions of their respective judges on the bench (Gros and Fitzmaurice), a fact commented upon by the President of the UN Council for Namibia, *ibid.*, p. 46. Both states also emphasized the nonbinding nature of advisory opinions.

[117] UN Doc. S/PV.1598, 20 October 1971, pp. 4–5; cf. the statement of the United Kingdom representative (who also abstained in the vote), *ibid.*, p. 12.

[118] The Somali representative (one of the cosponsors of the resolution) explained the reasons for the substitution as follows: (1) "Endorse" might connote a relationship of subordination between the two UN organs (Council and Court). (2) Endorsement might imply a higher degree of involvement, thereby making the draft unacceptable to certain states. *Ibid.*, p. 13.

gratitude to the Court, however, it also "took note with appreciation" of the opinion as a whole.[119]

The Court's opinion, it seems, had little effect on the Council's continued consideration of the Namibia issue. As in the pre-request stage, the Council remained deadlocked over the issue of invoking Chapter VII; and, as for measures short of Chapter VII, these had practically been exhausted in any case. The opinion may, in a sense, have had a cathartic effect, for the Council now appeared more open to suggestions for a kind of "dialogue" (though the word was not used) with South Africa on the Namibia issue.[120] In this respect, the Council seemed willing to retreat from a dogmatic insistence on the Court's conclusions. The Council's aim, of course, was still to bring the Namibian population to self-determination and independence; but the fact that, in place of a simple demand that the South African authorities "withdraw their illegal presence," contacts were to be made with those authorities, was significant. A proposal to have the Secretary-General initiate such contacts was raised by Argentina in October 1971 and adopted by the Council at its Addis Ababa meeting in February 1972.[121] At the same time, however, the Council reaffirmed its former resolutions, called again for immediate South African withdrawal, and threatened to take "effective steps or measures, in accordance with the relevant Chapters of the Charter, to secure the full and speedy implementation" of the new resolution.[122] In what direction the Council will ultimately move, what the results will be, and what effect the Court's opinion will have in the long run—all are, at the moment of writing, still open questions.

Compliance with the two opinions given within the framework of Article 96(2) of the Charter presented no particular problems. In the *UNESCO* case, the opinion was binding under the terms of Article XII of the ILO Adminis-

---

The Council's reluctance to accept the legal premises of the opinion meant that the Council was not prepared to view those of its decisions that were taken outside the framework of Chapter VII as binding. If so, Resolution 301, in which the Council "agreed with" the opinion's conclusions, did not create any legal obligation for states to accept those conclusions.

[119] See the explanation of the Argentine representative, UN Doc. S/PV.1593, 13 October 1971, pp. 11–12; and UN Doc. S/PV.1595, 15 October 1971, p. 66.

[120] The need for a more "realistic" and gradual approach was emphasized by several representatives. See, e.g., the statements of Japan (UN Doc. S/PV.1589, 6 October 1971, p. 41), Italy (*ibid.*, p. 52), and Argentina (UN Doc. S/PV.1595, 15 October 1971, pp. 68–71).

[121] SC Resolution 309, 4 February 1972. The purpose of the contacts was "to enable the people of Namibia . . . to exercise their right to self-determination and independence, in accordance with the Charter of the United Nations." The Secretary-General was to report to the Council by 31 July 1972.

[122] SC Resolution 310, 4 February 1972.

trative Tribunal Statute. Accordingly, the Executive Board took note of the Court's opinion and approved a proposal by the Director-General regarding payment of the awards granted by the ILO Administrative Tribunal.[123] The opinion in the *IMCO* case also was speedily complied with. The previous Maritime Safety Committee was dissolved, and a new one was constituted, in accordance with Article 28 of the IMCO Convention, "as interpreted by the International Court of Justice in its Advisory Opinion."[124]

In contrast with the League period—when post-opinion discussions tended to be brief, the definitiveness of the Court's opinion usually was assumed, and the post-opinion course of action generally was speedily agreed to—in the UN period the authoritativeness of the opinion, the terminology of the resolution regarding the opinion, and the action to be taken on the opinion all became, in many instances, the focus of sharp debate. Rival draft resolutions, reflecting varying measures of satisfaction with the opinion, were frequent phenomena.[125] Expressions of displeasure at, and criticism of, the Court's pronouncements were commonplace.[126] Nor were these expressions the monopoly of the Soviet bloc. However, the criticisms of other states tended to be more subdued in tone and tended to culminate in abstentions rather

---

[123] UNESCO, 45 EX/17, 1 November 1956; 45 EX/Decisions, p. 14, item 11.1; and 45 EX/SR.9, 6 November 1956, p. 57. The United States representative criticized the Court's opinion but agreed not to contest it. UNESCO, 45 EX/SR.9, 6 November 1956, p. 50.

[124] IMCO Assembly Resolution A.II/Res.21, 6 April 1961. In the same resolution, the measures taken by the Maritime Safety Committee from 1959 to 1961 were adopted and confirmed. New elections took place on 13 April 1961.

For discussions of the Court's opinion, see IMCO/A.II/SR.4, 6 April 1961. For a penetrating analysis of the post-opinion actions in the *IMCO* case, see Eli Lauterpacht, "The Legal Effect of Illegal Acts of International Organisations," *Cambridge Essays in International Law* (London: Stevens, 1965), pp. 100–106. As Lauterpacht points out, compliance with the opinion was the more noteworthy in the *IMCO* case, since, for the first time in the history of the Court (or its predecessor), the Court had deemed the action of a plenary organ of an international organization to be *un*constitutional. *Ibid.*, p. 100.

[125] Competing draft resolutions were presented in connection with the *Admission, Reparation, South West Africa (Status), Reservations,* and *Expenses* cases. Cf. also the final version of the post-opinion resolution on Namibia with the formulation in the original draft resolution.

[126] In support of their criticisms, UN members frequently drew upon dissenting judicial opinions, since these were in almost all instances available. Whereas fifteen of the PCIJ opinions were rendered by a unanimous Court, only one ICJ opinion was so rendered—that in the *South West Africa (Voting)* case. (In the *Reparation* and *South West Africa [Status]* cases, the Court attained unanimity only with respect to certain questions.) Furthermore, while in all thirteen nonunanimous ICJ opinions explanations of dissent were appended, in three of the twelve nonunanimous PCIJ opinions—Nos. 2, 5, and 25—the reasons for dissent were not given.

than in outright opposition to acceptance of an opinion. And while many non-Soviet states did, on occasion, defer to the Court's views,[127] no corresponding deference was ever forthcoming from the Soviet bloc.[128]

The question of what force and effect was to be attributed to advisory opinions was most thoroughly debated in connection with the *Admission*, *Reparation*, and *Expenses* cases.

In the discussions surrounding reception of the *Admission* opinion, three distinct points of view were represented in the General Assembly. (1) A majority of the membership favored Assembly recommendations based on implicit acceptance and approval of the Court's opinion. (2) Some states—most notably, France and Sweden—would have limited Assembly action to "taking note of" the opinion and would have eliminated any implication of Assembly endorsement of the opinion from the resolutions. (3) And, finally, the Soviet bloc would have expunged from the resolutions all references to the advisory opinion.[129]

The first group of states emphasized the authoritative nature of the Court's opinion[130] and cited constant League practice with regard to PCIJ advisory opinions.[131]

On the other hand, Sweden and France stressed the nonbinding nature of the opinion and the right of member states to criticize and oppose the Court's views.[132] In addition, noting the divergence of opinion within the Court, the

---

[127]The following examples are illustrative: (1) the willingness of the United States, Greece, and others to accept the Court's answer to question 1(b) in the *Reparation* case; (2) United States acquiescence in the *UN Administrative Tribunal* opinion; (3) the readiness of the United Kingdom, France, and others to apply the Court's *Reservations* rule to the Genocide Convention; (4) acceptance of the *IMCO* opinion by all concerned; (5) and the shift in the position of certain Latin American states in the wake of the *Expenses* opinion.

[128]However, the Soviet Union was not averse to invoking judicial authority when it suited its purpose to do so.

[129]As a minimum, the Soviet Union wished to see certain passages taken from the Court's reasoning cited alongside those taken from the opinion's operative part.

[130]The Court's interpretation was referred to, alternatively, as "official and authentic" and "authoritative." See the remarks of the representatives of the Netherlands, India, and the United Kingdom, GAOR (III/I), Ad Hoc Pol. Ctte., 6th Mtg., 22 November 1948, p. 59; and 9th Mtg., 23 November 1948, pp. 89–90, 95, On the other hand, the Australian representative implied that Assembly ratification of the Court's interpretation would alone make that interpretation "authoritative in the future." *Ibid.*, 12th Mtg., 25 November 1948, p. 131.

[131]Statements of Australia and the United Kingdom, *ibid.*, 6th Mtg., 22 November 1948, p. 58; and 9th Mtg., 23 November 1948, p. 95.

[132]For the Swedish statements, see *ibid.*, 9th Mtg., 23 November 1948, pp. 101–2; and Plenary, 175th Mtg., 8 December 1948, p. 769. For the French views, see *ibid.*, Ad

Swedish representative concluded that the Committee ought not—and, indeed, need not—determine "which judge of the Court had presented the best argument." What was involved, he said, "was not a question of a concrete dispute between two parties in which the General Assembly had to consider a specific opinion of the Court, but a matter of the general interpretation of Article 4." Nor could he agree that the Assembly possessed the requisite competence to give an "authentic and compulsory interpretation of the Charter." By confining itself to "taking note of" the opinion, the Assembly would avoid "passing any judgments on the various opinions expressed."[133]

Members of the Soviet bloc went even further. They denied entirely the existence of an advisory opinion in this case. The separate opinions of Judges Alvarez and Azevedo, they argued, placed those judges with the "minority" rather than with the "so-called majority" within the Court. Consequently, the 9 to 6 vote by which the opinion was supported ought to have been construed as an 8 to 7 vote in favor of the "minority" view.[134] Other arguments presented by these states included the following. (1) The Court itself had stressed the "abstract" nature of the opinion, and it would therefore be wrong to apply that opinion to concrete cases.[135] (2) The request should

---

Hoc Pol. Ctte., 11th Mtg., 24 November 1948, pp. 117–18; 13th Mtg., 26 November 1948, pp. 141–42; 15th Mtg., 27 November 1948, pp. 178–79; and Plenary, 176th Mtg., 8 December 1948, pp. 785–86.

Before the Court, however, France had expressed its willingness to accept in advance any Court opinion. *Admission* case, ICJ Pleadings, 1948, p. 63.

[133]GAOR (III/1), Ad Hoc Pol. Ctte., 9th Mtg., 23 November 1948, pp. 101–2. France, too, was anxious to avoid any implication of approval of the Court's opinion. That opinion ought to be merely one of several "relevant documents" to be studied by the Security Council.

For a summary of the various draft resolutions bearing on the Court's opinion, see *UN Repertory*, Art. 96, pars. 161–62.

[134]See the statements of the U.S.S.R., GAOR (III/1), Ad Hoc Pol. Ctte., 7th Mtg., 22 November 1948, pp. 67–68, 74; 11th Mtg., 24 November 1948, pp. 125–27; and Plenary, 176th Mtg., 8 December 1948, pp. 795–96. Cf. the remarks of the Polish representative, *ibid.*, Ad Hoc Pol. Ctte., 8th Mtg., 23 November 1948, pp. 82–83; 12th Mtg., 25 November 1948, p. 133; and Plenary, 176th Mtg., 8 December 1948, p. 781.

On the other hand, it was argued that the Court alone could determine how the votes of judges should be counted. See, e.g., the remarks of the United States representative, *ibid.*, Ad Hoc Pol. Ctte., 7th Mtg., 22 November 1948, p. 77.

The views of Judge Alvarez do, indeed, appear to coincide more fully with those of the minority. However, this would still leave an 8 to 7 majority. See the remarks of the Canadian representative, *ibid.*, p. 75.

[135]According to Mr. Vyshinsky, the judges "had cautioned the General Assembly that the abstract form of the question excluded the possibility of applying their advisory opinion to any concrete political question. The Court had said that nothing contained in its advisory opinion referred either directly or indirectly to concrete cases or to particular circumstances. The . . . Committee should therefore consider the . . . opinion . . . as an abstract statement." *Ibid.*, pp. 69–70. And, in the words of the Polish delegate, "To apply the . . . opinion to concrete cases, regardless of the Court's own intentions, would

never have been addressed to the Court, since the matter at issue was entirely "political."[136] (3) The Court had been incompetent to give the opinion.[137] (4) Even the Court's interpretation permitted states to take political considerations into account in matters of admission.[138] (5) The judges in the minority were more "eminent" than those in the majority.[139] (6) In any event, the opinion was merely advisory and was not binding.[140] (It is noteworthy that this last argument was only one—and not even the principal one—of the arguments presented.)

As has already been seen, the Assembly's recommendations immediately following the *Admission* opinion were, in fact, based on full acceptance of the opinion.

The starting point of the extensive debates regarding reception of the *Reparation* opinion was a draft resolution under whose terms the Assembly would have accepted the opinion "as an authoritative expression of international law on the questions considered."[141] A Belgian amendment would have had the Assembly express its agreement only with the *replies* given by the Court to the questions submitted to it.[142] And a French amendment would

---

deal a blow at the Court's authority." *Ibid.*, 12th Mtg., 25 November 1948, p. 134. But, as noted by the representative of the United Kingdom, "abstract" was not the equivalent of "meaningless." An "abstract" opinion was nevertheless applicable to particular cases. *Ibid.*, 9th Mtg., 23 November 1948, p. 94. Cf. the statements of Bolivia and Australia, *ibid.*, 10th Mtg., 24 November 1948, p. 112; and 12th Mtg., 25 November 1948, p. 131.

[136]*Ibid.*, 8th Mtg., 23 November 1948, p. 82; 10th Mtg., 24 November 1948, pp. 104, 113; 12th Mtg., 25 November 1948, p. 134; and Plenary, 176th Mtg., 8 December 1948, pp. 781, 788–89..

[137]*Ibid.*, Plenary, 176th Mtg., 8 December 1948, p. 791.

[138]Mr. Vyshinsky cited, in particular, the following passage from the Court's opinion: "Article 4 does not forbid the taking into account of any factor which it is possible reasonably and in good faith to connect with the conditions laid down in that Article. The taking into account of such factors is implied in the very wide and very elastic nature of the prescribed conditions; no relevant political factor—that is to say, none connected with the conditions of admission—is excluded." ICJ Reports, 1948, p. 63. If reference to the opinion were, indeed, to be made, the *entire* opinion, and not merely the Court's conclusions, should be included in the reference, Mr. Vyshinsky insisted. GAOR (III/1), Ad Hoc Pol. Ctte., 12th Mtg., 25 November 1948, p. 137; and Plenary, 176th Mtg., 8 December 1948, p. 796.

[139]See, e.g., *ibid.*, Ad Hoc Pol. Ctte., 7th Mtg., 22 November 1948, p. 68; and Plenary, 176th Mtg., 8 December 1948, p. 795. Cf. the statement of France, *ibid.*, Ad Hoc Pol. Ctte., 11th Mtg., 24 November 1948, p. 117.

[140]See, e.g., *ibid.*, 8th Mtg., 23 November 1948, p. 83; and 13th Mtg., 26 November 1948, p. 141.

[141]UN Doc. A/C.6/L.51, 26 October 1949. (The draft was sponsored by Brazil, India, Iran, and the United States.) This terminology was taken verbatim from a proposal submitted by the Secretary-General. UN Doc. A/955, 23 August 1949, par. 15.

[142]UN Doc. A/C.6/L.57, 3 November 1949.

merely have prefaced the directives to the Secretary-General with the phrase: "Having regard to the advisory opinion rendered by the International Court of Justice on 11 April 1949."[143] The Assembly's substantive directives to the Secretary-General would have remained the same under all three proposals.

The two amendments must be seen in the context of the severe criticism which greeted some of the Court's reasoning,[144] and of the newness and controversial nature of the Court's reply to question 1(b) of the request (namely, the organization's capacity to bring a claim for damage caused to the victim).[145] In these circumstances, acceptance of the Court's replies alone—or, better yet, tacit acceptance of those replies—was deemed more likely to forestall a long debate. Both Belgium and France pointed to this expediential consideration in arguing for their respective amendments.[146] Nevertheless, a long debate did, in fact, ensue, centering upon such questions as the "authoritativeness" of the Court's opinion, the implications of that "authoritativeness" for the Assembly, and the difference between the "authoritativeness" of an opinion and the "binding force" of a judgment.

Some states clearly considered that the Court's opinion possessed something very close to "binding force"—if not from the "legal," then from the "moral," point of view. League practice was cited in support of this stand.[147]

On the other hand, the view most current in Sixth Committee discussions was that the "authoritativeness" of an opinion as a statement of law had to be distinguished from the "binding force" of a judgment. The Assembly was not "bound" to base its recommendations on the Court's opinion. It might,

[143] UN Doc. A/C.6/L.68, 3 November 1949.

[144] See, in particular, the remarks of the Netherlands representative, GAOR (IV), 6th Ctte., 183rd Mtg., 3 November 1949, pp. 273–74.

[145] The Soviet bloc, Mexico, and Peru were among those who objected to this part of the opinion as involving the creation of new law. In particular, they objected to the possibility that the organization might exercise "functional" protection vis-à-vis the victim's own state. Ibid., Mtgs. 183–87, 3–9 November 1949, pp. 272–302 passim.

[146] Ibid., 183rd Mtg., 3 November 1949, pp. 275–76. In addition, the following considerations of principle were put forward. (1) Assembly acceptance of the opinion as "an authoritative expression of international law" might be construed to imply Assembly competence to adopt an authentic interpretation of the Charter on behalf of the UN. (2) The authoritativeness and legal validity of the Court's opinion were intrinsic, and it was not for the Assembly to proclaim the opinion's conformity with international law. The Assembly's task was merely to determine its own future course of action. (3) Following the Admission opinion, the Assembly had merely "noted" the opinion. Acceptance of the present opinion as "authoritative" might, then, give rise to an argument a contrario with respect to the previous opinion, and might necessitate the inclusion of similar qualifications in all future resolutions concerning advisory opinions. GAOR (IV), 6th Ctte., 184th Mtg., 4 November 1949, p. 282.

[147] See the statements of the Uruguayan and Greek representatives, ibid., 186th Mtg., 8 November 1949, p. 297; and Plenary, 262nd Mtg., 1 December 1949, pp. 446–47. The United States view was apparently similar. Ibid., 6th Ctte., 183rd Mtg., 3 November 1949, p. 227; and 185th Mtg., 7 November 1949, p. 293. Cf. the views of Australia, ibid., 184th Mtg., 4 November 1949, p. 287.

at its discretion, take other, nonlegal factors into account; and it might also reject the Court's opinion. What it could not do was affirm or deny the "authoritativeness" of the opinion on the findings of law. That "authoritativeness" was intrinsic to the opinion because, on matters of law, the Court was supreme. For the Assembly even to discuss the merits of the opinion—let alone approve or disapprove them—would imply that the Assembly was competent to act as a court of appeal against the legal pronouncements of the Court. The Assembly should therefore confine itself to determining what action it should take in light of the Court's opinion.[148]

The Soviet bloc and a few other states attributed neither "binding force" nor "authoritativeness"—in the sense set forth above—to the Court's opinion.[149] Not only did the Assembly have the right not to follow the Court's advice; it was also competent to discuss, analyze, and criticize the Court's conclusions and reasoning. "The Court was composed of men no less fallible than others." Only if an opinion was unanimous, "leaving no doubt on the question involved," could the opinion possess "moral value and persuasive authority." Moreover, in the words of the Polish representative:

A judicial organ, called upon to give an opinion, could only do so on the basis of existing rules of law; in no circumstances could it be allowed to create new law. Furthermore, the creation of new law through judgments was limited under Article 59 of the Statute of the Court to the parties to the dispute; that was to say, it became *lex inter partes*. An advisory opinion could never become *lex inter partes*; if it did, that opinion would be much greater in scope than a judgment since, if accepted, it would be binding upon all Member States. . . . If it were admitted . . . that the Court could create law and that the General Assembly could not even discuss the substance of that law, that would mean that all organs of the United Nations would have to submit blindly to all changes of law the Court might suggest, and that eventually the whole development of international law would be exclusively in the hands of the Court. . . . Such a theory of the creation of law without the consent of the Member States might affect the very existence of the States, and was obviously unacceptable.[150]

[148] See, especially, the statements of Belgium (*ibid.*, 183rd Mtg., 3 November 1949, p. 275), France (*ibid.*, p. 276; and Plenary, 262nd Mtg., 1 December 1949, pp. 444–45), and the United Kingdom (*ibid.*, 6th Ctte., 184th Mtg., 4 November 1949, pp. 280–82). In other contexts, however, these states did not hesitate to discuss and criticize the substance of the Court's opinions.

[149] *Ibid.*, 183rd Mtg., 3 November 1949, pp. 278–79 (the U.S.S.R.); *ibid.*, 184th Mtg., 4 November 1949, pp. 279–80 (Poland); *ibid.*, pp. 282–83 (Mexico); *ibid.*, pp. 285–86 (Czechoslovakia); and *ibid.*, 185th Mtg., 7 November 1949, p. 292 (Poland).

[150] *Ibid.*, 185th Mtg., 7 November 1949, p. 292; cf. the Czechoslovakian statement, *ibid.*, 184th Mtg., 4 November 1949, p. 286.

The consensus in the Committee was that the French amendment might be substituted for the original draft, thus replacing explicit acceptance of the Court's opinion with tacit acceptance. At the same time, in line with a Cuban suggestion[151] (concurred in by France),[152] the following explanation was inserted into the Sixth Committee's report.

> With regard to the draft resolution proposed by France it was stated that, in omitting the paragraph reading *"Resolves* that it accepts the advisory opinion . . . as an authoritative expression of international law on the questions considered" . . . it was not intended to cast doubt upon the authority of the Court's opinion; however, in view of the procedure followed previously by the General Assembly with regard to advisory opinions, it was considered that a statement to that effect in the resolution was unnecessary. It was specifically requested that the report to the General Assembly should make it clear that, in accepting the French draft resolution, those who had supported the . . . joint draft resolution had not changed their view, but had merely considered that the authoritative nature of the advisory opinion should be taken for granted.[153]

As noted above, the substantive recommendations adopted would have been the same had the opinion been explicitly accepted as binding.

In the *Expenses* case, as already noted, the issue of Article 19 added particular significance to the debate regarding Assembly action on the opinion. That debate revolved around the question whether the opinion should be "accepted" or merely "taken note of."

For "accepting" the opinion, the following arguments were presented, *inter alia*. (1) The Assembly had established a uniform practice of accepting or acting upon the Court's opinions, and to break with that tradition "would inflict a serious blow on the prestige of the Court and would sap the vitality of international law."[154] (2) Although the Court's opinion was not binding, it

---

[151]*Ibid.*, 184th Mtg., 4 November 1949, pp. 283–84. Earlier, the United States representative had voiced the fear that suppression of the phrase at issue might give rise to arguments *a contrario. Ibid.*, 183rd Mtg., 3 November 1949, p. 277.

[152]*Ibid.*, 186th Mtg., 8 November 1949, p. 300.

[153]UN Doc. A/1101 and Corr. 1, 16 and 17 November 1949, par. 7.

[154]GAOR (XVII), 5th Ctte., 961st Mtg., 3 December 1962, pp. 277–78 (statement of the United States). Most other representatives who spoke in favor of "accepting" the opinion emphasized one or both of these motifs—maintaining past tradition and upholding the Court's prestige and authority. Cf. the statement of the Secretary-General, p. 351, n. 109, above. The relevant remarks are contained in GAOR (XVII), 5th Ctte., Mtgs. 961–73, 3–12 December 1962, pp. 275–352 *passim.*

did constitute an authoritative statement of the law. The Assembly was free to accept or reject the opinion, but "it could not say that the Court was wrong from the legal standpoint or that the Assembly did not agree with its findings, because the Assembly had no competence to agree or disagree with the Court on a point of law, as the Court was the highest authority on matters of international law, and its findings were necessarily authoritative."[155] (3) Acceptance of the opinion would not only uphold the authority of the Court; it would make the opinion part of the "law recognized by the United Nations."[156] (4) "It would be absurd for the Assembly merely to note the opinion of the Court when it had expressly asked for authoritative legal guidance. Moreover, the use of the phrase 'takes note of' in a General Assembly resolution was usually interpreted to mean a negative or at least indifferent reception."[157]

Those who opposed accepting the Court's advisory opinion consisted basically of two groups of states. The first, comprised mainly of France and the Soviet bloc, emphasized their disagreement with the Court's substantive views and with the Court's consenting altogether to render an opinion in this case. The second group, led by Jordan, tended to emphasize the expediential grounds for not accepting the opinion. The initiative for the move to have the Assembly merely "take note of" the opinion came from the second group but had the blessings of the first.

Among the most important arguments presented by the opponents of "acceptance" of the opinion were the following. (1) An advisory opinion, as the Court itself emphasized, is purely advisory and nonbinding. Indeed, to treat the opinion as binding would be contrary to international law.[158]

---

[155] Statement of the United States representative, who was citing the United Kingdom view in the *Reparation* case. *Ibid.*, 961st Mtg., 3 December 1962, p. 277. In a similar vein, the Danish representative remarked: "What must be avoided at all costs was that a political organ like the General Assembly should set itself up as a court of appeal and consider itself more competent than the International Court to give opinions on legal questions." *Ibid.* Cf. the statement of Sweden, *ibid.*, 963rd Mtg., 5 December 1962, p. 289. For the view that the Court's opinion should be considered binding, see the statement of Colombia, *ibid.*, 972nd Mtg., p. 345.

[156] *Ibid.*, 962nd Mtg., 4 December 1962, p. 282 (statement of the United Kingdom). The remarks of Judge Lauterpacht in the *South West Africa (Committee)* opinion were cited in this regard. See ICJ Reports, 1956, p. 46.

[157] GAOR (XVII), 5th Ctte., 962nd Mtg., 4 December 1962, p. 283. The view that adoption of the Jordanian amendment would be tantamount to implicit rejection of the Court's opinion was widely held and had considerable influence in defeating that amendment. See, e.g., the statements of Liberia (*ibid.*, 972nd Mtg., 12 December 1962, p. 344) and Uruguay (*ibid.*, 973rd Mtg., 12 December 1962, p. 347).

[158] See, in particular, the remarks of the following: France (*ibid.*, 962nd Mtg., 4 December 1962, p. 284); Jordan (*ibid.*, 964th Mtg., 6 December 1962, p. 291; and 969th Mtg., 11 December 1962, pp. 326–27); Poland (*ibid.*, 964th Mtg., 6 December 1962, p. 292); and Hungary (*ibid.*, 966th Mtg., 7 December 1962, p. 308).

(2) Moreover, by accepting the Court's opinion, the Assembly could not endow that opinion with binding force. For, if it could, it would possess the power to revise the Charter de facto, and "the jurisdiction of the Court would be admitted as binding in a matter in which its competence had been expressly denied by the drafters of the United Nations Charter."[159] (3) The crux of the problem before the Assembly was political, not legal. As a legal document, the Court's opinion could be only one of the factors taken into account in guiding the Assembly. By taking note of the opinion, the Assembly would be acknowledging this fact.[160] (4) In deciding to "take note of" the opinion, the Assembly would not be evincing lack of respect for the Court. On the contrary, by thus minimizing the number of negative votes on the resolution, the Assembly would enhance the Court's prestige.[161] (5) The authority of the organization was likely to be most gravely impaired in the event the Assembly adopted a resolution which it later found itself incapable of implementing.[162] (6) An even greater danger, to be avoided at all costs, was the possibility that the attempt to implement the present resolution would lead to the use of Article 19 against a major group of states. Such a move would threaten the organization's very existence.[163] (7) "Taking note of" the opinion would fully conform with past Assembly practice.[164] (8) Acceptance of the opinion by the Fifth Committee would imply that the Committee was a higher authority than the Court, and this would tend to undermine the Court's authority.[165]

[159] *Ibid.*, 962nd Mtg., 4 December 1962, p. 284 (France); 964th Mtg., 6 December 1962, pp. 291–92 (Jordan and Poland); and 965th Mtg., 7 December 1962, pp. 300–301 (Czechoslovakia).

[160] See, especially, the statements of Jordan (*ibid.*, 964th Mtg., 6 December 1962, p. 291) and Algeria (*ibid.*, 971st Mtg., 11 December 1962, p. 340; and 972nd Mtg., 12 December 1962, p. 341). The views thus expressed accorded with some of those voiced by several Western states in the *Admission* and *Reparation* cases.

[161] *Ibid.*, 972nd Mtg., 12 December 1962, p. 341 (Algeria); cf. the statements of Iraq and France, *ibid.*, 971st Mtg., 11 December 1962, pp. 338–39.

[162] *Ibid.*, 969th Mtg., 11 December 1962, p. 327 (Jordan). This argument raises a rather interesting question which has been all but neglected in post-opinion debates. Where it is clear that attempted implementation of an opinion will meet with resistance on the part of important states, will the Court's prestige necessarily be harmed by failure of the requesting organ to base its action on the opinion? Or is the Court's prestige perhaps harmed more by open defiance of the Court's opinion following acceptance of the opinion by the Assembly?

[163] *Ibid.*, 964th Mtg., 6 December 1962, p. 291 (Jordan); 965th and 971st Mtgs., 7 and 11 December 1962, pp. 301, 339–40 (Czechoslovakia); 969th Mtg., 11 December 1962, p. 329 (Syria); and 972nd Mtg., 12 December 1962, p. 343 (Indonesia).

[164] *Ibid.*, 973rd Mtg., 12 December 1962, pp. 347–48. The Jordanian representative pointed out that his delegation's amendment "was by no means revolutionary in its wording." In previous instances, too, the Court's opinion had merely been "taken note of." "Acceptance" was the exception rather than the rule.

[165] *Ibid.*, 967th Mtg., 10 December 1962, p. 311 (the Ukrainian S.S.R.).

As noted above, the Assembly did, in fact, "accept" the Court's opinion, but it subsequently shied away from pressing forward with the implications of this "acceptance."

Thus, it can be seen that, despite frequent challenges to the authority of the Court's opinions, the requesting organ, for its part, has consistently sought to uphold that authority and to implement the Court's advice to the fullest. However, the action of the requesting organ has not, in all instances, been sufficient to make an opinion truly effective. In certain cases, such effectiveness has hinged on the attitudes of one or more key states, whose cooperation in implementing the opinion was not forthcoming. Given the majority system of voting, it has been possible to consult the Court without the consent of these key states, but requests made under these conditions have been predictably futile exercises. In the words of Leo Gross: "What the departure from unanimity has accomplished is that the United Nations now has at its disposal an effective procedure for requesting advisory opinions but not a procedure for effective advisory opinions."[166]

The most effective and useful of the Court's opinions were those rendered in the *Reparation, Reservations, UN Administrative Tribunal, UNESCO*, and *IMCO* cases. In each of these cases, the prognosis for acceptance of the opinion and for the opinion's aiding in the solution of the basic problem involved was favorable at the pre-request phase.[167]

In the *Reparation* case, the request for the Court's opinion was made unanimously and amid general agreement as to the desirability of affording some form of protection to UN agents. While in the post-opinion phase there was some resistance to accepting the Court's opinion in its entirety, this resistance did not prevent the Assembly from giving the Secretary-General the necessary authority to pursue claims on behalf of the United Nations. It was open to individual respondent states to deny the organization's right to present claims, but, apparently, no such denial was forthcoming. Of the states against whom claims were presented in the immediate aftermath of the opinion, Israel alone paid compensation, but the other states did not base their refusals to pay on nonrecognition of the principle of the organization's right to present claims.[168]

---

[166] Leo Gross, "The International Court of Justice and the United Nations," *RC*, 121 (1967-II): 369.

[167] See Chapter III.

[168] In later UN claims, the Secretary-General succeeded in obtaining satisfaction from other states as well. An account of the claims presented and of the action taken on those claims is recorded in the *Annual Reports of the Secretary-General on the Work of the Organization* (Supp. No. 1 of the General Assembly's *Official Records*). See, especially,

Implementation of the *Reservations* opinion did not depend on the acquiescence of particular states. Directives to the Secretary-General concerning his depositary practice could be given by majority vote, a fact which was obvious at both the pre-request and post-opinion phases. Furthermore, no state considered that it had a vital stake in blocking implementation of the opinion.[169] Basically, a general question of treaty law, involving the conflicting requirements of certainty versus flexibility, was at issue. As noted above, the Court's ruling gained currency with time, because, with the expansion of the international community, the need for flexibility in treaty law became paramount.

Again, in the *UN Administrative Tribunal* case, the Assembly majority was competent to order payment of the contested awards. Moreover, given the United States stand in the pre-request phase, American acquiescence in the opinion might be anticipated.[170] In the aftermath of the opinion, the United States endorsed the Assembly's decision to honor the awards,[171] but at the same time pressed for the adoption of a review procedure for future Administrative Tribunal judgments.

Each of the two opinions which related to specialized agencies could be implemented by a majority vote of the requesting organ.

In all of the above cases, the Court's advice proved helpful in resolving the difficulties which had prompted consultation of the Court.

The same cannot be said of the second major group of cases—namely, the *Admission, Peace Treaties* (First Phase), *South West Africa (Status)*, and *Expenses* cases (and probably, the *Namibia* case as well). Here, the opposition of certain states rendered the opinions either irrelevant or—even worse—harmful.

The request in the *Admission* case was made in the face of the certainty that the Soviet Union would not accept an opinion which failed to corroborate its own views. On this ground alone, the opinion was doomed at the outset, as many states recognized at the time the decision to consult the Court was made. Beyond this, as noted above,[172] no interpretation of Article

---

the Reports for the 5th to 10th sessions, UN Docs. A/1287, pp. 124–25; A/1844, pp. 188–89, A/2141, pp. 160–61; A/2404, pp. 144–45; A/2663, pp. 101–2; and A/2911, p. 109. See also UN Docs. S/7867, S/7873, S/7882, and S/7886. One of the claims paid by Israel, it might be noted, involved injury caused to a person entitled through the victim, as well as injury caused to the organization.

[169] The Soviet Union might have considered that it had such a stake, had the Court's opinion upheld the unanimity rule, for Assembly endorsement of the opinion would then have entailed nonacceptance of the Soviet Union as a party to the Genocide Convention.

[170] The United States attitude was one of "benevolent abstention." As noted earlier, it may have welcomed the opportunity to have the Court decide the matter. See Chapter III.

[171] At the insistence of the United States, payment was made out of a special indemnity fund.

[172] See the discussion of the *Admission* case in Chapter III.

4(1), even if accepted, could have gone far toward breaking the admission deadlock. It was hardly accidental that both the majority and minority opinions were predicated on the exercise of good faith.[173]

As seen earlier, the admission deadlock was finally broken when the Court's advisory opinion was ignored. Whether the effect of the Court's pronouncement was to retard agreement between the two blocs in the UN is a matter of conjecture. It would appear, however, that fluctuations in the temperature of the Cold War were determinative, and that the Court's opinion was merely irrelevant—not detrimental—to the final solution of the admission problem.

Similarly irrelevant was the Court's opinion in the first phase of the *Peace Treaties* case. Questions III and IV of the request were, of course, based on the expectation that Bulgaria, Hungary, and Rumania would *not*, in fact, comply with the Court's ruling. By its negative answer to question III, the Court effectively put an end to further futile endeavors in the matter. The pronouncements of two-man treaty commissions on the merits of the human rights issues involved might have yielded some further propaganda dividends for the West, but they could hardly have had much effect on the observance of human rights in the three communist countries.

The effect of the *South West Africa (Status)* opinion is more difficult to gauge. But it is entirely likely that, at least in the initial post-opinion period, the prospects for a solution to the South West Africa problem were to some extent hindered by the Court's pronouncement.

South Africa's attitude in the pre-request phase,[174] and even in the immediate post-opinion discussions,[175] was not quite as intransigent as it was later to become. While South Africa was clearly unwilling to concede all of the rights which the Court held the UN to possess in respect of South West Africa, it was prepared to negotiate with the UN and to accept some form of accountability for its administration of the territory—albeit that accountability would have been accepted vis-à-vis a mere fragment of the international community. Without a Court opinion, South Africa might not have ventured even this far; so, to this extent, the opinion was potentially helpful in facilitating a solution to the problem of the territory. At the same time, however,

---

[173] See, on this point, Lauterpacht, *International Court*, p. 50, n. 40, and pp. 149–52; and Lissitzyn, *International Court*, p. 91. Cf. the statement of France in the Assembly to the effect that the difference between majority and minority opinions was merely semantic, and was "largely based on a quibble." GAOR (III/1), Ad Hoc Pol. Ctte., 11th Mtg., 24 November 1948, p. 117; *ibid.* (IV), Plenary, 251st Mtg., 22 November 1949, p. 316.

[174] See Chapter III.

[175] See, e.g., the South African statement in GAOR (V), 4th Ctte., 191st Mtg., 30 November 1950, p. 319.

the opinion served to solidify the UN position and to establish a bedrock minimum below which no state would dare suggest that the UN go. The trouble was that this minimum was still far beyond South Africa's maximum. In these circumstances, compromise became impossible. By helping to rigidify the UN stand, the opinion also played a part in precluding a negotiated solution with South Africa.

However, even with the 1950 opinion in hand, a more realistic attitude might have led the UN to beat a tactical retreat from absolute insistence on all the rights spelled out in the Court's opinion and to accept "half-a-loaf." After all, in the game that was being played, South Africa held all the cards. Instead, the organization deluded itself into thinking that South Africa could be coerced, and that international supervision of the administration of South West Africa could be meaningful even without South African cooperation.

Whatever the effect of the Court's opinion in the initial period, with the passage of time and the influx of African states into the UN, the opinion became rather more irrelevant than harmful.[176] As South Africa retreated into self-imposed isolation, the UN fell back upon a form of escalating utopianism. The times became ever less propitious for compromise solutions—opinion or no opinion.

The *Expenses* opinion was as ineffective as the *South West Africa (Status)* opinion in facilitating a solution of the underlying problem which gave rise to the request. Moreover, the detrimental consequences of the *Expenses* opinion were even more evident.

That neither the Soviet Union nor France would voluntarily agree to pay the controversial assessments, even after a Court opinion, was a foregone conclusion. And the threat of invoking Article 19 against a Great Power was not, in the last analysis, a credible one. The threat did nothing to alleviate the organization's financial crisis, but it did much to precipitate the institutional crisis which culminated in the "lost" nineteenth Assembly session. Undoubtedly, in the absence of a supportive advisory opinion, matters would never have been brought to such a head. The opinion allowed Assembly members temporarily to lose sight of political realities. When vision was restored, the institutional crisis was, at least in its acute manifestations, overcome. The financial crisis remained unaffected.[177]

[176]The opinion may be said to have had this minimal effect: South Africa did not proceed with its plans to annex the territory of South West Africa outright. This was scant consolation for the UN, however, since it was still barred from exercising any effective control over the administration of the territory.

[177]In some respects the latter crisis worsened after delivery of the opinion. Even the integrity of the regular budget began to be affected. See Russell, *op. cit.*, p. 81. It is not clear, however, that the Court's opinion played any role in these developments.

It is too early to predict what the ultimate effect (if any) of the *Namibia* opinion on the root problem will be, but it seems probable that the opinion will be as irrelevant in the long term as it has been in the short term.[178] In the immediate aftermath of the opinion it was clear that the states the Security Council resolutions had failed to persuade—most notably, South Africa, France, and the United Kingdom—remained unmoved by the Court's opinion.[179] (In fact, these states may have been strengthened in their pre-existing attitudes by the powerful judicial dissents entered on the issue of mandate revocation.) The Council's own actions also were probably little affected by the opinion. With or without the opinion, the process of verbal escalation by resolution would have proceeded apace, and the impasse over Chapter VII would have continued unabated. In one sense, as already noted, the opinion may have produced a cathartic effect (perhaps on the South African side as well) and opened up prospects for a negotiated solution to the Namibian question. Whether this proves to be so remains to be seen. However, in the long run, it would seem that internal pressures within the territory (such as the stirrings among the Ovambo) will be more important than external pressures, and that, among the external pressures, the weight of the Court's opinion will be, at best, very minor.

In brief, in the UN period, the relationship between a Court opinion and the fundamental problem from which it had sprung was as follows. Frequently the opinion was helpful; often it was irrelevant; and at times it was positively harmful.

CONCLUSIONS

In both the League and UN periods, the Court's opinions were treated with the utmost respect by the organs which solicited them. Post-opinion recommendations were normally based on full acceptance of the Court's views on the points of law submitted to it. But, in the UN period, such acceptance was frequently preceded by extensive debates over the authority and effect of advisory opinions and over the terminology of post-opinion resolutions.

---

[178] In one respect, the opinion may have accomplished the goal set for it by many Council members—namely, the rehabilitation of the Court's image in the eyes of the Third World. See the statement of Burundi, UN Doc. S/PV.1584, 27 September 1971, pp. 23-30.

[179] See the statements of the South African foreign minister (*ibid.*, pp. 38-62) and the representatives of France (UN Doc. S/PV.1588, 5 October 1971, pp. 7-15) and the United Kingdom (UN Doc. S/PV.1589, 6 October 1971, pp. 23-33).

More significant, however, was the difference in the reaction of individual states to the Court's opinions. In the course of the League's consideration of the nature of the vote required for requests,[180] proponents of the unanimity rule often warned of the dire consequences which adoption of the majority rule might have for the prestige of the Court and for the authority of its opinions.[181] In the UN period, these prophecies were to a great extent fulfilled. Far too many opinions turned out to be nothing more than interesting academic exercises which reflected little credit on the organization and did little to enhance the Court's prestige. And this typical UN phenomenon was a direct consequence of the inequivalence between the vote needed to request an opinion and the crucial "vote" needed to make the opinion effective. The attempts to use the Court to bail the organization out of its own ineffectuality or to score propaganda victories had denouements which were entirely predictable. From a practical standpoint, state consent was as indispensable in the UN era as it had been in the League era.

In certain UN cases, of course, an equivalence between the two votes—that required for requesting an opinion and that required for implementing it—*did* exist. And, in these cases, the advisory function was used to greatest advantage. Similarly effective were those opinions in which no vital state interests were felt to be adversely affected.

The question of the binding force of advisory opinions has been the focus of much theorizing ever since the introduction of the advisory jurisdiction of the Permanent Court.[182] Apart from doctrinal writings, statements on the question abound in League discussions on the vote required for requests and on United States accession to the Court's Statute; in the pre-request discus-

---

[180] See Chapter IV, pp. 213-21.

[181] See, e.g., the remarks of Sir Cecil Hurst (LN, Records of the 9th Ass., 1st Ctte., 1928, p. 45) and M. Politis (LN, Records of the 16th Ass., 1st Ctte., 1935, p. 59). Cf. the statement of M. Titulesco in the *Salamis* case, LNOJ, 1927, p. 1474.

[182] See, e.g., the following: Ake Hammarskjöld, *Juridiction Internationale* (Leiden: Sijthoff, 1938), pp. 289-91. D. Negulesco, "L'évolution de la procédure des avis consultatifs de la Cour Permanente de Justice Internationale," *RC*, 57 (1936-III): 64-80; Goodrich, "The Nature of the Advisory Opinions of the Permanent Court of International Justice," pp. 738-58; Hudson, *Permanent Court*, pp. 511-13; Charles de Visscher, "Les avis consultatifs de la Cour Permanente de Justice Internationale," *RC*, 26 (1929-I): 23 ff.; and Salo Engel, "La force obligatoire des avis consultatifs de la Cour Permanente de Justice Internationale," *Revue de Droit International et de Législation Comparée*, 3rd Ser., 17 (1936): 768-800. Most of the above, with the notable exception of Hudson (who states: "An advisory opinion is what it purports to be. It is advisory.") and Engel, attributed a degree of binding force to the PCIJ's opinions. On the UN period, cf. the views of Rosenne, *Law and Practice*, 2: 744-47, with those of Leo Gross, "The International Court of Justice and the United Nations," pp. 415-21.

sions in both periods; in the debates surrounding "stillborn" requests; in pleadings before the ICJ; in post-opinion discussions in the UN era; and in majority and individual opinions within the ICJ.

Even when they originate with the same source, however, these statements are conflicting and contradictory. The particular context in which a statement is made is frequently determinative in this regard. Thus, e.g., a state that seeks judicial clarification will normally emphasize the "advisory" nature of the opinion in the pre-request phase and (provided the state is satisfied with the opinion rendered) the "authoritative" nature of the opinion in the post-opinion phase. On the other hand, a state opposed to the request or the opinion will tend to argue the reverse.[183]

For its part, the ICJ has often underscored the nonbinding nature of advisory opinions—especially in cases where the Court's competence to give an opinion has been challenged.[184] Individual judges, however, have been more willing to concede to advisory opinions an effect very close to that of actual judgments.[185]

In realistic terms, it is difficult to point to any opinion whose fate would have been different had it been an actual judgment. Certainly, the treatment accorded by the requesting organs could hardly have been more deferential.

---

[183] See Chapter IV. Even the Soviet bloc has not hesitated, in certain contexts, to stress the "binding" nature which opinions have assumed in practice. See, e.g., the Oral Statement of Czechoslovakia in the *Admission* case, ICJ Pleadings, 1948, p. 114; and cf. the dissenting opinion of Judge Krylov in the *Peace Treaties* case, ICJ Reports, 1950, p. 105.

On occasion, the *non*binding nature of advisory opinions has been adduced as a consideration against seeking an opinion. The usual argument then is that an opinion, being merely "advisory," would leave the basic problem unaffected. See, e.g., the Rumanian explanation during the League Council's initial consideration of the Hungarian optants case, LNOJ, 1923, p. 609; and cf. the Philippine objection to the request in the *Reservations* case, GAOR (V), 6th Ctte., 225th Mtg., 20 October 1950, p. 86.

[184] Thus, in the *Peace Treaties* case, the Court stated: "The Court's reply is only of an advisory character: as such, it has no binding force." ICJ Reports, 1950, p. 71. See also *ibid.*, 1956, p. 84; and 1962, p. 168. It is noteworthy that in the *Namibia* case, despite challenges to its competence, the Court did not emphasize the advisory nature of the opinion.

[185] See, especially, the three dissenting opinions in the *Peace Treaties* case, as well as the separate opinion of Judge Azevedo, ICJ Reports, 1950, pp. 80-81, 84-87, 91-92, 101-2, and 105. Cf., in the *Expenses* case, the dissenting opinions of Judges Moreno Quintana, Koretsky, and Bustamante, *ibid.*, 1962, pp. 240, 254, and 304. See, in this connection, the following observation by Leo Gross: "The Court [in the *Peace Treaties* case] wrote a prologue for the future, the minority wrote an epilogue for the past." "The International Court of Justice and the United Nations," p. 416.

In the *South West Africa (Committee)* case, Judge Lauterpacht expressed the view that the 1950 opinion was "the law recognized by the United Nations," but conceded that this did not necessarily entail any legal obligations for South Africa. ICJ Reports, 1956, pp. 46-47. Cf. the criticism of Judge Lauterpacht's views in Gross, "The International Court of Justice and the United Nations," p. 418.

Moreover, the action of these organs appears in many cases to have been based on a feeling of obligation, and not solely on considerations of political expediency.[186] As for the action of individual states, again, the assumption that a particular opinion would have been more effective had it been embodied in a binding judgment remains unproved. Indeed, this was one of the assumptions upon which the UN proceeded in encouraging the institution of contentious proceedings against South West Africa. But, to this extent, the entire costly effort to get a binding judgment against South Africa was, it is submitted, misconceived. It was not the "advisory" nature of the 1950 opinion which was to blame for South African recalcitrance. South Africa clearly would have been as unwilling to accept *any* adverse judicial ruling in a matter which it believed affected its vital interests. Perhaps South Africa's own statements deluded the Assembly majority into believing otherwise, for, in the South African repertoire of justifications for noncompliance with the 1950 opinion, the "advisory" nature of that opinion assumed a prominent place. (There was, of course, another, more important, reason for the move to invoke the Court's compulsory jurisdiction—namely, the possibility of recourse to Article 94 of the Charter. But, again, the expectation that a Court judgment would really be determinative in the matter of whether or not to use enforcement action against South Africa was probably unwarranted.)[187]

In a state's decision to comply or not to comply with a Court pronouncement, it appears that the "advisory" or "binding" nature of the pronouncement is not the crucial factor. What is crucial is that state's willingness to acquiesce in an adverse judicial ruling—of whatever sort.[188] Such willingness depends on many other factors, such as the importance of the interests which are at stake, confidence in the impartiality and fairness of the Court, the place of observance of international law in a state's hierarchy of values, and the ability and willingness of other states to exercise meaningful coercion to ensure compliance. Before deciding to request opinions, authorized organs might do well to assess these factors.

---

[186] Speaking of the UN period, Rosenne observed: "The succession of resolutions [adopted upon receipt of the Court's opinions] ... cannot be explained away in political terms only: the constant repetition of almost stereotyped formulas indicates at least an *opinio juris*." *Law and Practice*, 2: 747, n. 2.

[187] See Julius Stone, "Realism and Apartheid," *The Australian*, 26 September 1966, p. 9; and Slonim, *op. cit.*, Conclusions. Had the Security Council so desired, it might have taken enforcement action on the basis of the threat to the peace which the South West Africa question was declared by Assembly resolutions to pose. As noted, the Security Council remains, to date, deadlocked over the issue of invoking Chapter VII.

[188] The fact that the *Corfu Channel* case was a judgment did not make it any more acceptable to Albania. Cf. Stone, "Realism and Apartheid."

CONCLUDING
OBSERVATIONS

The experience of half a century with the advisory jurisdiction has surely served to underscore once again what has become self-evident and axiomatic to a generation of "realists"—namely, that recourse to judicial processes (of whatever sort) is primarily a function of the political context. Certainly the key to the dramatic contrasts between the uses of the advisory jurisdiction in the League and UN eras must be sought, first of all, in the political framework within which each world organization operated.

The context in which the League functioned, at least in the early period of its existence, was that of a stable peace settlement. Under such conditions, judicial solutions could, and did, assume a prominent place. As Lord Robert Cecil foretold in 1919:

> It seems probable . . . that in normal times the Permanent Court would have work to do. And almost certainly there will be a great many cases arising out of the Peace Settlement for which an International Court will be required. This was the case after the Congress of Vienna; and if it so happened now, the Permanent Court might very quickly establish for itself an extremely important and valuable position.[1]

Lord Cecil was referring in this passage to the Court's contentious jurisdiction. In practice, however, the Court came to play the role of Interpreter and Final Arbiter of the Peace Settlement in its advisory capacity at least as much as in its contentious capacity.[2] Upon encountering difficulties of interpretation, the various agencies set up by the Great Powers to supervise and implement the peace settlement—and, among these agencies, the League Council

[1] Cited in Miller, *Covenant*, 1: 63-64.
[2] As noted above (Chapter III), a certain interchangeability developed between the two jurisdictions of the Court.

itself occupied a focal position[3]—frequently resorted to the Court's advisory jurisdiction as the most efficacious means of clarifying the matters in dispute. The absence of an "organic connection" between the PCIJ and the League was, in practice, largely irrelevant.[4]

As long as the consensus which underlay the peace settlement lasted, and as long as the status quo enshrined in that settlement could be forcibly maintained, legal and judicial methods of dispute settlement were deemed appropriate. Once the peace settlement began to disintegrate, however, "political" rather than "legal" solutions became the order of the day. Significantly, the last PCIJ advisory opinion was rendered in 1935.[5]

From its very inception, the UN operated under conditions which were radically different from those of its forebear. No general peace settlement attended its birth.[6] The attainment of a stable and legitimized status quo eludes the organization yet. So, too, does the achievement of a meaningful consensus in a world torn by East-West and North-South cleavages. Within this political context, almost every dispute handled by the UN—and, *a fortiori*, by the Security Council—became, understandably, too "hot" and too volatile for effective application of judicial procedures. Many of the questions connected with such matters as decolonization, racial conflict, and the Cold War were particularly unamenable to "legal" solutions. (In fact, these questions proved to be unamenable to "political" solutions by the UN as well.)

In the absence of a stable peace settlement, all issues tended to become "politicized." The UN Charter—the one most important embodiment of East-West consensus in the post-World War II world—also was swept up in the general "politicization." When the world organization was established in 1945, it was expected that, with the "tools" forged at San Francisco, the consensus necessary to generate a final peace settlement would be fashioned.[7] Instead, the same lack of consensus which barred general stabilization caused

---

[3] The League Assembly's role in supervising the peace settlement was, by comparison, minor, and this fact may have had something to do with its nonuse of the Court's advisory function.

[4] There is much validity in the following comment by Leo Gross: "While the integration between the Permanent Court and the League might have been useful but was in fact not necessary, the integration of the International Court into the United Nations was neither necessary nor useful." "The International Court of Justice and the United Nations," *RC*, 121 (1967-II): 331.

[5] See, on this point, Lissitzyn, *International Court*, pp. 73, 90. In 1939, the League Council voted to request an opinion in the matter of ex-officials of the Saar, but the request was never filed in Court.

[6] Even those peace treaties which were concluded did not (at least insofar as they encompassed the Soviet bloc countries) embody more than a fleeting consensus (if that). Cf., in this connection, the pre-request history of the *Peace Treaties* case in Chapter III.

[7] See Ruth B. Russell, assisted by Jeannette E. Muther, *A History of the United Nations Charter* (Washington, D.C.: The Brookings Institution, 1958), p. 953.

even the organizational machinery to become a bone of contention in the Cold War and in the struggle over decolonization. In these circumstances, requests for judicial clarification of Charter provisions represented nothing but attempts by one side in the controversy to secure ineffective judicial sanction for its views—often for the sole purpose of scoring a propaganda victory over its opponent.

However, most suggestions for requesting judicial interpretation of Charter provisions were never accepted by the UN political organs in any case. These organs jealously guarded their right to interpret the Charter independently, and, in particular, their right to determine questions relating to their own competence. Already at San Francisco, and especially in the terminology of Article 2(7), the desire for greater freedom from regulation by legal norms and by "legal" agencies was indicated. With time, this desire became more pronounced; nor was it confined to provisions and issues of a more "political" content. The reluctance of UN organs to cede any measure of decision-making to the Court extended even to issues traditionally embraced within the realm of international law. It is in terms of the attitudes of states toward international law, and particularly in terms of the present-day "crisis" in international law,[8] that the perspective of UN organs in this regard becomes more explicable.

Until the latter part of the League era, when ideological rifts began to tear the fabric of the organization asunder, the League was characterized by a large measure of agreement regarding the governing norms of international law. The fact that the League was almost exclusively European undoubtedly worked to reinforce this consensus. With agreement on the substantive norms went a degree of willingness to see matters adjudicated by third parties (including the Court) on the basis of existing law.

In the UN era, on the other hand, vigorous challenges to traditional international law norms have come from two quarters, the Soviet Union and the states of the Third World. The challenge of the former is based on ideological and pragmatic grounds,[9] while that of the latter is based primarily on dissatisfaction with pre-existing norms which they had no voice in shaping.[10] Given these negative attitudes toward traditional international law, the attempt to minimize the role of the Court—the organ whose task it is to apply existing norms—has followed as a corollary. The League preference for judicial clarifi-

[8]See, in general, Oliver J. Lissitzyn, *International Law Today and Tomorrow* (Dobbs Ferry, N.Y.: Oceana, 1965), and the works cited therein.

[9]*Ibid.*, pp. 46–71.

[10]*Ibid.*, pp. 72–101. Cf. the Report of the 1966 Special Committee on Friendly Relations, UN Doc. A/6230, 27 June 1966, par. 219; and the discussions in GAOR (XXV), 6th Ctte., Mtgs. 1210–18, 29 October–5 November 1970, and Mtgs. 1224–30, 12–18 November 1970, *passim*, on the review of the role of the Court.

cation has been replaced by a marked UN preference for "legislation by codification" (an area in which the League was signally unsuccessful)[11] and "quasi legislation by declaration." By these processes, the Third World has attempted to employ its numerical strength to generate a new, more universal, consensus in place of the former "European" consensus. Perhaps once this evolution is completed and the new norms become part of the established corpus of law applied by the Court, a greater willingness to resort to judicial procedures will be forthcoming. (Perhaps, too, the "traditional" supporters of increased use of the Court—the Western states—will then defect, and the roles of proponent and opponent of recourse to the Court will be permanently reversed.)

Apart from the issue of the norms applied by the Court, there have been additional grounds for the opposition of the Soviet Union and the Afro-Asian states to judicial solutions. As is well known, the Soviet Union has always denied the possibility of having impartial, neutral arbitrators between the Soviet and non-Soviet worlds.[12] As for the Afro-Asian states, in the pre-1966 period the great disparity between their numerical strength in the General Assembly and their representation on the Court undoubtedly led them to prefer the former body over the latter and to view the Court with a measure of wariness and reserve. In the aftermath of the surprising 1966 *South West Africa* judgment, the earlier reserve gave way to positive antagonism and hostility. So deep was the disillusionment with the Court that, despite the steady increase in Afro-Asian representation on that body since 1966, Third World suspicion of the Court continued unabated for several years. By 1970, however, the "trauma of 1966" had weakened sufficiently for the Afro-Asian states to countenance submission of a "test case" to the Court in its new composition. This "test" the Court passed "with flying colors." Nevertheless, in terms of the future role of the Court, the "test" may have raised more questions than it answered.

What, for example, does this revival of the Court's advisory function augur for the future? Will it be the harbinger of a significant stimulation of the volume of the Court's advisory business? If so—and more important—what will be the nature of the new requests sent to the Court? Will the Court increasingly be called upon to add judicial legitimization to the collective legitimization processes of the UN political organs? And, if the Court is used in this manner, how will its prestige be affected in the long run?

It is certainly premature at this point to hazard predictions regarding such future probabilities. However, with respect to the last question posed, past experience would seem to indicate that indiscriminate stimulation of the

[11] See A. E. Gotlieb, "The International Law Commission," *Canadian Yearbook of International Law*, 4 (1966): 65; Gross, *op. cit.*, p. 336, n. 38.

[12] See the statement of Maxim Litvinov, cited in Lissitzyn, *International Law Today and Tomorrow*, p. 63.

Court's advisory business may well prove counterproductive—both for the requesting organ and for the Court—and that the nonuse of the Court's advisory function may be less lamentable than its abuse. Obviously, the desideratum must be a fruitful reactivation of the Court, not simply reactivation *per se*. And, if this is so, then organs contemplating requesting advisory opinions must carefully assess the probable effects of their moves on the solutions of the root problems involved as well as on the Court's prestige. (Given the Court's reluctance to take its prestige too much into account,[13] and given the delicate position of the Court in the international arena, the responsibility for shielding the Court from harmful requests must fall to the organs authorized to request advisory opinions. In point of fact, considerations related to problem-solving and those related to the Court's prestige are, in any case, closely interconnected.) The crucial questions to be asked before soliciting judicial advice are not simply whether the issues are "legal" or "political," "justiciable" or "nonjusticiable." The multiple connotations enveloping these terms have rendered them virtually meaningless. Rather, more specific questions, along the order of the following, might profitably be posed. How is a judicial pronouncement—regardless of its content—likely to affect the root problem before the organization? Is a Court opinion likely to meet with the acceptance of those organs and states in whose power it lies to implement the opinion? Will a Court opinion tend to aggravate the basic difficulty by unduly rigidifying the stand of one of the disputants? Does the organ seeking the Court's advice sincerely desire judicial clarification, or is it interested merely in obtaining judicial support for a particular position?

When the desire of an organ for a *particular* answer is strong and manifest—and perhaps nowhere was it as manifest as in the *Namibia* case, in which the UN (represented by the Secretary-General) assumed the role of a "quasi Applicant" against a member state—then the Court should probably be spared involvement. For, in such cases, the Court may be "damned if it does and damned if it doesn't." If it refuses to join in the legitimization process, it may unleash upon itself the wrath of the requesting organ; and, if it offers the desired support, the short-term gain for the Court in plaudits from the UN majority may not be worth the long-term debit of a possible question mark as to its true impartiality. (Although the objection regarding "political pressure" was dimissed by the Court in the *Namibia* case as unentertainable, the objection was not totally without foundation.) Judicial pronouncements rendered under such circumstances are in danger of being not only truly "advisory" (as the ICJ has repeatedly insisted its opinions are, in any case), but, far worse, superfluous political baggage.[14]

---

[13] See Chapter V.

[14] Cf. Rosenne's query whether some states today do not want "an organ to formulate texts having the appearance of a judgment but which would in reality be no more

If requests for advisory opinions are carefully screened for appropriateness (in the manner suggested above), the Court will undoubtedly be consigned to a less significant advisory role than the one its predecessor enjoyed in the League period and the one envisaged for it at San Francisco. But this is not necessarily a cause for pessimism. There is still room for requests of the kind involved in such "successful" opinions as the *Reparation, Reservations,* and *UN Administrative Tribunal* opinions—i.e., requests related to organizational and international law questions in which no really vital state interests are implicated. Furthermore, following the *IMCO* precedent, the specialized agencies might certainly utilize to greater advantage their hard-won authorizations to consult the Court on constitutional and other legal difficulties which may arise from time to time.

In the course of the recent stock-taking on the role of the Court, many suggestions for expanding the Court's advisory business have been put forward by states[15] and by writers.[16] In contrast with past efforts to enhance the Court's effectiveness,[17] the present attempt is characterized by a greater awareness of the limitations of artificial expedients and a keener appreciation of the more fundamental factors which impede greater use of the Court—the over-all political context and the confidence of states in the Court and in the law which it applies. Nevertheless, certain innovations which have been proposed appear to be rather unrealistic, undesirable, or unnecessary—or all three at once. Thus, the suggestion that states be empowered to request opinions[18]—a suggestion which was rejected in 1920 and again in 1945—appears to be unrealistic because it would require an amendment of the Charter and Statute, a process to which the Soviet bloc is at the moment adamantly opposed; undesirable because it might tend to convert the Court into a mere

---

than an *ex post facto* attempt at legal justification for policy decisions reached elsewhere." "The International Court at Fifty," *Israel Law Review,* 2 (1972): 183.

[15] See the citation of Sixth Committee discussions in n. 10; and see the Report of the Secretary-General on the Review of the Role of the Court, UN Doc. A/8382, 15 September 1971, and Add. 1-4, 30 September-12 November 1971.

[16] See, especially, Leo Gross, "The International Court of Justice: Consideration of Requirements for Enhancing Its Role in the International Legal Order," *AJIL,* 65 (1971): 253.

[17] On the Australian initiative which resulted in the adoption of Resolution 171A (II) (the text of which appears in Appendix 3), see, e.g., Manley O. Hudson, "The Twenty-eighth Year of the World Court," *AJIL,* 44 (1950): 36. The effort in the later years of the League to clarify the nature of the vote required for requests was similarly an attempt to "artificially" induce greater use of the advisory function. See pp. 213-21 above.

[18] See the Sixth Committee discussions cited in n. 10; especially the statement of Senator Javits at the Committee's 1211th Mtg., 29 October 1970; and UN Doc. A/8382, 15 September 1971, *passim.*

"legal consultation office,"[19] or, even worse, a propaganda tool indiscriminately used by one or more states against other states;[20] and unnecessary because, if two or more states in dispute genuinely wish to have an issue judicially clarified, the present advisory and contentious jurisdictions are probably flexible enough to allow them to do so—either by requesting the General Assembly to forward their request to the Court,[21] or by eliciting from the Court in contentious procedure a declaratory judgment very much akin to an advisory opinion.[22] For similar reasons, widening the circle of intergovernmental organizations empowered to request advisory opinions does not seem warranted at this juncture. (Much less does the suggestion that nongovernmental organizations be authorized to request opinions.)[23] The advisory jurisdiction in the UN period has suffered from underutilization, not from "underavailability." The aim should be, first of all, increased employment (in appropriate cases) of the already extensive facilities for activating the Court's advisory jurisdiction. As for intergovernmental organizations that are not empowered to address requests to the Court, the possibility of using the General Assembly as a conduit (even as the League Council was used in its time) remains, to date, totally untapped.[24]

Among the suggestions which deserve more serious consideration, even though they would entail Charter or Statute amendment, are those which would open up the advisory jurisdiction to judicial tribunals—whether na-

[19]Statement of the Soviet Union, GAOR (XXV), 6th Ctte., 1212th Mtg., 30 October 1970 (UN Doc. A/C.6/SR.1212, p. 5).

[20]Cf. the reply of France in UN Doc. A/8382, 15 September 1971, pp. 99–100; and the further objections to empowering states in the reply of Switzerland, ibid., pp. 94–95. Other states also voiced reservations in this regard. Ibid., passim.

[21]In several cases—most notably, in the Tunis-Morocco and Jaworzina cases—the League Council acted as a transmission belt for states in dispute. The United States and several other states recently recommended the establishment of a special committee (similar to the Committee on Applications for Review of Administrative Tribunal Judgments) which might be authorized to forward to the Court requests on behalf of intergovernmental organizations not empowered to request advisory opinions (including regional organizations) and on behalf of two or more states who voluntarily agree to submit their dispute to the Court for an advisory opinion. UN Doc. A/8382, 15 September 1971, pp. 92–93; see also the Canadian statement, ibid., p. 98. However, the assumption underlying the proposal—namely, that the authorization of the projected committee would fall within the ambit of Article 96(2) of the Charter and would not require Charter amendment—may not be warranted. See Chapter I. There would be less legal objection were the suggested committee to serve as a mere screening and recommendatory body for the General Assembly, which would reserve to itself the right to forward (or to refuse to forward) the request to the Court.

[22]Cf. the North Sea Continental Shelf cases, cited by Senator Javits, in GAOR (XXV), 6th Ctte., 1211th Mtg., 29 October 1970 (UN Doc. A/C.6/SR.1211, p. 5).

[23]See the suggestion by Senator Javits, ibid., and the reaction of the Soviet Union, ibid., 1212th Mtg., 30 October 1970 (UN Doc. A/C.6/SR.1212, p. 5).

[24]On the suggested special Assembly committee to forward requests by international organizations to the Court, see n. 21.

tional, regional, or international—for the purpose of facilitating greater uniformity both in treaty interpretation and in the application of customary rules of international law.[25] A Statute amendment which would ensure complete equality between an international organization and its officials in all phases of advisory proceedings also would be most desirable.[26]

Under the present circumstances, the goal of rejuvenating the advisory function may perhaps be best pursued in more limited ways. By utilizing the Court for those cases in which its opinions are likely to be heeded and effective, confidence in the Court may be built up for the day when greater stabilization of the world situation will permit wider application of judicial solutions. In the meantime, while the issues submitted to the Court will not be the most important issues of the day (in relation to which the UN is impotent in any case), neither must they be the most trivial.[27]

[25] See Leo Gross's suggestion regarding a "preliminary decision procedure," in "The International Court of Justice: Requirements for Enhancing Its Role," pp. 309–13. And cf. the suggestions of Sweden and Austria in UN Doc. A/8382, 15 September 1971, pp. 98 and 101, in which the idea is applied to advisory procedure. It is quite conceivable that, if and when the Soviet Union modifies its objection to Charter and Statute revision, it will view the authorization of judicial tribunals to request advisory opinions more favorably than the authorization of states and regional organizations directly.

[26] See Leo Gross, "The International Court of Justice: Requirements for Enhancing Its Role," p. 323. Cf. the discussion of the equality of the parties in Chapter V.

[27] See the address by Edvard Hambro, *Proceedings of the American Society of International Law*, 62 (1968): 272; and cf. Charles de Visscher, *Aspects récents du Droit Procédural de la Cour Internationale de Justice* (Paris: Pedone, 1966), p. 198.

Appendix

1

PROVISIONS GOVERNING THE ADVISORY JURISDICTION

Covenant of the League of Nations

Article 14

The Council shall formulate and submit to the Members of the League for adoption plans for the establishment of a Permanent Court of International Justice. The Court shall be competent to hear and determine any dispute of an international character which the parties thereto submit to it. The Court may also give an advisory opinion upon any dispute or question referred to it by the Council or by the Assembly.

Statute of the PCIJ as Amended in 1936

Article 65

Questions upon which the advisory opinion of the Court is asked shall be laid before the Court by means of a written request, signed either by the President of the Assembly or the President of the Council of the League of Nations, or by the Secretary-General of the League under instructions from the Assembly or the Council.

The request shall contain an exact statement of the question upon which an opinion is required, and shall be accompanied by all documents likely to throw light upon the question.

Article 66

1. The Registrar shall forthwith give notice of the request for an advisory opinion to the Members of the League of Nations, through the Secretary-General of the League, and to any States entitled to appear before the Court.

The Registrar shall also, by means of a special and direct communication, notify any Member of the League or State admitted to appear before the Court or international organization considered by the Court (or, should it not be sitting, by the President) as likely to be able to furnish information on the question, that the Court will be prepared to receive, within a time-limit to be fixed by the President, written statements, or to hear, at a public sitting to be held for the purpose, oral statements relating to the question.

Should any Member or State referred to in the first paragraph have failed to receive the communication specified above, such Member or State may express a desire to submit a written statement, or to be heard; and the Court will decide.

2. Members, States, and organizations having presented written or oral statements or both shall be admitted to comment on the statements made by other Members, States, or organizations in the form, to the extent and within the time-limits which the Court, or, should it not be sitting, the President, shall decide in each particular case. Accordingly, the Registrar shall in due time communicate any such written statements to Members, States, and organizations having submitted similar statements.

Article 67

The Court shall deliver its advisory opinions in open Court, notice having been given to the Secretary-General of the League of Nations and to the representatives of Members of the League, of States and of international organizations immediately concerned.

Article 68

In the exercise of its advisory functions, the Court shall further be guided by the provisions of the Statute which apply in contentious cases to the extent to which it recognises them to be applicable.

Rules of Court, 1922-1936

Article 71

[1922 text]

Advisory opinions shall be given after deliberation by the full Court.

The opinions of dissenting judges may, at their request, be attached to the opinion of the Court.

[1926 text]

Advisory opinions shall be given after deliberation by the full Court. They shall mention the number of the judges constituting the majority.

Dissenting judges may, if they so desire, attach to the opinion of the Court either an exposition of their individual opinion or the statement of their dissent.

[1927 amendment, new second paragraph]

On a question relating to an existing dispute between two or more States or Members of the League of Nations, Article 31 of the Statute shall apply.[1] In case of doubt the Court shall decide.

Article 72

Questions upon which the advisory opinion of the Court is asked shall be laid before the Court by means of a written request, signed either by the President of the Assembly or the President of the Council of the League of Nations, or by the Secretary-General of the League under instructions from the Assembly or the Council.

The request shall contain an exact statement of the question upon which an opinion is required, and shall be accompanied by all documents likely to throw light upon the question.

Article 73

[1922 text]

The Registrar shall forthwith give notice of the request for an advisory opinion to the members of the Court, and to the Members of the League of Nations, through the Secretary-General of the League, and to the States mentioned in the Annex to the Covenant.

Notice of such request shall also be given to any international organizations which are likely to be able to furnish information on the question.

[1926 text]

1. The Registrar shall forthwith give notice of the request for an advisory opinion to the members of the Court, to the Members of the League of Nations, through the Secretary-General of the League, and to any States entitled to appear before the Court.

The Registrar shall also, by means of a special and direct communication, notify any Member of the League or States admitted to appear before the Court or international organizations considered by the Court (or, should it not be sitting, by the President) as likely to be able to furnish information on the question, that the Court will be prepared to receive, within a time limit to be fixed by the President, written statements, or to hear, at a public sitting to be held for the purpose, oral statements relating to the question.

Should any State or Member referred to in the first paragraph have failed to receive the communication specified above, such State or Member may express a desire to submit a written statement, or to be heard; and the Court will decide.

2. States, Members and organizations having presented written or oral statements or both shall be admitted to comment on the statements made by

[1] [Author's note: Article 31 of the Statute deals, *inter alia*, with the right of states, parties to a dispute, to appoint judges ad hoc].

other States, Members or organizations, in the form, to the extent and within the time limits which the Court or, should it not be sitting, the President shall decide in each particular case. Accordingly, the Registrar shall in due time communicate any such written statements to States, Members and organizations having submitted similar statements.

Article 74

[1922 text]

Any advisory opinion which may be given by the Court and the request in response to which it was given, shall be printed and published in a special collection for which the Registrar shall be responsible.

[1926 text]

Advisory opinions shall be read in open Court, notice having been given to the Secretary-General of the League of Nations and to the representatives of States, of Members of the League and of international organizations immediately concerned. The Registrar shall take the necessary steps in order to ensure that the text of the advisory opinion is in the hands of the Secretary-General at the seat of the League at the date and hour fixed for the meeting held for the reading of the opinion.

Signed and sealed original copies of advisory opinions shall be placed in the archives of the Court and of the Secretariat of the League. Certified copies thereof shall be transmitted by the Registrar to States, to Members of the League, and to international organizations immediately concerned.

Any advisory opinion which may be given by the Court and the request in response to which it is given, shall be printed and published in a special collection for which the Registrar shall be responsible. [This paragraph was deleted in 1931.]

Rules of Court, 1936

Article 82

In proceedings in regard to advisory opinions, the Court shall, in addition to the provisions of Chapter IV of the Statute of the Court, apply the provisions of the articles hereinafter set out. It shall also be guided by the provisions of the present Rules which apply in contentious cases to the extent to which it recognizes them to be applicable, according as the advisory opinion for which the Court is asked relates, in the terms of Article 14 of the Covenant of the League of Nations, to a "dispute" or to a "question."

Article 83

If the question upon which an advisory opinion is requested relates to an existing dispute between two or more Members of the League of Nations or

States, Article 31 of the Statute of the Court shall apply,[2] as also the provisions of the present Rules concerning the application of that Article.

Article 84

1. Advisory opinions shall be given after deliberation by the full Court. They shall mention the number of judges constituting the majority.

2. Dissenting judges may, if they so desire, attach to the opinion of the Court either an exposition of their individual opinion or the statement of their dissent.

Article 85

1. The Registrar shall take the necessary steps in order to ensure that the text of the advisory opinion is in the hands of the Secretary-General at the seat of the League of Nations at the date and hour fixed for the sitting to be held for the reading of the opinion.

2. One original copy, duly signed and sealed, of every advisory opinion shall be placed in the archives of the Court and another in those of the Secretariat of the League of Nations. Certified copies thereof shall be transmitted by the Registrar to Members of the League of Nations, to States and to international organizations directly concerned.

THE UNITED NATIONS – THE ICJ

Charter of the United Nations

Article 92

The International Court of Justice shall be the principal judicial organ of the United Nations. It shall function in accordance with the annexed Statute, which is based upon the Statute of the Permanent Court of International Justice and forms an integral part of the present Charter.

Article 96

1. The General Assembly or the Security Council may request the International Court of Justice to give an advisory opinion on any legal question.

2. Other organs of the United Nations and specialized agencies, which may at any time be so authorized by the General Assembly, may also request advisory opinions of the Court on legal questions arising within the scope of their activities.

[2] [See n. 1.]

Statute of the ICJ

Article 65

1. The Court may give an advisory opinion on any legal question at the request of whatever body may be authorized by or in accordance with the Charter of the United Nations to make such a request.

2. Questions upon which the advisory opinion of the Court is asked shall be laid before the Court by means of a written request containing an exact statement of the question upon which an opinion is required, and accompanied by all documents likely to throw light upon the question.

Article 66

1. The Registrar shall forthwith give notice of the request for an advisory opinion to all states entitled to appear before the Court.

2. The Registrar shall also, by means of a special and direct communication, notify any state entitled to appear before the Court or international organization considered by the Court, or, should it not be sitting, by the President, as likely to be able to furnish information on the question, that the Court will be prepared to receive, within a time limit to be fixed by the President, written statements, or to hear, at a public sitting to be held for the purpose, oral statements relating to the question.

3. Should any such state entitled to appear before the Court have failed to receive the special communication referred to in paragraph 2 of this Article, such state may express a desire to submit a written statement or to be heard; and the Court will decide.

4. States and organizations having presented written or oral statements or both shall be permitted to comment on the statements made by other states or organizations in the form, to the extent, and within the time limits which the Court, or, should it not be sitting, the President, shall decide in each particular case. Accordingly, the Registrar shall in due time communicate any such written statements to states and organizations having submitted similar statements.

Article 67

The Court shall deliver its advisory opinions in open Court, notice having been given to the Secretary-General and to the representatives of Members of the United Nations, of other states and of international organizations immediately concerned.

Article 68

In the exercise of its advisory functions the Court shall further be guided by the provisions of the present Statute which apply in contentious cases to the extent to which it recognizes them to be applicable.

Rules of Court, 1946

Article 82

1. In proceedings in regard to advisory opinions, the Court shall, in addition to the provisions of Article 96 of the Charter and Chapter IV of the Statute, apply the provisions of the Articles which follow. It shall also be guided by the provisions of these Rules which apply in contentious cases to the extent to which it recognizes them to be applicable; for this purpose it shall above all consider whether the request for the advisory opinion relates to a legal question actually pending between two or more States.

2. If the Court is of the opinion that a request for an advisory opinion necessitates an early answer, it shall take the necessary steps to accelerate the procedure.

Article 83

If the advisory opinion is requested upon a legal question actually pending between two or more States, Article 31 of the Statute shall apply,[3] as also the provisions of these Rules concerning the application of that Article.

Article 84

1. Advisory opinions shall be given after deliberation by the Court. They shall mention the number of judges constituting the majority.

2. Any judge may, if he so desires, attach his individual opinion to the advisory opinion of the Court, whether he dissents from the majority or not, or a bare statement of his dissent.

Article 85

1. The Registrar will in due time inform the Secretary-General of the United Nations and the appropriate organ of the institution, if any, which requested the advisory opinion, as to the date and the hour fixed for the sitting to be held for the reading of the opinion.

2. One original copy of the advisory opinion, duly signed and sealed, shall be placed in the Archives of the Court and another shall be sent to the Secretariat of the United Nations. Certified copies shall be sent by the Registrar to Members of the United Nations and to the States, specialized agencies and public international organizations directly concerned.

---

[3] [See n. 1.]

Appendix

2

PROVISIONS FOR BINDING OPINIONS

CONVENTION ON PRIVILEGES AND IMMUNITIES OF THE UNITED NATIONS, ADOPTED 13 FEBRUARY 1946

Article VIII—Settlement of Disputes

Section 30

All differences arising out of the interpretation or application of the present Convention shall be referred to the International Court of Justice, unless in any case it is agreed by the Parties to have recourse to another mode of settlement. If a difference arises between the United Nations on the one hand and a Member on the other hand, a request shall be made for an advisory opinion on any legal question involved in accordance with Article 96 of the Charter and Article 65 of the Statute of the Court. The opinion given by the Court shall be accepted as decisive by the Parties.

AGREEMENT BETWEEN THE UNITED NATIONS AND THE UNITED STATES OF AMERICA REGARDING THE HEADQUARTERS OF THE UNITED NATIONS, SIGNED ON 26 JUNE 1947

Article VIII

Section 21

(a) Any dispute between the United Nations and the United States concerning the interpretation or application of this Agreement or of any supplemental agreement, which is not settled by negotiation or other agreed mode of settlement, shall be referred for final decision to a tribunal of three arbitrators, one to be named by the Secretary-General, one to be named by the

Secretary of State of the United States, and the third to be chosen by the two, or, if they should fail to agree upon a third, then by the President of the International Court of Justice.

(b) The Secretary-General or the United States may ask the General Assembly to request of the International Court of Justice an advisory opinion on any legal question arising in the course of such proceedings. Pending the receipt of the opinion of the Court, an interim decision of the arbitral tribunal shall be observed by both Parties. Thereafter, the arbitral tribunal shall render a final decision, having regard to the opinion of the Court.

ARTICLE XII OF THE STATUTE OF THE I.L.O. ADMINISTRATIVE TRIBUNAL

1. In any case in which the Executive Board of an international organization which has made the declaration specified in Article II, paragraph 5, of the Statute of the Tribunal[1] challenges a decision of the Tribunal confirming its jurisdiction, or considers that a decision of the Tribunal is vitiated by a fundamental fault in the procedure followed, the question of the validity of the decision given by the Tribunal shall be submitted by the Executive Board concerned, for an advisory opinion, to the International Court of Justice.

2. The opinion given by the Court shall be binding.

ARTICLES 11 AND 12 OF THE U.N. ADMINISTRATIVE TRIBUNAL STATUTE AS AMENDED BY G.A. RESOLUTION 957 (X), OF 8 NOVEMBER 1955

Article 11

1. If a Member State, the Secretary-General or a person in respect of whom a judgment has been rendered by the Tribunal (including any one who has succeeded to that person's rights on his death) objects to the judgment on the ground that the Tribunal has exceeded its jurisdiction or competence or that the Tribunal has failed to exercise jurisdiction vested in it, or has erred on a question of law relating to the provisions of the Charter of the United Nations, or has committed a fundamental error in procedure which has occasioned a failure of justice, such Member State, the Secretary-General or the

---

[1] [Paragraph 5 of Article II reads as follows: "The Tribunal shall also be competent to hear complaints alleging non-observance, in substance or in form, of the terms of appointment of officials and of provisions of the Staff Regulations of any other intergovernmental international organisation approved by the Governing Body which has addressed to the Director-General a declaration recognising, in accordance with its Constitution or internal administrative rules, the jurisdiction of the Tribunal for this purpose, as well as its Rules of Procedure."]

person concerned may, within thirty days from the date of the judgment, make a written application to the Committee established by paragraph 4 of this article asking the Committee to request an advisory opinion of the International Court of Justice on the matter.

2. Within thirty days from the receipt of an application under paragraph 1 of this article, the Committee shall decide whether or not there is a substantial basis for the application. If the Committee decides that such a basis exists, it shall request an advisory opinion of the Court, and the Secretary-General shall arrange to transmit to the Court the views of the person referred to in paragraph 1.

3. If no application is made under paragraph 1 of this article, or if a decision to request an advisory opinion has not been taken by the Committee, within periods prescribed in this article, the judgment of the Tribunal shall become final. In any case in which a request has been made for an advisory opinion, the Secretary-General shall either give effect to the opinion of the Court, or request the Tribunal to convene specially in order that it shall confirm its original judgment, or give a new judgment, in conformity with the opinion of the Court. If not requested to convene specially, the Tribunal shall at its next session confirm its judgment or bring it into conformity with the opinion of the Court.

4. For the purpose of this article, a Committee is established and authorized under paragraph 2 of Article 96 of the Charter to request advisory opinions of the Court. The Committee shall be composed of the Member States the representatives of which have served on the General Committee of the most recent regular session of the General Assembly. The Committee shall meet at United Nations Headquarters and shall establish its own rules.

. . . .

Article 12

. . . .

2. *Recommends* that Member States and the Secretary-General should not make oral statements before the International Court of Justice in any proceedings under the new article 11 of the Statute of the Administrative Tribunal adopted under the present resolution.

Appendix

3

GENERAL ASSEMBLY RESOLUTION 171A (II), 14 NOVEMBER 1947

NEED FOR GREATER USE BY THE UNITED NATIONS AND ITS ORGANS OF THE INTERNATIONAL COURT OF JUSTICE

The General Assembly,

Considering that it is a responsibility of the United Nations to encourage the progressive development of international law;

Considering that it is of paramount importance that the interpretation of the Charter of the United Nations and the constitutions of the specialized agencies should be based on recognized principles of international law;

Considering that the International Court of Justice is the principal judicial organ of the United Nations;

Considering that it is also of paramount importance that the Court should be utilized to the greatest practicable extent in the progressive development of international law, both in regard to legal issues between States and in regard to constitutional interpretation,

Recommends that organs of the United Nations and the specialized agencies should, from time to time, review the difficult and important points of law within the jurisdiction of the International Court of Justice which have arisen in the course of their activities and involve questions of principle which it is desirable to have settled, including points of law relating to the interpretation of the Charter of the United Nations or the constitutions of the specialized agencies, and, if duly authorized according to Article 96, paragraph 2, of the Charter, should refer them to the International Court of Justice for an advisory opinion.

Appendix

GENERAL ASSEMBLY RESOLUTION 684 (VII), 6 NOVEMBER 1952

METHODS AND PROCEDURES OF THE GENERAL ASSEMBLY FOR DEALING WITH LEGAL AND DRAFTING QUESTIONS

The General Assembly,

Considering that it is desirable to introduce adequate methods and procedures for dealing with the legal questions with which it is concerned, while leaving its Committees sufficient latitude for conducting their proceedings concerning matters within their competence,

Taking note of the report[1] and recommendations of the Special Committee established under resolution 597 (VI) of 20 December 1951,

1. *Recommends:*

(a) That, whenever any Committee contemplates making a recommendation to the General Assembly to request an advisory opinion from the International Court of Justice, the matter may, at some appropriate stage of its consideration by that Committee, be referred to the Sixth Committee for advice on the legal aspects and on the drafting of the request, or the Committee concerned may propose that the matter should be considered by a joint Committee of itself and the Sixth Committee;

(b) That, whenever any Committee contemplates making a recommendation to the General Assembly to refer a matter to the International Law Commission, the Committee may, at some appropriate stage of its consideration, consult the Sixth Committee as to the advisability of such a reference and on its drafting;

[1] [See UN Doc. A/2174.]

. . . .

(d) That, when a Committee considers the legal aspects of a question important, the Committee should refer it for legal advice to the Sixth Committee or propose that the question should be considered by a joint Committee of itself and the Sixth Committee;

2. *Directs*:

(a) That the terms of the foregoing recommendations shall be embodied as an annex to the rules of procedure of the General Assembly;

. . . .

Appendix

5

CHRONOLOGICAL LIST
OF OPINIONS RENDERED

THE PCIJ

CASE	DATE OF COUNCIL REQUEST	DATE OF COURT OPINION
1. Netherlands Workers' Delegate	12 May 1922	31 July 1922
2. ILO and Agricultural Labor	12 May 1922	12 August 1922
3. ILO and Agricultural Production	18 July 1922	12 August 1922
4. Tunis-Morocco	4 October 1922	7 February 1923
5. Eastern Carelia	21 April 1923	23 July 1923
6. German Settlers in Poland	3 February 1923	10 September 1923
7. Acquisition of Polish Nationality	7 July 1923	15 September 1923
8. Jaworzina	27 September 1923	6 December 1923
9. Monastery of Saint-Naoum	17 June 1924	4 September 1924
10. Exchange of Greek and Turkish Populations	13 December 1924	21 February 1925
11. Polish Postal Service in Danzig	13 March 1925	16 May 1925
12. Mosul	19 September 1925	21 November 1925
13. ILO and the Employer	17 March 1926	23 July 1926
14. Danube Commission	9 December 1926	8 December 1927
15. Jurisdiction of the Danzig Courts	22 September 1927	3 March 1928
16. Greco-Turkish Agreement	5 June 1928	28 August 1928
17. Greco-Bulgarian Communities	16 January 1930	31 July 1930

18. Danzig and the ILO	15 May 1930	26 August 1930
19. German Minority Schools in Upper Silesia	24 January 1931	15 May 1931
20. Customs Union	19 May 1931	5 September 1931
21. Railway Traffic between Lithuania and Poland	24 January 1931	15 October 1931
22. Polish War Vessels in Danzig	19 September 1931	11 December 1931
23. Polish Nationals in Danzig	22 May 1931	4 February 1932
24. Caphandaris-Molloff Agreement	19 September 1931	8 March 1932
25. Employment of Women during the Night	9 May 1932	15 November 1932
26. Minority Schools in Albania	18 January 1935	6 April 1935
27. Danzig Legislative Decrees	23 September 1935	4 December 1935

THE ICJ

CASE	DATE OF ADOPTION OF REQUEST	DATE OF COURT OPINION
Admission	17 November 1947	28 May 1948
Reparation	3 December 1948	11 April 1949
Competence	22 November 1949	3 March 1950
Peace Treaties (I)	22 October 1949	30 March 1950
Peace Treaties (II)	22 October 1949	18 July 1950
South West Africa (Status)	6 December 1949	11 July 1950
Reservations	16 November 1950	28 May 1951
UN Administrative Tribunal	9 December 1953	13 July 1954
South West Africa (Voting)	23 November 1954	7 June 1955
South West Africa (Committee)	3 December 1955	1 June 1956
UNESCO	25 November 1955	23 October 1956
IMCO	19 January 1959	8 June 1960
Expenses	20 December 1961	20 July 1962
Namibia	29 July 1970	21 June 1971

Appendix

PARTICIPATION
OF STATES
IN ADVISORY
PROCEEDINGS

THE PCIJ–PARTICIPATION BY CASE

CASE NO.	STATES PARTICIPATING IN WRITTEN PROCEEDINGS	STATES PARTICIPATING IN ORAL PROCEEDINGS
1	The Netherlands, Sweden	Great Britain, the Netherlands
2	Italy, Sweden	France, Great Britain, Hungary, Portugal
3	Sweden	France
4	France, Great Britain	France, Great Britain
5	Finland	Finland
6	Poland, Germany	Poland, Germany
7	Poland, Germany	Poland, Germany
8	Czechoslovakia, Poland	Czechoslovakia, Poland
9	Albania, the Serb-Croat-Slovene state	Albania, the Serb-Croat-Slovene state, Greece
10	Greece, Turkey	Greece, Turkey
11	Poland, Danzig	None[1]
12	Great Britain[2]	Great Britain
13	None[3]	None
14	France, Great Britain, Italy, Rumania	France, Great Britain, Italy, Rumania

[1] A second round of written documents was substituted for oral proceedings in this case.

[2] The Turkish government did, however, reply to certain questions put to it by the Court.

[3] Several international organizations were represented in both the oral and the written proceedings.

15	Poland, Danzig	Poland, Danzig
16	Greece, Turkey	Greece, Turkey
17	Greece, Bulgaria	Greece, Bulgaria
18	Poland, Danzig	Poland, Danzig
19	Poland, Germany	Poland, Germany
20	Austria, Czechoslovakia, France, Germany, Italy	Austria, Czechoslovakia, France, Germany, Italy
21	Poland, Lithuania	Poland, Lithuania
22	Poland, Danzig	Poland, Danzig
23	Poland, Danzig	Poland, Danzig
24	Bulgaria, Greece	Bulgaria, Greece
25	Great Britain, Germany	Great Britain, Germany
26	Albania, Greece	Albania, Greece
27	Danzig	Danzig

THE PCIJ–PARTICIPATION BY STATE

W = Participation in Written Proceedings
O = Participation in Oral Proceedings

STATE	CASES IN WHICH PARTICIPATED
Albania	No. 9 (W,O)
	No. 26 (W,O)
Austria	No. 20 (W,O)
Bulgaria	No. 17 (W,O)
	No. 24 (W,O)
Czechoslovakia	No. 8 (W,O)
	No. 20 (W,O)
Danzig	No. 11 (W)[4]
	No. 15 (W,O)
	No. 18 (W,O)
	No. 22 (W,O)
	No. 23 (W,O)
	No. 27 (W,O)
Finland	No. 5 (W,O)
France	No. 2 (O)
	No. 3 (O)
	No. 4 (W,O)
	No. 14 (W,O)
	No. 20 (W,O)

[4] As noted above, there were no oral proceedings in this case.

STATE	CASES IN WHICH PARTICIPATED
Germany	No. 6 (W,O)
	No. 7 (W,O)
	No. 19 (W,O)
	No. 20 (W,O)
	No. 25 (W,O)
Great Britain	No. 1 (O)
	No. 2 (O)
	No. 4 (W,O)
	No. 12 (W,O)
	No. 14 (W,O)
	No. 25 (W,O)
Greece	No. 9 (O)
	No. 10 (W,O)
	No. 16 (W,O)
	No. 17 (W,O)
	No. 24 (W,O)
	No. 26 (W,O)
Hungary	No. 2 (O)
Italy	No. 2 (W)
	No. 14 (W,O)
	No. 20 (W,O)
Lithuania	No. 21 (W,O)
The Netherlands	No. 1 (W,O)
Poland	No. 6 (W,O)
	No. 7 (W,O)
	No. 8 (W,O)
	No. 11 (W)
	No. 15 (W,O)
	No. 18 (W,O)
	No. 19 (W,O)
	No. 21 (W,O)
	No. 22 (W,O)
	No. 23 (W,O)
Portugal	No. 2 (O)
Rumania	No. 14 (W,O)
The Serb-Croat-Slovene state	No. 9 (W,O)
Sweden	No. 1 (W)
	No. 2 (W)
	No. 3 (W)

Turkey

No. 10 (W,O)
No. 16 (W,O)

THE ICJ–PARTICIPATION BY CASE[5]

CASE	STATES PARTICIPATING IN WRITTEN PROCEEDINGS	STATES PARTICIPATING IN ORAL PROCEEDINGS
Admission	Australia, Belgium, Canada, China, El Salvador, Greece, Guatemala, Honduras, India, Iraq, Thailand, the Ukrainian S.S.R., the U.S.S.R., the United States, Yugoslavia	Belgium, Czechoslovakia, France, Poland, Yugoslavia
Reparation	China, France, India, the United Kingdom, the United States	Belgium, France, the United Kingdom
Competence	Argentina, the Byelorussian S.S.R., Czechoslovakia, Egypt, the Ukrainian S.S.R., the U.S.S.R., the United States, Venezuela	France
Peace Treaties (I)	Australia, Bulgaria, the Byelorussian S.S.R., Czechoslovakia, Hungary, Rumania, the Ukrainian S.S.R., the U.S.S.R., the United Kingdom, the United States	The United Kingdom, the United States
Peace Treaties (II)	The United Kingdom,[6] the United States	The United Kingdom, the United States

[5] Many of the written statements emanating from the Soviet bloc were directed primarily at challenging the Court's right to exercise its advisory jurisdiction.

The following tabulation does not include as participants in a case those states which, in their communications to the Court, confined themselves to drawing the Court's attention to their previously stated positions.

[6] The written statement submitted to the Court in the first phase included a discussion of questions III and IV of the Assembly's request.

CASE	STATES PARTICIPATING IN WRITTEN PROCEEDINGS	STATES PARTICIPATING IN ORAL PROCEEDINGS
South West Africa (Status)	Egypt, India, Poland, South Africa, the United States	The Philippines, South Africa
Reservations	Bulgaria, the Byelorussian S.S.R., Czechoslovakia, Israel, Jordan, the Netherlands, the Philippines, Poland, Rumania, the Ukrainian S.S.R., the U.S.S.R., the United Kingdom, the United States	France, Israel, the United Kingdom
UN Administrative Tribunal	Chile, China, Ecuador, France, Greece, Guatemala, Iraq, Mexico, the Netherlands, the Philippines, Sweden, Turkey, the United Kingdom, the United States	France, Greece, the Netherlands, the United Kingdom, the United States
South West Africa (Voting)	India, Poland, the United States	None
South West Africa (Committee)	China, the United States	The United Kingdom
UNESCO	China, France, the United Kingdom, the United States	None[7]

[7]Oral hearings were dispensed with in this case in order to ensure a measure of equality between the parties. See Chapter V.

IMCO	Belgium, China, Denmark, France, India, Italy, Liberia, the Netherlands, Norway, Panama, Switzerland, the United Kingdom, the United States	Italy, Liberia, the Netherlands, Norway, Panama, the United Kingdom, the United States
Expenses	Australia, Bulgaria, the Byelorussian S.S.R., Canada, Czechoslovakia, Denmark, France, Ireland, Italy, Japan, the Netherlands, Portugal, Rumania, South Africa, Spain, the Ukrainian S.S.R., the U.S.S.R., the United Kingdom, the United States, Upper Volta	Australia, Canada, Ireland, Italy, the Netherlands, Norway, the U.S.S.R., the United Kingdom, the United States
Namibia	Czechoslovakia, Finland, France, Hungary, India, the Netherlands, Nigeria,[8] Pakistan, Poland, South Africa, the United States, Yugoslavia	Finland, India, the Netherlands, Nigeria,[8] Pakistan, South Africa, Vietnam (Republic of), the United States

THE ICJ–PARTICIPATION BY STATES

W = Participation in Written Proceedings
O = Participation in Oral Proceedings

STATE	CASES IN WHICH PARTICIPATED
Australia	Admission (W) Peace Treaties (I) (W) Expenses (W,O)
Argentina	Competence (W)
Belgium	Admission (W,O) Reparation (O) IMCO (W)

[8] Nigeria adopted the Written and Oral Statements presented by the Organization of African Unity.

STATE	CASES IN WHICH PARTICIPATED
Bulgaria	Peace Treaties (I) (W) Reservations (W) Expenses (W)
The Byelorussian S.S.R.	Competence (W) Peace Treaties (I) (W) Reservations (W) Expenses (W)
Canada	Admission (W) Expenses (W,O)
Chile	UN Administrative Tribunal (W)
China	Admission (W) Reparation (W) UN Administrative Tribunal (W) South West Africa (Committee) (W) UNESCO (W) · IMCO (W)
Czechoslovakia	Admission (O) Competence (W) Peace Treaties (I) (W) Reservations (W) Expenses (W) Namibia (W)
Denmark	IMCO (W) Expenses (W)
Ecuador	UN Administrative Tribunal (W)
Egypt	Competence (W) South West Africa (Status) (W)
El Salvador	Admission (W)
Finland	Namibia (W,O)
France	Admission (O) Reparation (W,O) Competence (O) Reservations (W,O)

UN Administrative Tribunal (W,O)
UNESCO (W)
IMCO (W)
Expenses (W)
Namibia (W)

Greece

Admission (W)
UN Administrative Tribunal (W,O)

Guatemala

Admission (W)
UN Administrative Tribunal (W)

Honduras

Admission (W)

Hungary

Peace Treaties (I) (W)
Namibia (W)

India

Admission (W)
Reparation (W)
South West Africa (Status) (W)
South West Africa (Voting) (W)
IMCO (W)
Namibia (W,O)

Iraq

Admission (W)
UN Administrative Tribunal (W)

Ireland

Expenses (W,O)

Israel

Reservations (W,O)

Italy

IMCO (W,O)
Expenses (W,O)

Japan

Expenses (W)

Jordan

Reservations (W)

Liberia

IMCO (W,O)

Mexico

UN Administrative Tribunal (W)

The Netherlands

Reservations (W)
UN Administrative Tribunal (W,O)
IMCO (W,O)

STATE	CASES IN WHICH PARTICIPATED
	Expenses (W,O)
	Namibia (W,O)
Nigeria[9]	Namibia (W,O)
Norway	IMCO (W,O)
	Expenses (O)
Pakistan	Namibia (W,O)
Panama	IMCO (W,O)
The Philippines	South West Africa (Status) (O)
	Reservations (W)
	UN Administrative Tribunal (W)
Poland	Admission (O)
	South West Africa (Status) (W)
	Reservations (W)
	South West Africa (Voting) (W)
	Namibia (W)
Portugal	Expenses (W)
Rumania	Peace Treaties (I) (W)
	Reservations (W)
	Expenses (W)
South Africa	South West Africa (Status) (W,O)
	Expenses (W)
	Namibia (W,O)
Spain	Expenses (W)
Sweden	UN Administrative Tribunal (W)
Switzerland	IMCO (W)
Thailand	Admission (W)
Turkey	UN Administrative Tribunal (W)
The Ukrainian S.S.R.	Admission (W)
	Competence (W)

[9] See n. 8.

	Peace Treaties (I) (W)
	Reservations (W)
	Expenses (W)

The U.S.S.R.

Admission (W)
Competence (W)
Peace Treaties (I) (W)
Reservations (W)
Expenses (W,O)

The United Kingdom

Reparation (W,O)
Peace Treaties (I) (W,O)
Peace Treaties (II) (W,[10]O)
Reservations (W,O)
UN Administrative Tribunal (W,O)
South West Africa (Committee) (O)
UNESCO (W)
IMCO (W,O)
Expenses (W,O)

The United States

Admission (W)
Reparation (W)
Competence (W)
Peace Treaties (I) (W,O)
Peace Treaties (II) (W,O)
South West Africa (Status) (W)
Reservations (W)
UN Administrative Tribunal (W,O)
South West Africa (Voting) (W)
South West Africa (Committee) (W)
UNESCO (W)
IMCO (W,O)
Expenses (W,O)
Namibia (W,O)

Upper Volta

Expenses (W)

Venezuela

Competence (W)

Vietnam (Republic of)

Namibia (O)

Yugoslavia

Admission (W,O)
Namibia (W)

[10]The written statement submitted to the Court in the first phase included a discussion of questions III and IV of the Assembly's request.

SELECTED
BIBLIOGRAPHY

OFFICIAL PUBLICATIONS

League of Nations

Official Journal. February 1920–March 1940.
Records of the Assembly. 1920–46. Published as *Special Supplements* to the *Official Journal.*
Treaty Series.
Advisory Committee of Jurists. *Procés-Verbaux of the Proceedings of the Committee.* LN Doc. V.Legal.1920, vol. 2.
Documents concerning the Action Taken by the Council of the League of Nations under Article 14 of the Covenant and the Adoption by the Assembly of the Statute of the Permanent Court. LN Doc. V.Legal.1920, vol. 3.
Minutes of the Conference of States Signatories of the Protocol of Signature of the Permanent Court of International Justice, 1–23 September 1926. LN Doc. V.Legal.1926.V.26.
Committee of Jurists on the Statute of the Permanent Court of International Justice. *Minutes of the Session Held at Geneva, 11–19 March 1929.* LN Doc. C.166.M.66.1929.V.
Minutes of the Conference regarding the Revision of the Statute of the Permanent Court of International Justice and the Accession of the United States of America to the Protocol of Signature of that Statute, 4–12 September 1929. LN Doc. C.514.M.173.1929.V.
Permanent Mandates Commission. *Minutes.* 16th Sess., 1929.
Secretariat, Information Section. *Political Activities.* 2 vols. Geneva, 1925 and 1928.
––––. *The Council of the League of Nations: Composition, Competence, Procedure.* Geneva, 1938.

Permanent Court of International Justice

Publications. Series A: *Judgments and Orders.* Nos. 1–24, 1922–30.
_____. Series B: *Advisory Opinions.* Nos. 1–18, 1922– 30.
_____. Series A/B: *Judgments, Orders, and Advisory Opinions.* Nos. 40–80, 1931–40.
_____. Series C: *Acts and Documents relating to Judgments and Advisory Opinions.* Nos. 1–19, 1922–30; Nos. 52–87, 1931–39.
_____. Series D: *Acts and Documents concerning the Organization of the Court.* Nos. 1–6, 1922–40.
_____. Series E: *Annual Reports.* Nos. 1–15, 1925–39.
_____. Series F: *General Indexes.* Nos. 1–4, 1922–36.

United Nations

Report of the Preparatory Commission of the United Nations. UN Doc. PC/20, 23 December 1945.
Documents of the United Nations Conference on International Organization, San Francisco, 1945. 16 vols. New York and London: United Nations Information Organizations, 1945–46.
Repertoire of the Practice of the Security Council, 1946–1951 (1954). Supp. No. 1, *1952–1955* (1958); Supp. No. 2, *1956–1958* (1959); Supp. No. 3, *1959–1963* (1965); Supp. No. 4, *1964–65* (1968); Supp. No. 5, *1966–1968* (1971).
Repertory of Practice of United Nations Organs. 6 vols., 1955; Supp. No. 1, 2 vols., 1958; Supp. No. 2, 3 vols., 1963.
Yearbook of the United Nations.
Economic and Social Council. *Official Records.*
General Assembly. *Official Records.*
Security Council. *Official Records.*
Trusteeship Council. *Official Records.*

International Court of Justice

The Bibliography of the International Court of Justice. Nos. 19–. Nos. 1–18 formed Chapter IX of the appropriate *Yearbook.*
Documents concerning the organization of the Court. 1946 and 1947.
Pleadings, Oral Arguments, and Documents.
Reports of Judgments, Advisory Opinions, and Orders.
Yearbook.

Other Documents

Great Britain. *Parliamentary Papers,* Miscellaneous No. 2 (1944). "Report of the Informal Inter-Allied Committee on the Future of the Permanent Court of International Justice," Cmd. 6531, 10 February 1944.

International Maritime Consultative Organization, Assembly Meetings. 1st Sess. *Summary Records.*
_____. 1st Sess., Legal Committee. *Summary Records.*
_____. 2nd Sess. *Resolutions.*
_____. 2nd Sess. *Summary Records.*
Union of South Africa. *Report by the Government of the Union of South Africa on the Administration of South West Africa for the Year 1946.* Pretoria: Government Printer, 1947.
United Nations Educational, Scientific, and Cultural Organization, Executive Board. 42nd Sess. *Summary Records.*
_____. 45th Sess. *Summary Records.*
_____. 70th Sess. *Summary Records.*
_____. 71st Sess. *Summary Records.*
_____, General Conference, 14th Sess. *Resolutions.*
_____. 14th Sess., Legal Committee. *Summary Records.*
_____. 14th Sess., Plenary. *Proceedings.*
United States, Congress, Senate, Committee on Foreign Relations. *Hearings on the Charter of the United Nations.* 79th Cong., 1st Sess., 1945.
United States, Department of State. *The United States and the Permanent Court of International Justice.* Pub. No. 44. Washington, D.C.: Government Printing Office, 1930.
_____. *Charter of the United Nations: Report to the President on the Results of the San Francisco Conference by the Chairman of the United States Delegation, the Secretary of State.* Pub. No. 2349. Washington, D.C.: Government Printing Office, 1945.
_____. *The International Court of Justice: Selected Documents relating to the Drafting of the Statute.* Pub. No. 2491. Washington, D.C.: Government Printing Office, 1946.

BOOKS

Abi-Saab, Georges. *Les exceptions préliminaires dans la procédure de la Cour Internationale.* Paris: Pedone, 1967.
Anand, R. P. *Compulsory Jurisdiction of the International Court of Justice.* London: Asia Publishing House, 1961.
_____. *Studies in International Adjudication.* Delhi: Vikas; Dobbs Ferry, N.Y.: Oceana, 1969.
Beuve-Méry, M. *La compétence consultative de la Cour Permanente de Justice Internationale.* Paris: Pedone, 1926.
Bonvalot, Gerard. *Les avis consultatifs de la Cour Permanente de Justice Internationale.* Paris: Pichon et Durand-Auzias, 1925.
Borchard, Edwin M. *Declaratory Judgments.* 2nd ed. Cleveland: Banks-Baldwin, 1941.
Brierly, J. L. *The Outlook for International Law.* Oxford: Clarendon Press, 1944.
Burton, Margaret E. *The Assembly of the League of Nations.* Chicago: University of Chicago Press, 1941.

Carnegie Endowment for International Peace. *Israel and the United Nations: Report of a Study Group Set Up by the Hebrew University of Jerusalem.* National Studies on International Organization. New York: Manhattan Publishing Co., 1956.

Castañeda, Jorge. *Legal Effects of United Nations Resolutions.* Translated by Alba Amoia. New York: Columbia University Press, 1969.

Cecil, Sir Robert. *A Great Experiment.* New York: Oxford University Press, 1941.

Clark, Grenville, and Sohn, Louis B. *World Peace Through World Law.* 2nd ed. Cambridge, Mass.: Harvard University Press, 1960.

Colijn, H. A. *La décision de la Société des Nations concernant les îles d'Aland.* Amsterdam: By the author, 1923.

Conwell-Evans, T. P. *The League Council in Action.* London: Oxford University Press, 1939.

Dallin, A. *The Soviet Union at the United Nations.* New York: Praeger, 1962.

Deák, Francis. *The Hungarian-Rumanian Land Dispute.* New York: Columbia University Press, 1928.

De Bustamante, Antonio S. *The World Court.* Translated by Elizabeth F. Read. New York: Macmillan, 1925.

De Visscher, Charles. *Aspects récents du droit procédural de la Cour Internationale de Justice.* Paris: Pedone, 1966.

_____. *Problèmes d'interprétation judiciaire en droit international public.* Paris: Pedone, 1963.

_____. *Théories et réalités en droit international public.* 4th ed. Paris: Pedone, 1970.

Dexter, Byron. *The Years of Opportunity: The League of Nations, 1920-1926.* New York: Viking, 1967.

Di Qual, L. *Les effets des resolutions des Nations Unies.* Paris: Pichon et Durand-Auzias, 1967.

Douma, J. *Bibliography on the International Court including the Permanent Court, 1918-1964.* Leiden: Sijthoff, 1966.

Dubisson, Michel. *La Cour Internationale de Justice.* Paris: Pichon et Durand-Auzias, 1964.

Engel, Salo. *Art. 5 und Art. 14 Satz 3 der Völkerbundsatzung.* Annemasse, France: Rosnoblet, 1936.

Engel, Salo, and Métall, Rudolf A., eds. *Law, State, and International Legal Order: Essays in Honor of Hans Kelsen.* Knoxville: University of Tennessee Press, 1964.

Fachiri, Alexander P. *The Permanent Court of International Justice.* 2nd ed. London: Oxford University Press, 1932.

Feinberg, Nathan. *La juridiction de la Cour Permanente de Justice dans le systeme de la protection internationale des minorités.* Paris: Rousseau, 1931.

Fischer, Georges. *Les rapports entre l'Organisation Internationale du Travail et la Cour Permanente de Justice Internationale.* Paris: Pedone, 1946.

Fleming, Denna F. *The United States and the World Court.* New York: Doubleday, Doran, 1945.

_____. *The United States and the World Court, 1920-1966.* Rev. ed. New York: Russell & Russell, 1968.

Friedmann, Wolfgang. *The Changing Structure of International Law.* New York: Columbia University Press; London: Stevens, 1964.

Goodrich, Leland M., and Hambro, Edvard. *Charter of the United Nations: Commentary and Documents.* 2nd rev. ed. Boston: World Peace Foundation, 1949.

Goodrich, Leland M.; Hambro, Edvard; and Simons, Anne P. *Charter of the United Nations: Commentary and Documents.* 3rd rev. ed. New York and London: Columbia University Press, 1969.

Goodrich, Leland M., and Simons, Anne P. *The United Nations and the Maintenance of International Peace and Security.* Washington, D.C.: The Brookings Institution, 1955

Hammarskjöld, Ake. *Juridiction Internationale.* Leiden: Sijthoff, 1938.

Henkin, Louis. *How Nations Behave: Law and Foreign Policy.* New York: Praeger, 1968.

Higgins, Rosalyn. *The Development of International Law through the Political Organs of the United Nations.* London: Oxford University Press, 1963.

Hudson, Manley O. *International Tribunals: Past and Future.* Washington, D.C.: Carnegie Endowment for International Peace, 1944.

_____. *The Permanent Court of International Justice, 1920-1942.* New York: Macmillan, 1943.

Hurewitz, J. C. *The Struggle for Palestine.* New York: Norton, 1950.

Jenks, C. Wilfred. *The Prospects of International Adjudication.* London: Stevens, 1964.

Jessup, Philip C. *A Modern Law of Nations.* New York: Macmillan, 1948.

_____. *The Use of International Law.* Ann Arbor: University of Michigan Law School, 1959.

Jiménez de Arechaga, Eduardo. *Voting and the Handling of Disputes in the Security Council.* New York: Carnegie Endowment for International Peace, 1950.

Kahng, Tae Jin. *Law, Politics, and the Security Council.* The Hague: Nijhoff, 1964.

Katz, Milton. *The Relevance of International Adjudication.* Cambridge, Mass.: Harvard University Press, 1968.

Keith, Kenneth J. *The Extent of the Advisory Jurisdiction of the International Court of Justice.* Leiden: Sijthoff, 1971.

Kellor, Frances, and Hatvany, Antonia. *The United States Senate and the International Court.* New York: Seltzer, 1925.

Kelsen, Hans. *Law and Peace in International Relations.* Cambridge, Mass.: Harvard University Press, 1942.

_____. *The Law of the United Nations.* London: Stevens, 1950.

_____. *Peace Through Law.* Chapel Hill: University of North Carolina Press, 1944.

Kluyver, Clasina A. *Documents on the League of Nations.* Leiden: Sijthoff, 1920.

Ladas, Stephen P. *The Exchange of Minorities: Bulgaria, Greece, and Turkey.* New York: Macmillan, 1932.

Lammasch, Heinrich. *Der Völkerbund zur Bewahrung des Friedens.* Olten, Switzerland: Trosch, 1918.

Lauterpacht, Hersch. *The Development of International Law by the International Court.* London: Stevens, 1958.

_____. *The Function of Law in the International Community.* Oxford: Clarendon Press, 1933.

Lipsky, George A., ed. *Law and Politics in the World Community.* Berkeley and Los Angeles: University of California Press, 1953.

Lissitzyn, Oliver J. *The International Court of Justice.* New York: Carnegie Endowment for International Peace, 1951.

_____. *International Law Today and Tomorrow.* Dobbs Ferry, N.Y.: Oceana, 1965.

MacIver, Robert M. *The Nations and the United Nations.* New York: Manhattan Publishing Co., 1959.

Mason, John Brown. *The Danzig Dilemma: A Study in Peacemaking by Compromise.* Stanford, Calif.: Stanford University Press, 1946.

Merillat, Herbert C., ed. *Legal Advisors and International Organizations.* Dobbs Ferry, N.Y.: Oceana, 1966.

Miller, David Hunter. *Drafting of the Covenant.* 2 vols. New York: Putnam, 1928.

Morley, Felix. *The Society of Nations: Its Organization and Constitutional Development.* Washington, D.C.: The Brookings Institution, 1932.

Morrow, Ian F. D., and Sieveking, L. M. *The Peace Settlement in the German-Polish Borderlands.* London: Oxford University Press, 1936.

Nantwi, E. K. *The Enforcement of International Judicial Decisions and Arbitral Awards in Public International Law.* Leiden: Sijthoff, 1966.

Philipse, A. H. *Les fonctions consultatives de la Cour Permanente de Justice Internationale.* Lausanne, Switzerland: Payot, 1928.

Politis, N. *La Justice Internationale.* Paris: Hachette, 1924.

Rajan, M. S. *United Nations and Domestic Jurisdiction.* 2nd ed. London: Asia Publishing House, 1961.

Remlinger, E. *Les avis consultatifs de la Cour Permanente de Justice Internationale.* Paris: Pedone, 1938.

Riches, Cromwell A. *The Unanimity Rule and the League of Nations.* Baltimore: The Johns Hopkins Press, 1933.

Rideau, Joël. *Juridictions internationales et contrôle du respect des traités constitutifs des organisations internationales.* Paris: Pichon et Durand-Auzias, 1969.

Röling, B. V. A. *International Law in an Expanded World.* Amsterdam: Djambatan, 1960.

Rosenne, Shabtai. *The Law and Practice of the International Court.* 2 vols. Leiden: Sijthoff, 1965.

Russell, Ruth B., assisted by Muther, Jeannette E. *A History of the United Nations Charter: The Role of the United States, 1940-1945.* Washington, D.C.: The Brookings Institution, 1958.

Schwarzenberger, Georg. *International Law as Applied by International Courts and Tribunals,* vol. 1. 3rd ed. London: Stevens, 1957.

Scott, James Brown. *The Project of a Permanent Court of International Justice and Resolutions of the Advisory Committee of Jurists.* Washington, D.C.: The Endowment, 1920.

Shihata, Ibrahim F. *The Power of the International Court to Determine Its own Jurisdiction: Compétence de la Compétence.* The Hague: Nijhoff, 1965.

Shotwell, James T., and Salvin, Marina. *Lessons on Security and Disarmament from the History of the League of Nations.* New York: Carnegie Endowment for International Peace, 1949.

Slonim, Solomon. *South West Africa and the United Nations: An International Mandate in Dispute.* Baltimore, Md.: The Johns Hopkins Press, 1973.

Stoessinger, John G., et al. *Financing the United Nations System.* Washington, D.C.: The Brookings Institution, 1964.

Stone, Julius. *Aggression and World Order.* London: Stevens, 1958.

_____. *International Guarantees of Minority Rights.* London: Oxford University Press, 1932.

_____. *Legal Controls of International Conflict.* 2nd ed. London: Stevens, 1959.

_____. *Quest for Survival: The Role of Law and Foreign Policy.* Cambridge, Mass.: Harvard University Press, 1961.

Syatauw, J. J. G. *Some Newly Established Asian States and the Development of International Law.* The Hague: Nijhoff, 1961.

Taracouzio, T. A. *The Soviet Union and International Law.* New York: Macmillan, 1935.

Taylor, Alastair M. *Indonesian Independence and the United Nations.* Ithaca, N.Y.: Cornell University Press, 1960.

Van der Molen, G. H. J.; Pompe, W. P. J.; and Verzijl, J. H. W., eds. *The United Nations Ten Years' Legal Progress.* The Hague: Nederlandse Studentenvereniging voor Wereldrechtsorde, 1956.

Verzijl, J. H. W. *The Jurisprudence of the World Court: A Case by Case Commentary.* 2 vols. Leiden: Sijthoff, 1965.

Walters, Francis P. *A History of the League of Nations.* 2 vols. London: Oxford University Press, 1952.

Weiler, Lawrence D., and Simons, Anne P. *The United States and the United Nations: The Search for International Peace and Security.* Carnegie Endowment for International Peace, National Studies on International Organization. New York: Manhattan Publishing Co., 1967.

Zimmern, Alfred. *The League of Nations and the Rule of Law, 1918-1935.* London: Macmillan, 1936.

ARTICLES AND PAMPHLETS

Alexey, Helmut. "Die Inanspruchnahme des IGH durch die Organe der Vereinten Nationen." *Zeitschrift für ausländisches Recht und Völkerrecht,* 21 (1961): 473.

Anand, R. P. "Attitude of the 'New' Asian-African Countries toward the International Court of Justice." *International Studies* (New Delhi), 4 (1962): 119.

_____. "The Role of Individual and Dissenting Opinions in International Organizations." *International and Comparative Law Quarterly,* 14 (1965): 788.

_____. "Role of the 'New' Asian-African Countries in the Present International Legal Order." *American Journal of International Law,* 56 (1962): 383.

Anderson, C. P. "The Basis of an Advisory Opinion by the World Court on the Proposed Austro-German Customs Union." *American Journal of International Law,* 25 (1931): 504.

Asamoah, Obed. "The Legal Effect of the Resolutions of the General Assembly." *Columbia Journal of Transnational Law,* 3 (1965): 210.

Baker, P. J. "The Permanent Court of International Justice." In *A History of the Peace Conference of Paris.* Edited by H. W. V. Temperley. Vol. 6. London: Frowde, Hodder & Stoughton, 1924.

Bastid, S. "De quelques problèmes juridiques posés par le développement des organisations internationales." *Les problèmes fondamentaux du droit international: Mélanges en l'honneur de J. Spiropoulos.* Bonn: Schimmelbusch, 1957.

Becker, André. "La Cour Permanente de Justice Internationale en 1930–1931." *Revue de Droit International et de Législation Comparée,* 3rd ser., 13 (1932): 524.

Beckett, W. E. "Decisions of the Permanent Court of International Justice on Points of Law and Procedure." *British Year Book of International Law,* 11 (1930): 1.

Bindschedler, R.L. "La délimitation des compétences des Nations Unies." *Recueil des Cours,* 108 (1963-I): 307.

Bloomfield, Lincoln. "Law, Politics, and International Disputes." *International Conciliation,* No. 516 (January 1958).

Bok, William Curtis. "The United States and the World Court: The Austro-German Customs Union Case." *University of Pennsylvania Law Review,* 80 (1932): 335.

Borchard, Edwin M. "The Customs Union Advisory Opinion." *American Journal of International Law,* 25 (1931): 711.

_____. "Declaratory Judgments in International Law." *American Journal of International Law,* 29 (1935): 488.

_____. "The Distinction between Legal and Political Questions." *Proceedings of the American Society of International Law,* 18 (1924): 50.

Brierly, J. L. "The Advisory Opinion of the Permanent Court on the Customs Regime between Germany and Austria." *Zeitschrift für ausländisches öffentliches Recht und Völkerrecht*, 3 (1932): 68.

Briggs, Herbert W. "The United Nations and Political Decision of Legal Questions." *Proceedings of the American Society of International Law*, 42 (1948): 42.

Brown, Philip Marshall. "The Anschluss and the Permanent Court of International Justice." *American Journal of International Law*, 25 (1931): 508.

———. "The Rule of Unanimity and the Fifth Reservation to American Adherence to the Permanent Court." *American Journal of International Law*, 22 (1928): 599.

Brownlie, Ian. "The Individuals before Tribunals Exercising International Jurisdiction." *International and Comparative Law Quarterly*, 2 (1962): 701.

———. "The Justiciability of Disputes and Issues in International Relations." *British Year Book of International Law*, 42 (1967): 123.

Cassidy, Lewis C. "The Advisory Opinion Concerning the Austro-German Protocol for the Establishment of a Customs Union." *Georgetown Law Journal*, 20 (1931): 57.

Castañeda, Jorge. "The Underdeveloped Nations and the Development of International Law." *International Organization*, 15 (1961): 38.

Cheng, Bin. "International Law in the United Nations." *Year Book of World Affairs*, 8 (1954): 170.

Claude, Inis L., Jr. "The OAS, the UN, and the United States." *International Conciliation*, No. 547 (March 1964).

———. "The Political Framework of the United Nations' Financial Problems." *International Organization*, 17 (1963): 831.

———. "States and the World Court: The Politics of Neglect." *Virginia Journal of International Law*, 11 (1971): 344.

Cohen, Benjamin V. "The United Nations in Its Twentieth Year." *International Organization*, 20 (1966): 185.

Collins, J. Foster. "The United Nations and Indonesia." *International Conciliation*, No. 459 (March 1950).

Currey, Muriel. *The Hungaro-Rumanian Dispute: The Optants' Case before the League, Part II*. London: Information Service on International Affairs, 1929.

Dalfen, Charles M. "The World Court in Idle Splendour: The Basis of States' Attitudes." *International Journal* (Toronto), 23 (1967–68): 124.

———. "The World Court: Reform or Re-Appraisal." *Canadian Yearbook of International Law*, 6 (1968): 212.

Davis, John W. "The World Court Settles the Question." *Atlantic Monthly*, 149 (January 1932): 119.

De Visscher, Charles. "Les avis consultatifs de la Cour Permanente de Justice Internationale." *Recueil des Cours*, 26 (1929-I): 5.

Dugard, John. "The Revocation of the Mandate for South West Africa." *American Journal of International Law*, 62 (1968): 78.

Dugdale, Mrs. Edgar. *The Hungaro-Rumanian Dispute: The Optants' Case before the League.* London: Association for International Understanding, 1928.

Engel, Salo. "La force obligatoire des avis consultatifs de la Cour Permanente de Justice Internationale." *Revue de Droit International et de Législation Comparée,* 3rd ser., 17 (1936): 768.

_____. " 'Living' International Constitutions and the World Court: The Subsequent Practice of International Organs under Their Constituent Instruments." *International and Comparative Law Quarterly,* 16 (1967): 865.

_____. "Procedures for the *De Facto* Revision of the Charter." *Proceedings of the American Society of International Law,* 59 (1965): 108.

Erich, R. "La question de la Carélie Orientale." *Revue de Droit International et de Législation Comparée,* 3rd Ser., 3 (1922): 1.

_____. "La question de la Carélie Orientale soumise pour avis a la Cour Permanente de Justice Internationale." *Revue de Droit International et de Legislation Comparée,* 3rd Ser., 4 (1923): 227.

Fachiri, Alexander P. "The Austro-German Customs Union Case." *British Year Book of International Law,* 13 (1932): 68.

Fawcett, J. E. S. "The Place of Law in an International Organization." *British Year Book of International Law,* 36 (1960): 321.

Feinberg, Nathan. "La juridiction et la jurisprudence de la Cour Permanente de Justice Internationale en matière de mandats et de minorités." *Recueil des Cours,* 59 (1937-I): 591.

Fitzmaurice, Sir Gerald. "Hersch Lauterpacht: The Scholar as Judge, Part I." *British Year Book of International Law,* 37 (1961): 1. Part II, *ibid.,* 38 (1962): 1. Part III, *ibid.,* 39 (1963): 133.

_____. "Judicial Innovation—Its Uses and Its Perils—As Exemplified in Some of the Work of the International Court of Justice during Lord McNair's Period of Office." *Cambridge Essays in International Law.* London: Stevens, 1965.

_____. "The Law and Procedure of the International Court of Justice: General Principles and Substantive Law." *British Year Book of International Law,* 27 (1950): 1.

_____. "The Law and Procedure of the International Court of Justice: Treaty Interpretation and Certain Other Treaty Points." *British Year Book of International Law,* 28 (1951): 1.

_____. "The Law and Procedure of the International Court of Justice: International Organizations and Tribunals." *British Year Book of International Law,* 29 (1952): 1.

_____. "The Law and Procedure of the International Court of Justice, 1951–4: Questions of Jurisdiction, Competence, and Procedure." *British Year Book of International Law,* 34 (1958): 1.

_____. "The Law and Procedure of the International Court of Justice, 1954–9: General Principles and Sources of International Law." *British Year Book of International Law,* 35 (1959): 183.

_____. "Reservations to Multilateral Conventions." *International and Comparative Law Quarterly,* 2 (1953): 1.

Frankfurter, Felix. "Advisory Opinions." In *Encyclopedia of the Social Sciences*, 1: 475–78.
_____. "A Note on Advisory Opinions." *Harvard Law Review*, 37 (1924): 1002.
Gilmore, Grant. "The International Court of Justice." *Yale Law Journal*, 55 (1946): 1049.
Gilmour, David R. "Article 2(7) of the United Nations Charter and the Practice of the Permanent Members of the Security Council." *Australian Year Book of International Law*, 3 (1967): 153.
Goodrich, Leland M. "The Nature of the Advisory Opinions of the Permanent Court of International Justice." *American Journal of International Law*, 32 (1938): 738.
_____. "The United Nations and Domestic Jurisdiction." *International Organization*, 3 (1949): 14.
Gordon, Edward. "The World Court and the Interpretation of Constitutive Treaties." *American Journal of International Law*, 59 (1965): 794.
Green, L. C. "The United Nations, South West Africa and the World Court." *Indian Journal of International Law*, 7 (1967): 491.
Greig, D. W. "The Advisory Jurisdiction of the International Court and the Settlement of Disputes between States." *International and Comparative Law Quarterly*, 15 (1966): 325.
Gross, Leo. "Expenses of the United Nations for Peace-Keeping Operations: The Advisory Opinion of the International Court of Justice." *International Organization*, 17 (1963): 1.
_____. "The International Court of Justice: Consideration of Requirements for Enhancing Its Role in the International Legal Order." *American Journal of International Law*, 65 (1971): 253.
_____. "The International Court of Justice and the United Nations." *Recueil des Cours*, 121 (1967-II): 314.
_____. "Limitations upon the Judicial Function." *American Journal of International Law*, 58 (1964): 415.
_____. "Participation of Individuals in Advisory Proceedings before the International Court of Justice: Question of Equality between the Parties." *American Journal of International Law*, 52 (1958): 16.
_____. "Problems of International Adjudication and Compliance with International Law: Some Simple Solutions." *American Journal of International Law*, 59 (1965): 48.
_____. "Some Observations on the International Court of Justice." *American Journal of International Law*, 56 (1962): 33.
_____. "States as Organs of International Law and the Problem of Auto-interpretation." In *Law and Politics in the World Community*. Edited by George A. Lipsky. Berkeley and Los Angeles: University of California Press, 1953.
_____. "The United Nations and the Role of Law." *International Organization*, 19 (1965): 537.
Hambro, Edvard. Address to the American Society of International Law, *Proceedings of the American Society of International Law*, 62 (1968): 269.

_____. "The Authority of the Advisory Opinions of the International Court of Justice." *International and Comparative Law Quarterly*, 3 (1954): 2.

_____. "The Jurisdiction of the International Court of Justice." *Recueil des Cours*, 76 (1950-I): 125.

_____. "Some Observations on the Compulsory Jurisdiction of the International Court of Justice." *British Year Book of International Law*, 25 (1948): 133.

Hammarskjöld, Ake. "The Early Work of the Permanent Court of International Justice." *Harvard Law Review*, 36 (1923): 704.

_____. "The Permanent Court of International Justice and the Development of International Law." *International Affairs*, 14 (1935): 797.

_____. "Quelques aspects de la fonction consultative de la Cour Permanente de Justice Internationale." In *Festgabe für Max Huber zum sechsigsten Geburtstag, 28 Dezember 1934*. Zurich: Schulthess, 1934.

_____. "Sidelights on the Permanent Court of International Justice." *Michigan Law Review*, 25 (1927): 327.

Head, Ivan L. "The Contribution of the International Court of Justice to the Development of International Organizations." *Proceedings of the American Society of International Law*, 59 (1965): 177.

Henkin, Louis. "The United Nations, 24th Session. Introduction: The United Nations and the Rules of Law." *Harvard International Law Journal*, 11 (1970): 428.

Hexner, Ervin P. "Interpretation by Public International Organizations of their Basic Instruments." *American Journal of International Law*, 53 (1959): 341.

Higgins, Rosalyn. "The Development of International Law by the Political Organs of the United Nations." *Proceedings of the American Society of International Law*, 59 (1965): 116.

_____. "The Place of International Law in the Settlement of Disputes by the Security Council." *American Journal of International Law*, 64 (1970): 1.

_____. "Policy Considerations and the International Judicial Process." *International and Comparative Law Quarterly*, 17 (1968): 58.

Hoffmann, Stanley. "A World Divided and a World Court Confused: The World Court's Opinion on U.N. Financing." In *International Law and Political Crisis: An Analytic Casebook*. Edited by Lawrence Scheinman and David Wilkinson. Boston: Little, Brown & Co., 1968.

Honig, F. "The Diminishing Role of the World Court." *International Affairs*, 34 (1958): 184.

Houben, Piet-Hein. "Principles of International Law Concerning Friendly Relations and Co-operation among States." *American Journal of International Law*, 61 (1967): 703.

Hudson, Manley O. Annual articles on the Court in the January issues of the *American Journal of International Law*, particularly "The Twenty-third Year of the Permanent Court of International Justice and Its Future," 39 (1945): 1; "The Twenty-fourth Year of the World Court," 40 (1946): 1; and "The Twenty-eighth Year of the World Court," 44 (1950): 1.

_____. "Advisory Opinions: Contributions of the Permanent Court of International Justice to the Development of International Law." *Proceedings of the American Society of International Law*, 24 (1930): 30.

_____. "Advisory Opinions of National and International Courts." *Harvard Law Review*, 37 (1924): 970.

_____. "The Advisory Opinions of the Permanent Court of International Justice." *International Conciliation*, No. 214 (November 1925).

_____. "The American Reservations and the Permanent Court of International Justice." *American Journal of International Law*, 22 (1928): 776.

_____. "Les avis consultatifs de la Cour Permanente de Justice Internationale." *Recueil des Cours*, 8 (1925-III): 345.

_____. "The Effect of Advisory Opinions of the World Court." *American Journal of International Law*, 42 (1948): 630.

_____. "Legal and Political Questions." *Proceedings of the American Society of International Law*, 18 (1924): 126.

_____. "Two Problems of Approach to the Permanent Court of International Justice." *American Journal of International Law*, 29 (1935): 636.

_____. "The World Court and the Austro-German Customs Regime." *American Bar Association Journal*, 17 (1931): 791.

Hurst, Cecil J. B. "The Permanent Court of International Justice," *Law Quarterly Review*, 59 (1943): 312.

Jenks, C. Wilfred. "Some Constitutional Problems of International Organizations." *British Year Book of International Law*, 22 (1945): 11.

_____. "The Status of International Organizations in Relation to the International Court of Justice." *Transactions of the Grotius Society*, 32 (1946): 1.

Jennings, R. Y. "The International Court's Advisory Opinion on the Voting Procedure on Questions concerning South West Africa." *Transactions of the Grotius Society*, 42 (1956): 85.

Jessup, Philip C. "The Court as an Organ of the United Nations." *Foreign Affairs*, 23 (1945): 233.

_____. "The Customs Union Advisory Opinion." *American Journal of International Law*, 26 (1932): 105.

_____. "The International Court of Justice and Legal Matters." *Illinois Law Review*, 42 (1947): 273.

_____. "The International Court of Justice Revisited." *Virginia Journal of International Law*, 11 (1971): 299.

_____. *The United States and the World Court*. Boston: World Peace Foundation, 1929.

Johnson, D. H. N. "The Effect of Resolutions of the General Assembly of the United Nations." *British Year Book of International Law*, 32 (1955–56): 97.

Jokl, M. "La Ville Libre de Dantzig devant la Cour Permanente de Justice Internationale." *Revue de Droit International et de Législation Comparée*, 3rd Ser., 17 (1936): 759.

Kane, Albert E. "The Unanimity Rule as Applied to Requests for Advisory Opinions from the World Court." *China Law Review*, 6 (1933): 185.

Kelsen, Hans. "Compulsory Adjudication of International Disputes." *American Journal of International Law*, 37 (1943): 397.

Keohane, Robert O. "Political Influence in the General Assembly." *International Conciliation*, no. 557 (March 1966).

Kerno, Ivan S. "L'Organisation des Nations Unies et la Cour Internationale de Justice." *Recueil des Cours*, 78 (1951-I): 511.

Khan, Rahmatullah, and Kaur, Satpal. "The Deadlock over South-West Africa." *Indian Journal of International Law*, 8 (1968): 179.

Kunz, J. L. "Compulsory International Adjudication and the Maintenance of Peace." *American Journal of International Law*, 38 (1944): 673.

Lalive, J. F. "Bulletin de jurisprudence de la Cour Internationale de Justice (1950)." *Journal du Droit International*, 77 (1950): 1228.

Larson, Arthur. "Peace Through Law: The Role and Limits of Adjudication—Some Contemporary Applications." *Proceedings of the American Society of International Law*, 54 (1960): 8.

Lauterpacht, Eli. "The Legal Effect of Illegal Acts of International Organisations." *Cambridge Essays in International Law*. London: Stevens, 1965.

Lauterpacht, Hersch. "Codification and Development of International Law." *American Journal of International Law*, 49 (1955): 16.

––––––. "Some Observations on the Prohibition of 'Non Liquet' and the Completeness of the Law." *Symbolae Verzijl*. The Hague: Nijhoff, 1958.

Leonard, L. Larry. "The United Nations and Palestine." *International Conciliation*, no. 454 (October 1949).

Liang, Y. L. "Interpretation of the Charter and Greater Use of the International Court of Justice." *American Journal of International Law*, 42 (1948): 439.

––––––. "The Settlement of Disputes in the Security Council: The Yalta Voting Formula." *British Year Book of International Law*, 24 (1947): 330.

McNair, Arnold D. "The Council's Request for an Advisory Opinion from the Permanent Court of International Justice." *British Year Book of International Law*, 7 (1926): 1.

McWhinney, Edward. "The 'New' Countries and the 'New' International Law: The United Nations' Special Conference on Friendly Relations and Co-operation among States." *American Journal of International Law*, 60 (1966): 1.

Mandelstam, A. N. "La conciliation internationale d'apres le pacte et la jurisprudence du Conseil de la Société des Nations." *Recueil des Cours*, 14 (1926-IV): 337.

Manning, C. A. W. "The Permanent Court and the Customs Union." *New York University Law Review*, 9 (1932): 339.

Mathews, Robert E. "Judicial Attitudes in the Customs-Union Case." *Michigan Law Review*, 30 (1932): 699.

Nathanson, Nathaniel L. "Constitutional Crisis at the United Nations: The Price of Peace Keeping, I." *University of Chicago Law Review*, 32 (1965): 621; II, *ibid.*, 33 (1966): 249.

Negulesco, D. "L'évolution de la procédure des avis consultatifs de la Cour Permanente de Justice Internationale." *Recueil des Cours*, 57 (1936-III): 5.

_____. "La Nature Juridique des avis consultatifs de la Cour Permanente de Justice Internationale, leur valeur et leur portée en Droit International." *Annuaire de l'Institut de Droit International*, 40 (1937): 1-7, 164-82, 245-47.

Nicholas, H. G. "The United Nations in Crisis." *International Affairs*, 41 (1965): 441.

Nisot, Joseph. "The Advisory Opinion of the International Court of Justice on the International Status of South-West Africa." *South African Law Journal*, 68 (1951): 274.

Pollux [pseud.]. "The Interpretation of the Charter." *British Year Book of International Law*, 23 (1946): 54.

Preuss, L. "Article 2, Paragraph 7, of the Charter of the United Nations and Matters of Domestic Jurisdiction." *Recueil des Cours*, 74 (1949-I): 547.

Rogers, William P. "The Rule of Law and the Settlement of International Disputes." *American Journal of International Law* (*Proceedings of the American Society of International Law*), 64, no. 4 (September 1970): 285.

Root, Elihu. "The Permanent Court of International Justice." *Proceedings of the American Society of International Law*, 17 (1923): 1.

Rosenne, Shabtai. "The Advisory Competence of the International Court of Justice." *Revue de Droit International de Sciences Diplomatiques et Politiques*, 30 (1952): 10.

_____. "La Cour internationale de justice en 1962." *Revue Générale de Droit International Public*, 67 (1963): 737.

_____. "La Cour internationale de justice en 1963." *Revue Générale de Droit International Public*, 68 (1964): 858.

_____. "La Cour internationale de justice en 1966." *Revue Générale de Droit International Public*, 71 (1967): 853.

_____. "The Court and the Judicial Process." *International Organization*, 19 (1965): 518.

_____. "The International Court and the United Nations: Reflections on the Period 1946-1954." *International Organization*, 9 (1955): 244.

_____. "The International Court at Fifty," *Israel Law Review*, 7 (1972): 175.

_____. "On the Non-Use of the Advisory Competence of the International Court of Justice." *British Year Book of International Law*, 39 (1963): 1.

_____. "Sir Hersch Lauterpacht's Concept of the Task of the International Judge." *American Journal of International Law*, 55 (1961): 825.

Russell, Ruth B. "United Nations Financing and the 'Law of the Charter.' " *Columbia Journal of Transnational Law*, 5 (1966): 68.

Schachter, Oscar. "The Development of International Law through the Legal Opinions of the United Nations Secretariat." *British Year Book of International Law*, 25 (1948): 91.

_____. "The Relation of Law, Politics, and Action in the United Nations." *Recueil des Cours*, 109 (1963-II): 169.

Schwartz, William. "The International Court's Role as an Adviser to the United Nations: A Study in Retrogressive Development." *Boston University Law Review*, 37 (1957): 404.

Seyersted, Finn. "Settlement of Internal Disputes of Intergovernmental Organizations by Internal and External Courts." *Zeitschrift für Öffentliches Recht und Völkerrecht*, 24 (1964): 1.

Shihata, Ibrahim F. I. "The Attitude of New States toward the International Court of Justice." *International Organization*, 19 (1965): 203.

Sloan, F. Blaine. "Advisory Jurisdiction of the International Court of Justice." *California Law Review*, 38 (1950): 830.

_____. "The Binding Force of a 'Recommendation' of the General Assembly of the United Nations." *British Year Book of International Law*, 25 (1948): 1.

Slonim, S. "The Advisory Opinion of the International Court of Justice on Certain Expenses of the United Nations: A Critical Analysis." *Howard Law Journal*, 10 (1964): 227.

Sohn, Louis B. "Exclusion of Political Disputes from Judicial Settlement." *American Journal of International Law*, 38 (1944): 694.

Sorenson, Max. "The International Court of Justice: Its Role in Contemporary International Relations." *International Organization*, 14 (1960): 261.

Stone, Julius. "A Common Law for Mankind?" *International Studies* (New Delhi), 1 (1960): 414.

_____. "The International Court and World Crisis." *International Conciliation*, No. 536 (January 1962).

_____. "*Non Liquet* and the Function of Law in the International Community." *British Year Book of International Law*, 35 (1959): 124.

Vallat, Francis A. "The Competence of the United Nations General Assembly." *Recueil des Cours*, 97 (1959-II): 207.

_____. "The Peaceful Settlement of Disputes." *Cambridge Essays in International Law*. London: Stevens, 1965.

Van Der Molen, Gesina H. J. "The Present Crisis in the Law of Nations." In *Symbolae Verzijl*. The Hague: Nijhoff, 1958.

Van Hamel, J. A. "Danzig and the Polish Problem." *International Conciliation*, No. 288 (March 1933).

Waldock, C. H. M. "Decline of the Optional Clause." *British Year Book of International Law*, 32 (1956): 244.

_____. "The Plea of Domestic Jurisdiction before International Legal Tribunals." *British Year Book of International Law*, 31 (1954): 96.

Wehle, Louis B. "The United Nations By-Passes the International Court as the Council's Adviser: A Study in Contrived Frustration." *University of Pennsylvania Law Review*, 98 (1950): 285.

Wilkinson, David. "The Article 17 Crisis: The Dispute over Financing the United Nations." In *International Law and Political Crisis: An Analytic Casebook*. Edited by Lawrence Scheinman and David Wilkinson. Boston: Little, Brown & Co., 1968.

Windass, S. "Indonesia and the UN: Legalism, Politics, and Law." *International Relations*, 3, No. 8 (November 1969): 578.

Wright, Quincy. "The United States and the Permanent Court of International Justice." *American Journal of International Law*, 21 (1927): 1.

UNPUBLISHED MATERIAL

Krishna, Rao K. "The International Court of Justice and the Advisory Jurisdiction." LL.D. dissertation, New York University, 1955.

INDEX OF CASES

INDEX OF SUBJECTS
AND NAMES